Handbook of
Management
Information
Systems
A Managerial Perspective

Handbook of
Management
Information
Systems

A Managerial Perspective

Hossein Bidgoli
School of Business and Public Administration
California State University
Bakersfield, California

ACADEMIC PRESS
San Diego   London   Boston   New York   Sydney   Tokyo   Toronto

Academic Press
a division of Harcourt Brace & Company
525 B Street, Suite 1900, San Diego, California 92101-4495, USA
http://www.apnet.com

Academic Press
24-28 Oval Road, London NW1 7DX, UK
http://www.hbuk.co.uk/ap/

Library of Congress Catalog Card Number: 98-87237

International Standard Book Number: 0-12-095975-5

PRINTED IN THE UNITED STATES OF AMERICA
98 99 00 01 02 03 EB 9 8 7 6 5 4 3 2 1

To so many fine memories of my brother,
Mohsen,
for his uncompromising belief in the power of education

Contents in Brief

Part IV
Information Systems in Action

Part V
Emerging Technologies and Applications in the Information Systems Environment

Contents

Chapter 2

Hardware and Software Concepts

Chapter 3

Database Concepts

Chapter 4

Organizational, Social, and Legal Impacts
of Information Systems

Part II
Data Communications and the Internet

Chapter 5

Data Communications Concepts

Chapter 6

Security Issues and Measures

Chapter 7

The Information Superhighway and Global Information Systems

Chapter 8

The Intranet: The Internet of Your Own

Part III

Building and Utilizing Effective Information Systems

Chapter 9

Tools and Techniques for Building Information Systems

Chapter 10

Total Quality Management and Information Systems Reengineering

Chapter 11

Building Effective Information Systems in Functional Areas

Part IV
Information Systems in Action

Chapter 14

Group Support Systems: Collaborative Computing Has Started

Chapter 15

Geographic Information Systems

Chapter 16

Multimedia and Virtual Reality Information Systems

Part V
Emerging Technologies and Applications in the Information Systems Environment

Chapter 20

Neural Networks: Computers That Learn by Doing

Chapter 21

Natural Language Processing:
The Ultimate User/System Interface

Preface

Cost reduction and significant improvement in all areas of computer technology have made computers a viable alternative in the decision-making process. During the past decade, microcomputer technology has grown extensively. Today, an executive can connect to a wealth of information through a desktop computer. The growth of the Internet, the Intranet, the Extranet, and the information superhighway has added more excitement to this expanding technology. Specific improvement in networking, database design, input/output devices, graphical user interface (GUI), and so on have made computers a true decision-maker's companion. Computers are becoming easier to use, more affordable, and more powerful.

To be able to design and utilize a computer-based information system (CBIS), two important concepts must be understood. First, the philosophical aspects of CBIS must be examined. Second, the architecture of a CBIS must be understood, and the philosophical issues must be integrated into the architecture.

This book incorporates the philosophical foundations as well as the practical issues regarding CBIS design, implementation, and utilization. The book covers the existing technology of CBIS, and it then explores future applications by introducing information systems reengineering, total quality management, the information superhighway, global information systems, executive information systems, decision support systems, group support systems, geographic information systems, multimedia, virtual reality, and artificial intelligence. The book is divided into five parts, which include twenty-one chapters.

Part I begins with a general dicussion of the past, present, and future of information systems technologies and then introduces a detailed discussion of hardware, software, and databases in the business world. This part examines the negative and positive impacts of information systems, and it concludes with a discussion of the social and ethical impacts of information systems. Part I sets the stage for the rest of the book.

Part II examines in detail the growing field of data communications and the Internet. It provides a general background for data communications technologies, and it explores computer security and measures. Part II also discusses the information superhighway and the Intranet.

Part III discusses systems analysis and design in information systems. It provides guidelines for establishing a successful information system, it discusses tools and techniques for design and implementation of an information system, and it introduces the principles of total quality management and reengineering for developing effective information systems. Part III introduces the important issues for planning and management of information systems, and it concludes with a detailed discussion of the competitive advantage gained by using information systems.

Part IV introduces in detail five of the most important and rapidly growing technologies in the information systems field. These technologies are gaining in popularity, and they show tremendous potential for improving the efficiency and effectiveness of business decision making. They include electronic data interchange (EDI), decision support and executive information systems, group support systems, geographic information systems, and multimedia information systems.

In Part V several recent issues related to information systems design and utilization are discussed. These include artificial intelligence, expert systems, neural computing, fuzzy logic, and natural language processing systems. Research data show that these issues and technologies are gaining in popularity. A thorough treatment of these topics should prepare information systems users for the challenges of tomorrow.

The text includes the following unique features:

1. For the first time, this book presents comprehensive coverage of the popular information systems technology within the context of information systems. Using this approach we have investigated all the important issues surrounding the design and implementation of information systems, including microcomputers, security issues, data communications, and group support systems.

2. The text presents numerous information systems applications in functional areas of business. This approach places our discussion in perspective, and the reader will have an easier time understanding our presentation.

3. The new and future issues related to successful information systems design are carefully examined. These include multimedia, global information systems, the information superhighway, the Intranet, electronic data interchange, total quality management, and applied artificial intelligence. This discussion should prepare the reader to understand emerging technologies.

4. The book places a heavy emphasis on human issues and the user perspective. This approach should provide current and future executives with the necessary background to deal with problems related to information systems design and utilization from the user's perspective.

5. The book presents a complete discussion of information systems design, implementation, and applications, thereby providing the foundation necessary to understand the next logical progression—expert systems design and implementation.

6. Important topics with significant decision-making applications that are not covered in other books are thoroughly covered in this text. In this book an entire chapter is devoted to each of the following topics: security issues and measures, the Internet, the Intranet, electronic data interchange, fuzzy logic, neural networks, and natural language processing systems. A thorough understanding of these important topics should help decision makers to take advantage of these growing technologies.

7. A comprehensive discussion of the organizational, social, and legal impacts of information systems appears early in the text (Chapter 4). The early presentation of this very important topic provides the reader with an understanding and appreciation of both the positive and the negative impacts of information systems.

8. Each chapter begins with a brief introduction that "warms up" the reader and lists the topics that are covered. Each ends with a summary that provides the reader with the essence of the particular chapter, leaving the reader with a clear understanding of the topics discussed. Each chapter includes learning objectives that provide a measurable goal to be achieved after studying the chapter.

9. Each chapter concludes with 20 to 25 review questions. These reinforce the topics covered. At the end of each chapter we introduce five to seven projects that can be used as class assignments or to further investigate a particular topic. Each chapter includes a list of the key terms and a comprehensive reference list.

10. There is a vast array of software products on the market. Several of these products can enhance and facilitate information systems design and utilization. Where appropriate throughout the book we introduce these products for both micro- and mainframe computers. This information should facilitate the actual information design and utilization.

11. This book presets numerous real-life applications of information systems in the business world. This presentation further illustrates the practical applications of various information systems technologies in the business world.

Hossein Bidgoli

About the Author

Hossein Bidgoli, Ph.D., is professor of management information systems at California State University, Bakersfield. Dr. Bidgoli helped set up the first PC lab in the United States. He is the author of 40 textbooks, 26 manuals, and more than three dozen technical articles and papers on various aspects of computer applications and information systems that have been published and presented throughout the world.

Dr. Bidgoli is a two-time winner of Meritorious Performance and Professional Promise Award for 1985–86 and 1988–89, School of Business and Public Administration, California State University, Bakersfield.

Acknowledgments

Several colleagues reviewed different versions of this manuscript and made constructive suggestions. Without their assistance the text could not have been in its present shape. Their help and comments are greatly appreciated.

Many different groups assisted me in completing this project. I am grateful to the students in my undergraduate and graduate classes who provided feedback. Also, executives who attended my seminars in information systems provided me with insights regarding the practicality of the materials. They helped me fine-tune the manuscript during its various stages. My friend and colleague Andrew Prestage assisted me with some of the art presented in the text, and my colleague Johanna Alexander assisted me in various library searches. As always, their support is appreciated. My old friend Assad Karimi deserves special recognition for providing moral support throughout the years.

A group of professionals from the Academic Press assisted me in various stages in completing this text. First and foremost, Dr. J. Scott Bentley, my senior editor, assisted me in various stages of the development process and refining the project. His timely review process kept the project ahead of schedule. Kay Sasser, the production editor, and her team did a fantastic job on the production of the manuscript, Karen Frost provided editorial assistance, and Karen Steele, product marketing manager, and her professional team provided superb marketing assistance. I appreciate their help.

Last, but not least, I thank my wonderful wife Nooshin and my two lovely children, Mohsen and Morvareed, for being so patient during this venture. Also, my two sisters Azam and Akram provided moral support as always. I am grateful to all for their support.

Part I

Information Systems Basics

Part I begins with a general discussion of the past, present, and future of information systems technologies, and it then introduces a detailed discussion of hardware, software, and databases in the business world. Part I examines the negative and positive impacts of information systems and it concludes with a discussion of the social and ethical impacts of information systems. This part sets the stage for the rest of the book.

Chapter 1

Information Systems:
An Overview

Learning Objectives

After studying this chapter, you should be able to:

- Define a computer-based information system (CBIS).
- Elaborate on the components of a CBIS.
- Define various types of information systems.
- Elaborate on artificial intelligence and its related technologies.
- Highlight the importance of a CBIS in an organization.
- Explore the future trends in CBISs.

1-1 INTRODUCTION

This chapter reviews the basics of a computer-based information system (CBIS) and looks at the components and objectives of such systems. The chapter considers different classes of CBISs: electronic data processing systems (EDP), management information systems (MISs), decision support systems (DSSs), and executive information systems (EISs). Group support systems (GSSs) and geographic information systems (GISs) as other types of information systems will be introduced. The chapter includes a brief discussion of artificial intelligence and its related technologies, including expert systems, natural language processing, robotics, neural networks, fuzzy logic and intelligent agents. The chapter concludes with a discussion of the importance and versatility of CBISs and introduces an outlook for future trends in CBISs. These topics will be further explained in the future chapters.

1-2 COMPUTER-BASED INFORMATION SYSTEMS (CBISs)

A computer-based information system (CBIS) is an organized integration of hardware and software technologies, data, procedure, and human elements designed to produce timely, integrated, accurate, and useful information for decision-making purposes.

The hardware elements that will be discussed in Chapter 2 include input, output, and memory devices. The type of device used in a CBIS varies from one application to the next and from one organization to the next.

The software used in a CBIS can include commercial programs, software developed in-house, or both. The particular application or organization determines the type of software employed. These various software will be discussed in Chapter 2.

The human element includes users, programmers, systems analysts, and other technical personnel. This text puts a heavy emphasis on the users of these systems.

In designing a CBIS, the first task is to clearly define the objective(s) of the system. Then data must be collected and analyzed. Finally, information must be provided in a useful format for decision-making purposes.

There are many CBIS applications in both private and public organizations, such as a CBIS for inventory control. This system provides information about inventory, so that the inventory manager can know how much of each product is on hand, what items have been ordered, and what items are back-ordered. Another CBIS may forecast sales volume for the next period in a typical business organization. This CBIS uses the most recent past data and some types of mathematical or statistical models to provide the best possible forecast. A sales manager can use this information for planning purposes. A CBIS for cash-flow analysis provides information to the financial manager regarding all the cash inflows and outflows. The manager can use this information to establish a balance between the incoming and outgoing cash. A final example of a CBIS is one for a police department. This CBIS could provide information such as crime statistics, crime forecasts, and police protection allocation. By examining these statistics a fast-growing or a slow-growing crime in a city can be spotted and analyzed.

1-3 A CBIS MODEL

A typical CBIS includes seven components: data, database, process, information, information systems life cycle (ISLC), environment, and design specifications. Figure 1-1 shows this model [4].

1-3-1 DATA

The information needed by the user directly affects the type of data used in a CBIS. If an organization has defined its strategic goals, objectives, and critical success factors to ensure a viable and growing company, the data component can be structured rather easily and the CBIS has potential for success. On the other hand, if there are conflicting goals and objectives, or if the company is not aware of which factors are critical to its success, many problems can occur to destroy the confidence in a CBIS or minimize its effectiveness. If the CBIS is not designed

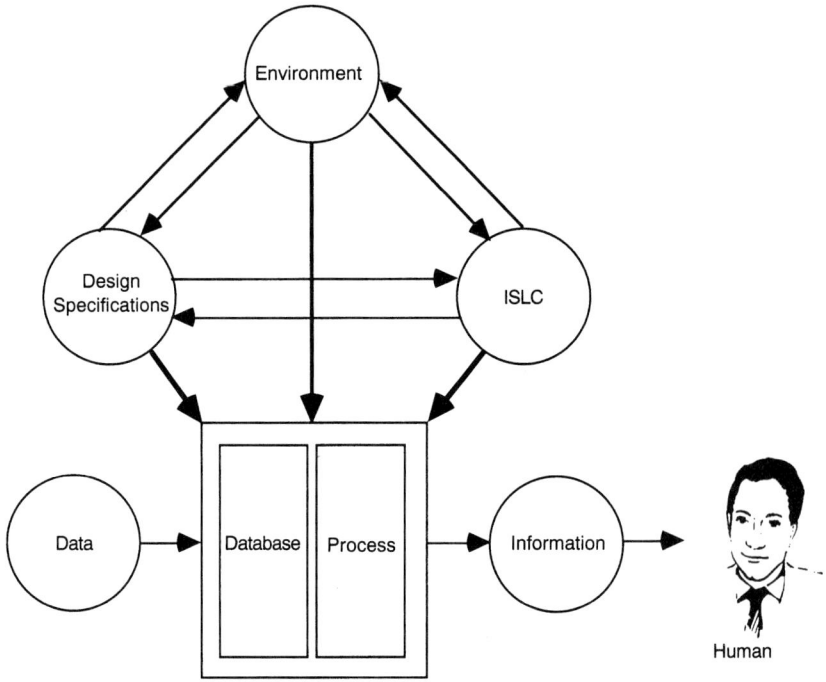

Figure 1-1   Conceptual model for a CBIS.

to evolve as changes (both internal and external) take place, then the system may do more damage than good.

Of course, the objectives of the organization ultimately resolve the questions of the sources of data—external or internal sources—and whether the data is past- (performance), present- (operational), or future- (budget or cash flow) oriented. The urgency of need and the availability of data in many forms, including aggregated (lump sum) or disaggregated (itemized), can then be addressed. Disaggregated data is needed when, for instance, sales are analyzed by product, territory, or salesperson, and costs are analyzed by cost center or product. Aggregated data limits the decision maker's ability to focus on specific factors. Figure 1-2 illustrates external factors that must be constantly monitored by a CBIS. A CBIS must collect and analyze the data related to the factors illustrated in Figure 1-2 and inform the decision makers about their consequences and impacts on the organization.

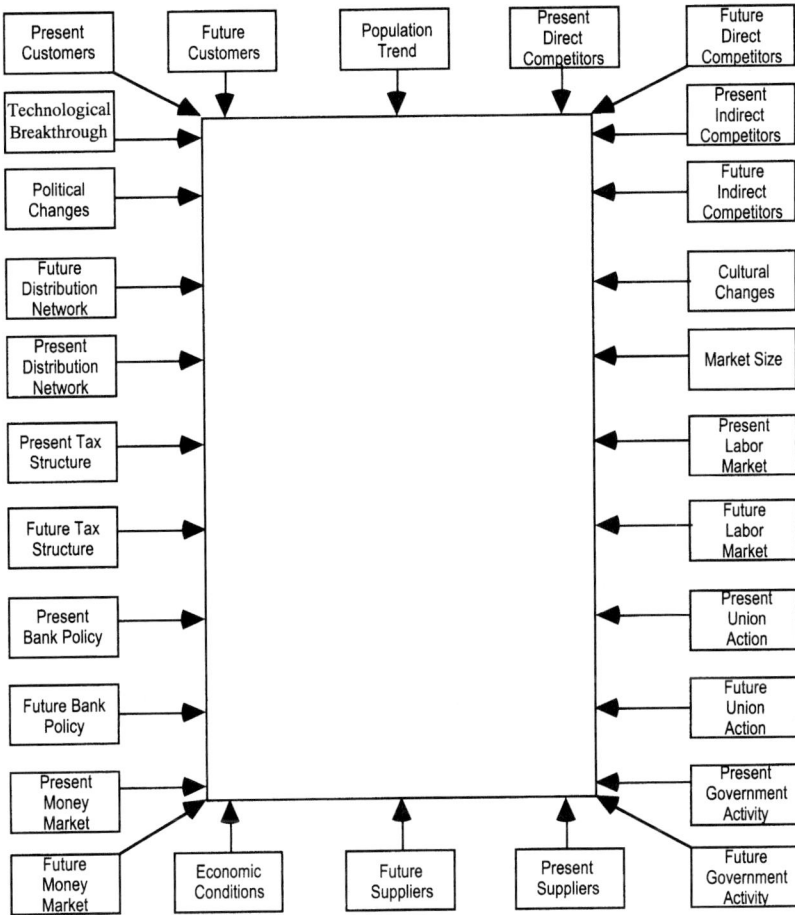

Figure 1-2 External factors to be considered and monitored by a CBIS.

1-3-2 DATABASE

The type of database is not important to the user; only the existence and availability of the database is the issue. A database is a collection of all relevant data organized in a series of integrated files. We will discuss different types of database models and various database concepts in Chapter 3. If the CBIS does not provide what the user wants, the success of the system is questionable.

In addition, managers at higher levels are less willing to expend valuable personal or staff time to manually gather, process, and interpret available data. Thus, data needs to be treated as a common resource so that it can be used readily. As you will see in Chapter 3, a comprehensive database is essential for the success of a CBIS.

1-3-3 PROCESS

Development of a CBIS generally includes a wide range of transaction-processing reports and some models for decision analysis. In many cases, the models are built into the system or can be accessed from external sources. Also, many of the commercial software packages employed in a CBIS include various modeling techniques.

Formal information is generated by a CBIS. Informal information is generated by informal channels, which may include rumors, unconfirmed reports, and stories. The user should have both formal and informal information available for decision making. A comprehensive CBIS should enable the user to work with both kinds of information when solving problems.

A CBIS could, therefore, include a wide range of models to support all levels of decision making. Users should be able to inquiry a CBIS and generate various reports. The capability to grow with the system requires that the initial CBIS enable the user to redefine, generate, restructure, and incorporate new information into the modeling analysis. Eventually, the purpose of the process component of the CBIS is generation of the most useful type of information for decision-making purposes.

1-3-4 INFORMATION

The nature of information is determined by its usefulness to the user. It is the usefulness of information that determines the success of a CBIS. The information must be responsive to the user in four main areas. It must be timely, integrated with other data and information, consistent and accurate, and relevant. If the information lacks any of these basic features, then incorrect decisions, misallocation of resources, and overlooked windows of opportunity will result. If the system cannot provide a minimum level of confidence, then the CBIS will not be used or the system will be severely discounted. Perhaps the greatest requirement for information is that it provide a fundamental base from which the user can explore different options, or better yet, gain an insight into the particular task at hand.

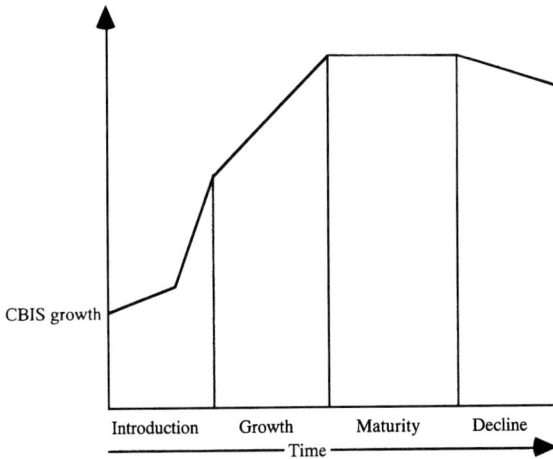

Figure 1-3   Four stages of a CBIS life cycle.

The user-system interface must be flexible and easy to use. Menu-driven systems and graphical user interfaces (GUIs) have attracted much attention in recent years. These systems provide flexibility and ease of use, particularly to those with a limited computer background. The CBIS should provide information in diverse formats, including graphic, tabular, and exception type. Graphic reports highlight the business situation in an easy-to-understand pictorial fashion. Exception reports highlight situations that are outside of the specified range. A CBIS that has many options for receiving or gaining access to information has a better chance for success because it uses methods of information transfer that are better understood by the user.

1-3-5 INFORMATION SYSTEMS LIFE CYCLE

As with all systems, a CBIS has a well-defined life cycle—the information systems life cycle (ISLC). Unless a system has a radical transformation, each information system experiences four distinct phases: introduction, growth, maturity, and decline. Figure 1-3 illustrates the four stages of the life cycle.

A CBIS has a life cycle because of technological growth, organizational growth and changing information needs due to changing government regulations, and other internal and external factors. Within the system itself, each subsystem has its own life cycle. The introduction stage is crucial to the acceptance of the CBIS (but not necessarily to its success). The growth period may be slowed by delays in the expansion of the CBIS, technical problems, the availability of the

CBIS to users, and the reluctance by the users to accept the CBIS. If the delays can be overcome, the growth period of the CBIS offers a great opportunity for it to be accepted. Finally, if the CBIS improves the quality of the work accomplished, searches of new areas and new ways to service users, and lowers the cost of providing information, it will also be more readily accepted.

In the maturity stage, the usage and reputation of the CBIS should be increased through quality and improvement of features such as graphics and external databases, which provide greater flexibility and create greater user enthusiasm.

The final stage in the information systems life cycle is the decline period. This stage can be crucial to an organization's success. If there is not a planned overhaul or review, the organization may be saddled with a CBIS that takes a disproportionate amount of the organization's resources relative to its contributions. A periodic review may force the current CBIS to be drastically overhauled or eliminated in favor of a new system.

1-3-6 ENVIRONMENT

Users of computer-based information systems occupy three organizational levels: top management (strategic), middle management (tactical), and lower management (operational). Each organizational level assumes a different role in the development and use of a CBIS.

Support in the form of financial, policies, and encouragement from top management is necessary for a CBIS to be successful. General resistance to a CBIS at all levels of the organization can be seen in habits, lack of familiarity with the system, and feelings of insecurity about the system. For example, people are accustomed to receiving hard copy reports regarding company polices, financial status, and progress status. So visualization of data on a CRT may be new and unfamiliar to many people. Learning how to access a computer is also an activity that may evoke user insecurity. Resistance is further compounded by the routine nature of data input, extraction, and all the mechanical elements associated with operating the computer. Designers of CBIS should consider these factors. By involving users early and often in the design process and by providing on-going education CBIS designers can try to minimize the resistance issues of CBIS design.

1-3-7 DESIGN SPECIFICATIONS

After a careful review of the information system's life cycle and a precise definition of the environment of a particular CBIS, the design specifications should be decided. Comprehensive design specifications play a crucial role in the CBIS. They should create consistency in computer use, increase the adaptability of the existing CBIS to growing technology, increase the chances of acceptance by the users, and, finally, they should serve as a guideline for CBIS use. The most important design specification variables are types of design (task force versus individual), provision for change (modularity in design), functional specifications and performance criteria, and system documentation.

Traditionally, a CBIS was designed largely by data processing personnel. As a result, the design did not always gain the full support of the users. The emerging issue of design by task force emphasizes the participation of all affected personnel in the design of the CBIS. This method could increase the commitment of users and give them a chance to express their views regarding the use of the CBIS.

Acquisition and use of computer technology should not be a one-shot operation. Rather, it should be a continuous and evolutionary process. Design specifications of the CBIS should consider the ways and methods by which a particular organization might adapt to changing technology. Modularity in design could provide such an opportunity. Modularity should be considered in relation to hardware acquisition, software acquisition, systems design principles, and, most importantly, software development. To achieve this goal, an organization needs a master plan for its CBIS applications. The master plan should include all the related activities for the next 3 to 5 years, and it should be reviewed and revised continuously. The master plan should clearly specify where the organization is with regard to its CBIS projects and where it is planning to be. All affected personnel should have input to the CBIS master plan.

To stay within the predefined objectives of the CBIS, the designer should keep in mind the functional specifications of the system. Functional specifications include the following:

- Time, cost, and other resource estimations (how much time and money are needed to design and implement a particular CBIS).
- Specific objectives of the CBIS.
- Input and output specifications.
- A description of system functions and characteristics.
- Accuracy of reports.
- Reliability of reports.

A comprehensive written document that describes the details and the step-by-step operation of the CBIS can be very helpful. This document may also aid in improving the performance of the existing system.

1-4 CLASSES OF CBISs

Different types of computer-based information systems have been designed to provide specific information. Based on their objectives, the intended audiences, and the technology used, systems have been classified as electronic data processing (EDP), management information systems (MISs), decision support systems (DSSs), and executive information systems (EISs). Each system addresses a specific type of decision.

Organizational decisions can be classified into three groups. **Structured decisions,** or programmable tasks, do not need a decision maker for implementation. Instead, a well-defined, standard operating procedure exists for the execution of these types of decisions. Record-keeping operations, payrolls, and simple inventory problems are examples of this type of task. Electronic data processing and management information systems are mostly associated with this level.

Semistructured decisions are those that are not quite as well defined by standard operating procedures as are structured decisions due to an uncertain decision environment and the complexity of decision variables. However, these decisions are a mix of structured aspects that benefit from information retrieval and unstructured aspects that can be dealt through mathematical and statistical models and human intuition and judgment. Sales forecasting, cash flow, and capital acquisition analyses are some decisions within this group.

Unstructured decisions are unique in nature, are mostly nonrecurring, and have no standard operating procedure that pertains to their implementation. In these circumstances, the decision maker's intuition plays the most significant role, and computer technology offers the least support. There are many instances of this type of decision: research and development, hiring and firing, and introduction of a new product. Future developments in artificial intelligence (as discussed later in this chapter) may be of great assistance to organizations confronted with these qualitative decisions.

Figure 1-4 shows various organizational levels and the types of decisions made at each level. This figure highlights the potential and applications of information technology in all levels of an organization [1].

1-4-1 ELECTRONIC DATA PROCESSING (EDP)

For the past 50 years, **electronic data processing** (EDP), or transaction processing systems (TPSs), has been applied to such structured tasks as record keeping, simple clerical operations, and inventory control. Payroll, for example, was one of the first applications to be automated. The emphasis of these systems has been on data collection and data processing. Cost reduction is the major objective for the implementation of these systems.

A closer investigation of structured tasks reveals that computers provide the most benefit for this group of data processing operations. These tasks are either repetitive, such as printing numerous checks, or they involve enormous volumes of data, such as inventory control of a multinational textile company. When these systems are automated, the human involvement becomes minimal. For example,

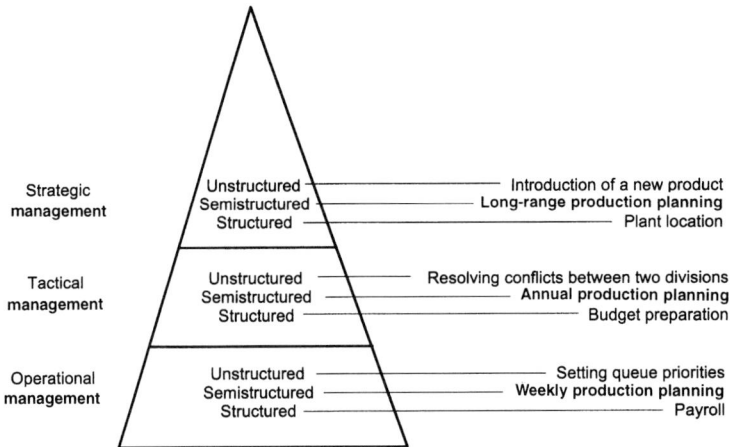

Figure 1-4   Organizational levels and types of decisions.

when a payroll system is automated, many checks are printed and sent to the recipients—there is no need for managerial judgment here.

1-4-2 MANAGEMENT INFORMATION SYSTEMS (MISs)

Since their inception in the mid-1960s, **management information systems** (MISs) have been used to inform what has happened between two points in time. The objective of these systems has been the production of timely, accurate, and useful information for middle management on a scheduled basis, such as weekly, biweekly, or monthly. Although an MIS supplies more aggregated information, it lacks flexibility and is not suitable for ad hoc applications.

There are many MIS applications in both private and public organizations. An automated budgeting system, annual income statements, annual balance sheets, a cash flow system, and sources and uses of funds statements are some examples. Although cost reduction is an important factor for designing these systems, other factors, such as employee satisfaction and customer service, play an important role.

1-4-3 DECISION SUPPORT SYSTEMS (DSSs)

We define a DSS as an interactive computer-based information system consisting of hardware, software (modeling and data analysis), and the human element designed to assist any decision maker at any organizational level with emphasis on semistructured and unstructured tasks. This simple definition underscores several requirements for a DSS [5]:

- A DSS requires hardware, software, and human elements (designers and users). The software include both modeling and data analysis capabilities.
- A DSS is designed to support decision making.
- A DSS should help decision makers at all organizational levels.
- A DSS emphasizes semistructured and unstructured tasks.
- A DSS is designed to improve effectiveness of decision-making process.

A DSS differs from an EDP and MIS in several aspects: a DSS uses both internal and external data, it emphasizes the present and future, and it uses mathematical and statistical models. Because a DSS is easier to use, the user is more actively involved in its design, implementation, and utilization. A DSS is designed to serve as a decision companion. These systems and decision makers work together to implement a decision. Wherever decisions are being made in an organization, there is a need for a DSS. We will discuss DSSs in more detail in Chapter 13.

1-4-4 EXECUTIVE INFORMATION SYSTEMS (EISs)

In recent years, some new systems have been introduced to the field of information systems: executive information systems (EISs), executive support systems (ESSs), and executive management systems (EMSs). Although their definitions and place among EDP, MISs, and DSSs are still evolving, we consider these systems a branch of DSSs. However, these systems have very little modeling capabilities. At the center of the system there is always a microcomputer that serves as an intelligent terminal. The microcomputer can serve as a stand-alone system or it can be used as a workstation to connect the executive decision maker to a wealth of information from both internal and external databases.

An **executive information system** (EIS) attempts to deliver only information that is critical to a decision maker and is user- or business-problem-driven. There is a heavy emphasis on providing an easily understood format in which executives use this information. One of the primary objectives of these systems is to eliminate and aggregate the vast amounts of information that bombards executives. This objective is accomplished with exception reports and by reporting only the critical information. An EIS combines the decision maker's imagination and judgment with the computer's ability to store, retrieve, manipulate, compute, and report internal and external information [11].

Executive information systems use integrated office technologies for planning, forecasting, and controlling managerial tasks. This kind of system may use the following:

- Touch screen;
- Mouse and Graphical User Interface (GUI);
- Menu-driven interfaces;
- Color screen;
- Key commands (such as SOLVE, DISPLAY, DRAW, and PLOT);
- Local area network (LAN);
- Wide area network (WAN);
- Metropolitan area network (MAN);
- Electronic mail;
- Facsimile equipment;
- Voice mail;
- Electronic message distribution;
- Teleconferencing (audio,video and computer);
- Graphics;
- Spreadsheets;
- Laptop computers;
- Scanners;
- Integration of voice, data, and images through ISDNs (integrated services digital networks, which are discussed in Chapter 5);
- Image transmission systems through facsimile.

In comparing an EIS with a DSS, some specific advantages can be highlighted. An EIS provides:

- Easier user-system interface;
- More timely delivery of highly condensed internal and external information;
- More understandable format for the information provided;
- Increased executive productivity by reporting on key items;
- A better understanding of the information and its interrelationships;
- Access to a large amount of internal and external data.

We will discuss data communications in Chapter 5. For now, remember that through communications systems, an organization can share the same information among many decision makers in an efficient manner. By using a communications system, an executive can access the wealth of information in public and private databases. We will discuss EISs in more detail in Chapter 13.

1-5 COMPARATIVE ANALYSIS OF EDP, MISs, DSSs, AND EISs

EDP, MISs, DSSs, and EISs are not unique technologies. Each technology addresses a particular user group. Table 1-1 provides a comparative summary of these four technologies.

Table 1-1

Comparison of EDP, MIS, DSS, and EIS Technologies

Key factor	EDP	MIS	DSS	EIS
Problem addressed	Structured	Structured	Structured and semistructured	Structured and semistructured
User	Lower management	Middle management	All management	Top management
Purpose	To inform what is happening	To inform what has happened	To inform what might happen	To diagnose organization malfunctions
Design team	Mostly DP professional	DP professional and the user	The user and DP professional	Top management and DP professional
Design tools	Mostly high-level language	High-level language and packages	Mostly packages	Mostly packages
Data used	Internal	Internal	Internal and external	Internal and mostly external
Interface mode	Batch and interactive	Batch and interactive	Interactive	Interactive

EDP, MISs, DSSs, and EISs can be developed from a series of design tools. Design tools are software technologies used to design and construct a CBIS. They can be either high-level programming languages (such as BASIC, FORTRAN, or C) or computer packages, 4GL (fourth-generation languages), or DSS generators. The 4GL and DSS generators (such as FOCUS, ORACLE, IFPS, NOMAD, Excel, Lotus 1-2-3, or Paradox) are more user-friendly and powerful than traditional programming languages.

A CBIS uses internal or external data—different systems use different proportions. The interface mode is either batch or interactive. In the batch mode, periodic reports are generated. In an interactive mode, the user receives instant response from the system.

1-6 OTHER CLASSES OF INFORMATION SYSTEMS

In addition to the above-mentioned types of information systems there are other types of information systems that are becoming popular. Among these are group support systems and geographic information systems. The following are brief descriptions of these two popular information systems.

1-6-1 GROUP SUPPORT SYSTEMS (GSSS)

In today's business environment, decision makers increasingly work in group situations. Group or collaborative computing is a new type of system. All major software vendors are competing to either enter into or increase their share in this growing market. Within this collaborative environment, there has been an increase in the use of computer-aided group support technologies. Group decision support systems (GDSSs), a subfield of decision support systems (DSSs), have evolved over the past decade. More recently, technologies such as electronic meeting systems (EMSs) and GroupWare have found their way into the workplace. We call these various technologies group support systems (GSSs). GSSs are intended to assist a group of decision makers who are working together on a certain task to make a decision or a better decision. These systems utilize computer and communications technologies in order to help a group of decision makers generate idea and decision alternatives and rank them.

Computer-aided decision support such as group decision support systems (GDSSs) can be considered a kind of intervention technology that can help to overcome the limitations of group interaction. A group decision support system is introduced to support a group's natural decision-making processes. The intervention feature of GDSSs reduces communication barriers and introduces order and efficiency into situations that are inherently disorderly and inefficient. Thus, a GDSS facilitates the process of group decision making by providing a clear focus for group discussion, minimizing politicking, and organizing attention around the critical issues. The effective outcome of this intervention depends on [7]:

1. Successfully matching the level and sophistication of the GDSS and its collaborative tools with the appropriate size of the group, scope of the task, and proximity of the decision-making environment.

2. Providing supportive management (specially at the CEO level) who are willing to "champion" the application of group decision support systems (GDSSs) within the organization.

Other computer-aided technologies that have emerged in the 1990s for group support are electronic meeting systems (EMSs) and GroupWare. Even though these systems are not considered "full-functionality GDSSs" due to their decision-making tool limitations, they are less expensive and they provide the communication and problem-solving mechanisms necessary for effective team management in a collaborative environment.

DSSs are usually designed to be used by a particular decision maker. A decision is made basically from the inputs given by this particular person. Group DSSs are designed to be used by more than one decision maker. These systems are useful for committees, review panels, board meetings, task forces, and decision-making sessions that require the input from several decision makers. Locating a new plant, introducing a new product, or participating in an international bid are three good examples of useful applications. We will discuss GSSs in detail in Chapter 14.

1-6-2 GEOGRAPHIC INFORMATION SYSTEMS (GISs)

Executives in a growing number of organizations are faced with questions such as [6]:

- Where should we locate a fire station?
- Where should we locate a fast-food restaurant?
- Where should we locate a new school?
- Where should we locate a new airport for minimal environmental impact?
- What route should our delivery truck follow for a minimum of driving time?

A properly designed geographic information system (GIS) can answer these questions and more. A GIS utilizes spatial and nonspatial data and specialized techniques for storing the coordinates of complex geographic objects, including networks of lines (roads, rivers, streets) and reporting zones (zip codes, cities, counties, or states).

There are numerous definitions for the GIS. The Environment Systems Research Institute, in Redlands, California, one of the major vendors of the GIS, provides this definition:

> A GIS is an organized collection of computer hardware, software, geographic data and personnel, designed to effectively capture, store, update, manipulate, analyze and display all forms of geographically referenced information.

A GIS integrates and analyzes spatial data from a variety of sources. The increasing power of the microcomputer and the significant cost reduction in computing equipment makes the GIS an attractive alternative for all types of organizations.

GISs have been around for almost 30 years. Their major applications have been in government and utility companies, mostly for analyzing census data. As will be explained in Chapter 15, GISs increasingly are utilized by various business organizations, particularly in marketing, manufacturing, and real estate.

A typical GIS is able to perform the following tasks:

- Enables the user to digitize maps.
- Associates spatial attributes with points, lines and polygons on the maps.
- Integrates the maps and database data with queries.

- The query language available in GIS supports sophisticated query operations. This includes the single criterion search—all the customers with income over $100,000—and the multiple criteria search—all the female customers with income over $100,000 who live in the southwest part of the city. It also includes searches with logical operators (AND, OR, and NOT—all the customers who are either female or have an income below $30,000. All the male customers except those who make over $200,000).

1-7 THE ARTIFICIAL INTELLIGENCE (AI) ERA

Artificial intelligence (AI) refers to a series of related technologies that try to simulate and reproduce human thought behavior, including thinking, speaking, feeling, and reasoning.

AI technology applies computers to areas that require knowledge, perception, reasoning, understanding, and cognitive abilities. To achieve this, computers must:

- Understand "common sense;"
- Understand facts and manipulate qualitative data;
- Deal with exceptions;
- Understand relationships among the facts;
- Interface with humans in a free-format fashion (natural language);
- Be able to deal with new situations based on previous learning;
- Be able to learn from experience.

Whereas traditional computer-based information systems are concerned with storage, retrieval, manipulation, and display of data, AI systems are concerned with the reproduction and display of knowledge and facts. In traditional computer-based information systems, programmers and systems analysts design and implement systems that help decision makers by providing timely, relevant, accurate, and integrated information. In the AI field, "knowledge engineers" are trying to discover rules of thumb, or **heuristics,** that will enable computers to perform tasks usually performed by humans or enable computers to duplicate human mental tasks, such as association and reasoning. Rules employed in AI technology come from a diverse group of experts in such areas as mathematics, computer science, psychology, economics, anthropology, medicine, engineering, and physics.

Some AI experts believe that AI is more of a concept than a solid field. AI encompasses a group of related technologies, including expert systems, natural language processing, speech recognition, vision recognition, robotics, neural networks, and fuzzy logic (to a degree). We will continue our discussion of AI in Chapter 17.

1-8 AI-RELATED TECHNOLOGIES

Of all the AI related technologies, expert systems, natural language processing, robotics, neural networks, fuzzy logic, and intelligent agents have attracted the most attention.

1-8-1 EXPERT SYSTEMS

Expert systems mimic human expertise in a narrow domain to solve a specific problem in a well-defined area. If a problem is not specific and it has not been solved previously by an expert or a series of experts, that problem is not suitable for expert system implementation.

Although traditional computer-based information systems generate information by using data and models and a well-defined algorithm, expert systems work with heuristics. Heuristics are sometimes referred to as the general knowledge available in a discipline. Heuristic reasoning does not imply formal knowledge, but rather considers binding a solution to a problem without following a rigorous algorithm. For example, if someone tells you that a canary is a bird, you know that a canary knows how to fly because it is a bird. If someone tells you John owns a horse, you quickly include this animal with other horses and separate them from millions of other animals.

Expert systems have been around since the 1960s and have improved continually during the past 30 years. A variety of expert systems are available commercially. News about expert systems is kept somewhat secret. Developers of the systems do not reveal detailed information regarding technical capabilities of these systems until their final release. Practitioners and companies that use the systems are also reluctant to reveal all the successes achieved by the systems because of the competitive advantages that may be gained by other users of the systems.

R1/XCON, developed by Digital Equipment Corporation (DEC) in a joint effort with Carnegie Mellon University, has been used by DEC for configuring VAX computers. This system uses more than 10,000 rules and more than 6000 product descriptions to configure the specific components of VAX systems based on a particular customer order. When the specifications are defined, the system generates a series of diagrams highlighting the electrical connections and the layout for the 50 to 150 components in a typical VAX order. The system has been continuously improved by modifying the quality and quantity of the rules employed by the system. In most cases XCON has been 99% accurate. All the correction incidents involved cases in which a seldom-used component was part of the system [12].

Dipmeter Adviser, developed by Schlumberger corporation, is another successful operational expert system. This system uses oil well log data and the geological characteristics of a well to provide recommendations concerning the possible location of oil in that region.

In the microcomputer environment, Expert Ease, developed by Human Edge Software corporation for IBM PCs and PC compatibles, has demonstrated significant success. With this system, Westinghouse has increased productivity in one factory by more than $10 million per year.

SRI International, working with the U.S. Geological Survey, has designed the Prospector system. This system provides advice and consultation to field teams during mineral exploration. It predicted a deposit of molybdenum in the Cascade Mountains in northern California that is expected to yield more than $100 million. We will discuss expert systems in more detail in Chapters 17 and 18.

1-8-2 NATURAL LANGUAGE PROCESSING (NLP)

Computer-based information systems have been designed to be used by those who are somewhat computer literate. No matter how flexible and user-friendly these systems are, a specific method must be followed to operate them or perform queries.

As will be discussed in Chapter 2, four classes of computer languages have evolved. The first class, a machine language, is a binary system consisting of 1s and 0s. It is the closest to the computer and the farthest from human language. The second class, assembly language, consists of a series of short codes (mnemonics) that represent instructions to the computer. The third class is high-level languages. They are more application- and user-oriented and more English-like than previous languages. The fourth class, fourth-generation languages (4GLs), are more forgiving than high-level languages and, most importantly, they are nonprocedural. The nonprocedural quality means that the user does not need to follow a rigid structure to communicate with a computer. The fifth class, natural languages, are the ideal languages from a user's point of view. These languages are supposed to enable a computer user to communicate with the computer in his or her native language.

The goal of **natural language processing** (NLP) is to provide a method for interface that is very similar to our native language. NLP provides a free-format question-and-answer situation for a typical user. Several NLPs are commercially available. These natural or artificial languages include CLOUT for database management systems, LADDER for ship identification and location, and TDUS for electromechanical repair. Currently, none of these products is capable of providing a dialog comparable to a conversation between humans.

There are several obstacles that have to be overcome before a natural language interface can be developed. Among these problems are ambiguity in our native language (one word may have several meanings), problems with ellipses (incomplete sentences), problems with metaphors (you say something and you mean something else), idioms, and similar-sounding words.

At this time, NLP systems have been successful only when they are used within a well-defined context; however, research continues. We will discuss NLP in detail in Chapter 21.

1-8-3 ROBOTICS

Robots and **robotics** are some of the most successful applications of AI. Today's robots are the ones seen mostly in movies and factories. They are far from intelligent, but progress has been steady. At the present time, most are slow, clumsy, blind, and mostly stupid! Their major applications have been on assembly lines in factories where they are used as a part of computer-integrated manufacturing (CIM).

Industrial robots cost between $100,000 and $250,000. Their mobility is limited. A serious challenge that still exists is teaching robots how to walk. How does a robot learn to walk on a soft surface? Which foot has to go first? Even with all these problems, robots have been used successfully by the Japanese and in some American factories. At the present time, most robots are operating on assembly lines. A typical robot has a fixed arm that moves objects from point A to point B. Some robots have some vision, and they can locate objects and pick them up as long as the desired objects are isolated from other objects.

The operation of a robot is controlled by a computer and a program. A computer program written for a robot includes such commands as when and how far to reach, in which direction to go or turn, when to grasp an object, and how much pressure to apply. There are many computer languages for robot programming: T3, RCL, AL, AML, and PAL are just a few. Naturally, these languages are associated with a particular manufacturer of robots.

Personal robots have attracted a lot of attention in recent years. These robots have limited mobility, limited vision, and some speech capability. Currently, they are used mostly as toys. Improvement in speech and vision recognition should enhance the usefulness of these robots.

Robots have some unique advantages compared with human in the workplace:

- They do not fall in love.
- They never ask for a raise.
- They do not ask for a room with a window.
- They are not moody.

- They are consistent.
- They do not take coffee or meal breaks.
- They do not argue with the boss.
- They do not join unions.
- They cannot be hurt emotionally.
- They do not become insulted.
- They can be used in environments that are hazardous to humans, such as the spray painting of autos or radioactive work.
- They do not spy for your competitors.

Developments in AI-related fields such as expert systems, natural language processing, vision, and hearing will have a definite effect on future developments in the robotics industry.

1-8-4 NEURAL NETWORKS

Neural computing or neural networks is one of the new multidisciplinary research fields that has grown because of the study of the brain and its potential for solving ill-structured business problems. Neural networks are capable of performing tasks that conventional computers find hard to do. Neural computing technology is also known as connectionism and parallel distributed processing. The reason for these names comes from the fact that a neural network connects a number of independent CPUs (central processing units) to perform a task. This is very similar to the human brain, which uses numerous neurons to perform a task. The computers that we come into contact with in our daily lives are based on the architecture developed by John Von Neuman.

Like expert systems, neural computing is used for poorly structured problems. Unlike expert systems, neural computing is not able to explain its solution. This is because neural computing uses "patterns" as opposed to "rules" used by expert systems. A neural network uses a large number of connected microprocessors and software that tackles a problem in a unified rather than a sequential manner. A neural network learns by doing various tasks. They achieve the learning process by creating a model based on its input and output. For example, in a loan application problem the input data are income, assets, number of dependents, job history, and residential status. The acceptance or rejection of the loan applications is the output data. By using many of these loan applications, the neural network establishes a pattern for an application to be approved or rejected. Other areas of applications for neural computing include characteristics of potential oil fields, diagnosing automobile engine problems, and the analysis of price and volume patterns in stock trading. Neural computing is suitable in applications in which data are fuzzy and uncertainty is involved.

To be precise, a neural network is the complex system of interconnected nerve cells that communicates, processes, and stores information in all animals. While natural neural networks form the conceptual basis for the current flurry of research into this subcategory of the broad field of artificial intelligence, it is artificial neural networks (ANNs) that are the real focus of this attention. Indeed, while the natural neural network is composed of the brain as well as the skeletal nervous system, current research in artificial neural networks seems to have focused completely on imitating brain functions.

Artificial neural networks are an attempt to imitate the structure and function of a natural neural network in computer hardware and software. Many authors equate neural networks with "neural computers" on the basis of their apparent belief that special purpose computers (typically multiprocessor-based) are required to implement neural networks. To others neural networks are a form of logical information processing architecture that can be implemented on any computer. For practical, real-world applications, the business requirements will dictate the processing speed. This is necessary to accomplish the desired task (such as detecting explosives in airport baggage or detecting the fingerprint of a particular suspect among millions of fingerprints stored in a database). This speed or throughput requirement will dictate the processing power needed to drive the network hardware and software. Any computer that can provide the necessary power can be considered a candidate for implementing the neural network. By applying this description we can say that massive parallel processor computers are a reasonable candidate for the implementation of neural computing [2]. We will discuss neural networks in detail in Chapter 20.

1-8-5 FUZZY LOGIC

Have you ever been given a questionnaire that asks ambiguous questions and then expects you to give a straightforward yes or no response? Did you wish that you could use words such as "usually," "often," "sometimes," "it depends," "probably," "only if," or "most likely"? You probably have had this feeling, but you still answered the questions with "yes" or "no" because you know that the survey could not be analyzed if only descriptive answers were given. The computers that the surveyor uses to analyze the questionnaire simply cannot deal with anything but clear-cut, black-and-white and yes-and-no answers. Today, this is no longer true; computers can analyze information to whatever degree of accuracy you wish. It is done with the help of fuzzy logic.

Earl Cox, one of the pioneers in fuzzy logic, states: "Boolean logic is to fuzzy logic as a light switch is to a dimmer switch." By using this analogy, the author demonstrates the essential differences between the traditional mind-set and the evolving phenomenon of fuzzy logic. Traditional logic categorizes everything as being "yes" or "no," "on"or "off," "1" or "0," "pass" or "fail." Fuzzy logic allows the computer to reason in a fashion that is similar to humans. Traditionally, a computer would analyze problems using straight forward AND, OR, and NOT functions, providing true or false or 0 or 1 answers from clearly defined inputs. With fuzzy logic, one can use approximations and vague data and yet produce clear, definable answers.

You should bear in mind that fuzzy logic can produce exact results. Fuzzy logic can deal with any degree of precision from input data, and it can react just as precisely in returning the results or processed information [3].

Fuzzy logic systems have been utilized in a variety of applications, including transportation, home appliances, risk management, robotics, financial management, forecasting, and database management systems. The outlook for fuzzy logic is very promising and we should see more applications of fuzzy logic in the near future. We will discuss fuzzy logic in detail in Chapter 19.

1-8-6 INTELLIGENT AGENTS

Intelligent agents are gaining in popularity as another application of artificial intelligence. Imagine yourself as a busy executive returning from a business trip and to find out there are more than 60 e-mail (electronic mail) messages waiting for you. What do you do with all these e-mail messages? Let's say you have time to go through seven of these messages now—what would be the seven most important e-mail messages that you should choose from these 60? An intelligent agent might come to your rescue. A sophisticated mail agent can prioritize all your e-mail messages and it can even respond to some of them while you are gone. It can sort your messages by date, name, or subject. The messages can also be sorted into different folders. Some mail agents can even call the user's pocket pager to alert her that a particular e-mail message has arrived.

So what is an intelligent agent? Different people define intelligent agents differently. For the purposes of this book we define an intelligent agent as combination of hardware and software that is capable of reasoning and that has rule-based capability. For example, in our e-mail example, the agent may delete a message if it was received before or after certain dates or if it was related to a specific topic or came from a particular source.

There are several categories of intelligent agents on the market. Some of the popular types are:

- Mail agents;
- World Wide Web navigation agents;
- Usenet and newsgroup agents;

- Business and economic agents;
- Shopping agents.

World Wide Web navigation agents allow the user to navigate through the vast resources available on the Internet, providing better results in finding information. These agents can quickly navigate the Internet and gather more consistent information. They can be search engines, site reminder, and personal surfing assistants. **Usenet and newsgroup agents** have features that are specific to newsgroups. They provide sorting and filtering functions. They can access specific groups and send and receive information. **Business and economic agents** have diverse applications. One of the most important tasks performed by these agents is to filter news from premium new providers. These agents allow users to receive customized news from the mainstream media without having to sift through all of the news stories generated each day [9]. **Shopping agents** are capable of doing comparison shopping and finding the best price for a specific item. One of the best-known shopping agents on the Internet is the Bargain Finder from Andersen Consulting. This agent performs price comparison shopping for compact disks.

1-9 DO COMPUTERS THINK?

The issue of computer "intelligence" has been around since the early 1950s. This is a controversial issue, and experts have different opinions. Computers play chess and can even win a game against a chess player, as in the famous match in April 1997 between the master chess player, Garry Kasparov, and the IBM chess program, Deep Blue 2. After several challenging matches, the IBM program was named the winner. The question remains the same: When a computer plays a chess game, is it thinking? When a computer plays a chess game, there is more intelligence involved than when it prints a paycheck. Is it really thinking? In our opinion, no. The algorithm, or road map, for thinking has been given to the computer. Because computers possess extensive memory and are extremely fast, they can play a chess game and win when facing a human player.

To make a computer a thinking machine, it must behave and simulate the human brain. To date, we have not been able to fully understand how the brain functions, let alone how to design a computer that operates similarly to the human brain.

AI research in both the United States and Japan has been steady. Billions of dollars are being spent on it throughout the world. The results of this research undoubtedly will assist us in designing more intelligent computers. The outcome of this research will improve the quality and effectiveness of robots, natural language processors, and expert systems.

1-10 WILL COMPUTERS REPLACE US?

This question is also difficult to answer. Certainly, computers have replaced many workers, mostly clerical, during the past 50 years. Robots have and will replace many workers on assembly lines. More and more corporations, such as AT&T, Ford, General Motors, and Chrysler, are using computer technologies in various stages of their operations to improve efficiency and effectiveness.

Word processing programs have almost made typewriter technology obsolete. Fax, voice mail, and electronic mail may soon take over a large portion of mail services. Teleshopping and Internet shopping may replace many of the traditional shopping arrangements. Automatic point-of-sale terminals and the UPC (universal product code) have eliminated certain clerical jobs by providing faster service with fewer employees.

In our opinion, for the foreseeable future, humans still will be the key players in all aspects of CBIS design and use. Programmers will be required to write most of the computer codes, analysts will be needed to design systems, and users will be needed to utilize and interpret the information provided by a CBIS.

1-11 THE IMPORTANCE OF CBISs

Information is the second most important resource (after the human element) in any organization. Timely and accurate information is a critical tool used by key decision makers to enhance their competitive position in the marketplace. This important resource enables a decision maker to manage the other crucial resources in the organization. Information is used to manage the four Ms of resources in the organization: manpower, machinery, materials, and money.

To manage each of these resources, a specific information system has evolved. A **personnel information system** (PIS) or human resource information system (HRIS) is designed to provide information to assist decisionmakers in the personnel department in carrying out their tasks in a more effective way.

A **logistic information system** (LIS) is designed to manage all the machinery and equipment in the organization. The logistic information system is a sophisticated, automated database that provides the decision maker with timely and accurate information, including the date of purchase, when a machine was last serviced, when it again needs service, its price, and when it should be replaced. Such a system can save money by providing timely information regarding the repair or replacement of a piece of equipment.

A **manufacturing information system** (MFIS) is primarily used by managers responsible for managing manufacturing resources. Its objective is to reduce the total manufacturing costs to the lowest level that is consistent with the company's desired level of service, while increasing the quality of products.

The goal of a **financial information system** (FIS) is to provide diverse financial information to finance executives in a timely manner. A FIS uses internal and external data, mathematical and statistical models, and a user-friendly interface to achieve this goal.

1-12 FUTURE OUTLOOK

By examining some of the important factors surrounding the design, implementation and utilization of a CBIS, it is possible to make some predictions. Although it is very difficult to provide a long-range projection, we can make a projection that should put us into the beginning of the 21st century. By that time, the status of the AI projects and the information superhighway will be clearer, and a more decisive trend for the future can be ascertained.

1. The cost of hardware and software will continue to decline. In other words, it will be cheaper to process one unit of information in the future than it is today. This should make CBISs a more affordable alternative to all organizations regardless of their size and financial status.

2. AI technology and its related fields will continue to grow. This enhancement will have a definite impact on CBISs. Further development in natural language processing should make CBISs easier to use for a typical user.

3. User awareness and computer literacy for typical CBIS users will improve. The basics of computers will be taught in the majority of elementary and grade schools.

4. Networking technology will improve. This means it will become easier to connect computers to each other and it will become faster to send one unit of information from one location to another. Issues of compatibility will become more manageable. This means that computers from different manufacturers will have an easier time communicating with one another than is now the case. The quality of communication will improve as voice, data, and images are integrated.

5. Microcomputers will continue to improve in power and quality. A majority of CBIS software will run on microcomputers without any significant problems. This trend should make CBISs more affordable, more maintainable, and more appealing to diverse organizations.

6. Fourth-generation languages will be improved and they should become more attractive to organizations of all sizes. Enhanced productivity by users employing these languages is already well documented in the literature. This positive trend will continue due to ease of use, less training for computer novices, faster application development, and the enhanced power of these languages. These factors will promote CBIS use by organizations of all sizes.

7. The information superhighway will become more acceptable. This will promote database access throughout the world and will place small and large organizations on the same footing regardless of their financial status.

8. Computer criminals will become more sophisticated and it will become more difficult to protect the privacy of ordinary citizens.

As a closing statement for this chapter, we believe that CBISs will become an integral part of computer applications and will grow in popularity. It would be rare to find an organization that is not using this powerful technology.

SUMMARY

This chapter reviewed the fundamentals of computer-based information systems. Different classes of such systems, including EDP, MISs, DSSs, EISs, GSSs, and GISs, were discussed. The chapter introduced artificial intelligence as a growing trend in the information systems field. Expert systems, natural language processing, robotics, neural networks, fuzzy logic, and intelligent agents are promising applications of AI technology. The chapter introduced a discussion of the importance of computer-based information systems in the business world. The chapter concluded with an outlook for future trends in the CBIS field.

REVIEW QUESTIONS

1. What is a CBIS? What are seven major components of a CBIS?
2. What are some examples of a CBIS?
3. What are four classes of computer-based information systems?
4. How is EDP different than a MIS?
5. How is a MIS different than a DSS?
6. If we introduce the three focal points—data, information, and decision—which system (EDP, MIS, DSS) emphasizes each focal point? Explain.
7. What is an EIS?
8. How is an EIS different than a DSS?
9. What are some of the technologies used by an EIS?
10. What are two unique characteristics of each of the four technologies: EDP, MIS, DSS, and EIS? What is a GSS? What are some of the applications of a GIS?
11. What is AI? Is AI a solid discipline or is it a concept? Discuss.
12. What are some of the successful applications within the AI discipline?
13. What should an AI computer do? How are these computers different than the traditional computers?
14. How do you define an expert system? Why are they called expert systems?

15. What are some of the applications of expert systems? What are some successful examples?

16. What is NLP? How is NLP different than traditional computer languages?

17. What are robots? Where would a robot be a good substitute for humans? What are neural networks? What are fuzzy logic systems? Intelligent agents?

18. Will computers really think? Discuss.

19. Will computers replace us? Discuss.

20. Why is a CBIS important?

21. What are the four Ms?

22. How will a CBIS manage the four Ms?

23. What are some CBIS applications in a university? In a bank? In a law firm? In a CPA firm?

24. Let us say you have been asked to establish a CBIS for the president of a state university. The main objective of this system is to monitor student enrollment. What are the seven components of this system as discussed in this chapter? What specific information will be generated by this system?

25. Why will a CBIS experience a life cycle that is similar to a product life cycle? What factors cause such a cycle?

26. What are some of the future trends in CBISs? It is a general belief that the cost of hardware and software will decline. Do you agree with this assessment? Discuss.

PROJECTS

1. Comshare corporation markets a system under the EIS name. Conduct research on this system. What are some of the specific tasks performed by this system? Who should be using this system?

2. By consulting MIS journals, research two of the commercial expert systems on the market. What are some of the unique applications of these systems? Who should be using this system?

3. There are several commercial natural languages on the market. Research two of these products. What are some of the unique advantages of these products compared to traditional high-level languages? What is performed by a natural language? Why are they called natural languages?

4. Research a commercial robot. What can a robot do that a human cannot? Why are the Japanese using so many robots in their assembly lines? Discuss.

5. Computers play chess. Is this an AI application? Can they beat a master chess player? Discuss.

6. Identify one example of EDP, MIS, and DSS in a typical college or university. What is the basis of your classification? What are the differences in these applications as far as the users are concerned?

7. Consult the city or the county in which you live and investigate various applications of a GIS. Who would benefit from these systems?

8. Lotus Development Corporation markets a successful GroupWare called Lotus Notes. Investigate the applications of this popular software.

KEY TERMS

Artificial intelligence, 19
Computer-based information system,
 4–11
Decision support system, 13–14
Electronic data processing, 12–13
Executive information system, 14–15
Expert system, 20–21
Financial information system, 28
Fuzzy logic, 24–25
Group support system, 17–18
Geographic information system,
 18–19

Intelligent agent, 25–26
Logistic information system, 27
Management information system, 13
Manufacturing information system, 27
Natural language processing, 21–22
Neural networks, 23–24
Personnel information system, 27
Robotics, 22–23
Semistructured decisions, 12
Structured decisions, 12
Unstructured decisions, 12

REFERENCES

[1] Anthony, R.N. (1965). Planning and control systems: A framework for analysis. Cambridge, MA: Harvard University Press.

[2] Azoff, E. M. (January/February 1995). Extracting meaning from neural network solution. *Neurove $ Journal*, 7–10.

[3] Barron, J. J. (April 1993). Putting fuzzy logic into focus. *BYTE,* 111–118.

[4] Bidgoli, H. (1997). *Modern information systems for managers.* San Diego: Academic Press.

[5] Bidgoli, H. (1989). *Decision support systems: Principles and practice.* Minneapolis: West Publishing Company.

[6] Bidgoli, H. (May/June 1995). Geographic information systems : A new strategic tool for the 90's & beyond. *Journal of Systems Management,* 24–28.

[7] Bidgoli, H. (July/August 1996). Group support systems: A new productivity tool for the 90's. *Journal of Systems Management,* 56–62.

[8] Hedberg, S. (April 1995). Where's AI hiding. *AI EXPERT,* 17–20.

[9] Indermaur, K. (March 1995). Baby steps. *BYTE,* 97–104.

[10] Minsky, M. (October 1994). Will Robots Inherit the Earth? *Scientific American,* 109–113.

[11] Rockart, J. F. and DeLong, D. W. (1988). Executive support systems: The emergence of top management computer use. Homewood, IL: Dow-Jones Irwin.

[12] Sviokla, J. J. (June 1990). An examination of the impact of expert systems on the firm: The case for XCON. *MIS Quarterly,* 127–140.

[13] Treadwell, W. A. (January/February 1995) Fuzzy set theory movement in the social sciences. *Public Administration Review,* Vol. 55, No. 1, 91–96.

[14] Wong, B. K. and Monaco, J. A. (1995). Expert systems applications: A review and analysis of the literature. *Information & Management* 29, 141–152.

Chapter 2

Hardware and Software Concepts

Learning Objectives

After studying this chapter, you should be able to:

- Discuss various types of input and output devices.
- Understand various types of memory devices.
- Describe operating systems for both micro and mainframe computers.
- Discuss various types of computers
- Define a computer program.
- Review different classes of software for microcomputers.
- Discuss different programming languages.

2-1 INTRODUCTION

This chapter discusses the different types of hardware and software commonly used in day-to-day operations. The chapter explains input, output, and memory devices. Computer classifications based on size, speed, and sophistication are also explained. The chapter introduces eleven classes of software for microcomputers and it concludes with a brief survey of some of the popular computer languages used with micro and mainframe computers.

2-2 INPUT DEVICES

Input devices send data and information to the computer. Throughout the years, input devices have been improved to make the data input task easier. Commonly used input devices today include a keyboard, mouse, trackball, touch screen, light pen, scanner, and data tablet. Earlier, the punch card and joystick were more prevalent [1,2,3,4,5,6,7].

2-2-1 KEYBOARD

Keyboards are the most widely used input device. Originally, keyboards were designed with a configuration very similar to that of a typewriter. In recent years, there have been several modifications. To make the user's task easier, most keyboards include control keys, arrow keys, function keys, and several special keys. Keyboards are capable of performing most computer input tasks. For some special tasks, however, a scanner or a mouse is faster and more accurate. Figure 2-1 shows an enhanced keyboard. As you can see, the enhanced keyboard includes 12 function keys across the top and it also includes a dedicated arrow movement key toward the lower right side.

2-2-2 TOUCH SCREEN

Touch screens, which work with menus, are actually a combination of several input devices. Some touch screens rely on light detection to determine which item from the menu has been selected; others are pressure sensitive. Touch screens may be easier to use than keyboards; however, in some cases they may not be as accurate because they can misread the chosen instruction.

2-2-3 LIGHT PEN

Light pens are similar to conventional pens and are connected to the terminal with a cable. They are particularly useful to engineers, draftsmen, and designers for graphic applications. When the pen is placed on a location on the screen, the data in this spot is sent to the system. The data can be characters, lines, or blocks. A light pen is easy to use, inexpensive, and accurate.

Figure 2-1 An enhanced keyboard. (Courtesy of International Business Machines Corporation. Unauthorized use not permitted.)

2-2-4 MOUSE

A **mouse** allows a rapid cursor movement. You move the mouse until the cursor is on the desired item; then you push a button to enter a command or an instruction. The cursor is a special character that indicates your position on the computer screen or acts as an indicator (pointer) to focus attention on a specific point on the monitor. With a graphical environment such as Microsoft Windows and IBM OS/2, the mouse has become the input device of choice. Commands and instructions can be sent to the computer using a mouse.

2-2-5 TRACKBALL

The **trackball** is another input device. The ball is kept in a stationary location, but it can be rolled in different directions by hand. When you roll the ball, a pointer or icon on a display monitor moves in a direction and distance similar to the rolling of the ball. The trackball is convenient because it occupies less space than a mouse, thereby giving you more room on your computer table. Trackballs are becoming more common in notebook and subnotebook computers because users take these computers everywhere, including planes and buses.

2-2-6 DATA TABLET

A **data tablet** consists of a small pad and a pen. Menus are presented on the tablet, and you make selections with the pen. Currently, the data tablet is most widely used in CAD (computer-aided design) and CAM (computer-aided manufacturing). In these applications, the user draws on the tablet with the pen rather than using a CRT or a light pen.

2-2-7 BAR CODE READER

Bar code readers are optical scanners that use laser light to read codes in bar form. These devices are very fast and accurate, and they have many applications in inventory systems, data entry, and tracking systems. They are used mostly with UPC (universal product code) systems in grocery stores.

2-2-8 OPTICAL CHARACTER READER

Optical character readers (OCRs) work on the same principle as optical scanners. Because the OCR must recognize special characters, uppercase and lowercase characters, and special spacing, using an OCR is more difficult than using a bar code reader. Nevertheless, OCR systems have achieved remarkable success and are steadily improving.

Magnetic ink character recognition (MICR) and optical mark recognition (OMR) are two other scanner methods. A MICR system reads characters printed with magnetic ink. MICR systems are used primarily by banks for reading the information on the bottom of checks. An OMR system is sometimes called "mark sensing" because the machine senses marks on a piece of paper. Multiple-choice and true/false tests often are graded by this type of device. Figure 2-2 illustrates some commonly used input devices.

2-3 OUTPUT DEVICES

Many **output devices** are available for both mainframe and microcomputers. The most common output devices are the **CRT** (cathode ray tube) or VDT (video display terminal) for soft copies and **printers** for hard copies. CRTs are either color or monochrome (one color) and some of them have graphics capabilities. Printers come in different sizes and shapes, and typically are either dot matrix or letter quality.

A dot-matrix printer forms letters or images with a group of dots. Although the print quality is not particularly high, the cost is relatively low. Although the quality of dot-matrix printers has been improving steadily, letter-quality, laser, ink jet, thermal, and electrostatic printers deliver a much higher quality of print; consequently, they are favored for business correspondence. Printer speeds vary from a few hundred to several thousand characters per minute. When selecting a printer, users should consider cost, quality, noise level, and speed.

Other output devices include plotters, for converting computer output to graphics, and voice synthesizers, for converting computer output to voice. Voice synthesization is gaining in popularity. For example, when you call telephone directory assistance, the number given to you may be produced by a computer. Voice output also is being used as a marketing device (to the concern of many). A computer can dial a long list of phone numbers and give a message. If the phone is busy, the computer makes a note and dials the number later. Voice output also is being used in grocery stores at the cash register station for repeating the price of items purchased. We will talk about voice input and output and other natural input/output devices in detail in Chapter 21. Figure 2-3 shows some typical output devices.

2-4 MEMORY DEVICES

Two types of memories are common to any computer: main memory and secondary memory. As the name suggests, the main memory of the computer is

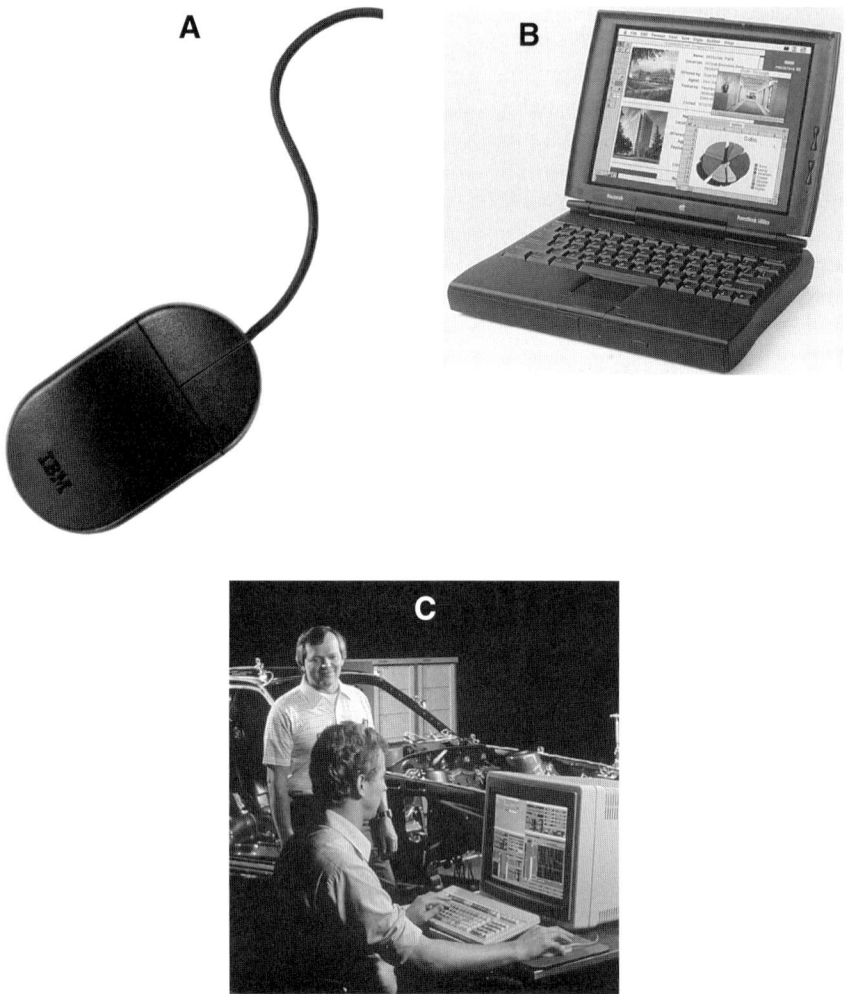

Figure 2-2   Commonly used input devices. (A) Mouse. (Courtesy of International Business Machines Corporation. Unauthorized use not permitted.) (B) Macintosh Powerbook 1400c. (Photography by John Greenleigh. Courtesy of Apple Computer, Inc.) (C) A computer-based signal acquisition and analysis system; (D) An industrial touch terminal; (E) Omnibook 2000 PC. [(C)–(E) courtesy of Hewlett-Packard Company.]

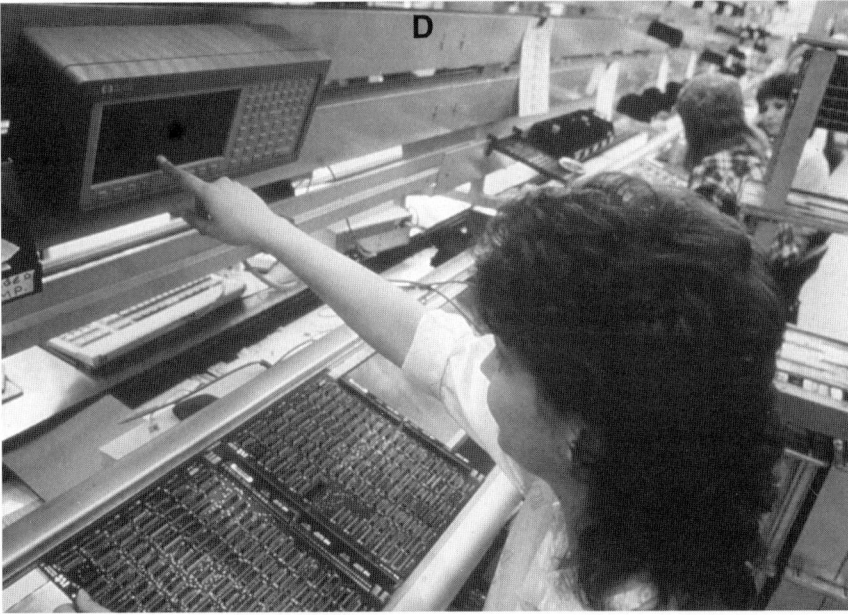

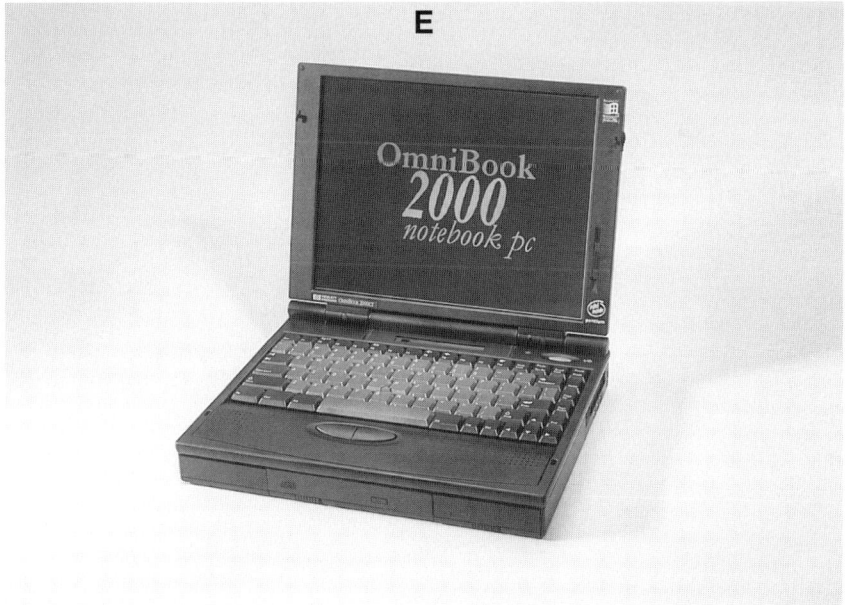

Figure 2-2 *(continued)*

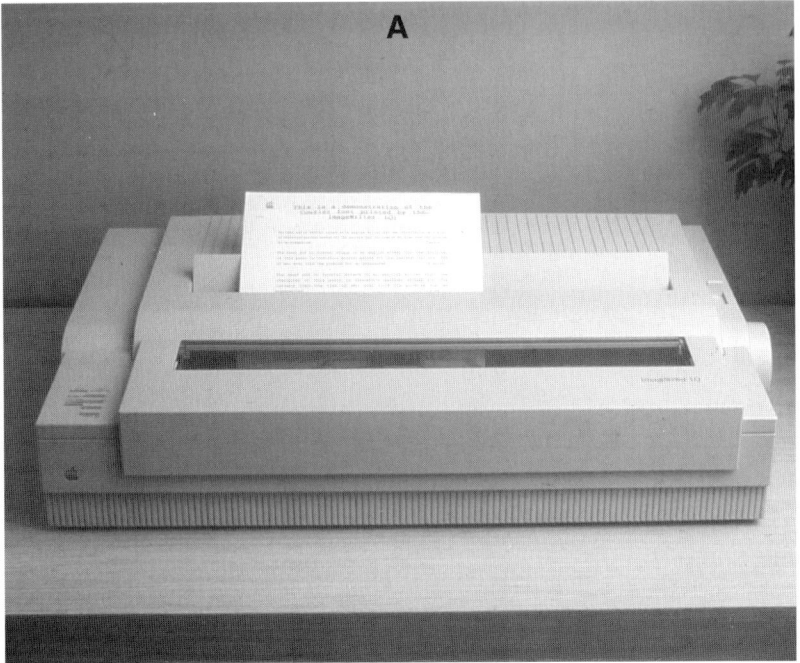

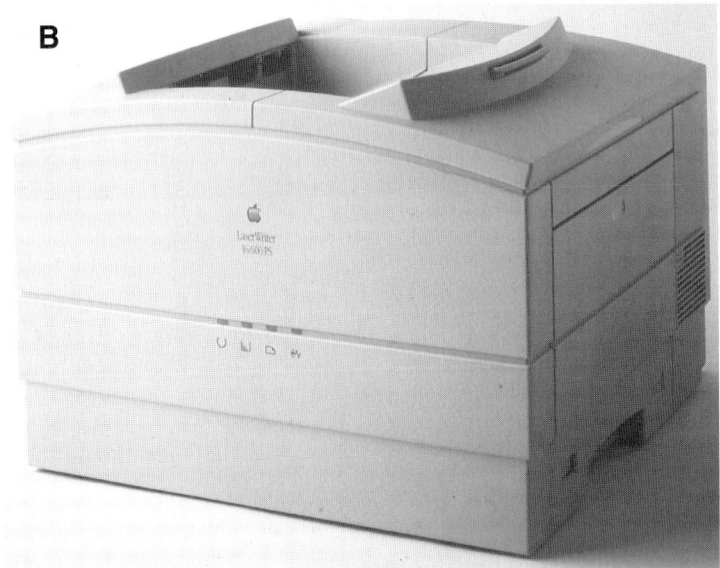

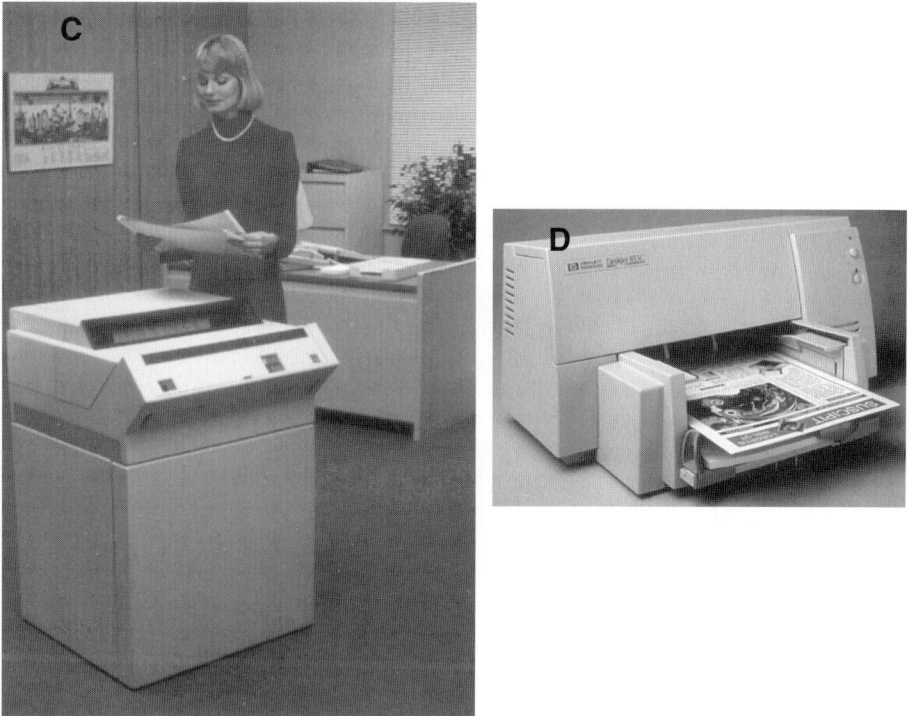

Figure 2-3 Typical output devices. (A) ImageWriter LQ Printer. (Photography by Will Mosgrove. Courtesy of Apple Computer, Inc.) (B) LaserWriter 16/600 (Photography by John Greenleigh. Courtesy of Apple Computer, Inc.) (C) Line printer (Courtesy of International Business Machines Corporation. Unauthorized use not permitted.) (D) Deskjet 855C printer; (E) Designjet 350 C large-format inkjet plotter; (F) Designjet 750C plotter; (G) Deskjet 400 printer; (H) 5000 series printers. These printers can produce from 100 to 210 printed pages per minute (ppm). [(D)–(H) courtesy of Hewlett-Packard Company.]

part of the central processing unit (CPU) ; it stores data and information. This memory is usually volatile, meaning it loses its contents when the electrical source is disconnected. Secondary memory, which is nonvolatile, serves mostly as an archival device.

2-4-1 MAIN MEMORY DEVICES

At present, two types of main memory devices exist: semiconductor and bubble memory. Semiconductor memory chips are made of silicon. Silicon is found nat-

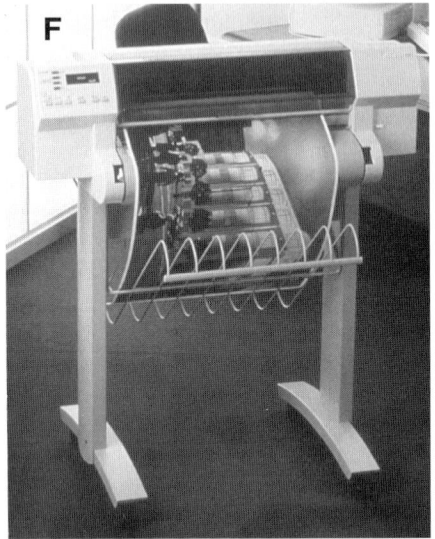

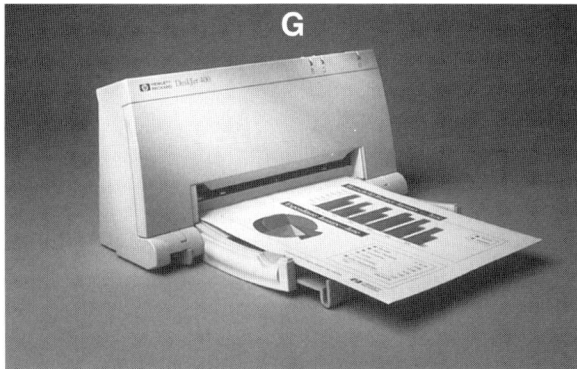

Figure 2-3   *(continued)*

urally in quartz; however, the silicon used for chips is manufactured synthetically. A **semiconductor memory** device can be either volatile or nonvolatile. When volatile, it is called random-access memory (RAM). A better name for RAM would be read-write memory. It means you can read from it and also write to it. When nonvolatile, it is called ROM (read-only memory). In ROM memory, you can only read from it; you cannot write to it.

Because silicon technology is not able to emit light and because it has speed limitations, computer designers have concentrated on gallium arsenide technology. Electrons move almost five times faster in gallium arsenide than they do in silicon. Devices made with this synthetic compound can emit light, withstand higher temperatures, and survive much higher doses of radiation than can silicon devices.

The major problems associated with gallium arsenide are the difficulties in mass production and in working with it. Gallium arsenide is soft and fragile compare to silicon; it breaks more easily during slicing and polishing. At present, because of high costs and difficulty of production, military systems are the major users of this technology. However, research continues to eliminate some of the shortcomings of this impressive technology.

Bubble memory is built on a thin crystalline film (mineral garment). By polarizing the bubbles, data is presented on this nonvolatile memory. The presence of a bubble represents a 1, and the absence of a bubble represents a 0. This kind of memory has 2 drawbacks: its high cost and its relatively low speed.

2-4-2 SECONDARY MEMORY DEVICES

Secondary memory devices are nonvolatile and are used for storing large volumes of data for long periods of time. There are three primary types of secondary memory devices: magnetic tape, magnetic disk, and optical disk.

Magnetic tape, which is made of plastic material, resembles a cassette tape. Data is stored sequentially on the tape. Records can be stored in a block or separately, and there is a gap between each record or each block. This space is called the inter-record gap (IRG). Magnetic tape usually is used to store historical data for back up purposes.

Magnetic disk is used for random-access processing. The disk is made of mylar or is a metallic platter. Magnetic disks are similar to a phonograph record in that data can be accessed in any order, regardless of the order on the surface. Compared with magnetic tape, a disk is much faster and more expensive.

Optical disks use laser beams, highly concentrated beams of light, to access and store data. This technology can store vast amounts of data and is durable. However, because optical technology is relatively new, it is expensive. Three types of optical storage have attracted much attention in recent years: CD-ROM, WORM, and erasable optical disk.

CD-ROM (compact disk read-only memory), as the name implies, is a read-only media. To record information, CD-ROM drives use disk-mastering machines. CD-ROM is similar to an audio compact disk. A CD-ROM disk can be duplicated and distributed throughout the organization. Its major application is for large permanent databases; for example, public domain databases such as libraries, real estate information, and corporate financial information. With multimedia applications (discussed in Chapter 16), CD-ROMs have become very popular. At the present time the majority of software vendors distribute their software products on CD-ROM. This technology is cheaper than floppy disks and it occupies less space and holds much more information than do floppy disks.

WORM (write once, read many) is also a permanent device. Information can be recorded once and cannot be altered. A major drawback compared to a CD-ROM is that you cannot duplicate a worm disk. Its major application is for storing information that must be kept permanently; for example, information related to annual reports, nuclear power plants, airports, and railroads.

An **erasable optical disk** is used when high-volume storage and updating are essential. The information can be recorded and erased repeatedly. Figure 2-4 illustrates an Apple Computer CD-ROM.

2-5 CLASSES OF COMPUTERS

Computers can be classified in several ways. Usually, computers are classified based on cost, memory size, speed, and sophistication (single-tasking versus multitasking). A single-tasking computer performs one task at a time; a multitasking computer performs several tasks at a time. Using these criteria, computers are classified into micro, mini, mainframe, and super computers. This means super computers are more expensive and faster, and they possess much more memory than do microcomputers, minis, or mainframes. This justification applies to other class of computers as well.

Applications for these computers include anything from homework (microcomputer) to space shuttle launches (super computer). Because the speed and sophistication of microcomputers are steadily increasing, it is difficult to draw a clear line between the different classes. A microcomputer of today has more power than a mainframe of the 1970s, and all indications suggest that this trend will continue.

2-6 DEFINING A COMPUTER PROGRAM

A computer program is a series of instructions. It tells a computer what specific steps must be taken to solve a problem.

Figure 2-4   Apple CD-ROM. (Photograph by Peter Fox. Courtesy Apple Computer, Inc.)

To write a computer program, you first must know what needs to be done, and then you must plan a method to accomplish it. You also must choose the proper language for the task. Many computer languages are available—the language you choose depends on the problem under consideration and the type of computer that you are using.

Regardless of the language used, the program that you write is called the source code. This source code must be translated into object code, that is, the code that the computer will be able to understand and use. The object code is always in 0s and 1s (the binary system).

A program that translates your program from source code to object code is called a compiler. If your source code is written in an assembly language (see Section 2-9), the translator is called an assembler. Some languages use interpreters, which are similar to compilers; however, interpreters are slower and less sophisticated. The major difference between a compiler and an interpreter is that a compiler offers the user a choice between executing or saving the object code version of a program; an interpreter does not. An interpreter converts a program to machine language and executes it statement by statement. It does not wait for the entire program to be entered. Interpreters usually are used when an interactive

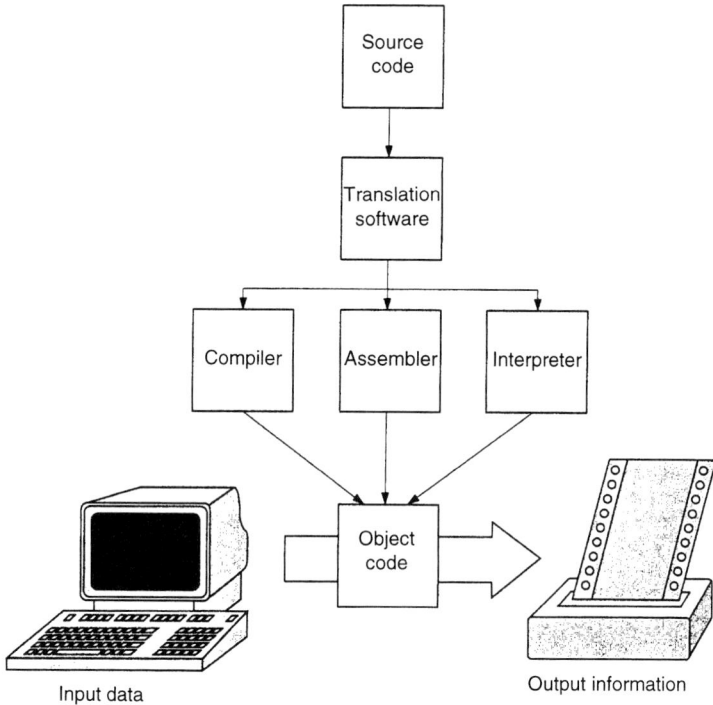

Figure 2-5   Program translation process.

process occurs between the user and the computer. In this a case, the user receives immediate feedback. Figure 2-5 illustrates the program translation process.

The following is a simple program written in BASIC (Beginner's All Purpose Symbolic Instruction Code):

```
10  A = 20
20  B = 30
30  C = A+B
40  PRINT C
50  END
```

In lines 10 and 20, values are assigned to two different addresses: A and B. In line 30, the values are added and the result is stored in a location (address) called C. An address is similar to an empty bucket and it holds one value at a time. A new value replaces the old one. Line 40 tells the computer to print the value in location C. Line 50 tells the computer that it has reached the end of the program.

2-7 OPERATING SYSTEMS

An **operating system** is a set of programs that controls and supervises computer hardware and software. An operating system provides an interface between a computer and its user. An operating system increases computer efficiency by helping users share computer resources and by performing repetitive tasks that otherwise would be performed by the users. A typical operating system consists of two sets of programs: control programs and supervisor programs.

Control programs manage the computer hardware and resources, including job management, resource allocation, data management, and data communication. Job (program) management controls different jobs performed by the CPU. It tells the CPU in which order jobs should be processed. The resource allocation function exercises a tight control over the existing computer resources. It tells the CPU, for example, which printer should be assigned to which job. The data management function controls the accuracy of the data. The communication function controls the transfer of data among different sections of the computer system.

The supervisor program, also known as the kernel, is responsible for controlling all the other programs within the operating system. These other programs include compilers, interpreters, assemblers, and utility programs for performing special tasks.

Many types of operating systems are available. In addition to single-tasking and multitasking systems, some are time-shared systems, meaning they allow several people to use the computer resources at the same time.

The majority of the operating systems for microcomputers, such as MS-DOS, Apple PRODOS, and Apple Macintosh, are single-tasking operating systems. However, OS/2, a newer operating system from IBM, and different versions of the UNIX and Microsoft Windows operating systems are designed to perform multitasking operations. Figure 2-6 summarizes the functions of an operating system.

2-8 APPLICATION SOFTWARE FOR MICROCOMPUTERS

A microcomputer can perform a variety of tasks by either using commercial software or software developed in-house. In-house developed software is usually more expensive than commercial software. However, in-house developed software is more customized and may better fit the users' needs. There are several thousand software packages available for PCs. For almost any task that you can think of, there is a software package on the market. The following are typical commercial packages and applications available for microcomputers.

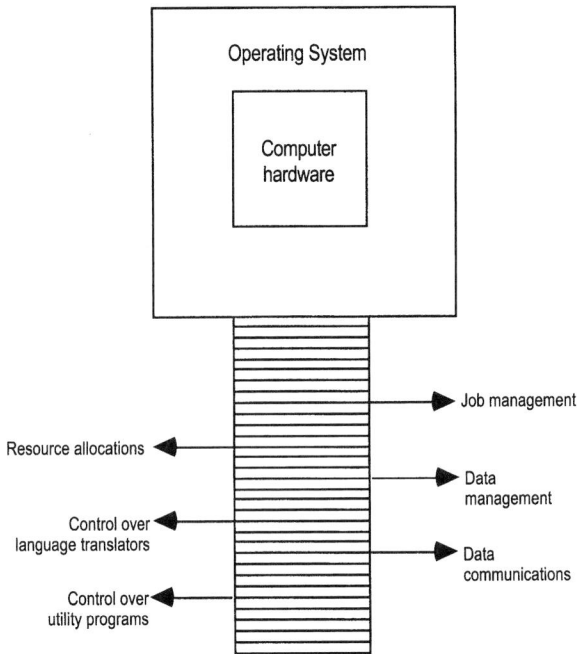

Figure 2-6   Different functions of an operating system.

2-8-1 WORD PROCESSING SOFTWARE

A microcomputer used as a word processor is similar to a typewriter with a memory. With such a facility, you can generate documents, reports, brochures, make deletions and insertions, and cut and past. Word processing programs are becoming more sophisticated. Some of these programs provide sophisticated graphics and data management features. Using word processing programs, hundreds of hours can be saved by not typing the same document repeatedly. Organizations often send the same letter to many of their customers. The only difference in these letters is the names and addresses of the customers. Word processing programs include a mail merge feature that allows and expedites mass mailing. The majority of word processors now include spelling checkers that are able to correct most of the misspelled words a document. The next challenge is to create documents that include correct verbs, subjects, adjectives, and a smooth style. Grammar checkers are able to correct grammatical errors. Also, the creation of simple, easy-to-read sentences is of prime importance. Grammar-checking software promotes good writing techniques.

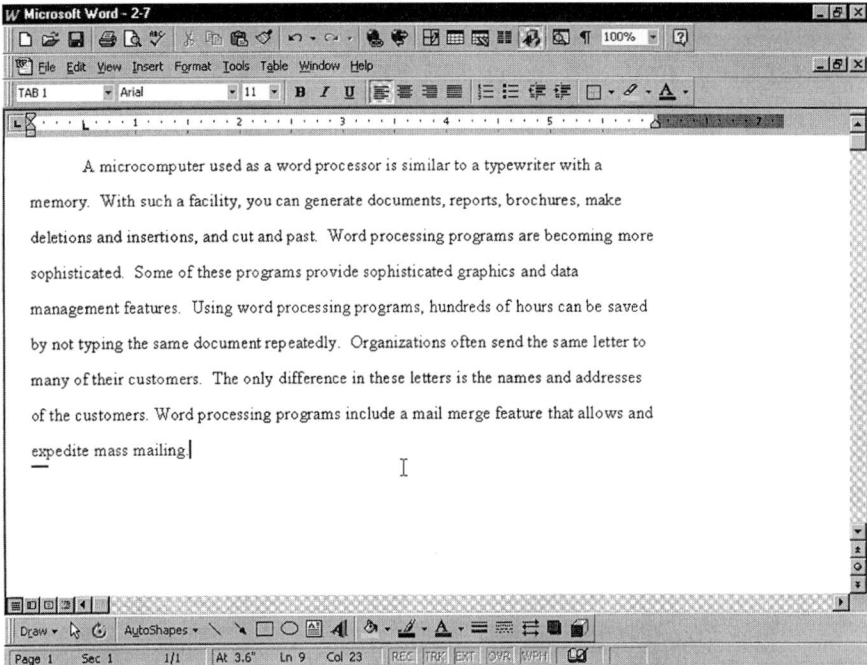

Figure 2-7 A Microsoft Word screen.

Grammar checkers perform text analyses by using linguistic analysis, parsing, and rule matching. Parsing, or simply breaking the long sentences into shorter ones, is done by using a parser. Grammar checkers play an especially important role when multiple authors are involved in a project. In such cases grammar-checking software creates uniformity of tone, reading level, style, and usage. Grammar checking software is not yet perfect, but it has come a long way.

Numerous word processing programs are on the market. Some of the popular ones are WordPerfect by Corel corporation, Word by Microsoft, and Word Pro by Lotus Development. Figure 2-7 illustrates a Microsoft Word screen.

2-8-2 SPREADSHEET SOFTWARE

A spreadsheet is a table of rows and columns. A typical spreadsheet software program is capable of performing numerous tasks. Excel by Microsoft Corporation, for example, is capable of performing spreadsheet functions as well as data-

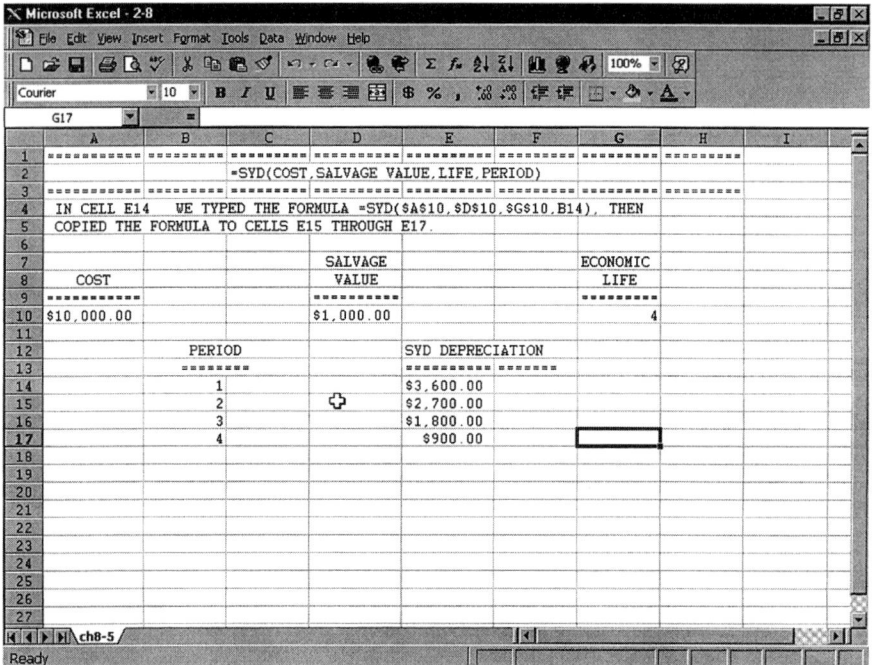

Figure 2-8   A Microsoft Excel screen.

base and graphics functions. Other popular spreadsheet packages include Lotus
1-2-3 by Lotus Development and Quattro Pro by Corel Corporation.

An unlimited number of tasks can be performed by a spreadsheet program.
Any application suitable for row and column analysis is a candidate for a typical
spreadsheet. For example, you may use a spreadsheet to prepare a budget. When
you are done with the budget you can perform some impressive "What-if" analysis. This means you can manipulate variables on the spreadsheet. For example,
reduce your income by 2% and direct the spreadsheet to calculate the effect of
this change on other items. Or you may want to see the effect of 2% reduction on
the interest rate on your house mortgage. Figure 2-8 shows a Microsoft Excel
spreadsheet.

2-8-3 DATABASE SOFTWARE

Database software is designed to perform database operations such as file
creation, deletion, modification, search, sort, merge, and join (combining two files

or tables based on a common key). A file is a collection of records, a record is a collection of fields, and a field is a collection of characters. Popular database programs for microcomputers include dBASE and Paradox by Borland International, FoxBASE+, FoxPro and Access by Microsoft, Q&A by Symantec, and R-Base by Microrim Corporation. High-end database software include Oracle by Oracle Corporation, Sybase by Sybase Corporation DB2 by IBM and Informix by Informix Corporation.

A database can also be compared to a table of rows and columns. The rows correspond to records and the columns correspond to the fields (attributes) within the record. Two common applications of a database software are to sort and search records. In sort operations the user enters a series of records in any order and then asks the database management program to sort the records in ascending or descending order, based on the data in the fields. Search operations are even more interesting. You can search for data items that meet certain criteria. For example, you can search for all MIS students who have GPAs greater than 3.60 and are under 20 years of age. Some database management systems (such as Q&A) allow you to search for key words within a text file. This type of application is common when you perform a literature search. Figure 2-9 shows a Microsoft Access database.

2-8-4 GRAPHICS SOFTWARE

Graphics software is designed to present data in graphic format. Data can be converted into a line graph to show a trend, to a pie chart to highlight the components of a data item, and to other types of graphs for various analyses. Masses of data can be converted to a graph and, in an instant, the user can discover the general pattern of the data. Graphs can easily highlight patterns and the correlation among data items. They also make data presentation a more manageable job. Graphics are done either by integrated packages such as Excel, Lotus 1-2-3, or Quattro Pro, or by dedicated graphics packages. Three popular graphics packages include Harvard Graphics by Software Publishing Corporation; Freelance by Lotus Development, and PowerPoint by Microsoft. Figure 2-10 shows a graph generated by Microsoft Excel.

2-8-5 COMMUNICATIONS SOFTWARE

By using a modem and communications software, your microcomputer can easily connect you to a wealth of information that is available in public and private databases. Several executives can simultaneously work on the same report in several different states or countries by using communications software. The report

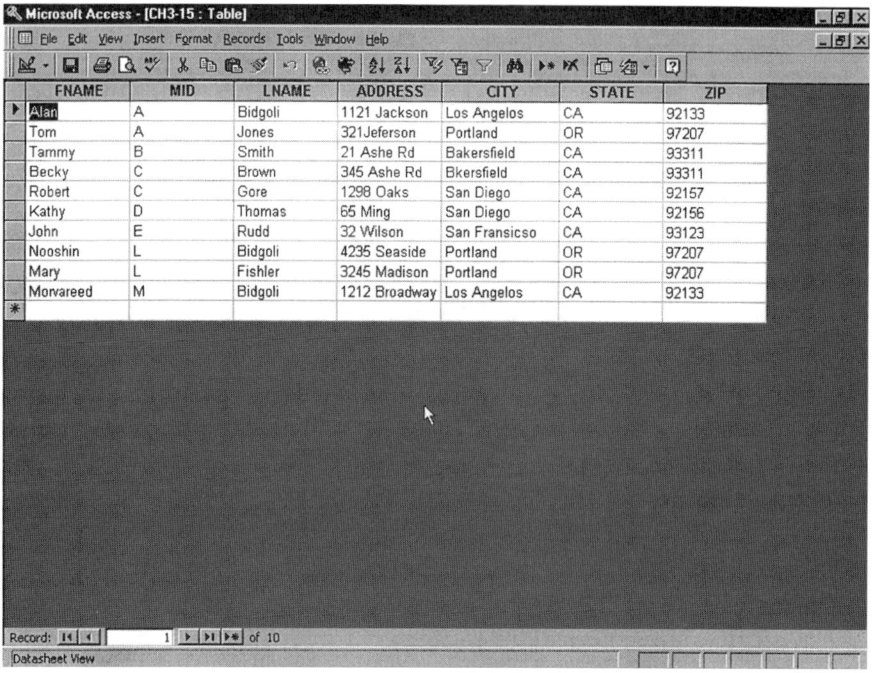
Microsoft Access - [CH3-15 : Table]
File Edit View Insert Format Records Tools Window Help
FNAME MID LNAME ADDRESS CITY STATE ZIP
Alan A Bidgoli 1121 Jackson Los Angelos CA 92133
Tom A Jones 321Jeferson Portland OR 97207
Tammy B Smith 21 Ashe Rd Bakersfield CA 93311
Becky C Brown 345 Ashe Rd Bkersfield CA 93311
Robert C Gore 1298 Oaks San Diego CA 92157
Kathy D Thomas 65 Ming San Diego CA 92156
John E Rudd 32 Wilson San Fransicso CA 93123
Nooshin L Bidgoli 4235 Seaside Portland OR 97207
Mary L Fishler 3245 Madison Portland OR 97207
Morvareed M Bidgoli 1212 Broadway Los Angelos CA 92133
Record: 1 of 10
Datasheet View

Figure 2-9 A Microsoft Access screen.

is sent back and forth to each location until it is completed. By using communications software and a modem, remote job entry becomes an easy task. A modem is used to convert computer signals (digital signals) to signals that are transferable on a telephone line (analog signals). There are many communications software products on the market, including Crosstalk by Microstuf, Inc., On-Line by Micro-Systems Software, Inc., and Smartcom by Hayes Microcomputer Products, Inc. We will discuss data communications in detail in Chapter 5.

2-8-6 Desktop Publishing Software

Desktop publishing is used to produce professional-quality documents (with or without graphics) using relatively inexpensive hardware and software. All that is needed is a PC, a desktop publishing software package, and a laser or letter quality printer. Desktop publishing has evolved as a result of three major factors: (1) inexpensive PCs; (2) inexpensive laser printers; and (3) sophisticated and easy-to-use desktop publishing software.

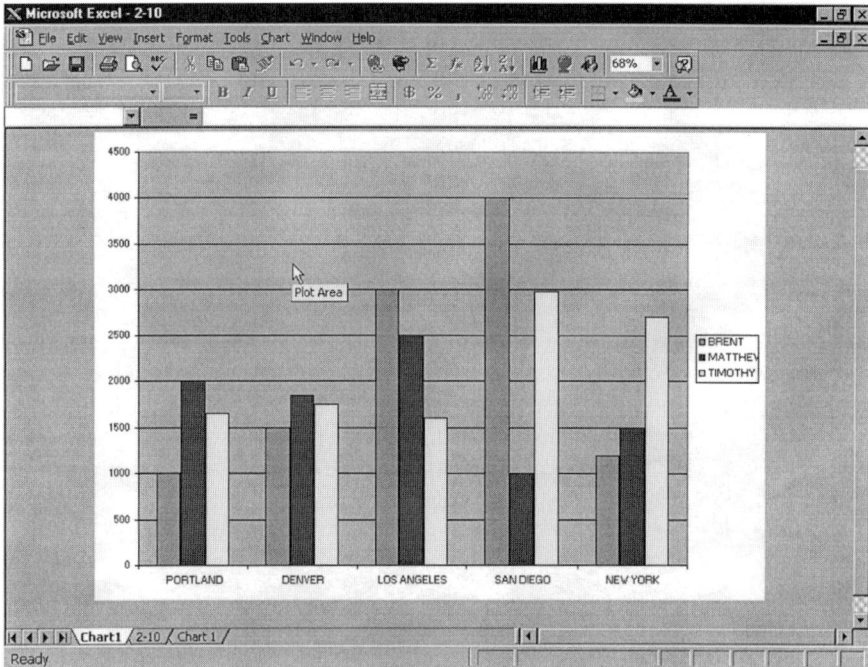

Figure 2-10   A graph generated by Microsoft Excel.

Desktop publishing enables a user to produce high-quality screen output and then transfer it to the printer, using the "what you see is what you get" or WYSIWYG concept. Major applications of desktop publishing include creating newsletters, brochures, training manuals, transparencies, posters, and books. There are several desktop publishing software packages available on the market. PageMaker by Aldus and Ventura Publisher by Xerox Corporation are two popular ones. Recent versions of Word, WordPerfect, and Word Pro also include the basic desktop publishing features.

2-8-7 FINANCIAL PLANNING SOFTWARE

Financial planning software works with large amounts of data and performs diverse financial analyses. These analyses include present value, future value, rate of return, cash flow analyses, depreciation analyses, retirement planning, and budgeting analyses. There are several packages for financial planning on the market. Among them is Javelin by Javelin Software, and Quicken by Intuit, Inc.

By using these packages you can plan and analyze your financial situation. For example, you will know how much your $2000 IRA will be worth at 7% interest in 30 years and you can discount all future cash flows into today's dollars. You will know how much you have to deposit in the bank in order to have $150,000 in 18 years for your child's education.

2-8-8 ACCOUNTING SOFTWARE

Besides spreadsheet software that has widespread applications in the accounting field, there are dedicated accounting software programs that are able to perform numerous accounting tasks. The tasks performed by these software programs include general ledgers, accounts receivable, accounts payable, payrolls, balance sheets, and income statements. Depending on the price, these software programs vary in sophistication. Some of the popular accounting software packages include 4-in-1 Basic Accounting by Real World Corporation, Peachtree by Peachtree Software, Inc., and DacEasy Accounting by Dac Software, Inc.

2-8-9 PROJECT MANAGEMENT SOFTWARE

A project consists of a series of related activities. Building a house, designing an order entry system, or writing a thesis are examples of projects. The goal of project management software is to help project managers keep time and the budget under control by resolving scheduling problems. Project management software helps managers to plan and set achievable goals. Project management software highlights the bottlenecks and the relationships among different activities. These software programs allow the user to study the cost and the time and resource impact of any change in the schedule. There are several project management software packages on the market, including Harvard Total Project Manager by Software Publishing Corporation, Micro Planner by Micro Planning International, and Microsoft Project by Microsoft.

2-8-10 COMPUTER-AIDED DESIGN (CAD) SOFTWARE

CAD software is used for drafting and design. CAD has replaced the traditional tools of drafting and design such as the T-square, triangle, paper, and pencil. It is used extensively in the architectural and engineering industries. CAD software no longer belongs just to large corporations. With powerful PCs and significant price reductions, small companies and individuals can afford this software.

New PCs with their enhanced power and sophistication are able to take advantage of the majority of features offered by CAD programs. The home use of CAD software may include diverse architectural and engineering applications. There are several CAD programs on the market. AutoCAD by Autodesk, Cadkey by Cadkey, and VersaCAD by VersaCAD are some examples.

2-8-11 OTHER POPULAR SOFTWARE FOR MICROCOMPUTERS

In addition to the first 10 groups of software, there is other commonly used software for microcomputers. Let us briefly introduce this software.

2-8-11-1 Utility Software

These programs or utilities provide various disk operating system (DOS) operations. Their goal is to simplify DOS operations for PC users. Depending on the sophistication of the program they offer various tasks, including hard disk management, recovering a damaged disk or file, menu design, condensing data, and so forth. In recent years vendors have begun offering Windows utilities as well.

2-8-11-2 Terminate and Stay Resident (TSR) Software

These programs are loaded when you start your computer and stay in the background while other software applications are being used. A "hot-key" combination instantly recalls the TSR to the screen so that you can use it. These programs offer various features including screen printing, calendar, memo pad and online calculator functions.

2-8-11-3 Tax Preparation Software

Tax software helps a PC user prepare her tax return in a fairly straightforward manner. Some of these software packages enable the user to electronically transmit the prepared tax forms to the taxing authority. Others provide advice regarding various tax-saving alternatives.

2-9 COMPUTER LANGUAGES

Computer languages have developed through four generations, and soon the fifth generation will appear in the marketplace.

The first generation of computer language is called **machine language.** Machine language consists of a series of 0s and 1s that represent data or instructions.

Machine language, as the name indicates, is machine dependent—a code written for one computer will not work on another computer. It is a time-consuming process to write a machine language program.

The second generation of computer language is called **assembly language.** Assembly language is a higher level language than is machine language, but it is also machine dependent. It uses a series of short codes, or mnemonics, to present data or instructions. Compared with machine language, it is easier to write programs in assembly language. Some of the commands used by a typical assembly language may include ADD, SUBTRACT, and LDA (load register A, meaning store a value in a location called A).

The third generation of computer languages are machine *independent* and are called **high-level languages.** Many high-level languages are available, and each is designed with a unique objective. For example, COBOL is used mostly for business data processing, and FORTRAN is used for scientific applications. High-level languages are more English-like, are mostly self-documenting, and are easier to learn and code than were earlier generations. Self-documenting means that codes written in these languages are pretty much understandable as you read them and usually do not need additional documentation to explain them. A strict format must be followed to successfully implement a program written in these languages.

The **fourth-generation languages,** or 4GLs as they are known, are the easiest computer languages on the marketplace from a user's point of view. These languages are user-friendly, and the commands are powerful and easy to learn, particularly for people with minimal computer training. Sometimes 4GLs are called nonprocedural languages. This means the user does not need to follow a rigorous format while using them.

The 4GLs use macro codes—codes that can take the place of several programming lines. For example, in a 4GL you might issue the PLOT command, which is a macro code. This command may take the place of 100 or more lines of a program in a high-level language. If you want to draw a fancy graph in a high-level language, you might have to write hundreds of lines of code. In a 4GL, one simple command will do the job for you. Many 4GLs are now available. IFPS Plus (interactive financial planning system), NOMAD, and FOCUS are some examples.

The fifth-generation languages, also called natural language processing (NLP), are the ideal computer languages for people with minimal computer training. These languages are designed to facilitate a free-form conversation between you and the computer. Just imagine if you could say to your computer, "What product generated the highest sales last year?" Your computer, equipped with a voice synthesizer, could respond, "Product X." CLOUT, INTELLECT, and Q&A are some examples of this type of language. Research continues to be steady in this area because of the already promising results. We will discuss natural language processing systems in detail in Chapter 21.

2-10 HIGH-LEVEL LANGUAGES

There are several hundred computer languages available. The reason for such diversity is the specific application of each language in a given discipline. Some are for business, some for science, and some for other specific uses. The following is a brief description of six of the most popular high-level languages.

2-10-1 FORTRAN

FORTRAN (FORmula TRANslator) was invented in 1954. It is the oldest procedural language. FORTRAN is generally used for scientific applications; however, recent versions have been used successfully for business applications as well. Because of its long history, many applications have been written in this language.

A FORTRAN program consists of a series of statements. A FORTRAN statement contains a key word, variable names, and a symbol. A key word is a command that tells the computer to do a certain task. READ, WRITE, and DO are examples of FORTRAN key words. Variable names are addresses or locations that store data. For example, in the statement

$$A = 20$$

A is a variable that contains the value 20. Symbols, such as + (addition), − (subtraction), * (multiplication), and / (division) are used for mathematical operations.

A FORTRAN program usually consists of executable and nonexecutable statements. Executable statements are either assignment, control, or input/output statements. Assignment statements, as the name indicates, assign a value to a variable. For example, the statement

$$A = 55$$

assigns the value 55 to variable A. Control, branch, or loop statements either change the normal operation of a program, such as to transfer the control from one location to another (the GOTO command), or they execute a certain portion of a program for a specific number of times (the DO and IF-THEN-ELSE commands.) Input/output statements control the input and output of data in the program. For example, READ sends information to the computer, and WRITE sends information out of the computer.

Nonexecutable statements are used for declaration purposes. For example, at the beginning of a FORTRAN program, you must declare your data types as integer, real, or character. Integer data are whole numbers, such as 59, 62, and 35. Real data uses decimal points, such as 299.65 and 1.57. Character data is a combination of digits and characters, such as Bob and 16ABC. The FORMAT command is another example of a nonexecutable statement. This command tells the computer how to print a line or how to read from an input medium such as a magnetic tape.

2-10-2 COBOL

COBOL (COmmon Business Oriented Language) has been in use since the early 1960s. It has gone through several variations, but now it is fairly standard and portable. Portability means that a program written for one computer will work on another computer with either no changes or with minimal modifications. COBOL is English-like and self-documenting. Programs written in COBOL are much easier to read than those written in FORTRAN. COBOL is more suitable for business data processing because of its character-handling and report-generating facilities.

A COBOL program is divided into four major parts, called divisions. The identification division includes the name of the program, name of the programmer, and the date. This section is useful for future reference and changes to the program. The environment division includes input/output (I/O) support. This division identifies the type of computer and I/O devices that were used to read and compile the program. The data division identifies record layouts for both input and output records. The exact formats of data are identified in this division. The procedure division tells the computer what operations must be performed.

Like to FORTRAN, COBOL includes commands for assignment, control, and I/O operation. For example, the statement

MOVE 30 to HOURLY-PAY

is an example of an assignment statement in COBOL. This statement assigns the value 30 to a variable called HOURLY-PAY. Commands such as IF and PERFORM are used for control operations. READ and WRITE are used for I/O operations. In COBOL, a statement consists of three parts: words, symbols, and phrases beginning with a COBOL word. There are three types of COBOL words:

- Reserved words, such as ADD, SUBTRACT, PERFORM, and MOVE, have special meaning to the COBOL compiler and cannot be used by the program as variable names.
- User-defined words are different variables and addresses created by a programmer. For example, STATE-TAX, HOURLY-PAY, and COMMISSION-RATE.
- System names are supplied by the manufacturer of a particular computer. For example, a code name for a particular card reader, tape drive, or a printer.

COBOL, aside from being wordy, is an ideal language for business data processing. It is not suitable for scientific applications.

2-10-3 BASIC

Since **BASIC** was invented in 1964 at Dartmouth College, it has gone through many revisions. The BASIC language is available for most computers regardless of their size or sophistication. BASIC has not targeted a specific application area. It was designed to be used in an interactive conversational mode, and it is useful for both scientific and business applications.

BASIC includes statements for assignment, control, and I/O operations. The assignment operation is done by the LET statement. For example, the statement

$$LET A = 55$$

assigns the value 55 to an address called A. The LET statement is not needed in the majority of BASIC versions: just A = 55 will do the job.

Control operations are performed by commands such as GOTO, IF-THEN, and FOR-NEXT. The GOTO statement is used to transfer control from one location to another. The IF-THEN statement is used for conditional transfer. In the statement

$$IF\ HOURS > 40\ THEN\ 100$$

if the number of hours worked is greater than 40, the computer performs line 100. The FOR-NEXT statement is used for performing a task a certain number of times. For example, the code

$$FOR\ X = 1\ TO\ 100$$
.
.
.
$$NEXT\ X$$

performs the tasks between the FOR and NEXT statements 100 times.

Input/output operations are done by the READ and PRINT commands. The READ statement either reads data from a data line or from a data file. The PRINT statement is used to display the output either to a CRT, printer, or to another file.

BASIC comes with many built-in functions. You can also define your own functions to perform a specific task. The most attractive feature of BASIC is its simplicity and ease of use. Its most serious drawbacks are lack of portability and structure. This means that there are many different versions of BASIC and only limited types of data can be handled by this language. Numbers and characters are the only types of data BASIC can handle.

2-10-4 PASCAL

PASCAL was named for Blaise Pascal, the French mathematician who was a pioneer in computer development history. PASCAL was first implemented in 1970. Ever since, it has been a widely used language, especially in the academic environment.

The major objective of PASCAL is to promote well-structured and readable programs. This language tries to eliminate or at least minimize the number of GOTO statements in a program. Programs with too many GOTO statements are difficult to debug.

PASCAL is a block-structured language. A block starts with BEGIN and ends with END. Data definition is accomplished with a VAR statement. In PASCAL, the programmer can define any type of data such as integer, real, and character.

Assignments are accomplished with the : = sign combination. For example,

$$A: = 23;$$

assigns the value 23 to variable A. The assignment statement must end with a semicolon (;).

Control statements in PASCAL use IF-THEN-ELSE, DO-WHILE, PER-FORM-UNTIL, and CASE commands. The CASE statement is equivalent to a series of IF-THEN-ELSE statements.

The I/O operations are done by the READ, READLN, WRITE, and WRITELN commands.

By use of rigorous data type declaration and the block structure features, PASCAL delivers readable and easy to understand programs. PASCAL is particularly suitable for microcomputer implementation because of its processing speeds and its reasonable memory requirements. Relatively poor character handling is its major drawback.

2-10-5 C

The **C** programming language was developed at Bell Laboratories by Dennis Ritchie in 1972. It enables a programmer to exercise substantial control over the computer hardware. It is English-like and includes an excellent data structure, which is the capability of defining any type of data such as integer, real, and character.

C was first used for developing system software such as the UNIX operating system. Recently it has been used for application development. Many of the application software described in Section 2-8 have been rewritten in C.

C includes diverse data types such as integer, character, and real that are similar to other languages discussed earlier. It has its own format for assignment statements, for example, Total = 10;. Each statement must end with a semi-colon (;).

C includes several commands for branching and looping. Among these are WHILE, DO WHILE, FOR, and SWITCH-CASE.

Input/output operations are done by using PRINTF (print format) for displaying the output and GETS for reading input data to the computer.

C is extremely portable, concise, and flexible. Understandably, it has become quite popular. Newer versions of C such as C++ and Visual C++ are becoming very popular.

2-10-6 JAVA

Traditionally, applications have run on personal computers utilizing complex operating systems requiring lots of memory and local storage. However, many tasks do not require high-powered PCs. This is where Java computing comes in. Java, developed by Sun Microsystems in 1995, is a user-friendly language that allows the writing of software applications that can run on many platforms. It was derived from C++, a popular object-oriented programming language. It is some-times called the Internet programming language. A platform is a combination of hardware and software that comprise the basic functionality of a computer. At present, the most popular platform is Wintel, for the combination of the Microsoft Windows operating system and Intel's microprocessor. Software developers who write programs in other programming languages have to write a different version of each program for different operating systems. This is not the case in Java.

Java is an applications development platform that replaces PCs with simple network computers equipped with little memory and that often have no hard drive. Java applications normally reside on a server and are delivered to the client as needed, which centralizes data storage and eases client-computer administration.

Java downloads nuggets of application code, known as applets, from server to client on demand, regardless of computer platform. Java accomplishes this by running on top of other platforms and by using generic codes, called bytecodes, which are not specific to any physical machine or platform. Bytecodes are instruc-tions written for the Java Virtual Machine. Programs written in the Java language can run anywhere a Java Virtual Machine is present, regardless of the underlying operating system.

Java applets are different than ordinary applications in that they reside on centralized servers. Applets are delivered over the network to the user on request. The dancing cartoon character, a voice clip that starts giving you vocal instruc-tions as soon as you click on it, and the bouncing balls are examples of applets developed by using Java. Many of the impressive animation and sound elements of today's Web sites would be impossible without Java.

For example, let's say that you want to check your bank account balance before transferring funds from savings to checking. After dialing in to your financial institution you would use your Web browser to log into the bank's system. The bank account balance information would be transmitted to you along with the Java applet required to view it. The bank system would also transmit an applet to electronically transfer funds between the two accounts. The applets are cached into your system as needed, eliminating the need for local storage. In a Java environment, memory-intensive applications requiring large amounts of local data manipulation and storage would still be run on PCs or Macintoshes.

At the beginning of the Internet development era, the Internet designers and Web masters started moving printed documents to the Web. Of course, these documents were not dynamic. These were plain text or graphics migrated from papers to the Web. Java changed all of this in a very short period.

So how does Java accomplish this multiplatform status? The programs that programmers write in Java can be understood by a universal platform, called the Java platform. This platform resides atop a computer's regular platform. This universal platform is an extra layer of software that has been accepted as a standard by most of the major players of the computer industry. The Java platform translates Java instructions into instructions that the platform underneath can understand. This is the major difference between Java and all the other languages discussed in this chapter. There is no compiler here.

There are several reasons for the Java's success. Cost of ownership is a major reason for the transition from traditional PC client machines to network computers. The total cost of owning a networked, Windows-based PC exceeds the total cost of owning a networked computer utilizing Java. All network and application management in Java computing is accomplished at the server rather than at each individual desktop. Software updates and upgrades, configuration assistance, technical troubleshooting, and user support are easier to provide in a Java environment.

Another reason for Java's success is its success in simplifying the creation and deployment of applications. Applications created in Java can run on any computing platform, thus saving the costs associated with developing software for multiple platforms. Also, because the applications are stored on centralized servers, there is no longer a need to have people insert disks or ship CDs to update a user's software.

A third reason for Java's success is that it is based on the same protocol as the World Wide Web (TCP/IP). Java is widely accepted and has attracted attention for its ability to tap the full potential of the Internet. As more internal networks are deployed using TCP/IP, Java usage will increase. By using these networks, known as intranets, Java solves the problems of information system incompatibility and user isolation. Intranets will be discussed in Chapter 8.

SUMMARY

This chapter reviewed the hardware and software components used in a typical computerized information system. A variety of input and output devices, including CRTs, printers, and plotters, were introduced. Different memory devices for both main and secondary storage were explained. Eleven groups of software for microcomputers were introduced. The chapter explored the criteria for computer classification and it briefly discussed operating systems. The chapter concluded with a discussion of computer software, including a survey of six of the most popular computer languages.

REVIEW QUESTIONS

1. What is the most popular input device? Why?
2. What is the difference between a keyboard and a typewriter?
3. What are some of the applications of a touch screen? A mouse?
4. What are some of the obstacles in using a voice recognition system as an input device?
5. What are some of the applications of data tablets?
6. What are the differences between main and secondary memory?
7. What are two types of main memories?
8. Which main memory device is volatile? Which one is nonvolatile?
9. What is a secondary memory made of?
10. What are some of the common examples of secondary storage devices?
11. In choosing a printer, what criteria should be considered?
12. How are computers classified?
13. What are the differences between a microcomputer and a mainframe?
15. Why is it difficult to draw a clear line between these computers?
16. What are some of the classes of computer languages? Which class is closest to the computer? To human language?
17. What are some examples of software for microcomputers?
18. What is an operating system? What are its functions?
19. What are some of the unique features of FORTRAN?
20. Why is COBOL most suitable for business data processing?
21. What are some of the limitations of BASIC?

22. What are some of the unique features of PASCAL? Of C?

23. Visit a computer lab. What kinds of input devices are available? What are some of the output devices?

24. Visit a local bank. Ask about the applications of the MICR device.

25. Ask your instructor or the lab supervisor to tell you how multiple-choice and true and false questions are graded. Besides speed, what are some other advantages of using computers to grade tests?

26. What is the fastest printer on your campus or in an organization in your area? What are some of the applications of high-speed printers?

27. What input device is typically used in a computerized grocery store? In a department store?

28. What types of secondary storage devices are available on your campus or an organization in your area? What device is used mostly by mainframe computers? By micros?

29. Using the classifications of computers presented in this chapter, what types of computers are available on your campus or in an organization that you are familiar with?

30. What operating system is used by the mainframe computer(s) on your campus or an organization in your area? What are the functions of an operating system?

31. What computer languages are taught on your campus or at the community college in your area? What language is the most popular for business majors? For engineering majors?

32. Ask your instructor or the computer lab supervisor to compare and contrast the computer languages introduced in this chapter.

33. Why has Java become so popular? What is the most important difference between Java and other programming languages discussed in this chapter?

PROJECTS

1. Visit a local bank and investigate the various input and output devices used. How are the checks processed? How is your credit limit checked?

2. By contacting the data processing department of the city or county in which you live, investigate various types of input and output devices in use. What are some of the applications of CAD programs for the city or county? What programming languages are in use?

3. Contact the library of a college or university in your area and investigate the applications of optical technologies. Why is CD-ROM becoming so popular?

4. Among the 11 classes of software for microcomputers introduced in this chapter, which one do you know? Why have spreadsheet programs become so popular? What are the applications of a database program in your personal life?

5. Natural language input and output devices have received a lot of attention in recent years. Investigate some of the applications of this growing technology. What are the strengths and limitation of this technology? What are some of the advantages of a voice activated VCR system? What are some of the disadvantages? Discuss

KEY TERMS

Assembly language, 56
Bar code, 36
BASIC, 59
Bubble memory, 43
C, 60–61
CD-ROM, 44–45
COBOL, 58–59
CRT, 37
Data tablet, 36
Erasable optical disk, 44
FORTRAN, 57–58
Fourth-generation language, 56
High-level language, 56
Input device, 34–37
Java, 61–62

Keyboard, 34–35
Light pen, 35
Machine language, 55–56
Magnetic disk, 43
Magnetic tape, 43
Mouse, 36
Operating system, 47
Optical character reader, 36–37
Optical disk, 43–44
Output device, 37
PASCAL, 60
Printer, 37
Semiconductor memory, 41, 43
Touch screen, 35
WORM optical disk, 44

REFERENCES

[1] Anonymous (February 1991). The changing world of input devices. *PC Novice,* 34–37.
[2] Bidgoli, H. (1997). *Modern Information Systems for Managers.* San Diego: Academic Press.
[3] Caudill, M. (April 1992). Kinder, gentler computing. *BYTE,* 135–150.
[4] Jacobson, B. (April 1992). The ultimate user interface. *BYTE,* 175–182.
[5] May, K. M. (October 1991). The next wave in AI. *Best's Review,* 118–127.
[6] Nigenbaum, P. (Winter 1994). Building flexible user interfaces. *Information Systems Management,* 62–67.
[7] Zarowin, S. (April 1995). Touchless typing. *Journal of Accountancy,* 63–65.

Chapter 3

Database Concepts

Learning Objectives

After studying this chapter, you should be able to:

- Define a database and database management systems.
- Discuss various types of data models.
- Elaborate on the importance of a database for the development of an effective information system.
- Discuss various methods for accessing files and databases.
- Explain SQL and QBE as two important methods for querying a database.
- Discuss new trends in database design including distributed database, client/server database, object-oriented database and database machines.

3-1 INTRODUCTION

This chapter provides an overview of database and database management systems (DBMSs). The types of data used in the information systems environment will be discussed and several views for database design will be provided. Data can be presented in different formats within a database. We refer to these varying formats as database models, and we briefly explain three models that are commonly used. The chapter discusses the importance of the data component of a database and various methods for accessing and querying a database. The chapter concludes this discussion by introducing new trends in the database environment, including distributed databases, client/sever databases object-oriented databases, and database machines. The discussion in this chapter should clearly highlight the importance of a comprehensive database for the successful design and implementation of an information system.

3-2 WHAT IS A DATABASE?

A database is simply a collection of relevant data. These relevant data can be stored in a central location or in multiple locations. Database and database designs are by no means new topics in the computer field. These topics have been discussed thoroughly by several authors [5,7]. In this chapter we would like to provide an overview of this important component of an information system along with guidelines and instructions for the design and implementation of a database in the information systems environment.

Databases have been utilized even in manual systems. A file cabinet is a good example of a database. Various information and data are stored using a series of drawers and manila folders. However, in this type of database, speed and accuracy are not high. In this chapter we are interested exclusively in computerized databases in order to satisfy the specific needs of an information system.

In computer terminology, a database is defined as a series of integrated files (although a database can include only a single file). A file is a series of related records, while a record is a series of related fields. This is called data hierarchy. Figure 3-1 illustrates data hierarchy. For example, in a university database a student's name, social security number, major, and age are examples of fields. All the information for Mary Smith constitutes the record for Mary Smith. All the records for all the students constitute the student file. The university database may include several files, including a student file, a staff file, and a faculty file. The collection of these files constitutes the university database. In a database environment all of these files are integrated. This means that information can be cross-referenced. For example, you should be able to retrieve all of the students who are enrolled in MIS 480 in Professor Thomas' section.

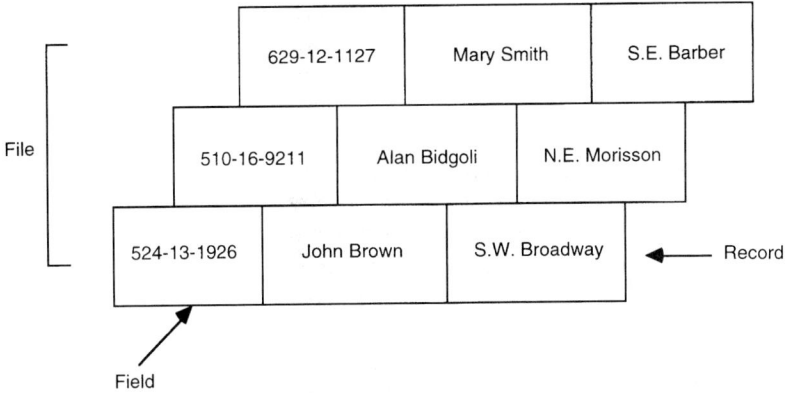

Figure 3-1 Data hierarchy.

A database is a critical component of any information system. As will be discussed in Chapter 13, a database is necessary to support modeling analysis as well as data analysis performed by any computer-based information system, including decision support systems.

A database is closely associated with database management systems (DBMS). A DBMS is a set of computer programs that create, store, maintain, and access database files. The features offered depend on the type and level of sophistication of the DBMS. Figure 3-2 illustrates the relationship of the user, DBMS, and database. For example, the user issues a request for a listing of all the MIS majors with a GPA greater than 3.6. The DBMS searches the database and provides a listing of the qualified candidates on a display terminal or in a printed format.

Traditionally, data have been stored in a series of files. These files or flat files can include redundant data. Redundancy in data can result in conflicting reports and it is also costly. The update procedure in a flat file environment can also be a time-consuming process.

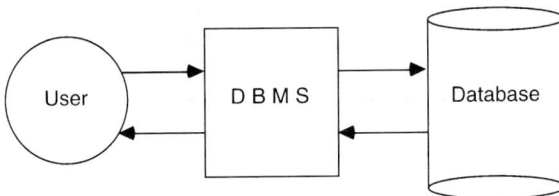

Figure 3-2 Relationship of user, DBMS, and database.

The database environment, compared to a flat file environment, offers a series of unique advantages:

- More information can be generated from the same sets of data.
- Ad hoc and one of a kind requests can be easily fulfilled.
- Data duplication is minimal.
- Programs and data are independent. This means that more than one program can use the same set of data.
- Data management is enhanced and improved.
- More sophisticated programming is affordable and feasible.
- Various data relationships can be presented and maintained easily.
- More sophisticated security measures can be implemented.
- Less space is needed for data maintenance.

As you will see, these features are very important in an information systems environment. One cannot establish an effective functional information system without having a comprehensive database in place.

3-3 TYPES OF DATA IN THE INFORMATION SYSTEMS ENVIRONMENT

To function as a support system for operational management, management control and strategic planning, an information system must have access to two types of data: internal and external.

Internal data, as the name implies, is generated and collected internally. This can be transaction data, which is usually supported by an accounting subsystem in an organization, or other types of data collected internally from other subsystems such as marketing, manufacturing, personnel, and finance. An accounting information system serves as the basis for other functional information systems in the organization by collecting and maintaining all the internal data. This may include payroll, accounts receivable, accounts payable, purchasing and receiving, fixed assets, and general ledgers.

An information system, if it is designed to support strategic planning, must also have access to data, which cannot be generated internally. These are external data and they may come from various sources. Table 3-1 summarizes these sources. These sources will play different roles in various information systems. The specific objective of an information system determines the sources of data to be considered in database design.

3-4 DATABASE DESIGN: AN OVERVIEW

In designing a database two views are recognized: the managerial view and the technical view.

Table 3-1

Sources for the External Data

Bank policies

Competitors

Consumer behaviors

Cultural change indicators

Customers

Distribution networks

Economic indicators (e.g. consumer price index, producer price index, and so forth.)

Government activities

Labor markets

Labor union activities

Money markets

Political climates and changes in these climates

Population trends

Suppliers

Tax structures

Technological breakthroughs

The **managerial view** of a database emphasizes issues concerning the user of a database and the way in which the user views the data. This view may also be concerned with the necessity and justification of establishing the database in the first place. From this perspective, the methods of collecting data and the types, sources, and nature of the data to be collected are important. This view also may emphasize issues such as the maintenance and storage of data within the database.

- Should data be aggregated (lump sum) or disaggregated (itemized)? For example, should the sales data for the last quarter in the northwest region be added to show a single number or should it be reported by sales territory, by product, and by salesperson?
- How should data be organized? For example, should it be organized by territory, product, or salesperson?
- How often should a database be updated? For example, how often should the suppliers' file with all the products that they offer be updated—monthly, quarterly, and so forth?
- What sources of data should be considered? For example, for external data should you consider government agencies, financial communities, or third party independent providers, or a combination of all of them?
- What method of data collection should be used? For example, should you use questionnaires, observations, or interviews?

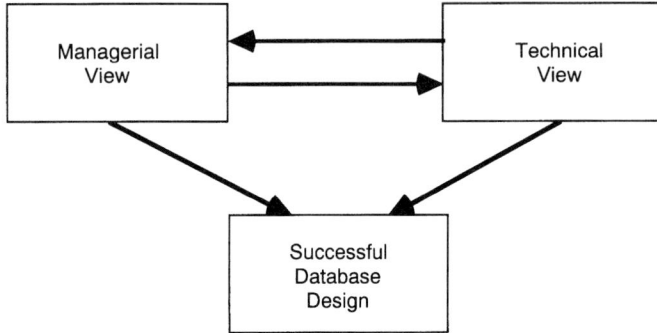

Figure 3-3   Two views in database design.

On the other hand, the **technical view** of a database is concerned with the technical issues associated with database design and maintenance. Some of the important issues in a technical view may be as follows:

- What type of access method must be implemented (on-line, batch, or both)?
- How can an effective security measure be implemented (passwords, encryption, or biometrics)? We discuss security measures and issues in detail in Chapter 6. For now, remember that encryption uses coding and decoding to protect the data from unauthorized access. Biometrics involves the use of a part of the human body in the security measure, such as a fingerprint or the retina of the human eye.
- How must backup and recovery procedures (in case of failure) be implemented?

For design and implementation of an effective database, both views are important and each must be carefully investigated. Figure 3-3 shows these views graphically. The database administrator (discussed in Section 3-8) should consider the views of both of these parties to be able to design an effective database.

3-5 DATABASE DESIGN: A FUNCTIONAL VIEW

The data in a manufacturing corporation usually comes from one of the four major functional areas:

- accounting and finance;
- manufacturing;
- marketing;
- personnel.

Table 3-2

Data in Major Functional Areas of a Manufacturing Business

Functional area	Data to be collected and maintained
Accounting and finance	Payroll
	Cost of raw materials
	Taxes
	Income and loss statements
	Balance sheets
	Cash flow
	Sources of funds
	Uses of funds
Manufacturing	Warehousing
	Transportation
	Purchasing
	Inventory
	Production
	Technology
	Legal environment
	Economy
Marketing	Consumer behavior
	Competitors
	Sales
	Promotional activities
	Advertising
Personnel	Wages and salaries
	Contracts
	Skills inventory
	Personal history
	Training
	Government regulations
	Affirmative action statistics

Table 3-2 highlights detailed data items that should be maintained in these individual databases. As you will learn in Chapter 11, each functional information system utilizes these specific data in order to provide timely, accurate, and relevant information for a perspective decision maker.

3-6 ISSUES RELATED TO THE DATA COMPONENT OF A DATABASE

Regardless of the sophistication of the database and DBMS, an information system may not be effective if the data contained in the database are not properly

Table 3-3

Possible Data Problems

Data are not correct.

Data are not timely.

Data are not measured properly.

Too much data are needed.

Needed data simply do not exist in the database.

---

gathered, organized, and stored. There are a series of issues known as "data problems," which must be carefully analyzed and resolved prior to the design of the database. These problems and issues are summarized in Table 3-3 [1]:

1. The data are not correct. This may be caused by entering inaccurate data (typing error) or data that were wrong initially. More rigorous collection, verification, and entry procedures may resolve this issue. In the old days of punch card machines, the verifier machine was used to double-check the accuracy of the data. However, if the wrong data have been collected in the first place, verification will not eliminate errors. Standard procedures must be carefully developed to ensure collection of the correct data. The sources of data must be identified, and their validity must also be verified.

2. The data are not timely. No matter how sophisticated an information system is, if it cannot generate timely information, its effectiveness will be jeopardized. Data collection and entry procedures and data validation methods must be monitored and periodically analyzed in order to assure timeliness of data.

3. The data are not measured properly. This problem is less serious than the ones mentioned earlier. Designers and users of information systems should be able to develop a system for measuring the data in order to meet the requirements of the information system. For example, if two tables are compared for sales analysis purposes, they must use the same scale.

4. Too much data are needed. Sometimes an information system may require a series of data values for a single variable in order to produce relevant information. A forecast of total sales based on the sales performance in previous years would highlight this potential problem. In another case, a model may include several variables for which the database does not include values. If the user and designer define the objectives of the information system, a comprehensive database should be able to resolve the first problem by maintaining adequate data related to all-important variables. The second problem may be resolved by using alternative models that require fewer variables. For example, choosing a multiple linear regression model that requires fewer variables than the original model.

5. Needed data simply do not exist in the database. This may be caused by improper definition of the objectives of an information system. A simple oversight of the user and designer of the system may be another cause for this problem. From an economic feasibility viewpoint, the benefits associated with data collection must outweigh the associated costs. In any event, the needed data must be identified, gathered, and stored for future use.

3-7 CONCEPTUAL DESIGN OF A DATABASE

After a general understanding of what a database is and different functional views of a database, we now discuss how a database is designed and we introduce different formats for storing data in the database.

First, a data model will be defined. A data model is a procedure for creating, representing, organizing, and maintaining data in a computer system. Usually a data model includes three components:

1. *Data structure.* This includes one or more data structures such as relations, hierarchies, or networks.
2. *Operations offered by a data model.* This includes a variety of operations such as database creation, update, and query.
3. *Integrity rules.* This feature defines the boundaries of a database. Examples include maximum and minimum for values, different constraints, and different types of access procedures.

Let us now define different data models in the information system environment.

3-7-1 THE RELATIONAL MODEL

A relational model uses a mathematical construct called a relation (table). A relation is simply a table of rows and columns of data. Rows are records (tuples) and columns are fields (attributes).

There are three major relational operators used in the majority of relational database management systems on the market. These are select, project, and join. Selecting means searching a table by eliminating rows (records) according to a criterion or a series of criteria. To make this discussion more clear, consider Table 3-4. Using the select operator we have generated a table that shows only the MIS majors. The criterion used here is "Major=MIS." Table 3-5 shows the results of the select operation on Table 3-4.

Projecting refers to paring down a table by eliminating columns (fields or attributes) according to a criterion or a series of criteria. By applying the project

Table 3-4

An Example of a Student Table

Name	Major	Age	GPA
Mary	MIS	25	4.00
Sue	CS	21	3.60
Debra	MGT	26	3.50
Bob	MKT	22	3.40
George	MIS	28	3.70

Table 3-5

The Results of the Select Operator on Table 3-4

Name	Major	Age	GPA
Mary	MIS	25	4.00
George	MIS	28	3.70

operator to Table 3-4 we have generated Table 3-6, which includes only the name, major, and GPA fields.

Joining means combining two tables based on a common field. By using the customer number we have combined (joined) Tables 3-7 and 3-8. The result is shown in Table 3-9.

The relational model is relatively straightforward. The creation and maintenance of this type of database is relatively easier to accomplish than with other data models. The addition and deletion of records are straightforward. Overall, relational models offer a great degree of flexibility. A major shortcoming of this model can be found in complex database operations such as in the areas of computer-aided design (CAD), computer-aided manufacturing (CAM), and computer-aided system (software) engineering (CASE). Substantial disk space may be required when many relations must be established and with the key included in all of these relations. Also, modification may be time-consuming. Compared with hierarchical and network models (discussed later), this model may impose limitation and complexity on the insertion of new records, and it may also be slow in complex operations. Overall, the relational model is easier to use and development time is shorter than other data models.

Table 3-6

**The Results of the Project Operator
on Table 3-4**

Name	Major	GPA
Mary	MIS	4.00
Sue	CS	3.60
Debra	MGT	3.50
Bob	MKT	3.40
George	MIS	3.70

Table 3-7

A Customer Table

Customer number	Name	Address
2000	ABC	Broadway
3000	XYZ	Jefferson
9000	TRY	Madison

Table 3-8

An Invoice Table

Invoice number	Customer number	Amount	Method of payment
111	2000	$2000.00	Cash
222	3000	$4000.00	Credit
333	3000	$1500.00	Cash
444	9000	$6400.00	Cash
555	9000	$7000.00	Credit

3-7-2 THE HIERARCHICAL MODEL

As in the relational model, a hierarchical data model is made up of records. Like the relational model, a record can have several fields. In this model relationships between records form a hierarchy or treelike structure. The records are called nodes, and the relationships between them are called branches. The node at

Table 3-9

Invoice and Customer Relations Are Joined by Using Customer Number

Invoice	Cust. no.	Amount	Method of payment	Name	Address
111	2000	$2000.00	Cash	ABC	Broadway
222	3000	$4000.00	Credit	XYZ	Jefferson
333	3000	$1500.00	Cash	XYZ	Jefferson
444	9000	$6400.00	Cash	TRY	Madison
555	9000	$7000.00	Credit	TRY	Madison

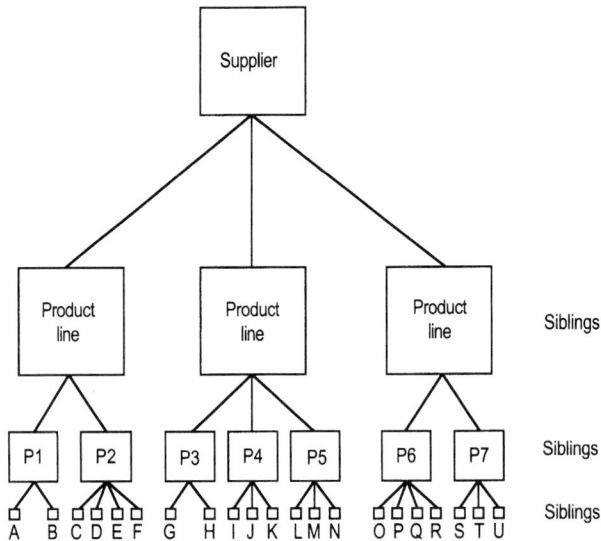

Figure 3-4   An example of the hierarchical model.

the top of the hierarchy is called the root. Every node of the tree except the root node has a parent. The nodes with the same parents are called twins or siblings. For example, P1 and P2 in Figure 3-4 are twins.

In the relational model, as discussed earlier, the connections among the tables (relations) are based on a common key field. In the hierarchical model records in various files are linked to records in other files by using pointers. Pointers are data stored by the computer system to establish links between records.

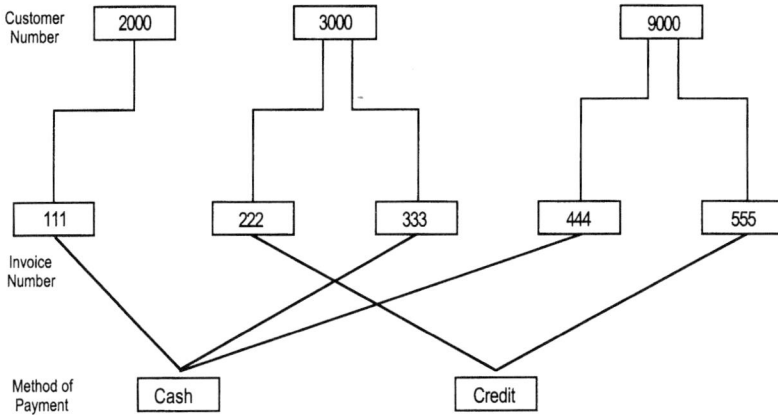

Figure 3-5 An example of a simple network model.

The hierarchical model is sometimes called an upside-down tree (a tree with its roots up). Any data element can be accessed by moving progressively downward from a root and along the branches of the tree until the desired record is reached. Figure 3-4 illustrates an example of a hierarchical model, which shows that a supplier may supply three different families of products. In each family, there may be several different product categories. As an example, Supplier X may provide soap, shampoo, and toothpaste. Within each product category there may be several brands of the same product such as 10 different shampoos or 5 different toothpastes. The node at the top is called the parent (supplier). The nodes at the bottom are called children.

This data model has a one-to-many relationship. This means that a parent can have many children; however, each child has only one parent. In the hierarchical model a search in the parent node can lead you to children nodes and vice versa. Any updating in a parent node should automatically update the children nodes. When compared with the relational data model, the hierarchical data model is less flexible. However, for certain applications this data model may be faster than a relational model.

3-7-3 THE NETWORK MODEL

The network model is very similar to the hierarchical model. However, the records and fields of a network model are organized differently. Figure 3-5 illustrates the customer and invoice relations in a network model.

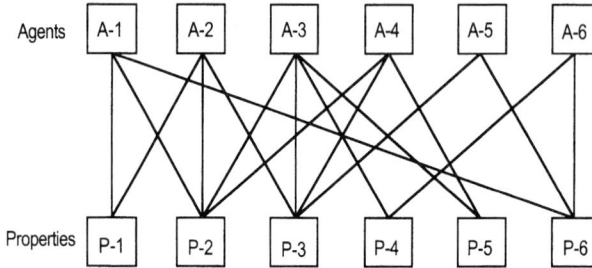

Figure 3-6   An example of a complex network model.

In place of related key fields, we see that there is a link between the invoice number, the customer number, and the method of payment. In this case the customer number no longer needs to remain in the invoice record. As Figure 3-5 illustrates, invoice numbers are linked to the header link in the same order in which they were entered (from Table 3-8).

The network model is not as flexible as the relational model. One can say that the network model is an enhanced version of the hierarchical model. In this data model the relationship can be either one-to-many (simple network) or many-to-many (complex network). Figure 3-5 illustrates a one-to-many relationship. Each parent (invoice) has two children (method of payment and customer number). Figure 3-6 illustrates a many-to-many relationship. In a real estate organization, each agent is selling several properties. For example, agent A-1 sells properties P-1, P-2, and P-6. At the same time, property P-1 has been listed under Agent A-1 and as well as Agent A-2. In a many-to-many relationship, the parent/child relationship breaks down. Which node is the parent and which node is the child becomes optional.

3-8 DATABASE ADMINISTRATOR

In large organizations, the design and implementation of a database is performed by an individual(s) called a database administrator (DBA). The scope of the responsibility of this person(s) depends on the complexity of the database. Some organizations, such as large banks, devote an entire office to database design and maintenance. In smaller organizations one individual may carry full responsibility for database design and maintenance. The following are some of the responsibilities of a DBA:

- Designing and implementing a database;
- Establishing security measures—who has access to what;
- Establishing the recovery procedures in case data is lost or corrupted;
- Documenting the database;
- Establishing database performance evaluation;
- Adding new database functions;
- Fine-tuning the existing database functions.

In the database environment, a database administrator and database administration are critical. Careful consideration is needed in order to establish an effective database administration office and a database administrator.

Establishing a database will increase costs and complexity in the operation. However, you should remember that the implementation of an effective information system requires a comprehensive database regardless of its costs and complexity.

3-9 METHODS FOR ACCESSING FILES AND DATABASES

In the database environment, files and databases are accessed by using one of the following methods: sequential, random, and indexed sequential. In a **sequential** file structure records are organized and processed sequentially. The storage medium used for sequential files is usually magnetic tape. Files are organized based on a key. Social security and account numbers are types of keys. For example, in order to access record number 10, all records before this one either must be read or skipped in order to reach this particular record. This type of access method is very effective when a large number of records are processed on a periodic basis.

In a **random** access file a record can be accessed in any order regardless of its physical location. These files are usually stored on magnetic disk. This method of access is very effective when a small number of records are processed on a regular basis.

By using the **indexed sequential access method** (ISAM) files can be accessed either sequentially or randomly. The random access method is used to process a small number of records, and for processing a large number of records the sequential access method is used. This file organization is similar to a card catalog system in a library. The card catalog tells you where a particular book is located. The index of this book is another example of this file organization. To find a specific topic you refer to the index, which provides the page number where the topic was introduced.

Table 3-10

An Example of SQL Query

SELECT NAME,SSN,TITLE,GENDER,SALARY
FROM EMPLOYEE, PAYROLL
WHERE EMPLOYEE.SSN=PARROLL.SSN AND TITLE="ENGINEER"

3-10 QUERYING A DATABASE

There are two popular methods used by the majority of popular database management systems to query a database: **structured query language (SQL)** and **query by example (QBE).** The basic format of an SQL query is:

SELECT . . . FROM . . . WHERE . . .

After SELECT, you list the fields that you want to retrieve. After FROM, you list the files or tables that the data must be retrieved from. After WHERE, you list one or more conditions. Table 3-10 illustrates an example of an SQL query. This query retrieves the name, social security number, job title, gender, and salary from the EMPLOYEE and PAROLL files for all the employees whose job title is "engineer."

Using query by example you request specific data from a database by constructing a query statement made of one or more query forms. In today's graphical databases this is achieved by the "point-and-click " technique. This is easier than using SQL where you have to remember specific commands. The conditional AND, OR, and NOT criteria can be added to the QBE form to enhance the capability of this query method. When using the AND operator, all of the conditions must be met (for example, a student who is MIS major, female, and with a GPA greater than 3.8). When using the OR operator, only one of the conditions must be met (for example, either MIS or ACCOUNTING majors). The NOT operator searches for the opposite condition (for example all the employees except the engineers). Figures 3-7 and 3-8 illustrate two examples of QBE by using Paradox for Windows. Under MAJOR in Figure 3-7 we entered ACC OR MGT (this means either accounting or management majors). Under AGE in Figure 3-8 we entered <25 (meaning students under 25 years of age) and under MAJOR we entered MIS (meaning management information systems majors).

3-11 NEW TRENDS IN DATABASE DESIGN AND UTILIZATION

In recent years several new trends have developed in database design and utilization. Natural language processing, distributed databases, client/server da-

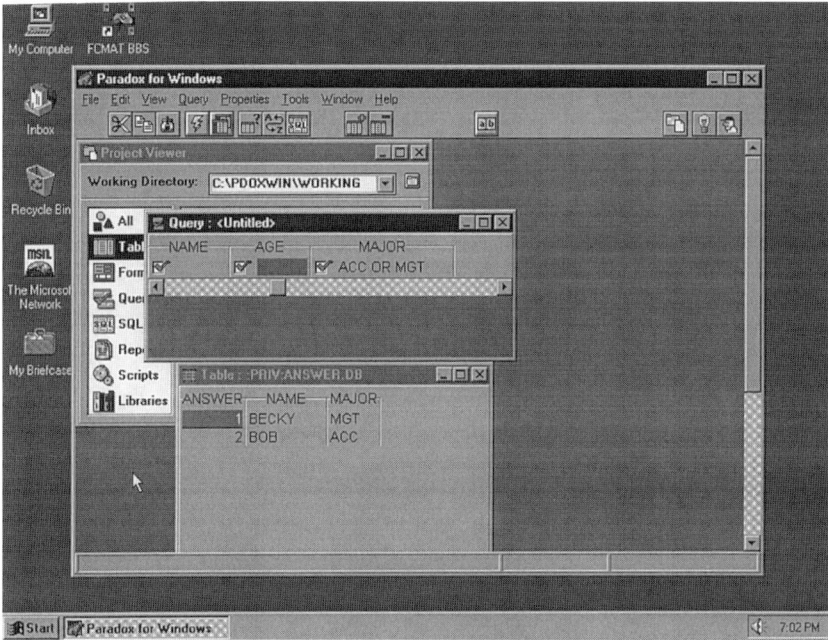

Figure 3-7   A listing of all students majoring in accounting or management.

tabases, object-oriented databases, and database machines are all part of these developments. Advances in artificial intelligence and natural language processing will have a definite impact on the design and utilization of databases [11]. AI technology should facilitate the construction of a database. Natural language processing should allow easier access for the information system's user by providing an interface that is more similar to the user's native language. Currently, these issues may be of limited practical importance; however, they may be quite significant in the near future, and this may have a direct impact on the design and utilization of information systems. We discussed natural language processing briefly in Chapter 1. A detail discussion of this topic will be given in Chapter 21. We will briefly explain these other new trends here.

3-11-1 DISTRIBUTED DATABASE

So far in our discussion, we have assumed a central database for all the users of an information system. However, a number of factors challenge this centralized operation of a database and prescribe one that is distributed throughout an orga-

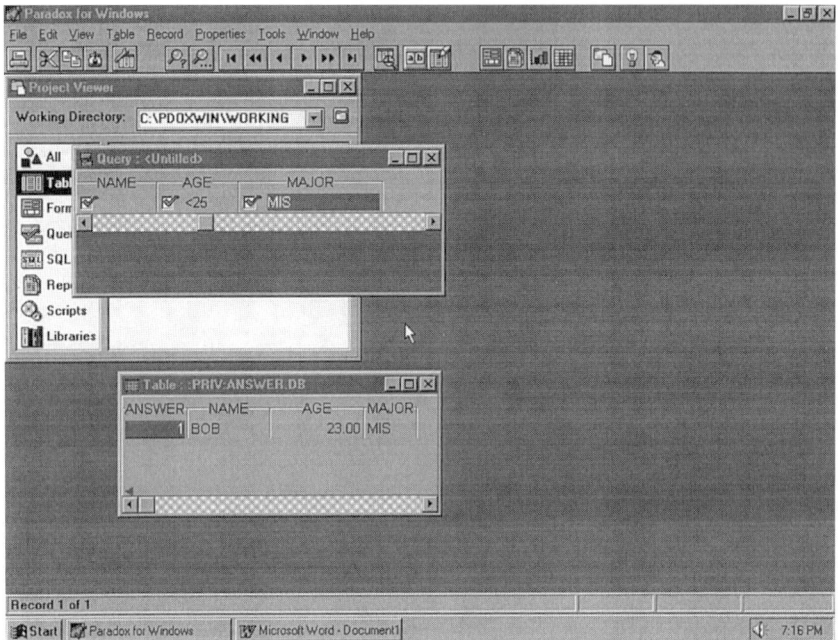

Figure 3-8   A listing of MIS majors who are under age 25.

nization. A distributed database is a collection of data distributed over different computers in a network. These factors include [2]:

• *Economic constraints.* For remote users of an information system (those users who are not located in the same place where the system is located) it may not be economically feasible to access the central database all the time. It may be more economical to store some of the data at the remote site(s). The manager of the remote site may have to spend a lot of money on communications costs in order to access the data from the central site.

• *Lack of responsiveness.* Centralized databases may not be responsive to the immediate needs of the users who are in the remote sites.

• *Enhanced sophistication in microcomputers.* The increasing sophistication and the decreasing cost of microcomputers has made distributed processing more feasible and the utilization of these computers a more viable option in a distributed environment.

• *Change in the data processing organizational structure.* Since the mid 1970s there has been a trend toward distributed processing, which certainly includes database design and implementation. Apparently, the responsiveness of this type of system is higher than a centralized system when considering the user's needs.

These issues advocate a distributed DBMS (DDBMS). In a distributed database the data are not resident at the same site where the user and the computer are located. There are three approaches for implementing distributed database systems. The degree to which these approaches are combined is a critical factor in determining the data communications requirement of any DDBMS. Each approach meets a different data communications requirement. These three approaches are fragmentation, replication, and allocation [2].

Fragmentation deals with how a table is broken up and divided among multiple locations. Horizontal fragmentation breaks a table into rows, storing all of the fields (columns) in different locations. How many rows will be stored in each location varies from organization to organization and from application to application. In vertical fragmentation a subset of columns is stored in different locations. Mixed fragmentation combines both vertical and horizontal fragmentation. By using this method only site-specific data is stored at each location. If data are needed from other sites, the DDBMS retrieves it by using communications systems.

Replication stores an exact copy of data at multiple sites. This method achieves maximum availability by providing the entire data to each site and can be used to provide backup copies for different sites. However, this method may be costly.

Allocation is a combination of fragmentation and replication. Records are stored at locations with the highest use of the data. This method maximizes local processing of data.

Ranch-Hindin [9] identifies some specific advantages for a distributed DBMS:

- The design reflects an organization's structure. For example, how data are distributed depends on the number of branches and offices of a particular organization.
- Local storage of data decreases response time and communications costs.
- Data distribution throughout multiple sites limits the effects of a computer breakdown to its point of occurrence.
- The size and number of users are not limited by one computer's size or its processing power.
- Multiple, integrated small systems might cost less than one large computer.
- Most important of all, a distributed database need not be constrained by the physical organization of data.

This type of database may follow one of the data models discussed earlier. Security issues are more challenging in a distributed environment due to multiple access points from both inside and outside of the organization. Security policies must be clearly defined and the authorized users must be identified. The scope of user access and access times must also be clearly defined. We will discuss security issues and measures in detail in Chapter 6.

The designer(s) of a database must bear in mind that not all applications are suitable for distributed processing. The designer must always ask the question, "Is it really needed?" A distributed database may be designed in several config- urations. Figure 3-9 illustrates one example of this type of database.

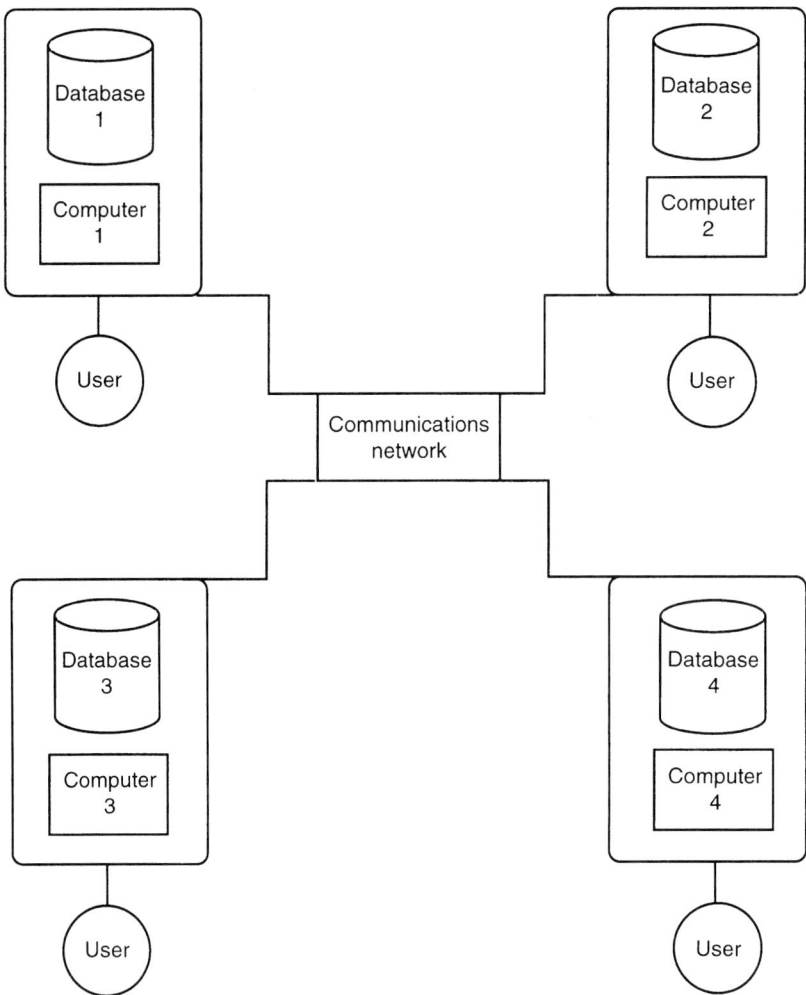

Figure 3-9   An example of a distributed database.

3-11-2 CLIENT/SERVER DATABASE

With the increase in the power and the reduction in the cost of microcomputers and workstations, client/server database processing has attracted a lot of attention in recent years. In this type of database processing the computers are linked together in a local area network in which several clients may share the services of a single server. A server is a software application that provides files and services to requesting clients. In this case the service will be data management functions. A client is an individual or a software application that requests services from one or more servers. The server application (the database server in Figure 3-10a) is located on a separate computer on the network [7].

A traditional LAN (Local Area Network) approach has been the file/server approach. In this architecture a central computer acts as an extended disk drive. In file/server architecture data may reside on the server for access by the individual user. When data are required, the entire file is transmitted over the LAN to the workstation to be processed at the local site. The file server does not perform any processing task. It simply sends the entire data set over the network to the requesting site. An example of this kind of data set is the entire student table in a university database.

In client/server architecture, specific requests are transmitted to the server, the server processes the request, and returns only those records that match the original request. An example is a listing of all MIS majors who speak Spanish and have a GPA greater that 3.8.

Client/server computing is rapidly becoming the essential part for enterprise-wide computing systems in a growing number of organizations. Figure 3-10 illustrates two architectures for client/server computing [7].

3-11-3 OBJECT-ORIENTED DATABASE

A relatively new type of data model called an object-oriented data model is gaining in popularity [4]. This is an extension of object-oriented programming. Conventional database management systems such as the relational model have been designed to deal with homogeneous data that are organized in fields and records. In today's multimedia environment this type of data model may not be as effective for certain applications. Object-oriented database models can manage numbers and characters as well as drawings, images, photographs, voice, and full-motion video. This may be an attractive application in medical fields where a doctor can access a database that contains a patient's medical history accompanied by X-rays, notes, and a graph of vital signs.

This model reduces the semantic gap between complex business applications and the data storage that supports these applications. This data model carries the

A

B

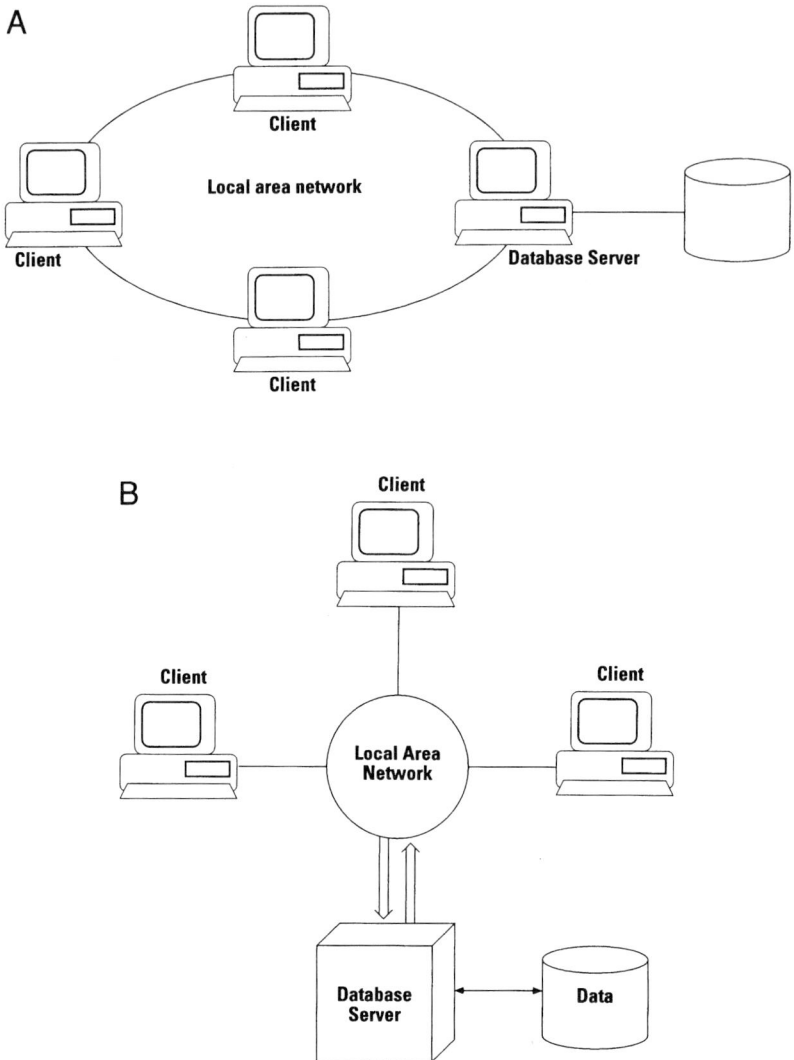

Figure 3-10   Two possible architectures for a client/server computing network. [The first architecture uses a Ring network (A), and the second one uses a star network (B). Both of these architectures will be discussed in Chapter 5.]

relational model one step farther, providing support for more complex data management applications. This should make it easier to model the complex real-world business problems. This model represents an object in the real world with a corresponding object in the database. This is a more realistic way of modeling a reallife system. There should be many new DBMSs that are based on this model in the near future.

A relational database is characterized by a simple data structure. Relationships between tables (files) are based on a common value (the key). This architecture allows a great deal of flexibility in terms of system development and data access and retrieval. There remain, though, some applications for which the acceptable performance proves elusive. These applications are characterized by complex data structures. For instance, one complex table that required about 40 hours to load using a relational DBMS took only a few minutes using an object-oriented database management system (OODBMS) [4].

An object consists of data values describing the attributes of an entity, plus the operations that can be performed on the data (see Figure 3-11). This capability is called encapsulation, and it allows an OODBMS to better handle more complex types of data such as text, images, and graphs. The OODBMS also supports inheritance; that is, new objects can be automatically created by replacing some or all of the characteristics of one or more parent objects. In Figure 3-11, for example, in the VEHICLE object class license, year, make, and model can be replaced by new data to represent a new object such as a BMW or a Honda.

An OODBMS uses object, type, and class to perform database management tasks. An object corresponds to an entity's occurrence, while the nature of the object is called type. A type is the general specification of the entity, whereas a class is a rule for building occurrences. Unlike a relational table's primary key, objects have object identifiers. Objects can be more than simple attributes (fields) and tuples (records); they are collections of other objects as well. An unordered collection is called a set, while an ordered collection is called a list. Collections can improve performance by providing an explicit link between objects and information to cluster data.

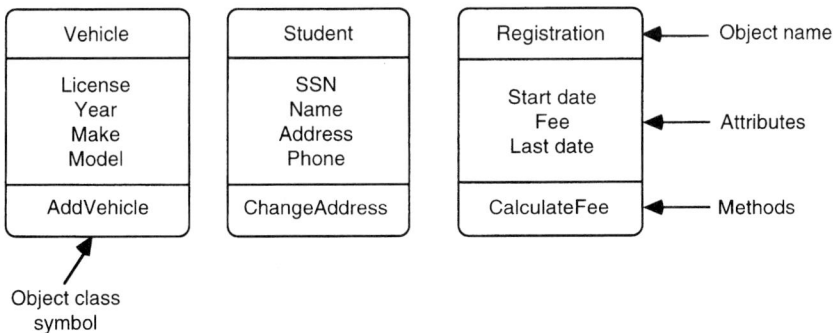

Figure 3-11 Sample objects and object classes.

The interaction between a relational database and the user is through a query language, usually SQL (structured query language). In OODBMSs, interaction is performed through predefined procedures called methods, which are invoked by sending a message to the object. Usually, messages are generated by an "event" of some kind. A simple event may be that the user has pressed the Enter key or pushed the left mouse button. A complex event may trigger into action a set of predefined methods. The implementation of this method provides a high degree of data independence. Instead of SQL, in OODBMSs a high-level language, mostly C++, is used to design methods. Object-oriented technology is well supported by companies such as IBM, HP, Microsoft, Apple, and Borland International. Some of the current object-oriented database management systems on the market include POET by BKS Software, Guppy by Guppy Technologies, and Hyperdesk Distributed Object Management by Hyperdesk Incorporated. Figure 3-11 illustrates a sample representation of objects and object classes.

3-11-4 DATABASE MACHINES

Database machines also have attracted some attention in recent years. Database machines simply serve as a backend processor to the main computer system. The main advantage of this type of database processing is that it provides enhanced efficiency. Because a second processor handles the entire operation related to the DBMS, the first processor (the main computer system) can be dedicated to the application programs. In other words, database machines provide an environment for parallel processing. Because this technology has not been around long enough, we cannot make a decisive judgment about its effectiveness. It seems that this type•of data processing has its own merits in complex business environments. However, its real effectiveness is yet to be seen. Figure 3-12 illustrates the typical architecture of a system that uses a back-end computer as a database machine [10].

SUMMARY

This chapter introduced and discussed databases as one of the major components of an information system. Different views related to database design, types of data, and problems associated with data were explored. Different database models used in information systems design were also discussed. The latter part of this chapter concentrated on functions and operations supported by a DBMS. An understanding of these functions should help the information system user and designer to choose a more suitable DBMS. Finally, the chapter introduced and highlighted some of the new trends in the database environment, including distrib-

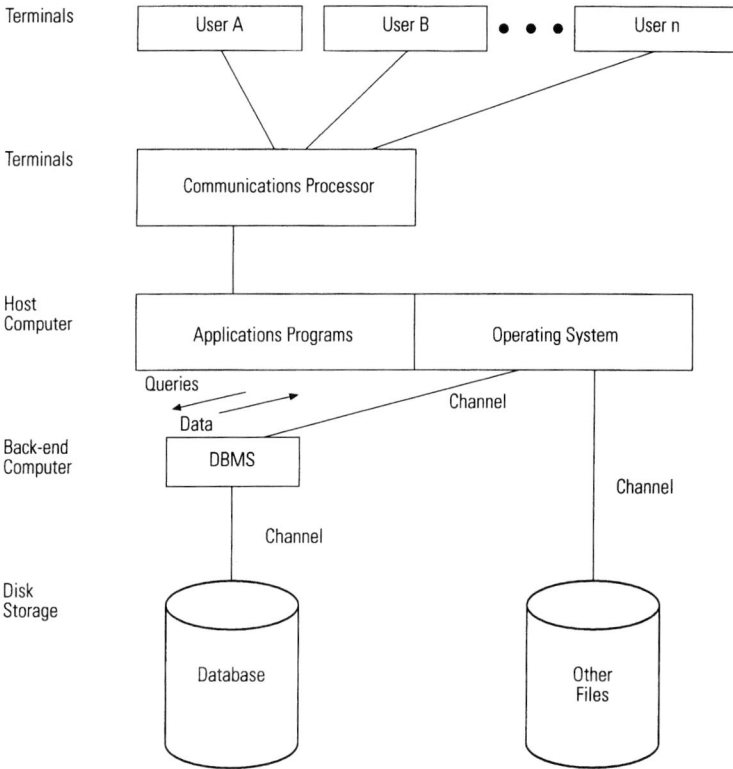

Figure 3-12 A typical architecture of a system with front- and back-end processors.

uted databases, client/server databases, object-oriented databases, and database machines. These new trends should play an important role in information systems design and utilization in the near future.

Table 3-11 illustrates some examples of popular DBMSs and data models used by these systems.

REVIEW QUESTIONS

1. What is a database?
2. What is the difference between an automated database and a manual database?

Table 3-11

Examples of DBMS and Data Models Used

Name/vendor	Data model	Hardware support
Paradox for DOS and Windows by Borland International	Relational	IBM-PC and compatibles
Access and FoxPro by MicrosoftCorp.	Relational	IBM-PC and compatibles
dBASE by Borland International	Relational	IBM-PC and compatibles
IDMS/R by Cullinet Software, Inc.	Network	IBM mainframe
IBM/VS-DB by IBM	Hierarchical	IBM mainframe
DB2 by IBM	Relational	IBM mainframe
System 2000 by Intel Corp.	Hierarchical	IBM mainframe
IDM 500 by Britton-Lee, Inc.	Database machine	Any computer
Oracle by Oracle Corp.	Relational	Any computer
POET by BKS Software	Object-oriented	IBM-PC and compatibles
Guppy by Guppy Technologies	Object-oriented	IBM-PC and compatibles

3. What are some of the advantages of a database compared with a flat file system?

4. What are the different types of data used in an information system design?

5. Mention some external sources for data used in an information system environment.

6. What is a functional view of database design?

7. Why is a database so crucial to information systems design?

8. What types of analyses are supported by a database?

9. Give some examples of data used in the finance, manufacturing, marketing, and personnel departments of an organization.

10. What are "data problems" as discussed in the chapter? How can these problems be resolved?

11. What is a data model? What does a data model support?

12. Briefly discuss three types of data models discussed in this chapter: relational, hierarchical, and network.

13. What are some of the limitations of each data model?

14. What are some of the advantages of the relational data model compared with the others?

15. Why is the relational data model more popular than the others?

16. Why is the object-oriented data model gaining in popularity?

17. List major operations supported by a relational data model.

18. What is an example of a projection operation?

19. What is the difference between the select and join operations?

20. What is SQL? QBE?

21. What is a distributed database?

22. What are some of the advantages of a distributed database?

23. What is the difference between a file/server and client/server environment?

24. What are database machines? What are some of the advantages of this type of processing?

25. What are three approaches for designing a distributed database system?

26. What is the difference between replication and fragmentation in a distributed database environment?

PROJECTS

1. There are 20 students in our information systems class. For each student we keep track of 8 fields: first name, last name, social security number, major, GPA, age, nationality, and status (freshman, sophomore, etc.) Organize this sample database in a relational format. What operations can be performed by such a database? Using a DBMS package that you are familiar with generate the following:
   a. A listing of all the MIS majors.
   b. A listing of all the MIS majors with a GPA grater than 3.7.
   c. A listing of all the MIS majors with a GPA greater than 3.7 who are Spanish.
   d. A listing of all the MIS or accounting majors.
   e. A listing of all the students except the MIS majors.

2. The Corner Grocery store is planning to establish a database that will be used to keep track of customers for various promotional activities. The manager of this grocery store has asked your advice. What will you tell this manager to improve the chances of success for this database design?

3. Microsoft Access is a well-known DBMS for microcomputers. Investigate the strengths and weaknesses of this DBMS.

4. Table 3-11 presents some popular DBMS on the market. Research DB2 by IBM and IDM 500 by Britton-Lee, Inc. Both of these systems offer relational

DBMSs. Compare and contrast these two. What are the unique features of a database machine not found in a regular DBMS?

KEY TERMS

Client/server database, 87–88
Conceptual design, 75
Data model, 75
Data problems, 73–75
Database, 68–70
Database administrator, 80–81
Database machines, 90–91
Database management systems
   (DBMSs), 68–70
Distributed database, 83–86
External data, 71
Flat file, 69
Functional view, 72–73

Hierarchical model, 77–79
Internal data, 70
Join operation, 76
Managerial view, 71–72
Natural language processing, 82–83
Network model, 79–80
Object-oriented model, 87–90
Projection operation, 75–76
QBE (query by example), 82
Query operation, 82
Relational model, 75–77
SQL (structured query language), 82
Technical view, 72

REFERENCES

[1] Alter, S. L. (1980). *Decision support systems: Current practice and continuing challenges,* pp. 127–132. Reading, MA: Addison-Wesley Publishing Company, Inc.
[2] Brueggen, D. and Lee, S. (Spring 1995). Distributed data base systems: Accessing data more efficiently. *Information Systems Management,* 15–20.
[3] Bidgoli, H. (1997). *Modern information systems for managers.* San Diego: Academic Press.
[4] Edelstein, H. (November 1991). Relational vs. object-oriented. *DBMS,* 68+.
[5] Kroenke, D. M. (1994). *Database processing,* 5th ed. New York: Macmillan Publishing Company.
[6] Linthicum, D. S. (February 1995). Make bulletproof SQL queries. *BYTE,* 111–113.
[7] McFadden, F. R. and Hoffer, J. A. (1994). *Modern database management,* 4th ed. Menlo Park, CA: The Benjamin/Cummings Publishing Company.
[8] Moad, J. (February 1991). What IBM says about client–server. *Datamation,* 53–58.
[9] Rauch-Hindin, W. (May 1987). True distributed DBMS's presage big dividends. *MiniMicro Systems,* 65–73.
[10] Ricardo, C. (1990). *Database systems: Principles, design, & implementation.* New York, NY: Macmillan Publishing Company.
[11] Storey, V. C., and Goldstein, R. C. (March 1993). Knowledge-based approaches to database design. *MIS Quarterly,* 25–32.

Chapter 4

Organizational, Social, and Legal Impacts of Information Systems

Learning Objectives

After studying this chapter, you should be able to:

- Explain various negative impacts of information systems.
- Explain the impact of information systems on the structure and function of an organization.
- Discuss telecommuting and virtual organizations.
- Discuss copyrights and patents issues.
- Explain legal issues of expert systems.

4-1 INTRODUCTION

We begin with a discussion of the negative effects of information systems. This includes information systems effects on the workplace, privacy, crime, fraud, and health issues. We then discuss the impacts of information systems on organization structure and function. This includes the information system's impact on the traditional organization structure, telecommuting, virtual organization, middle management, and decentralization issues. The last part of this chapter concentrates on copyrights, patents, piracy, and legal issues of expert systems. The materials presented in this chapter should be carefully examined before the introduction of any information systems application to an organization. The consideration of these issues should improve the chances for success of information systems implementation and it should reduce the negative issues of this powerful technology.

4-2 NEGATIVE EFFECTS OF INFORMATION SYSTEMS: AN OVERVIEW

In earlier chapters, we discussed the positive effects of information systems. No one can discount the positive impact of information systems, which are well documented throughout the literature. Organizations around the world spend billions of dollars every year on information systems to stay ahead of the competition. Nevertheless, some negative issues of the computerized environment deserve careful attention. These social and health issues are not so severe as to require banning information systems, but any undesirable aspects should be addressed. To eliminate or reduce the negative effects, careful planning is required. Figure 4-1 illustrates these issues [6].

4-2-1 Information Systems Effects on the Workplace

There is no doubt that information systems have eliminated some clerical jobs. At the same time, information systems have created many new jobs for programmers, systems analysts, database administrators, LAN managers, and technicians. In the field of artificial intelligence (AI) new jobs such as knowledge engineer, robotics technician, and AI programmer have been created. In the Inter-

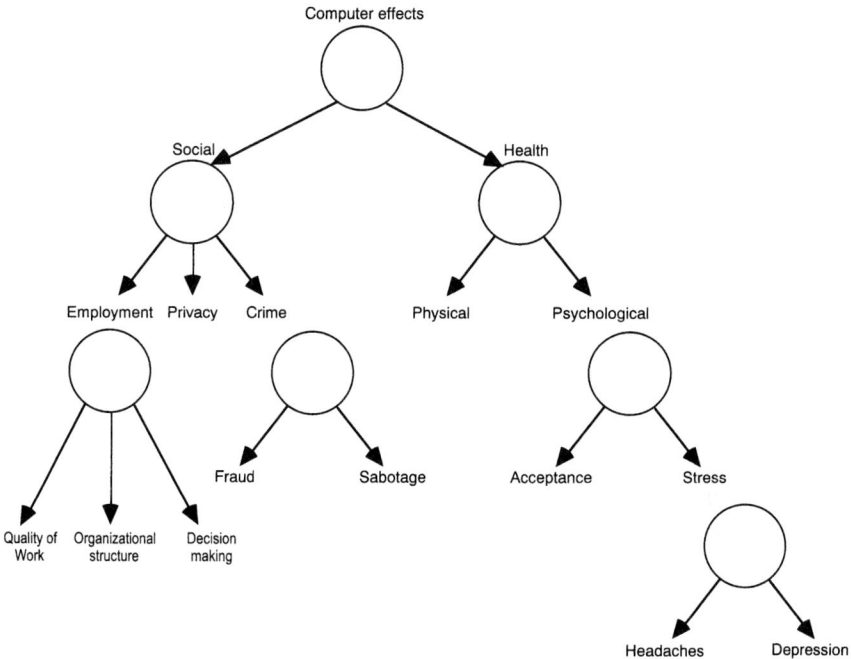

Figure 4-1 Information systems issues in the workplace.

net world new jobs such as web designer, home page developer, and web trouble shooter have been created. Some argue that the jobs that are eliminated are clerical, while the jobs created are mostly technical and require extensive training. Others maintain that information systems have reduced production costs and, therefore, have improved and increased the purchasing power of consumers, resulting in a stronger economy.

Information systems definitely have a direct effect on the nature of the jobs performed by different workers. Telecommuting, for example, will enable a significant portion of the work force to perform their duties from their homes. By means of telecommunications technology, a worker can use a personal computer and send and receive data to and from the main office. Information systems have made some jobs more interesting by taking over the repetitive and boring tasks. As a result, information systems have enabled some workers to be more satisfied with their jobs.

Information systems have created "job de-skilling" by performing technical tasks such as CAD for designers. In some situations, job skill content decreases over time as in the case of a machinist who depends on information systems to perform the technical aspects of the job. At the same time, information systems have created "job upgrading"; think of the secretaries who now use computers to perform word processing tasks. One skilled worker may end up doing the job of several workers. For example, by using word processing and mail merge programs, a secretary can generate thousands of letters, thereby eliminating the need for additional secretaries. In cases of job upgrading, the ideal is to train some of the existing employees to perform the newly created jobs. However, this is only possible to a degree. It would probably be very difficult to retrain a clerical worker as a systems programmer.

The effect of information systems on organizational structure may be varied. Information systems can change the organizational structure of a company from a pyramid to a diamond structure. In a pyramid structure, three distinct layers of management exist: lower (operational), middle (tactical), and upper (strategic). A diamond structure consists of only decision makers and unskilled labor; it eliminates middle management personnel. In this case, information systems perform the jobs of middle managers. In another instance, information systems may reinforce the existing structure (the pyramid) by providing timely and accurate information for the key decision makers. We will discuss this issue further in Section 4-3-1.

You have seen all along that information systems can provide timely and accurate information that facilitates decision making and, at the same time, creates a better control mechanism for the decision makers. This may lead to a highly centralized organization.

4-2-2 PRIVACY ISSUES

Managers in some organizations are now able to monitor an employee's performance, the number of errors made, the speed of work, and time away from the desk by using computerized systems. Electronic mail has added a new dimension to the meaning of privacy and private information in the office. Naturally, some workers are concerned about their privacy [16].

Much private data is left at doctors' and attorneys' offices, and financial institutions. This information is entered into computerized databases. Misuse and abuse of this information can have serious consequences. The question of who should have access to this information and to what extent is a difficult one for information systems practitioners. Organizations should establish a tight security system as will be discussed in Chapter 6.

When we think of what privacy means, most of us can give examples of things that we have become accustomed to. This includes such things as personal mail, bank account balances, and telephone conversations, especially since most of us now have private lines. We also assume that our personal life, as opposed to our career image, is private. In general, it is difficult to define privacy. In terms of electronic information, we probably all agree that a person should be able to keep personal affairs to herself. We also would like to know how information about us is used. By using this somewhat elusive definition of what we think should be private, the uses of electronic databases by the federal and state governments, credit agencies, and marketing companies have invaded our privacy. Unfortunately, information systems have been in the center of all of these important issues.

The number of computerized databases is increasing rapidly. In the United States, the top three credit rating companies, TRW, Equifax, and Trans Union Credit Information, have records for more than 160 million individuals (and the number is increasing). About 85 federal databases have more than 300 million records on 120 million people. Although these companies are fairly reputable, that is, they supply information only to people who will use it for the intended purpose, there are a number of smaller companies that buy the information from one of the big three and match it in ways that were never intended. These credit agencies, called "superbureaus," will sell information to anyone who will pay for it. This is clearly illegal but enforcement of federal laws has been very lax. It is quite likely that you have experience with an organization that you have recently joined. After joining this particular organization, let's say a credit agency, you begin receiving letters and other communications from other organizations, which makes you wonder how they got your address.

As a result, advances in computer technology are making it easy to do what was impossible not long ago. Information in many databases can be cross-matched to create "profiles" of individuals and to even predict their behavior. This behavior is determined by individual transactions with various educational, financial, governmental, professional, and judicial institutions. Major uses of this information include direct marketing and credit check services for potential borrowers or renters.

The social security number is the most common way to index and link these databases. However, a person's name can be used as well. A consumer's credit card purchases, charitable contributions, insurance information, movie rentals, mail order pharmacies, and other services that do not require a person's social security number can be tracked. Through credit bureaus, the social security number can be determined and a wealth of information may be obtained. This too is mainly used by direct marketing agencies.

To the individual, the result of all this information sharing is most commonly seen as increased "junk mail." There are much more serious privacy issues to be considered. Should the information provided to, for example, XYZ Bank to help a customer establish a credit record be repackaged (i.e., linked with other databases) and end up being used for less noble uses?

The first governmental linking of large databases took place in 1977. The Department of Health, Education, and Welfare (HEW) decided to root out those people collecting welfare who were also working for the government. (It is illegal to collect welfare while being employed.) By comparing records of welfare payments and government payroll records, officials were able to identify these individuals. In this case, those persons abusing the system were discovered, so it can be concluded that the system worked.

Governmental effects to match computer database records have expanded to more than 2 billion records in 110 programs. The Housing and Urban Development Department (HUD) has records that indicate if mortgage borrowers are in default on federal loans. This information was made available to large banking institutions such as Citibank to add to their credit files on individuals. This led Congress to pass the first of several laws intended to protect individual rights of privacy of credit records.

There are several federal laws that regulate the collection and more specifically the use of information on individuals and corporations. However, these laws are all very narrow in scope and full of loopholes.

The 1970 Fair Credit Reporting act bars credit agencies from sharing credit information with anyone but "authorized customers." An "authorized customer" is anyone with a "legitimate need." Legitimate is not defined in the Act [1, 23].

4-2-3 COMPUTER CRIME AND FRAUD

Computer viruses have made headlines worldwide. One virus attacked more than 6000 computer installations. Viruses have brought to the forefront the necessity of protecting computers from hackers, crackers, extremists, and computer criminals. Billions of dollars are stolen every year by computer criminals. Many organizations are reluctant to report their losses because they do not want to be recognized as vulnerable. With the popularity of the information superhighway, this problem will only become worse.

Computer fraud is the unauthorized use of computer data for personal gain. This includes transferring money from one account to another or charging expenses to an account that did not use the service or product. Computer sabotage can involve destruction, disruption, and disclosure of computer services. Computer criminals are those who modify, change, eliminate, hide, or use computer files for personal gain. They include insiders, extremists, and hackers. Hackers usually break into computer systems for personal satisfaction. Other computer criminals seek financial gain.

More than 80% of computer crimes are committed by insiders. This presents an even more difficult challenge when protecting information systems resources.

In an interesting article Belden Menkus states eight facts about computer fraud and eight factors contributing to computer fraud. These factors bring the crime and fraud issues to the forefront of information systems applications [18].

Eight facts about computer fraud:

1. Computer fraud exists.
2. The nature of computer fraud is not well understood by either data processors or auditors.
3. Computer fraud is difficult to discover in the conventional audit process.
4. Most auditors are not prepared by training and attitude to engage in computer fraud detection.
5. Most discovered computer frauds reflect inadequate information system design.
6. Most discovered computer frauds have persisted for some time—and may be part of a group of concurrent frauds within the same organization.
7. Management is often reluctant to prosecute discovered computer frauds— or even to admit publicly that they have occurred.
8. The public legislators and regulators all seem to believe that auditors can and will discover computer fraud in the normal course of their work.

Eight factors contributing to computer fraud:

1. Inadequate design of the information system.
2. Aggregation of the information system's transaction processing steps so that a review of what is taking place becomes impossible.
3. Insufficient discrimination as to the legitimacy of the transactions processed by the information system.
4. Toleration of errors by the information systems—either in data content or processing results.
5. Detachment of the information system's ongoing operation from the physical or functional reality that it is supposed to reflect.
6. Unrestrained, unmediated remote access to an information system that is subject to possible compromise or manipulation.
7. Restricted ability to collect sufficient knowledge about the fraud itself— especially its scope and the extent of the loss that has occurred.
8. And finally limits in the investigative tools for analyzing the knowledge that auditors may gain about the fraud.

These factors should assist the designers and users of information systems to guard against these serious problems. Careful information systems planning and following the guidelines introduced in Chapters 6, 9,10 and 11 should minimize these problems.

4-2-4 HEALTH ISSUES

The health-related issues of computers, particularly VDTs (video display terminals), have been reported in recent years. There is, however, no conclusive study to indicate that VDTs have caused health problems, despite the many complaints about them. Work habits and how workers interact with VDTs do cause some physical problems but health problems are not linked to the unit itself. More likely they are associated with the environment in which computers are located. Static electricity, inadequate ventilation, poor lighting, a dry atmosphere, inappropriate furniture, and too few rest breaks are all possible causes of the problems.

Some of the health problems reported include eye and vision problems, such as fatigue, itching, and blurred vision; musculoskeletal problems, such as back strain and wrist pain; skin problems, such as rashes; reproductive problems, such as miscarriage; and stress-related problems, such as headaches and depression. The majority of these problems can be resolved by properly designed computer rooms.

The psychological problems associated with computer technology are primarily related to "resistance to change" attitudes—employees resist the new system in favor of the old. This resistance is due to various reasons, among them economic concerns, uncertainty, and fear of losing a job. Experts in the field believe that the majority of health issues of information systems can be resolved by a sound ergonomics program.

Ergonomics is not a new concept. It is not even a new word in the English language. It seems, however, that it is finally getting the recognition it deserves due to rising worker's compensation claims and the large amount of money that has become involved.

In Greek ergonomics means work. In modern times, it is referred to as the implementation of safe work practices between humans and machines. These machines can be parts of assembly lines, point of sale monitors, or, for the purposes of this book, a PC or a workstation that runs information systems applications.

These problems most commonly effect the hands, arms, back, and eyes. Eye strain is commonly due to poor illumination, lighting, glare, and workstation set-up. The back is affected when the user sits for long periods of time in postures that are not conductive to this type of work. The arms, wrists and hands suffer from a condition known as carpal tunnel syndrome. This is a repetitive-strain injury that is caused by improperly bending the wrists for long periods of time while using a keyboard to enter data [13].

David Harvey [9] equates carpal tunnel syndrome to the bending of a garden hose. When the hose is crimped, no water can travel through the tube. The same is true when the wrists are bent. The neural impulses, along with blood flow, cannot get to the thumb and first three fingers of the hand, which often causes very painful and disabling results. This is due to the construction of the carpal tunnel, a canal that houses a number of ligaments and blood vessels that connect the wrists and hand with the rest of the body. The prolonged bending causes the blood vessels and ligaments to become irritated and swell in the carpal tunnel.

They then press on the nerve, causing severe pain and other problems. Cases have been known to be so severe that surgery is required to correct the problem. The good news is that recovery is generally complete.

Another problem with prolonged usage of CRTs is the concern over exposure to electromagnetic fields and radiation. In the early 1980s there was a report that an unusually high rate of babies born to a group of women who worked extensively with computer equipment suffered some type of birth defect. At that time the employer supplied these workers with lead aprons in an attempt to prevent this problem. This is not a common practice; however, at this time there is still no conclusive evidence as to the effect of this low-level radiation on the user. It is believed that most of the problems with the radiation are taken care of by placement of the workstations. It has been found that most of the radiation is emitted from the back and sides of the machines and is diffused within a foot and a half or two feet of the VDT [17].

4-3 INFORMATION SYSTEM IMPACTS ON THE ORGANIZATION STRUCTURE AND FUNCTION

In this section we explore the effects of information systems on the structure and function of the traditional organization. This will include the transformation from a pyramid-shaped to a diamond structure, the increase in telecommuting, the creation of a virtual organization, the impact on middle management, and decentralization issues.

4-3-1 INFORMATION SYSTEM IMPACTS ON THE ORGANIZATION'S TRADITIONAL STRUCTURE

Information technology has already led to the reengineering or restructuring of many organizations. This is possible as information systems perform more and more of the middle management jobs. This transformation has resulted in the development of flatter, less hierarchical organizational structures [10]. The traditional corporate pyramid and functional structure will probably become obsolete as information technology promotes a more diamond-shaped structure as seen in Figures 4-2 and 4-3. A management core will probably give direction to various technical arms, such as R&D, production, personnel, marketing, accounting, and finance, which, with the help of information systems, may be made up of only few people.

A viable alternative to having these "arms" in-house, (functional departments) is outsourcing. The statistics regarding outsourcing are very significant. "Consulting revenue in the United States is expected to nearly double from roughly

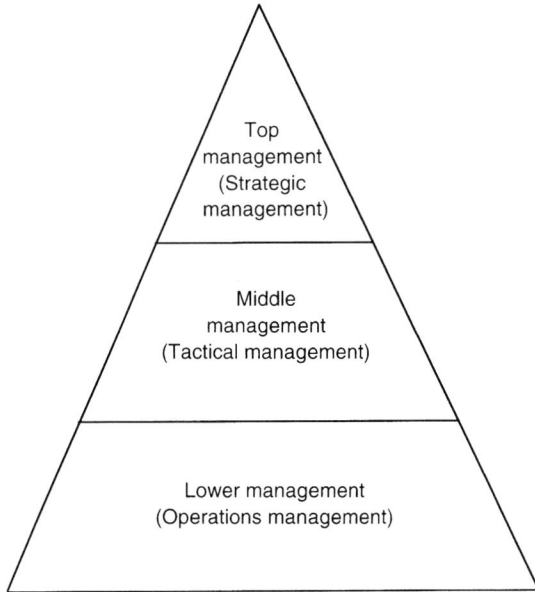

Figure 4-2   Traditional pyramid structure.

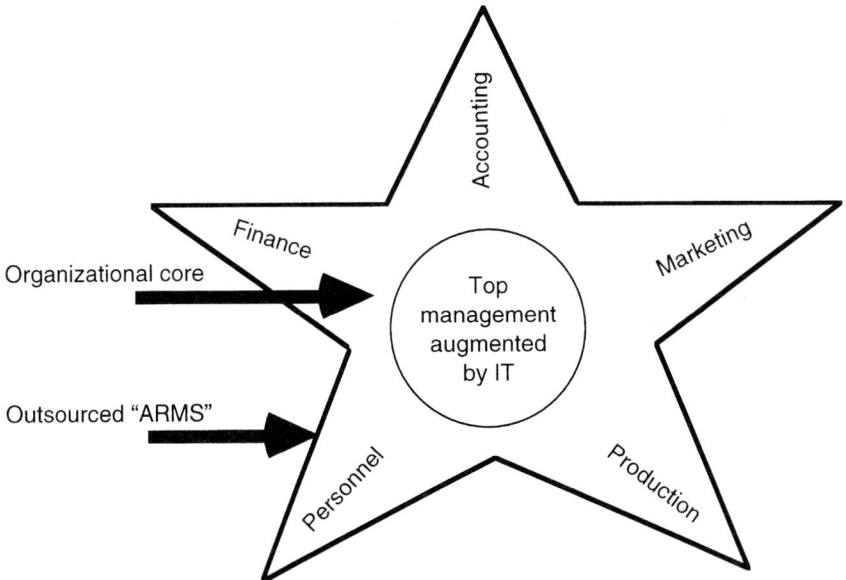

Figure 4-3   Diamond-shaped structure.

$8 billion in 1994 to $15 billion 1999," and "from 1993 to 1994, global spending for outside services grew 7.6%, reaching $165 billion" [2]. Because of the linkages made possible through information systems, it is often both cheaper and faster to hire specialists to do work outside of the organization's core expertise. Organizations may become smaller and smaller, yet the number of specialized organizations will increase. More and more companies will probably go the way of the virtual organization.

The virtual organization is a short-term project partnership, made up of several organizations for a specified length of time. A corporation could be made up of literally one or two people who outsource their accounting, manufacturing, and marketing to other firms to manage. These arms may be in action far remote from the managing corporation, but they would be allowed temporarily to send and download relevant information to and from the host computer. The advancement in various communications technologies such as WANs, LANs, MANs, and the Internet has established a true connection regardless of the geographical distribution of the employees and the organization.

The realm of security issues is an area that will directly impact organizations with regard to information systems. With so much of the organization's relevant data stored in one central location, the chances for information theft definitely will be consequential. With larger numbers of employees telecommuting from home or remote offices, access to an organization's databases could become a central focus for dishonest competitors, and even organized crime. Temporary access by other arms of the virtual corporation could result in unauthorized retrieval scenarios. Organizations will have to employ tight security measures in order to guard against unauthorized transmission of sensitive information from their corporate databases.

Humans as a workforce will never be replaced—just reshuffled. The use of computer-aided decision making will increase productivity, liberate the employee to serve customers, and reduce and improve the learning curves [10]. While any new technology can be threatening to those whom it may potentially effect, it must be regarded solely as a tool to benefit humanity. The real goal of information systems is to increase a decision-maker effectiveness and efficiency. Yet, many aspects of information systems will force employees to become smarter to remain functional and irreplaceable.

4-3-2 TELECOMMUTING: REDUCING THE ORGANIZATION'S PHYSICAL SIZE

Telecommuting and telecommuting technologies are changing the workplace. Telecommuting simply means conducting the normal office duties from anywhere except the office itself. An employee may utilize various computers and communications technologies for an effective telecommuting program. There are five types of telecommuting or teleworking [22].

1. Electronic home working, where an employee works out of her house utilizing data and phone lines to do her work.
2. Telecottages and neighborhood centers that are centered close to employees' homes and offer shared multimedia services. By using this alternative the employee may reduces her travel distance to and from work.
3. The mobile or nomadic worker. By using this type of telecommuting employees can operate from their homes or from the road.
4. Group or team telework. Just as there are "virtual offices" these are "virtual teams," using communications technology to bring them together.
5. The call center and remote offices. Businesses are separating production functions and have a separate office to handle the normal office functions.

Typical technologies utilized for a successful implementation of a telecommuting program are:

- Fax machines;
- Electronic mail;
- Voice/data PBX;
- Local area networks (LANs);
- Wide area networks (WANs);
- Metropolitan area networks (MANs);
- Intelligent/mobile phones;
- Integrated digital services networks (ISDNs);
- Video, data, and computer conferencing;
- The Internet.

There are many incentives driving companies and employees toward telecommuting as an attractive option. Table 4-1 [14] lists the strengths of telecommuting. The federal incentive to reduce air pollution is one example. The Clean Air Act of 1990 requires companies to reduce single-car commuting. More attractive incentives come from within the company itself. Corporate efforts to cut expenses result in reduced office space requirements. Another driving force is the corporate need to hire key talent. Many people do not want to relocate and are able to do their office duties out of their homes. Also, many employees want or need to spend more time with their families, and employers are realizing that ignoring employee needs hurts the company.

Sometimes telecommuting is the result of a disaster such as the Northridge earthquake. Los Angeles experienced an instant boom in the number of people telecommuting because of the disrupted transportation system. A mix-up in the design of Georgia Power's new office left the company without enough office space. This error saved the company $100,000 in rent alone in the first year.

Table 4-1

Potential Benefits of Telecommuting

Ability to oversee dependent children and adults
Ability to wear more comfortable clothes
Achieve increased productivity
Avoid a commute
Compliance with air-quality mandates
Conserve energy
Decrease transportation demand
Improved quality of life
May reduce neighborhood crime by increasing daytime population
Overcome limitations of distance and time
Provide 24-hour service from home terminals
Reach employees with special skills
Reduce air pollution
Reduce turnover and absenteeism
Save costs of meals, clothing, and commuting
Save office space and costs
Work in more pleasant surroundings
Work with fewer interruptions

Georgia Power has set up two telework centers. They have experienced productivity increases of more than 10% as well as savings of 600 miles of commuter travel every day.

Some of the companies that have successfully implemented telecommuting include American Express whose 240-member core sales staff at American Express Travel Related Services Co. are all telecommuters [5]. Compaq Computer closed its sales offices and instructed sales people to work out of their homes. In slightly more than two years, with a sales force reduced to two-thirds of its original size, and after the unit prices were cut in half, Compaq has doubled its revenue, with each sales representative selling six times the number of computers as before. Transquick Corporation has approximately 20% of their 150 transcriptionists working as telecommuters. Because of the ability to work without all the office disruptions, they have increased their productivity by more than 25%. The accounting firm of Ernst & Young has slashed office requirements by two million square feet, resulting in savings of approximately $25 million a year. These are all the results of a successful telecommuting program.

4-3-2-1 Strengths and Weaknesses of Telecommuting

Tables 4-1 and 4-2 [14, 26] provide a listing of some of the benefits and weaknesses of a telecommuting program. These strengths and weaknesses may not be apparent in all cases and they vary from organization to organization.

Table 4-2

Potential Weaknesses of Telecommuting

Become workaholics
Dislike not having a regular work routine
Have less interaction with co-workers
Have no separation of work and home life
It may raise some legal issues regarding workers' injuries
May have too many family interruptions and household distractions
May not have necessary supplies or equipment
May set up a two-tiered workforce: telecommuters and on-site workers
Miss the office politics
Not all jobs are suitable for telecommuting

4-3-2-2 Implementing a Successful Telecommuting Program

Before the implementation of a telecommuting program, an organization must first determine how to take full advantage of this type of work arrangement and what measures must be taken in order to make this policy effective.

According to John Curran [3], business systems analyst at the management consulting firm of Saltzer, Sutton and Endicott, companies can achieve the most productivity from telecommuting by following the "three Rs":

1. *The right reasons.* The fundamental problem is that telecommuting is viewed as an accommodation and a benefit instead of a business strategy to increase productivity. Among the reasons businesses should implement telecommuting are: increased productivity, reduced need for office space, increased customer contact by the sales force, and increased use of highly qualified people who are not available or affordable on a full-time basis.

2. *The right job.* The first step is to examine the nature of tasks that employees perform. Work that involves individual rather than team contributions is best suited for telecommuting. Examples include sales, telemarketing, writing, programming, editing, data manipulation, and research. However, many office tasks are not accomplished by the effort of one employee. Many jobs are interrelated and can be accomplished only after much consultation with co-workers. In this case, the employee can work some days at home and for those tasks requiring group coordination can be conducted at the central site. One-on-one meetings can be held effectively and inexpensively over the telephone with information shared through e-mail or fax. Group meetings can be conducted using videoconferencing, which allows employees to see and hear others while working at their home computers. All the technologies discussed in Chapter 14 for group support systems can be utilized here.

3. *The right people.* Even though the type of work may be suitable for tele-commuting, that does not necessarily guarantee an individual will be self-structured and self-motivated enough to become a successful telecommuter. There must be a right match between the job and the worker for a successful telecom-muting program.

However, the "three Rs" alone are not enough to ensure a successful tele-commuting program. Management must change what it is managing. Manage-ment must move from managing attendance to managing performance. Manag-ers need to eliminate the false sense of security they get when they observe workers who appear busy at their assigned places in the office. Also, employees who work in-house must realize that fewer managers will be supervising them. Senior management can encourage these changes in management style in several ways. Managers can shift the focus of their own expectations away from atten-dance at meetings and report presentations and toward performance. They should evaluate and change performance appraisals as necessary to accommo-date telecommuting considerations. They should also make sure that middle managers are given some form of training in working with telecommuters and it should be made clear by these managers what is expected from the tele-commuters [3].

4-3-3 VIRTUAL ORGANIZATION: BREAKING THE TRADITIONAL BARRIERS

The ever-increasing popular virtual organization concept refers to the network of independent companies, suppliers, customers, and so forth connected by vari-ous information systems technologies to share skills, costs, and access to one anther's markets [7]. A virtual corporation is a temporary network of several companies assembled to exploit a specific opportunity. No hierarchy, no central offices, and no organizational chart are necessary.

The virtual corporation is a temporary network of companies that come to-gether quickly to exploit fast-changing opportunities, costs, talents, resources, and access to global markets. In such a scenario, each participant can contribute based on their expertise. The technology for implementation of a virtual corporation is very similar to telecommuting facilities. It utilizes various communications and computer technologies.

The virtual corporation delivers its products to the customers with the appear-ance of a highly integrated company. The virtual corporation, in fact, consists of a company that faces the customer and a network of other companies that coop-erate to achieve what none of them would achieve alone. Using this strategy, each participant concentrates on what they do best. This limits the risks and investment necessary to finish a project. Some of the advantages of the virtual corporation concept include [11]:

- Greater customer focus;
- Higher customer responsiveness;
- Reduced cycle times for new product introduction;
- Lower cost;
- Customization of mass-market products for every customer;
- Financial flexibility;
- A company can change its parents in the virtual coalition. This has operational flexibility.

Companies such as MCI, Xerox, and Apple Computer have already used virtual organization concepts. This concept has assisted them in bringing new products to market faster and generating higher sales per employee. Banks also use virtual organizations to market their financial products to diverse customers. Banks underwrite certificates of deposits, brokerages underwrite securities, and insurers underwrite annuities. Here, the bank can act as a virtual corporation and provide these services by making arrangements with these parties. If properly structured, the virtual corporation should provide benefits to all parties that participate [11].

4-3-4 INFORMATION SYSTEM IMPACTS ON MIDDLE MANAGEMENT

The debate has been long lasting on whether information systems have eliminated or increased the middle management's jobs. According to Pinsonneault [21, p. 271]. "It has been estimated that information technology has eliminated almost a third of the middle managers jobs in the U.S., or about two million managers. A reduction of over 60 percent of the middle management workforce has been forecasted for the next decade. In the UK, recent lay-offs 11,000 at Nat West, 6,000 at Lloyds, 5,000 at British Telecom, 4,500 at Philips, 4,300 at Barclays, and 1,000 at British Petroleum—are attributed mainly to information technology." In the United States massive lay-offs have been reported in corporations such as AT&T, IBM, Apple Computer, and others. Proponents of the statement that the decrease in jobs for middle managers is not due to information technology argue that organizations are moving toward a lean-and-mean structure in an increasingly competitive world, and that information technology merely facilitates but is not the cause of these changes.

The rationale for the belief that information systems decrease jobs for middle management is that the main objective for middle managers has been to provide an informational connection between operation management and top management. Since information systems are taking over this function, middle managers are likely to be diffused into the operational level. In addition, information systems centralize the organization by merging business units together and by forcing decision-making authority to the highest level of the organization. Thus, the organizational chart will include a few top management positions, and a large base of operational line workers (refer back to Fig. 4-3). Information systems can either reduce the real total number of middle managers, or decrease their decision-making authority. This agrees with our earlier discussion of the impacts of information systems on the organization structure and the transformation of a pyramid-shaped structure to a diamond-shaped structure.

In contrast, researchers have found that information systems increase the number of middle management jobs and decentralize decision making. The rational for this view is the belief that middle management is not a mere link of information between top management and lower levels; rather, middle managers fulfill decisions and interpersonal roles as well. In addition, information systems could be an information bombardment for top management, extending the role of middle managers in sorting and highlighting the relevant information. Thus, the richness of information causes middle managers to analyze even more situations, hereby increasing their decision-making authority. Studies show that "computerized information systems were found to decrease clerical manpower by 17 percent, and increase managerial manpower by more than 5 percent." [21, p. 277] Other studies found that the impact of information systems on middle managers gave them more responsibility, authority, flexibility, and status within the organization.

We believe that information systems have and will reduce the number of traditional middle management jobs by providing more information to top management. The ever-increasing concept of downsizing and rightsizing in the United States supports this theory.

4-3-5 INFORMATION SYSTEMS AND DECENTRALIZATION

One of the outcomes of downsizing or rightsizing is that the information systems department is being dissolved into business units. Traditionally, information systems departments were located at the corporate headquarters. With the popular appeal of decentralization, the number of information systems employees is reduced and they are relocated throughout the organization.

A solution to the decentralization problem is the hybrid approach to information systems structure: both the benefits of a business unit and a central unit are accomplished. At TransCanada Pipelines, a natural gas distributor, the information systems department is located in business units, but they report to a central information systems department. According to Eric Baerg [4, p. 62] "This approach helps the information systems staff build strong links among business units without sacrificing training and career-planning support or adherence to the company-wide information systems architecture." TransCanada separated information systems between so-called "functional systems teams," assigned to 21 business units, and a central "shared resource group," assigned to 21 business units. Functional systems team responsibilities include requirements, application development, and systems support. The shared resource group controls the information systems budget, sets standards, and has responsibility for training and human resource issues. People are transferred between the business unit and the central unit on a continuous basis to gain different experiences and to remain up-to-date within their field. Benefits of this approach include enforcement of corporate technology standards, simplified accounting for information systems expenditures, and preservation of networking and career advancement opportunities.

4-4 SOCIAL AND LEGAL ISSUES OF INFORMATION SYSTEMS

In this section we concentrate on copyrights, patents, piracy, and legal issues of information systems in general and expert systems in particular. With the proliferation of PC-based information systems applications these issues will become even more important in the near future. Users and top management should investigate these issues carefully and they should try to inform all employees to be aware of these important issues.

4-4-1 COPYRIGHTS, PATENTS, AND PIRACY

While rapid technological changes have expanded a firm's information needs from internally derived and managed data to a broad spectrum of information and choices, laws relating to information use have struggled to keep up. Management, however, is still responsible for the misuse and abuse of its information; and litigation in this area is on the rise.

There are three main areas of concern for the management in this area [25].

1. provision of functionality without impinging on the intellectual property rights of external program creators (piracy);
2. acquisition and utilization of external information without violation of copyright or licensing agreements (proprietary databases); and
3. utilization of information about individuals without violation of persons' rights (privacy).

There has been, and will continue to be, much industry infighting over intellectual property rights. Intellectual property is a legal umbrella that covers protections involving copyrights, trademarks, trade secrets, and patents. These are intangible properties that individuals or corporations have developed. Although there has been a trend toward legal protectionism—very few cases have actually been settled. This issue is widespread throughout the world. World leaders have made several unsuccessful attempts to resolve it [8].

A now-famous example of this type lawsuit was the Apple Computer copyright infringement suit against Microsoft Corporation and the Hewlett-Packard Company. The lawsuit sought to protect the so-called "look and feel" of user interfaces—specifically, icon-based windowing environments. The lawsuit brought by Lotus Development Corporation against Borland International is another example.

Eliot [8] offers the following cautions due to the widespread variation in definitions and legal interpretations: Trademarks protect product names and identifying marks. Smaller and newer companies have tended to pick a cute name that sometimes mimics that of a larger competitor or product. The courts have taken a dim view of this. Much confusion exists in the area of software copyright; the protection is supposed to be limited to an author's expression of ideas—not to the ideas themselves. As an example, there is no agreement in either the courts or the industry as to whether icons are ideas or expressions of ideas. The same principle applies to pull-down menus, keystroke sequences, and dialog boxes. Lawsuits are being used in the industry to simply scare off competitors, due to their length and expense. The benefits of obtaining a copyright, however, are substantial. A corporate copyright lasts 75 years.

It is likely that patents are a better way to go for the software industry. A patent protects new and useful processes, but is extremely difficult to obtain. It generally takes several years to obtain a patent—with only a fifty-fifty chance that the courts will uphold it. The rewards are worth it, however, as patents grant a virtual monopoly for 17 years. Nestor, Inc., has obtained patents on several neural network products. Eliot advises firms to involve attorneys at each step of product development, and to assume both offensive and defensive positions [8].

Samuelson [24] details industry arguments for and against patenting program algorithms. In a survey with 667 respondents, there was overwhelming support for source and object code protection; strong objection to "look and feel" protection, and some support for algorithm patenting. The Supreme Court has generally said that algorithms are comparable to a law of nature or a scientific principle—and, since they do not involve transformations of matter, they do qualify for patent protection. Most insiders feel that these rulings are based on outmoded technology, and should be reversed.

In discussing the subject of legal issues in these areas in general, Krass [12] states that while software developers are now firmly enforcing trade secrets, copyrights, and patents—and utilizing "legions of lawyers" to do so—these protections also stifle innovation and should be eliminated or, at least, controlled.

Since the early 1980s the government and courts have expanded protection of software copyrights for macrocodes, operating system programs, and source and object codes. Lotus and Apple are now trying for "look and feel" patent protection for commercial software, screen displays, and graphical icons. According to Krass, many legal experts think that most of these are simply "trivial" improvements on industry common knowledge—and that they will be overturned.

There are a number of important considerations that relate to patents and copyrights: the limits are not yet established; litigation is an effective competitive weapon; judges and attorneys have limited technical knowledge; the length and expense of litigation; the specter of loss can devastate a small company; and these protections can limit innovation and stifle competition [12].

Laws concerning software piracy appears to be the most straightforward. The 1980 revisions to the Copyright Act of 1976 explicitly include computer programs. Both the individual and the organization can be held liable for unauthorized duplication and use of copyrighted programs. Contracts have been used to supplement copyrights in specific cases. These contracts are tailored to a particular program and provide additional protection for the originator. Trade secret laws—covering ideas, information, and innovations—are also being utilized as supplemental protection.

Straub and Collins [25] also refer to the potential liabilities involved in downloading information from proprietary databases, combining such data with internal information, and reusing such recombined data. In some cases this information can be uploaded back to the network under a new author. The law and precedent are still particularly unclear in this area; but several recent rulings suggest copyright infringement has resulted from such actions. Specific contracts between database vendors and subscribers appear to be the solution in current use.

Privacy is another important issue as discussed earlier. The threat of the misuse of stored information about an individual in various databases is, perhaps, the general public's greatest fear engendered by the information revolution. The capability of computers for matching records from different databases and for statistical inference increases this perceived threat.

Some of this "information paranoia" is valid—since virtually every aspect of our lives is now routinely stored on various databases; and the potential for misuse is very high. Misuse of extremely sensitive information—such as AIDS-related information—could serve to deny an individual employment, health insurance, and housing. There is legal recourse available, but it is, of course, both costly and, usually, too late—the damage has already been done.

It is incumbent upon management to develop specific policies and procedures to protect the collected data from abuse and misuse. Information liability and responsibility should be designated to a specific person—preferably one with strong connections to functional managers. Security controls, ongoing steward-ship of personal data, and careful and limited dissemination of such information are paramount. As will be discussed in Chapter 6, organizations must establish tight security measures in order to protect sensitive information.

4-4-2 LEGAL ISSUES OF EXPERT SYSTEMS

As discussed briefly in Chapter 1, expert systems are one of the successful applications of artificial intelligence that apply human expertise to a well-defined problem. Expert systems offer significant decision support capabilities, but also the great potential risk of liability. Since expert systems are relatively new, few lawsuits have been filed, but with all likelihood the number of these lawsuits will increase in the near future.

Since expert systems try to mimic the human expert, it is quite likely that an expert system will suffer from many of the same problems as its human counter-part: it will make mistakes.

One of the major questions in this area of risk is who will be liable when the lawsuits start. Experts in the field believe that everyone involved with an expert system has potential liability: the knowledge engineer (the individual who acquire the knowledge from the expert), the domain expert (the expert whose expertise becomes the basis of the expert system judgment), the user, the individual who inputs raw data, and, ultimately, the corporation.

The knowledge engineer is the actual developer of the expert system. The knowledge engineer is unfamiliar with the specific domain of the system, but is the critical link to the domain expert. Potential pitfalls delineated for the knowl-edge engineers are [20]:

- Due to the lengthy development time required—sometimes several years— the knowledge engineer is in danger of thinking he has "learned" the do-main. He could then make faulty inferences based on his "expertise." Causal knowledge does not make someone an expert—no matter how lengthy.
- The knowledge engineer could misunderstand the heuristic knowledge of the domain expert. Heuristic knowledge, by definition, is developed through actual experience. A misunderstanding of the heuristics, intentional or not, could expose the knowledge engineer to charges of active or concurrent negligence.
- The personal feelings and opinions of the knowledge engineer could influ-ence the way decisions are made by the system, and could contaminate the knowledge base.
- As "pure" a communication link as possible is necessary between the knowledge engineer and the domain expert.

- The problem posed by the multiple knowledge engineer. To save money, shorten development time, and validate the expertise, an organization might assign more than one knowledge engineer to the project. The problems listed above would then simply be multiplied—as misinterpretation possibilities would increase with each additional person involved.

The domain expert is the expert in the necessary area and, as such, could be liable for the validity of his expertise. Experts are viewed with wide variability by the courts. There is no reason to think that this would not extend to expertise in an expert system, which will be challenged in court by experts with an opposing view.

The reliance by some firms on in-house experts also could cause problems in the domain expert area. If the employee is unwilling, reluctant, or hostile (overtly or covertly), the entire project could fail. Because of the potential liability, many employees are not willing to be the domain experts without being provided expensive malpractice insurance.

As with the knowledge engineer, the complexity of the task multiplies if a firm chooses multiple domain experts. Most of what the domain expert provides is in the form of heuristics—which are based on individual experience, intuition, and instincts [20].

Another potential legal problem facing domain experts is detailed by Lynn and Bockanic: how long is the domain expert responsible for maintenance and monitoring of the expert system developed—when the environment, including the humans involved, the organizational policies, and the law are constantly hanging? Will he be liable if another domain expert modifies the system and produces unexpected results due to differing heuristics? Will he be liable forever [15]?

The user is generally seen in the literature as an unwitting victim—but the user is also exposed to potential legal action in connection with expert systems. A user, such as a physician, who does not use an existing system—which may have provided a better patient outcome—may be negligent by omission (affirmative duty). The user is also in danger of misapplication of the system if he is not thoroughly trained. There are no opportunities for questions at this level—he is simply using a "black-box"; and he cannot make unknown inferences regarding it. There is no iterative process involved, as there usually is in human decision making. Therefore, user expertise must be defined; and the user must be experienced in the domain—the expert system is not designed to instruct. If his questions and responses with the system cause bad conclusions, the user could also be held liable [20].

In all cases, the organization is most likely to be ultimately responsible, in whole or in part. A critical issue for developers of expert systems is whether the system is classified as a product or a service. This has not been substantially decided in the courts as yet.

Several industry opinions include:

- The system should be regarded as a new hybrid of product and service.
- The system should be classified by how it is marketed. If mass-marketed, it should be a product; and if custom-designed, it should be a service.
- The system should be a product, as you are selling a concrete set of instructions—not just a set of ideas.
- The system should be a product, as it is sold, owned, and transported via magnetic tape or disks. A critical issue is whether the liability is treated as negligence or as a strict liability.

Expert system lawsuits fall under the tort system. A tort is a wrongful act subject to civil but not to criminal action. If the expert system is considered a product, there is no need for the plaintiff to prove negligence on part of the provider. Products are subject to the Strict Liability Act covered by the Uniform Commercial Code. In essence, this act states that if you sell a product, you are responsible for any harm done by it.

If, however, the expert system is considered a service—or a hybrid—the plaintiff may have to prove negligence by one or all parties. Malpractice, which is considered a form of negligence, applies to any business—not just to medicine as commonly understood. Affirmative duty (mentioned earlier) is considered negligence by omission.

As a sort of pre-protection, some organizations utilize warranties and disclaimers on their expert systems, but legal experts feel the court has a history of disregarding these when harm has been done. You probably have seen some of these disclaimers printed in the first or second page of many computer texts.

Several legal precedents have been set that could apply to expert systems—but only one case has been specifically settled a company that sold readouts of navigational aids for pilots—in which the information was supplied by the Federal Aviation Administration—was found liable when the information proved to be faulty. A pilot death was involved, and the company was found liable for not verifying the information and instead simply relying on the FAA information. This case was treated as a strict liability case dealing with the provision of an unreasonably dangerous product—regardless of conduct or care taken.

The legal waters remain mostly untested and extremely murky, however developers of expert systems should beware of the following [20]:
Organizations

- Organizations should research court decisions for relevance to their products in development. Decisions could impact current development, testing, design, and engineering.
- Organizations should develop "worst-case" scenarios—they should try to anticipate what could go wrong.

- Organizations should be aware of their own marketing department and public overenthusiasm. Market expert systems realistically—do not promise magic.
- Organizations should monitor the use of the system by the public, defining specific problems, and identifying and correcting possible threats; and an organization should be willing to pull the product from the market if necessary.
- The organization should modify standards, policies, and procedures, based on evolving law.
- The organization should have the public well-being as its primary concern.

Individual domain experts

- Individual domain experts are advised to be wary.
- Individual domain experts should carry sufficient liability and/or malpractice insurance.
- Individual domain experts should draft "hold-harmless" agreements with their employer prior to aiding in expert systems development—although it is uncertain whether the courts would honor these.
- Individual entrepreneurs (domain experts) should, where possible, incorporate or create limited partnership—to limit personal liability.
- Individual domain experts should determine proper use of disclaimers and warranties that could offer some limited protection.

SUMMARY

This chapter provided a detailed discussion on social, organizational, and legal impacts of information systems. The presentation examined the impact of information systems on the workplace, and on privacy, crime, and health issues. The chapter examined the impact of information systems on the structure and function of an organization, including the transformation from a pyramid-shaped to a diamond-shaped organization, and the impact on middle management, telecommuting, and the virtual organization. The chapter concluded with a discussion of social and legal issues of expert systems. A careful examination of these issues should increase the chances for success for any information systems introduction to an organization and it should reduce the legal issues of this growing technology.

REVIEW QUESTIONS

1. What are some of the potential negative impacts of information systems?
2. What are the information systems impacts on the workplace?

3. Information systems may improve the quality of certain jobs. What are some examples of these types of jobs?

4. What are some of the privacy issues and examples of how information systems might invade our privacy?

5. What are some examples of computer crimes?

6. How can we control computer crimes?

7. Many experts in the field believe that the pyramid shape of a typical organization will be changed to a diamond shape. How is this claim true? Discuss.

8. What is telecommuting? How will telecommuting change the physical structure and function of an organization?

9. What are some potential strengths of telecommuting? What are some of its weaknesses?

10. What are some guidelines for the successful implementation of a telecommuting program?

11. What is a virtual organization? What are some of the technologies used in a virtual organization? What type of industry might benefit from the virtual organization concept?

12. What are some of the impacts of information systems on the middle management? What are some of the reasons that support a complete or at least a partial replacement of middle management?

13. What is the relationship between information systems and decentralization?

14. What are some of the laws for copyrights? Patents?

15. How can we stop or reduce piracy?

16. What are some of the legal issues of expert systems?

17. Do you consider an expert system to be a product or a service? Discuss.

18. What are some of the legal responsibilities of knowledge engineers?

19. Who is responsible if something goes wrong while using an expert system?

20. What are some of management responsibilities as they relate to the legal issues concerning expert systems?

21. How can we protect ourselves from the legal issues concerning expert systems?

22. In your opinion, will the legal issues increase or decrease in the near future? Discuss.

PROJECTS

1. Throughout the MIS and computer literature there are numerous cases of computer crimes and frauds. Investigate one of these cases and come up with a possible solution that might have stopped the crime or fraud before it occurred.

2. Several companies, including Compaq Computer, Shiva Corporation, and the Los Angeles County Affirmative Action program have implemented a successful telecommuting program. Investigate one of these organizations and find out how have they were able to achieve success.

3. By referring to the references provided, investigate the legal issues of expert systems. How an organization would be able to eliminate or minimize these issues.

4. There has been a long debate concerning a lawsuit between Lotus Development Corporation and Borland International on copyright infringement. Investigate this claim. In your opinion, is this a unique situation or can it happen frequently?

5. A mail order company that sells personal computers and peripheral is planning to utilize telecommuting. What advice will you give this company for a successful telecommuting program? What are some of the drawbacks of telecommuting? Discuss.

KEY TERMS

Computer crime, 100–101
Computer fraud, 100–101
Copyrights, 112–115
Decentralization, 111–112
Diamond-shape structure, 103–105
Health issues, 101–103
Legal issues, 112–118

Middle management, 110–111
Patents, 112–115
Piracy, 112–115
Privacy issues, 98–100
Pyramid-shape structure, 103–105
Telecommuting, 105–109
Virtual organization, 109–110

REFERENCES

[1] Anonymous (September 4, 1989). Is nothing private? *Business Week,* 74–82.
[2] Anonymous (February 24, 1995). Closer is better: Success in IT services entail new strategy. *International Data Corporation,* Vol. 3, No. 6, 1.
[3] Anonymous (January, 1995). The far out success of teleworking. *Supervisory Management,* 1.
[4] Baerg, E. (July 15, 1994). Toss dispersed is a safety net. *Datamation,* Vol. 40, 61–63.
[5] Baig, E. C. (June 26, 1995). Welcome to the officeless office. *Business Week,* 104.
[6] Bidgoli, H. (1997). *Modern information systems for managers.* San Diego: Academic Press, Inc.

[7]   Brousell, D. R. (April 15, 1993). The virtual data center, *Datamation,* 104.

[8]   Elliot, L. B. (September 1989). Patent pending and other legal threats. *AI Expert,* 13.

[9]   Harvey, D. A. (October 1991). Health and safety first. *Byte,* 119–128.

[10] Heygate, R. (September 22, 1994). Being intelligent about intelligent technology. *The McKinsey Quarterly,* 137.

[11] Klein, M. M. (October 1994). The virtue of being a virtual corporation. *Best Review,* 88–94.

[12] Krass, P. (June 3, 1991). Why so many lawsuits? *Information Week,* 40.

[13] Labar, G. (October 1997). Ergonomics for the virtual office. *Managing Office Technology,* 22–24.

[14] Lavalle, W. J. (December 1993). Telecommuting still limited, but growing. *Communications News,* 30.

[15] Lynn, M. P. and Bockanic, W. N. (November 1993). Legal liability of the domain expert. *Journal of Systems Management,* 44.

[16] Martin, J. A., Gibbs, G., and Grossman, G. (November 1997). Are you being watched? *PC World,* 245–258.

[17] McQuick, W. (March 19, 1984). Easing tensions between man and machine. *Fortune Magazine,* 58–66.

[18] Menkus, B. (June 1990). Eight unfortunate facts about computer fraud. *Internal Auditor,* 70–73.

[19] Mykytyn, P. P., and Mykytyn, K. (December 1991). Legal perspectives on expert systems. *AI Expert,* 40.

[20] Mykytyn, K., Mykytyn, P. P., and Slinkman, C. W. (March 1990). Expert systems: A question of liability? *MIS Quarterly,* 26–42.

[21] Pinsonneault, A. (September 1993). The impact of information technology on middle managers. *MIS Quarterly,* 271–292.

[22] Prile, C. (June 15, 1995). Survey of telecommunications in business, *Financial Times,* xi.

[23] Pritchard, T. (April 1991). The linear file. *Database,* 6–8.

[24] Samuelson, P. (August 1990). Should program algorithms be patented? *Communications of the ACM,* 23.

[25] Straub Jr., D. W. and Collins, R. W. (June 1990). Key information liability issues facing managers: Software piracy, proprietary databases, and individual rights to privacy. *MIS Quarterly,* 143–155.

[26] Westfall, R. D. (Fall 1997). The telecommuting paradox. *Information Systems Management,* 15–20.

Part II

Data Communications and the Internet

Part II examines in detail the growing field of data communications and the Internet. It first provides a general background for data communications technologies and it then explores computer security and measures. This part also discusses the information superhighway and the Intranet.

Chapter 5

Data Communications Concepts

Learning Objectives

After studying this chapter, you should be able to:

- Define a data communications system.
- Elaborate on the components of a data communications system.
- Describe various data processing configurations.
- Discuss various types of network systems.
- Understand important concepts in the data communications environment.
- Discuss some of the popular applications of data communications.

5-1 INTRODUCTION

This chapter discusses principles of data communications. The chapter looks at the components, topologies, and different types of networking systems, and it discusses the role of data communications in a computer-based information system (CBIS) environment. Important concepts in data communications environment will be reviewed. Office automation and remote job entry, as two important applications of data communications, will be briefly discussed. The chapter concludes with a brief discussion of PBX and ISDN as two important types of network systems.

5-2 DEFINING DATA COMMUNICATIONS

The electronic transfer of data from one location to another is called data communications. The efficiency and effectiveness of any computer-based information system (CBIS) are measured in terms of the timely delivery of relevant information [1,4]. Data communications enable a CBIS to deliver information where and when it is needed.

In today's national and international organizations data may be collected in different cities, states, and even countries. If an effective data communications system is in place, geographic organizational distribution does not impose any problems in the collection and distribution of relevant information. Data can be collected anywhere, processed, and delivered to any location throughout the world. An effective data communications system can significantly improve the effectiveness of a CBIS by improving the flexibility of data collection and transmission. By using a portable computer and a communications system, an executive can communicate with her office at any time and from any location.

Data communications is the fundamental basis of the virtual organizations of tomorrow. This new trend indicates that an organization is not limited to its physical boundary. Various functions can be outsourced and the results can be delivered to the organization in a timely manner by using a data communications system. Data communications systems are the backbone of the growing phenomena of the information superhighway. The information superhighway will be discussed in detail in Chapter 7.

5-3 COMPONENTS OF A DATA COMMUNICATIONS SYSTEM

A typical data communications system may include the following components:

- Sender and receiver devices;
- Modems;
- Communications media;
- Communications software;
- Communications control unit;

Figure 5-1 illustrates a basic configuration of a data communications system.

5-3-1 SENDER AND RECEIVER DEVICES

The sender or receiver device may include one of the following devices:

- An input/output device, or a dumb terminal, which is used only for sending or receiving information and has no processing power.
- A smart terminal, which is an input/output device with a limited degree of processing capability. This device can perform certain processing tasks; however, it is not a full-featured computer. This type of device is used on factory floors and assembly lines for data collection and transmission to the main computer system.
- An intelligent terminal, a workstation, or a microcomputer, which serves as an input/output device and also as a stand-alone system. Using this type of device, the remote site is able to perform processing tasks without the support of the main computer system.
- Other types of computers (mini, mainframe, or super computers).

5-3-2 MODEMS

A **modem** (modulator-demodulator) converts digital signals to analog signals that can be transferred over an analog telephone line. Analog signals are

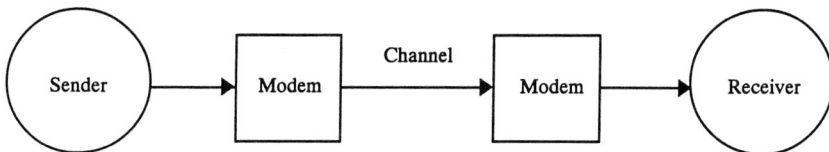

Figure 5-1   A basic data communications system.

continuous wave patterns, such as the human voice. Digital signals are distinct electrical signals. Figure 5-2 illustrates these two different signals.Once the analog signals arrive at their destination, another modem converts them back to digital signals before they enter the receiving computer. Figure 5-3 illustrates a high-speed modem.

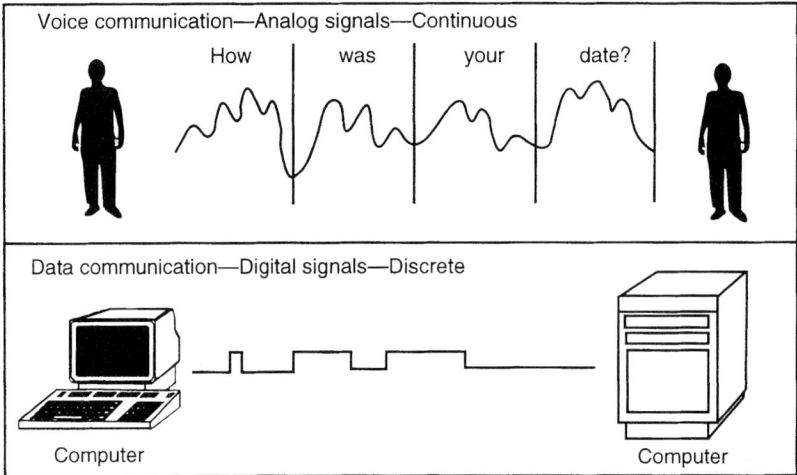

Figure 5-2   Digital and analog signals.

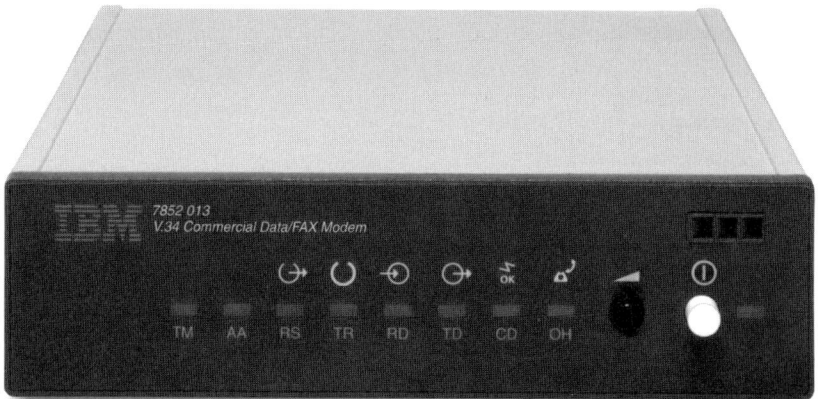

Figure 5-3   High-speed modem. (Courtesy of International Business Machines Corporation. Unauthorized use not permitted.)

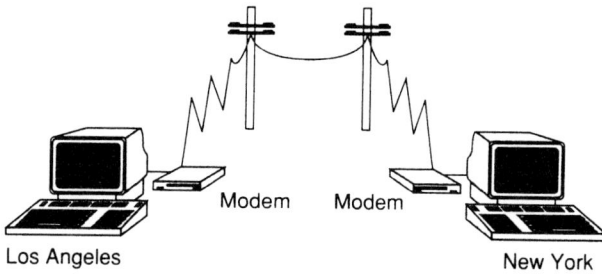

Figure 5-4   Micro-to-micro network system.

Modems generally are classified as dumb or smart. With a dumb modem, you must dial the number yourself from the telephone. With a smart modem, you can dial the number from the keyboard. Some modems include an auto-dial feature that directly dials a number for you. With some modems, you can store several phone numbers in memory and have the modem automatically dial the number for you. Some smart modems include an auto-answering feature that enables them to receive the incoming call and direct it to your computer. They automatically disconnect when the communication is terminated.

To establish a communications link, the two devices must be synchronized. This means both devices must start and stop at the same point. Synchronization is achieved through protocols—rules that govern a communications system. Protocols provide compatibility among different manufacturers' devices. Figure 5-4 illustrates a micro-to-micro network system [5].

5-3-3 COMMUNICATIONS MEDIA

Communications media, or channels, connect the sender and receiver. Communications media can be any one or a combination of regular telephone lines (or twisted pair), coaxial cables, microwaves, satellites, and fiber optics. Each has its advantages and disadvantages. When choosing a communications medium, you should consider the quality of transmission, security of the medium, throughput of the medium (how much information can be transferred at a time—measured in bits per second, or bps), and the transmission range (the distance of transmission) of the medium.

Telephone lines have been the major method of communications to date, because the system is already well established. However, speed and security issues make this medium less attractive than other options, particularly since the telephone lines are not suitable for continent-to-continent transmission.

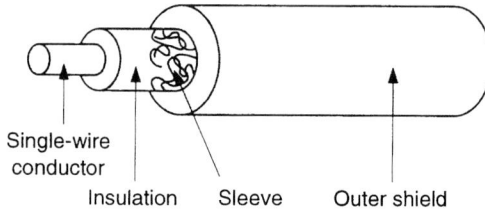

Figure 5-5   Coaxial cable.

The ordinary telephone line is sometimes called a dial-up system, meaning you dial a number to establish a communications link. Telephone services are offered through common carriers, such as AT&T, Sprint, and MCI. Telephone lines are reasonably inexpensive, but they can be slow and often are busy during prime time. An alternative to an ordinary telephone line is a leased line, which is a dedicated line. A leased line is more reliable and faster, and is always available. It is, however, more expensive than the common carriers.

Coaxial cables are thick cables that can be used for both data and voice transmissions. They also can be used as underwater cables for continent-to-continent communications. They are mostly used with local area networks (LANs), discussed later in this chapter. Figure 5-5 illustrates a coaxial cable.

Satellite systems cover a broad geographical range, but they are not completely secure. Messages are sent through an Earth station to the satellite (uplink) and the satellite sends the messages to a dish antenna (downlink). Satellite channels are fast and have very high capacities—one satellite is equivalent to over 100,000 voice telephone lines.

Microwave systems have a shorter range, similar to radio signals, and they suffer from the same problems as the satellite. They are used for short distance transmission.

Fiber optics communications appear to be the wave of the future. In fiber optics technology, tubes of glass half the diameter of a human hair form a light path through wire cables. This method is capable of high-quality transmission, high throughput, and very high security.

Other communications media include broadcast radio. The primary application of broadcast radio are in paging terminals (the devices carried by professionals, such as doctors or attorneys, who are on call); for cellular radio telephones; and in wireless local area networks. For high-speed transmission T1, T2, T3, and T4 lines will be used. Table 5-1 summarizes the speed of these lines.

A communications medium can be either a point-to-point or a multipoint medium. In a point-to-point system, only one device uses the medium. In a multipoint system, several devices share the same medium. All of these communications

Table 5-1

Transmission Speed of Various T Lines

T1 or DS-1 signaling up to 1.544 million bits per second (Mbps)
T2 or DS-2 signaling up to 6.3 Mbps
T3 or DS-3 signaling up to 45 Mbps
T4 or DS-4 signaling up to 274 Mbps

media may be used at the same time in a complex network system such as an airline reservation system.

5-3-4 COMMUNICATIONS SOFTWARE

Communications software is a dedicated program that enables a user to send or receive messages from one site to another. Several of these types of software were mentioned in Chapter 2.

5-3-5 COMMUNICATIONS CONTROL UNIT

The communications control unit (CCU) is usually a minicomputer or micro-computer that serves as a front-end processor in a data communications system. The CCU performs some processing tasks, such as data condensation, error check-ing, and simple processing, for the host computer. In a data communications system, this unit improves the effectiveness of the host computer by enabling the host to concentrate on the important networking tasks.

5-4 DATA PROCESSING CONFIGURATIONS

During the past 50 years as the computer field has advanced, three types of data processing configurations have emerged: centralized, decentralized, and dis-tributed data processing. Figure 5-6 illustrates these three types of data processing configurations.

5-4-1 CENTRALIZED

In a **centralized data processing** system, one central location performs all data processing tasks. In the early days of computer technology, this type of

Centralized data processing

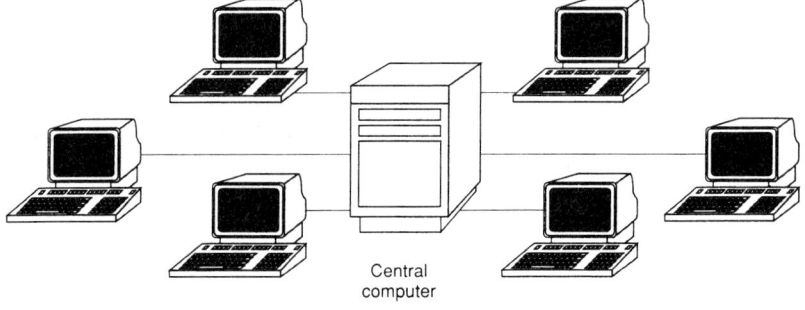

Central
computer

Decentralized data processing

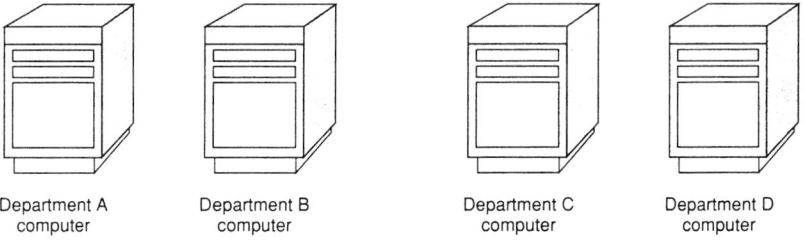

Department A   Department B   Department C   Department D
computer   computer   computer   computer

Distributed data processing

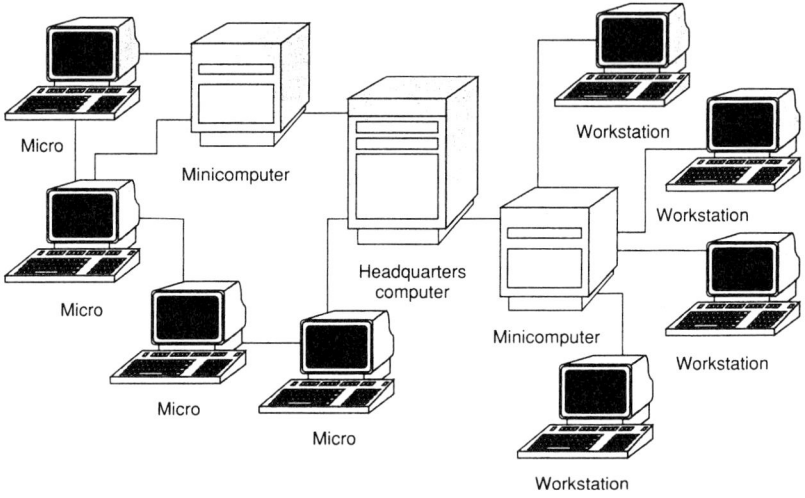

Micro

Minicomputer

Micro

Headquarters
computer

Micro

Micro

Workstation

Workstation

Minicomputer

Workstation

Workstation

Figure 5-6   Three data-processing configurations.

processing was justified because data processing personnel were in short supply; economy of scale, both in hardware and software, could be realized; and only large organizations could afford computers.

5-4-2 DECENTRALIZED

In a **decentralized data processing** system, each office, department, or division has its own computer. All data processing tasks can be implemented within each separate organizational unit. A decentralized data processing system is certainly more responsive to the user than centralized processing. Nevertheless, there are some problems with decentralized systems, including lack of coordination among organizational units, the excessive costs of having many systems, and duplication of efforts.

5-4-3 DISTRIBUTED DATA PROCESSING

Distributed data processing (DDP) solves two of the major problems associated with the first two types of data processing configurations: lack of responsiveness in centralized processing, and lack of coordination in decentralized processing. Distributed data processing has overcome these problems by maintaining centralized control and decentralized operations.

In DDP, the processing power is distributed among several locations. Databases, processing units, or input/output devices may be distributed. A good example is a newspaper publishing business, in which reporters and editors are scattered throughout the world. Reporters gather news stories throughout the world, enter them into their terminals, edit them, and using a communications medium, forward them to the editor in charge. The reporter and the editor can be thousands of miles apart. Since the mid-1970s, with advancements in networking and microcomputers, this type of data processing configuration has gained popularity.

Some of the unique advantages of a DDP system includes:

- Design modularity—computer power can be added or deleted based on the needs;
- System reliability—failure of a system can be limited to only one site;
- User orientation—the system is more responsive to user needs;
- Redundant resources as a security measure—if one component fails, a redundant component will take over;
- Access to unused processing power by an overused location.

5-5 IMPORTANT CONCEPTS
IN DATA COMMUNICATIONS

To better understand a data communications system and its operations, several keywords and concepts should be defined.

Transmission modes include synchronous, asynchronous and isochronous. In **synchronous transmission,** several characters are blocked together for transmission. At the beginning and end of each block there are empty bits, but these bits make up a small percentage of the total number of messages. Synchronous transmission is used to reduce overall communications costs.

In **asynchronous transmission,** each character is sent through a medium as an independent message. Each message is one character long, and the character is preceded by a start bit and ended with a stop bit. This type of transmission is more expensive than synchronous transmission; however, it may be more accurate. Figure 5-7 illustrates an asynchronous configuration.

In **isochronous transmission** the elements of both synchronous and asynchronous are combined. Each character is required to have both a start bit and a stop bit; however, as in synchronous data transmission, the sender and receiver are synchronized.

The three elementary types of data flow are: simplex, full duplex, and half duplex. In a **simplex transmission,** communications can take place in only one direction—a warehouse sending its daily transactions to the main office, for example. Also radio and television transmissions are examples of simplex transmission. In a **half-duplex transmission,** communications take place in both directions, but not at the same time—a warehouse sending its daily transactions to the main office and then receiving the main office inventory status. In a **full-duplex transmission,** communications can take place in both directions at the same time. Figure 5-8 illustrates these configurations.

Improving line efficiency is done either by multiplexing or concentration. **Multiplexing** takes place when a high-speed line is shared by multiple devices or users through a device called a multiplexer. If multiple devices can share one line, then only one line may be necessary. For example, two lines at 3200 bits per second can be combined by a multiplexer on a single 6400-bps line, or three 2400 bps can be combined in a 6400 pbs using statistical time division multiplexing.

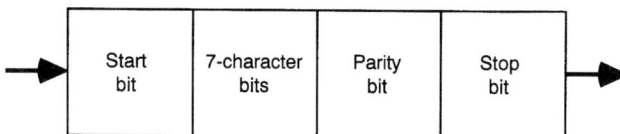

Start bit	7-character bits	Parity bit	Stop bit

Figure 5-7   Asynchronous transmission.

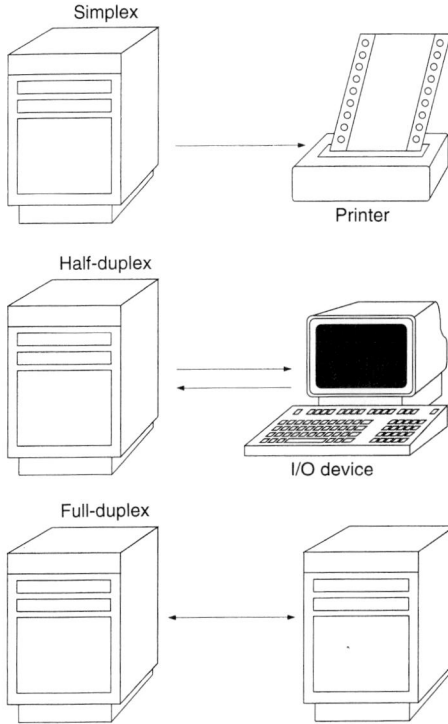

Figure 5-8   Three types of data flow.

Concentration is a more advanced feature than multiplexing. It enables a greater number of input channels to be combined in one output channel through a device called a concentrator. For example, four 3200-bps lines could share a 6400-bps line using a concentrator. A concentrator may store and later forward some of the communications traffic. This storage function is not possible with a multiplexer. However, using statistical time division multiplexing the storage function is a possibility.

Other concepts in data communications include the following:

• *Bridge*   The interface used to connect network systems using similar protocols.

• *Client/server computing*   A server is a software application that provides files and services to requesting clients. In a client/server architecture, specific requests are transmitted to the server, the server processes the request, and returns only those records that match the original request

• *Fault tolerance*   The combination of hardware and software technologies and procedures that improve the reliability of a system.

- *Gateway* The interface used to connect two dissimilar network systems.
- *International standards organization (ISO)* An organization that sets data communications standards.
- *Mean time between failure (MTBF)* A measure of the average amount of time that a given component is expected to operate before it fails.
- *Mean time to repair (MTTR)* The average amount of time that it takes to repair a failed component.
- *Open system interconnection (OSI) reference model* A seven-layered architecture for transmission of data from one location to another. Each layer in the architecture performs a specific task. (1) The application layer, it is application dependent, it performs different tasks in different applications. (2) The presentation layer addresses message formats. (3) The session layer is responsible for establishing a dialogue between applications. (4) The transport layer is responsible for generating the receiver's address and ensuring the integrity of the messages sent. (5)The network layer is responsible for message routing. (6) The data link layer oversees the establishment and control of communications link. (7) The physical layers specifies the electrical connections between the transmission medium and the receiving system.
- *Protocol* Convention and rules that govern a data communications system. They cover error detection, message length, speed of transmission, and so forth.
- *Response time* The amount of time required for a user to receive a reply to a request. This is the elapsed time between your last key stroke or click of the mouse until you see the first character of the response.
- *Router* A network interconnection device and related software that connects two network systems. The two systems being connected can be different. However, they must use a common routing protocol.
- *Security* A combination of hardware, software and personnel that collectively protect the computing resources from unauthorized access. Security issues and measures will be discussed in detail in Chapter 6.
- *Throughput* The amount of information that passes through a communications media per unit of time. For example, 56,000 bps (bits per second) is the speed of modern modems

5-6 NETWORK TYPES

There are three major types of network systems: LAN (local area network), WAN (wide area network), and MAN (metropolitan area network).

LANs have received a great deal of attention in recent years. A LAN system connects peripheral equipment in close proximity. Usually this kind of system is limited to a certain geographical area, such as a building, and it is usually owned by one company. Some systems, however, cover a broad geographical range and are still referred to as LANs. The geographical scope of a LAN can be from a single office, to a building, to an entire campus. The speed of LANs varies from 10 million bits per second (Mbps) to 1 trillion bits per second (Gbps). A LAN is usually a prerequisite for an automated office. In an automated office, word processing, electronic mail, and electronic message distribution are integrated by means of a LAN system. (We discuss office automation later in this chapter.) To establish a LAN system, careful planning and a thorough assessment of the information needs of a particular organization are required.

A **WAN** system does not limit itself to a certain geographical area. It may be in several cities, states, or even countries. Usually it is owned by several different parties. The geographical scope of a WAN can be from intercity to international boarders. The speed of WANs varies from 28,800 bps to 100 Mbps. As an example of a WAN system, consider a company that has its headquarters in Washington, D.C., and 30 offices in 30 states. With a WAN system, all these offices can be in continuous contact with the headquarters and can send and receive information. Remote data entry becomes a real possibility in a WAN system. An airline reservation system is another example of a WAN. You can reserve an airline ticket in the United States and pick it up in Asia or Africa. A WAN system may use all the technologies discussed earlier. For example, it may use all the different communication media, terminals of different sizes and sophistication, and a multiplexer. Figure 5-9 illustrates a WAN system.

A committee of the Electrical and Electronic Engineers group has developed specifications for a public, independent, high-speed network that connects a variety of data communications systems, including LANs and WANs in metropolitan areas. This new set of standards is called a **metropolitan area network** (MAN). This network is designed to deliver data, video, and digital voice to all organizations within a metropolitan area. The geographical scope of a MAN usually covers a city and contiguous cities. The speed of MANs varies from 1Mbps to 100Mbps. Several companies are involved in developing the MAN system; among them are Bell Atlantic, AT&T, and QPSX Communications, Ltd., of Australia.

5-7 NETWORK TOPOLOGIES

There are several architectures (**topologies**) for a network system, each with its own advantages and disadvantages. Depending on the organizational structure, functions, and needs, one or several of these architectures may be implemented. The commonly used topologies are star, ring, bus, tree, and web networks.

5-7-1 STAR NETWORK

The star network usually consists of a central computer (host computer) and a series of nodes (terminals). The main processing power is supplied by the host

Data communications options

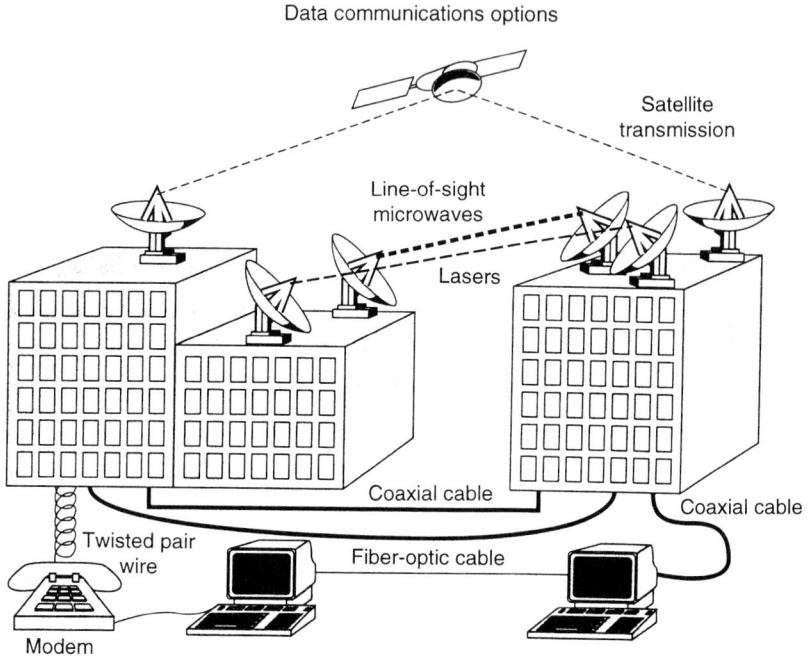

Figure 5-9   Example of a WAN system.

computer. The breakdown of any of the nodes does not affect the operation of the entire network; however, if the host computer goes down, the entire network is no longer operable. Figure 5-10 illustrates a star network.

5-7-2 RING NETWORK

A ring network does not have a central host computer. A variety of computers and input/output devices may be used in this architecture. If any one of the nodes or computers goes down, the network will go down. Figure 5-11 illustrates this type of network.

5-7-3 BUS NETWORK

The bus network, which is commonly used in a LAN system, connects a series of different nodes (see Figure 5-12). The failure of any of the nodes does not have an effect on any other node. This type of network is usually used for resource

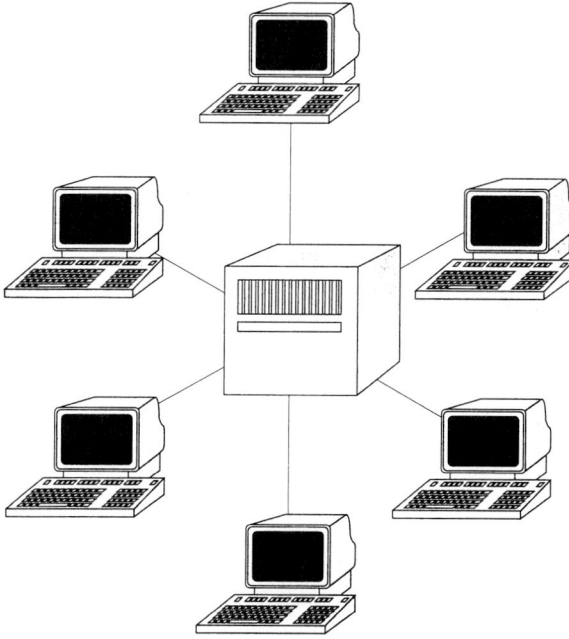

Figure 5-10 Star network.

sharing in an organization. For example, a bus network can enable 20 PCs to use one high-speed laser printer or a hard disk with 200 gigabyte (GB) of memory.

5-7-4 TREE NETWORK

A tree (hierarchy) network combines computers with different powers in different organizational levels (see Figure 5-13). This network may use microcomputers at the bottom, minicomputers at the middle, and a mainframe computer at the top. Companies that are organized in a tree (hierarchical) fashion are the main candidates for this type of network.

Failure of nodes at the bottom may not have a significant effect on the performance of the entire network; however, the middle nodes and, especially, the top node—which has control over the entire operation of the network—are extremely important for the operation of the network.

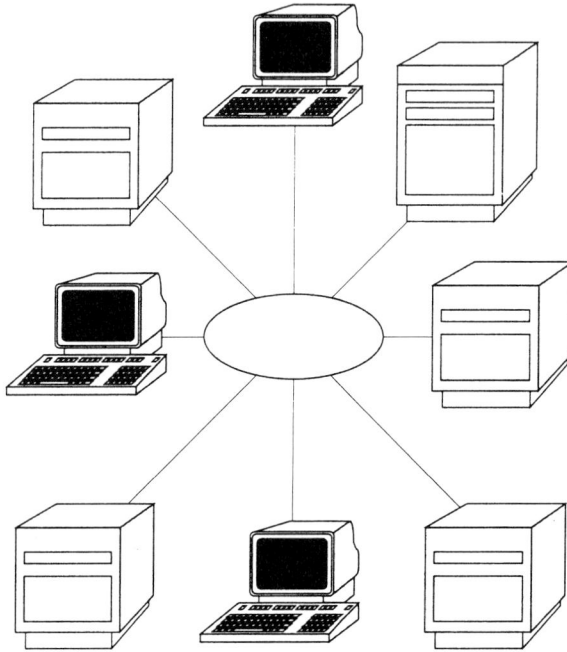

Figure 5-11   Ring network.

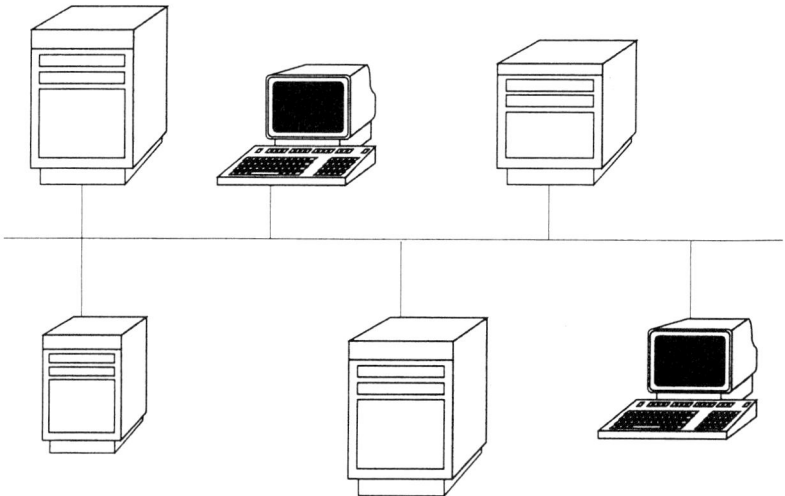

Figure 5-12   Bus network.

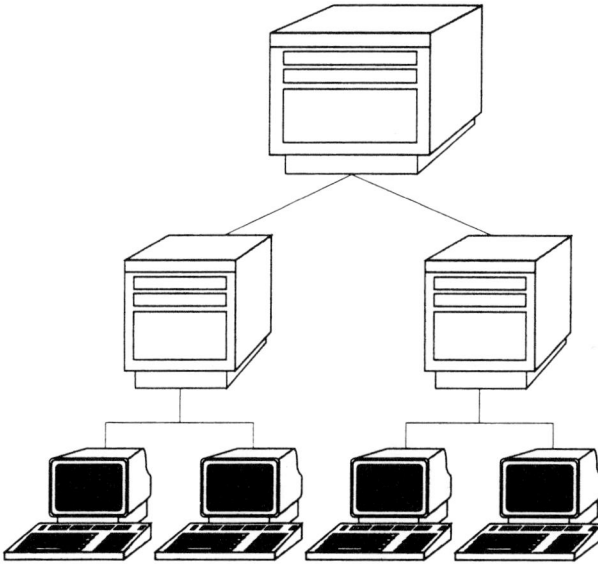

Figure 5-13 Tree (or hierarchy) network.

5-7-5 WEB NETWORK

In a web (or a fully connected) network, every node (which may differ in size and configuration from the others) is connected to every other node (see Figure 5-14). This type of architecture is the most reliable. Failure of one or a few of the nodes may not cause a major problem to the entire network operation. However, this type of architecture is costly and difficult to maintain.

5-8 APPLICATIONS OF DATA COMMUNICATIONS

Chapters 7, 8 and 12 explore several applications of data communications in detail. For now we would like to briefly introduce two popular applications of data communications: Office automation and remote job entry.

Office automation, or office automated systems, consists of a series of related technologies, such as electronic message distribution, text processing and reprographics, voice mail, micrographics, and facsimile.

An electronic mail (e-mail) system delivers messages electronically. An e-mail system reduces the amount of paper flow throughout the organization and expedites information delivery by disseminating the information to all authorized users

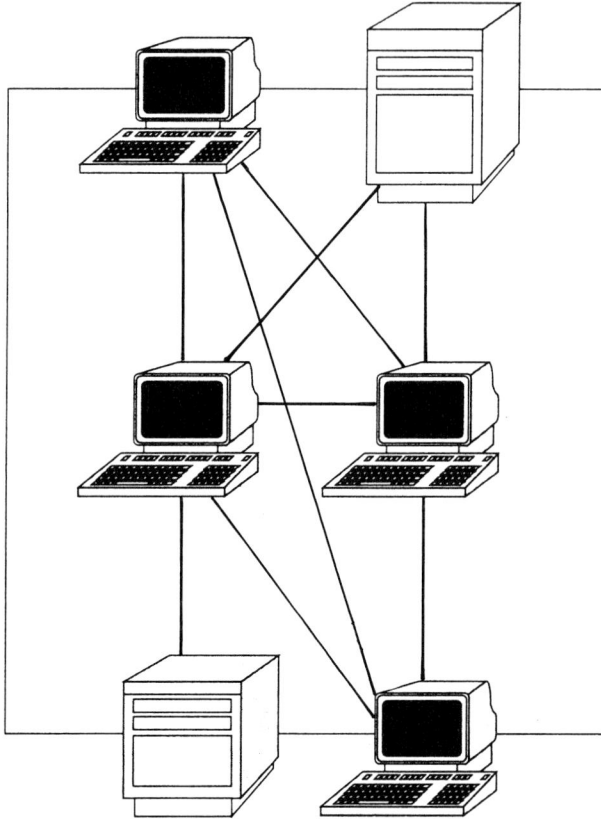

Figure 5-14   Web network.

immediately. With an e-mail system, a decision maker can send and receive messages, copy messages, save them on computer files, and set up private and public
mailing lists. An e-mail system enables the user to deliver a message to the
recipient without a third-party intervention, which enhances the privacy of communication. This type of system also improves the effectiveness of communication by delivering a message to the right person.

Electronic message distribution is similar to an e-mail system. You can send a
message to several employees through your computer terminal. You also can
request a reply from the recipients. We will talk about these applications in more
detail in Chapter 7.

Text processing and reprographics include creation and dissemination of forms and documents electronically. This includes all the features of word processing such as document creation, modification, cut and past, and mail merge operations.

Voice mail is an enhanced version of a telephone answering machine. You send and receive your voice messages through a telephone system within or outside your office. You can forward a message as it was received or add to it, and then forward it to one or several recipients.

Micrographics is the process of reducing texts and graphs on hard copy documents to a fraction of their size and storing these documents on film. The micrographics process helps an organization save space, which results in significant cost savings.

Facsimile, or fax, machines send a hard copy document from one location to another through an ordinary telephone line. Fax machines can be integrated with PCs and laser printers in an automated office. This means the output from a PC can be directly faxed to another location or to another computer without producing a hard copy.

The goal of the automated office is to use all these technologies to make the office operation more effective. In a sophisticated office, voice, data, and images are transmitted on a single line. This capability improves the quality of information processing. The automated office should improve the effectiveness of decision makers by providing timely access to the information needed for decision-making purposes. The technology is available in the form of integrated services digital networks (ISDNs), which is discussed later in this chapter. When costs are reduced and data communications systems are further improved, we should see more applications of office automation.

Remote job entry is one of the oldest applications of data communications. Using this feature batches of data are collected at a remote site, let's say a warehouse in Denver, Colorado, and transmitted to a host computer for processing. In our example the host computer may be in Los Angeles, California.

5-9 PBX NETWORK

A **private branch exchange** (PBX) is a computer system that switches telephone signals in an organization. A PBX system replaces the same equipment available from the local telephone companies. There are several advantages to establishing a PBX system privately. First, the costs may be less. Second, a PBX provides services that may not be available through the local telephone company. These services may include voice mail, networking microcomputers, and combining voice and data messages.

Most local telephone companies offer services that provide many of the benefits of PBX for additional fees. The CENTREX service for example, offers call forwarding, call waiting, conference calling, paging, automatic call backs, and much more. For those organizations that do not want to pay the initial cost of a PBX, these services can be very valuable.

5-10 ISDN NETWORK

Until the advent of the **integrated services digital network** (ISDN), the computer user had to have separate lines for voice, data, and images. An ISDN allows the networking of telephones, PCs, mainframes, printers, and fax machines. It uses an ordinary twisted-pair telephone line and digital transmission technology to send voice, data, and image information over the same line [2, 3,6].

The ISDN will make analog modems obsolete. Today's fastest modems transmit data at 56,000 bits per second. A broadband ISDN, on the other hand, can transmit data over 2,000,000 bits per second (2 Mbps), and that speed will improve as the technology advances. An ISDN line available through major carriers can transmit up to 128K (kilobit per second). This would be an attractive alternative for those users who need faster data transmission from their home PCs. Figure 5-15 illustrates an ISDN network.

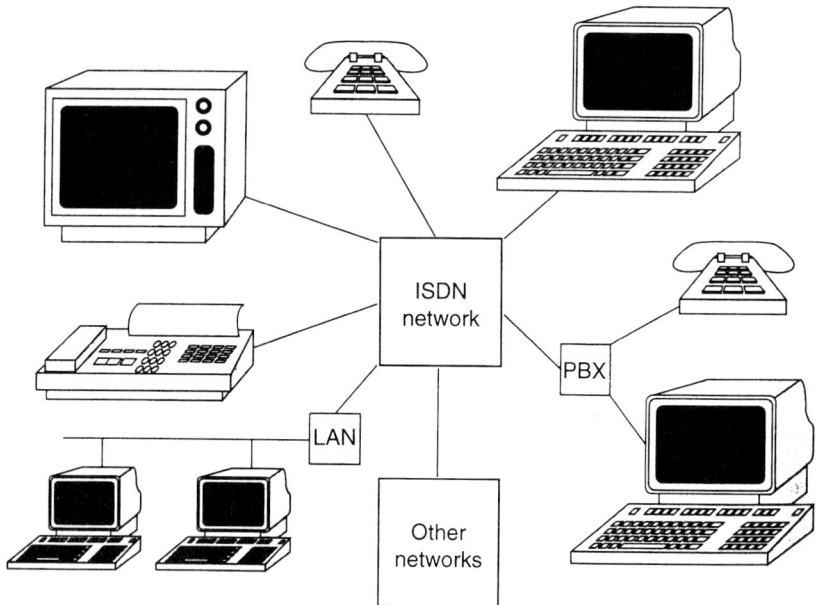

Figure 5-15   Example of an ISDN network.

SUMMARY

This chapter discussed data communications and networking principles. Components of a data communications system, types of networks, and network topologies were explained. The chapter introduced some of the important keywords and concepts in data communications field. The chapter also looked at office automation and remote job entry as examples of popular applications of data communications. The chapter concluded with a brief discussion of PBX and ISDN networks.

REVIEW QUESTIONS

1. What is data communications?
2. Why is data communications needed?
3. What are the major components of a data communications system?
4. What is a modem?
5. Is a modem always needed in a data communications system?
6. What is modulation? Demodulation?
7. What are five major communications media? Which medium is the most secure? Which medium is the least secure? Which costs the most? Which has the longest transmission range?
8. Why has fiber optic become so popular?
9. What are three types of data processing configurations? What are some of the advantages of each?
10. What is distributed processing?
11. What is a local area network?
12. What is a wide area network? What are some of the differences between LANs and WANs?
13. What are some of the applications of WANs?
14. What are five major network topologies?
15. What is multiplexing? Why is it used?
16. What are three elementary types of data flow?
17. What is synchronous transmission? Asynchronous?
18. What is client/server computing?
19. What is fault tolerance?
20. What is MTBF? MTTR?

21. How many layers are in the open system interconnection reference model?

22. What are protocols?

23. What is the response time of a data communications system? How do measure the response time of a data communications system?

24. What is computer security?

25. What is throughput? How do you measure the throughput of a data communications system?

26. What is office automation? What are the components of an automated office?

27. What is a PBX?

28. What is an ISDN?

29. What are some of the applications of an ISDN network?

PROJECTS

1. It has been estimated that a significant portion of the work force will work at home using communications systems by the year 2005. This phenomenon is known as telecommuting. Discuss the pros and cons of telecommuting. What types of jobs are the most suitable for telecommuting?

2. Consult computer magazines and find out who are the major vendors of modems. Why is there such a price range for modems? What is the difference between a $49 modem and a $300 modem?

3. It has been said that fiber optics is the communications medium of the future. Why is this statement true? Discuss.

4. Compare and contrast the five communications media. What are the major advantages of each? The disadvantages of each?

5. Visit a business organization in your area. What type of network system does it have? What are the applications of a LAN system in this organization?

6. Discuss the advantages and disadvantages of each network topology. Which application is the most suitable for each type? Discuss.

7. Visit an organization that has implemented an automated office. What are some of the unique advantages of an automated office? What functions are performed by an automated office? What equipment is used in an automated office?

8. Compare and contrast LANs, WANs, and MANs. What are some of the key factors that separate these networks from each other? Discuss.

KEY TERMS

Asynchronous, 134
Bridge, 135
Centralized data processing, 131–132
Coaxial cable, 130
Communications media, 129–131
Computer security, 136
Concentrator, 135
Decentralized data processing, 132–133
Distributed data processing, 132–133
Fiber optics, 130
Full-duplex data flow, 134–135
Gateway, 136
Half-duplex data flow, 134–135
Integrated services digital network, 144
Isochronous, 134
Local area network (LAN), 136–137

Metropolitan area network (MAN), 136–137
Microwave, 130
Modem, 127–128
Multiplexing, 134
Network topology, 137–141
Office automation, 141–143
Private branch exchange (PBX), 143–144
Protocol, 136
Remote job entry, 143
Router, 136
Satellite, 130
Simplex data flow, 134–135
Synchronous, 134
Throughput, 136
Wide area network (WAN), 136–137

REFERENCES

[1] Bidgoli, H. (1997). Modern information systems for managers. San Diego: Academic Press.
[2] Budwey, J. N. (March 1990). ISDN progress in the USA. *Telecommunications,* Vol. 24, No. 3.
[3] Jcob, A. (9 October 1997). Data network speak up. *BYTE,* 107–112.
[4] Johnson, J. T. (December 1992). Rebuilding the world's public network. *Data Communications,* Vol. 21, No. 18.
[5] Margolin, B. (August 1997). Chip makers keeping pace with changing modem technologies. *Computer Design,* 101–102.
[6] Romei, L. K. (May 1997). Networking connectivity gains momentum. *Managing Office Technology,* 16–18.

Chapter 6

Security Issues and Measures

Learning Objectives

After studying this chapter, you should be able to:

- Define computer security and its important aspects.
- Identify computer threats (natural and others).
- Describe security measures.
- Distinguish biometric and nonbiometric security measures.
- Understand the roles of firewalls and data encryption in protecting data resources.
- Discuss a comprehensive security policy in an organization.
- Explain measures that should be taken if disaster strikes.

6-1 INTRODUCTION

This chapter discusses security issues and measures. A comprehensive security system can protect data resources, the second most important resource (after human resources) in an organization. The chapter identifies important computer threats, including natural, man-made, intentional, and unintentional. Security measures including general security, physical security and software security will be explained. The chapter introduces firewalls as the newest security system in the Internet environment and it presents a series of guidelines for establishing a comprehensive security plan. The chapter concludes with actions that should be taken if disaster strikes.

6-2 WHAT IS COMPUTER SECURITY ANYWAY?

Computer hackers and criminals are making national and international news. It's no wonder that executives in private and public organizations are taking computer security very seriously. A comprehensive security system protects buildings, terminals, printers, CPUs, cables, and other hardware and software in an organization. Moreover, a computer security plan protects data resources, the second most important resource (after human resources) in an organization. The data resources can be an e-mail message from a division supervisor to the CEO, the blueprint for a new product design, a new advertising strategy, or financial statements. Security threats exceed simply stealing data; they include everything from sharing passwords with a co-worker to spilling coffee on a keyboard. A comprehensive security system includes hardware, software, procedures, and personnel that collectively protect a computer system and keep intruders and hackers at bay.

Computer security is broken down into three important aspects: secrecy, accuracy, and availability [9]. Let us briefly explain each aspect.

A **secret** system must not allow information to be disclosed to anyone who is not authorized to access it. In highly secure government agencies (Department of Defense, the CIA, and the IRS) secrecy ensures that only the users that are supposed to have access be given that access. In business organizations, confidentiality ensures the protection of private information (payroll, personnel, and corporate data).

Accuracy ensures the integrity of data resources within the organization. This means that the security system must not allow the data to be corrupted or allow any unauthorized changes to the corporate database. Database administrators must establish comprehensive security systems for corporate databases. Authorized users must be identified and they must be given the proper access codes. Just imagine that the addition or elimination of a zero would be the difference between $100,000 and $10,000. In financial institutions accuracy is probably the most important aspect of a security system.

Availability ensures the efficient and effective operation of a computer system. A secure computer system must make information available to its authorized users. It should also ensure a quick recovery of the system to its normal operation in case of a disaster. In many cases, availability is the baseline security need for all authorized users. If the system is not accessible to its authorized users, the secrecy and accuracy objectives of the system cannot be properly assessed.

6-3 SECURITY ISSUES AND CONSIDERATIONS

Computer security is an important managerial and technical issue, and organizations should be aware of the underlying factors. Computer security is concerned with unauthorized access to important data resources. Some computer threats are controllable, some are partially controllable, and some are completely uncontrollable. Some are intentional while some are made unintentionally. Table 6-1 summarizes several potential computer threats.

The majority of computer threats are created by insiders. This makes the design and implementation of a comprehensive security policy a challenging task. Some security threats are intentionally created by insiders or outsiders; for example, spreading a computer virus by a hacker or a disenchanted programmer. Some security threats are unintentional. For example, an employee may erase a computer file or format a data disk unintentionally. Some security threats such as earthquakes are natural and are not controllable (or partially controllable). A comprehensive security system should allow only authorized employees to have access to computer facilities. Table 6-2 summarizes the threats posed by insiders.

The damage from natural disasters is somewhat controllable. Buildings with special designs for earthquake protection are now available, and flood damage

Table 6-1
Potential Computer Threats

Natural disasters	Other disasters
Cold weather	Blackouts
Earthquakes	Fires
Floods	Gas leaks
Hot weather	Neighborhood hazards
Hurricanes	Nuclear attacks
Ice storms	Oil leaks
Ocean waves	Power failure
Severe dust	Power fluctuations
Snow	Radioactive fallout
Tornadoes	Structural failure

Table 6-2
Internal Computer Threats and Vulnerability

			Sources of Threats			
Type of threat	I/O operator	supervisor	Programmer	Systems engineer/ technician	User	Competitor
Changing codes	X		X			
Copying files	X		X			
Destroying files	X	X	X		X	X
Embezzlement			X	X		X
Espionage	X	X	X			X
Installing bugs			X	X		X
Sabotage	X		X	X		X
Selling data	X	X	X		X	
Theft		X	X		X	X

usually can be controlled. Frequently, computer rooms are designed separately from the rest of a structure to minimize potential hazards. Wiring, air conditioning, and fire protection should be of special concern. Locks and physical deterrents should prevent most computer thefts.

6-4 INTENTIONAL COMPUTER THREATS

Intentional computer threats usually fall into one of the following:

- Computer virus;
- Trojan horse;
- Logic bombs;
- Trap doors.

The newest and most highly publicized computer threat is the computer virus. A **computer virus** is a series of self-propagating program codes that is triggered by a specified time or event within the computer system. When the program or the operating system containing the virus is used again, the virus latches onto another program and the cycle continues. The seriousness of computer viruses varies. It ranges from springing a joke on a user to completely destroying a computer program and data. Computer viruses are relatively new in the United States, but they have been around much longer in European countries.

Virus infections also can be transmitted through a network. Probably the most dangerous type of virus infection comes from a bulletin board; this type of virus can infect any system that accesses the bulletin board. Bulletin boards are computer systems to which different individuals can post messages or computer programs that can be downloaded by others. Experts feel that the greatest national risks come from infecting large computers, such as those governing air traffic control systems, those concerned with public safety, security, and defense, and those used by NASA. Computer viruses have been observed in many countries, including the United States, Germany, Switzerland, Italy, Great Britain, and Israel. Computer viruses can be installed or programmed into a disk controller, a hard disk, an operating system, or simply a floppy disk. The following are some indications that your computer may have been infected by a computer virus:

- Unusual messages appear on the screen;
- Data disintegrates;
- Keyboard locks;
- Screen freezes (no cursor movement);
- Unexpected disk activity;
- Your computer takes too much time to boot;
- Hard disk space diminishes significantly;
- Certain programs are bigger than normal.

Table 6-3 highlights some of the popular antivirus programs on the market.

A **worm** is similar to a computer virus. It is called worm because it travels like a worm from one computer in a network to another computer or site. A worm usually does not erase the data. It either corrupts the data or it copies itself to a full-blown version that eats up the entire computing resources. Eventually, it will bring the computer to a halt. The most popular example of a computer worm is the one unleashed by Robert Morris in November 2,1988, that brought more than 6000 computers in a network to a halt.

A **Trojan horse** program contains codes intended to disrupt a computer system. Trojan horse programs are usually hidden inside a popular useful program. Historically, Trojan horse programs have been created by disenchanted pro-

Table 6-3

Popular Antivirus Programs on the Market

Dr. Solomins's Antivirus Toolkit
IBM Antivirus
McAfee Virus Scan
Norton Antivirus
Thunder Byte Antivirus Utilities

grammers who are trying to get even with an organization. These programs may erase accounting, personnel, and financial data. Unlike computer viruses and worms a Trojan horse program does not replicate itself. Although a Trojan horse program functions differently than viruses and worms, the end results are basically the same—damage and interruption of the computer system.

A **logic bomb** is a type of Trojan horse that is used to release a virus, a worm, or some other destructive code. Logic bombs are triggered at a certain point in time, or by an event or an action performed by a user. An action can include pressing certain keystrokes or running a specific program. An event may be the birthday of a famous person.

A **trap door** (also called a back door) is a routine that is built into a system by its designer or programmer. This routine allows the designer or the programmer to sneak back into the system to access software or specific programs. A trap door is usually activated by the individual (or her agent) who designed the system. Usually the user is not aware of the problem, a keystroke or a specific login may set it off.

Figure 6-1 illustrates major components of a computer-based information system (CBIS) and Table 6-4 summarizes different threats associated with different components of a CBIS. Careful security planning may keep computer hackers at bay.

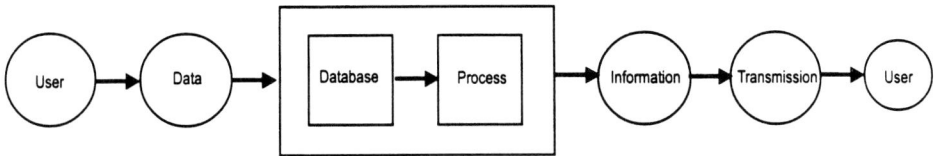

Figure 6-1   Major components of a computer-based information system.

Table 6-4
CBIS Components and Security Problems

Input/Database	Process	Output	Transmission
Deleting data	Installing bugs	Selling output	Sending wrong data
Entering wrong data	Changing programs	Searching and using waste-baskets	Sending incomplete data
Copying data	Erasing programs	Changing output Erasing output	Sending data to unauthorized users
Selling or changing data	Selling programs	Generating wrong output	

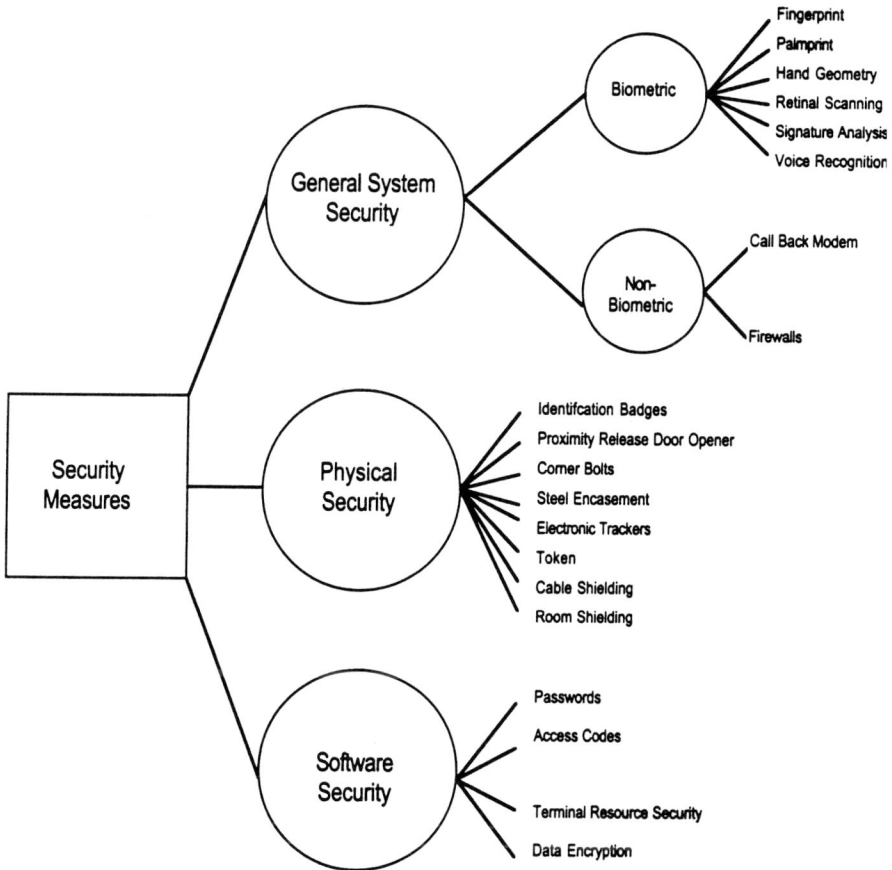

Figure 6-2   Security measures.

6-5 SECURITY MEASURES

The first step toward securing a computer operation is to generate a backup of each data resource. The backup files must be kept in a location away from the computer room. A comprehensive security system should include the following (see Figure 6-2):

- General system security;
- Physical security;
- Software security.

6-5-1 GENERAL SYSTEM SECURITY

General system security is broadly classified under biometric and nonbiometric measures.

6-5-1-1 Biometric Security Measures

Biometric security measures involve an element from the human body in order to enhance security measures. Biometric security measures include:

- Fingerprint;
- Palmprint;
- Hand geometry;
- Retinal scanning;
- Signature analysis;
- Voice recognition.

Let us briefly explain these security measures.

• *Fingerprint* Whenever a user tries to access the system, his or her fingerprint is checked by scanning and is verified against the print stored in a file. If there is a match, access is given. If there is no match, access is rejected.

• *Palmprint* The individual characteristics of the palm are used to identify the user.

• *Hand geometry* Hand geometry uses the length of the five fingers on each hand as well as the translucence of the fingertips and the webbing.

• *Retinal scanning* Retinal scanning is one of the most successful methods for security application. It employs scanning by using a binocular eye camera. Identification of the user is verified by the data stored in a computer file.

• *Signature analysis* Signature analysis uses the signature as well as the user's pattern, pressure deviation, acceleration, and the length of the time needed for the user to sign his or her name.

• *Voice recognition* Voice recognition translates words into digital patterns for transmission to the host computer. Voice patterns are recorded and examined by tone, pitch, and so forth. This technique is relatively new and research is ongoing.

These different biometric techniques have been very effective in protecting the security of a computer system. They may not currently be justified financially for all organizations. However, with rapid cost reduction and improvement in quality, they present a viable alternative to traditional security systems for the near future.

6-5-1-2 Nonbiometric Security Measures

In this group, call-back modems and firewalls are the two prominent security measures. Let us explain each technique.

• *Call-back modems* Using a call-back modem the system tries to verify the validity of a particular access by logging the user off and calling the user back. By doing this the system identifies the authorized user from an unauthorized user.

• *Firewalls* As it will be explained in detail in Chapter 7, use of the Internet for business is expanding. Nearly all large businesses have already installed Internet servers or plan to do so. Along with this growth, there are security issues that companies must address. Internal networks are extremely vulnerable to unauthorized access once a gateway to the Internet has been opened. Firewalls are part of the solution to this threat. A firewall is a combination of hardware and software that acts as a dedicated computer that serves as a gateway between the private network and the Internet. Predefined access and scope of use are required, and all other requests are blocked. Figure 6-3 shows a basic firewall configuration.

An effective firewall should protect both the export and import of data from and to the private network. Some organizations are so concerned with security threats that they choose to use the Internet by indirect connection. To use this option a service provider such as America Online, CompuServe, or Delphi may be chosen. Indirect connection is the most effective for those organizations that wish to gather periodic information through the Internet and provide a minimum Internet capability such as e-mail for their employees. This limited access involves the least amount of risk. This indirect connection links the organization's computers to a remote computer called a host. The only way a user can access the Internet is through the host computer. A typical user can use the resources available on the host to retrieve files, perform searches, and send and receive e-mail. Other companies place an isolated server on the Internet that is not connected to their private network with marketing data and questionnaires as the only contents. They find this approach acceptable because it is inexpensive to reload the nonproprietary data if there is a problem. Some companies may think they have avoided Internet security issues by not connecting. However, all it takes is one employee with a PC and modem to access the Internet via an online service and the internal security can be compromised. Therefore, businesses need to proactively address security [5].

However, since the indirect connection offers limited features and is somewhat inflexible, most medium-sized and large organizations choose direct access. Using a direct connection allows organizations to establish a "virtual office" so that they can do business on the Internet [8]. Despite the added benefits that a direct

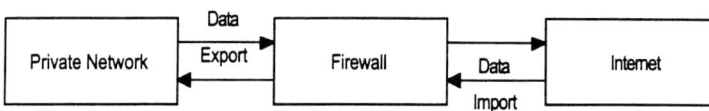

Figure 6-3   A basic firewall configuration.

connection offers, it also allows computer hackers to have direct access to the organization's important data.

The protection a firewall provides is similar to a house with walls, windows, and doors. The walls and doors of the house prevent unauthorized people from getting in, while the windows still allow those in the house to see the outside. However, as we all know, houses with walls and doors can be entered by those who really wish to.

If designed effectively, a firewall can look at every piece of data that passes into or out of a private network and can decide whether to allow passage based on the following:

- User identification;
- Point of origin;
- Point of destination;
- The information contents.

By careful examination of the packet that is trying to exit from or enter into the private network a firewall can choose one of the following actions:

- It can reject the incoming packet.
- It can send a warning to the network administrator.
- It can send a message to the sender of the message that the attempt has failed.
- It can allow the message to enter the private network.

Based on their functions firewalls have been broadly classified into two groups [4,7]:

- Router-based Internet protocol level (also called screening routers);
- Host-based application level (also called basion hosts).

The difference between these two types of firewalls is narrowing, leaving the user to wonder about the function of each type. **Router-based firewalls** control the data traffic (the export and import of data) based on packets. Packets are the basic units of communications in TCP/IP, the most popular protocol on the Internet. A router-based firewall either accepts or rejects a packet based on the packet's header.

A router's function is to direct packets of information from network to network. Rockwell Automation-Allen Bradley uses this approach. At the other end of the continuum is a design with three computers: internal network, a router communicating with the Internet, and a third retranslating data from PC to PC. Some businesses simply lease Internet access from a service provider to avoid opening a gateway to their internal network.

Programmable routers as firewalls can be purchased and have been compared to the club car antitheft device. Digital Equipment Corporation markets a SEAL system. This is a sophisticated system that includes hardware, software, and consulting. All incoming connections are recorded and an unsuccessful try might be a warning sign of an unauthorized attempt.

Advanced Network & Services, Inc., markets a firewall called Interlock. Users and the type of authorized interactive session can be predefined. This product utilizes a device the size of a credit card powered by a battery that changes the password every 60 seconds [10]. IBM provides "smart cards" to traveling employees, and the firewall is able to recognize their accesses as valid. In addition to firewalls, passwords and vigorous auditing of network activity are necessary to ensure security of internal networks.

Factors that influence the rejection or acceptance of a packet are based on the network application requested, protocol type, and the source and destination of the packet. A firewall can be programmed to accept or reject a packet based on the host that initiated the packet. Router-based firewalls may not be very efficient since they have to examine each packet one-by-one, and they may be difficult to install. They may provide a false sense of security, and they usually cannot accurately record all of the actions taking place at the firewall. This makes it difficult for the network administrators to find out how intruders are trying to break into the private network. However, the arrival of the self-programmed routers may solve some of these problems.

Host-based firewalls are regarded as more secure and flexible, and are naturally more expensive than the router-based firewalls. These firewalls are installed in the host computer. A dedicated PC or a workstation may perform this task. A host-based firewall controls the private network applications such as e-mail, Telnet, and FTP at the individual or group level by focusing on the type of action and the time period in which the action is taking place. By concentrating on the time period these firewalls can be very effective since many unauthorized attempts take place at night or after hours. Host-based firewalls are able to log actions that take place at the firewall. By using this data network administrators are able to identify potential breaches to security that may be directed to the private network.

6-5-1-3 Choosing a Firewall

The discussion about firewalls should not lead you to believe that firewalls provide complete security. This is far from true. Sophisticated hackers and computer criminals are able to threaten any security measure if they are taken individually. Major break-ins have recently occurred at NASA, NATO, and General Electric. GE even had a firewall installed. In January 1995, Stanford University was attacked by a hacker using an "IP spoofing" technique, which makes private networks think that hackers are legitimate users. IP spoofing is the equivalent of forgery. Filtering software is available from major vendors of networking equipment. This filtering software will not allow access from an outside source to any internal data. Therefore, firewalls should be used with other security measures and policies we will discuss later.

To improve the chances of success when choosing a firewall, a prospective organization should analyze the following factors:

1. The organization should first identify its objectives and the data that is trying to secure against intruders and computer criminals. A risk analysis should also be performed at this stage in order to assess the costs and benefits of a firewall.

2. The options and capabilities of the firewall candidates must be identified and analyzed against the organization needs. For example, if e-mail, Usenet, and FTP are some of the typical applications of the Internet for a typical organization, then the firewall chosen must support at least these activities.

3. The organization must decide between the two most commonly used types of firewalls, router-based and host-based, and then compare and contrast the features of each type against its security needs and goals.

4. The cost of firewalls with their features and capabilities must be identified and analyzed. The cost of a firewall varies significantly. Organizations should also remember that the most expensive firewall is not necessarily the best. Some organizations (depending on their specific needs) may be able to obtain a reasonable security measure by a cheaper router-based firewall.

5. A balance between security and user friendliness must be found. Some firewalls are designed by placing accuracy and security ahead of ease of use and functionality. Others try to build their firewalls by putting user friendliness before security while trying to provide a good entry level solution. An acceptable design is a matter of tradeoffs and the best policy is to design a system that best matches the organization's needs and objectives.

Table 6-5

Popular Firewalls on the Market

AltaVista Firewall (Digital Equipment Corp.)
Black Hole (Miikyway Networks, Inc.)
BorderWare (Secure Computing Corp.)
CrptoWall (Radguard Ltd.)
CyberGuard Firewall (CyberGuard Corp.)
FireWall-1 (CheckPoint Software Technologies, Inc.)
GFX Internet Firewall System (Global Technology Associates, Inc.)
Interceptor (Technologic, Inc.)
On Guard (On Technology Corp.)
PrivateNet (NEC Technologies, Inc.)
Secured Network Gateway (IBM)
TurnStyle Firewall System (Atlantic Systems Group)

6. The vendor's reputation, support staff and maintenance, and update policies are important issues that must be identified and analyzed before making the final decision. Because of the significant increase in demand for firewalls the number of vendors is steadily increasing. Not all of these vendors offer quality products. The type of user support offered by these vendors is an essential criterion before choosing a firewall.

7. To build a firewall from scratch is a viable option for some organizations. Although this option maybe more expensive than choosing a readily available product, the tailor-made feature and the flexibility offered by a firewall developed in-house may outweigh its costs.

Table 6-5 introduces some of the popular firewalls on the market.

6-5-2 PHYSICAL SECURITY

Physical security primarily addresses the concerns of access control to computers as well as the devices available to secure computers from acts of theft. Physical security is achieved through the following:

- Identification badges;
- Proximity-release door openers;
- Corner bolts;
- Steel encasements;
- Electronic trackers;
- Token;
- Cable shielding;
- Room shielding.

Let us briefly explain these measures.

- *Identification badges* Identification badges are checked against a list of authorized personnel. Checks must be done on a regular basis so that any change in personnel is noted.
- *Proximity-release door openers* The proximity-release door opener is an effective way to control access to the computer room. Access to the computer area is gained through the use of a small radio transmitter located in the authorized employees' identification badges. When the authorized person comes to within a predetermined distance of the entry door, a radio signal sends a key number to the receiver, which opens the door for admittance.
- *Corner bolts* Corner bolts and steel bolts are inexpensive methods of securing a microcomputer to a desktop or counter. These devices are a combination of locks and cables. Steel bolts are used to secure micros to a heavy-duty locking

plate, which is then bonded to an anchor pad that has adhesive on both sides. The pad is then adhered to a desk or counter.

• *Steel encasements* Steel encasements are designed to fit over the entire computer. The encasement is made of heavy-gauge welded steel. The encasement is kept locked and the security administrator or another designated person has control of the key.

• *Electronic trackers* Electronic trackers are secured to the computer at the AC power insert point. If the power cord is disconnected, a coded transmitter sends a message to an alarm, which sounds, and/or a camera, which is activated to record the disturbance.

• *Token* A token is a transmission device worn around the user's neck. The device activates the computer only when a user wearing a token is seated in front of the screen.

• *Cable shielding* Cable shielding is accomplished by braiding layers of the conductors to form a braided shield. This scheme protects the data from electromagnetic emanations. This is done by either shielding or by using a conduit. Shielding is more difficult with hardware devices than with cables.

• *Room shielding* Room shielding is done by spraying a conductive material in the computer room. This material reduces the number of signals being transmitted, or it completely confines the signals to the computer rooms.

6-5-3 SOFTWARE SECURITY

Software security is designed to protect the system from data integrity loss and unauthorized access, and to provide data security. Software security is accomplished by one of the following:

- Passwords;
- Access codes;
- Terminal resource security;
- Data encryption.

These measures are explained below.

• *Passwords* Passwords are sets of numbers, characters, words, or combinations of these that must be entered into the system for access. Passwords are the most basic access controls, and their length and composition determines their vulnerability to discovery by unauthorized users. The human element, which plays a major role in the success of the password control, is one of the most notable weaknesses of the password security system.

• *Access codes* Access codes are the simplest form of access control, and the most basic security method is the missing-character code. Files and/or programs are listed in the directory incompletely. In order for the user to access the data, he or she must fill in the missing character(s). The challenge is that the authorized user remembers the missing characters.

• *Terminal resource security* Terminal resource security is a software capability that erases the screen automatically and signs the user off after a predetermined length of inactivity. There are also programs that allow the users to access data only during certain time slots. Any attempts to access the system other than during the predetermined times results in the denial of access.

• *Data encryption* Data encryption transforms original information called plain text or clear text into transformed information, called cipher text or cipher, which usually has the appearance of random, nonreadable data. The transformed information is called the cryptogram. The rules selected for encryption, known as the encryption algorithm, determine how simple or how complex the transformation process should be.

Simply put, data encryption means to scramble the original data to a form not understandable by the user and sending it to its destination. At the receiving point the user will descramble the data to its original form by using a key. There are many different algorithms for encrypting data. One of the oldest encryption techniques was developed by Julius Caesar. Caesar used a simple substitution algorithm in which each letter in the original message was replaced by the letter three positions further in the alphabet. For example, the word *top* will be transmitted as *wrs*. Figure 6-4 shows a simple example of this encryption technique.

Endorsement of the Clipper chip by the Clinton administration has sparked business interest in the development of encryption technology. A National Security Agency hardware security device, the Clipper chip would enable the government to decode computer or telephone communications since they would hold the master key. Apparently, the purpose would be for use in FBI or other governmental investigations.

Encryption is basically the process of encoding and decoding data. It can also be used to provide digital signatures to authenticate sender identities and to verify that the message has not been altered. Digital signatures are vital to the success of online financial transactions [1].

An alliance formed between Microsoft and Visa in November 1994 is aimed at developing a secure-transaction software to authenticate buyers and sellers in the Visanet payment system. Visa believes corporate customers will "shop till they drop on the Internet." This will include everything from placement of bids to negotiation of deals [1].

Affordable hardware encryption is also being pursued by a number of companies; this is noted for being faster and more secure than software encryption.

A number of competitors like Visa and MasterCard are working together to develop specifications for smart cards. Smart cards are a hardware platform that

```
┌─────────────────────────────────┐
│        Original Message         │
│         This Is A Secret        │
└─────────────────────────────────┘
                 │
                 ▼
┌─────────────────────────────────┐
│          Encryption             │
│          Algorithm              │
└─────────────────────────────────┘
                 │
                 ▼
┌─────────────────────────────────┐
│      Transmitted Message        │
│        WKLV LV D VHFUHW         │
└─────────────────────────────────┘
                 │
                 ▼
┌─────────────────────────────────┐
│       Decryption Algorithm      │
└─────────────────────────────────┘
                 │
                 ▼
┌─────────────────────────────────┐
│        The Final Message        │
│         This Is A Secret        │
└─────────────────────────────────┘
```

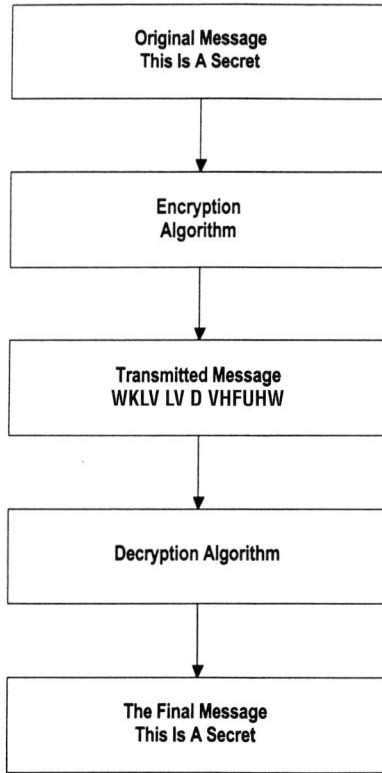

Figure 6-4   A simple encryption technique.

contain miniature math coprocessors. They will be used for encryption of telephones, computers, and interactive TVs. To date, however, they have not been fully field tested and remain expensive for the majority of consumers.

Cryptographic techniques of private and public keys rather than platform type are expected to be at the heart of the encryption debate. With private key encryption, both sender and receiver use the same key. This implies a one-to-one relationship and a unique set of private keys for each relationship with each party holding a copy of the private key. Banks currently use a method called Data Encryption Standard (DES) that incorporates a private key to conduct financial transactions on private networks. There are limitations because a prior relationship of trust must already have been established. Also, it would be cumbersome to send private keys to all parties with whom a user may want to communicate. Therefore, instantaneous communications or sending communications to more than one person, which both happen on the Internet, would not work with private key encryption.

Public key encryption probably works better for public networks such as the Internet where each business would receive a private key and a public key. This implies a one-to-many relationship, with a business holding the only copy of the private key. A business selling on a public network could publish its public keys as it would a telephone number. Customers would then have the capability to send their credit card numbers over the network using the public key. At the receiving end, a business would decrypt the message with its private key.

In addition to encryption and certification, three other areas of consideration are vital for electronic commerce: authentication, confirmation, and nonrepudiation. The mere possession of a credit card number does not ensure a legitimate user. Two factors are crucial in authentication: what a receiver knows to be accurate and what a sender is providing to them. Passwords and personal information such as mother's maiden name, social security number, date of birth, and so on can be successfully used for authentication. Physical proof, such as fingerprints or retina scans, works even better. Order confirmation and notice of receipt of goods must be incorporated into the electronic commerce framework. Nonrepudiation is also necessary to bind trading partners to a deal. Before businesses expose themselves and ship expensive merchandise long distances, they are going to want assurance that the other party will abide by the agreement. Currently, this feature is missing in the proposed electronic commerce plans [6].

6-6 GUIDELINES FOR A COMPREHENSIVE SECURITY SYSTEM

Security measures can be improved with moderate expense. To establish a comprehensive security plan inexpensively, an organization can utilize its existing resources. The following suggestions should assist an organization in establishing security guidelines [2,3].

1. Organize a security committee. The committee will be responsible for the following:
   A. Setting security policies and procedures. A clear and precise network policy plays a significant role in an organization. A lack of such policies and procedures may result in the failure of employees to understand what undesirable activities are and, consequently, the inability of the organization to prosecute abusers.
   B. Assessing the effect of system security in the organization periodically.
   C. Distributing passwords and account numbers.
   D. Providing security training for key decision makers and computer users.

    E. Establishing the necessary protection plan for the computer-based information system.

    F. Developing a regular audit procedure for log-in and system use.

    G. Obtaining employee and top management support for security policy enforcement.

    H. Evaluating and revising the security policies constantly.

    I. Labeling hardware and software with warning stickers.

    J. Overseeing the security policy enforcement.

    K. Designing color-coded disks.

    L. Advocating the use of paper shredders for computer waste papers.

    M. Designing an audit trail procedure for both input and output.

    N. Designing a computer operation log to record the log-on and log-off times for different users.

    O. Defining employee duties related to security enforcement.

    P. Documenting and labeling all hardware and software components.

2. Post the organization's security policies in a visible place and/or in front of any entry port (log-in station). The signs should state the organization's policies on security.

3. Encourage employee sensitivity to security problems.

4. Keep security codes strictly secret.

5. Revoke terminated employee's passwords and badges immediately so that a malicious ex-employee cannot be destructive.

6. Keep sensitive data, software and printouts locked up to reduce the chance of accessing, stealing, or altering the information.

7. Exit from the programs and systems promptly. Log off and turn off the computer. This prohibits unauthorized access to vulnerable files.

8. Limit the employee access to files to reduce system access opportunities.

9. Limit computer access to authorized personnel only. Curious personnel must be kept away from the system.

10. Consider unlisted telephone numbers. An unlisted number deters hackers and intruders to some degree.

11. Compare the communication log with communication billing periodically. The log should contain all of the outgoing calls with the users' name and call destinations and time in and out. Also, keep a log of calls in and out. Billing discrepancies should be investigated.

12. Be prepared for computer virus attacks by using antivirus utility programs and consider the following:

    A. Boot your computer with a known, write-protected operating system floppy disk.

    B. Install only licensed software purchased from reputable vendors. After installation store the original copies in a secure off-site location.

    C. Do not use software that arrives with its packaging open.

    D. Do not install software brought to the office from a home computer.

    E. Install only the needed software on each computer.

    F. Be aware of the beta version and shareware and freeware programs. Do not be the first person to try these programs.

    G. Whenever downloading or copying a file (from the Internet or from other sources) check it first for a possible virus.

13. Observe the following against various computer threats:

    A. Install smoke detectors in the computer rooms.

    B. Keep fire extinguishers in and near computer rooms.

    C. Maintain no-smoking policies.

    D. Install alarm systems for fire and smokes.

    E. Maintain a steady temperature in the computer rooms.

    F. Maintain humidity level between 20 and 80%.

    G. Equip the heating and cooling systems with air filters to protect against dust.

    H. Keep computers away from glass windows and high surfaces, particularly if you are in high-risk earthquake region.

    I. Secure computer equipment against strong vibrations and make sure that other objects will not fall on them in case of strong vibrations.

    J. If a computer gets wet, let it dry thoroughly before it is used again.

    K. Too much or too little electricity can destroy a computer. Install surge protectors.

    L. If lightning storm strikes, turn off all computers and then unplug them. To protect backup tapes from the magnetic field created by lightning, store all the tape backups as far away as possible from a building's steel structure. In mountain areas install lightning arrestors.

    M. Install antistatic carpeting in the computer rooms.

14. Observe the following physical security measures:

    A. The simplest way to keep someone from walking out the door with your computer is to bolt it down.

    B. Use ID badges and a token in order to screen out unauthorized users.

15. When using the Internet, establish firewall.

These steps should be used as a guideline. Not every organization will need to implement every step; however, some may need to include even more steps to fit their needs.

6-7 PREPARING FOR A DISASTER

As discussed earlier the sources for computer threats are numerous, they are controllable and uncontrollable, they are done by accident, either intentionally and unintentionally. In any event, an organization must be prepared to respond to a disaster if it occurs. One of the best security measures is to plan for disaster. The response process known as the disaster recovery planning system can play a major role in putting the organization back on its feet.

A disaster recovery plan is useful because it gives the organization a place to begin bringing the operation back to normal. It lists the tasks that must be performed and includes a map for recovery. Disaster may strike in one of the following forms:

- Hardware and software failures;
- Human error;
- Sabotage;
- Natural and other disaster (refer back to Table 6-1);
- Power failure;
- Theft;
- Environmental contamination.

It has been reported that more than half of all the organizations throughout the world do not have a disaster recovery plan in place. Many of these organizations are not able to return to normal if disaster strikes. To guard against disaster, the following steps must be taken before a disaster strikes:

- Back up all of your computer files.
- Periodically review security and fire standards for your computer facilities.
- Make sure the staff is properly trained and that they are aware of the consequences of possible disaster and what actions need to be taken to prevent such disasters.
- Regularly test your disaster recovery plan with trial data.
- Identify all of the vendors and manufacturers of the software and hardware used in the organization. Record their most recent addresses and phone numbers.
- Document all changes done to the initial hardware and software.
- Get a comprehensive insurance policy for your computer facilities.
- Use hot sites—separate computer facilities with all the needed equipment.
- Use cold sites—rooms with raised floors, air conditioning, and humidity control without the computer itself.
- Share ownership of back-up facilities.
- Use decentralized computer facilities.
- Arrange a reciprocal agreement with another installation.
- Maintain minimal cash on site.
- Check and recheck the sprinkler systems and fire extinguishers.
- Review the insurance policy to make sure that the coverage is adequate.

6-8 STEPS TO TAKE WHEN A DISASTER STRIKES

You have taken all the security measures and you have prepared for a disaster, and then disaster strikes. The following are some of the important steps that must be taken in order to bring the operation back to normal:

1. Contact the insurance company to confirm the agreement regarding the implementation of the recovery plan.
2. Restore the telephone lines and other communication systems.
3. Notify all the impacted people including customers, suppliers, and employees.
4. Implement a help desk for assisting the impacted people.
5. Put together a management crisis team to oversee the recovery plan.
6. Notify the impacted people that the recovery is underway.
7. Document all the actions taken for getting back to normal.

SUMMARY

This chapter discussed security issues and measures in a network environment. Computer threats were identified as natural, intentional, and unintentional. Security measures were discussed in terms of general security, physical security, and software security. Firewalls and data encryption were discussed in detail as two important types of security measures. The chapter presented detailed guidelines for establishing a comprehensive security system and it concluded with a series of guidelines for preparing for a disaster with the steps to be taken if a disaster strikes.

REVIEW QUESTIONS

1. What is computer security?
2. Why must security issues be taken seriously?
3. What are the important aspects of a security system?
4. What are some examples of natural threats to a computer system?
5. What are some examples of other threats to a computer system?
6. What are some examples of intentional threats?
7. What are some example of unintentional threats? How can an organization guard against these threats?

8. What is a computer virus?

9. How does a computer virus spread?

10. What are some of the sources for computer viruses?

11. How do you guard against a computer virus?

12. What are some of the popular antivirus programs on the market?

13. What is a Trojan horse?

14. What is a computer worm?

15. What are biometric security measures?

16. Compare and contrast biometric and nonbiometric security measures.

17. Why aren't we using more biometric security measures to protect our data resources? Discuss.

18. What are some examples of physical security measures?

19. What are some examples of software security measures?

20. What is a firewall?

21. What are two important types of firewalls?

22. Generally speaking which type of a firewall is more effective? Discuss.

23. What are some examples of the commercial firewalls on the market?

24. What are some of the causes for a computer disaster?

25. How do you choose a firewall?

26. Do security risks increase in a distributed system? If yes, how? What can be done to avoid security loss?

27. What are some of the computer threats associated with each component of a CBIS? How are they prevented?

28. What is a disaster recovery plan?

29. What are the components of a comprehensive disaster recovery plan?

PROJECTS

1. How are we going to protect our computers? Can we really implement a tight security system? Consult with the computer center of your school or an organization that you are familiar with. Has it had any problem with computer security? What type of security system is in place? Which is easier to implement, system security or physical security? Discuss.

2. You have been asked to put together a security policy for a local bank. What will you include in this document? What are the major sources of computer

threats for this bank? How should the bank guard against the insider threats? What are the major outsider threats? Discuss.

3. How do you protect the security of your own PC? How do you deal with a computer virus? What are the steps that you should follow before you copy a file from a bulletin board? Among the guidelines introduced in Section 6-6, which one(s) apply to you as a student? What should you do to protect your password?

4. What should a local CPA firm do in order to prepare for a disaster? What should be included in a disaster recovery plan?

5. By consulting the computer and MIS journals identify two of the effective antivirus software programs on the market. How do these software programs deal with unknown viruses? Discuss.

6. By consulting the computer and MIS journals compare and contrast a router-based and a host-based firewall. What are the major differences between these two classes of firewalls? Why are there such price differences among these software programs? Discuss.

7. The chapter listed a number of physical security devices. Visit the computer center of your school or an organization that you are familiar with and see which devices are being used. Why won't physical security alone provide comprehensive security for your computer system? Discuss.

KEY TERMS

Accuracy, 150
Access codes, 162–163
Availability, 150–151
Cable shielding, 162
Call-back modems, 157
Computer security, 150–152
Computer virus, 152–155
Corner bolts, 161–162
Data encryption, 163–165
Electronic trackers, 162
Fingerprint, 156
Firewalls, 157–161
Hand geometry, 156
Host-based firewall, 158–159
Identification badges, 161
Logic bombs, 154

Palmprint, 156
Passwords, 162
Proximity-release door openers, 161
Retinal scanning, 156
Room shielding, 162
Router-based firewalls, 158–159
Secrecy, 150
Signature analysis, 156
Steel encasements, 162
Terminal resource security, 163
Token, 162
Trap doors, 154
Trojan horse, 153–154
Voice recognition, 156
Worms, 153

REFERENCES

[1] Appleby, C. (January 2, 1995). Making security a reality for all. *Information Week,* 38–40.

[2] Bidgoli, H. (1997). *Modern information systems for managers.* San Diego: Academic Press.

[3] Bidgoli, H., and Azarmsa, R. (October 1989). Computer security: New managerial concern for 80's and beyond. *Journal of Systems Management,* 21–27.

[4] Garfield, M. J. (Winter 1997). Planning for Internet security. *Information Systems Management,* 40–46.

[5] Groenfeldt, T. (January 30, 1995). The online safety net. *Information Week,* 74–84.

[6] Marion, L. (February 15, 1995). Who's guarding the till at the cyber mall. *Datamation,* 38–41.

[7] McCarthy, V. (May 1996). Building a firewall. *Datamation,* 74–76.

[8] Ranum, M. J. (July 1995). Create walls of fire. *Security Management,* 131–132+.

[9] Sanders, S. (January 1996). Putting a lock on corporate data. *Data Communications,* 78–80.

[10] Wilder, C. (January 23, 1995). Online security push. *Information Week,* 24.

Chapter 7

The Information Superhighway and Global Information Systems

Learning Objectives

After studying this chapter, you should be able to:

- Define Internet as the backbone for the information superhighway.
- Review the history of the Internet.
- Define some Internet terminology.
- Outline international participation in Internet.
- Review popular Internet applications.
- Discuss global information systems.
- Elaborate on the components and applications of global information systems.
- Define popular Internet tools and navigational techniques.
- Explore security, economic, and social issues of the information superhighway.

7-9   Internet Applications
    7-9-1   Marketing
    7-9-2   Online Employment
    7-9-3   Banking
    7-9-4   Online Software
    7-9-5   Politics
    7-9-6   Healthcare
    7-9-7   Miscellaneous Applications
7-10   Global Information Systems: An Overview
7-11   Definitions and Requirements of Global Computer-Based Information Systems (GCBISs)
7-12   Components of a Global Information System
7-13   Organizational Structure and Global Information Systems
7-14   Global Information Systems in Action
    7-14-1 Digital Equipment Corporation
    7-14-2 Frank Russell Corporation
7-15   Obstacles in Designing Global Information Systems
7-16   Economic Issues
7-17   Social Implications
7-18   Future Development

7-1 INTRODUCTION

This chapter reviews the basics of the Internet as the backbone of the information superhighway. It provides a brief history of Internet development, and it reviews Internet access options, navigational tools, and basic terminology. The chapter discusses international participation in the Internet and it explains some current and future Internet applications. Global information systems as a growing technology will be reviewed. Definitions, components, organizational structures, and applications of global information systems will be discussed. Economic and social implications of the Internet will be explored. The chapter concludes with a review of the future development of the information superhighway.

7-2 THE INFORMATION SUPERHIGHWAY: AN OVERVIEW

The backbone of the information superhighway is the Internet. The Internet is a collection of thousands of computers and network systems of all sizes. We can simply refer to the Internet as the network of networks. No one actually owns or runs it. Each network is locally administered and funded, in some cases by volunteers. It is estimated that more than 200 countries are directly or indirectly involved in the Internet. This number is increasing on a daily basis.

The Internet started in 1969 as a Defense Department Advanced Research Projects Agency project called ARPANET. ARPANET was an experimental project to link remote computers for national security in the event that a nuclear war destroyed communication lines. Since starting the Internet in 1987, the network has grown more than 20 times in size. Table 7-1 [8] provides a review of the major events in the Internet's development.

ARPANET evolved into NSFNET (National Science Foundation Network) in 1987 that was the initial Internet backbone. Internet was derived from the term "internetworking," which signified the networking of networks. NSFNET connected four supercomputers located at San Diego, Cornell, Pittsburgh, and Illinois to form the backbone. Other universities and government labs were subsequently added to the network. Federal subsidiaries are currently being phased out and three commercial fiber-optic backbones have been created: AlterNet, PSInet, and SprintLink. These backbones link all the networks in a three-level structure: backbones, regional networks, and local area networks (LANs). Backbones provide connectivity to other international backbones. Local area networks provide the standard user interface. Phone lines (twisted pair), coaxial cables, microwaves, satellites, and other communications media are used to connect local area networks to the regional networks. TCP/IP (transmission control protocol/Internet protocol) is the language of the Internet that allows the networked systems to understand each other. Regional networks have been subsidized by the NSF and state governments. NSFNET's acceptable application policy initially restricted the Internet to research and educational institutions; commercial use was not allowed.

Due to increasing demand, additional backbones were allowed to connect to NSFNET and commercial applications began. Initial NSFNET throughput (the amount of information that can go through) was 45 Mbps (million bits per second). The current throughput is more than 600 Mbps. TCP/IP divides network traffic into individually addressed packets that are routed over different paths.

7-3 INTERNET ACCESS OPTIONS

Four types of Internet access options are currently available: terminal or shell accounts, dial-up protocol service, direct connections, and online services as the latest addition. Terminal or shell accounts and dial-up protocols are the two primary Internet access options for personal computers. Terminal accounts require a modem and communications software to dial a host computer that is connected to the Internet. With this access method, a personal computer serves as a dumb terminal. This means it sends and receives information with no processing power

Table 7-1

Major Events in the Internet Development

Date	Event
September 1, 1969	ARPANET is born.
1984	William Gibson coins the term "cyberspace".
1987	Backbone to the National Research and Education Network is created by the National Science Foundation. It is called NSFNET and signifies the birth of the Internet.
November 2, 1988	Worm virus attacks over 6000 computers connected to the Internet, including Department of Defense.
February 11, 1991	Bush administration approves Senator Al Gore's idea to develop a high-speed national computer and the term "information superhighway" first appears.
January 1992	High Performance Computing Act signed into law.
April 1993	Birth of Internet Talk Radio—weekly, half-hour show.
June 1, 1993	President Clinton and Vice President Gore receive Internet e-mail addresses.
November 1993	Pacific Bell publicizes plan to spend $16 billion on the information superhighway.
January 1994	MCI announces six-year plan to spend $20 billion on an international information highway.
October 1994	White House home page established on the Internet.
November 1994	A consortium of companies beginning to do business on the Internet called CommerceNet receives a $520,000 grant to apply toward Internet connectivity and electronic commerce.
1995	The World Wide Web Consortium is formed.
April 1995	Netscape becomes the most popular graphical navigator for surfing the Web.
August 1995	Microsoft releases the first version of the Internet Explorer.
April 1996	Yahoo, the most popular search engine, goes public.
January 1997	Microsoft releases Office 97 with major Internet support.
1998	Microsoft Internet Explorer becomes a major player in the browser market.

of its own. Since most host computers are UNIX-based, this option can be complicated because of the commands required to navigate the net. Another drawback is that the users are restricted to host computer options that may be limited. However, this is the least expensive access option.

Dial-up protocol is an option that gives a user full access to the Internet. A computer can be connected to the Internet via a telephone line utilizing a high-speed modem. In addition, TCP/IP software is installed on the PC to provide an interface. There are two types of dial-up protocols: serial line Internet protocol

(SLIP) or point-to-point protocol (PPP). With SLIP connections, packets travel faster; however, reliability is lower because packets are not evaluated as they are sent. The PPP option on the other hand, is a newer protocol that monitors packet traffic to ensure the accuracy of packets received. The PPP option may be a slower method of transmission but it is more reliable.

There are more than 200 U.S. commercial access providers on the market now and the number is increasing. Price, reputation of the provider and reliability of service should be considered in selecting a provider. Local providers can eliminate the cost of long-distance phone calls. Fixed rates for unlimited connect time can also pay off. Access may be limited if users frequently receive busy signals when attempting to connect to the Internet. Therefore, the quality of service should be examined before choosing one of these options. User support is also essential for navigating the complex paths of the Internet.

Direct connections are the most expensive access option. Accordingly, this option is normally limited to large networks that have UNIX operating systems. Both SLIP and PPP accounts and direct connections require that TCP/IP software be installed on each computer in the network.

Online services such as America Online, Prodigy, Genie, Delphi, and CompuServe also offer Internet access. Initially their services were quite minimal and limited to e-mail, newsgroups, and basic file transfer options. However, they are adding more options to their offerings.

7-4 DOMAIN NAME SYSTEMS

Before a user can begin to navigate the Internet, an understanding of the domain name systems (DNSs) (also called domain name server) is essential. Domain names are unique identifiers of computer or network addresses on the Internet. They come in two forms: English-like names and numeric or IP (Internet protocol) addresses. The Internet Assigned Numbers Authority (IANA) assigns and keeps track of these addresses. Users can obtain addresses from network administrators.

IP addresses are inconvenient because numbers seem to be harder to remember. The English-like names are electronically converted to IP addresses for routing. Domain names are structured as follows: *machine.subdomain.organization. domain;* however, it can contain as few as two alphanumeric fields separated by periods (pronounced "dot"). Combinations of the letters of the alphabet as well as the numbers 0 through 9 can be used. The hyphen is the only other character utilized; spaces are not allowed.

The top-level domain is the field on the far most right. It refers to the type of organization or country. Top-level domains are divided into organizational and geographic domains as follows:

Organizational domains

.com	Commercial organizations (e.g., Microsoft)
.edu	Education and academic organizations (e.g., California State University)
.int	International organizations (e.g., United Nations)
.mil	U.S. military organizations (e.g., U.S. Army)
.gov	U.S. government organizations (e.g., Internal Revenue Service)
.net	Backbone, regional, and commercial networks (e.g., The National Science Foundation's Internet Network Information Center)
.org	Other organizations such as research and nonprofit (e.g., The Internet Town Hall)

Geographic domains

.au	Australia
.br	Brazil
.ca	Canada
.fr	France
.de	Germany
.hk	Hong Kong
.il	Israel
.jp	Japan
.kr	Korea (Republic)
.ru	Russia
.es	Spain
.uk	United Kingdom
.us	United States
.va	Vatican City State
.zw	Zimbabwe

This system makes it easy to identify the type or location of the organization by looking at the last section of the domain name. Organization, which is the second field from the right, simply refers to the name of the organization. A name for a small company is as easy as a company name. The two left-most fields of the domain name refer to the computer. This is relevant for large organizations with several levels of sub-domains. For example, my home page address at California State University, Bakersfield, is:

http://www.csubak.edu/~hbidgoli.

A more complete Internet address is the address of a document in the Virtual Tourist site as follows:

http://www.vtourist.com/vt/usa.htm

A brief explanation from left to right follows:

http Means of access, HyperText Transfer Protocol. This is how the majority of the documents in the Web are transferred.

www.vtourist.com This is the address of a Web site. It is uniquely defined and differentiated from any other Web site.

vt This is a path or directory. A server may be divided into a series of directories for a better organization.

usa.htm This is the document itself. The htm extension indicates that this is a html (Hypertext Markup Language) document. All hypermedia documents are written in HTML format. Servers that do no support long extensions display htm, other servers display html.

7-5 NAVIGATIONAL TOOLS

Navigating the Internet can be a challenging task. Several navigational tools are available but they may confuse beginners. Names such as Telnet, FTP, Archie, Gopher, Veronica, World Wide Web (WWW), Lynx, Netscape, Yahoo, and Mosaic make it confusing to decide which one to use and for what purpose.

Let's provide a brief description of these various tools. Telnet and FTP (File Transfer Protocol) were developed around the same time and are among the rudimentary navigational tools. Telnet is used for remote dial-in and allows a user to gain remote access. The Telnet command followed by a space and the computer name will connect a user to a remote computer. Upon connection, which can be a matter of seconds, the user is presented with the remote computer's menu system and the user can start navigating the Internet.

FTP is a tool by which specific files are transferred from one computer to another. Again, the FTP command followed by a space and the computer name will connect a user to a remote site. Visitors are normally allowed to log in as "anonymous" by using "guest" as a password. From this point, it's just a matter of navigating the various directory levels to locate the desired files. FTP requires that users have a basic knowledge of DOS or UNIX. UNIX is a case-sensitive operating system. Users must know the computer and file names in advance.

Archie is a search engine or file-finding utility for FTP; it tells a user where to locate a file. Again, file names must be known in advance. It was developed at the McGill University School of Computer Science in Montreal. Archie does not inform the user what the contents of the file are. WAIS (wide area information server) was designed for that purpose. By simply identifying a few keywords, WAIS searches the contents of several hundred databases and identifies which files contain specific data; however, WAIS has not been widely implemented yet so it is not always available for use [24].

Gopher is a hierarchical menu-driven system that was developed at the University of Minnesota. As recently as 1992, there were only 100 Gopher servers in existence. At the present time, there are more than several thousand. Gopher allows a user to navigate through a hierarchical menu system, or to link to other computers or services such as online library catalogs. Gopher combines the Telnet and FTP tools into a menu-driven system where a user can either select a menu number, move to a desired selection, or click on an icon rather than using DOS or UNIX-like commands. It is much more user-friendly and is more suitable for searching for broad information rather than for specific files.

Veronica is the search engine for Gopher. Developed at the University of Nevada, Veronica can be accessed as a Gopher menu item. Users provide keywords and Veronica searches and provides a Gopher menu with resource items containing those keywords. Resources can be directories, text files, binary files, graphic files, or sound images. Selecting the desired menu item and pressing the equal sign will identify what host computer contains the resource.

The World Wide Web (WWW or the Web) changed all of this by introducing a true graphical environment. The WWW is one of the latest generation of Internet navigational tools. It has been around since 1989. It combines the attributes of the Gopher system with hypertext. The WWW consists of a large portion of the Internet that contains hypermedia documents. Hypermedia is an extension of hypertext. Hypertext allows a user to follow a desired path by highlighting or clicking on bolded text to follow a particular "thread" or topic. This involves accessing files, applications, and computers in a nonsequential fashion. It combines text, images, sounds, and full-motion video in the same document. It allows information retrieval with a click of a button. Hypertext is an approach to data management in which data are stored in a network of nodes connected by links. The nodes are designed to be accessed through an interactive browsing system. A hypertext document includes node links and supporting indexes for a particular topic. A hypertext document may include data, voice, images, and video. This type of document is usually called hypermedia. In hypertext documents the physical and logical layouts are usually different. This is not the case in a paper document. In a paper document the order is established by the author of the paper.

A hypertext system provides users with nonsequential paths to access information. This means that information does not have to be accessed sequentially as in a book. A hypertext system allows the user to make any request that the author or designer of the hypertext provides through links. These links choices are similar to lists of indexes.

Any computer that stores hypermedia documents and makes them available to the other computers in the Web is called a server or a Web server. The computers that request these documents are called clients. A client can be your PC at home or a node in a local area network at your university or at the organization where you work. The most exciting feature about the Internet and the WWW is that these hypermedia documents can be stored anywhere in the world. A user can practically jump from a site in the United States to a site in Paris, France, in a few seconds.

Lynx is a text-based browser available for the WWW. It was developed at the University of Kansas. You can log onto the UNIX computer with a Telnet session, type Lynx at the UNIX prompt, and use the keyboard to navigate the Web. However, a user must know the specific commands, so it is not especially user friendly.

Netscape, Mosaic, and Microsoft Internet Explorer are the hottest new graphical browsers available for navigating the WWW. Each of these browsers combines graphics with audio and visual capabilities. Each Web server has a "home page" that publishes information about the location. Using Lynx, a user will find this information in text-form, while graphical browsers such as Netscape and Mosaic provide images, sound clips, and video clips as well.

Internet Phone by VocalTec was released in February 1995. It provides telephone-like communication over the Internet. Long-distance costs were traded for an Internet access fee. An Internet Phone kit complete with speaker phone, handset, and PC sound card are commercially available now. Internet Phone quality is similar to a CB radio, in that users experience one or two second delays, communication is limited to individuals who have access to the same hardware and software, and only one person can speak at a time [36].

Netscape has become the leading Web browser in a short time. Netscape is available for both Windows and Macintosh platforms. It is relatively easy to use and install. Netscape provides a true graphical environment that allows the user to surf the Net using a mouse and the point-and-click technique. Similar to other Windows applications, Netscape features a standard menu bar and toolbar buttons for frequently used commands.

The Microsoft Internet Explorer is yet another graphical browser that has attracted much attention in recent years. It provides the same type of interface that Netscape does. With strong marketing support from Microsoft and improvement in the features, the Internet Explorer has become a major player in the browser market.

Yahoo is one of the best-known search engines on the Web that can be used for searching categories or individual documents. Categories such as art, business, and entertainment are organized by topic. The user can go to a category and then navigate for specific information. Yahoo also includes an internal search engine that can expedite the search process.

7-6 BASIC TERMINOLOGY

To be able to understand the Internet and information superhighway literature a basic understanding of the following vocabulary is necessary.

Backbone   High-capacity links, microwaves, fiber optics, and satellites used as information
                  carrying channels for the Internet.

Bandwidth   Information carrying capacity of the communication medium.

Cyberspace	The land of knowledge, the collective environments or places created by computer networks.
FAQ	Frequently asked questions, a document that contains questions and answers regarding a specific topic, application, or Internet service. Before asking questions or posting a message, it is a good idea to read the FAQ of a given site.
F2F	Face-to-face as opposed to communication in Cyberspace.
Flame	Insult—a slang term used on the Internet to mean an emotional or inflammatory note, usually written in response to another message.
Home Page	Starting point for each WWW server that contains information about the location including textual, graphical, and audio and visual formats. Just about all major organizations in the United States now have their own home page.
HTTP	HyperText Transfer Protocol is a set of standards known as protocols to govern the way data are transmitted across the World Wide Web.
Hypermedia	An information storage system in which each page of information can include embedded references to images, texts, sounds, or video clips.
Hypertext	Provides links between files, applications and computers. Using this feature, the user can search in any direction.
IMHO	In My Humble Opinion.
IMO	In My Opinion.
Internauts	Users of the Internet.
Lurk	To read, without posting, messages to a news group or an e-mail discussion list. Recommended behavior for individuals new to a list or group.
Net	Internet.
Netiquette	Etiquette appropriate for Internet use. A list of suggestions for how to behave when using the Internet.
Netizens	Users of the Internet.
PMJI	Pardon My Jumping In.
RTFAQ	Read The Frequently Asked Questions. Read the FAQ document before posting messages that waste time or they have already been answered.
RTM	Read The Manual. A polite suggestion to refer to on-line help or the manual before posting the question.
Surf	To browse the Internet without any particular goal in mind.
SYSOP	System Operator.
TCP/IP	Transmission Control Protocol / Internet Protocol, the standard and software that divide data into packets and forward the packets to the IP protocol layer in the TCP/IP stacks.
TIA	Thanks In Advance. A pleasant touch at the end of a response or request for assistance.
URL	Uniform Resource Locator (new naming convention that includes application: double slash "//", user log-in name and password, host domain name, port number and path). For example http.//www_isu.csubak.edu/. In this example, **http** stands for Hypertext Transfer Protocol, or the rules used to create hypertext pages on the Web. The //**www_isu.cusbak.edu** is the domain address for one Web server at California State University-Bakersfield.

7-7 NETIQUETTE

An understanding of "netiquette" can be crucial to survival on the Internet. Due to the limited resources of the Internet, shorter is better than longer. The use of as few words as possible can improve efficiency and effectiveness in using the Internet. Replies to e-mail messages should not exceed one half the length of the original message. Never reference incorrect grammar or spelling, or flaming may result. Emotion can be shown in various ways. The use of capital letters indicates shouting. Keyboard symbols can be grouped together as "smileys" for the following purposes:

:-) Denotes humor or sarcasm;
;-) Denotes winking;
:-(Denotes a sad face;
:-O Denotes surprise.

Smileys can be used as flame retardant but should not be overused. Internet beginners should read the FAQs before attempting to join any discussion or ask questions. There is nothing that veteran Internet users despise more than receiving questions that have already been answered in a FAQ. FAQs are posted on-line under the same name. As a common courtesy, users should attempt to access networks that are geographically closer to home and after regular business hours (unless access is attempted for a business purpose). Downloading large files over long distances can put a load on Internet resources and is considered an abuse. Finally, do not take insults personally, especially when they respond to a memo you wrote. Remember that the writer does not know you and may not respect your title or position.

7-8 INTERNET SERVICES

In this section we provide a quick review of some of the most popular services available in the Internet. These are electronic mail (e-mail), news and discussion groups, file transfer using FTP, Telnet, and the Internet Relay Chat.

7-8-1 ELECTRONIC MAIL (E-MAIL)

We briefly explained electronic mail in chapter 5. With the introduction of Internet this application has become very popular. Electronic mail or e-mail is one of the most popular services available on the Internet. Using e-mail you create a letter electronically and send it over the communications media. The message stays in the recipient computer until it is read. In many e-mail systems, the receiver is able to store the e-mail message in an electronic folder for future reference. E-mail is fast and will get to the recipient's computer in a matter of seconds or minutes. All you need to send an e-mail message is the Internet address of the recipient. You can send an e-mail message to a group of people at the same time. You can apply all the word processing tasks such as spell checking and grammar correction before you send the e-mail message. You can also attach document files to your e-mail message and you can ask for delivery notification. Using e-mail you can establish various folders with different contents and send a particular e-mail to a specific group. Using e-mail enables you to establish an effective message distribution system.

7-8-2 NEWS GROUPS AND DISCUSSIONS

The Internet brings people with diverse backgrounds and interests together. This is done through discussion groups that share opinions and ideas. Every person in a discussion group can post messages or articles that can be accessed and read by others in the group. News groups can get together for just fun and entertainment. For example, you may join a news group that is interested in ancient civilization. Or you may join a news group that can help you to write and debug a computer program in a specific programming language.

7-8-3 TRANSFERRING FILES WITH FTP

There are many useful programs and files available to the Internet users. These programs and data files are usually available free of charge. FTP, or file transfer protocol, represents the set of standards for performing the file transfer tasks. This feature can be particularly helpful when two users write and share programs across a long distance. File transfer can be done using ASCII (American Standard Code for Information Interchange) or in binary forms. Using ASCII, files are transferred in standard text format. Binary files contain special character codes that are only understood by computers.

7-8-4 TELNET

As we mentioned previously, early Internet users employed dial-up connections to establish a terminal session with a remote computer. A terminal session or Telnet is a connection to an Internet server that simulates (emulates or mimics) a terminal directly attached to the computer. A terminal is basically an input/ output device with no processing power. To do so, a terminal program such as

HyperTerminal in Windows 95 must be run in the connecting PC. This enables the user to establish a Telnet session with the desired Internet server.

After a connection, the system prompts you to enter your user ID and password. The prompt $ or % indicates that a user has successfully established a Telnet session. Again this is a text-based environment and everything will be communicated in plain text.

7-8-5 INTERNET RELAY CHAT (IRC)

Th Internet relay chat (IRC) enables you to communicate in a written form with anybody in the world. It is similar to a coffee shop that people sit around a table and start chatting. The major difference between this electronic coffee shop and the real coffee shop is that there is no coffee. However, you are able to participate in many different discussions with people anywhere in the world who share the same interest.

To start the electronic conversation, you start the IRC program on your PC, and then you choose a channel in which to participate. Everyone in that particular channel will see all the messages that you send and you will see all the messages that they send to you. You can choose to respond or not to respond to a message or a series of messages. You can also become involved in more than one conversation by joining multiple channels. This is done by switching back and forth. If you are reluctant to give your real name you can remain anonymous in IRC by using a nickname that is not being used by anybody else during the course of that conversation. The nickname of all the participants will be displayed on the right side of the screen. Therefore you know all the people with whom you are conversing. The IRC can be used for a serious discussion and exchange of ideas, or it can be used for fun, for finding new friends, and for getting to know people with the same interest.

7-9 INTERNET APPLICATIONS

In this section we review some of the leading applications of the Internet. Some of these applications are already very popular, such as using the Internet for marketing. Others are starting to gain popularity, such as using the Internet for health care management. A review of these applications should justify the popularity of the Internet.

7-9-1 MARKETING

Marketing is perhaps best suited to utilize the Internet. The Internet puts large and small organizations on the same footing. Regardless of its size and financial strengths, any business can sell goods and services through the Internet. Users have already divided themselves into interest or newsgroups complete with e-mail addresses. However, the traditional approach to marketing will not work on the Internet. Because of the democratic atmosphere, consumers are on the plus side of the power balance. They can respond individually to a marketing attempt or they can spread the word to their associates. If they approve, everything is fine; however, if they disapprove, consumers have the power in this medium to wreak havoc with an ill-fated marketing attempt. Users unhappy at receiving material from catalog companies have flooded them with messages not to do it again. Marketers, therefore, should only post concise messages to applicable newsgroups that are relevant to a company's campaign. Appropriate newsgroups should be identified before attempting contact.

Martin Nisenholtz has suggested the following six guidelines for Internet advertising [11].

1. Never send intrusive messages.
2. Express permission of the user is required prior to selling consumer data.
3. Advertise only in designated newsgroups.
4. Use full disclosure to conduct direct selling or promotions.
5. Obtain the consumer's informed consent when conducting research.
6. Internet communications should never be used to conceal activities.

Passive advertising is being used successfully by businesses. Bulletin boards can be set up and minimal investment is required to cover the hardware and software costs. An alternative would be to publish advertisements through a service provider.

The medium that is perhaps best suited for advertising is that of the World Wide Web, by establishing a home page. Thousands of companies, including Cadillac, Microsoft, Novell, Cisco, and IBM have established home pages for corporate and corporate-sponsored advertising. On April 1, 1995, Cadillac inaugurated its first Internet marketing program. By utilizing the America's Cup server, Cadillac sponsored information about the America's Cup yacht races, including updates, pictures, and special reports. Cadillac's home page, called "Hard Drive," contains both "on the water" information about the team and "on the road" information about their products. Cadillac plans to keep this information available throughout the America's Cup races.

Club Med's home page directs prospective vacationers to an appropriate online brochure after responding to a few brief questions about the type of vacation they would like to take. Customers simply have to point and click on appealing photographs or phrases to explore further. The advantage is that marketing messages are individually tailored for each customer. Major textbook publishers in the United States have their home pages now. A student or a professor can read the major features of the forthcoming books or the books in print before ordering them. Some publishers even include a sample chapter from specific books on the WWW.

Other companies such as Apple, IBM, Novell, Microsoft, and Schlumberger are making product information, press releases, e-mail directories, and financial information available via the Net. Digital Equipment has improved on this concept, and it allows potential clients to remotely "test drive" two of their new Alpha computers. Customers log on through the Internet and run their own software on Digital's computers. Results have been astounding. Several thousand customers have tested their computers. Some of the soft drink manufacturers now include a URL address on their cans or bottles that a customer can access for additional information on the product such as information related to the ingredients, nutritional facts, and so forth.

Major universities also have home pages. You can go on a tour of the university, and read about different departments and programs, faculty, and academic resources.

Global Network Navigator is a free service offered by O'Reilly & Associates and includes two types of ads: GNN Marketplace and GNN Magazine. The marketplace portion lists ads from various companies such as Digital Equipment, a children's catalog called Hand in Hand, and so on. Readers can click to get further information. The magazine portion is more like the actual print media magazines. More than a dozen Internet-related topics are included, as well as advertisements. In the particular issue referenced, MIT Press was the advertiser. Interested customers simply had to point and click to find out more about one of their books and how to order it.

Real Estate Connection in Austin, Texas, has established a Web presence. Home buying information includes builders, mortgage companies, attorneys, and title companies as well as property photographs. The Homes and Land Publishing Corp.'s Web site contains a nationwide listing of homes by state and city. For Michigan alone, 110 cities are listed [35].

On-line malls or shopping centers are growing in number. Cybermalls of Vermont opened for business on-line in October 1994. It includes almost 60 businesses, from a coffee store to a marine equipment shop. Free information on ski conditions has bolstered the traffic.

Open Market, another such mall, went on-line on the Web in January 1995 with 30 stores. Jem Computers, one of the sellers, plans to liquidate excess computer equipment with "interactive pricing." Considering the economic principles of supply and demand, prices will remain low as long as large volumes of goods are unsold. However, prices can change immediately if sales pick up and inventory levels drop [38]. Harcourt Brace, a seller of books on-line, allows customers to purchase portions rather than the entire book. Applications such as these are allowing companies to reengineer the way they do business.

Business use of the Web is still very much in the introductory stage; to date, small advertisers are producing the majority of on-line advertising and the present situation has been compared to the early days of cable TV. However, by the introduction of Web television (WTV), video on demand, and cable modems, this business will gain great popularity.

Newsgroups are one of the best areas on the Internet available to the advertisers. For example, if a business wanted to advertise a dog food, they should post their advertisement in newsgroups that are interested in dogs.

7-9-2 ONLINE EMPLOYMENT

Employment service providers have established a Web presence. Career Mosaic, Monster Board, E-Span, Online Career Center, and others are the way to find or recruit for a job, especially if it involves information technology. Most companies provide classified ads and job search information but they differ in the software tools they offer. Career Connections allows companies to hold online job fairs by leasing their Internet site.

Seagate Technology, Inc. paid Career Mosaic $18,000 for a 22-page Web site. This figure is equal to what would be paid for a full-page Sunday ad in the local newspaper. Included in the Web site is information about Seagate's goals and culture [9].

On-line shelf life is longer than with newspaper ads. When you run an ad in the newspaper, you receive the bulk of your responses in the first two or three days after it appears. When you put something on-line, you get responses for three or four weeks [9].

Home pages for recruiting should contain company information, including objectives and culture, employee benefits, and job opportunities. An all-text home page with basic graphics can be designed for as little as $50. Home pages with hyperlinks can be included for a total cost of around $200. An elegant version can cost as much as $25,000 and would likely include hyperlinks, color graphics, full-motion video, and hi-fi sound [9]. With competition on the rise these prices will further decline. There are also readily available tools that a user with minimal computer skills can use in order to design her own home page. Microsoft Front-Page, Netscape Navigator Gold, and Macromedia Backstage Designer are examples of these tools.

7-9-3 BANKING

Even though current security technology is not yet ready for banking on the Internet, many banking-related resources are being utilized. For example, e-mail is used by Northern Trust Bank to communicate with its corporate customers. The Chicago Bank has found e-mail to be a less expensive alternative to a WATS line. Quarterly financial reports for banks can be easily distributed via e-mail to mutual-fund investors or customers. Newsgroups have been used by programmers at Northern Trust to confer with customers and vendors about new applications. A newsgroup for employment issues for the handicapped was joined by the bank's disabilities act coordinator. Internet databases also provide valuable information such as federal employment statistics for economists. SEC financial information is also available to portfolio managers through a free source called EDGAR [30].

The banking industry's ultimate goal is to carry out many of their transactions through the Internet. The issue of security is the only factor that has kept this business from exploding. It is generally believed that a secure nationwide electronic banking system is almost in place. Soon people will use their PCs to write personal checks and send check information electronically to vendors. Digital signatures are a key technology for this project. The American Bank Association (ABA) is working on standards to support these new technologies. There is general agreement that the payoffs of electronic commerce are so great that there will never be a shortage of investment dollars to finance expansion when it is needed [30]. The current mergers and acquisitions that are taking place in the banking industry and frequent downsizing strongly support Internet banking.

7-9-4 ONLINE SOFTWARE

Several major software vendors offer on-line software on the Internet. Customers will be able to view listings of software available, and order and designate an installation time.

Microsoft already offers free software on the Web: Internet Assistant for Microsoft Word and Viewer for Word to assist Internet users to publish and read documents in Word format. Both of these are relatively small programs. In contrast is the Microsoft Office Suite, which would take significantly longer to download via an on-line service. Program size will definitely pose a challenge to online distribution.

Bryan Fukuda of Dataquest thinks that companies will lose the marketing benefits of software packaging. "I can't imagine electronic software distribution will take off among consumers. They want something tangible that they can go into a store and buy." McAfee Associates sells software on-line via the honor system. Most customers do not want to violate antipiracy laws and they do pay. The development of on-line copyright protection continues to be a challenging problem. If users need an encryption code to "unlock" software, backups may not be possible. However, the odds may be in favor of electronic software distribution as it provides an inexpensive, convenient, and speedy method of purchase [19].

7-9-5 POLITICS

Empowering voters and revitalizing democracy may be facilitated by the Information superhighway. Twenty-first century citizens may vote with modems, resulting in increased participation. Part-time legislators may have remote access to Washington and they may be able to remain geographically close to their constituents. Of course, an identification system will have to be in place, which could very likely use voice identification, face scan, finger image, or some other technology. Currently, the speaker of the House, Newt Gingrich, is attempting to put all pending legislation on-line.

7-9-6 HEALTHCARE

Electronic patient records on the "information superhighway" could provide complete medical information and allow physicians to order lab tests, admit patients to hospitals, refer patients, and order prescriptions. Test and consultation results would be directed automatically to patient records. The advantages of this approach include the fact that all patient information would be accessible in one central location. Another positive side of this application is that it would allow easy access to critical health information. Imagine a person who is far away from home and runs into a serious health problem due to injury or other causes. Any doctor in any location will be able to download the complete medical history of this individual and prescribe a suitable treatment in a short period [10].

Telemedicine may provide remote consultation, diagnosis, and conferencing. This could result in a major annual savings in travel costs and overhead for medical care professionals. As part of the information superhighway, a personal health information system (PHIS) could feasibly provide interactive medicine tools to the public. Public kiosks located in shopping malls would be equipped with user-friendly computer equipment for network access. Patients would be prompted through the diagnosis by a series of questions. Premature onset of disease could be minimized with this proactive approach [2].

Virtual medicine on the Internet may allow specialists at major hospitals to operate on patients remotely. Telepresence surgery, as this is called, would allow specialists to operate all over the world without physically traveling anywhere. A robot would perform the surgery based on the digitized information sent by the specialist over the Internet. Robots would have stereoscopic cameras to create three-dimensional images for the surgeon's virtual reality goggles. Doctors would operate in a virtual operating room. Tactile sensors on the robot would provide position information to the surgeon so that she can feel what the robot feels [7].

7-9-7 MISCELLANEOUS APPLICATIONS

Businesses are using the Internet in a multitude of creative ways. The owner of a New York neon sign company found needed African power transformer specifications by conducting a Gopher search at an electrical engineering college in South Africa. E-mail is being used extensively for business applications. IBM engineers use the Internet to communicate with other companies on development work rather than driving to each other's labs. Cross-functional teams are enhanced by using the Internet. In today's increasingly global environment, teams can be geographically dispersed and incredibly flexible. The Internet will serve as a powerful tool to bring these teams together with minimal cost.

Fidelity Investments has established a WWW home page to provide mutual fund information, interactive financial planning modules, and other services. Using the system, mutual funds, bonds, options, and margin accounts are offered. Major brokerage houses are offering Internet trading. They provide quotations for stocks, bonds, and other securities. To encourage more customers to use these services, they offer discounts.

Presidential documents can be found on the Net. Full-text versions of speeches, proclamations, executive orders, press briefings, daily schedules, the proposed federal budget, health care reform documents, and the Economic Report of the President are available. There are a number of repositories of this information. They can be found via Archie, Veronica, WAIS, and WWW searches.

Since 1991 the Internet Weather Channel has provided weather observations and forecasts by the University of Michigan. The information available includes temperature highs and lows, precipitation, sunrise and sunset, forecasts and extended forecasts, hurricane advisories, earthquake locations, tornado path reports, images of the latest eclipse, videos of famous blizzards, and air pollution modeling software. Both textual and graphical formats are available. In addition, Canadian and international reports are included [29].

Senior citizens are finding extended family on the Internet. A newsgroup called SeniorNet has 15,000 participants, and seniors go on-line to chat with others and to obtain a rich new source of friends. Connecting with younger generations has been facilitated by Internet links to schoolchildren. SeniorNet has been likened to the "equivalent of the old folks sitting around the village square." This "intellectual mobility" is particularly important for nonmobile seniors who are physically restricted. Two million seniors were recently identified as computer users. They are also using the Internet to monitor investments, to track genealogy, to produce memoirs, and to perform Internet research as a business [13].

7-10 GLOBAL INFORMATION SYSTEMS: AN OVERVIEW

The global economy is producing global customers that demand integrated worldwide services. Airlines, hotels, rental car companies, and credit card services all require worldwide databases to service their customers more effectively and efficiently [22]. Global products are becoming increasingly important in international marketing efforts. The global product is either standardized for all markets or manufactured incrementally throughout subsidiaries. A manufacturer may rationalize operations, due to comparative advantages in different regions of the world. Access to raw materials may be easier and cheaper in Indonesia than in Singapore. Specialized skills needed for production may be available in India, but not in Brazil.

The growing trend toward global customers and products generates additional drivers that necessitate globalization. Worldwide purchasing gives the global organization a great deal of leverage over suppliers: the supplier must not be concerned only with domestic competition, but with foreign suppliers as well. Furthermore, large global firms can achieve economies of scale in purchasing, manufacturing, and distribution. Joint resources, duplicate facilities, and risk management are all popular drivers caused by the globalization of the customer and product [14,26].

International organizations are forced to adopt global information technologies capable of sharing scarce resources across many borders. These systems range from simple 2400 BPS modems at each location to multimillion dollar global networks integrating all major applications of CBISs. The Internet and the information superhighway have created a major boost for this growing trend. Global information systems facilitate international communication between a headquarters and its foreign subsidiaries. Global information systems, in theory, have no cultural or national boundaries. An ideal global information system contributes to achieving a firm's global business strategy by using information technology platforms to store, transmit, and manipulate data across cultural environments [14].

Strategic planning is one of the core functions of global information systems. The information shared between locations is fundamental to the success of a global company. Tracking performance criteria, production schedules, shipping alternatives, and various accounting entities using a global computer based information system permits top management to align master plans and business objectives on an international scale.

A globally designed information system integrated with contemporary business methodology offers organizations an opportunity to increase control and enhance coordination, while opening access to new global markets and businesses [22]. However, implementing such a system has its shortcomings. Differences in culture, politics, social and economic infrastructures, and business methods impede the successful development of a global system. International policy discrepancies exacerbate the communication and standardization process. Thus, compatibility problems arise. Furthermore, some argue that a truly global corporation does not exist, much less a global information system to support its operations.

A global information system cannot simply be injected into the existing organization. Several issues must be answered before a globalized system is implemented [17,31].

1. Business opportunities specific to the organization must be identified in the global marketplace.
2. Global information systems require substantial resource commitments, usually years in advance. Thus, investment in global systems must be justified by all relevant departments and decision makers.
3. Implementing global information systems is far more challenging than traditional CBIS. Consequently, information systems personnel within the organization need to be screened for technical, as well as business expertise required to design and implement such a system.
4. Finally, migration to the new global system should be carefully orchestrated to allow the impacted personnel to successfully move from the old familiar system to the fresh, new, and challenging one.

Clearly, information technology generates opportunities with an international scope. However, obstacles prevent corporations from utilizing the full benefits that technology has to offer. Utilizing information systems on a global scale presents management with problems that are far more challenging than those encountered in sharing systems across domestic boundaries. A global information system can reduce managerial discrepancies by eliminating time and space differences in the distribution of the information commodity, only if that system transcends national boundaries.

In order to address some of the fundamentals surrounding global information systems, executives must first apprehend the kind of information international corporations need and share. Regardless of the architecture adopted by the organization, top management can no longer follow the make-and-sell strategy because of rapidly changing customer needs [17]. Considering the operational efficiency of the entire organization is critical in coordinating multicountry productivity and profitability. Corporations that have not successfully implemented information systems to respond to the global market most probably will lose market share.

Communication systems have generated opportunities for companies to use e-mail instead of the post office or to transfer files on-line rather than shipping magnetic tapes and disks. Clearly, networks have attractive characteristics. An integrated network enhances managerial control, shortens product and service development life cycles, and provides better information to those who need it most. Most importantly, an integrated network is a crucial part of an organization's international information systems infrastructure.

Global information systems can be categorized in several different ways, depending on their function or application. Global marketing information systems, strategic intelligent systems, transnational management support systems, and global competitive intelligent systems are some of the current divisions among global systems. Regardless of its name, the global system must achieve resource sharing across borders. Ideally, the global system should be transparent to the user. However, the complexity and capital investment required to implement such a system may not be feasible from an economic standpoint.

7-11 DEFINITIONS AND REQUIREMENTS OF GLOBAL COMPUTER-BASED INFORMATION SYSTEMS (GCBISs)

What makes a CBIS global? The essential role of the global CBIS is to support global decisions that are multifaceted and relatively complex. This multidimensional complexity stems from the multiplicity of the global environments in which multinational corporations (MNCs) operate. The global environment consists of legal (patent and trademark laws, laws affecting multinational operations, etc.), cultural (languages, value systems, religious beliefs, etc.), economic (currency, tax structure, interest rates, monetary and fiscal policy, etc.) and political (type and stability of government, governmental policy toward MNCs, etc.) forces [14, 15].

In international business planning, it is crucial to understand several important global risks that are unique to the operation of the MNC. These include political risks, foreign exchange risks, and market risks. A global decision will contain some or all risks. Each decision alternative may have different degrees of composite risk levels. In addition, the management of global operations requires the consideration of potential conflicts of interest among the parent government, the host government, the parent company, and foreign subsidiaries.

A GCBIS is defined as an information system to manage (plan, staff, organize, control, direct, coordinate, and motivate) global operations of MNCs, to support the MNCs' decision-making process, and to deal with variables that constitute the multidimensional complexities of global decision making. This definition differentiates a GCBIS from a CBIS operating in a domestic corporation. Three different levels of management can further classify GCBISs: operational, tactical, and strategic.

There are several functional requirements of the GCBIS, distinguishable from those of a domestic CBIS. The complexities of global decision making necessitate several distinctive functional requirements of the GCBIS in addition to the generic functional requirements of a CBIS in a domestic environment. These are classified as operational (requirements 1 through 4) and tactical/strategic (requirements 5 through 9) [14,15]. Let's briefly explain these requirements:

1. *Global data access.* The unrestricted on-line access to information from a company location anywhere in the organization is an important requirement. This allows the corporate managers to monitor global operations from company headquarters. Ideally, global networks of MNCs will provide a real-time communication link with foreign and domestic subsidiaries around the globe through an all-digital system integrating voice, data, and video. Several MNCs such as Compaq Computer, General Electric, Texas Instruments, and Hewlett Packard, to name a few, have either completed or are moving toward the complete worldwide linkage of corporate databases.

2. *Global consolidated reporting.* Consolidated global reporting is a crucial tool for a successful management of overseas subsidiaries. Accounting and financial reports (and in some cases manufacturing reports) need to be integrated in a global consolidated report. Consolidating financial statements is a vital activity for any global decision. These are the reports that highlight the profitability of the corporation throughout the world and they must be analyzed carefully. Other reports for internal control include inventories, account receivables, sales, cash flow by currency, capital expenditure budgets, and product line income statements for each foreign subsidiary of the parent company and the consolidated organization. In addition to the consolidated reporting, GCBISs should allow MNCs to compare financial accounting data between foreign subsidiaries. Due to the differences in accounting procedures and practices and regulatory policies special care must be given to such comparisons.

3. *Providing effective means of communication between the MNC headquarters and its subsidiaries.* To facilitate the organizationwide decision-making and planning process, GCBISs should provide an effective means of communication between the MNC headquarters and its subsidiaries.

4. *Short-term global foreign exchange risk management support.* A mix of freely floating (without any government intervention), managed floating, and fixed exchange rates characterizes today's international monetary systems. Relative value of a currency compared with other currencies might change on a daily basis. Consequently, an essential task of the management of global corporations is to minimize the negative impact of fluctuations among the currencies of country of the parent company and the other operating countries. To effectively manage foreign exchange risks, many companies developed and deployed expert decision support systems. Morgan Stanley's Trade Analysis and Processing Systems

(TAPS) and Manufacturers Honover Trust's Technical Analysis and Reasoning Assistant (TARA), for example, are tracing in real time the corporation's inventory of financial instruments such as bonds, equity, interest rates, and currency exposure in multiple currencies.

5. *Strategic planning support.* Supporting the strategic management processes is the core of any GCBIS. The strategic planning and control systems of MNCs aim at rationalizing resources more effectively on a global basis to respond to rapid environmental changes, such as increased political and foreign exchange risks and global competition.

6. *Conflicts and political risk management support.* A major difference in the decision making of MNCs and a domestic company is that global decisions of an MNC must always take into consideration the conflicting objectives of MNCs, national governments, and multinational organizations. Conflict management in MNCs is critical for multinational corporate survival. The focus of conflict management in MNCs is not conflicts between individual managers, or interpersonal conflicts among executives, or intraorganizational conflicts within a firm. Rather, it is on interorganizational conflict among MNCs, host governments, home governments, and multinational organizations.

7. *Long-term foreign exchange risk management support.* Many MNCs have developed more integrated strategic planning systems to rationalize resources more effectively on a global basis to respond to rapid environmental changes, such as increases political and foreign exchange risk and global competition [14,15]. When formulating a worldwide financing strategy, financial managers of MNCs must resolve several issues, including long-term foreign exchange risk management. There are three fundamental issues in global financing decisions:

    a. the conflicting nature of financing objectives;

    b. financial market imperfections and effective management of foreign exchange risks; and

    c. the corporation's financial structure.

8. *Global tax risk management support.* Global tax planning has been an extremely important topic in international financial management. Effectively, designing tax-risk management systems requires a detailed knowledge of international finance, international monetary systems, and international tax law concerning the legal structure of parent and subsidiaries.

9. *Global joint decision support between headquarters and overseas subsidiaries.* A central issue that the managers of MNCs face is headquarters' control over subsidiary activities. The nature and the extent of the control vary depending on the type of global corporation as will be discussed in Section 7-13. Therefore, a critical responsibility of MNCs' top management is to structure a decision-making process between headquarters and its subsidiaries, through which an appropriate balance between national responsiveness and multinational integration can be reached.

7-12 COMPONENTS OF A GLOBAL INFORMATION SYSTEM

As mentioned earlier, a firm with a global objective may implement various technologies to achieve an integrated global information system. Small firms may outsource for expertise that is not available within the company. On the other hand, larger firms with the resources and technical expertise may develop custom applications to be shared across borders. Depending on the system's use, relative to their business objective, a global system may consist of a network that encompasses e-mail, remote data entry, video and computer conferencing, or distributed databases. However, smaller companies may take advantage of existing public network providers, such as the Internet or value-added-networks to achieve multi-country communication [3]. Value-added networks are private mutipoint, data-only third party managed networks that are used by multiple organizations on a subscription basis. Businesses of all sizes are utilizing the Internet to conduct international business. Bank of America and Novell have recently signed contracts with Netscape Communications, an Internet access provider, to expand some of their business operations. Bank of America is using the Internet to enhance international communication. No matter the size or scope of an organization, an integrated network is the foundation for any global system. An integrated network allows global control over the organization's entire resources.

An information systems manager is faced with a plenty of design and implementation issues when developing a global network. The components of global networks are the same as with domestic ones, with the addition of the bridges, routers, and gateways necessary for worldwide interconnection. These components consist of:

- data terminal equipment;
- modems;
- network interface equipment;
- switching nodes;
- and communications media.

Dumb terminals, workstations, and hosts are examples of data terminal equipment that communicates with other terminals through radio frequency, or fixed or conventional modems. Bridges, routers, and gateways allow the interconnection of several networks, and switching nodes guide the packets to its destination. We discussed these components in Chapter 5.

An information systems manager must also determine the optimal physical medium or communications medium to meet specific performance and traffic levels, such as fiber-optics, satellite, microwave, or conventional phone lines. The more common measuring devices for selecting the optimal medium are bandwidth, range, noise, and cost. The bandwidth is a measure of the medium's capacity, while the range is a measure of the geographical distance in which the medium is expected to travel. Clearly, the range becomes a critical factor on a global scale. However, when leasing dedicated transmission lines from popular providers such as Sprintnet, Tymnet, Datapac, AT&T, and MCI, communication consultants ease the burden regarding range specifications. The medium's immunity to noise is another critical determinant of the type of medium to use or lease. However, a balance between components, installation, and leasing costs should be optimal in performance and minimal in costs.

Additionally, an information systems manager should spend considerable time choosing the best transmission technology for the specific needs of the global network. The network does not have any value without reliable transmission. Current transmission technologies available are synchronous (transmits in blocks), asynchronous (transmits one character at a time), multiplexing, digital (baseband), and analog (broadband). However, an organization implementing a global information system is restricted to transmission technologies supported by the telecommunication infrastructures of the countries in which the subsidiaries are located. The appropriate protocols and type of links to manage contention and minimize error rates must also be considered when establishing a functional global interconnection.

The objectives and strategy pursued by the organization determine the architecture of the network. If international communication requirements suggest only simple file sharing and the response time is not a critical factor, then a half-duplex transmission (one direction at a time) in conjunction with a value-added network would probably be sufficient. However, if multimedia applications are to be utilized, encompassing video conferencing or electronic meeting systems in addition to normal file or database sharing, then full-duplex transmission (both directions simultaneously) would not only be more efficient, but it would be necessary for the real-time processing requirements of image transfers. Further, a private network or dedicated leased lines would provide stability in transmission protocols, because of poor public telecommunication infrastructures in developing countries in most of Africa, the Middle East, and Latin America.

Once an integrated network is in place, public or private, a global organization must decide on the type of information-sharing technologies to utilize, such as electronic meeting technology (EMT) or video conferencing, group support systems, e-mail, file transfer protocol, and/or application sharing. It cannot be stressed enough that these technologies should be consistent with the overall business objective and organizational structure. Standardized software and hardware are always ideal where common applications are concerned, although not always feasible. Hardware, for example, seems simple enough to duplicate in various countries, but unfortunately that is misleading. It is not as simple as shipping the same kind of system to Cairo and plugging it in. Vendors may not support Cairo, or electrical standards may differ significantly. Duplicating software becomes much more complicated due to differences in language, business methods, and transborder data flow (TDF), restricting what type of data can be captured and transmitted. However, these problems are becoming more manageable due to the ever-increasing cooperation and coordination among the countries around the world.

7-13 ORGANIZATIONAL STRUCTURE AND GLOBAL INFORMATION SYSTEMS

There are four commonly accepted types of global organizations:

- multinational;
- domestic exporter (International);
- franchiser (Global);
- transnational.

The drivers that encourage global expansion also facilitate global technologies. Most often the organizational structure will determine the architecture of the global system. There are fundamental differences among the four popular structures that will significantly change the architecture. For example, if an organization follows a multinational structure the subsidiaries operate autonomously, with heavy reporting requirements to the parent company. This reduces the need for communication between the subsidiaries and the headquarters, because the subsidiaries can make many of the decisions without consulting the parent first. Production, sales, and marketing are decentralized while financial management and control remain the parent's responsibility. The focus is clearly on local responsiveness [23]. The multinational structure sometimes hinders globalizing efforts because common systems are very rare. Multinational corporations implement either decentralized or networked systems, with the former the more popular of the two. Local hardware and software vendors influence the applications choices so that national communications standards are consistent with the systems chosen. Inevitably, each subsidiary operates on different platforms and interorganizational linkage becomes economically impractical. Thus, very little communication takes place between headquarters and its subsidiaries' systems. However, new methodologies are altering the definition of multinational corporations by decentralizing all the other functions except information systems. For example, Tyco Corporation follows a multinational structure as described above, but has centralized its global information systems development to maintain control over integration efforts [34].

An organization may also adopt an international structure. International organizations, or domestic exporters, operate much like multinational corporations;

however, the subsidiaries are more dependent on headquarters for process and production decisions. The potential for interorganizational linkage is greater for international corporations, because the subsidiaries may be influenced, rather than forced, to implement information systems consistent with that of headquarters. Information systems personnel are regularly exchanged between locations to encourage joint applications development. This facilitates a cooperative culture among geographically dispersed personnel. Implementing global information systems to support an international structure is more feasible due to this cooperative nature. Their systems are either centralized or decentralized depending on the extent to which they cooperate. The objective of the global information system in this environment is to rapidly disseminate corporate innovation while providing the flexibility to be responsive to local business entities [22,25].

Third, an organization may follow a global or headquarters-driven structure. A corporation adopting a global structure, sometimes called franchisers, manages highly centralized corporatewide information systems. The objective of these corporations is worldwide efficiency in support of a global product [22]. Its subsidiaries have very little autonomy, and rely on headquarters for all process and control decisions, as well as systems design and implementation. Consequently, an extensive communications network is necessary to centrally manage this type of organization. A global information system fits well into this structure. Unfortunately, the integration necessary to manage and control global factors of production becomes difficult and impractical because of the heavy reliance on headquarters for new products and ideas. So, to manage the organization as efficiently and effectively as possible, duplicated or decentralized systems are developed and implemented. The chemistry between the global system's decentralized architecture and the centralized organizational structure inherently breeds inefficiencies and possible mismanagement of information commodities [16].

Since the product is created, designed, financed, and initially produced in the home country or the country where headquarters is located, subsidiaries have the responsibility of sales and marketing for their country. Foreign personnel are used to achieve these efforts, in addition to finalizing the production process and tailoring the product to local requirements and tastes. McDonald's, Mrs. Field's Cookies, and Kentucky Fried Chicken are examples of corporations that follow this structure [25].

Finally, an organization may adopt a transnational structure. Transnational organizations do not have national headquarters, but instead have several regional divisions that share authority and responsibility. A transnational corporation is truly stateless. Business activities are managed from a global perspective without reference to national borders [25]. Optimizing sources of supply and demand and taking advantage of any local comparative advantage are the objectives of a transnational organization. In short, transnational organizations attempt to do everything by encompassing the characteristics of multinational, international, and global structures. Again, global information systems fit extremely well into this structure by integrating global activities through cooperation and information sharing among all the headquarters and foreign subsidiaries.

The architecture of the global information systems in a transnational structure, requires a higher level of standardization and uniformity for global efficiency, while maintaining local responsiveness. The development of international standards for homogeneous architectures will make global coordination easier and allow common systems solutions. Universal data dictionaries and standard databases would also enhance information systems integration on a global scale.

At this time only a few companies have actually attained transnational status. The level of cooperation and worldwide coordination needed to facilitate a transnational structure does not yet exist in the global environment. However, as cultural sensitivity increases and business methodologies' progress toward a common worldview, transnational corporations will become increasingly more common. Citicorp, Sony, and Ford recognize the benefits of adopting a transnational structure and are attempting the transition currently. In fact, the globalizing trend described earlier is forcing many organizations to gravitate toward transnational structures. Competition with those who are already receiving comparative advantage benefits by sharing innovation across borders, maximizing efficiency by achieving economies of scale, and maintaining local responsiveness induces rapid movements toward transnational structures. Consequently, the need for fully integrated global information systems becomes imminent [23].

7-14 GLOBAL INFORMATION SYSTEMS IN ACTION

There are numerous corporations that have used various applications of global information systems. The following are two of the popular ones.

7-14-1 DIGITAL EQUIPMENT CORPORATION

Digital Equipment Corporation provides an example of how networking technology can impact business productivity. Digital has implemented one of the largest distributed global networks in the world. Their global network integrates voice, data, and image transmission, linking more than 500 sites around the world [6]. Digital adopted an open network architecture that includes over 70,000 DECnets, 15,000 TCP/IP hosts, and 1351 AppleTalk hosts. Although the hardware is a critical element in their global network, the conceptual design is far more important to their business management models and business applications. Those applications include engineering, sales and marketing, asset and materials management, and finance. Their global network has enabled engineering staff to operate as a unit, even though critical participants are geographically dispersed. The global network enables the unit to be responsible for the entire development life cycle, including design, manufacturing, marketing and delivering the product to customers. Each member of the team, regardless of location, participates in the process through computer conferencing, videotext, and voice-mail supported by the network.

In sales and marketing, Digital has developed an on-line shopping center using the network. The Electronic Store's core function is to assist in sales and marketing efforts for every product that Digital manufactures. The on-line shopping and information center allows customers to view or obtain information regarding a product before actually purchasing it. This service provided by their global network not only assists the engineering teams in their responsibilities, but it also frees additional employees who would normally fill these positions to pursue other critical matters within the organization.

Order processing and inventory control are critical success factors in the computer industry. An organization will fail if it cannot manufacture and deliver their products in a timely fashion. With its globally integrated network, Digital has eliminated most of the logistical problems associated with global manufacturing and order processing. The order processing system, an integrated portion of the network, collects orders throughout the world for more than 25,000 products and services, it guides them through the manufacturing plants and service delivery channels across the globe, and it then ensures delivery to a worldwide customer base [6].

The use of networks for financial reporting is not new. However, Digital added another dimension to its financial organization. To consolidate the finances of a global corporation is highly complex and time consuming. Digital's finance department eliminated most of the redundant systems and integrated them into the new system. Using the integrated global network, Digital can now consolidate its global financial position in less than one hour by transmitting all relevant information to one of six financial centers for compilation and analysis. After this process, the detailed management information is transmitted back to the individual sites for review and implementation. Consequently, external reporting was made easier and financial decisions can be made faster.

As a result, Digital's inventory turnover ratio increased from 2 to 4.6, the quarterly closing cycle time was shortened by more than two weeks, and time-to-market cycles with new products and services have declined. Moreover, Digital has been able to serve its customers faster and more effectively by giving people more timely access to the information they need, via the global network.

7-14-2 FRANK RUSSELL CORPORATION

Frank Russell financial corporation, based in Tacoma, Washington, recognized the significance in which a global system supports its main function; to watch and rank the men and women who manage hundreds of billions of dollars of invested money. Until recently, Frank Russell Corporation communicated with their foreign locations via 2400 BPS modems. At present the Tacoma headquarters functions as the hub of an international network with offices in New York City, Toronto, London, Sydney, Tokyo, and Zurich [12].

Their success in developing a global system is attributed to their implementation procedures. Conversion strategies often determine whether a system is accepted and utilized to its maximum potential, or rejected, thereby increasing the communication difficulties between headquarters and foreign subsidiaries. By following a phase-in-phase-out approach, (discussed in Chapter 9) the information systems staff at Frank Russell implemented various data communications technologies without the fanfare of major projects and sudden large expenditures.

7-15 OBSTACLES IN DESIGNING GLOBAL INFORMATION SYSTEMS

It has been demonstrated that global information systems have significant advantages in terms of global coordination, managing the globalizing drivers, and maintaining a sustainable competitive advantage by supporting the strategic planning process. However, like any other CBIS, implementing and maintaining a global information system has its own problems that must be overcome. Factors that impede the advancement of global information systems include a lack of standardization, poor telecommunications infrastructures, a lack of skilled analysts and programmers, diverse regulatory practices, and a lack of empowerment. Also, differences in cultures, work practices, and politics play important roles in the development of a successful global information system.

Standardization can impact the development of global information systems on two fronts. First, the lack of international standards impedes the development of a cohesive system that is capable of sharing the information commodity across borders. Different electronic data exchange (EDI), e-mail, and telecommunications standards exist throughout the world. Consideration of all of them becomes impractical. Although open systems are increasing in popularity and the technology required to link diverse systems is present, few organizations have the working capital to absorb the expenditures necessary to integrate the various platforms. Consequently, the lack of appropriate international systems development standards prevents a large number of organizations from implementing global information systems.

Second, too much standardization can exacerbate the necessary flexibility for responding to local tastes and preferences, as well as time differences. For example, an operations system implemented in the United States may use the standard measuring system and the metric system in European facilities. For integration to be successful, additional development is necessary to provide conversion for comparative purposes. Additionally, information systems personnel managing a centralized global information system under international standards that share the information commodity across time zones may encounter difficulties in finding the appropriate time to bring the system off-line for backup and maintenance [21]. A balance between international systems development standards, allowing ease of integration, and modularization, enabling custom tailoring of systems and applications for local responsiveness, must be realized.

The sharing of software becomes difficult and impractical when these factors are considered. It has been estimated that only 5% to 15% of a company's applications are truly global in nature. Most applications are local in nature and cannot be integrated into global information systems infrastructure. Even if the software can be fully integrated globally, support and maintenance problems may be created. If the network goes down, who is responsible for bringing the system back on-line? Moreover, if an employee who speaks only Greek calls a user support line for the shared software, it lends an entirely new meaning to the concept of "help desk" So, coordination and planning for variations in local needs impede the adoption of a truly integrated global information system [1].

As mentioned earlier, an organization that implements a global information system must take into consideration the telecommunication infrastructures of the countries in which their subsidiaries reside. The organization may have the capital, the talent, and the motivation to implement a worldwide integrated system, but it cannot bring some locations into the loop because the telecommunications infrastructure at that location cannot support the organization's requirements. Furthermore, the differences in telecommunications systems around the world make these systems difficult to consolidate. For example, implementing a global system that encompasses 15 different countries becomes expensive and cumbersome when each country may have different service offerings, price schedules, and policies.

Diverse regulatory practices also impede the integration process. This does not necessarily apply to regulation on TDFs (transboarder data flows) , but rather it applies to policy regarding business practices and technological use. TDF regulation is not as large of a problem as was once thought, because of the enforcers' unfamiliarity of the technologies. As a result, many organizations dictate to the appropriate authorities what their technology will be, totally disregarding formal regulation. Many countries also restrict the type of hardware and software utilized within that country. Additionally, some countries may not be serviced by the distributor or vendor with which the organization normally deals. The adoption of open systems technology may eliminate a large portion of this problem. However, as mentioned earlier, very few organizations are capable of adopting such systems.

Access to skilled analysts and consultants with the technical and conceptual knowledge to implement a global system is one of the more critical factors that can impede successful development. When forming the integrated teams mentioned earlier, one must consider the nature of each culture; there are distinct differences in skill sets across national boundaries [21]. For example, experts from Singapore and Korea have been regarded as the best consultants in Asia, due to their work ethic and their broad skill base. Germans are recognized for their project management skills, while Japanese are known for their quality process controls. Ideally, an organization would link various skills sets to form a sort of "dream team." However, cultural conflicts, politics, regionalism, and nationalism eliminate the cooperative environment necessary to achieve global integration.

A more subtle, American-based, shortcoming to global information systems development is the unwillingness to release control and to distribute authority. To achieve true information systems integration on an international scale, corporate information systems executives must empower key geographically dispersed personnel and rely on feedback and information sharing technologies to maintain their global perspective.

7-16 ECONOMIC ISSUES

The lack of capacity may soon become an issue with the increasing number of users and memory intensive applications such as the World Wide Web. New multimedia capabilities such as transmitting live videos will consume extensive Internet resources. At this rate, it would not take many users performing like activities to exceed the information-carrying capacity of the Internet. Even with the new vBNS backbone with capacities of up to 600 Mbps, more bandwidth will be needed.

Up until now, the ad hoc management of the Internet has been sufficient because applications were mainly text-based. However, that is quickly changing. With the growing popularity of memory-intensive applications such as the WWW that incorporate text, graphic, and audio and visual capabilities, we may see frequent crashes of the Internet. Estimates are that the bandwidth capacity of the Internet needs to increase by a factor of thousands to accommodate these applications and that the new vBNS backbone will fall short of that figure [20].

Current Internet pricing usually involves a fixed rate for unlimited throughput. With no pricing controls, users can exploit the maximum capacity. Unlike the highway system where a single driver can only put one automobile on the road at a time, the Internet allows a single user to send a widely varying amount of traffic ranging from a small e-mail message to hundreds of memory-intensive applications.

To prioritize different types of Internet traffic is impractical. It is impossible to distinguish between types of users. Voluntary efforts at controlling congestion are proving unsuccessful. In 1994, the Internet was unable to air a previously scheduled Finnish University audio broadcast when a single user blocked transmission by concurrently sending a 350-450 Kbps audio-video test pattern. Protests resulted in the disconnection of the user. This case illustrates the severe congestion that results from improper use [27].

The mechanism used to this point on the Internet is overprovisioning. To continue this approach, vast new infrastructures are necessary to exceed current and future demands. This will only be feasible if the cost of capacity falls faster than growth.

One proposal is to route Internet traffic based on type: e-mail, file transfer, real-time voice and video broadcasts, and so forth. E-mail and file transfer can tolerate delays but require accuracy. Real-time voice broadcasts generate more throughput but can tolerate distortion. Real-time video tolerates neither distortion nor delay. The key to successful implementation of such a proposal would be correct identification of traffic by users. However, they may be motivated to label all traffic as real-time video to obtain the highest quality of service [27].

Usage-based pricing may be the answer; however, even this approach offers significant problems. Compare the accounting for a single phone call. One entry is required. A comparable one-minute Internet message may consist of 4000 or more individual packets. The resulting accounting entries are overwhelming. Each month, NSFNET alone handles 60 billion packets [38]. Another impediment is the inability to identify the source of the traffic at any level lower than the originating host computer. This is analogous to the telephone system, where phone numbers rather than callers are tracked.

Current Internet routing is based on FIFO principle—first in first out. However, increasing privatization may force implementation of allocation and pricing mechanisms. Matching prices to costs on the Internet would involve in three areas: cost of connection, cost of additional capacity, and the social cost of congestion. Direct cost of usage is not considered because of the associated burdensome accounting previously mentioned. Connection charges can easily be assigned; however, incremental capacity is not so easily charged. A peak demand pricing scheme similar to electrical usage would work except for the fact that there are no off-peak hours with the global nature of the Internet. Congestion costs are measured in terms of delays or packet losses experienced by other users. The prioritization of packets based on bids may be a solution. As an incentive, packets are not priced at the user's bid but rather at the bid equivalent to the lowest priority packet accepted for throughput. Users inflating the priority of their packets will pay accordingly. With the open access capabilities of the Internet, should the sender or the receiver be billed? Unsolicited file transfers and other requests may dearly cost those institutions that provide free services if they are charged as senders of information [27].

The pricing of Internet services poses a significant challenge. The growing demand for services that exceeds volunteer network-available resources may force the issue. Due to the decentralized nature of the Internet, the creation of billing accounts is impractical because information may be obtained from thousands of different computers. It would be too burdensome to establish a user account at each computer site. Pricing by replication will not work with information commodity. The value is not in the transport but in the information being transported. Software is a good example. Once it has been developed, the replication costs are minimal. Therefore, what will prevent someone from electronically obtaining software and redistributing it in an unauthorized manner? These and other issues will have to be resolved in the near future [27].

7-17 SOCIAL IMPLICATIONS

The Information Age may be creating a society of "haves" and "have-nots." Early in the next century, the network will become the major channel through which we conduct our lives. Any disenfranchisement will be very severe. The computer is quickly becoming as standard a feature as is television in American homes. However, those who are unable to afford to tap into the information superhighway may be left behind. Imagine all of the educational, business, and entertainment services that will be offered through the information superhighway in the near future. People with no access to the Internet will not have the opportunity to even see and feel these offerings. This may very well create a subclass within our society. Proper precautions must be taken before we create the educated and economically privileged information haves and have-nots. A related statistic reveals that employees with computer skills earn 15% more than those without similar skills [33].

At the heart of the controversy is how to address this problem of unequal access. In the past, telecommunications companies have bypassed the poorer areas and initially implemented new information services in the more affluent areas. Even if services were simultaneously provided to underprivileged and affluent areas, the problem of affordability and knowledge of personal computer operation by the undereducated is a significant issue.

The expansion of the concept of universal telephone service to the information superhighway is being debated in Washington. Plans are being discussed to provide wider access to computers and Internet connections in public places such as libraries and post offices. Then those without computers at home would be able to tap into the highway. Many such projects are already underway. Other proposals include creation of public trust funds financed by service providers for subsequent use as subsidies.

7-18 FUTURE DEVELOPMENT

Jim Clark and Marc Andreessen, co-founders of Mosaic, which then became Netscape Corporation, predict that in the next 3 to 5 years, the Internet will change completely and will become like a phone system with incredibly easy connection. Internet services will be obtained from both cable and telephone providers, and the separate networks will have exchange agreements. In addition, they predict that long distance voice and data communications will be consolidated into one model. Users will pay service providers rather than on-line services. Included will be the equivalent of printing and postal distribution services. Both feel that the Internet will become the information superhighway. With so much infrastructure already in place, a corporate attempt to duplicate and compete with this worldwide network would be impossible. E-mail will be the catalyst for Internet growth, and multimedia will shift the traditional print media paradigm to that of electronic storage and retrieval. Andreessen also predicts that the PC rather than TV will "end up being the core of future consumer devices" [18].

Philip Quigley, chairperson of the board and CEO of Pacific Telesis Group, predicts that the information superhighway will be the convergence of computer, telecommunications, and video technologies. Computer databases and video libraries will be as accessible as making a phone call. "The common phone call will be enriched, offering callers the option of sharing pictures and computer data as they speak." He envisions the telephone of the future as an advanced form of the present-day personal computer. These applications, however, require vast infrastructure upgrades to the tune of $200 billion for the roadway alone [32]. Ultimate success, however, will depend on the desirability of applications to consumers.

What will the "Nextnet" be called? The three most popular names are: MBone, Giganet, and NII (National Information Infrastructure). MBone, an acronym for multicast backbone, is videoconferencing routing software for the Internet. Giganet is derived from the Gigabit Testbed Initiative that is currently testing billion-bit-per-second transmission at five U.S. computer sites. The NII is the Clinton administration's vision of making the highway accessible to all citizens [4].

A recent development in the Internet world is the Internet 2 or I2. The Internet 2 is a collaborative effort by over 120 major universities in the United States and several corporations including AT&T, IBM, Microsoft, and Cisco Systems to develop advanced Internet technology and applications essential to the research and education missions of higher education. The I2 project started in 1987. The I2 project has been envisioned as a decentralized network where participating universities in the same geographic region will form an alliance to create and found a local connection point-of-presence called gigapop. One of the major objectives of the I2 project is to demonstrate new applications that can significantly enhance researchers' ability to collaborate and conduct experiments.

Whatever the name might be, the Internet is here to stay. More people will be using the Net for their daily activities. The quality and quantity of service will improve and it will become an inseparable part of our lives in years to come.

SUMMARY

This chapter provided an overview of the Internet as the foundation of the information superhighway. A brief history of the Internet was provided. The chapter reviewed various access options, domain name systems, navigational tools, and basic terminology. Commonly accepted netiquette for using the Internet was introduced. Popular Internet services were briefly mentioned. The chapter introduced several current and upcoming Internet applications. Global information systems, their components, and applications were introduced. The chapter touched on economic and social implications of the information superhighway and concluded with an outlook for the future development of the Internet.

REVIEW QUESTIONS

1. How did the Internet start? What is ARPANET? Who sponsored ARPANET? Discuss.

2. What are some of the popular Internet access options? What are the differences between these various options?

3. What are domain name systems? How are educational institutions identified? The military? The U.S. Government?

4. What are some examples of navigational tools? What is WWW? What is Netscape? Why has Netscape gained so much popularity? What has been the trend in designing navigational tools?

5. What is some of the popular Internet terminology? What is an FAQ? A FTP? A home page? Hypertext?

6. What is the Internet netiquette? What is a flame? How do you avoid receiving a flame?

7. What are some of the popular Internet services? What is an e-mail?

8. Compare and contrast e-mail with regular mail. What are some advantages of e-mail over regular mail? Discuss.

9. What are news and discussion groups? What is their purpose?

10. What are two basic formats used by FTP?

11. What are some applications of the Internet in the marketing field? Discuss.

12. How can employment opportunities be explored through the Internet? What are some of the advantages of using the Internet for seeking jobs?

13. What are some journalism applications of the Internet? Discuss.

14. How do banks utilize the Internet? Discuss.

15. In addition to the popular business applications of the Internet, what other applications can be identified?

16. How do politicians utilize the Internet?

17. What are some of the advantages and disadvantages of selling software through the Internet? Discuss.

18. What are some of the health care applications of the Internet?

19. What are some of the drawbacks of providing medical histories through the Internet? Discuss.

20. Why are global information systems gaining in popularity? Discuss.

21. What are some of the typical components of a global information system?

22. What is the relationship between the types of global information systems and the organization structures?

23. What are some examples of global information systems discussed in this chapter? Discuss.

24. What are some of the obstacles in designing and utilizing a global information system? Discuss.

25. How and why might the Internet expedite the popularity of global information systems? Discuss.

26. What are some of the social implications of the Internet? How might the Internet create a subclass within society? Discuss.

27. What are some of the economic issues of the Internet?

28. What are some of the future development trends in the Internet environment? What is Internet 2? Discuss.

PROJECTS

1. There are several e-mail packages on the market. These packages vary in price and sophistication. Investigate a couple of these packages and find out some of the capabilities of each. Why are they so different in price?

2. Netscape, as a graphical navigator, has been one of the success stories of recent times. Investigate this package. What is being offered by this product that was not available through its predecessors? Discuss.

3. Compare and contrast Netscape with the Microsoft Internet Explorer. Why has Microsoft been gaining market share in recent years? Discuss.

4. Numerous corporations are reluctant to conduct business using the information superhighway. Why is this claim true? Discuss.

5. It has been said that the information superhighway may create a subclass within society. How and why is this claim true? How may this issue be resolved? Discuss.

6. The banking industry may become one of the major users of the Internet. Compare and contrast regular banking and banking through the Internet. Why aren't more banks using the Internet at the present time? Discuss.

7. West Talk, a manufacturer of PCs and peripherals, is planning to expand its market share by establishing a global information system. Prepare a cost and benefit analysis for this company. What are some of the major issues to be considered here? What are some of the benefits of global information systems? Discuss.

KEY TERMS

ARPANET, 175
Domestic exporter, 199
Economic issues, 205–207
Electronic mail, 183–184
Franchiser, 200
Global information systems, 192–205
Information superhighway, 174–177

Internet, 174–177
Internet 2, 208–209
Multinational, 199
Navigational tools, 179–181
Netiquette, 183
Social issues, 207–208
Transnational, 200–201

REFERENCES

[1] Ambrosio, J. (August 2, 1993). Global software?; When does it make sense to share software with offshore units? *Computerworld,* 74–77.
[2] Anonymous. (August 1994). Health care on the information superhighway poses advantages and challenges. *Employee Benefit Review,* 24–29.
[3] Bar, F., and Borrus, M. (1992). Information networks and competitive advantage: issues for government policy and corporate strategy. *International Journal of Technology Management,* v7, No 6–8, 398–408.
[4] Begley, S., and Rogers, A. (February 27, 1995). MBones and giganets. *Newsweek,* 58.

[5] Bidgoli, H. (1997). *Modern information systems for managers,* San Diego: Academic Press, Inc.

[6] Brown, P. (April 1992). Business productivity through networking (DEC's global network). *Telecommunications,* v. 26, 8–10.

[7] Burke, R. R. (March/April 1996), Virtual shopping: Breakthrough in marketing research. *Harvard Business Review,* 120–130.

[8] Callaway, E. (December 26, 1994, and January 3, 1995). Chronology of significant events regarding the Internet. *ComputerWorld,* 20–24.

[9] Chabrow, E. R. (January 3, 1995). Online employment. *Information Week,* 38–45.

[10] Corcoran, C. T. (May 1997). Cutting-edge health care. *BYTE,* 86–88.

[11] Cross, R. (October 1994). Internet: The missing marketing medium found. *Direct Marketing,* 20–23.

[12] Davis, D. (May 1993). Building a global network on a shoestring. *Datamation,* v. 39, 59–63.

[13] Dickerson, J. F. (Spring 1995). Never too old. *Time,* 41.

[14] Eom, S. B. (Spring 1994). Transnational management systems: An emerging tool for global strategic management. *Advanced Management Journal,* v. 59, No. 2, 22–27.

[15] Eom, S. B. (Spring 1996). Global management support systems: The new frontiers. In P. C. Plavia, S. C. Palvia, and E. C. Roche, Eds., *Global Information Technology and Systems Management,* pp. 441–460. Nashua, New Hampshire: Ivy League Publishing.

[16] Fleenor, D. (December 22, 1993). The coming and going of the global corporation. *Columbia Journal of World Business,* v.28, 6–10.

[17] Haeckel, S., and Nolan, R. (Sept./Oct. 1993). Managing by wire (enterprise models driving strategic information technology). *Harvard Business Review,* v.71, 122–132.

[18] Haight, T. (November 15, 1994). The pattern in the mosaic. *Network Computing,* 44–47.

[19] Hayes, M. (January 2, 1995). Online shopping for software. *Information Week,* 23–24.

[20] Hudgins-Bonafield, C. (March 1, 1995). How will the Internet grow? *Network Computing,* 80–90.

[21] Huff, S. (Autumn 1991). Managing global information technology. *Business Quarterly,* v.56, 71–75.

[22] Ives, B., and Jarvenpaa, S. (March 1991). Application of global information technology: Key issues for management. *Management Information Systems Quarterly,* v.15, 33–49.

[23] Kettinger, W., G. Varun, and G. Subashish (March 1994). Strategic information systems revisited: A study in sustainability and performance. *Management Information Systems Quarterly,* v.18, 31–58.

[24] LaQuey, T. (1994). The Internet companion: A beginner's guide to global networking, p. 262. Reading: Addison-Wesley Publishing Company.

[25] Laudon, K., and Laudon, J. (1996). Management information systems: Organization and technology, pp. 668–692. Upper Saddle River, NJ: Prentice-Hall.

[26] Lucas, H. (1994). Information systems concepts for managers, pp. 137–152 and 289–315. San Francisco: McGraw-Hill Inc.

[27] Mackie-Mason, J. K. and Varian, H. (Summer 1994). Economic FAQs about the Internet. *Journal of Economic Perspective,* Vol. 8, No. 3, 75–96.

[28] Notess, G. R. (April 1994). The Clinton review: Presidential documents on the Net. *Database,* Vol. 17, No. 2, 80.

[29] Notess, G. R. (October 1994). The Internet weather channel. *Database,* Vol. 17, No. 5, 95.

[30] Orr, B. (November 1994). Banking on the Internet. *ABA Banking Journal,* 65–75.

[31] Passino, J., and Severance, D. (Spring 1990). Harnessing the potential of information technology for support of the new global organization. *Human Resource Management,* Vol. 57, 69–76.

[32] Quigley, P. J. (Summer/Fall 1994). What the info superhighway means for business. *Business Forum,* 5–7.

[33] Ratan, S. (Spring 1995). A new divide between haves and have-nots. *Time,* 25–26.

[34] Schatz, W. (August 30, 1993). Scatter-shot systems: There are lots of ways to buy and manage technology in a decentralized environment. *Computerworld,* 75–79.

[35] Seaman, B. (Spring 1995). The future is already here. *Time,* 30–33.

[36] Wilder, C. (February 27, 1995). Pulling in the Net. *Information Week,* 96.

[37] Wilder, C. (January 16, 1995). An electronic bridge to customers. *Information Week,* 38–39.

[38] Wilder, C. (January 23, 1995). Online security push. *Information Week,* 24.

Chapter 8

The Intranet: The Internet of Your Own

Learning Objectives

After studying this chapter, you should be able to:

- Define Intranet and compare and contrast it with the Internet and with Extranets.
- Outline major phases for the construction and successful maintenance of an Intranet site.
- Discuss the importance of security and privacy issues in Intranet development.
- Elaborate on various platforms for Intranet implementation.
- Discuss Intranet site marketing for promoting Intranet utilization.
- Compare and contrast the Intranet with GroupWare.
- Discuss several major applications of the Intranet.

8-1 INTRODUCTION

This chapter provides a detailed discussion on Intranets as one of the growing applications of the Internet and Web technology. The chapter contains several definitions of the Intranet, which is compared and contrasted with the Internet and the Extranet. We discuss in detail eight major steps for the development and maintenance of a successful Intranet program. These steps include problem definition, cost and benefit analysis, formation of the task force, construction of a prototype, assessing security and privacy issues, tool selection, implementation, and postimplementation audit. The chapter compares and contrasts the Intranet and GroupWare, and it concludes with a detailed discussion of various applications of the Intranet.

8-2 INTERNET VERSUS INTRANET

In Chapter 7 we explained the Internet in detail. In this section we briefly highlight the similarities and dissimilarities between the Internet and the Intranet. The Internet is a public network. Any user can access the Internet assuming the user has an account with an Internet service provider (ISP). The Internet is a worldwide network, whereas the Intranets are private and are not necessarily connected to the World Wide Web (WWW). Intranets are connected to a specific company network and usually the users are the company's employees. An Intranet is separated from the Internet through a firewall (or several firewalls).

Intranets usually have higher speed than the Internet; improving the efficiency of the Intranet is always an available choice if the organization is willing to spend additional resources. Intranets are usually more secure than the Internet

Table 8-1

The Internet versus Intranet

Key feature	Internet	Intranet
User	Anybody	Employees only
Geographical scope	Unlimited	Limited
Speed	Lower than Intranet	Higher than Internet
Security	Lower than Intranet	Higher than Internet
Technology used	TCP/IP	TCP/IP
Document format	HTML and Java scripts	HTML and Java scripts
Multimedia capability	Could be lower than Intranet	Could be higher than Internet

Apart from the above-mentioned dissimilarities, the two have a lot in common. They both use TCP/IP and they both use browsers such as Netscape navigator or Microsoft Internet Explorer. They both use documents in HTML format and they both are capable of carrying documents in multimedia format. Also, they both use the Java programming language for developing applications. Table 8-1 summarizes the similarities and dissimilarities of these two technologies.

8-3 WHAT IS AN INTRANET?

The excitement created by the Internet has been transferred to another growing application called Intranet. In simple terms, whatever that you do with the Internet you should be able to do it with an organization's private network, the Intranet. The latest survey indicates that all the fortune 500 companies either have established an Intranet or are planning to establish one shortly.

Since the computer's inception in 1946, medium-sized and large organizations have used these machines to access timely, accurate, and meaningful information to gain competitive advantage. By providing timely and accurate information information systems have improved the efficiency and effectiveness of employees. Until 1995 the client/server model that promoted intracompany collaborative capabilities such as e-mail and newsgroups was the approach of choice for companies to support their growth. The Internet technology has provided a worldwide connectivity for all types of organizations. The point-and-click approach for finding information has been well received by workers and decision makers.

The Intranet is the next logical step in client/server technology. The Intranet provides users with easy-to-use access that can operate on any computer regardless of the operating systems in use. Intranet technology helps companies to disseminate information faster and more easily to both vendors and customers. Intranet technology can be of benefit to the internal operations of the organization. Although the Intranet is fairly new, it its short life has attracted a lot of attention. So what is the Intranet?

The Intranet ethnology uses the Internet and Web technologies to solve organizational problems traditionally solved by proprietary databases, GroupWare, scheduling and workflow applications. One should understand that the Intranet is different from LAN and WAN although it uses the same physical connection. The Intranet is only logically internal to the organization. It can physically span the globe , as long as access is specifically defined and limited to the specific organization's community of users behind the firewall or behind a series of firewalls.

Figure 8-1 illustrates a simple Intranet configuration. As this figure indicates, all users in the organization have access to all the Web servers. The degree of access for each user must be defined by the system administrator. Users can constantly communicate with one another and post information on their departmental Web servers. Within these departmental Web servers, individual employees can have their own Web pages. However, as the figure shows a firewall (or several firewalls) separate these internal networks from the Internet (the worldwide network).

There are several definitions of Intranet. In simple terms, Intranets are networks within the organization that use the Internet and Web technologies for collecting, storing, and disseminating useful information throughout the organization. Other definitions of Intranets are:

• A computer network connecting a series of clients (users) using standard Internet protocols such as TCP/IP and HTTP. As will be explained later in the chapter, TCP/IP (Transmission Control Protocol/Internet Protocol) is a series of protocols (rules) that specify how computers communicate on the Internet. Also, TCP/IP refers to the software that implements the protocols. HTTP (HperText Transport Protocol) is the specific protocol used to access World Wide Web (WWW) documents.

• An IP-based interconnection of nodes behind a firewall or behind several firewalls that is connected by secure networks. Therefore, as explained in Chapter 6, you can assume that everything behind the firewall is the Intranet and everything on the other side of the firewall is the Internet. A properly designed Intranet should only allow authorized employees within the organization to access their computers. These employees should have access to the Intranet from the outside of the organization as well.

• An internal Internet, a network of computers that communicates using TCP/IP as the primary protocol, FTP (File Transfer Protocol) for file transfer between dissimilar networks, SMPT (Simple Mail Transfer Protocol) for electronic mail delivery, and HTTP and HTML for WWW services [21].

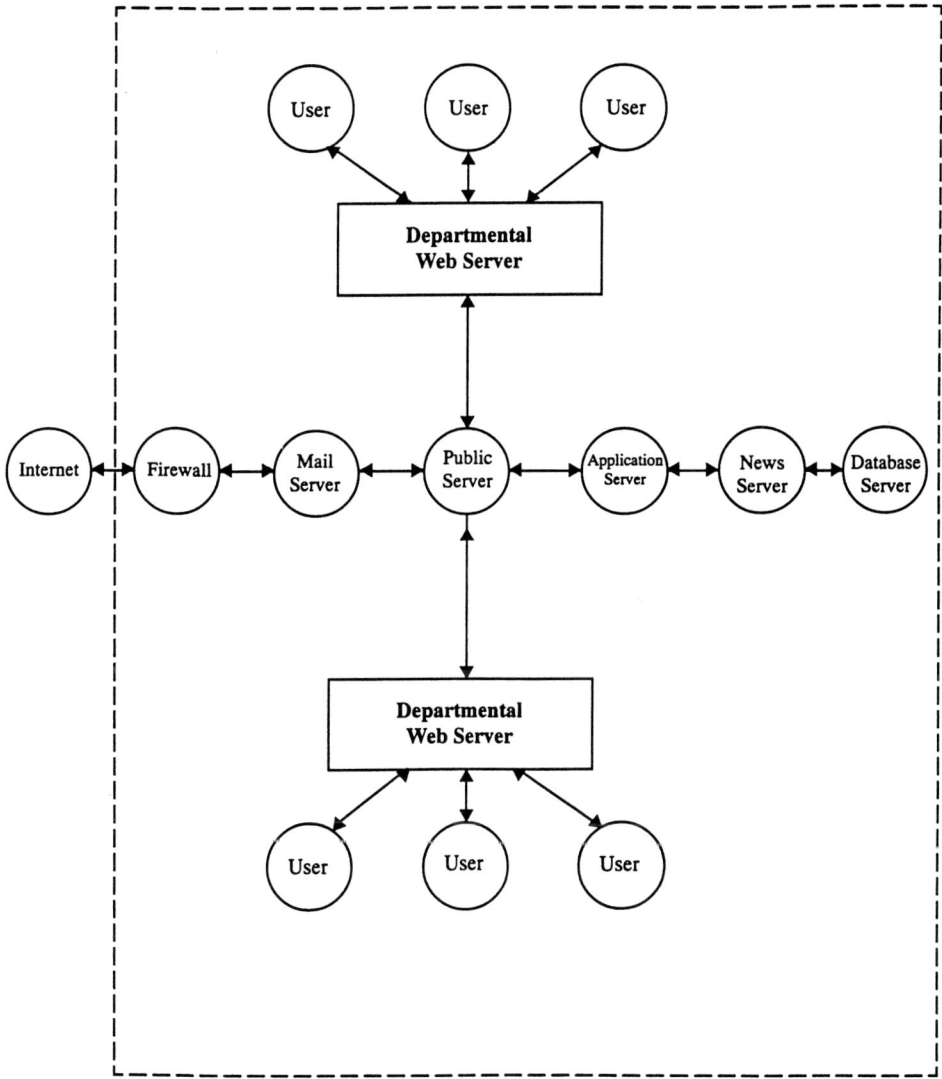

Figure 8-1 A simple Intranet configuration.

• Internet technology is used inside organizational boundaries to improve employee efficiency and effectiveness in storing, searching, creating, and distributing relevant information in a timely manner.

Employees can find internal information and they can bookmark important sites by using an Intranet. Furthermore, individual departments can create their own Web sites to educate or inform other employees about their departments by implementing Intranet technology. For example, marketing can present the latest product information, while manufacturing can post the shipping schedules and new product designs. The personnel department can post new jobs, benefit information, new promotions, and the 401K plans. The finance and accounting departments can post cost information and other financial reports on their sites. And yet the president's office might post the next company picnic on its site.

8-4 WHAT ARE EXTRANETS?

Some organizations allow some of their customers and business partners to access their Intranets for specific business purposes. For example, a supplier may want to check the inventory status or a customer may want to check his account balances. These networks are referred to as Extranets. It should be noted that an organization usually makes a portion of its Intranet accessible to these external parties. Also, tight security measures must ensure that access is given only to authorized parties.

Mobile Corporation, based in Fairfax, Virginia, designed an Extranet application that allows distributors throughout the world to submit purchase order [15]. By doing this the company increases the efficiency of the operation significantly. It also expedites the delivery of goods and services.

8-5 DEVELOPING AN INTRANET SITE

Developing an Intranet is similar to other information systems applications. This means that a formal life-cycle approach similar to the one introduced in Chapter 9 should be followed. Since the technology is new and the applications are somewhat different than with traditional information systems, the life cycle changes direction slightly. The following phases are used to develop an Intranet site:

- Problem definition
- Costs and benefit analysis
- Formation of the task force
- Construction of a prototype
- Assessing the security and privacy issues
- Tool selection
- Implementation
- Postimplementation audit: Intranet site marketing

In the following pages we explain in detail these steps.

8-5-1 PROBLEM DEFINITION

There are several ways in which to develop the Intranet site for an organization. An Intranet can start small and grow. A company can try out an Intranet pilot to publish a limited amount of information on, let us say, personnel policy, on a single platform and measure the results. If the pilot is successful then additional content can be added and more departments and organizational units can participate.

During the problem definition phase for building an Intranet site a likely area for deployment must be identified. The information flow and the needs within the organization must be identified. An area that has appeal to a broad user group should be chosen. This can be done by examining the company's newsletter, human resources procedural handbooks, employee benefits handbook, competitive sales information, and so forth. The next step is to identify the content source or authors who will be responsible for the intelligence behind the information and for delivering it on paper. Some of this information may already be available in written form; in other cases the entire content may have to be developed from scratch. To identify where the information resides is always a challenging task. Is it in a series of word processing documents? In spreadsheet forms? Or in database documents? Does it exists in the heads and minds of the employees? Should it be collected from external sources?

8-5-2 COST AND BENEFIT ANALYSIS

Most organizations already have some kind of infrastructure in place. When this is the case, additional costs are minimal. However, if the infrastructure is not in place, this will be a major cost. We will discuss this later in the chapter. Table 8-2 summarizes the major costs associated with Intranet development.

In most cases the benefits that an effective Intranet provide outweigh its costs. An Intranet can serve as a dynamic platform for collecting and disseminating critical information throughout the organization. This may improve the efficiency and effectiveness of all the employees and it may also improve moral.

Intranet technology can help employees reduce paper reports and unnecessary information. In a typical office duplicated documents are floating around. With the Intranet only one copy, let us say a training manual, can be posted on the Web server, and anybody interested can access the document electronically. Intranet technology allows different individuals to create and maintain relevant information and then make it available to all interested parties.

One of the most important benefits of the Intranet is its ability to shift the control of information flow from the information creators to the information users. Intranet technology enhances information access by individual users from their

Table 8-2

Major Costs for Intranet Development

Application maintenance
Initial content development
Further content development
Monthly maintenance
Network costs
Personnel development
Server hardware
Software (network software and browsers)
Telecommunications hardware
Web site software
Workstations and PCs

desktops. This information may be standard forms, reports, minutes of meetings, new advertising campaigns, or the company's mission statement to name but a few.

The information transfer can also include the dissemination of training manuals and educational documents. Traditionally, organizations have spent significant time and money to train and educate their employees on new products, new software, and new procedures. With the Intranet technology, information can be found efficiently and distributed on demand, which will lead to changing the traditional education and training model. If the appropriate infrastructure is in place, current information content can be found and accessed when and where it is needed. As a result, the Intranet can reduce both the time needed for training and the amount of information an employee is required to absorb at once [20]. We will talk about the training applications of the Intranet later in the chapter.

The Intranet is based on the pull technology through which employees and interested parties extract exactly what they need and where they need it. This is the opposite of the traditional push technology in which information is delivered without asking for it. Too often the workers are bombarded by the information overload that they cannot absorb [7]. Intranets can even reduce the flow of e-mail throughout the organization. For example, instead of sending an e-mail to all employees, the president of the company can post a message on the president's page and the employees can read it if they need to.

8-5-3 FORMATION OF THE TASK FORCE

Similar to the development of other information systems, the development of the Intranet should include a task force. The task force creates broad support for this new technology and it provides an opportunity for the involved parties to express their views. The participants of the task force should include representatives from the following departments and user groups:

- Art department
- Hardware group
- Legal department
- Software group
- Top management representative
- User group (including finance, accounting, marketing, manufacturing and personnel)

Each group should express its views and needs regarding Intranet development. The representative from the art department should provide advice regarding the look and feel and the esthetic of the Internet site. A more professional looking site will probably be better received by typical users. The legal department should provide advice regarding legal issues, privacy, and security problems. The representative from top management needs to provide encouragement for the entire organization and for financial support. Hardware and software specialists provide technical advice regarding the proper implementation and utilization of the system. They also help with the technical aspects of the security issues.

8-5-4 CONSTRUCTION OF A PROTOTYPE: PILOT IMPLEMENTATION

As with other information systems, the development of the Intranet site must start small or it must be implemented in a pilot project and then it can be introduced to the entire organization. Organizations must determine whether information should be made available via a Web server, via e-mail, or through some other means. Many companies find that building Web interfaces to legacy information systems is a key application. With tools such as Purveyor's Data Wizard and HTML Transit, endusers can build simple point-and-click access to legacy information systems without programming, making it available to nontechnical users through their Web browser. Key database applications, including customer records, product information, and technical problem tracking are good exercises for the pilot project.

Typically, organizations begin a pilot with existing content that is delivered via paper. It is important, for the sake of the pilot, to choose a candidate by which both the costs and results can be tracked and measured accurately. A company usually can directly measure the cost of duplicating and distributing copies of its employee benefits manual. When this traditional process is moved over to an

Intranet site, the savings in direct costs can be taken directly to the bottom line, and the incremental costs of managing the content on the Intranet server can be calculated and easily justified.

However, the costs of informal information publishing, such as a memo or a table that provides a competitive product analysis, may not be directly measurable. In many organizations, these competitive tables are developed and distributed by staff people rather than production departments, and the direct costs are buried in other overhead expenses. Therefore, the move from traditional paper-based information flow to the Intranet may not result in direct measurable cost savings. Once the value of the Intranet technology has been established through such a pilot, it can be expanded into other departments and functions. In addition, access to other legacy information systems can be provided, so that employees can search and update customer databases, check 401K balances, vacation days, or can register for training classes. This pilot project should provide the entire organization with an idea regarding the usefulness of this powerful technology. It also provides the design team with an opportunity regarding any possible problem before a full-scale implementation takes place.

8-5-5 ASSESSING THE SECURITY AND PRIVACY ISSUES

The development of the Intranet will bring up certain organizational challenges, including security and privacy issues. We discussed these issues in detail in Chapters 4 and 6. Due to the importance of these issues we would like to visit them once again.

Security can be defined as providing access for authorized personnel to the organization information commodity. In the case of the Intranet, these authorized accesses are given to the nodes (workstations or PCs) connected to the organizational Intranet. At the same time a comprehensive security system should deny access to all others. Web servers allow systems administrators to limit access rights by specific IP addresses for individual pages. This capability would potentially allow the systems administrators to set access to financial records or personnel files only for the personal computers of relevant staff members. Access can be barred to all other users or groups, keeping unauthorized personnel from gaining access to sensitive financial or personal data.

Security may include encryption at several levels. Web servers offer encryption for communications between the server and browser, effectively scrambling the message and preventing its interception. Encryption may also play a major role if the Intranet application spans multiple organizations or locations. As discussed in Chapter 6, firewalls can provide comprehensive security measures, protecting the Intranet from unauthorized users from outside of the organization who try to access the system. Many companies require employees to use personal identification numbers and passwords that limit access to their information. Enrollment receipts and confirmation e-mail sent automatically after any transaction can also guard against tampering.

Firewalls as discussed in Chapter 6 are among the most effective security measures for an Intranet. Firewalls are a combination of hardware and software systems that protect one part of a network from another, or protect an internal network from the outside world. A firewall can determine who will cross a network boundary. The organization can further control security by restricting file and directory level access using standard user privileges.

Hackers, and other computer criminals, who are usually technically savvy outsiders, are the most serious threat to an Intranet security. A hacker may break into a corporate Intranet just for fun or for a challenge. A cracker, who is sometimes an expert retained by a competitor to wreak havoc on a company's Intranet, is another outside threat. In addition to outside threats, there is an increasing trend toward security breaches initiated by current and former employees [5]. As mentioned in chapter 6, more than 80% of security threats are committed by insiders. This makes the job of security protection a challenging one.

Intranet applications can either assist in maintaining an employee's privacy, or they can have the potential to invade her privacy if the designer is not careful. Privacy can be enhanced by the use of Intranet applications for delivering sensitive information in an anonymous manner. For example, new raises or an overseas assignment can be delivered confidentially to the employee workstation. While the interoffice mail staff may pick through a document when they deliver a memo that is marked confidential, the Intranet server treats all pages without similar bias or prejudgement. Employees can feel free to review the employee assistance program information at their desktops. They may browse information on maternity leave or sabbatical programs without fear of raising concerns of their supervisors or of personnel representatives. However, in a loosely secured network, all of this information and much more can get into the hands of unauthorized personnel. For these reasons, security issues and measures must be taken seriously. Guidelines introduced in Chapter 6 must be followed in order to keep the intruders at bay.

8-5-6 TOOL SELECTION

Numerous basic Intranet publishing tools are available. Web servers, for instance, are available for a variety of platforms found in a typical organization, including Windows 3.1, Windows 95/98, Windows NT, Macintosh, NetWare, VMS, UNIX, OS/2, and many others. An increasing number of tools enable the user to create HTML for Intranet applications. Many tools allow documents to be saved in HTML and tools are entering the market that allow the large-scale

Table 8-3

Web Publishing Software

Adobe PageMill
Macromedia Backstage Designer
Microsoft FrontPage
Netscape Navigator Gold
SoftQuad HotMetaL Pro

migration of content from traditional word processing format to HTML. For example, documents created in Microsoft Word can be saved in HTML format. Slides created in Microsoft PowerPoint can be saved in HTML format. These tools allow the nontechnical users to continue to create content in their familiar application and to transfer this content to the server without having to manipulate each file or document. Table 8-3 presents a list of some of the popular Web publishing programs that can be used at a moderate cost.

More sophisticated users can write codes directly in HTML format for creating customized applications. Organizations can also use Java to develop software applications that can run on any computer. Java is an object-oriented programming language similar to Visual BASIC or C++ that can deliver the software functionality for a specific task as a small applet downloaded from a network. Java can run on any computer and operating system. It can run on a personal digital assistant (PDA), a subnotebook, or a mainframe. The operating systems include Windows, UNIX, and Macintosh OS.

To run Java applets, a computer needs a Java Virtual Machine (JVM). The JVM is a small program, embedded in an operating system such as Windows 95/98, Windows NT, or UNIX that enables the computer to run Java applications. For example, a JVM is incorporated into Netscape Web browser software. The JVM interprets and executes the Java applets one-by-one and then performs the commands. Java capabilities allow the Web server to pass information taken from HTML pages to programs that run outside of the server.

8-5-7 IMPLEMENTATION

There are three main activities during the implementation phase of Intranet development [23]:

1. Build the infrastructure. This includes the interconnection among the nodes, and installing the software and browsers.

2. Choose and set up the network operating system (NOS). This may include one of the popular operating systems such as Windows NT, Novell NetWare, IBM OS/2 , Macintosh OS, and so forth.
3. Overlay the Intranet onto the NOS. This involves installing TCP/IP and browsers such as Netscape Navigator, Microsoft Internet Explorer, and so forth.

The Internet usually will run in a LAN or a client/server environment using TCP/IP protocol. Let's briefly explain these three technologies

8-5-7-1 What Is TCP/IP?

TCP/IP (Transmission Control Protocol/Internet Protocol) is the Internet protocol that organizes computers and data communications equipment into computer networks. The U.S. Department of Defense, developed TCP/IP to interconnect hosts on ARPANET (Advanced Research Project Agency Network), PRNET (packet radio), and SATNET (packet satellite). After these three networks were phased out, TCP/IP grew in use due to its flexibility and ease of use.

TCP/IP now can be found on almost every type and size of computer. TCP/IP is the most important component of the Internet and Intranet technology. Internet servers use a group of Internet protocol (IP) applications. IP assigns a unique Internet address that is managed by the IP layer for each computer. This address is used by IP protocol to allow hosts and workstations to communicate with each other. The IP application on the computer maintains a log of all IP addresses known to that computer. The log information maintained by the computer is the unique IP address converted from the name to a number, which is easier for a computer to manage and understand. The computer changes this log into a routing table. A computer uses IP to access the Internet. Each computer connected to the Internet has a list of closely located computers saved in a routing table that is continually updated. This table maps the network topology by storing how far away the network is and which router the computer needs to use in order to send a packet to a network that is not directly connected to it. A packet is the unit of data sent across a network. An Internet packet is usually called an IP datagram. Address resolution protocol (APR) is the actual mechanism that maps the IP address to physical addresses. APR will find the new location and change this location in its table if a server is moved. This way client does not need to know where sites are located or how to get to a site.

The TCP segment of the protocol makes sure that commands get through to the other end. TCP keeps track of what is sent, and retransmits anything that did not get through. If any text is too large for one datagram (the text being sent), TCP will split it up into several datagrams to make sure that all the datagrams arrive correctly.

TCP/IP has a hierarchy of servers. A root server is at the top of hierarchy, followed by a domain server, the local server, and finally the client. Clients are limited by the size of the connection of servers they need to go through. For example, a client might have fast access to any information within his local server, but he might have slow access when getting information from a domain such as com, edu, or gov [17]. For a detailed discussion on domain name systems consult Chapter 7.

8-5-7-2 Wide and Local Area Networks

We briefly explained local area networks (LANs) and wide area networks (WANs) in Chapter 5. Because of their importance for the Intranet implementation, we would like to visit them again and introduce some of their additional features. A LAN provides the means for communication of one computer with another within a limited geographical area through twisted pair, fibers, coaxes, and radios. When buildings are constructed, computer-grade wires should be installed along with the phone wiring. WANs services are provided by service providers such as telephone companies, cable companies, or private satellite companies. These networks are not limited to a certain geographic region and can span the globe.

As discussed in Chapter 5, there are three commonly used topologies of LANs: bus, ring, and star. Using the **bus** topology, all personnel computers and nodes are connected directly to the network. The data link layer of the protocol manages the communications in the following manner:

- Before sending information, one node has to make sure that no one else is using the network.
- When two nodes send information simultaneously, a collision occurs. The sending station detects this collision and sends a jam signal to all nodes on the network.
- The two nodes pause and retry automatically to connect several times before giving up. At this point, the user is not notified that the transmission has failed. The main advantage of the bus topology is its reliability. If one node fails other nodes continue operating with no problem.

In **ring** topology each node is connected to the network to form a ring-shaped structure. All nodes have a table identifying the names of the other nodes. Each node sends the information to its adjacent node and the adjacent node then examines the message to find out whether the information has been addressed to it. If not, this node will pass the message on to the next node, and the process continues. A token-passing network passes a token around the ring. Nodes can only transmit information when they have the token. Ring topology tends to be more expensive than bus topology. Token rings do not collide, but they will fail if any segment in the ring is disconnected.

In **star** topology every node is connected to a central server. The central server has all the intelligence and processing power. Nodes send information to the central server. The central server then sends the information to a destination node. Star topology may be expensive because a computer must be dedicated to managing the network. Upgrades also tend to be expensive since each node needs to be wired into the central computer. If the central server fails, the network can fail unless a backup has been established. Star topology is relatively reliable. The IBM mainframe systems network architecture (SNA) uses star topology.
WANs can be set up as point-to-point or multipoint architecture:

1. Point-to-point architecture allows one node to connect directly to another node using a WAN service provider.
2. Multipoint architecture allows several nodes to share one communications link. This configuration can be used to minimize costs on long distance lines to remote but clustered locations.

WAN data link protocols describe how information is transferred between nodes on a single data link. These protocols are designed to operate over dedicated point-to-point and multipoint facilities based on dedicated facilities and multi-access switched services such as frame relay. Frame relay is a type of packet switching technology that transmits data faster than the X.25 standard. WANs have their own topologies and protocols.

8-5-7-3 Client/Server Model

A client/server model is relatively straightforward. A client runs on the local computer, let's say at your desktop, and it communicates with the remote server, requesting for information. A server is a remote computer somewhere on the network that provides information based on request. As an example, consider the request that I make from my PC on my desk to the campus database server. My request is, "DISPLAY THE NAME OF ALL THE MIS MAJORS WITH A GPA GREATER THAN 3.8." The database server receives my request and processes it, and it might respond with the following three names:

Alan Bidgoli
Morvareed Bidgoli
Robert Brown

An Intranet can be implemented using the client/server model. A Web browser will be installed on each of the employee's PC or workstation. The client computer would then access the company's Intranet Web site to gather information . The local office would have a mail and proxy server (software for replicating and filtering web content). Periodically the proxy server will call up the central enterprise server and download all the most-requested Web pages. A proxy server saves time and network costs. The mail server forwards all mail to the people located in the local office and saves all the mail addressed to people who are not available locally [18].

8-5-8 POSTIMPLEMENTATION AUDIT: INTRANET SITE MARKETING

Let's say an Intranet has been introduced and the initial results are positive. This last phase can assist the organization significantly enhance the efficiency and effectiveness of this new decision-making vehicle. The goal of selling an Intranet site or application is to encourage all employees to use the site as a central communications tool. The company should focus on educating its employees on how an Intranet will help them to do their jobs better. In another words, the Intranet site marketing should educate employees and show them how this new tool can make them more efficient and effective. There are four parts of a good marketing plan or a good postimplementation audit program [19]:

- Involve top management;
- Create awareness;
- Provide ongoing education;
- Introduce new features by active user participation.

8-5-8-1 Involve Top Management

As we have said all along, top executives and senior managers are among the most important groups of people who can make or break any information systems projects, including the introduction of the Intranet. These individuals can provide both encouragment and support regarding the success of the Intranet program. If these people use e-mail, for example, everybody else will start using e-mail. CEO and senior-level executives should be taught how to use the Intranet site. The importance of the Intranet must be explained to them. The benefits of using the Intranet have to be focused on their needs. Some of the specific benefits of an Intranet for executives may include:

- An efficient and effective way to communicate,
- An effective way to control the operation of the organization at all levels,
- A good way to keep in touch with the organization's operations while traveling.

However, as we will explain in Chapter 13, the complexity and technical operations of the Intranet should be de-emphasized for the executives. The executives do not have to know how this technology works. They should be taught how to navigate through the applications on the Intranet, which may include sending their reports or organizational notices using e-mail [10].

8-5-8-2 Enhance Awareness

Employees have to be told that the site or application is available. Effective awareness campaigns should focus on the benefits of this new tool. Introducing the Intranet as being similar to other technology applications may create resistance. The resistance can be expressed in a number of ways. Some employees may be skeptical; others will view the new tool as the latest toy; still others might complain that the new tool is one more thing added to their already overburdened workload. Ongoing education, encouraging active user participation, and including employees in the task force team should minimize these resistance issues. The existence of the site and its benefits should be advertised. Here are some methods for getting the word out [19]:

- Have the site featured in the company magazine and/or newsletter.
- Have the site's availability mentioned in staff meetings.
- Place a banner in the cafeteria and in other meeting places.
- Put a flyer in all employee mail boxes.
- Send an e-mail message to all employees.
- Set up meetings with division managers and supervisors and discuss the Intranet in detail.

8-5-8-3 Provide Ongoing Education

The role of education and ongoing education in improving system acceptance is well documented throughout the information systems literature. One organization in Southern California that the author has experience with has gone beyond traditional educational methods. The organization not only provides traditional education with instructor, lectures, and slides, they also provide CD-ROM-based education. They provide private tutorial on a one-and-one basis for employees who need this kind of personal attention. They have been very successful in introducing all types of information systems applications to a broad group of users with minimal technical background. As you will see later in this chapter, the Intranet itself is a great training tool that the organization can use for future projects and applications.

Generally speaking, education and training depends on company size and the location of employees. For a single-location company, a member of the information system staff can visit departmental meetings and present the site. The people should be grouped and taught how to use a browser and how to navigate through the company's web site. A brief document explaining the Intranet site should be passed out to all employees. The document should highlight the type of information that can be obtained from the site. Companies that have offices located throughout a large region should implement training through the Intranet from its headquarters by using the Internet. Training should be short and simple [19].

8-5-8-4 Introduce New Features by Active User Participation

As the Intranet grows, different departments will put their information on the company's Web site. As mentioned earlier, there are readily available Web publishing programs that enable employees to create their own Web pages without knowing HTML programming. One such package is the Microsoft FrontPage. Most organizations now have one or more Web masters who assist employees in publishing their own pages. The organization should distribute formal policies and procedures for publishing and maintaining Web materials. Guidelines such as the following may be helpful [19]:

- Use the established company style guide.
- Create documents that are grammatically correct and are in standard English
- Develop materials that are appropriate for viewing by the entire organization.
- If access to the information is limited, a user ID and password protection should be used.
- The information published must be legal and also should not be copy protected. In the case of copyrighted materials, the written permission of the copyright holder must be obtained.

8-6 INTRANET VERSUS GROUPWARE

We will discuss GroupWare in detail in Chapter 14. GroupWare is software systems that support a group of decision makers engaged in a common decision-making task by providing access to the same-shared environment and information. The shared environment may be a memo, a single file, or even an entire database. Lotus Notes, Microsoft Exchange, and Novell GroupWise are three popular examples of GroupWare on the market.

Intranets provide some of the capabilities of GroupWare programs such as sharing documents and accessing vital information throughout the organization. Intranets are cheaper and easier to use. However, GroupWare software offers certain features that are not available through the Intranet, such as replication capabilities, database support, and comprehensive security systems. Although Intranets are relatively secure from outside access through a firewall, there is not much security that can be implemented internally. For example, as soon as a document is loaded to the Web server, all employees may have access to the document. However, a user ID and password could provide adequate security. For confidential materials encryption technology should be used. The organization should also consider various levels of security protection for sensitive documents. One attractive feature of the Intranet is that it is operating system independent. It runs on almost all platforms. This is not the case with GroupWare, which is mostly vendor dependent.

8-7 APPLICATIONS OF THE INTRANET: AN OVERVIEW

A properly designed Intranet can make the type of information listed in Table 8-4 available to the entire organization in a timely manner.

Many internal applications in use today can be easily converted to an Intranet or can be supported using an Intranet. Human resources applications, such as job information, name and phone number lists, and medical benefits can be displayed on a human resources Web page. A finance Web site might present information on time cards, expense reports, or credit authorization. Employees can easily access the latest information on a server. With e-mail and chat lines, employees can easily archive meeting minutes.

The Intranet also allows organizations to evolve from a "calendar" or "schedule" based publishing strategy, to an "event-driven" or needs-based" publishing strategy. In the past, companies published an employee handbook once a year. Traditionally, the handbooks would not be updated until the following year even though they may have been outdated as soon as they arrived on the users' desks. The author has experience with several applications of this kind. Some of these organizations sent a few loose pages as an update every so often. The employee was supposed to add these additional pages to the binder. After a while these materials become difficult to go through to retrieve any specific information.

With an Intranet publishing strategy, information can be updated instantly. If the organization adds a new mutual fund to the 401K program, content on the benefits page can be updated immediately to reflect that change, and the company internal home page can include a brief announcement about the change. Then, the employees have the new information at their desktop as soon as they look up the 401K program.

Intranets dramatically reduce the costs and time of content development, duplication, distribution, and utilization. The traditional publication model includes a multistep process including:

Table 8-4

Possible Information Provided by the Intranet

401K plans
Budget planning
Calendar events
Call tracking
Company mission statement
Competition data regarding the latest actions taken by competitors
Contest results
Customer information
Employee stock options
Equipment inventory
Expense report
Facilities management
Industry news
Job postings
Leave of absence and sabbatical news
Medical benefits
Meeting minutes
New hire orientation materials
New product offerings
Newscast on demand to desktop, custom filtered to client profile
On-line training
Order placement
Order tracking
Organizational charts
Patient treatment sign-off
Personnel policy
Press releases
Product catalog
Sales tips
Software program tutorials
Suggestion box
Time cards
Training manuals
Training schedules
Travel authorization
Upcoming functions

- Creation of content;
- Migration of the content to desk publishing environment;
- Production of the draft;
- Revision of the draft;
- Final draft preparation;
- Duplication;
- Distribution.

However, the Intranet technology reduces the number of steps to only two:

- Creation of content,
- Migration of content to the Intranet environment.

8-8 TRAINING APPLICATIONS OF THE INTRANET

An increasing number of organizations are using the Intranet to train their employees on new software, new procedure, new products, and so forth. Some examples of the companies that have successfully used the Intranet for this purpose include Graybar, Hewlett-Packard, Intel, Lawrence Livermore National Laboratory, NCR, Oracle, Qualcomm, Silicon Graphics, and Sprint.

There are 10 good reasons to use Intranet for an effective training program [20]:

1. *Consistency:* With an Intranet, every employee can view the same training materials. This will create balanced training for all participants.

2. *Pull versus push approach:* Too often, the company provides employees with more information than they can possibly absorb. A 90-page training manual that the company passes to employees may be viewed with dread. However, an Intranet allows the company to provide access to as little or as much information as employees wish to pull onto their desktops.

3. *Interactivity:* The Intranets provide two-way communication tools to create discussion groups.

4. *Ease and low cost for updates:* The company can easily and inexpensively update on-line publications and training materials as frequently as needed by using various Web technologies.

5. *User-friendly interface:* If employees can easily get to the information they seek, they're much more likely to look for that information. The click-and-point approach provided by Intranet training makes it a user-friendly environment.

6. *Centralization:* With an Intranet, employees can access information from a central database at any time, and from any number of geographical locations. Self-training can be completed at home, in the office, or on the road. The process is also self-paced, which gives the trainee the opportunity to advance at her desired speed.

7. *Simplicity in creation and maintenance:* Intranet sites can be created and maintained with a minimum of programming expertise.

8. *Keeping up with the workforce:* As more and more young employees enter the workforce, keeping up with technology will become increasingly important. The young workforce is used to being intellectually stimulated through electronic media. Intranet training provides them with such opportunity.

9. *Flexibility:* An Intranet can be an ongoing work in process.

10. *Potential:* As the evolution of Intranet sites continues, more and more features will emerge that expand its functionality.

The Washington State Department of Personnel is handling human resources data consisting of more than 100 state agencies with 60,000 employees. Faced with increasing demand for reports containing analytical and operational data and the tight fiscal constraints, the human resources department set out in July 1995 to create a system using Web technology to access data easily from its data warehouse. As a result, the human resources department has received positive feedback from the client agencies. Carol Wyckoff, the department's human resource business representative, says "Most significantly, it has allowed a quick turnaround time in answering questions." Furthermore, other agencies said that Intranet technology has increased their administrative efficiency [6].

Thomson Consumer Electronics (TCE) developed its Intranet server. Gary Fields, senior systems consultant for Web technologies at TCE, spent about two-and-half years developing an Intranet solution. Doghouse, an Intranet server, helps TCE train its new employees by offering an essential source for information such as procedures, policies, and employee personal data pages including pictures [11].

Silicon Graphics, Inc. (SGI), a manufacturer of high-powered workstations, used to send thick, hard copy training manuals to all employees. Some employees did not find these materials useful, so simply they did not use them. Duplication and distribution of all these materials was a major expense for the company. The company solved the problem by using a CD-ROM. However, there was still a problem since not every desktop computer is equipped with a CD-ROM player. Therefore, Silicon Graphics has begun to replace the CD-ROM distribution method with distribution of training materials via an Intranet. Now everyone can access the programs whenever they want. The Intranets benefit the company in reducing reproduction costs of training manuals. If the company wants to make a change to the program, it can do so at a central location. With an Intranet, the company can make available all kinds of training documents, including product directions, sales tips, company history, new hire orientation materials, and software program tutorials [20].

Ramos & Associates, Inc., a workflow automation systems integrator, has used an Intranet to train its employees. Of the 170 employees in the company, only 10 of them do not travel regularly, and at any one time there are usually fewer than 20 people at the corporate office. The Intranet allows its people to access training materials whether they are at home or in a hotel room. In addition, the company can send audio interviews with top consultants and show video clips of new products and procedures [20].

Table 8-5

Applications of the Intranet in Specific Areas

General category	Specific applications
Sales	Provides instant access to product information. Places orders and check status quickly and efficiently. Provides technical background information regarding products, enabling sales agents to sell products with more confidence.
Human resources	On-line job postings. Employment applications. 401K programs. Training classes.
Customer service	Increase the processing speeds by providing on-line information to sales people. Provides up-to-date information on customer orders.
Health services	Increases effective communication among physicians, hospitals, labs, insurance, and drug companies.
Financial services	Saves the cost of printing and distributing human resource information. Provides the bulk of research reports and manuals on financial procedures.
Manufacturing	Reduces the preparation time for the assembly instructions. Improves effective problem solving in the assembly process. Carries data on quality measurement such as defects, rejects, maintenance, training schedules, sales history, purchase orders and quality. Distributes technical drawings.

8-9 MAJOR BUSINESS FUNCTION APPLICATIONS OF THE INTRANET

Table 8-5 provides several categories of popular Intranet applications. These are only sample applications. Organizations can develop further applications within each category [1,2,3,9,12,14,16,23].

8-10 APPLICATIONS OF THE INTRANET BY MAJOR COMPANIES

Table 8-6 presents a summary of some applications of the Internet by selected companies.

Table 8-6

Applications of the Internet by Selected Companies

Company	General applications
US West	The company utilizes its Global Village Intranets to streamline document distribution by sending e-mails and to integrate with a mainframe system to determine when new telephone facilities will be available.
Ford Motor Company	Provides information on benchmarking, auto shows, global market information, competitor news, global product-cycle plans and patent information.
Columbia/HCA Healthcare	Provides up-to-date corporate directory. Posts physician resumes submitted via the Intranet site. Trains employees on processes.
CIBA-GEIGY AG	Advertises surplus equipment, which will be available for other hospitals. Increases knowledge sharing among international units. Improves the company's corporate culture by fostering a feeling of connection that spans countries.
Fujitsu Corporation	Supports the needs of Fujitsu system engineers. Enables engineers in research and development as well as manufacturing to access a comprehensive set of resources. Provides an information service for Fujitsu's sales division.
Federal Express	Publishes internal technology reports, personnel guidelines, tax forms, employee evaluations, and project management documentation. Creates an adjunct help desk support application to streamline customer support by information system.
AT&T	Integrates disparate billing systems from various AT&T business units. Provides an interface to library services, internal research, and external news feeds. Provides a system for ordering office supplies. Provides an interface for employee contacts for more than 300,000 employees.

SUMMARY

This chapter introduced the Intranet as one of the growing applications of the Internet and Web technology. It compared and contrasted the Intranet with the Internet, Extranet, and GroupWare. The chapter provided a detailed discussion of the steps taken for the construction of an Intranet site. These included problem definition, cost and benefit analysis, formation of a task force, construction of a prototype, assessing the security and privacy issues, tool selection, implementation, and postimplementation audit. The chapter concluded with a detailed listing of various Intranet applications.

REVIEW QUESTIONS

1. What are three differences between the Internet and an Intranet?
2. Generally speaking is an Intranet faster than the Internet? If yes, why? Discuss.
3. Do the Internet and an Intranet use the same technology? Discuss.
4. How do you define an Intranet?
5. What is the role of TCP/IP in Intranet implementation?
6. What are the similarities and dissimilarities of the life cycle for developing an Intranet site versus developing a typical information system?
7. What takes place during the problem definition phase of Intranet development?
8. List three important costs and three important benefits of an Intranet program.
9. It is generally believed that the costs of developing an Intranet are relatively low compared with other information systems. Why is this claim true? Discuss.
10. Intranet technology is based on pull technology. What is the difference between this and the push technology? Why is pull technology more effective in the case of the Intranet? Discuss.
11. Who should participate in the task force for Intranet development?
12. Why should a representative from the legal department be included in the task force?
13. What is the role of the art department representative in the task force?
14. Why is it a good idea to design a prototype or introduce the Intranet as a pilot? What are some of the advantages of this approach?
15. Which security and privacy issues must be carefully examined in Intranet development?
16. How do we protect security and privacy issues? What are some of the available tools?
17. What are some examples of tools for developing the content of an Intranet site?
18. What are some of the activities that will take place during the implementation phase of Intranet development?

19. What are some examples of network configurations for Intranet development?
20. What are some of the unique features of the client/server model?
21. What are the purposes of Intranet site marketing?
22. Why should top executives be involved in the Intranet development process?
23. Compare and contrast the Intranet and GroupWare. Which is cheaper? Which is more powerful? Discuss.
24. List 10 popular applications of the Intranet.
25. What are the sales applications of the Intranet? What are its applications for human resources management?
26. Name some organizations that have been successfully using the Intranet.
27. What are some advantages of using the Intranet for training? Discuss.

PROJECTS

1. A large CPA firm is planning to establish an Intranet for its three local branches in Southern California. They need your advice. Provide a detailed cost and benefit analysis for this project. What are some possible applications of an Intranet for this firm? What are some of the ongoing costs?
2. In your opinion what are some of the advantages of an Extranet for a large textile company? What are some of the risks associated with using an Extranet? Discuss.
3. Java has received a lot of attention as a programming language in Internet and Intranet environments. Why is this claim true? What does this language offer that has not been offered by previous languages? Discuss.
4. Discuss in your own terms the implementation phase for the development of an Intranet site. What are some of the options available? What are some of the activities that must take place during this phase?
5. Compare and contrast training using traditional methods such as the instructor and classroom, the CD-ROM, and the Intranet. What are some of the advantages and disadvantage of each method? Discuss.

KEY TERMS

Client/server model, 229–230   FTP, 218
Costs and benefits, 221–222   GroupWare, 232–233
Extranets, 220   HTML, 225–226

REFERENCES

[1] Allerton, H. (February 1997). Intranet news, *Training & Development*, 55–56.

[2] Anonymous. (January 22, 1997). More firms use Intranets to distribute data. *Document Imaging Report.*

[3] Anthes, G. H. (January 6, 1997). Community Intranet gets real-world test. *Computerworld*, 55–56.

[4] Bacon, I. (August, 1996). Building an information empire. *Database Advisor*, 5.

[5] Canterucci, J. (February 1997). Intranet security. *Training & Development*, 47.

[6] Cheng, F. (September 29, 1997). State agency turns to an Intranet for easy access to its data warehouse. *Infoworld*, 100.

[7] Croft, B. (July 1996). Ten reasons to use Intranet for training. *Personnel Journal*, 28.

[8] Derfler, F. J., Jr. (April 23, 1995). Corporate Intranet strategies and you." *PC Magazine*, 106–107.

[9] DiDio, L. (January 27, 1997). Network gives resort a lift: Sundance taps IntranetWare for LAN links. *Computerworld*, 53, 56.

[10] Fletcher, T. (September 29, 1997). Intranet pays dividends in time and efficiency for investment giant. Infoworld, 84.

[11] Foster, A. (September 29, 1997). Worldwide Intranet sparks innovative and enthusiastic communication at TCE. *Infoworld*, 98.

[12] Hibbard, J. (April 7, 1997). Spreading knowledge: Intranet puts all of Arthur Andersen's know-how in hands of consultants at client sites. *Computerworld*, 63–64.

[13] Hibbard, J. (May 12, 1997). Intranet replaces CAD apps. *Computerworld*, 61–63.

[14] Hibbard, J. (January 20, 1997). GMAC takes Fast Ethernet route to multimedia Intranet. *Computerworld*, 8

[15] Maloff, J. (August,1997). Extranets: Stretching the Net to boost efficiency. *Net Guide Magazine*.

[16] Nash, K. S. (July 29, 1996). BIONET: Intranet helps researchers cross-pollinate. *Computerworld*, 59.

[17] Rosen, A. (1997). What is TCP/IP? *Looking into Intranets & the Internet*, pp. 34–37. New York: AMACOM.

[18] Rosen, A. (1997). Client-serve model. *Looking into Intranets & the Internet*, pp. 34–37. New York: AMACOM.

[19] Rosen, A. (1997). Intranet Site Marketing. *Looking into Intranets & the Internet*, pp. 170–174. New York: AMACOM.

[20] Stevens, L. (July 1996). The Intranet: Your newest training tool? *Personnel Journal*, 27–32.

[21] Swedeen, B. H. (August 1996). GroupWare/workflow application options for your intranet. *Database Adviser*, 54–57.

[22] Wagner, M. (March 10, 1997). Intranet 'pushes' data among departments. *Computerworld*, 61–62.

[23] Weinstein, P. (October 1996). Intranets: Time for a Web of your own. *Technology and Learning*, 50–57.

Part III

Building and Utilizing Effective Information Systems

Part III discusses systems analysis and design in information systems. It provides guidelines for establishing a successful information system, it discusses tools and techniques for design and implementation of an information system, and it introduces the principles of total quality management and reengineering for developing effective information systems. This part introduces the important issues for the planning and management of information systems and it concludes with a detailed discussion of the competitive advantages gained by using information systems.

Chapter 9

Tools and Techniques for Building Information Systems

Learning Objectives

After studying this chapter, you should be able to:

- Discuss the classic life-cycle approach as a design methodology.
- Explain the product life-cycle approach.
- Explain the role of CASE tools in information systems design.
- Discuss new design methodologies, including prototyping and iterative design.
- Elaborate on the integrated approach for information systems design.

9-1 INTRODUCTION

This chapter reviews the principles of systems analysis and design. The chapter begins with a discussion of the classic life-cycle approach. Different phases in this life cycle will be explained. Then the chapter discusses the product life cycle as it relates to the development of an information system. The chapter reviews various new methodologies for designing an information system, including computer-assisted systems engineering (CASE) and prototyping. By synthesizing these approaches the chapter provides an integrated approach, which is more suitable for the development of an information system in a rapidly changing environment. This chapter should provide a good background for building an effective information system, which will be discussed in Chapter 11.

9-2 THE CLASSIC LIFE-CYCLE APPROACH

This approach, which has been utilized for many years, includes a series of well-defined steps. Figure 9-1 illustrates the phases involved in the classic life-cycle approach. The phases in this approach are briefly explained below [2,7,12].

9-2-1 PROBLEM DEFINITION

During this stage the user and the designer of the system try to define and understand the problem faced by the organization. This very important step must be undertaken with great care. It is possible to mistakenly identify the symptoms

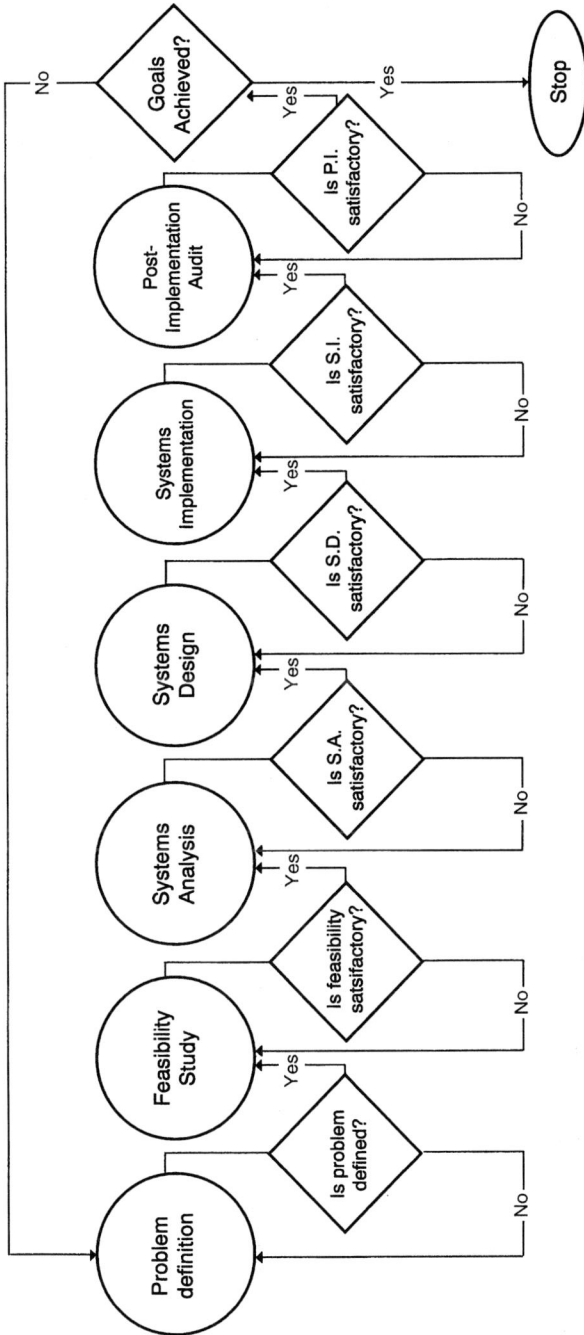

Figure 9-1 Phases involved in classic life-cycle approach.

of the problem instead of the problem itself. The resulting system may alleviate the symptoms without resolving the problem.

The problem may have been identified internally or it may have been brought to the attention of the organization by customers, suppliers, employees, external agencies, and so forth. The following are some examples of problems in a typical business organization:

Problem 1. Improper allocation of resources.
Problem 2. Inaccurate billing system.
Problem 3. Inefficient inventory system.
Problem 4. Inaccurate budgeting system.
Problem 5. Customer complaints regarding the timeliness of services.
Problem 6. Inaccurate sales forecasts.

In a real-life environment the problem may not be as well defined as these problems. For example, the problem may be the improvement of competitiveness in the marketplace or the employment of a new technology to analyze the environment of the organization more thoroughly. In today's competitive world a growing number of problems are usually novel, nonrecurring, and unstructured.

9-2-2 FEASIBILITY STUDY

A feasibility study is conducted to determine how desirable an information system project is while considering several factors. Before starting this phase, the objective of the new systems must be defined.

During this stage of the life cycle, the systems analyst or a team of systems analysts tries to investigate the feasibility of a solution that may resolve the problem. The feasibility study may include the following dimensions [4]:

Economic feasibility is concerned with the costs and benefits of the system. For example, if the net gain of the implementation of an inventory system is $250,000 and the system would cost $500,000 to implement, this system is not economically feasible. To conduct an economic feasibility study, the systems analyst team must identify all the costs and benefits of the proposed system. The costs and benefits may be either tangible or intangible. The tangible costs may include equipment, training, new employees, and so forth. The intangible cost may include the social issues related to automation such as privacy, security, and employee turnover.

The real challenge for the systems analyst team is an accurate assessment of the intangible costs. The systems analyst should attempt to estimate and attach a realistic monetary value to the intangible costs and then conduct an economic feasibility study.

When it comes to the benefits or potential benefits of a new system, the systems analyst is again faced with the same issue. The assessment of the tangible benefits is usually straightforward. These benefits usually include all the cost savings generated by the new system. The assessment of the intangible benefits is a challenging task. However, the systems analyst team should attempt to estimate and attach a monetary value to these intangible benefits and then conduct an economic feasibility study.

To make the assessment of intangible benefits more clear, let us give an example. Let us say that one of the intangible benefits of a new system is improved customer service. How do you assign a monetary value to this? One way to look at this issue is by quantification of the intangible benefit. Customer service means maintaining the present total sales and possibly increasing the total sales by a certain percentage in a business organization. If improved customer service means 10% growth, it means 10% of $15,000,000 for ABC Company. This means a $1,500,000 increase in sales. If ABC company has a 20% net margin, this means an additional $300,000 of net profit just by increasing the customer service. The same type of analysis can be performed for the assessment of intangible costs.

Technical feasibility is concerned with the technical aspects of the new system. One way to investigate the technical feasibility is to study the state of technology. A proposed solution may not be technically feasible for implementation. The technology may not exist for the implementation of the new system. For example, a full-featured, voice-activated monitoring system at this point is not technically feasible. However, given today's computer technology, this is not a major problem and the technical support is available for many proposed solutions.

A lack of technical feasibility may also stem from an organizational deficiency. A specific system may not be feasible because the organization lacks the expertise, time, or personnel required to implement the new system. This has been referred to as a lack of organizational readiness. If this is the case, the organization must first take the appropriate steps to prepare its employees and then consider the new system. This may be achieved by extensive training and on-going education for key personnel in all of the affected functional areas.

Social feasibility investigates the proposed system within the context of social issues. This dimension is generally concerned with the social issues of automation. This may include employee replacement, privacy issues, turnover, employee dissatisfaction, and so forth. An organization may choose not to implement a new system because of the social problems that may be caused by the new system. As discussed in Chapter 11 some of the social issues can be overcome by a series of design measures performed by the systems analyst team. However, some of these issues are an inherent part of any change, and there is no way for complete elimination of such problems. We discussed the social and ethical issues of information systems in detail in Chapter 4.

Finally, a feasibility study may be concerned with the *time* (schedule) factor. Let us say a system is feasible economically, technically, and socially; however, it will not be ready within the time frame needed by an organization. For example, an organization may critically need an automated payroll processing application

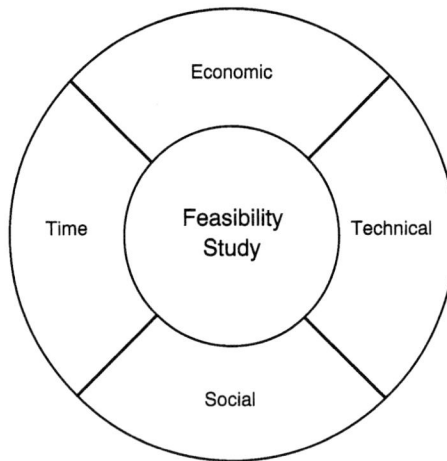

Figure 9-2   Different dimensions of feasibility study.

to reduce the overtime required to maintain the existing manual system. However, if the new system cannot be delivered in time, the drain on organization resources created by the excess overtime may force the organization out of business. If this is the case, you may say the proposed system is not feasible from the time-factor viewpoint. The issue of overtime and over budget is a common problem in the information systems field. By employing appropriate project management and project control tools and techniques the designer(s) of information systems can minimize this issue. We will discuss project control tools in Section 9-2-5-1. Figure 9-2 illustrates the four dimensions of a feasibility study.

9-2-3 SYSTEMS ANALYSIS

The third step in the life-cycle approach is systems analysis. In this phase, the systems analyst or a team of analysts specifically define the problem and generate alternatives for solving it. A variety of tools may be utilized during this phase. These may include:

- Interview
- Questionnaire
- Observation
- Statistical sampling
- Work measurement
- Form investigation and control

- Flow chart
- Data flow diagram (DFD)

The output of this phase will be a clear problem definition, one or several alternatives, and some initial documentation relating to the operation of the new system.

Interview, questionnaire, statistical sampling, and observation techniques are used to grasp a better understanding of the problem area. Graphical tools such as the flowchart and data flow diagram (DFD) are used for highlighting the problem area, so that a clear understanding of the input/process/output cycle and the bottlenecks encountered throughout the entire system operation can be gained. Flow charts usually show the *logic* involved in the system and highlight the detail by using special symbols. By using bubbles and arrows data flow diagrams show the *process* in the system and highlight the overall procedure and operations of the system. A DFD depicts the flow of data through a system and the work or processing performed by that system. Again, these tools are very useful when the prespecifications can be made. These tools may not be suitable if the problem under investigation is unstructured. Computer-assisted systems engineering (CASE) tools, as will be discussed in Section 9-6-1, will significantly improve systems analysis by providing various systems support. Figure 9-3 illustrates a typical flowchart and Figure 9-4 depicts a data flow diagram.

9-2-4 SYSTEMS DESIGN

During this phase the team of analysts tries to choose the alternative that is the most realistic and presents the highest payoff to the organization. At this point, the details of the proposed solution will be outlined. The output produced by the team would be a document very similar to a blueprint. This blueprint will include specifications for file and database design, form and report design, documentation design, procedure design, hardware and software specifications, networking requirements, and general system specifications.

9-2-5 SYSTEMS IMPLEMENTATION

During this phase, the solution is transferred from paper to action. A variety of tasks will take place while the implementation phase is underway. These may include:

- Acquisition of new equipment
- Hiring new employees
- Training new employees

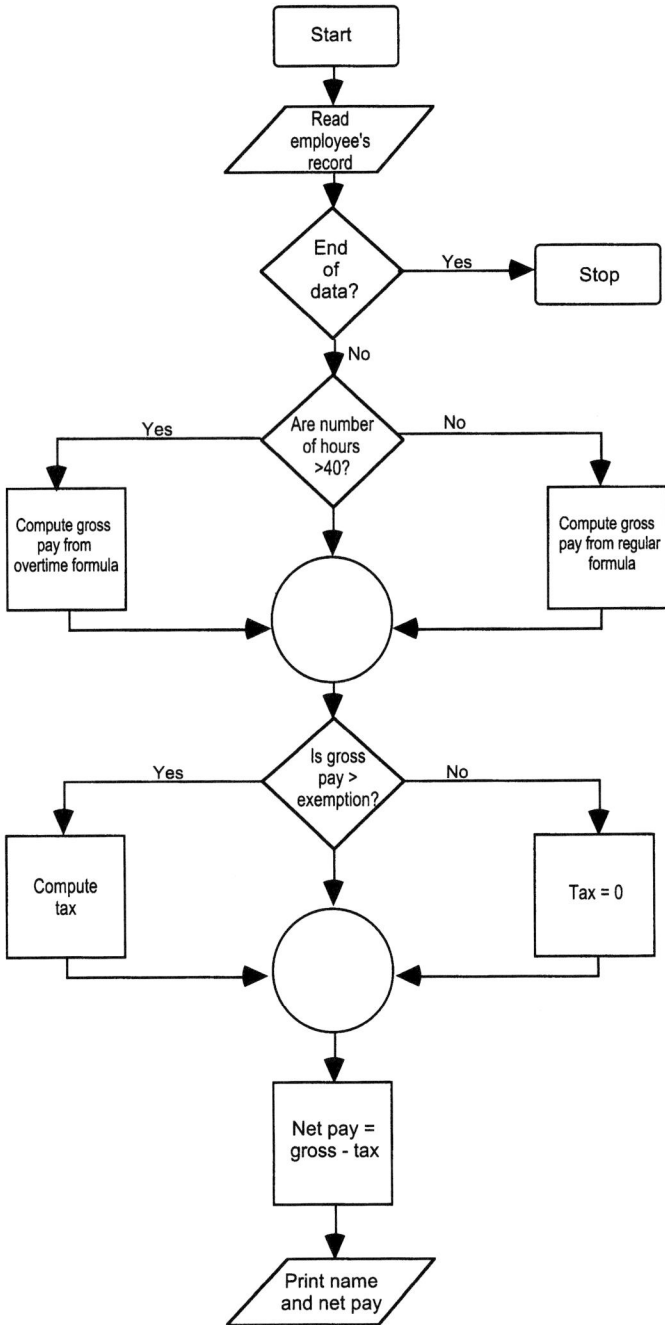

Figure 9-3   An example of a flowchart.

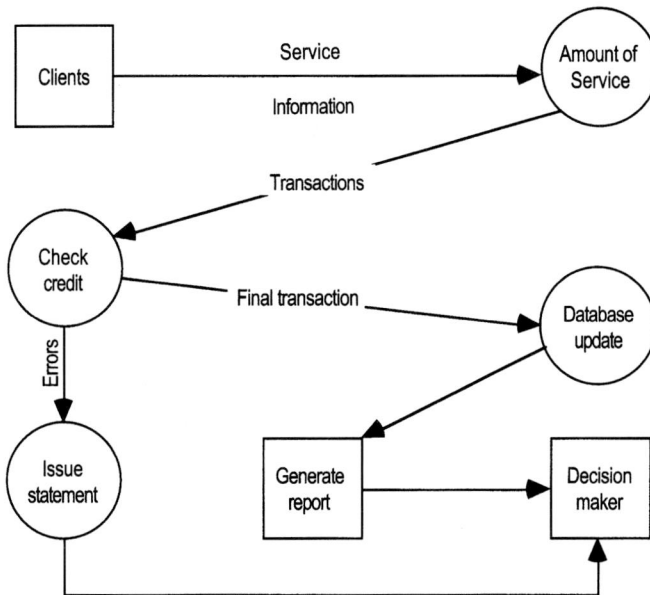

Figure 9-4   An example of a data flow diagram.

- Physical planning and layout design
- Coding
- Testing
- Security design
- Disaster recovery specification
- Conversion planning and documentation
- Communications requirements

When a system is ready to be converted, there are several options available to the designer. These include:

- Parallel conversion
- Phased-in-phased-out conversion
- Direct (crash) conversion
- Pilot conversion

Using the *parallel* conversion approach, the old and the new system are run simultaneously for a short time in order to ensure that the new system will operate properly. However, this approach is costly and will work only if an operational system is already in place.

Depending on the suitability of the system for such conversion, as each module of the new system is converted, the corresponding part of the old system is retired when using the *phased-in-phased-out* approach. This process will continue until the entire system is converted. This approach is not suitable for all applications. In accounting and finance areas, this approach may be very effective.

Using the *direct (crash)* conversion approach, the old system is stopped and the new system is implemented. This approach is risky; however, the organization may save a lot of money by not running the old and new systems concurrently.

Finally, using a *pilot* conversion approach, the analyst develops the system and introduces it only to a limited area of the organization, such as a division or a department. If the system works properly, it is made available to the rest of the organization. The installation may take place all at once in several stages.

9-2-5-1 Project Control Techniques

To manage the implementation of a CBIS, the systems analyst usually works with project control techniques. These techniques are used to control the budget and the implementation time. Three of these popular techniques are PERT (program evaluation review technique), CPM (critical path method), and the Gantt chart.

The PERT and CPM techniques determine the critical path for the completion of a series of interrelated activities. The critical path includes all those activities that are extremely crucial for the completion of the project. These activities include zero slack time. If any of these activities is delayed, the entire project is delayed. Other activities that are not on the critical path are more flexible and can be delayed without delaying the project.

To establish a PERT or CPM network, the analyst must identify all the activities needed for the completion of the project, identify and establish a prerequisite list (which activities are prerequisites to subsequent activities), and calculate the critical path duration.

Figure 9-5 shows several paths that lead from the beginning to the end of the project:

- $1 \to 2 \to 4 \to 6 \to 7 = 5 + 15 + 6 + 11 = 37$
- $1 \to 4 \to 6 \to 7 = 13 + 6 + 11 = 30$
- $1 \to 4 \to 5 \to 6 \to 7 = 13 + 9 + 10 + 11 = 43$
- $1 \to 3 \to 4 \to 5 \to 6 \to 7 = 7 + 10 + 9 + 10 + 11 = 47$
- $1 \to 3 \to 4 \to 6 \to 7 = 7 + 10 + 6 + 11 = 34$
- $1 \to 2 \to 4 \to 5 \to 6 \to 7 = 5 + 15 + 9 + 10 + 11 = 50$

In this example, the last path is the critical path because it takes the longest to be completed. While this path is being completed, the other paths will be completed as well. The activities on the other paths can be delayed for some time and the

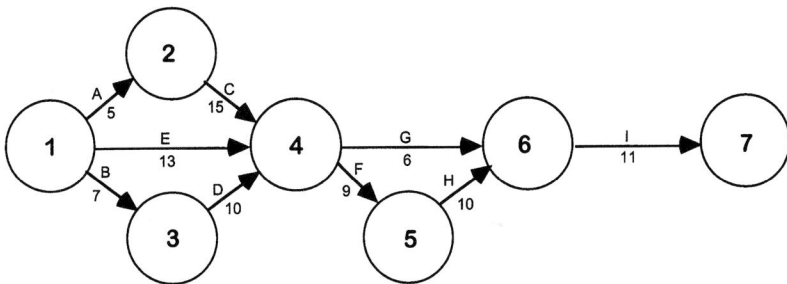

Figure 9-5 A PERT network.

project will still be completed on time. However all the activities on the last path must be completed on time if the project is to be finished on time.

Using the critical path, the analyst can establish a Gantt chart. A Gantt chart lists the completion time (sometimes called milestone) on the X-axis and all the activities on the Y-axis. Now the analyst can monitor the progress of the project and can see any delay in the daily operation of the project. If a delay is spotted, the analyst must consider additional resources if the project is expected to be completed on schedule. Figure 9-6 illustrates a Gantt chart.

9-2-6 POSTIMPLEMENTATION AUDIT

This last phase in the life-cycle approach attempts to verify the suitability of the system after the implementation. The team of analysts tries to collect data and talk with the users, customers, and other people affected by the new system to make sure that the system is doing what it was designed to do. If the objectives of the system have not been met, then the team of analysts must take corrective actions.

9-3 PRODUCT LIFE-CYCLE APPROACH

The design and implementation of computer-based information systems follow four stages similar to the product life cycle [3,6]. This means that these systems follow the four stages of the life cycle, including introduction, growth, maturity, and decline. An understanding of this life cycle is important and should help the designer of an information system with a series of tools that can be used to design a more successful system.

Activity

Define the problem

Conduct the feasibility

Redefine the problem

Create and evaluate
alternative solutions

Select new
hardware/software

Install new
hardware/software

Construct the prototype

Implement the new system

```
  1  2  3  4  5  6  7  8  9  10 11 12 13 14  15 16 17 18 19 20 21 22
```

Time

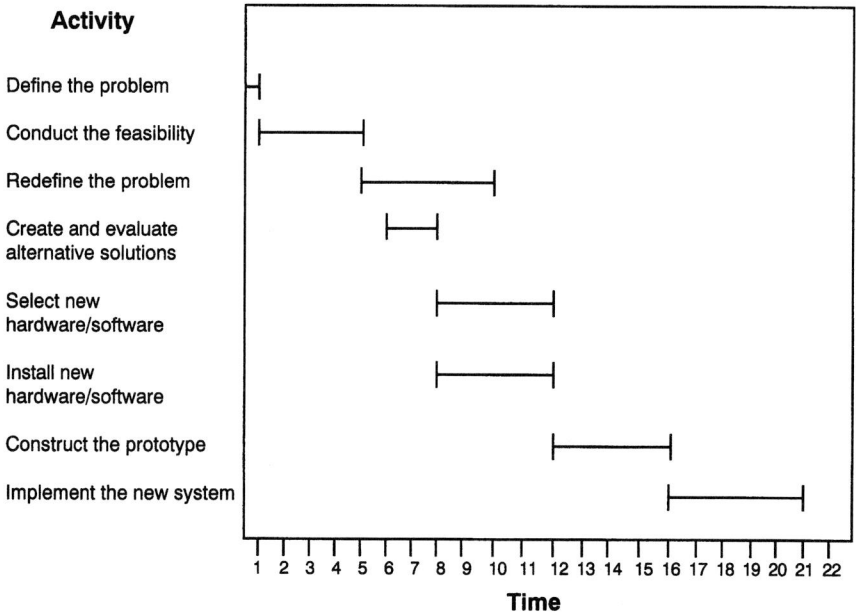

Figure 9-6   A Gantt chart.

Traditionally, "life cycle" has been discussed with respect to product obsolescence due to a number of reasons such as change in consumer preference, technological change, and so forth. Increasingly, the lifecycle concept is being defined more broadly. It has been applied to various professionals, including engineers and physicians [10], as well as to such unusual areas as organizational rules [8] and even to plant openings and closings [1]. Thus, it is not unusual to consider the "life cycle" (LC) concept in the design, implementation, and continuous evaluation of computer-based information systems (CBIS). As each of us has experienced, entropic processes (this may include changes in customer taste, technological breakthroughs, changes in market, etc.) adversely affect the life cycle of products, systems, and people. To manage these processes, we need to: 1. understand what affects the life cycle of these products, systems, and people; 2. determine what stage of the life cycle they are currently in; and 3. decide what interventions, if any, are appropriate for that particular stage. These interventions should be built into the information systems framework.

In order to meet these objectives or needs, the concept of a *CBIS* (computer-based information system) *life cycle* (*CBISLC*) must be defined. The CBISLC consists of the four specific stages of introduction, growth, maturity, and decline. These are similar to other life-cycle concepts but different in their application.

More specifically, the transformation of the CBISLC from infancy or introduction to decline and abandonment is affected mainly by technological advancements in hardware and software, rapidly changing environments, and continuous change in the information needs of the organization in general and the decision makers in particular. In addition, one could suggest that a CBIS actually experiences a half-life [10]. This is the amount of time in which the efficiency, effectiveness, and even relevance of these systems has been reduced to half of its original full value. The CBIS can, however, be modified to extend its full life. Despite this extended period, complete replacement of the existing system is inevitable and must be planned for a particular time frame.

As discussed later in this chapter, appropriate design tools such as prototyping, and iterative design help the information systems designer to carefully evaluate each stage of the information systems life cycle and determine its effectiveness. These appropriate measures may prevent an information system from experiencing a half-life.

The most important features of an information system life cycle (ISLC) are their characteristics that are unique or indigenous to different stages of the cycle. By understanding these characteristics or determinants, the CBIS user and designer will be able to identify not only the stage the CBIS is in (macro), but where it is within that stage (micro). This will help the designer take whatever action is appropriate at that particular time. We now discuss the stages of the ISLC and how they might be characterized.

9-3-1 INTRODUCTION

The introduction phase is characterized by a series of technical problems, unrealistic demand by users, lack of interest and familiarity, and so forth. There may even be adverse feelings or attitudes toward the introduction of this new technology due to individual, group, or organizational habit structures.

9-3-2 GROWTH

The growth phase is characterized by an increase in awareness and interest, multiplying usage, and new applications suggested and incorporated.

9-3-3 MATURITY

The maturity phase is characterized by a high degree of efficiency and effectiveness, a low cost/benefit ratio, and widespread satisfaction with "our" systems.

9-3-4 DECLINE

Although an information systems designer would want to anticipate the decline stage, many do not understand the human as well as technical responses to this process. Characteristics include lack of interest, slow response time to requests, and the inevitable bypassing of the system by using "personal" micros and individually contrived or procured databases, technological obsolescence, and so forth. Figure 9-7 illustrates the stages of the information systems life cycle. These characteristics will help information systems designers identify what stage the system is in and what action must be taken for resolving any possible problems.

The classic phases involved in building an information system as mentioned earlier include problem definition, analysis, design, implementation, and a post-implementation audit.

A careful examination of the variables involved in each phase should significantly improve the life cycle of the CBIS in the various stages of its life. This may result in a shorter introduction phase and a longer maturity phase, as well as a high quality of life for the system throughout the entire cycle. The use of appropriate tools, techniques, and methodologies in each phase or step should bring about a more successful information systems introduction. When these phases are applied to an information system they should include the following:

1. *The analysis phase* should include economic, technical, time, and human concerns. The user(s) of the system must be identified, and style, status, and preferences of these users must be considered. Quantitative as well as qualitative benefits of the system must be evaluated in this phase. Also, a combination of top-

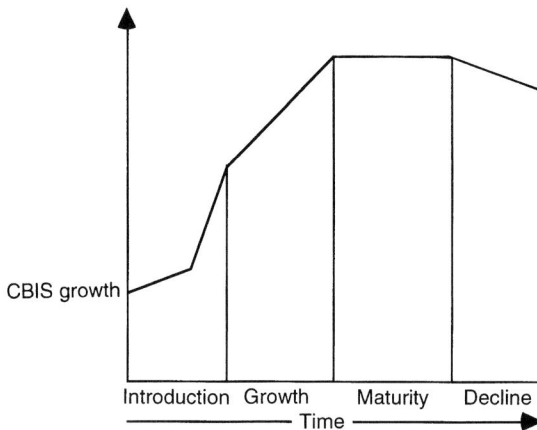

Figure 9-7   Stages of information systems life cycle.

down and bottom-up methodologies should be utilized. This means that the problem should be looked at as a whole and then the specific components must be analyzed.

2. *The design phase* should include more flexible methodologies such as iterative design, task force design, and/or modular design in order to reflect user information needs. This phase should also consider potential technological advancements and changing user needs.

3. *The implementation phase* provides the first impression of the information systems to the users. Fortunately or unfortunately, user acceptance is based to a great extent on the user's first impressions and is akin to a job interview for the system. In order to smooth the implementation process and minimize human resistance, the parallel conversion (if appropriate) may be considered the best conversion method. Parallel conversion provides the users with advantages including more on-the-job training than the other conversion methods and a safety net (physically and psychologically) in case of system failure. In the particular case of information systems, on-line prototyping may achieve the same goal as parallel conversion. Online prototyping provides the user with an idea regarding the operation of the system and makes it possible to integrate the views of the user into the system during the final stages of completion. This allows the user to suggest design changes and specifications and encourages user acceptance through increased participation and "buy in."

4. *The postimplementation audit* should continuously monitor the system. Implementation of an information system is no different than any other organizational change, which requires evaluation of operations as an absolute necessity. The behavior of the system *and* the users will indicate the stage in the ISLC. The designer must make appropriate decisions in each situation.

9-4 PRODUCT LIFE-CYCLE AND INFORMATION SYSTEMS DESIGN CONSIDERATIONS

The user(s), technology used, top management and the environment of an information system play a very important role in the success or failure of the system. Let us briefly explain these factors as they relate to the product life cycle.

9-4-1 USER

The user and his/her information needs are one of the most important elements that could expand or reduce the life expectancy of an information system. These needs may have been generated either by company requirements or industry pressure. A variety of attributes related to the user such as style, acceptance, convenience, and status are also important for an expanded and productive information systems life. A system that is not responsive to these factors will have a shorter life expectancy or reduced effectiveness.

9-4-2 TECHNOLOGY

Hardware and software technologies and their proper augmentation into the conceptual model for an information system are other important factors for an expanded and effective information systems life. In many cases information systems have failed to respond to user needs because of improper employment of either software and/or hardware technologies. Production of timely, integrated, and useful information, which is the prime objective of any information system, could have a significant impact on the proper employment of these technologies. The proper selection of these technologies has direct impact on the effective life of an information system.

9-4-3 TOP MANAGEMENT

Active involvement of top management in all phases of analysis, design, and implementation could facilitate the introduction of a more viable information system. This involvement could speed up the introduction phase and improve the cost and benefit ratio of the system during the growth and maturity phases. This involvement could also accelerate the planned abandonment of the system and consequently shorten the life cycle.

9-4-4 ENVIRONMENT

There are many elements outside the boundary of the information system that could have a significant impact on the life expectancy of such a system. Increasing business volume is one element that could shorten the life expectancy of an information system. There are several other factors within the environment that have direct or indirect impact on the life expectancy of an information system. These factors include changes in present and future competition, customer preferences, government action, suppliers, union activity, labor market, tax structure, and economic conditions.

9-5 MONITORING MECHANISMS FOR INFORMATION SYSTEMS IMPLEMENTATION

When considering the design and implementation of an information system, it is essential to establish monitoring mechanisms that gather information and evaluate the status of these internal and external determinants of the information system life cycle. If significant variance or change occurs in these determinants, the information system designer may need to take appropriate action to minimize any adverse impact of the change. This would be analogous to political risk analysis as a monitoring mechanism for the investment decision process with respect to a project in a foreign country. The investment process (or life cycle) could be abandoned or redesigned if the value of the investment project has changed significantly. This variance has, in effect, changed the potential or useful life of the project.

An example of external determinants would be a significant breakthrough in hardware technology. Microcomputer capacity has increased so significantly in the past few years that many companies that were using minicomputers are now able to use microcomputers for the same and even for expanded service capability. Some individual or individuals must be responsible for providing this continuous evaluation of the status of hardware and software technologies such that the abandonment of current technology can be anticipated prior to the actual decline phase of the information system life cycle.

With these monitoring mechanisms in place, the information systems designer can enhance the design and implementation of the information systems as well as manage its movement through its useful life cycle. These monitoring mechanisms should also tell the information systems designer where she is in the life cycle at any moment in time.

Some examples of monitoring mechanisms and how they might be used include the following:

1. *IF* the user need is not satisfied, *THEN* the information systems designer should change the data collection strategy in order to reflect the quality and quantity of collected data.

2. *IF* the information provided does not match the user's personal and organizational style and status, *THEN* the information systems designer should vary the format of provided information.

3. *IF* the user has problems with the acceptance of information systems, *THEN* the introduction phase should provide for on-going education, *OR* the information systems should hide the complexity (i.e., through use of a user-friendly system interface). In other phases, the redesign and/or planned abandonment should be considered.

4. *IF* the user is not comfortable in using the information systems, *THEN* the information systems designer should provide easy access to the system.

5. *IF* the information systems is not responsive to volume increase, *THEN* the information systems designer should upgrade the database, *OR* improve the data input/output channels.

6. *IF* the user is bombarded by the information provided, *THEN* the information systems designer should use intelligent filtering and exception reports.

7. *IF* the views of top management and/or user have not been considered in any phases of information systems design and implementation, *THEN* the information systems designer should use task force design *AND/OR* interactive design.

8. *IF* hardware/software components of information systems are not responsive to various needs of the user and/or environment, *THEN* the information systems designer should employ more suitable hardware/software *OR* upgrade these components *OR* plan abandonment.

9. *IF* information systems do not provide information related to the changing environment, *THEN* the information systems designer should modify the data collection strategy *AND/OR* redesign the database.

Numerous other examples that are related to the conceptual model of the information systems can also be generated.

9-6 RAPID SYSTEM DEVELOMENT

There are two major reasons that traditional design methodologies discussed so far may not be useful in some cases:

1. The problem under investigation may not be always well defined and the input-output process cannot be fully identified.
2. The user needs may be continuously changing; therefore a system may have to undergo several changes until it satisfies the unique user needs. Even the system may be suitable for a short range, but in the medium and long range, the system may not be suitable.

For these reasons more dynamic design tools need to be utilized. Computer-assisted systems engineering (CASE) and prototyping are two of these tools. The following is a brief discussion of these tools.

9-6-1 COMPUTER-ASSISTED SYSTEMS ENGINEERING

Computer-assisted systems engineering (CASE), also called computer-assisted (or aided) software engineering, refers to the tools used by systems analysts to automate parts of the application development process. **CASE** tools are a collection of computer programs similar to computer-aided design, which has been used by drafters and engineers for years. The capabilities of CASE tools vary from product to product, but some of the general capabilities offered by a typical CASE tool include the following:

- Graphic tools such as data flow diagrams, flowcharts, and structure charts to depict the entire system's operation graphically.
- Dictionary tools designed to record the operation of the system in detail.
- Prototyping tools for designing input and output formats, forms, and screens.
- Code generators to minimize or eliminate the programming efforts.
- Project management tools to help control the time and budget of the project.

Several CASE tools are currently available. Some of the most popular ones are Excelerator (Index Technology), Analyst/Designer Toolkit (Yourdon), System Developer's Prokit (McDonnell Douglas), and Information Engineering Facility (Texas Instrument).

CASE offers several advantages for systems analysis and design:

- Design errors can be spotted graphically.
- An analyst can design several alternatives. Addition and deletion are more manageable—there is no need to redraw the entire design after each change.
- CASE tools perform some of the repetitive tasks, freeing the analyst to concentrate on more important issues.
- Users can participate actively in the design process and express their opinions.
- CASE expedites prototyping.

9-6-2 PROTOTYPING

The prototyping methodology has been around for many years in physical science. It is easier and cheaper to build a prototype of a system first than to build the entire system. Throughout information systems history, we have learned that by building small models or prototypes and testing them, the problems and the solutions become more understandable. The knowledge gained by building, using, and modifying a prototype enables the designers to better understand the problems, the information related to the problems, alternative solutions, and perhaps choosing the best solution for a given situation.

Prototyping as a methodology for information systems construction has gained popularity in recent years. This popularity is mainly due to the changing information needs of decision makers and the lack of prespecification in some information systems projects. Since the construction of a complete system is time consuming, difficult, and expensive, a prototype of the system is developed first. A prototype is usually a small-scale version of the system under investigation. The small-scale system is significant enough in order to highlight the value of the information systems to the user. Also, prototyping makes it possible for the user to express her views regarding the final information systems. Prototyping is also the fastest way to put the information systems into operation [9].

A comprehensive survey of emerging prototyping methodologies defines the prototyping process in four steps [5]:

- Define initial requirements
- Develop initial prototype
- Review and evaluate the prototype
- Revise the prototype

Defining the initial requirements involves agreement between the user and the team of designers that a prototyping approach is the most suitable approach for solving the problem at hand. After agreeing on the approach, the user and designer team work together in order to gather information about the components of the prototype and how those components relate to one another. The team may decide on one of the following three approaches for the construction of the prototype: 1. using an external vendor to construct the prototype; 2. using application packages or fourth generation languages; and 3. using high level languages and developing the prototype from scratch.

It is extremely important to include the users of the information systems and top management in the construction phase of the prototype because problems may arise that only the user and top management will be able to resolve. The construction phase increases the knowledge gained of the problem(s) that the information systems will resolve. The team of users and analysts will learn a lot about the decision-making process of a given situation during the construction phase.

Upon completion of the prototype, the user begins to use the prototype to make decisions. With each use of the prototype, an evaluation is made by the user and analyst team to evaluate the prototype. This evaluation process may result in one of the following decisions:

1. Revision of the prototype;
2. Cancellation of the information systems project;
3. Developing an entirely new prototype; and
4. Building a complete system based on the prototype.

Regardless of the decision made, the prototype has provided useful information to the user and analyst team. At this point, the problem is better defined and the system's operations are more understandable.

There are four major types of prototyping used in the information systems field [5]:

- Illustrative or throwaway
- Simulated
- Functional
- Evolutionary

The **throwaway** or **illustrative prototype** is designed for the purposes of illustration and gaining feedback. If the user does not like the prototype, it will be thrown away and a new prototype may be designed. This may also result in the abandonment of the information systems project. If the user is happy with the prototype, this may either evolve to the final system or it may be used until a separate full-featured information system is constructed. In this methodology, sample screens and reports for user reviews are generated. It is usually a noniterative process that is used to enhance communication between the user and designer during the requirements definition and design phase. This is probably the most commonly used type of prototyping methodology.

The **simulated prototyping** methodology provides models that behave as if they were parts of the desired information systems. Simulated models appear to function similar to part(s) of the desired information systems, but simulate the interaction with other components of the final information systems such as the database and user/system interface. This model is interactive, since the model can be refined and enhanced.

The **functional prototyping** methodology is similar to the simulated methodology with one difference. It provides models that represent a more complete set of system functions. In other words, a functional prototype is a more realistic version of the actual information systems.

The **evolving prototype** starts from a small-scale system and evolves into the final system by continuously adding new features and upgrading the existing features. The model or models developed in this methodology is nondisposable and will be used in the final information systems. Evolutionary methodology is more suitable for systems whose requirements are poorly defined.

9-6-2-1 Prototyping Development Tools

To construct a prototype of a system, numerous tools can be utilized. Some of the most popular tools include spreadsheet packages such as Lotus 1-2-3 and Microsoft Excel, and database management packages such as Microsoft Access and Paradox. In recent years tools have been developed to provide rapid prototyping. Rapid prototyping is an approach to system development that uses prototypes to help both the designer and users to visualize the prototype system and depict its operations and properties in an interactive process [11].

Rapid prototyping makes use of computer-aided systems engineering (CASE) tools (discussed earlier) to quickly develop prototypes. However, any of the fourth generation languages or even third generation languages can be used to construct a prototype.

Some of the popular examples of prototype generators are computer-aided prototyping systems (CAPS), prototype system description language (PSDL), knowledge-based rapid prototyping systems (KBRPS) and framed-based software requirements specialization system (FSRSS).

9-6-2-2 Advantages and Disadvantages of Prototyping

As mentioned earlier, due to the lack of prespecifications and changing the information needs of decision makers, prototyping offers several unique advantages:

1. It provides a method to investigate an environment in which the problem is poorly defined, and information is difficult to gather.
2. It reduces the need for training of the information systems users because they are involved in development of the system.
3. It results in cost savings because it is cheaper to build a model of the system than to build the complete system. The prototype may result in the abandonment of the system, resulting in major savings.
4. It increases the chances of success by promoting the user's involvement.
5. Prototypes are easier to modify and maintain than the actual system.
6. Prototyping enhances the documentation process of the system by walking through several versions of the system.
7. It improves communications between users, top management, and information systems personnel.

With all these advantages, prototyping offers some disadvantages as well. Let us briefly introduce these disadvantages:

1. The uncontrolled use of the selected data for developing the prototype may result in incorrect decision.
2. The development of prototypes may require more user and top management support and assistance than they are willing to provide.
3. Prototypes may not reflect the actual operation of the final system.

9-7 SYSTEMS ANALYSIS AND DESIGN: AN INTEGRATED APPROACH

Because information systems are designed to be used by key decision makers, their involvement plays a major role in determining the success of these systems. Also, to follow the TQM principles (discussed in Chapter 10), the customers of the system must be involved in all phases of analysis, design, and implementation. The classic life-cycle approach changes direction in the dynamic world of business. Differences can be traced by examining the following steps.

9-7-1 PROBLEM DEFINITION

In this step, the objective of the system must be defined. The user must be informed and in agreement with the four Ws:

1. *Why issue.* Why is the system going to be designed? What decision(s) will be effected? How will the organization use this system?
2. *Who issue.* Who is going to use the system? Is it going to be used by one decision maker or a group of decision makers?
3. *When issue.* When will the system be operational? Until the final implementation, how will decisions affected by the information systems be made?
4. *What issue.* What kind of capabilities will be provided by the system? How will these different capabilities be used and how will the system provide these capabilities?

9-7-2 FORMATION OF THE TASK FORCE

For the continued success of the information systems, different users of the system must have input in the design and implementation of the system. Their views must be highly regarded. This issue will be of considerable significance, particularly *if* the system is going to be used by more than one user.

The task force should include representatives from different user departments, top management, and technical staff. Preferably, the task force should include the individuals presented in Figure 9-8. The task force team should work to define the user's needs as precisely as possible.

9-7-3 CONSTRUCTION OF AN ONLINE PROTOTYPE

To show the user how the system will work, a simple prototype greatly improves the chances of success. The on-line prototype gives the user a chance to see a small-scale version of the system in action. Also, the designer will find out the possible problems associated with the system. As discussed earlier, there are four types of prototypes. A prototype may even be developed into the final system.

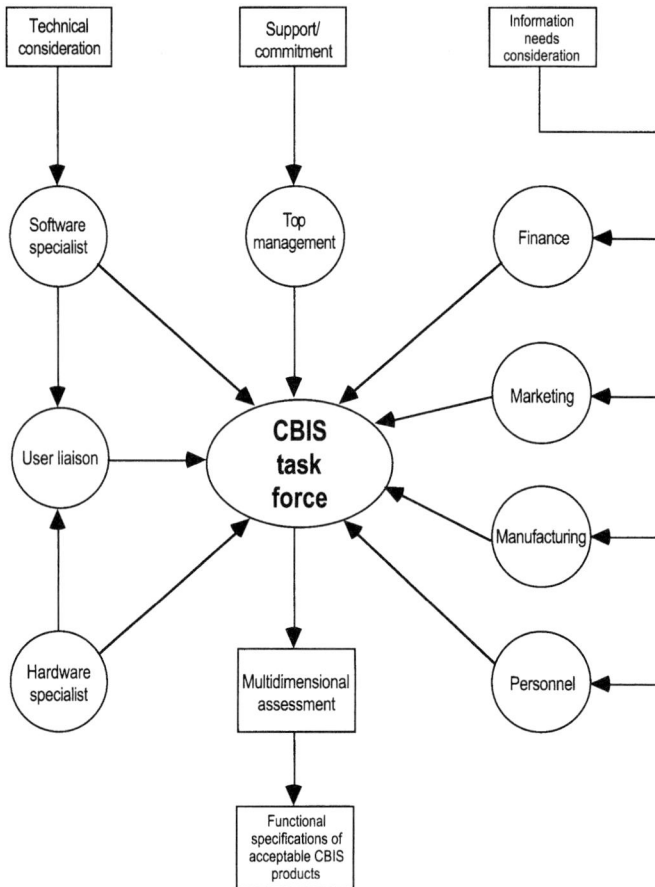

Figure 9-8   Information systems task force.

The process of prototype design and modification should continue until the user is satisfied with the prototype. Then the construction of the final system can be started.

9-7-4 EVALUATION

The evaluation of information systems should not only be based on the monetary benefits generated by the system. The impacts of the system on decision making, decision implementation, the learning impact of the system, and the overall effectiveness of the system are important concerns here.

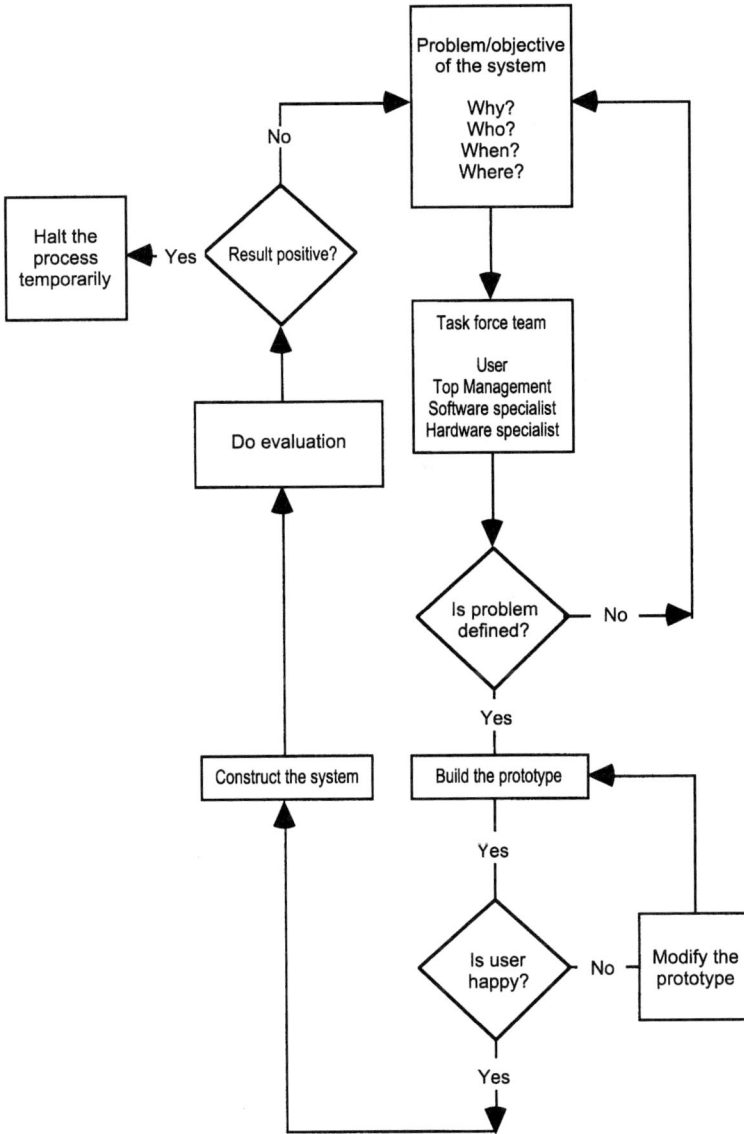

Figure 9-9   The iterative process of information systems design.

Based on the result of the evaluation, the process of modification may continue or may be halted temporarily until the user tries the new features of the system or new features are added to the system. Figure 9-9 illustrates this process. As this figure shows, all the phases of the classic life-cycle approach are combined into one phase, and this phase continues in an iterative manner until the system is constructed. After construction of the system, the monitoring mechanism improves the quality of life for the system and suggests any corrective action(s) that must be taken to guarantee the user's satisfaction.

SUMMARY

This chapter discussed systems analysis and design in the information systems environment. By explaining the classic life-cycle and the product life-cycle approaches we have combined and integrated these approaches, and we have proposed an integrated approach that is more suitable for information systems in a rapidly changing environment. This discussion should provide you with a good background for the process of building an effective information system that will be discussed in Chapter 11.

REVIEW QUESTIONS

1. What is the classic life-cycle approach?
2. What phases are included in this life cycle?
3. What is the outcome of the systems analysis phase?
4. What is a feasibility study?
5. What are the four major issues concerning feasibility?
6. Why is social feasibility important?
7. What are some of the tools used by a systems analyst in the systems analysis phase of the life cycle?
8. What is a data-flow diagram? What are flowcharts?
9. What are some of the tasks performed in the systems implementation phase?
10. What are the major types of conversion techniques?
11. Why might direct conversion be a right approach? What are some of the project control techniques introduced in this chapter? How can these techniques assist the systems analyst to control the implementation of a project?
12. Why is a postimplementation audit important?

13. What are CASE tools? What are some of the advantages of CASE tools? What are some of the commercial CASE tools on the market?

14. What are the four phases of the product life-cycle approach as it relates to the development of an information system?

15. What are the characteristics of each phase?

16. What should a systems analyst do in each phase?

17. What is a half-life? Does an information system experience a half-life? If yes, how? Discuss.

18. What are some of the characteristics of an information system in the maturity phase?

19. What are some of the monitoring mechanisms in the product life-cycle approach?

20. What is prototyping? Why is prototyping so important?

21. What are four types of prototyping methodologies?

22. What is iterative design? What is the difference between prototyping and iterative design?

23. What are some of the tools for constructing a prototype of an information system?

24. What is the integrated approach? What are the phases in the integrated approach?

PROJECTS

1. Southern Craft, a manufacturer of wood products, is implementing a cost-control information system. What are the phases of systems design in this project as it applies to the classic life cycle? What is the outcome of each phase? Prepare a feasibility study for the system. Which type of feasibility is the most important one in this particular case?

2. How do you apply the product life cycle to the Southern Craft problem? How do you establish a monitoring mechanism? How do you establish a planned abandonment?

3. Mention five monitoring mechanisms for Southern Craft as they utilize the cost-control information system.

4. The president of a state university needs advice for construction of a student-monitoring information system. This system should help the president to monitor all the students enrolled in different disciplines and display different graphs showing the number, age, nationality, and gender of the different students in

each discipline. The system should also generate exception reports regarding these four important variables. Apply systems analysis and design to this specific information system. Who should participate in the task force? What should the prototype show? How do you build the monitoring mechanism?

5. CASE tools are gaining popularity for various systems analyses and design projects. Investigate some of the capabilities of these tools. What are some of their limitations?

KEY TERMS

REFERENCES

[1] Anonymous. (October 24, 1983). Plant shutdowns: States take a new tack. *Business Week,* 73, 76.
[2] Bidgoli, H. (1997). Modern information systems for managers. San Diego: Academic Press, Inc.
[3] Bidgoli, H., and Rudd, H. (February-March 1985). Information systems life cycle as a tool for design and implementation of computer-based management information systems. *Proceedings S.E. DSI,* New Orleans, Louisiana, 316–318.

[4] DeKom, A. K. (June 1991). Systems feasibility: Studying the possibilities. *Journal of Systems Management,* 23–27.

[5] Doke, R. E. (1990). An industry survey of emerging prototyping methodologies. *Information & Management,* 18, 169–176.

[6] Gaydesch, A. Jr. (1982). *Principles of EDP Management,* pp. 79–90. Reston: Reston Publishing Company, Inc.

[7] Gore, M., and Stubbe, J. W. (1994). *Contemporary Systems Analysis,* Fifth Edition. Dubuque, Iowa: Wm. C. Brown, Publisher.

[8] Jackson, J. F., and Adams, S. W. (October 1979). The life cycle of rules. *Academy of Management Review,* 269–273.

[9] Jefferson, S. (October 1997). Cut and paste your way to a powerful prototype. *Datamation,* 104–107.

[10] Smith, E. P. (October 1978). Measuring professional obsolescence: A half-life model for the physician. *Academy of Management Review,* 914–917.

[11] Steiger, W. R., Lupi, and McDowell, J. (November 1991). CASE tool for reusable software component storage and retrieval in rapid prototyping. *Information and Software Technology,* Vol. 33, No. 9, 698–706.

[12] Whitten, J. L., and Bentley, L. D. (1998). *Systems Analysis & Design Methods.* Burr Ridge, Illinois: Irwin-McGraw-Hill.

Chapter 10

Total Quality Management and Information Systems Reengineering

Learning Objectives

After studying this chapter, you should be able to:

- Define total quality management (TQM).
- Elaborate on the key components of TQM.
- Explain the information systems role for an effective TQM program.
- Discuss TQM role in building effective information systems.
- Discuss some of the companies that have used TQM effectively.
- Elaborate on business process reengineering and its relationship to TQM.
- Discuss the synergy between TQM and information systems for improving productivity.

10-1 INTRODUCTION

This chapter provides a discussion of total quality management (TQM) and its role in designing quality information systems. The principles of TQM will be reviewed and its components will be elaborated upon. The chapter explains in detail the major contribution of TQM in various information systems applications, including CASE tools and group decision support systems. The chapter discusses business process reengineering principles and their relationship to TQM. Several corporations that have successfully implemented TQM are introduced. The chapter concludes with a discussion of the synergy that exists between TQM and information systems. TQM and information systems together can help organizations to achieve their goals in an effective and efficient manner.

10-2 TOTAL QUALITY MANAGEMENT (TQM): AN OVERVIEW

In the late 1970s and early 1980s many American corporations in several industries were losing significant market share. One such company was IBM, whose Japanese subsidiary lost its number one position in 1979 to Fujitsu and later fell to third, below NEC. Until the late 1970s IBM had been the dominate computer company in Japan [5].

IBM's story of losing market share to Japanese corporations was becoming epidemic. Not only were American corporations losing international market share, but they were losing market share in the United States as well. The "Buy American" slogan was used extensively to try to persuade American consumers to support American corporations. However, the slogan did not help to minimize consumer purchases of Japanese goods. American consumers were buying Japanese products simply because of their higher quality and cheaper price.

The question of how a country that must import a majority of its fuels, consumer goods, and materials could produce higher quality products at lower prices was difficult to answer. By the middle of the 1980s, it was painfully obvious that the Japanese were doing something right [13].

American business experts began to look for an explanation. Their studies showed that American companies had a higher return on investment, return on assets, and operating margins than did the Japanese companies. However the Japanese had higher market shares in many industries. Simply put, Japanese companies were selling more at lower costs; as a result they were generating more revenue. This gap was the result of the differences in management styles between the two countries. American corporations focused on stock prices and maximizing the stockholder's value, while the Japanese corporations focused on gaining market share. Another important factor has been the long-term focus in Japan versus short-term focus in the United States. This was obvious by comparing the R & D budget per capita in Japan versus the United States.

The Japanese corporations found that they could not compete in industry with the same focus as the American firms so they found a different way to compete. This was by gaining market share through the improved quality of goods and services.

Ironically, this Japanese philosophy was taught to Japanese corporations by Americans at the end of World War II. Dr. Edward Deming and Joseph M. Juran were two of the scientists who helped the Japanese rebuild their economy by teaching them how to make goods with a focus on quality.

Total quality management is the American-coined phrase to describe the philosophy used by Japanese corporations. To understand the philosophy of total quality management one must first define quality. Deming referred to quality as "continuous improvement" [25].

Computer-based information systems (CBIS) can be one of the most valuable tools in an organization for the implementation and continuous improvement of the total quality management process.

Total quality management is the organizational-wide focus on the continuous improvement of quality. This is achieved by the improvement in the efficiency of process, focusing on satisfying the external customer and empowering the internal customers—the employees. Continuous improvement is similar to the iterative process in information systems design (discussed in Chapter 9). This methodology tries to improve system quality by monitoring it and measuring its effectiveness. By doing so, more enhanced features are continuously added and the inefficient features are removed. This may be achieved by talking to the users and reflecting more on their needs.

10-3 PRINCIPLES OF TOTAL QUALITY MANAGEMENT

Deming emphasized the behavioral aspect in managing quality and identified seven deadly diseases in the United States quality crisis as follows [25, p.9]:

1. A lack of constancy of purpose.
2. An emphasis on short-term profits.

3. Evaluations of people by rating and annual reviews, therefore destroying teamwork and creating rivalry and fear.
4. Management mobility, leading to inadequate understanding of how the organization works and lack of incentive for long-term planning.
5. Managing the organization by visible numbers only.
6. Excessive employee healthcare costs.
7. Excessive warranty costs, encouraged by attorneys.

To solve these problems, Deming proposed the following 14 points that are his views of TQM [25, pp. 9-10]:

1. *Create constancy of purpose for improvement of product and service.* Deming suggests a radical new definition of a company's role. Rather than making money, it is to stay in business and provide jobs through innovation, research, constant improvement, and maintenance. This theory puts a heavy emphasis on R & D that has been very important in Japan.

2. *Adopt the new philosophy.* Americans are too tolerant of poor workmanship and low-quality service. We need a new religion in which mistakes and negativism are unacceptable.

3. *Cease dependence on mass inspection.* American firms typically inspect a product as it comes off the assembly line or at major stages in the assembly line. Defective products are either thrown out or reworked; both are expensive. In effect, a company is paying workers to make defects and then to correct them. Quality comes not from inspection but from improvement of the process. With inspection everyone can be enlisted in this improvement. In another words, a defect should not be introduced in the first place.

4. *End the practice of awarding business on price tag alone.* Purchasing departments customarily operate on orders to seek the lowest priced vendor. Frequently, this leads to suppliers of low-quality products that in turn results in low-quality output. Instead, they should seek the best quality and work to achieve it with a single supplier for any one item in a long-term relationship.

5. *Improve constantly and forever the system of production and service.* Improvement is not a one-time effort. Management is obligated to continually look for ways to reduce waste and improve quality.

6. *Institute training.* Too often, workers have learned their job from another worker who has never been trained properly. They are forced to follow instructions that have not been fully tested. They cannot do their jobs because no one tells them how.

7. *Institute leadership.* The job of a supervisor is not to tell people what to do or to punish them but to lead. Leading consists of helping people do a better job and of learning by objective methods who is in need of individual help.

8. *Drive out fear.* Many employees are afraid to ask questions or to take a position on an issue, even when they do not understand what the job is or what is right or wrong. People will continue to do things the wrong way, or not do them

at all. The economic loss from fear is appalling. It is necessary for better quality and productivity that people feel secure. This theory promotes an open style management.

9. *Break down barriers between staff areas.* Often staff areas such as departments, units, and divisions are competing with each other or have goals that conflict. They do not work as a team so they can solve or foresee problems. Worse, one department's goals may contradict those of another.

10. *Eliminate slogans, exhortations, and targets for the workforce.* These never helped anybody do a good job. Let people put up their own slogans.

11. *Eliminate numerical quotas.* Quotas take account only of numbers, not quality or methods. They are usually a guarantee of inefficiency and high cost. To hold onto a job, a person meets a quota at any cost, without regard to damage to the company or quality.

12. *Remove barriers that rob employees of their pride of workmanship.* People are eager to do a good job and are distressed when they cannot. Too often, misguided supervisors, faulty equipment, and defective materials stand in the way. These barriers must be removed.

13. *Institute a vigorous program of education and retraining.* Both management and the workforce will have to be educated in the new methods, including teamwork and statistical processes and techniques.

14. *Take action to accomplish the transformation.* It will take a special top management team with a plan of action to carry out the quality mission. Workers can not do it on their own, nor can managers. A critical mass of people in the company must understand the 14 points, and the seven deadly diseases.

These 14 points are applicable to every industry whether it is a service industry or manufacturing industry. There are seven categories that these 14 points fall into. These categories are [11]:

- Vision and values
- Commitment and participation
- Quality management
- Continuous improvement
- Human resource development
- Rewards
- Technology and systems

The following is a brief explanation of these seven categories.

10-3-1 VISIONS AND VALUES

The vision and values of the corporation are set by the top management. The vision is what drives an organization to strive for improvement. Top management sets down on paper where they envision the corporation is going to be in the future. Contained in the vision are the values that the company wishes to maintain. These values include the corporation's responsibility to its employees, customers, suppliers, and society. Most companies' visions entail the desire to be the highest quality producer and offer the highest potential growth to its employees.

Progressive organizations have an information systems master plan that achieves the same goal. The plan outlines the preset position of the organization with regard to the information systems technology and it depicts the future goal that must be achieved.

10-3-2 COMMITMENT AND PARTICIPATION

Once a vision is created, it must be ingrained in all employees of the organization. This means that it is important not only to inform the employees of the words and phrases contained in the vision statement, but to make them commit to the purpose of the corporation. This is one of the most important steps in the total quality management process. Participation by every employee in the organization is necessary in order to make the cultural change to quality in the corporation. In other words, TQM is an organization-wide effort. This commitment must begin with top management. Without their support, the TQM process has small chance of being fully implemented and successful.

10-3-3 QUALITY MEASUREMENT

Total quality management focuses on eliminating defects and on doing the job right the first time and every time. Processes must be stable, repeatable, visible, and measurable. Therefore, management, with the help of employees, must create goals to be measured that will help to ensure high quality in products and services. Many firms use benchmarking as a way to compare the corporation with its past performance and make comparisons with the operations of other corporations within a similar industry. Benchmarking provides a rational method to set performance goals and to gain market leadership and a broader, more accurate management perspective.

Benchmarking provides management with three valuable tools in the total quality management process [15]:

- It shows the improvement made within the firm towards its quality goals.
- It provides knowledge regarding the corporation position in its industry.
- It provides management with ideas used in other organizations that can help improve the efficiency of the firm's processes and in turn increases the perceived quality of the corporation by the customers.

Benchmarking techniques have also been used in information systems for many years. Benchmarking tools have helped information systems designers to continuously improve the system performance. Benchmarking tools can also help in screening top quality products among systems that are not as high quality.

10-3-4 CONTINUOUS IMPROVEMENT

Process improvement never stops. The process must be constantly nurtured through management involvement and employee empowerment. TQM recognizes that quality cannot be added to a product or service after its completion but must be designed into the work process from the beginning. Corporations need to begin implementing TQM by detailing who their customers are [17,22].

There are three groups of customers whose needs must be analyzed in order to implement and maintain the continuous improvement process. These are the external customers, the internal customers, and suppliers. Figure 10-1 illustrates these three groups of customers.

The first group of customers to be analyzed are the **external customers.** These customers should be surveyed to determine if they are satisfied with the product they have purchased as well as the service provided them by sales people, management, and delivery employees. Because quality is in the eye of the beholder, sometimes there are minor factors that differentiate a corporation from its competition. These minor factors need to be investigated to ensure that they will be maintained in the future. External customers also need to feel that management is

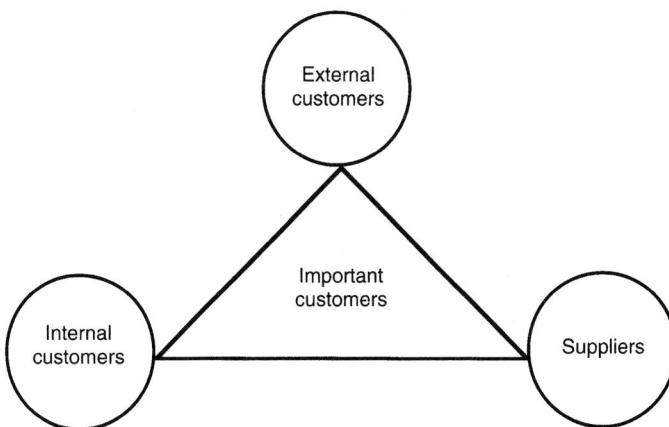

Figure 10-1   Three important categories of customers.

listening to their ideas; therefore, all suggestions made by this group need to be considered in order to keep the perceived quality of the corporation intact.

The second group of customers that corporations need to analyze are its **internal customers,** that is, employees. Employees are the most important resource in any organization. In analyzing employee needs the firm needs to question whether or not the current system empowers the employees to be productive. Are the employees given ample opportunities for professional development and promotion? Is adequate training provided? In order for employees to feel empowered, they should be an active participants in the total quality management process. Management needs to release power from the top and disburse it throughout the organization.

The third group of customers of a corporation is its **suppliers.** Suppliers should not be chosen on the basis of low cost but instead for providing consistently high-quality goods and services. If suppliers are unable to meet the requirement of the corporation, the corporate management should make every attempt to educate the supplier and provide them with the assistance necessary to meet the requirements. By increasing the quality of suppliers, the corporation is also increasing its own quality. This means that the supplier and the corporation are both active participants in a long-term partnership.

Top management must realize that total quality management is not an overnight cure. It is a long and challenging change in the culture of the organization. The planning and implementation of TQM should contain measures for overcoming resistance to the new corporate culture that is associated with the new philosophy. Open communication between top management and employees can eliminate or at least minimize the resistance-to-change issue.

10-3-5 HUMAN RESOURCE DEVELOPMENT

Much of the total quality management process surrounds people. This is why the development of human resources plays such an important role in the implementation and maintenance of TQM.

Pauline Brody, chairperson of Xerox's Quality Forum, explains the necessary changes that have to be made in the organization's culture in order for total quality management to succeed. TQM requires a change in organizational culture, a fundamental change in the way individuals and groups approach their work and their roles in the organization. Therefore, an organization should change from an environment of distrust and fear of reprisal to one of openness and trust where creativity can flourish; from working as individuals to working as teams; from protection of organizational turf to the breakdown of control to a softer style of team leader and coach; from power concentrated at the top to power shared with employees; from a focus on results to a focus on change; from making decisions based on

information systems are playing a vital role and contribution in almost every aspect of a successful TQM program.

Information systems can contribute to total quality management by helping other business functions perform their work more effectively, by helping to analyze and redesign the business process, by suggesting new ways to apply technology to enhance quality, and by sharing experience in qualifying and measuring procedures within the organization.

Information systems are involved in almost every department within an organization. For instance, information systems are involved in designing, developing, and supporting daily work in finance, accounting, sales, personnel, manufacturing, and strategic planning. (We will discuss these various applications of information systems in functional areas in Chapter 11.) In addition, information systems professionals have a unique knowledge of the different systems operating in every department. Functional information systems are indispensable in order to achieve any quality project. The information systems staff is the source of ideas on the application of technology to quality issues; often they are also the people who can make that technology available to the quality projects. For example, with the help of information systems departments statistical analysis software is becoming more widely used in achieving quality by performing statistical quality control.

Some of the most important contributions that information systems can provide to TQM are meeting benchmarking standards and improving customer services by expediting the delivery of goods and services. Another way in which information systems contribute to TQM is by installing information systems for the automation of paperwork to improve the processes involved for improving quality. In most cases reducing paperwork will result in faster service to the customers [20,22].

Information systems fit into every aspect of an organization and the total quality management process. Information systems are able to monitor the process of manufacturing assembly lines to enable the corporation to evaluate the efficiency of its automated processes. Information systems allow higher levels of customer service by allowing services to be provided twenty-four hours a day to its customers, and they can help solve problems that customers may have with the corporation's product. Information systems allow business transactions to occur at any time and anywhere. Information systems provide timely information with a higher level of accuracy. In the information superhighway era, information systems allow customers to access any type of product description or announcement at any time and anywhere.

The problem that often occurs is that TQM teams do not include information system departments in quality planning. Even though most measuring and benchmarking are done by using functional information systems. By including the information systems department in the quality process, corporations can gain a valuable tool for the implementation of TQM. Several tools can be used for problem solving and improving quality. These tools are scatter diagrams, histograms, check sheets, pareto diagrams, run charts, control charts, and cause and effect diagrams [11]. With effective information systems in place, these tools can be readily available and utilized in quality improvement process.

An example of the need for the information systems department to be an active participant in the quality teams is found in the concept of the paperless office and paperless manufacturing information systems. This technology would have never been introduced into these organizations if it were not for information systems participation in the total quality management process.

The concept of the paperless office is similar to manufacturing firms automating their production processes. Accounting firms are notorious for the amount of documentation they create, file, sort, and retrieve. This is a very costly venture. Another problem is the space required to store all of this paperwork.

Document management systems is the new technology to solve this problem. This technology uses document imaging, which scans paper documents in the same way fax machines transmit a document over telephone lines. The documents are then stored on optical disks that can hold more than 13,000 pages of information. By organizing the information, the retrieval process becomes much simpler. Documents that are ideal candidates for optical storage in accounting firms include income tax returns, time and billing reports, payroll records, bank statements, canceled checks, accounts receivable and accounts payable, confirmation requests and replies, and detailed physical inventory count sheets [24]. The imaging techniques along with computer designed financial statements will eliminate the problems associated with paper documents.

Once an image is stored in the system, retrieval of the information can be performed in minutes, not days as could be the case with paper documents. The information also could be sent to the customer electronically via a modem. The system even makes it easy to find missing material by conducting a computer search for key words in the document. This process can be made secure by adding passwords to some or to all the files in the system. Document imaging offers accounting firms more than just cost savings and increased productivity. This is quality that can be marketed to the customer and it also provides a perception of high quality because they do not have to wait while the paper document is retrieved or recreated if it cannot be located. This technology will save organizations a great deal of time and money.

A modified form of the paperless office is that of the paperless integrated manufacturing system that is in operation in Motorola's manufacturing process. The corporation designed a system to fulfill three needs: 1. Online access to factory information and data collection on the manufacturing process; 2. a means to easily input the necessary data through interfaces that were usable by all operators in all facilities; 3. a system that could track current and historical information of all production lots through the manufacturing process [9].

The early stage of this system operation was not very successful because the requirements of the system were not well defined by the factory users or the system developers. This points out another concept where systematic improvement requires the dedicated support of developers and managers. Obviously, Motorola needed to explore further the original planning and implementation of the paperless integrated manufacturing system.

10-5 TQM ROLE IN INFORMATION SYSTEMS DESIGN AND IMPLEMENTATION

The quality issue and developing high-quality systems is a common problem for many organizations. The reason is that information systems departments are so focused on meeting deadlines that they often deliver the system before it is ready and then try to fix it once it is in place. This way of thinking violates the principle stated by Philip Crosby, one of the pioneers in TQM development [25]. He states that quality cannot be added after the fact. The use of a quality focus in the planning and designing phase of a new system should work to minimize problems that may occur later, therefore allowing the successful design and on-time delivery of a quality system. Incomplete requirements, that is, items requested by internal or external customers, represent a large portion of errors that occur in information systems. Information systems that are not properly designed or maintained for quality create more costs and work than if the system had been behind schedule and then implemented.

The first step in implementing the total quality management principle in information systems is to define and identify the customer of the information systems departments. Most information systems departments do not know who their customers are. Customers may be external, such as an automated teller machine that provides information to the customers of a bank. The customers may be internal and may come from different divisions within the organization. When the company defines its customers, it can then investigate what information the customers need, what items could improve the employees' satisfaction, and what technologies could help in the continuous improvement of existing systems.

The information systems department then needs to evaluate the current system and make adjustments to create a quality system instead of a traditional system. The quality information system is based on the principle that all employees are active participants in the system development process.

The next step in the total quality management process is for the information systems department to create a vision and set goals that are congruent with the continual improvement of information systems. The goals for an information system should be made in order to point out processes that need to become more effective or efficient. Goals also allow an organization to link its activities to a vision. This helps employees maintain a continual focus on quality.

Ultimately, all goals should be monitored for continuous improvement. These can be monitored by choosing the quality concept and choosing a way to measure it. Some guidelines for measuring continuous improvement are:

- Define the process, then formulate the measures.
- Expect measurement to change.
- Measure all key variables numerically.
- Measurements should indicate progression toward goals.

Some suggested measurements of information systems quality are [8]:

- Programming-related incident reports;
- Cost of service provided for the end user;
- End-user satisfaction surveys;
- Time spent on quality;
- Number of problems resolved;
- Response time in meeting targets;
- Network response time in meeting targets;
- Total defects by group;
- Reduction in the number and quality of complaints.

An organization should constantly monitor its own industry and its competitive positions. It should look outside for solutions, listen to the marketplace, manage its essential resources, it should be precise in specifications and expectations, and it should be flexible in its expectations.

When the corporation has gathered the relevant information regarding its operations, it should be analyzed so that more improvements can be made (in continuous improvement, the cycle never stops). These improvements should always be focused toward quality improvement.

When considering the total quality management process in an organization it is important to remember the characteristics of a total quality management corporation. These are something that all information systems departments should strive to achieve:

1. The information systems must be customer driven.
2. Top management must be involved.
3. All employees must be involved and responsible.
4. There should be a strong effort in reducing response time.
5. The focus of the information systems department should be on prevention, not detection.
6. Information systems managers should use feedback information to measure progress.
7. The focus of the department should be on the present and also on the long range.

8. The information systems manager should promote the development of a partnership between suppliers, customers, and employees.
9. Management and the information systems department should maintain a high level of public responsibility.

These characteristics define what has made companies such as Xerox, Eastman Kodak, Toyota, and Motorola the market leaders in their industries. In the following pages, we further discuss role of TQM in specific information systems areas.

10-5-1 CONTINUOUS IMPROVEMENT IN INFORMATION SYSTEMS

Continuous improvement, one of the principal elements of TQM, can be successfully applied to information systems. A minimum set of stable and repeatable processes is required before systems development, maintenance, and operation can be effectively measured, controlled, and improved [22]. Furthermore, the information systems department must establish processes while developing systems. These processes must be stable, repeatable, visible, and measurable, and the standard must be "no defects." For example, when developing an order entry system, bugs should not be introduced in the first place. Debugging in later stages can be time-consuming and expensive. By using structured design methodology, top-down design, and modular programming, programmers are now able to deliver relatively error-free codes.

According to James Ward, many companies do not even have a minimum set of defined processes. The absolute minimum set of processes that must be defined and implemented in an information system organization are [22]:

• *Systems development life cycle (SDLC) methodology.* The SDLC should be applied and followed on all appropriate cases. We discussed this methodology in Chapter 9.

• *Project management methodology.* Project management tools such as PERT (program evaluation and review technique), CPM (critical path method), and the Gantt chart help systems analysts deliver timely systems. PERT and CPM techniques determine all the critical activities that must be performed on time in order not to delay the project. Gantt charts provide a monitoring mechanism for observing various activities involved in a project. We discussed these techniques in Chapter 9.

• *Quality assurance and testing methodology.* This allows feedback and control of the process.

These processes establish the basis for continuous improvement, one of the essential elements of TQM. Without standards, the quality assurance effort becomes subjective and arbitrary, which can quickly undermine any TQM effort.

The benefits from implementing continuous process improvement in information systems are the very same that an organization achieves from business process reengineering (BPR). These include work simplification, reduced cycle time, fewer defects, and lower error rates, which ultimately lead to a substantial cost reduction, higher quality, and increased customer satisfaction. We will discuss BPR later in this chapter.

Many TQM processes fail to achieve significant benefits. The reasons are always the same—lack of management understanding, commitment, and involvement. However, if the TQM program passes the first stage of its introduction, the chances for success are high.

Quality is not something that senior executives can order to occur. It cannot be achieved through promotional techniques that involve the use of posters and advertising. Quality is achieved when the environment is modified in the right fashion. Seven keys to realizing such a change in the atmosphere are [18]:

1. Commit to continuous quality improvement in both user service and end product.
2. Create a positive work environment.
3. Eliminate barriers between work group members and between the work group and those with whom it functions.
4. Discontinue merit ratings and numerical goal settings and performance measurement mechanisms.
5. Encourage continuing education and self-improvement.
6. Limit reliance on inspection to achieve quality.
7. Avoid concentrating on price when working with vendors, whether services, equipment, or software are involved.

10-5-2 TQM TECHNIQUES FOR INFORMATION SYSTEMS DEVELOPMENT

The increasing size and complexity of information systems often lead to larger teams and increasing communication difficulties. These problems sometimes continue to grow during system integration, or through the entire system development life cycle. In recent years, system size and complexity have driven major corporations to develop solutions such as the application software factory (ASF). Some of the causes for the increasing complexity are due to combining tools, languages, and design approaches. The ASF works through a combination of process flexibility and team discipline gained from a thorough team understanding of ASF principles. The overall purpose of this program is to first eliminate any unnecessary variation from program to program and then to reduce the necessary variation to its minimal acceptable level. This is in contrast to traditional software engineering approaches that attempt to empower the programmer or analyst by providing all the capabilities that he or she may want to use. Current 4GLs associated with ICASE (integrated CASE) products feature compilers and may be more flexible and adaptive to ASF requirements. As confidence grows, analysts find ways to improve and expand their use of the original ASF design team. By empowering the teamwork, members significantly improve their own work environment and productivity. The technology of generating and reducing codes is not enough to gain productivity improvements in many projects. Some of the processes for system quality improvements are [21]:

1. To eliminate any design or code that does not add real value to the final system functions.
2. To eliminate simplifying and then automating processes that could otherwise create flows in testing or bugs in the finished system.
3. To test and improve the process rather than the product (system). This eliminates error (bugs) and the opportunity to make those errors.
4. To emphasize training, discipline, and consistent standards.
5. To improve the entire team to build and improve the ASF rather than relying on a separate technical group of builders.
6. To foster a positive approach to prevent perceptions of "bad" ideas or failures.

10-5-3 TQM AND CASE TOOLS

The quality of a system should always be the most important and the first concern for the developer, as well as for the end user. Applying TQM concepts can aid in developing a timely, efficient, and error-free systems that meets the user's requirements through the life of the system. There are numerous reasons for information systems failure. Some of these reasons are:

- Not meeting the user requirements;
- Improper planning;
- Lack of user involvement;
- Inadequate analysis and design;
- Inflexibility of design;
- Long response time;
- Personnel turnover.

TQM philosophy, by emphasizing active user involvement and defining the requirements properly, can assist in developing high quality systems.

CASE (computer-assisted system engineering) probably offers the best set of tools for the implementation of TQM when developing software packages.

Integrated CASE (ICASE) contains tools applicable to all stages of the system development life cycle. Table 10-1 summarizes the role of CASE tools in implementing TQM concepts for avoiding failures in systems development. In addition, by using CASE tools the design team can develop systems that are efficient, relatively free from errors, and easy to modify. CASE tools streamline the entire development process by improving the planning phase. Planning tools are often used at the strategic level of the organization. At this stage a master plan is generated that proposes a set of systems projects to facilitate organizational goals and to help in achieving the critical success factors of the organization.

Another TQM strategy in the development of quality information systems is to get the user involved. After the lack of involvement in some data processing projects that failed to serve the needs of their users in the 1950s and 1960s, the

Table 10-1
CASE Tools to Implement TQM Concepts
for Removing Inadequacies in Systems Development

Inadequacies	TQM concepts	CASE tools
1. Improving planning and estimating	Management with metrics Continuous process improvement	Planning tools Standardized data modeling tools Structure analysis and design tools
2. Lack of user involvement	Continuous process improvement Quality by design Deployment of technology Employee participation	Diagramming tools Structure analysis and design tools Prototyping tools Requirements tools
3. Inadequate analysis and design	Customer orientation Employee participation Improved communication	Prototyping tools Detailed design Documentation tools Standardized data modeling tools
4. Inflexibility of design	Quality by design Deployment of technology Productivity improvement Continuous process improvement	Repository tools Structure analysis and design tools Diagramming tools Code-generation tools
5. Long lead time	Productivity improvement Deployment of technology	Repository tools Prototyping tools Code-generation tools
6. Turnover of personnel	Employee participation Deployment of technology	Repository tools Standardized data modeling tools Code-generation tools Prototyping tools

Source: Aggarwal, Rajesh, and Jong-Sung Lee, p. 17. Reprinted with permission.

field of information systems has become one of the firm advocates of involving end users in developing information systems.

Constant communication among developers and users is perhaps the best tool for creating quality software. The participation of the user in prototyping, in designing the specifications, and in creating the standardized data models is essential for the quality of software. Further, the involvement of users in the development of software can reduce error, as well as the need for modification, which can be done in the early stages of the development process.

10-5-4 TQM AND GROUP DECISION SUPPORT SYSTEMS

Quality improvement team and process improvement teams are a significant part of the TQM concept. Good communication is the key to successful teamwork. A comprehensive group support system (GSS) is one technology that can be used to enhance communication and decision making in quality groups [19]. This growing information system application improves the productivity of meetings, which in turn leads to an improvement in quality and productivity for the entire organization. A GSS increases team productivity and effectiveness within TQM framework. We will discuss the GSS in detail in Chapter 14.

The most frequently used applications of group support systems used in TQM process are:

- *Electronic brainstorming.* Allows group members to simultaneously and anonymously exchange ideas on specific topics presented to the group.
- *Idea organizing.* Lets group members or other staffers organize the comments generated during the brainstorming session into related topic areas.
- *Ranking and rating.* A GSS usually offers a group the means to express preferences through a voting program.
- *Anonymity.* Individuals feel less compelled to agree with the group's opinion.
- *Parallel communication.* A GSS allows everyone to exchange written comments simultaneously through a computer network, which increases participation.
- *Automated record keeping.* A GSS automatically records comments, votes, and other information shared by a group onto a disk file (it is no longer necessary to take notes).

10-6 BUSINESS PROCESS REENGINEERING

The term "business reengineering" or business process reengineering (BPR) seemed to appear in the American business world overnight. Now it is everywhere. However, many companies begin to play this new "game" without quite understanding it. No wonder failures in reengineering are heard from time to time [3].

Michael Hammer, a pioneer of the reengineering concept, believes that most reengineering failures are caused by a company's lack of understanding of the true nature of reengineering, combined with a less than total commitment to carrying it out.

Hammer and Champy, the creators of the term "reengineering," define business reengineering as [14]:

> The fundamental rethinking and radical redesign of business processes to achieve dramatic improvements in critical, contemporary measures of performance, such as cost, quality, service and speed.

They further define four key phrases in the reengineering process: fundamental, radical, dramatic and process.

1. *Fundamental.* Reengineering first should answer basic questions such as What must a company do to achieve its goals? How can a company perform these tasks? The company should ignore all the traditional values and beliefs. It should concentrate on "what should be" instead of "what is."

2. *Radical.* Reengineering goes to the root and bottom of the ways in which we work. Radical redesign of business processes means discarding conventional ways of working and replacing them with completely new ways. Reengineering is not business improvement, business enhancement, or business modification, but it is business reinvention.

3. *Dramatic.* Reengineering is not about making incremental or marginal improvements but about making magnitude breakthroughs in operating and financial performance. Reengineering should be adopted only where a need exists for major takeoff. Dramatic improvement demands discarding the old methods and replacing them with something new.

4. *Process.* A business process is a collection of activities and tasks that take one or more types of inputs and creates an output that is of value to the customers.

10-6-1 WHY REENGINEERING?

Today, the business environment is very different from that of the 1970s and 1980s. The hierarchically structured, command and control driven organizations of the past can no longer deliver the goods and services in an efficient and effective manner. To stay competitive businesses should deliver goods and services that are of high quality and reasonably priced, and in a timely manner. Business and government organizations are growing larger and larger, and they are becoming less responsive to the needs of their customers. These organizations face a major challenge in staying competitive, regardless of the kind of technology that they are using.

A quick fix for these organizations has been partially achieved by downsizing and restructuring. However, these changes have not led to significant improvement in the bottom line. A majority of the organizations that have tried to reduce costs by reducing the number of people have overburdened the employees who remain. The scenario of doing more with fewer people has become widespread.

How can the issue of productivity be resolved? Business process reengineering is an attractive solution. As mentioned earlier, reengineering means starting over, and starting from scratch. It touches the root or the heart of the business processes.

The result of reengineering is very impressive and encouraging. There are many success stories that illustrate this process. For example, by reengineering, IBM accomplished a 90% reduction in cycle time and a hundred fold improvement in productivity. Ford Motor accomplished a 75% reduction in its accounts payable staff, a simplification of material control, and improved accuracy in financial reporting. Of course, these are not the only firms that have gained major benefits from business process reengineering. Other success stories include AT&T, Digital Equipment, Mutual Benefit Life, Hallmark Cards, Zayre Corp., and Kentucky Fried Chicken [16].

10-6-2 THE ROLE OF INFORMATION SYSTEMS IN REENGINEERING

Information systems have changed a lot of the old rules in business. Some of the changes are:

- Information can be delivered simultaneously in as many places as is needed.
- A generalist can do the work of an expert.
- Decision making is part of everyone's job.
- Field personnel can send and receive information wherever they are.
- Organizational barriers are broken by the Internet and global information systems.

Information systems play a critical role in the reengineering process. Information systems make business process reengineering a reality. For example, personal computers and network technologies facilitate simplified processes, they promote decentralized decision making, and they empower front line employees.

To implement the reengineering process, information systems serve as powerful tools. They provide the support structure that allows companies to automate business processes that involve information. Personal computers, for example, are becoming the technology tool of choice. As the power of PCs increases and the price declines, more companies will be using this productivity tool. PC-based networks provide fast information retrieval, processing, and communication among employees, suppliers, and customers. This, in turn, makes most business processes amenable to reductions in cycle time, increased productivity, and quality improvement.

Wal-Mart Stores, for example, attributes much of its success to reengineering the processes used to procure and distribute mass market retail goods. One key to Wal-Mart's effectiveness is an enterprise-wide information system that directly connects each retail location to all Wal-Mart distribution warehouses and major suppliers. This system closely tracks daily sales and inputs them back to Wal-Mart distribution points and third-party manufacturers and suppliers.

Reengineering and information systems are so interrelated that some people define the term reengineering as the use of information technology to radically redesign business processes in order to achieve dramatic improvements in performance. However, information systems are not the entire solution for implementing the reengineering process. They only provide a series of tools.

An interview with senior executives responsible for reengineering efforts at 40 Fortune 500 companies showed the role of the information systems in the reengineering process. One of the questions asked was: "What are the most important success factors for a reengineering effort?" More than 50% of the participants in the interview believed that all reengineering efforts are initiated because of a perceived information systems opportunity. However, only 15% of the executives indicated that information systems proved to be a success factor. The success turns out to be more dependent on clear senior management leadership, vision, and the training and active involvement of a cross-functional employee. In other words, the actual technological solution is far less important than educating employees to use information systems as tools in the reengineering process [12].

There are several information systems applications that are particularly helpful in business process reengineering:

• *Electronic data interchange, or EDI.* This technology allows one company to interconnect with others such as its suppliers or customers, and to exchange information electronically. This eliminates the shuffling of paper documents. As a result this process can greatly speed up the flow of transactions among myriad companies. We will discuss EDI in detail in Chapter 12.

• *Image processing technologies.* Image processing technology exchanges data and documents within and outside of the organization electronically and therefore reduces paper processing and speeds up the delivery of information.

• *GroupWare.* As will be discussed in Chapter 14, GroupWare and group support systems allow teams of decision makers to function more effectively by breaking up the geographical boundaries.

• *Telecommunication and Internet technologies.* Electronic mail, computer conferencing, video conferencing, computer-assisted telephone interviewing (CATI) and other related technologies can make it possible for remote groups of people to function effectively.

• *Network systems.* Network technologies such as fiber optics and ISDN are providing the capacity to transmit quickly much higher volumes of data than in the past. The appearance of network systems such as LAN, WAN, and MAN have greatly improved the speed and volume of information exchange, both internally and externally.

These and other information systems technologies can be used to simplify the business process and information flow, thus making business process reengineering a reality.

Since every organization is unique in its business process, various methods are used to apply information systems to reengineering. Some companies change their process first, then bring the information systems support. Others bring the new information systems first, and then reengineer the process by maximum use of these systems. No matter which method is used, organizations should follow one important rule, which is to focus on process instead of on technology or function.

A good example is Wal-Mart. As mentioned before, Wal-Mart is very successful in its business process reengineering. In less than 30 years it has become the largest retailer in North America. What is instructive about the Wal-Mart success story is that the company did not simply use technology to find faster ways of performing its old processes or speeding up individual tasks. Instead, it improved its efficiency and effectiveness by using information systems to eliminate unnecessary tasks.

A common mistake made by many organizations is that they place a heavy emphasis on how technology is used instead of what it is used for. They simply computerize manual systems and do not take full advantage of the capabilities that information systems technologies provide. When information systems professionals design a new system, they usually design the system to fit into the existing organizational structure, operating procedures, and tasks. This tradition eventually leads to process reengineering.

Since information systems are very important in business process reengineering, the information systems department needs to participate in the company's reengineering program. First of all, information systems personnel should reeducate themselves. They must understand what business process reengineering is and they need to focus on the business process. Information systems should be used to eliminate unnecessary tasks and to simplify the existing processes. Otherwise, they might see process reengineering as simply re-implementing their old systems with new technology, without changing the business process. They might confuse business reengineering with software reengineering, therefore missing the main point.

Software reengineering helps systems builders reconfigure software to conform to structured design principles and to make it easier to maintain. Reengineering has several aspects from which quality professionals and their programs can benefit. Reengineering programs have a strong focus on achieving specific improvement levels in cycle-time process, cost, or output quality.

The TQM goal of productivity and reduction of errors in designing of new software projects can be accomplished by reusing proven software designs and methods. By reusing similar functions of a system after it has been tested, these functions and procedures can be stored in the CASE toolkit of the organization. Project development time can be significantly reduced when reusable designs, data models, or code are used. Projects created primarily with reusable software need significantly fewer resources than does designing software from scratch.

In summary, developers use reengineering to extract intelligence from existing systems, thereby creating new systems that are not started from scratch and are easier to maintain. IBM, for example, which has seen its work force fall by half since 1986, is taking a similar approach. IBM's most ambitious goal is to reconcile its massive reengineering program with its quality goals [10].

The dilemma facing managers is that total quality management emphasizes continuous, step-by-step improvement, while reengineering relies on a radical once-and-for-all scrapping of existing business processes. Organizations must carefully monitor their reengineering programs to ensure, at the very least, that each step of the process improves rather than worsens quality.

Total quality management and business process reengineering have emerged as important practices in major organizations. Both TQM and BPR rely on information technology to measure process times and outputs and to make process records available to all participants. Reengineering processes is not simply a matter of drawing new maps and introducing new technology. It is also a matter of reorganizing employees practices, habits, and self interest.

Reengineering affected by information systems is offered as a model to redesign business processes and to achieve quality. The primary role of information systems in the reengineering effort is to recognize business opportunities that are hidden in information technology. By providing fast processing and analytical capabilities, capturing important information at the source, and offering instantaneous data transmission, information systems play a central role in achieving aggressive reengineering improvement targets [2].

10-7   TQM IN ACTION

There are numerous companies that have been using TQM and TQM-related techniques with positive results. In the next few paragraphs, we introduce some of these companies.

Xerox regained its market share from Japanese corporations by applying the techniques used by the Japanese producers. Xerox used benchmarking to gain an advantage over Motorola and Cannon copiers.

AT&T regained much of the market share it had lost to Sprint and MCI. AT&T measures all of its quality program in terms of financial returns. AT&T found that when customers perceive improved quality, it shows up in better financial results 3 months later. This provides AT&T with the ability to benchmark its quality programs against itself to look for new areas of improvement [13].

UPS, which stresses prompt delivery at any cost, is giving drivers free time to talk to customers. This effort toward higher quality service should keep UPS ahead of its competition. Also, UPS spends a considerable amount of money every year on information technology to improve its quality of service.

IBM has made a dramatic comeback in the last couple of years. While IBM is still having trouble remaining competitive, it has begun to reengineer its corporate structure and improve its information system departments. Also, customer service has dramatically improved at IBM.

These corporations all have one thing in common—they recognize the value of the information systems departments and they treat them as a major component of the total quality management process. None of these companies could have made the changes that they have made without information systems support. IBM, Xerox, and Motorola are constantly looking for technologies that will help improve the flow of information and the monitoring of total quality management measures. Federal Express and UPS use computer systems to track the routes of packages in order to fulfill the needs of their customers. All of these companies are competitive market leaders in their industries due to the total quality management process.

Perhaps the best example of how information systems can be used in the total quality management process is that of the Internal Revenue Service. The Internal Revenue Service collects and accounts for more than $1 trillion in revenue each year. Surprisingly it is estimated that another $100 billion of taxes is owed each year and is not collected. In addition, millions of taxpayer contacts are made annually, requiring unnecessary taxpayers' time. The Internal Revenue Service was also lacking in the area of customer service. It was estimated that three out of four calls during tax season either were not answered at all or were answered with significant delay [7].

With all of the inefficiencies that were rampant in the Internal Revenue Service, the government decided to introduce a total quality management program into this organization. The Internal Revenue Service had three major goals:

1. To enhance quality and productivity through its business processes;
2. To reduce the taxpayer burden;
3. To improve voluntary compliance with tax regulations.

To meet these goals the Internal Revenue Service invested nearly $1 billion to start an information system, called tax system modernization, that may eventually cost $23 billion in total. However, due to the large quantity of information that the Internal Revenue Service handles, and their long-term commitment to quality, they feel that it is highly justified.

The goals of this system are to modernize tax document input, minimize paper processing, make taxpayer information readily accessible to Internal Revenue Service employees, reduce overhead costs, increase security of information, and provide flexibility for the future.

While this improvement process is being undertaken, the Internal Revenue Service is also implementing other principles of total quality management. Within the next 10 to 20 years, the American public should see an entirely new customer-oriented Internal Revenue Service.

10-8 SYNERGY BETWEEN TQM AND INFORMATION SYSTEMS

There are many new technologies that can improve the ability to implement total quality management programs in various organizations. The following technologies will save corporations time and money, which, in turn, will improve the quality of the services and products offered by a corporation.

Hypertext is a rapidly growing technology that employs a nonsequential search that can be used in whatever way the customer requires information. Hypermedia is an extension of hypertext that uses the linking of information from many different media types such as graphics, spreadsheets, full motion video, animation, and sound to provide the required information in the format that the customer desires. These technologies will be further discussed in Chapter 16.

Companies are no longer limited to the physical barrier of their buildings. Virtual organizations now allow a corporation to operate from anywhere in the world without the necessity of an office. The Internet and global information systems are adding to this growing trend. We explained the virtual organization concept in Chapter 4. The Internet and global information systems were discussed in Chapter 7.

GroupWare such as Lotus Notes, Microsoft Exchange, Team Focus, Group-System, and Vision Quest allows quality teams to be formed and companywide brainstorming to take place without having to be in the same general area. Quality teams that once were scattered geographically and were not able to work together can now use group support systems applications to hold meetings without having to leave their own offices. This technology will provide new ideas and also will save corporations time and the money that it would cost to physically bring these teams together. These various technologies will be discussed in Chapter 14.

Artificial Intelligence (discussed in Chapter 17) is being used by companies to decide what parts to ship, to make judgments about basic issues associated with billing, and to pay bills. Executive information systems (discussed in Chapter 13) are used in problem solving to help the quality teams in the continual improvement process.

Because of its high-level simulation capabilities, virtual reality (discussed in Chapter 16) allows business to try new processes in a test run before committing any capital resources. This will make it easier for management to try new total quality management concepts with minimal risk. It is also feasible that market studies could be conducted by way of virtual reality in order to test consumer reaction to new products.

SUMMARY

The chapter introduced total quality management (TQM) as a growing philosophy for increasing efficiency and effectiveness in today's competitive environment. The chapter introduced TQM principles and its role for developing effective information systems, and also outlined the role of information systems in the implementation of an effective TQM program. The chapter discussed business process reengineering and its relationship to information systems and TQM and concluded with a discussion of the synergy that exists between TQM and information systems. It would be very difficult to implement a successful TQM or business process reengineering program without having a comprehensive information system in place.

REVIEW QUESTIONS

1. What is total quality management?
2. Where did this philosophy originate?
3. Which country first applied this philosophy?
4. What are some of the key elements of an effective TQM program?
5. Who are some of pioneers of the TQM philosophy?
6. In your opinion what are some of the key factors of TQM that can help a business to become more competitive?
7. How is quality measured? What is benchmarking?

8. How many types of customers does a business organization have?

9. What is "universal responsibility"? Why is it important to have such a view?

10. What are some of the contributions made by information systems to TQM implementation?

11. What are some of the contributions of TQM to information systems design? Discuss.

12. What are some of the factors that illustrate the quality of an information system?

13. What is the relationship between TQM and CASE tools?

14. What is business process reengineering? Why do organizations spend so much money on reengineering?

15. Discuss how Wal-Mart Stores have become the largest retailer in North America.

16. Define these key words in business process reengineering: fundamental, radical, dramatic, and process.

17. What is the relationship between TQM and reengineering?

18. How can group support systems contribute to TQM process?

19. What are some of the companies that have successfully implemented TQM? Discuss.

20. What are some of the information systems technologies that can assist and simplify TQM implementation?

PROJECTS

1. You have been asked to apply the TQM principles in a 4-year college that is trying to improve the quality and quantity of its enrollment. Provide a two-page proposal regarding this process. Who should be involved? What would be the outcome? Discuss.

2. Discuss how applying TQM principles can improve the quality of an information system. What are some of the attributes of a quality information system? How do you measure quality?

3. What are some of the information systems technologies that can improve TQM implementation? Discuss.

4. Why do organizations spend so much money to implement the business reengineering process? Can all companies and processes be reengineered? What types of businesses will benefit the most from reengineering? Discuss.

KEY TERMS

Computer-assisted systems
  engineering (CASE), 291–293
Continuous improvement, 289–290
Customer service, 284–286
Group support systems, 293

Quality, 283–284
Reengineering, 293–298
Total quality management, 276–277
Universal responsibility, 284

REFERENCES

[1] Aggarwal, R., and Lee, J.-S. (Fall 1995). CASE and TQM for flexible systems. *Information Systems Management,* 15–19.
[2] Alavi, M., and Yoo, Y. (Fall 1995). Productivity gains of BRP. *Information Systems Management,* 43–47.
[3] Barrier, M. (February 1994). Reengineering your company. *Nation's Business,* 154.
[4] Bartel, T., and Finster, M. (Summer 1995). A TQM process for systems integration. *Information Systems Management,* 19–28.
[5] Bidgoli, H. (1997). *Modern information systems for managers,* San Diego: Academic Press, Inc.
[6] Blackburn, R., and Benson, R. (August 1993). Total quality and human resources management: Lessons learned from Baldridge-winning companies. *Academy of Management Executives,* 49+.
[7] Chen, A. Y. S., and Sawyers, R. B. (July 1994). TQM at the IRS. *Journal of Accountancy,* 774.
[8] Cordato, J. W. (1995). *TQM for information systems management.* New York: McGraw-Hill.
[9] Dawson, S. P. (Winter 1994). Continuous improvement in action. *Information Systems Management,* 314.
[10] English, L. P. (Winter 1996). Redefining information management. *Information Systems Management,* 65–67.
[11] Esichaikal, V., Medey, G. R., and Smith, R. D. (Winter 1994). Problem-solving support for TQM. *Information Systems Management,* 47+.
[12] Furey, T., Garlitz, J. L., and Kelleher, M. L. (December 1993). Applying information technology to reengineering. *Planning Review,* 224.
[13] Greising, D. (August 8, 1994). Quality: How to make it pay. *Business Week,* 54.
[14] Hammer, M., and Champy, J. (May 4, 1992). What is reengineering? *Information Week.*
[15] Haserot, P. W. (October 1993). Benchmarking: Learning from the best. *The CPA Manager,* 814.
[16] Huff, S. L. (January 1992). Reengineering the business: You and the computer. *Business Quarterly,* 38.
[17] Jeffords, R., and Thibadoux, G. (July 1993). TQM and CPA firms. *Journal of Accountancy,* 59–63.
[18] Menkus, B. (August 1991). Seven keys to achieving the quality. *Journal of Systems Management,* 19.
[19] Milam, A., Hasan, B., and Vanjani, M. (Winter 1996). Total quality management: A GDSS approach. *Information Systems Management,* 73–75.
[20] Peterson, D. (Spring 1991). Case study: Improving customer service through new technology. *Journal of Information Systems Management,* 284.
[21] Swanson, K., McComb, D., Smith, J., and McCubbrey, D. (December 1991). The applications software factory: Applying TQM techniques to systems development. *MIS Quarterly,* 567–577.

[22] Ward, J. (Spring 1994). Continuous process improvement. *Information Systems Management,* 744.

[23] Ward, J. A. (Summer 1994). Meeting customer requirements. *Information Systems Management,* 75–78.

[24] Weiss, M. J. (November 1994). The paperless office. *Journal of Accountancy,* 73–76.

[25] Zahedi, F. (1995). *Quality information systems.* Boston: Boyd and Fraser Publishing Company.

Chapter 11

Building Effective Information Systems in Functional Areas

Learning Objectives

After studying this chapter, you should be able to:

- Outline the steps for the construction of an information system.
- Discuss tools and software products needed to construct an information system.
- Discuss three approaches for constructing an information system, including the traditional approach, outsourcing, and end-user computing.
- Outline input and output of an information system in functional areas.
- Discuss guidelines for building successful information systems.

11-1 INTRODUCTION

This chapter reviews the process of building an information system. It emphasizes the methodology developed in the last two chapters, which stressed user involvement, utilization of prototypes, and development of quality information systems. The emphasis is placed on the managerial design of an information system. Tools and software products for building an effective information system are highlighted, and various approaches for building an information system are discussed. End-user computing is explained in detail and its advantages and disadvantages as a prominent alternative for building an information system are elaborated upon. The chapter concentrates on building information systems in the functional areas of a business. Five major areas of a business organization are chosen and the data and modeling requirements of these information systems are analyzed. These areas include manufacturing, marketing, personnel, financial, and strategic planning. The chapter explains the behavioral issues in information systems design and it identifies system characteristics for different levels of an organization. The chapter concludes with a series of guidelines for building an effective information system.

11-2 BUILDING INFORMATIONS SYSTEMS: AN OVERVIEW

To build an effective information system, we use the methodology that was introduced in Chapter 9 under the integrated approach:

- Problem definition
- Formation of the task force
- Construction of an online prototype
- Evaluation

In the problem definition phase, the team of designers (managerial and technical) must define the problem to be addressed by the information system. Although some of the problems in an information system environment are not fully defined and do not possess a well-defined structure, during the problem definition phase the need for the information system must be articulated. This phase should leave users with the distinct impression that there is a need for constructing the system.

In this phase a feasibility study should also be conducted, as explained in Chapter 9. The feasibility study should include economic, technical, social, and time issues. In this phase, the design team identifies the critical success factors of the organization and explains how the information system may generate information regarding these factors to assist the organization in achieving its goals and objectives. This phase should not leave any ambiguity about why the system has to be built, and the design team must ensure that all participants support the system.

In the second phase the task force is formed. As mentioned in Chapter 9, all the affected departments and user groups must have a representative on the task force. The task force must consider both the technical and the managerial issues of information systems construction. Each activity in the design of the information systems must be clearly defined, and the time requirements and interdependencies between tasks must be identified and communicated to all members of the task force. As we have emphasized all along, managerial and technical issues are equally important, and the task force must make sure that both dimensions are fully defined.

In the third phase, the design team should build a small-scale version of the system in a prototype form. The prototype must be significant enough to demonstrate the value of the information system. If the user is not satisfied with the prototype and the operation of the system that it represents, the system must be abandoned. However, if user reaction is positive, it is possible that the prototype may evolve into the final information system or may be used temporarily until the final information system is constructed.

In the fourth phase, which is the evaluation phase, an iterative approach is used to add or delete features until the user is fully satisfied with the system. As we mentioned in Chapter 9, the final construction may never be finished and the system may evolve in stages. Also, the continuous improvement process as one of the key components of TQM must be observed. The design team should remember that the effectiveness of the information systems must be evaluated within a certain time frame. For the short range the information systems may be responsive by utilizing its existing features. In the medium range (3 months to 1 year) features may have to be augmented in the architecture of the information systems to improve its effectiveness. However, in the long range (more than 2 years), the information systems may have to utilize a completely new technology. This may include new hardware and software tools.

11-3 TOOLS AND SOFTWARE PRODUCTS FOR BUILDING AN INFORMATION SYSTEM

There are a number of tools and software products available for building an information system. We summarize these tools and products below:

1. *Programming languages.* These include COBOL, Pascal, C, C++, and visual BASIC. It may be difficult and time consuming to develop an information system using these languages. However, the final product will be tailor-made for the specific needs of the user.

2. *Statistical analysis packages.* These packages can provide various statistical analyses such as finding correlation between advertising and total sales. In this group we can include Minitab, SPSS, and SAS.

3. *Forecasting packages.* These packages perform predictions assuming the past behavior somewhat will continue into the future. Many of the modeling products and spreadsheet programs such as Microsoft Excel, Lotus 1-2-3, and Quattro Pro are capable of performing forecasting tasks.

4. *Graphical packages.* These packages provide numerous types of graphs for better visualization of data. There are several dedicated graphics packages on the market such as Harvard Graphics, Freelance, and Microsoft PowerPoint. Also, spreadsheet programs such as Lotus 1-2-3, Microsoft Excel, and Quattro Pro are capable of creating sophisticated graphs.

5. *Database-oriented products.* These packages or products provide extensive data management facilities. As their names indicate, these packages are more suitable in cases that involve lots of data management tasks. In this group we can include DB2, Oracle, Microsoft Access, and Paradox.

6. *Modeling-oriented products.* These packages or products provide extensive number crunching and modeling analysis. IFPS PLUS, Lotus 1-2-3, and Microsoft Excel are some examples of these types of products.

11-4 THREE APPROACHES FOR BUILDING AN INFORMATION SYSTEM

There are three approaches for building an information system: traditional, outsourcing, and end user-computing. Figure 11-1 illustrates these three approaches.

In the **traditional** or the life-cycle approach the data processing department mainly constructs an information system with some input from the user group. This approach has its own advantages and disadvantages. Among the advantages are [5]:

- These systems are usually technically sound.
- These systems usually include appropriate security measures.
- These systems usually meet the information systems standards.

There are serious disadvantages with this approach because it is not tailored to the specific needs of the users and the time requirements of system construction are not always considered.

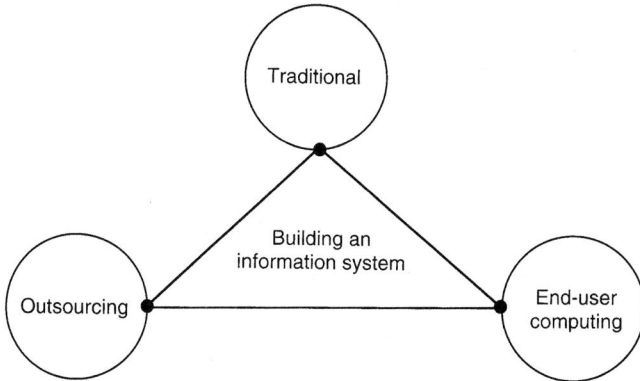

Figure 11-1   Three approaches for building an information system.

In using the **outsourcing** approach an organization may hire an external vendor or consultant(s) who specializes in providing these services. However, the outsourcing firm may choose to utilize a life-cycle approach for the implementation of the requested system. This approach has its own advantages and disadvantages. Among the advantages are:

- It may be cheaper.
- It may be more timely.
- It may provide flexibility for the organization to concentrate on other projects.

Some of the disadvantages of outsourcing include:

1. *Loss of control.* The organization may lose control over its information systems functions. The final system may not reflect the specific information requirements of the organization.
2. *Dependency.* The organization becomes dependent on the outsourcing company. A significant change in the financial or management status of the outsourcing company may reduce the quality of the information system that is provided.
3. *Vulnerability of strategic information.* The use of outsourcing may jeopardize important information and may leak information to competitors.

For these reasons, a number of users and organizations consider end-user computing (EUC) as an attractive approach for information systems construction. In the next section we provide a detailed discussion regarding this growing trend.

11-5 END-USER COMPUTING (EUC): A VIABLE ALTERNATIVE FOR INFORMATION SYSTEMS CONSTRUCTION

In recent years, a growing number of end users in various organizations have developed their own information systems with little or no formal assistance from the information systems group. These users occupy various positions such as accountants, bankers, lawyers, and other professionals who may not know how to write programming codes, but are eager and skilled enough to take off-the-shelf PC software such as spreadsheets and databases and produce custom-built applications [3,8,13,14]. This trend is called end-user computing (EUC), a development that results from lengthy system backlogs, the availability of affordable hardware and software, and the increasing dependency of business organizations on timely and relevant information. With the help of EUC tools such as query languages, report generators, and fourth generation languages end-user computing has become an active partner in sharing information systems functions and resources. EUC does have positive effects such as reducing application backlog, supporting user-defined systems analysis and development, and providing the flexibility in responding to users' unique information needs. In the meantime, EUC also brings challenges to managers who are concerned with the lack of adequate system analysis and design background, the loosening systems standards, and the proliferation of uncontrolled "private" data and applications.

The ever-increasing demand for timely and relevant information has placed great pressures on the organizations' information systems group. Already overloaded with the maintenance and enhancement of existing applications, information systems departments have been unable to satisfy new requirements from end users. For a large number of business organizations, the task of keeping the existing systems and applications running already consumes a large portion of computing resources and manpower, leaving very limited resources for developing new applications. User dissatisfaction has existed for years as a result of the inability of the information systems department to respond to their needs. Application backlog has become a common problem for many firms, affecting both poorly managed and well-managed organizations. The documented application backlogs, however, are just the tip of the iceberg. When the backlog list is long, end users do not even consider making new requests for many of the applications they need, because they believe that those requests would only make the list longer. The undocumented list of applications that go unrequested is often longer than the documented backlog, and it is rightly termed the "invisible" backlog.

In responding to user demands, information systems departments have tried in several ways to improve the productivity of their staffs. One way to do this is to expand the number of information systems professionals. This approach is not always welcomed by senior executives because many of them feel that the information systems department is already too large, and the budget set aside for information systems functions should not be increased. Even if the expansion of the information systems staff is authorized, it is sometimes impossible to hire a sufficient number of competent programmers and analysts. Many attempts have been made to improve the productivity of the organizations' existing information systems staff. Several new tools are used to facilitate the programmer's tasks and to shorten the completion time for each task. These tools include very high-level languages, development tool kits, and preprogrammed and reusable application modules. Recently, a new tool called the Application Re-Engineering Machine has become available on the software market. This type of software can read an old program (usually written in a third-generation language such as COBOL, FORTRAN, or C) and code it into a well-structured, modular program that can handle the same functions as the old one. Since modular programs are easier to maintain, this new tool can help improve programmers' productivity.

Despite the efforts to improve information systems department productivity, the imbalance between supply and demand is becoming steadily worse. Growing dissatisfaction with the inability of the information systems department to provide information has been one of the major factors contributing to the growth of user-developed information systems.

The continuing drop in computer hardware costs and the availability of user-friendly software have also contributed to the growth of EUC. During the last two decades, significant progress has been made in the field of computer technology, and while computers are becoming more and more powerful, they continue to shrink in both size and cost. Microcomputers are more affordable, and a variety of user-friendly software is available for users working in all business areas. All of these factors have given business organizations a promising solution to the application backlog: user-developed applications and information systems.

11-5-1 Advantages of EUC

EUC can benefit the organization in many ways. One of them is that application backlogs can be significantly reduced because end users now can develop their own applications, leaving only large-scale service requests that are impossible for end users to develop to be sent to information systems departments.

The improvement in the process of defining information requirements is another benefit offered by EUC. If users develop their own systems, there is less need to rely on information systems professionals for requirements analysis, and less chance that these requirements will be distorted by the large communications gap that exists between the end users and systems analysts. This is true because end users, who are experienced in certain business areas (accounting, finance,

Table 11-1

Advantages of EUC

Reducing the information systems department backlogs
Improving information requirements analysis
Creating ad hoc and one-of-a-kind reports

marketing, and manufacturing), have a better understanding of their information needs than do the technically oriented analysts; however, end users may fail to communicate their requirements in a way that the analysts can thoroughly understand. EUC, in effect, has changed the role of systems analysts to that of consultants, who help explain technical aspects of systems development to end users.

Another important benefit that EUC can offer is that the end user's ad hoc, one-of-a-kind information needs can be satisfied quickly through the modification or upgrading of the users' own information systems. This is possible because user-developed information systems are usually small and flexible. The prototyping approach is a popular systems development methodology that end users employ in developing their own systems. This approach allows continuous modifications and enhancements; therefore, the prototype system can be modified or enhanced to produce the unique information needed by users in a timely manner. Table 11-1 summarizes the advantages of EUC.

11-5-2 DISADVANTAGES OF EUC

While EUC offers significant benefits to business organizations, it does create some organizational risks because it has grown in an environment that is unfamiliar to the organizational mechanism for information systems management and control. The most critical issues regarding inherent problems of the EUC include the possible misuse of computing resources, the inadequacy of complete systems analysis and design, the lack of systems standards, and the proliferation of private systems, applications, and uncontrolled data.

Inadequacy of complete systems analysis and design in an EUC environment is due largely to the fact that the functions of the user and the analyst are no longer separate. Without the participation of the analyst in the development process, applications developed by end users have no independent reviews by outsiders. The applications, therefore, are often built with users' subjective perceptions and requirements. If analysts are allowed to participate in the development process, there is a good chance that user requirements are objectively analyzed and alternatives can be recommended to enhance the quality and workability of future applications.

Systems analysts can also serve as the enforcers of information systems standards and practices that an information system is expected to meet to assure its quality. User-developed systems are often built in a short time span by using the prototyping approach. While this approach offers productivity and design advantages over traditional systems development methodologies, a lack of systems standards and quality assurance can occur if these standards are not enforced. Systems standards include documentation, control facilities and procedures, testing procedures, input and output data validation, and linkage among various systems. The participation of systems analysts in the development of users' systems and applications is necessary to ensure that the future systems and applications will operate efficiently and effectively. EUC applications can have an adverse effect on the organization's information systems as a whole if system verification and validation are not a part of the systems development process. A user-developed system may not work at all if all aspects of systems design are not carefully studied. For example, a user-developed system designed to extract a subset of the corporate financial data for forecasting purposes was successfully tested with a test file stored in a hard disk. When the user's computer was connected to the mainframe, it was unable to access the needed data in the corporate database because they were stored in a different format, and the user's application had not been designed to handle this type of format. This simple example typifies the need for systems analysis and design work before and during the development of the application.

Another critical issue regarding EUC is the proliferation of "private" data, applications, and information systems. Users can create information systems that are totally out of sync with organizational objectives and policies. Such systems may be used to provide benefit and convenience to certain user groups at the expense of other business units. The uncontrolled proliferation of user-developed applications can be costly in terms of human and computing resources because of many duplicated efforts by end users from across the organization to develop applications that serve similar purposes. For example, the managers in both the marketing and finance departments might develop separate systems that extract the same data set from the corporate database to project the sales volume for coming years. Although their purposes can be different (one needs the data for marketing strategies, the other for investment plans), the methods they use to access and manipulate data are the same. Had they communicated with each other about their needs, a single application could have been built with their cooperation, and unnecessary expenses in time and money could have been avoided.

The proliferation of "private" data can cause serious problems to the integrity and reliability of corporate databases if control measures are not established. It is likely that users may create their own sets of data to be used by their own applications and to be accessed and updated by their own standards and methods. These

Table 11-2

Disadvantages of EUC

Possible misuse of computing resources
Inadequacy of complete systems analysis and design
Lack of systems standards
Proliferation of private systems, applications, and uncontrolled data
Lack of access to crucial data
Lack of proper documentation for the applications developed
Lack of security for the applications developed
Applications developed may not be up to information systems standards
Lack of support from top management
Lack of training for the perspective users

"private" data sets may have little in common with the corporate data and with one another. Because of this, unpredictable situations may occur when the figures on certain items presented by various functional areas such as marketing, finance, and accounting are not exactly the same, and they do not match the figures given by the corporate information systems department.

The author has experience with a large chemical company in Southern California that had a forecasting system that was developed by a few end users. At the beginning the user group had access to a correct set of data for generating the appropriate forecast. Later, the data set was updated at the corporate level and the user group, not knowing this fact, kept generating forecasts based on the old data set. As a result decisions made based on this data set generated erroneous results. Table 11-2 summarizes the disadvantages of EUC.

11-5-3 Successful Utilization of EUC

End-user computing gives end users the power to build their own applications in a short period of time and to create, access, manipulate, and alter data. This type of power can be destructive if the organization does not apply control and security measures over the EUC environment. One of the control issues involves computing resources. Computing resources are scarce, and they should be allocated in a way that best serves users without sacrificing the efficiency and effectiveness of the entire organization's information processing functions. Until now, the best approach is to let the information systems departments manage the allocation and distribution of computing resources because information systems staff consists of the most qualified people for the evaluation and definition of user computing requirements.

In preventing the proliferation of "private" information systems and applications, the organization should develop appropriate guidelines for systems and application development. Certain criteria should be established to evaluate, approve or reject, and prioritize appropriate projects. For example, questions such as "Can any of the existing applications generate the requested report?" or "Can we fulfill the requirements of two users by building a single application?" should be asked before a decision regarding a proposed application is made.

Classification and cataloguing of existing applications are necessary to minimize the costly redundant efforts of end-users in developing applications that basically handle the same functions. A small catalogue, in many cases, can save a great deal of human and computing resources for the organization in question.

Data administration should also be enforced to ensure data integrity and reliability. The creation of private data sets should be minimized if not eliminated. Sometimes, for the sake of efficient data processing, redundant data are allowed to exist; however, they should be managed tightly and continually. This control task is becoming increasingly difficult because the number of end users using diverse data is growing. The best approach to control the proliferation of invalid and inconsistent data into corporate databases is to control the flow of data at every gateway that leads to the corporate database. Certain data validation measures should be established and installed at these gateways to ensure that the incoming data is valid.

EUC is still in its infancy. Although unexpected developments in this field are likely, it is obvious that the role of EUC in business organizations will become more and more important. The computer industry has been making significant moves toward establishing a common computer hardware and software platform to increase the portability of computer applications between systems and to provide end users with a single interface regardless of what kind of computers they are using. IBM has introduced its systems application architecture (SAA) and common user interface (CUI) concepts hoping that hardware and software developers will follow suit. IBM's SAA refers to the standardization of computer systems and application development so that all computer programs can be executed by any computer system produced by any manufacturer. Common user access refers to the standardization of computer keyboard key combinations with which users access data and application programs. IBM, Apple, and Motorola have formed a joint venture company named Taligent. The objective of the new company is to build a computer system that combines IBM's reduced instruction set code (RISC) technology, Apple's graphical user interface, and Motorola's chip technology. The new computers are able to run both PC and Macintosh applications, creating a single system multiplatform approach that is bound to become increasingly popular in coming years.

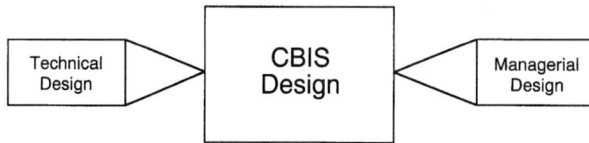

Figure 11-2   Two views in information systems design.

11-6 BUILDING EFFECTIVE INFORMATION SYSTEMS IN FUNCTIONAL AREAS

Three of the most important components of any information system are database, model base (process), and user-system interface (the method by which the user accesses the system). The user-system interface component can be designed by using the facility provided by software tools or products. Also, a high-level language such as C or Pascal can be used to develop the user-system interface. In this chapter, we would like to emphasize the database and model base components of an information system from a managerial designer's viewpoint. We attempt to identify the types of data, sources of data, types of analyses, and particular models needed to perform these analyses. Figure 11-2 illustrates the two views of information system design. The emphasis in this chapter is on the managerial design of a functional information system. Further, to establish a functional information system, we assume that the organization already has a comprehensive accounting information system (AIS) in place. This system will serve as one of the major input components to all information systems in different functional areas.

11-7 MANUFACTURING INFORMATION SYSTEMS (MFISs)

By using internal and external data, mathematical and statistical models with "what-if" and "goal seeking" capabilities, and a user-friendly interface, an MFIS can provide valuable information in all aspects of manufacturing operations. By using the what-if feature, the user can investigate the impact of one variable over the entire system. For example, the user can analyze the impact of a 7% increase of raw materials over the final cost of an item. The "goal seeking" feature allows the user to establish a goal and then the user can manipulate other variables in order to achieve that goal. For example, a user can determine how many assembly line workers are needed in order to generate 200 automobiles in the next 3 weeks. An MFIS should provide timely, accurate, and integrated information regarding production planning and control. To achieve this goal, the database component of

Table 11-3

Types of Data Needed by a MFIS in its Database

Area	Types of data needed	Sources of data
Accounting	Invoicing Order scheduling Credit control and collection	Accounting information systems
Warehousing	Receipt data Shipping Storage Replenishment Packing	Accounting information systems
Transportation	Loading Trip log Overall costs/units/miles Commodity movement information Carrier movement patterns	Accounting information systems Trade publications
Marketing	Current and potential customers Customer service demands Current and potential competitors Competitor strategies Market potential Market share Demographic profiles Regional changes and shifts	Marketing research Sales force reports Trade publications Syndicated services Census guide data Survey of buying power Marketing information guide
Purchasing/ inventory	Vendor file (lead time, price, and financial strength) Procurement Bidding Overall purchasing Inventory records Lot sizing	Accounting information systems Trade publications Securities and Exchange Commission reports

(continues)

the MFIS must collect and store different types of data, both internally and externally. The model base must include a number of mathematical and/or statistical models for diverse analyses. Table 11-3 illustrates types of data and Table 11-4 illustrates types of models for an effective MFIS.

11-7-1 MFISs AND INVENTORY CONTROL

Manufacturing management has always been responsible for inventory control. The objective is to reduce the total inventory costs to the lowest possible level

Table 11-3 *(continued)*

Area	Types of data needed	Sources of data
Production	Aggregate scheduling Priority planning Capacity planning Facility planning Production control Material planning Work force planning Shop floor data collection R & D planning Output design Layout of facilities Overall production management	Industrial engineering information systems Personnel information systems

Economy	General level of economic activity
	Economic activity within industry
		Economic indicators
		Survey of Current Business
		U.S. Industrial Outlook
		Standard & Poor's Industry
		  Survey
		Across the board trade
		  publications

Legal
  environment
	Changes impacting all businesses
	Changes impacting industry
		General business publications
		  such as *Business Week* and
		  The Wall Street Journal

Technology	Available technology and expected trends	Trade publications Trade shows

Source: "Developing an Effective Manufacturing Decision Support System," by Mohsen Attaran and Hossein Bidgoli, October-December, 1986. Reprinted with permission of *Business Magazine.*

consistent with the desired service. The total inventory costs consist of carrying or holding costs, which vary directly by inventory level, and purchasing or ordering costs, which vary inversely with the number of units ordered. The two key decisions in inventory management are when to order and how much to order.

If the demand for finished goods inventory is constant and known in advance, the economic order quantity (EOQ) model balances these two inventory costs and identifies the optimum order quantity.

These two decisions can be made with little management intervention by using the MFIS. Management uses the accounting, purchasing, and inventory files in the database to determine the total holding and ordering costs. The EOQ model will determine the optimal quantity to order. The specific vendor is then selected from information provided by the procurement or purchasing file.

Table 11-4

Types of Analysis and Models Needed for MFIS

Types of analyses	Description	Examples of models
Inventory	When to order and how much Cost calculations Safety stock Priorities for inventory management	EOQ (economic order quantity) ELS (economic lot size) MRP (material requirements planning) TPOP (time-phased order point)
Warehousing	Storage structures Space utilization analysis Control of equipment	AS/RS (automatic storage and retrieval systems) Simulation modeling
Procurement/ purchasing	The supplier rating/selection decision Vendor rating/selection decision Price change/discount analysis Bid evaluation	Vendor rating/selection models
Logistics and location	Distribution improvements Routing/scheduling Selection of modes of transportation Transportation budgeting Shipment planning Regional/International selection Community selection Site selection	Transportation model Center of gravity/incremental analysis Weighted-score model Break-even model
Transformation/ process design	Selection of the process Design of the transformation process Layout design Balancing a line	Computerized line balancing CPM/PERT CRAFT (computerized relative allocation of facilities)
	Tools/equipment/facilities selection	ALDEP (automated layout design program) CORELAP (computerized relationship program)

(continues)

Material requirement planning (MRP) is another area where MFISs can be helpful in inventory control decisions. MRP schedules "what we want" in each time period and plans the acquisition of the items. To derive maximum benefit from an MRP system, a comprehensive and integrated database is needed.

Table 11-4 *(continued)*

Types of analyses	Description	Examples of models
Capacity planning and scheduling	Short-term capacity planning Long-term capacity planning Capacity versus investment Aggregate scheduling Priority planning Sequencing Detailed scheduling What-if production/inventory tradeoffs	CPM/PERT GERT (graphical evaluation review technique) Learning curve Linear programming Decision tree Linear decision rule MRP II (manufacturing resource planning)
Quality control	Design quality Quality/Cost analysis Where to inspect/how to inspect Handling of defects Setting optimal control limits Process control Acceptance sampling	Fraction production charts (P charts) Number of defects (C charts)

Source: "Developing an Effective Manufacturing Decision Support System," by Mohsen Attaran and Hossein Bidgoli (October-December 1986). Reprinted with permission of *Business Magazine.*

The input requirement of the MRP model is information regarding what should be produced, when it is needed, and a record of the actual inventory level and lead times, product structure, raw materials, and components and subassemblies. These data can be obtained from various files in the MFIS database. For example, data regarding lead times and on-hand balance will be obtained from inventory files. The number of finished goods needed during each time period and the part number of components required to make each individual part will be obtained from production files.

Management will then use the MRP model (computer software) to determine the quantity to order and to generate management reports. The output usually includes (1) what should be ordered; (2) what order should be canceled; (3) exception reports (items that need management attention); and (4) how well the system is operating.

If properly designed and integrated, the MFIS is a powerful support tool that enhances the effectiveness and capabilities of today's decision makers in a manufacturing environment. By using an MFIS, it becomes easier to collect more data, to make forecasts, to schedule operations, to remove bottle-necks, to perform sensitivity, what-if, and goal seeking analyses, and to optimize, monitor, and control the system. These features offer today's production manager who is pressed more than ever to maximize efficiency, quality, and flexibility unprecedented benefits in the management of resources.

11-8 MARKETING INFORMATION SYSTEMS (MKISs)

The importance and versatility of computer applications in the marketing discipline are well documented in the literature [7, 12]. An effective MKIS should provide timely, accurate, and integrated information regarding the marketing mix (price, promotion, place, and product). To achieve this goal, the MKIS database must collect and store certain data. The model base component of this system should also be able to perform certain analyses. Table 11-5 illustrates the database component and Table 11-6 illustrates the model base components of an MKIS.

11-9 PERSONNEL INFORMATION SYSTEMS (PISs)

PISs are designed to provide information to assist decision makers in the personnel department to carry out their tasks in a more effective way. A PIS deals with the human element, the most valuable resource in the organization. Due to the complexity and diversity of skills utilized by a typical large organization, retention and promotion of a skilled labor force is a challenging task. Affirmative action decisions, minority employees, and manpower planning all have added more complexity to the management of human resources. An effective PIS, when designed properly, should be able to serve as a valuable tool for human resource directors [4,11]. The database component of a PIS should include the data presented in Table 11-7. The model base component should perform the analyses highlighted in Table 11-8.

11-10 FINANCIAL INFORMATION SYSTEMS (FISs)

By using internal and external data, mathematical and statistical models, and a user-friendly interface, FISs should be able to provide diverse financial information to financial executives in a timely manner. By using what-if, goal seeking, and sensitivity analyses, an FIS should be able to highlight and analyze various financial scenarios. To achieve the financial goals of an organization, the database component of an FIS should include the data presented in Table 11-9. For performing different analyses an FIS should include the models presented in Table 11-10.

Table 11-5

Types of Data Needed by a MKIS to be Stored in Its Database

Area	Type of data needed	Source of data
Economy	General level of economic activity Economic activity within industry	Economic indicators Survey of Current Business U.S. Industrial Outlook Standard and Poor's Industry Survey Conference Board Record Trade publications
Legal environment	Changes impacting all businesses Changes impacting industry	General business publications such as *Business Week* and *The Wall Street Journal* Trade publications
Technology	Available technology and expected trends	Trade publications Trade shows
Consumers	Current and potential customers Tastes and preferences Characteristics	Marketing research Sales force reports Census data *County and City Data Book* *A Guide to Consumer Markets* *The Average American Book* *Survey of Buying Power* *Commercial Atlas and Marketing Guide*

(continues)

11-11 STRATEGIC PLANNING INFORMATION SYSTEMS (SPISs)

SPISs should be able to help the chief executive make long-range strategic decisions [6]. Although the majority of strategic decisions are either semistructured or unstructured, an SPIS can still be of significant help. An SPIS can generate timely information regarding long-range planning, corporate planning, simulation, and decisions regarding new products and new plants. An SPIS utilizes the data presented in Table 11-11 from various functional areas; the models and analyses are presented in Table 11-12.

Table 11-5 *(continued)*

Area	Type of data needed	Source of data
Competition	Current and potential competitors Strengths and weaknesses Strategies Customers Sales	Marketing research Sales force reports Syndicated services Trade publications F & S Index of Industries and Corporations Standard and Poor's Register of Corporations Thomas Register of Manufacturers
Sales	Market Potential Market share Sales by product and customer	Sales force reports Market research Accounting information Systems Syndicated services
Markets	Size of various segments Demographic changes and shifts Regional changes and shifts Segment identification Market share Market position	Marketing research *Measuring Markets: A Guide to Federal and State Statistics* *Marketing Information Guide* *Marketing Information Professional Reference Guide*
Cost	Expense ratios Financial ratios	Accounting information systems

Source: "Marketing Decision Support Systems," by Hossein Bidgoli and Robert Harmon, Spring 1987, Vol. 3, No. 1. Reprinted with permission of *Business Insights*.

11-12 THE BEHAVIORAL ISSUES IN INFORMATION SYSTEMS

The design and implementation of any computer-based information system will impact different employees in the organization in different ways. The general issue of "resistance to change" may play an important role in the success or failure of such systems.

Resistance to change is directly related to the position of the employees within the organization (e.g., operational management, tactical management, and operational control) [9]. It is also related to the age and experience of the employees.

Table 11-6

Types of Analyses and Models Needed for MKISs

Types of analyses	Description	Examples of models
Market analysis	Study of the nature and composition of the market including market size, market segments and market potentials	Market demand function, demographic analysis
Market share analysis	Study of a firm's sales relative to competition	Market share determination, market response needs
Sales analysis	Study of the composition of a firm's sales by product, brand size, territory, customer type, and so on	Sales response function, territory analysis
Cost analysis	Study of a firm's expenses and financial position for the overall company and by products	Financial ratio analysis
Sales forecasting	Prediction and estimation of a firm's sales	Regression analysis, time series analysis, Box-Jenkins
Simulation	Performance of what-if analysis by simulating various decision-making situations	Competitive analysis, sales response, profit response
Comparative analysis	Simulation of various strategies and alternatives to compare outcomes of various decisions	
Sales force analysis	Study of the effectiveness and efficiency of sales staff	Scheduling and routing, sales force size, territory assignment, optimal number of customer calls
Media selection analysis	Comparison of alternative media choices	Linear programming, stepwise regression, simulation models, advertising allocation model
Price analysis	Determination of the elasticity of price changes on demand	Competitive bidding model, price change models, product line pricing models

Source: "Marketing Decision Support Systems," Vol. 3, No. 1 (Spring 1987) by Hossein Bidgoli and Robert Harmon. Reprinted with permission of *Business Insights.*

Table 11-7

Types of Data Needed by a PIS in Its Database

Types of data needed	Source of data
Employee personal data	Personnel files
Positions held in the organization	Personnel files
Skills	Personnel files
Employee work hours	Personnel files
Employee education	Personnel files
Employee work experience	Personnel files
Employee ethnic background	Personnel files
Training requirements	Personnel files
Labor union requirements	Labor union information
Job market data	Colleges, universities, trade schools and the Internet
Government requirements	Published government data
Affirmative action data	Published government data
Equal opportunity employment data	Published government data

Older employees may tend to be less receptive to new technology than are younger employees. Employees may show varied reactions to the introduction of new technology. Hostile reactions may appear as aggression, projection, and/or avoidance.

Employees who harbor aggression may go so far as to physically harm the system. Such an employee will take advantage of any opportunity to stop or sabotage the operation of the system. In the case of an avoidance reaction, the employee simply will not use the system and he may continue to use the old system until the new system fails. In the case of projection, the employee attributes real or imagined difficulty to the system.

These general resistance issues may be related to numerous factors. The employee may think that he may not be able to use the system, or the system may create time pressures, role ambiguity, feelings of insecurity, added complexity, and so forth. The employee may falsely conclude that his job is threatened.

The resistance issues may vary in different CBIS applications. For example, resistance will be more severe in EDP and MIS environments than in DSS. Because a DSS is usually designed to support a decision maker, and because it is not intended to replace the human element, such systems may encounter less resistance than do the EDP and MIS. However, by active user and management involvement, a clear definition of the objectives of the system, and the use of a

Table 11-8

Types of Analyses and Models Needed for PISs

Types of analysis	Description	Examples of models
Recruitment analysis	To choose the best candidate	Sort routine Simple statistical models Correlation analysis
Skills evaluation	To maintain and update the most recent skills of employees	Database management systems
Scheduling assignment	To schedule and assign employees to the most suitable assignments	Assignment models, simulation models
Job-appraisal	To promote the most competent employees	Correlation analysis Performance analysis
Job-pattern analysis	To trace the pattern of employee growth internally and externally	Markov analysis models
Achieving worker objectives	To achieve worker objectives within the internal and external constraints	Goal programming
Work force planning	To determine work-force requirements of the organization	Forecasting models
Training and skill development	To assess and implement the training needs of the organization	Forecasting and statistical models
Affirmative action requirements	To provide affirmative action reports	Statistical models
Resource allocation	To allocate human and financial resources	Budgeting models Linear programming models Simulation models

prototype, the designers of information systems may eliminate or at least minimize these troublesome issues.

Table 11-13 highlights some of the common problems associated with information technology and offers some suggested solutions. The consideration of these factors should help the design team to create a more successful information system.

11-13 INFORMATION SYSTEMS AND ORGANIZATIONAL LEVELS

The designer of an information system must distinguish the characteristics of information systems to be designed and utilized by each level of the organization.

Table 11-9
Types of Data Needed by a FIS in Its Database

Area	Type of data needed	Source of data
Accounting	Raw materials Labor Overhead	Accounting information systems
Budgeting	Sources and uses of funds including sales production and operating expenses	Accounting information systems
Auditing	Related audit data internally and externally	Accounting information systems External sources for the same industry
Internal financial data	Financial management and control	Accounting information systems
External financial data	Interest rate, financial regulation	Financial community, published government material, Federal Reserve Banking Index

Table 11-10
Types of Analyses and Models for FISs

Type of analysis	Description	Examples of models
What-if analysis	To allocate budget	Spreadsheet models
Financial forecast	To predict financial needs	Forecasting models, regression, exponential smoothing
Risk assessment	To minimize capital investment risks	Risk analysis models Expected value analysis models
Why and when analysis	To justify financial allocation	Expert systems and DSS
Cost analysis	To monitor cost trends	Forecasting models Correlation analysis
Financial management	To manage cash flows	Cash flow models
Financial control	To control financial resources	Financial ratio analysis (current ratio, acid test, and so on)
Investment analysis	To determine portfolio structure	Portfolio models
Borrowing analysis	To determine timing of borrowing decisions	Present value, future value, rate of return

Table 11-11

Types of Data Needed by a SPIS in Its Database

Area	Type of data needed	Source of data
Marketing	Customers Competition	Accounting information systems Marketing information systems
Corporate planning	Competition	Marketing information systems
Forecasting	Sales	Accounting information systems Marketing information systems
Finance	Funds management	Accounting information systems
Plant location	Production	Accounting information systems and manufacturing information systems
Product planning	Production	Marketing information systems and manufacturing information systems
Merger and acquisition	Financial Marketing	Financial information systems Marketing information systems
Personnel planning	Personnel	Personnel information systems

Table 11-12

Examples of Types of Analyses and Models Needed for SPISs

Types of analyses	Description	Examples of models
Finance	To analyze financial policy	Portfolio models Capital budgeting models Forecasting models
Marketing	To analyze marketing policy	Market analysis models Segmentation analysis models, simulation models
Manufacturing	To analyze production policy	Plant location models Product planning models Optimization models
Personnel	To analyze personnel policy	Statistical models Forecasting models

This is essential because the different levels of an organization have different needs and personal and organizational styles. This distinction will expedite the introduction and utilization of these systems. This is possible through identifica-

Table 11-13

Behavioral Problems and Suggested Solutions

Problem	Suggested solutions
Styles and status	Modify output format to suit the user's preference
Organizational roles or status	Modify input device to fit organizational roles or status
Habit, experience with the old system	Make use of the new system mandatory
Unfamiliarity with the new system	Sell the system by providing continuing education
Too technical for a typical user	Design a flexible and easy to use system
Problems with formal system	Use informal as well as formal channels of information
Ambiguity in the goals and objectives of the system	Define the goals of the system clearly
Information provided is too voluminous	Use exception-reporting system
The user does not know how his/her job would be improved by the system	Clarify and explain the mission of the system
Lack of flexibility in user/system interface	Provide several options for user/system interface
Threat to security and familiarity	Keep the impacted employee informed
Resistance to change	Spread the credit, get user and top management involved
System is more advanced than the user	Provide training and education
Turnover and organizational change	Provide comprehensive documentation, provide modularity in design
Organizational readiness	Start readiness (provide training first, then implement the system)
Gap between user and IS personnel	Use intermediary and task force design
Image problem	Use flexible user/system interface
Conflicts between different organizational units	User task force design

tion of sources of data, types of data, and output format. Table 11-14 summarizes the major attributes of an information system at different organizational levels [10].

The format of the information provided by the information system should be different at each level. For example, graphs have more usage in strategic planning than in operational control. It is easier to show trends and forecasts with graphs than with other types of data format. These features should be considered *if* an information system is going to be successful.

Table 11-14

Information Characteristics and Organizational Levels

Information systems attributes	Organizational levels		
	Operational management	Tactical management	Strategic planning
Currency of data	Highly current	Moderately current	Very old
Frequency of IS use	Very frequent	Semi-frequent	Infrequent
Level of data aggregation	No aggregation	Some aggregation	Very aggregated
Data accuracy	Very high	Moderately high	Low
Scope of collected data	Very narrow	Moderately narrow	Very wide
Sources of data	Mostly internal	Mixed (internal & external)	External
Time horizon emphasized by he system	Past	Mostly past, some future	Future
Output format	Detail reports	Detail & summary	Exception reports
Uses of graphs	Very small	Moderate	Large
General user/ system interface	Mostly scheduled reports	Scheduled reports and some exception reports	Exception, summary reports

11-14 GUIDELINES FOR BUILDING A SUCCESSFUL INFORMATION SYSTEM

To summarize the material presented in this chapter, we would like to provide you with a series of guidelines for building an effective information system. These guidelines may serve as a checklist and are summarized in Table 11-15.

SUMMARY

This chapter provided a series of guidelines for building information systems in different functional areas. We reviewed tools and software products for building an information system and we explained three approaches for building an information system: traditional, outsourcing, and end-user computing. Because end-user computing is gaining in popularity, it was explained in detail. To build an

Table 11-15

Guidelines for Building a Successful Information System

Consider the principles of TQM as discussed in Chapter 10

Consider the behavioral issues in information system design

Identify the information system attributes and the organizational levels that an information system is going to be utilized (Table 11-14)

Involve top management

Involve key users

Use a task-force design

Conduct critical-success factors analysis in conjunction with users' needs assessment

Try to use existing hardware and software technologies (if possible)

Develop the system in stages

Use prototypes

Use readily available software packages (if possible)

Clearly define goals and objectives of the information system

Ascertain that there is a need for the system

Provide training and education

Consider user requirements in the context of

- feasibility
- simplicity
- reliability
- accuracy
- economy
- compatibility

Establish effective communication both for motivation of the effected employees and information transfer

Keep the user/system interface simple

Let decision makers determine information usefulness

---

information system two important views must be carefully analyzed: managerial and technical. We emphasized the managerial view. If the components of an information system are designed from the managerial designer perspective, then the technical designer can take over and construct the system. We discussed the behavioral issues in information systems design and we reviewed information systems characteristics and their relationships to different organizational levels. The chapter concluded with a series of guidelines for building a successful information system.

REVIEW QUESTIONS

1. What is the objective of the problem definition phase for building an information system?

2. Why must a task force be formed prior to the construction of an information system?

3. Who are usually the members of the task force?

4. Why should top management have a representative on the task force?

5. Why must a prototype be designed before the final construction of an information system?

6. Will this prototype be converted into the final information system or will it be abandoned?

7. What kinds of tools are available for designing a prototype?

8. Where does an iterative design come into the design of an information system?

9. Why is the managerial designer's viewpoint so important?

10. What are the three approaches for building an information system?

11. What are some of the disadvantages of building an information system using only the information systems staff?

12. What is outsourcing?

13. What are some of the advantages of outsourcing?

14. What is end-user computing (EUC)?

15. What are some of the advantages and disadvantages of EUC?

16. How can you eliminate the shortcomings of EUC in the construction of an information system?

17. Discuss the input and output of a manufacturing information system.

18. Discuss the input and output of a marketing information system.

19. What are some of the internal data sources for a manufacturing information system? For a marketing information system?

20. What are some of the external data sources for a personnel information system? For a financial information system?

21. What is the role of a manufacturing information system in inventory control operations?

22. What are some of the decisions that may be supported by a personnel information system? By a financial information system?

23. How may strategic planning benefit from information systems?

24. Why are fourth generation languages preferred to third generation programming languages in building an information system?
25. What is the importance of critical success factors in building an information system?
26. How do you relate the critical success factors to user needs?
27. How do you conduct a cost and benefit analysis in building an information system?
28. What are the behavioral issues in information systems design? Why must the designer of an information system identify these issues?
29. What are information systems characteristics and their relationships with organizational levels? Why is such identification so crucial?

PROJECTS

1. A soft drink vendor is planning to establish a marketing information system to effectively market its products. Identify the type of data and modeling tools needed for this system. Which decisions are supported by this information system?
2. Neighbor Community Bank is planning to establish an information system for their credit department. They need your advice. What are five important suggestions that you might give to the bank prior to the construction of their information system in order to improve their chances for success?
3. Research an existing MRP system as an information system for the manufacturing discipline. What is the input/process/output of this system? What is needed to establish an MRP system? What are the strengths and weaknesses of a system of this type?
4. Research an organization of your choice. Conduct an interview with the chief financial officer. How does this individual make her financial decisions? Are there any information systems involved? If yes, what type of information is provided by this system?
5. Using any third or fourth generation language that you are familiar with, design a small-scale information system in finance, marketing, manufacturing, and personnel. What are the advantages of a system such as this? Can these small-scale systems be developed to a full-featured information system?
6. Using Microsoft Excel, design a balance sheet and an income statement for a company. Using six of the popular financial ratios, analyze the financial strengths of this company. By changing some of the figures in the balance sheet and the income statement perform several what-if analyses with these

ratios. What are these ratios telling you? Are they good indicators of the financial strengths of a company? Discuss.

7. The Internet has become a major source for personnel, marketing, and financial data. What are some of the advantages and disadvantages of this medium? What are some of the impacts of this medium on traditional, functional information systems? Discuss.

KEY TERMS

Behavioral issues, 323, 325–326, 329
Critical success factors, 306–307
Economic order quantity (EOQ), 318
External data, 316
Financial information system
  (FIS), 321, 327
Fourth generation languages, 310
Goal-seeking analyses, 316
Internal data, 316
Inventory control, 317–321
Managerial design, 306–307
Manufaturing information system
  (MFIS), 316–321
Marketing information system
  (MKIS), 321–324

Marketing mix, 321
Material requirement planning
  (MRP), 319–321
Personnel information system
  (PIS), 321, 325–326
Problem definition, 306–307
Prototype, 307
Strategic planning information system
  (SPIS), 322, 328
Task force, 307
Technical design, 316
Third generation languages, 308
Top management involvement, 331
User involvement, 331
What-if analysis, 316

REFERENCES

[1] Attaran, M., and Bidgoli, H. (October-December 1986). Developing an effective manufacturing decision support system. *Business,* 9–16.
[2] Attaran, M., and Bidgoli, H. (May 1988). CBMFIS: Core of the factory of the future. *Industrial Management & Data Systems,* 6–12.
[3] Benson, D. H. (December 1983). A field study of end user computing: Findings and issues. *MIS Quarterly,* 35–40.
[4] Berry, W. E. (Autumn 1993). HRIS can improve performance, empower and motivate knowledge workers. *Employment Relations Today,* 297–303.
[5] Bidgoli, H. (1997). *Modern Information Systems for Managers.* San Diego: Academic Press, Inc.
[6] Bidgoli, H., and Attaran, M. (June 1988). Improving the effectiveness of strategic decision making using an integrated decision support system. *Information and Software Technology,* 278–284.
[7] Bidgoli, H., and Harmon, R. R. (Spring 1987). Marketing decision support systems. *Business Insights,* Vol. 3, No. 1, 20–26.

[8] Boyer, G. L. (Spring 1990). Ten facts of end-user computing for every systems manager. *Journal of Systems Management,* 14.

[9] Dickson, G. W., and Simmons, J. K. (August 1970). The behavioral side of MIS. In *Marketing Information Systems: Selected Readings,* Charles D. Schewe, *American Marketing Association,* 1976, pp. 65–77.

[10] Gorry, G. A., and Scott-Morton, M. (Fall 1971). A framework for MIS. *Sloan Management Review,* Vol. 13, No. 1, 55–70.

[11] Greengard, S. (March 1994). The next generation. *Personnel Journal,* 40–46.

[12] Li, E. Y., *et al.* (Summer 1993). Marketing information systems in the fortune 500 companies: Past, present, and future. *Journal of Management Information System,* Vol. No. 1, 165–192.

[13] Plenert, G. (Spring 1996). Decision support in the lending industry: A case study of a user-developed system. *Information Systems Management,* 58–63.

[14] Tayntor, C. B. (Summer 1994). New challenges or the end of EUC. *Information Systems Management,* 86–88.

Part IV

Information Systems in Action

Part IV introduces in detail five of the most important and rapidly growing technologies in the information systems field. These technologies are gaining in popularity and they show tremendous potential for improving the efficiency and effectiveness of business decision making. They include electronic data interchange (EDI), decision support and executive information systems, group support systems, geographic information systems, and multimedia information systems.

Chapter 12

Electronic Data Interchange (EDI): A New Strategic Tool

Learning Objectives

After studying this chapter, you should be able to:

- Define electronic data interchange (EDI) as a growing applications of information systems.
- Discuss the historical development of EDI.
- Highlight the growth of EDI.
- Outline the six major steps for introducing EDI into an organization.
- Discuss some of the popular applications of EDI.

12-1 INTRODUCTION

This chapter discusses electronic data interchange as a growing application of information systems. The chapter provides a definition, the historical development, and the growth of EDI throughout the world, especially in North America. The chapter reviews six major steps for introducing EDI into an organization, including assessing the strategic value of EDI applications, analyzing the advantages and disadvantages of EDI applications, analyzing EDI costs, choosing a communication interface option, EDI standards, and EDI implementation. The chapter concludes with several popular applications of EDI and introduces several organizations that have been using EDI successfully.

12-2 WHAT IS ELECTRONIC DATA INTERCHANGE (EDI)?

Although computers have enabled companies to store, process, and retrieve data electronically since their inception, companies needed a more effective method to capture and transfer the data at the source. This method was implemented by the extensive use of data communications.

As discussed in Chapter 5, data communications can help companies transmit data electronically over telephone lines and other communications media. These data can be entered directly into a trading partner's business application. However, data communications can only solve a part of the problem. The data are captured first and then they are electronically transmitted. Some manual intervention will take place here.

Electronic data interchange (EDI) was initially developed to improve response time, to reduce paperwork, and to eliminate potential transcription errors. EDI represents the application of computer and communications technology to traditional paper-based business processes, supporting innovative changes in those processes. Similarly, EDI is the electronic exchange of business transactions, in a standard format, from one entity's computer to another entity's computer using a communications network.

In today's competitive business environment, most large companies and government agencies have made a commitment to reducing expenses, increasing efficiency, and improving their business relationships with a limited number of key suppliers. EDI is one of the main technologies that can help these organizations achieve these goals.

EDI is a comprehensive set of standards and protocols for the exchange of business transactions in a computer-understandable format. This may cover applications such as:

- Acknowledgments of business transactions
- Financial reporting
- Inquiries
- Invoices
- Order status
- Payments
- Pricing
- Purchasing
- Receiving
- Scheduling

EDI is commonly defined as an application-to-application transfer of business documents between computers while using industry-defined standards. EDI is the closest option to implementing paperless business transaction processing. Many businesses use EDI to substitute for their usual method of communication where paper documents such as purchase orders, invoices, and/or shipping notices were physically carried from department to department, mailed or faxed from one organization to another, or manually re-entered into the computer of the recipient. Also, organizations use EDI to electronically communicate, having documents and other types of information transmitted immediately and accurately into a computer-understandable format.

EDI is different than sending electronic mail or sharing files through a network (LANs, WANs, or MANs), or through an electronic bulletin board. When using these communications systems, the format of the transmitted document must be the same for the sender and the receiver. Otherwise, an effective communication will not take place.

When EDI is used, the format of the document does not need to be completely the same. When documents are transmitted, the translation software of EDI converts the document into an agreed-upon standard. Once the document is received, translation software changes the document into the appropriate standard. An EDI message is held within two parts, known as envelopes. One envelope, called the outside envelope, contains the interchange control information to address the message being transmitted. The outside envelope can be compared to a common paper envelope that contains a letter. Another part of the EDI message is known as the inside envelop (the content). The inside envelope consists of header information, which is the content of the document that is being transmitted, signature authentication, and error detection and correction information. This inside envelope can be compared to the content of the letter that is sent in the regular paper envelope.

For the purposes of this book we define EDI as follows:

> A computer-to-computer exchange of business documents in a public or industry standard format using public or private networks among trading partners. This may include requests for quotation, purchase orders, invoices, and transaction balances. As this definition indicates, the standard format plays an important role in EDI environment. Sending e-mail, faxes, or posting through bulletin boards does not require a specific format and standard.

12-3 THE HISTORY OF EDI

The growth of EDI is due mainly to the introduction and growth of data communications. EDI has been in existence since the late 1960s and has gained popularity ever since. With the improvements in the quality and affordability of data communications systems, EDI has become more attractive to all types of organizations. Experts in the field believe that the Internet will further enhance the applications and popularity of EDI in all types of organizations. Table 12-1 highlights some of the major events in the historical development of EDI applications [2,7,10,12,14,22].

12-4 THE GROWTH OF EDI

EDI has grown rapidly around the world, particularly in North America. According to an annual survey conducted by the EDI Group, Ltd., and published in *EDI Forum,* the EDI industry in 1990 reported a revenue increase of 40% over the previous year. A recent survey demonstrates that the growth in Canada should maintain a rate of 25% to 30% a year for several years. The survey reports that EDI is used for a wide range of transactions, the most common of which are purchase orders, invoicing, transportation documents, and financial statements [1,16].

The use of EDI in the United States has grown steadily. Nearly 25% of the organizations surveyed in 1993 anticipated implementing EDI within two years, and 20% were already using EDI. It is interesting to note that by 1993 the number of companies with no EDI plans fell dramatically. EDI was the second most common means of exchanging business documents in the United States. Paper remained the number one choice, but had fallen by nearly 50% since 1988. Despite the numerous benefits that EDI can provide, most companies implement EDI because a trading partner requires it. Conversely, the most common reason for not

Table 12-1

Major Events in the Historical Development of EDI Applications

Year	Event
1968	Ten California banks formed the Special Committee On Paperless Entries (SCOPE) to recommend specific rules and procedures for paperless payments and deposits using magnetic tapes. Transportation industry formed the Transportation Data Coordinating Committee (TDCC), having recognized the problem of communicating with different formats, protocols, and media speed.
Mid-1970s	National Data Corporation, General Electric, and several other companies developed systems using their time-sharing networks for banks to store and for customers to retrieve balance and transaction information.
1975	Automated Clearing House (ACH) network began to process Social Security payments. Other nationwide applications included veterans' payments and military payrolls. Insurance companies began to debit premiums and pay claims to individuals through the ACH.
1986	American Hospital Supply Corporation (now part of Baxter Healthcare Corporation) introduced ASAP, a proprietary computer order-entry system. Large suppliers such as Sears, J.C. Penney, and K-Mart developed proprietary standards for ordering from their suppliers.
1978	Federal Reserve implemented interregional exchange among automated clearing houses. The major trade associations in the grocery industry commissioned Arthur D. Little, Inc., to study the feasibility of electronic data interchange among food manufacturers, distributors, and brokers. The study analyzed how electronic communications could make basic ordering and invoicing functions more efficient. It recommended the use of a store-and-retrieve system for communications and grocery industry adaptation of the TDCC message format system.
1978/1979	American National Standards Institute (ANSI) formed Accredited Standards Committee (ASC) X.12 to develop uniform, variable-length, cross-industry standards. It built on the message format system developed by the TDCC. The Federal Reserve began processing debits through the night processing cycle, allowing companies to make deposits in remote locations late in the day, provided their banks with instructions to transfer funds through the ACH, and use those funds in their central accounts the next morning. National Automated Clearing House Association (NACHA) Board of Directors appointed a task force to study corporate trade payments.
1981	The Automobile Industry Action group, a nonprofit trade association, was formed by members of middle management in vehicle manufacturing companies and their suppliers. NACHA introduced the first corporate trade payment formats, Cash Concentration or Disbursement (CCD) and the Corporate Trade Payment (CTP). Banks began to sell corporate trade payments though the ACH network as an alternative to regular checks.
1982	Joint Electronic Data Interchange (JEDI) was formed to combine dictionaries. EDI pilots were developed in Canada under the auspices of the Grocery Products Manufacturers of Canada (GPMC) and another by the drug industry. The Public Warehousing Industry developed the Warehousing Industry Network Standards (WINS).

(continues)

Table 12-1 *(continued)*

Year	Event
1983	ANSI X.12 published first standards; ANSI X.12 standards became common standards for cross-country standards. Canadian grocery industry adopted modified version of UCS (Uniform Communications Standards) message standard (to allow metric trades).
1984	EDIFACT (Electronic Data Interchange For Administration, Commerce, and Transport) West European Technical Assessment Group produced an EDI Standard that later became the basis for EDIFACT.
1985	EDI Council of Canada formed.
1986	General Motors announced a program to pay its suppliers electronically.
1987	U.S. Treasury Department started a program to replace an annual volume of 80 million vendor check payments with ACH payments. NACHA (National Automated Clearing House Association) implemented Corporate Trade Exchange (CTX) format as a cooperative effort with ASC X.12. ASC X.12 and Grocery Industry Uniform Code Council (UCC) discussed possible merger. Warehousing Industry Network System (WINS) and UCC proposed merging standards. ISO 9737 (international syntax) was approved.
1988	The Auto Industry Action Group (AIAG) realized that the U.S. carmakers and their suppliers would need a standard, developed by ANSI.
1989	Canadian Inter-Financial Institutions EDI Committee formed, responsible for establishing standards for financial institutions exchanging transactions with each other through EDI.
1992	Canadian Payments Association approved standards and guidelines applicable to EDI Transactions. These standards collectively governed the exchange of EDI transactions between Canadian financial institutions that were members of the Canadian clearing system.
1993	The Department of Defense implemented a variety of pilot EDI systems at a number of buying installations. As a result of these early efforts, the Department of Defense has spearheaded the conversion effort at the federal level to EDI by developing the infrastructure for the process and would be conducting a variety of training events over the next 2 years.
1995	The ISO/IEC JTC1/SC30 (International Standards Organization/International Electrical Committee Joint Technical Committee/Standards Committee 30). ISO, representing more than 16 countries from Europe, Pan America, and Asia, announced the availability of a Reference Models for Open-EDI, which is the new framework for coordinating standards development. This Reference Model is an alternative method to the traditional EDI standards development process that is slow and cumbersome. The committee has worked on this project for 3 years, and has reached its first goal of making this Reference Model available for worldwide review and ballot. Reaching this milestone allows the Open-EDI concept to be openly shared and standards to be established in a structured manner.

(continues)

Table 12-1 *(continued)*

Year	Event
1996/1997	The UN's Center for Facilitation of Practices and Procedures for Administration, Commerce and Transport (CEFACT) and the ANSI's Accredited Standards Committee X.12 are creating prototypes of model-generated EDI standards and discussing the institutional changes necessary to implement a model-driven standards development and maintenance process.
1998/2000	The use of Internet for EDI transactions being considered as an alternative to traditional methods for communications.

implementing EDI is that a trading partner refuses to participate. Industry growth has reduced early concerns over costs and compatibility issues.

A recent report by Market Research Company Ovum revealed that EDI expenditure in Europe is growing at an annual compound rate of 21%. There are presently more than 30,000 users of EDI in Europe, participating in more than 500 large EDI communities, and that this will rise to 300,000 by the year 2000. It is expected that worldwide applications of EDI will continue at a rapid pace for the following reasons [1,16]:

- EDI is a major component of electronic commerce, as it provides benefits that are not matched by electronic mail or fax. Internet growth in conjunction with the growth of the electronic commerce would be one of the major reasons for the expansion of EDI.
- More organizations are becoming aware of the significant benefits that EDI can provide.
- Large corporations continue to push EDI down to new suppliers, creating networks of trading partners.

12-5 INTRODUCING EDI INTO YOUR ORGANIZATION

As mentioned earlier EDI can enhance an organization's competitiveness by expediting the delivery of information and reducing costs. Like other information systems applications, EDI utilization is a multifaceted process that involves detailed planning and considerations. The following are the major steps that must be analyzed for a proper introduction of EDI to an organization:

- Assessing the strategic value of EDI applications
- Analyzing the advantages and disadvantages of EDI applications
- Analyzing EDI costs
- Choosing a communication interface option

- Reviewing EDI standards
- EDI implementation

In the following pages we provide a detailed explanation of these steps.

12-5-1 ASSESSING THE STRATEGIC VALUE OF EDI APPLICATIONS

As we briefly mentioned in Chapter 10, EDI can be viewed as a part of total quality management (TQM) and business process reengineering (BPR) programs. TQM, BPR, and EDI are closely related. Organizations can benefit from recognizing this relationship. Total quality management (TQM) is a management philosophy aimed at creating an organization that it is committed to continuous process improvement and customer satisfaction. EDI represents an innovative method of meeting and exceeding customer expectations. Effective use of EDI by suppliers results in better availability of information and greater cost savings through operational efficiencies. EDI creates a link between suppliers and customers, reducing the time required to respond to changing market conditions [21].

Business process reengineering (BRP) typically involves close scrutiny of the core business activities and effective design of those activities. EDI represents a process change in the sense that electronic documents are used instead of paper documents. However, the effect of EDI on business processes is really much more pervasive and often requires changes in work practices. The successful implementation of EDI can involve redesigning other information systems applications and related work structures.

Given that EDI results in changes and modifications in hardware and software infrastructure for electronic business, this infrastructure can then be used to re-engineer organizational processes. The network between the companies resulting from EDI provides an opportunity for reengineering additional business processes to utilize the electronic channels. Electronic mail communication, alliances for marketing products, creation of the virtual organization, and product distribution are some applications that could benefit from this infrastructure.

EDI often requires that information systems personnel accompany sales personnel on customer visits to understand customer requirements, or to answer questions from customers regarding EDI. This change in roles of information systems personnel has implications for training. Information systems personnel must be trained in how to interact with customers and in other marketing issues. Marketing personnel, who must sell the EDI applications, must be trained in information systems issues. This training is critical to the success of the EDI partnership, both internal and external to the company. The full potential of EDI as a strategic tool is often overlooked since many firms view EDI a tool for maintaining market share. EDI is usually perceived as a method of reducing paperwork and inventory cost. Other impacts of EDI utilization include quick response time, greater accuracy gained from reduction in data entry, improved cash flow, improvements in the customer/supplier relationship, and improvements in productivity.

The development of EDI applications in the workplace has largely evolved from a desire to improve efficiency in order processing and billing. For these applications, management views the benefits gained from EDI utilization as operational in nature. The introduction of EDI provides a method of electronically handling the customer-supplier transfer of data. Customers request and/or receive goods, services, and data in a standardized format through established policies and procedures. Using electronic journals, companies can easily monitor the performance of suppliers in providing the goods and services requested.

Successful EDI implementation encourages better allocation of resources for the suppliers and customers because of the availability of timely information. Suppliers often adopt just-in-time processes along with EDI to serve customers. Information availability helps in tactical control of the manufacturing process at the supplier level and evaluation of supplier performance at the customer level. For EDI to be viewed strategically, companies must understand the significance of EDI as a competitive tool. The following strategies must be carefully evaluated [21]:

1. Differentiation strategy
2. Cost leadership strategy
3. Innovation strategy
4. Growth strategy
5. Alliance strategy

The following is a brief description of each strategy.

1. *Differentiation strategy.* The chemical industry has used EDI to offer inventory handling for its customers. The chemical supplier is connected directly to the customer's inventory database. Using a remote automated program, periodic checks by the supplier signal the customer's need for raw materials. These raw materials are then automatically ordered for the customer by the supplier's computer program. Delivery of the materials is handled by the supplier and subsequently billed electronically to the customer. By using this system, the supplier can anticipate shipment and the customer can reduce the chance of running out of inventory. Periodic review of the customer database for sales data helps the chemical company anticipate customer needs. Suppliers who are capable of such service may use this to differentiate themselves from those who do not. Naturally, a

broad range of businesses to achieve the same strategic objective can adopt this kind of application. As discussed in Chapter 8, some organizations are using Extranets to achieve the same objective.

2. *Cost leadership strategy.* EDI can provide low-cost delivery of products and services. At an operational level, EDI serves the company by providing paperless ordering and receiving applications. Time saving from the absence of re-keying equates to efficiency gains. Faster preparation and transfer of invoices and payments resulted in faster turnover of account receivables.

3. *Innovation strategy.* Financial institutions are constantly seeking methods of providing new services to their clients. The financial application in cash management can also be considered as an innovative strategy. A financial institution, for instance, initiated an EDI application to provide loan and scholarship payments for students. Students may receive money from several sources to complete their education, including scholarships and loans from private companies or government agencies. Many times these checks must go directly to the school to pay tuition, and transactions are handled manually. The balance then goes to the student for other related expenses. In an effort to simplify the process, the bank receives loan and scholarship payments from multiple sources to perform clearinghouse activities for educational institutions. Students receive their checks or direct deposits from one financial institution. After direct tuition payments have been made, the financial institution receives the benefits of having its name on all checks cut from this process and of acquiring the names and addresses of all students serviced. This activity represents a new service provided for the university (and existing customers) and an innovative method of obtaining a new student customer base for the financial institution.

4. *Growth strategy.* A chemical company is presently expanding its service. Faced with reduced staff and escalating business opportunities, the company is employing EDI to manage the changes. Manufacturing multiple products across dispersed geographical regions has forced the chemical company to develop a corporate growth strategy that includes implementation of EDI. EDI has facilitated the link between the different divisions of the company, allowing for economies of scale in purchasing across divisions. Some customers are also forcing the chemical company to be EDI proficient, awarding contracts to those companies that meet the stated EDI requirements with the fewest errors in processing. Thus, growth of business could be linked to EDI. Introduction of new EDI-based products and services by financial institutions can also be viewed as a growth strategy.

5. *Alliance strategy.* Financial institutions have taken a lead in developing alliance strategies. One company has formed an alliance with a value-added network (VAN) vendor to produce a financial EDI application. The application combines account payable and receivable with electronic funds transfer (EFT). This includes information exchange between banks or other financial institutions that

result in debits and credits, and an automated clearinghouse. The application will be jointly owned and operated for the benefit of both parties in the alliance, providing a complete package of products and services required by prospective financial EDI customers.

12-5-2 ANALYZING THE ADVANTAGES AND DISADVANTAGES OF EDI APPLICATIONS

Like other information systems applications, EDI presents a series of advantages and disadvantages to a typical organization. The extent of these advantages and disadvantages may vary from organization to organization and from application to application. However, for the most part an EDI application may include the following advantages and disadvantages:

12-5-2-1 Advantages of EDI

If properly designed and integrated EDI offers numerous benefits as outlined in Table 12-2 [4,15,18,22,25]:

12-5-2-2 Disadvantages of EDI

An EDI system may include some disadvantages compared with traditional systems. A proper implementation may eliminate or at least minimize some of these advantages. The flowing is a listing of some of these disadvantages [1,13]

- Concentration of control
- Data processing, application, and communications errors
- Potential loss of management and audit trails
- Reliance on third parties
- Reliance on trading partner's system
- Total systems dependence
- Unauthorized transactions and fraud

A brief description of these disadvantages follows:

1. *Concentration of control.* The strength of the internal control structure provided by a segregation of duties and structured management reporting may be reduced or weakened in an EDI environment because the number of people is reduced. EDI causes management to place a greater reliance on computer systems and concentrates control in the hands of fewer individuals, potentially increasing risk. While effective automated controls can reduce the potential for human error,

Table 12-2

EDI Advantages

Accelerates the order-invoice-payment cycle from days or weeks to hours or minutes

Decreases paperwork

Expands the organization customer base

Improves accuracy of information transfer

Improves customer service

Improves response and access to information

Improves communications

Improves cost efficiency

Improves customer service

Improves quality through improved record-keeping, fewer errors in data entry, reduced processing delays, less reliance on human interpretation of data, and minimized unproductive time

Improves the competitiveness of an organization

Improves the speed of transaction processing

Improves the speed of information transfer

Increases business opportunities through wider diffusion of procurement information

Offers process improvement and quality assurance benefits through improving the way in which companies handle information

Provides timely and accurate data for decision-making

Reduces data entry costs

Reduces inventory

Reduces mailing costs

Reduces personnel requirements

Simplifies order entry and processing

Simplifies accounting and billing

---

the impact of any control deficiencies will be greater and could include overpayment, over- and understocking, over- and underproduction.

2. *Data processing, application, and communications errors.* Errors in computer processing and communications systems may result in the transmission of incorrect trading information or the reporting of inaccurate information to management. Application errors or failures can also result in significant losses to trading partners.

3. *Potential loss of management and audit trails.* In some cases, EDI transaction data may not be maintained for a long period of time. Without proper consideration of legal an audit issues, the entity may not be able to provide adequate or appropriate evidence, in hard copy or on magnetic media, for the legal dispute to

be resolved favorably or the audit to be completed cost-effectively. Backup of the transactions must be made and maintained to guard against this possible problem.

4. *Reliance on third parties.* The organization will become more dependent on third parties to ensure security over transactions and continuity of processing. Also, EDI may share the same kinds of security threads associated with any electronic data communications. A number of potential risks include:

- Confidential information could be exposed to unauthorized third parties, possibly competitors.
- Third party staff could introduce invalid and/or unauthorized transactions.
- Transactions could be lost resulting from disruptions of data processing at third party network sites or on route to the recipient partner, causing business losses, and inaccurate financial reporting.

5. *Reliance on trading partner's system.* In facilitating just-in-time and quick response systems, EDI creates a dependence on the trading partner's computer system. Errors, security breaches, and processing disruptions in the trading partner's system may have an impact on the client's business operations.

6. *Total systems dependence.* All EDI transactions entered by an entity could be corrupted if the EDI-related application became corrupted. If the errors remained undetected, there could be an impact on cash flow, noncompliance with contractual obligations, and adverse publicity and loss of business confidence by customers and suppliers. Undetected errors in transactions received from trading partners could cause losses from inappropriate operating decisions.

7. *Unauthorized transactions and fraud.* Increased access to computer systems can increase the opportunities to change an entity's computer records and those of its trading partners, enabling significant fraud to be committed. Where payment transactions are automatically generated by the system, payments can be manipulated or diverted, or they can be generated in error or at the wrong time intervals. The benefit of human experience in identifying unusual or inconsistent transactions is reduced with electronic or EDI transactions, which are less subject to visual review. In the future some of these problems may be resolved by the integration of artificial intelligence and expert systems into EDI applications.

12-5-3 ANALYZING EDI COSTS

There are several different types of costs associated with implementation of EDI. Table 12-3 provides a summary of these costs [1,21].

12-5-4 CHOOSING A COMMUNICATION INTERFACE OPTION

EDI transactions are transmitted either directly between the organizations and their trading partners or through third parties called VANs (value-added networks)

Table 12-3

Major EDI Costs

Hardware costs associated with the installation of the system. This may vary from organization to organization and the type of hardware chosen including mainframes, minicomputers, or microcomputers.

Legal and other costs associated with setting up trading partner relationships.

Security costs.

Software costs associated with the installation. The costs of EDI software for a minicomputer or mainframe can be significant, depending on the comprehensiveness of the installation.

System development costs that vary according to the extent to which EDI is being implemented.

Telecommunications costs, accessing and using value-added or other types of networks.

Training, which includes training employees to change their existing work practices.

---

and public networks such as America Online, CompuServe, Prodigy, and the Internet. The VAN serves as an electronic clearinghouse or post office, routing messages between trading partners and holding them until the recipient is ready for them. The EDI transmission process commonly involves three phases [1,22]:

1. The application interface includes passing the electronic transactions to (or extracting them from) the appropriate business application system. It is the critical link between the EDI translator and the business's own internal processing.
2. The EDI translator performs formatting (or reformatting) the data into an agreed-upon EDI data format and passing them to the data communications interface. All transaction data must pass through this process to be sent from or received by the organization using EDI.
3. The communications interface includes the transmission and receiving of EDI documents electronically. It presents the media that all EDI transactions go through.

There are four common types of communications networks that a company can choose from. Which option should be selected depends on the strategic goals of a particular organization. These options include:

1. Point-to-point connection
2. Value-added networks (VANs)
3. Proprietary networks
4. Public networks

Let us briefly explain each option:

1. In point-to-point connection EDI partners establish a direct computer-to-computer link through a private network. In this case all partners must use the same standards and conventions for setting up formats for various transactions and conform to specified speed and are responsible for developing and monitoring their individual systems. This option has been popular with government agencies and U.S. carmakers. Table 12-4 summarizes the advantages of this option and Table 12-5 summarizes the disadvantages of this option.

2. In value-added network (VAN) EDI partners do not deliver messages directly to each other, instead they use a VAN as a sort of "post office" for holding and forwarding messages. The sender transmits data to the VAN; that, in turn, determines the intended recipient for the transaction and places the data in the recipient's electronic mailbox. The data remain in the mailbox until the intended recipient retrieves it. A VAN usually provides dependable and secure service. The VAN provides a more cost-effective alternative compared with a point-to-point connection. It also provides services such as storing and forwarding messages, detecting and correcting errors, and message encryption and decryption [1,27].

Value-added network (VAN) providers such as Sterling Commerce (Dublin, OH), GEIS, and IBM Global Networks are planning to introduce a new generation of IP-based EDI. This new EDI would interconnect legacy systems in industries

Table 12-4

Advantages of Point-to-Point Connection

It allows the organization to control the access to the network.

It allows the organization to use and enforce proprietary software standard in dealing with all trading partners.

The sponsoring organization controls the system. Therefore, there is no reliance on third parties for computer processing.

With the absence of a third party handling data, the timeliness of delivery can be improved.

Table 12-5

Disadvantages of Point-to-Point Connection

A higher initial cost for communication networks.

A need to establish the point-to-point connection with each trading partner.

Limited business partnership.

Computer scheduling issues.

Hardware and software compatibility.

Need for standard protocols.

Table 12-6

Advantages of VANs

In some cases, the VAN provides value-added services, such as converting the application format to a standard format; the partner sending the data does not have to reformat it.

It reduces communication and data protocol problems, since most VANs have the appropriate facilities to deal with diverse protocols. The fact that the sender and receiver are not directly connected eliminates the need to agree on and implement a common protocol.

It reduces scheduling problems, since sender and receiver do not directly communicate; the receiver can, at its convenience, request delivery of the information from the VAN.

The mailbox facility of the VAN allows one trader to deal with many partners without establishing numerous point-to-point connections.

The VAN can provide increased security and can act as a network firewall to protect the entity.

---

and companies that have not had the resources to utilize traditional EDI. For example, Sterling Commerce, which has 1600 employees, more than 30,000 EDI customer sites worldwide, and 20 years' experience in building EDI solutions recently started two new business units to implement Internet interface-based EDI solutions. The company has inexpensive PC-based software for a "Commerce Catalog," which can be used to build EDI-enabled, IP-based electronic catalogs. These can be used to develop EDI-customized order forms and other types of EDI-enabled documents [1,27].

Sterling has also developed the "Commerce Connection," a package of IP-based software applications for EDI materials. They have simple Internet-like browsers and offer quick IP-based network access. Web technology promises to eliminate many of the complications of EDI as it was implemented on mainframes in various flavors of UNIX and in proprietary VANs.

GEIS recently launched an initiative to establish a partnership with Netscape, called Actra, to integrate EDI with Netscape's Navigator browser technology. GEIS's role is to establish and stabilize the standards to add security, interoperability with EDI systems, and functions such as certification of Internet business-to-business transactions. These features should make EDI more acceptable over the Internet with a moderate cost.

Table 12-6 summarizes the advantages of VANs and Table 12-7 provides a listing of some of the disadvantages of VAN.

3. Proprietary networks are used in some situations, such as health care and banking. In these cases industry-specific networks have been developed that allow the transmission of EDI transactions [5].

4. The public networks option allows the use of public networks such as CompuServe, Prodigy, America Online, and the Internet to transmit EDI transactions is a growing new alternative to VANs and proprietary networks. The use of

Table 12-7

Disadvantages of VANs

Confidentially of data may be in jeopardy.
The organization becomes dependent on the VAN's computer systems and controls.

these networks for EDI exists but is not significant because of an overall lack of effective security for the organization, especially in the case of the Internet. However, the use of this option is growing and the security problems are becoming more manageable [30,32].

12-5-5 REVIEWING EDI STANDARDS

Standards are available in almost all information systems applications. These include standards for programming languages, standards for data transmissions and control, standards for software development, and so forth. In a growing economy, EDI standards are fundamental to enhancing development and to reducing the overall costs. EDI initially developed along specific-industry lines, with each industry developing its own standards. Due to the increased use of EDI, the cross-industry common standards became a necessity. The goal of standardization is to enable dissimilar computer systems, with dissimilar data structures and formats, to be able to communicate with a minimum human intervention. By agreeing to use common standards, companies can program their computers only once, per standard, to send messages, and once to receive. The larger the number of companies using common standards, the greater the benefits for all the participants [31].

Standards or protocols are the common language spoken when dealing with trading partners, defining the format of the transaction and the way in which the transaction is communicated. Generally speaking, it will be a generic, comprehensive protocol, agreed by a sufficiently wide group of user community. The alternative will be for each industry to support at least three standards: (1) the standard for its own industry; (2) the X.12 North American standard; and (3) the EDIFACT European standard. The two main EDI standards include ANSI X.12 and UN/EDIFACT.

ANSI (American National Standards Institute) X.12 was developed in 1978. Its goal was to establish EDI standards that would cross all industry segments. Various subcommittees were formed to develop standards that would accommodate and consolidate industry standards. Their overall goal was to emerge with one common, generic, and public standard. X.12 became the pervasive standard in North America. This standard allows different organizations to comprehend the same information. ANSI responded to the need for a uniform message format for specific industries. However, some problems arose, when communicating electronically with other countries (crossing national and international boundaries). Those businesses outside the United States found that the ANSI X.12 standards did not meet their specific needs. While X.12 is one of the oldest major standards, it is by no means the only one [31].

In 1988, the United Nations developed the UN/EDIFACT (Electronic Data Interchange For Administration, Commerce, and Transport), which would design international standards for EDI. This international development has created a significant increase in competitiveness, but UN/EDIFACT did promote trade with the European countries. EDIFACT has become to be known as the European Standard. The UN/EDIFACT standard is not restricted only to European countries, and it is expected to eventually become the predominant standard. Canada selected the UN/EDIFACT as its standard. There are many benefits to accepting the UN/EDIFACT as the universal standard. The benefits include overseas expansion, cost control, and eliminating the need for multiple formats. Therefore, at the present time, X.12 is primarily used in North America, while EDIFACT is used for European and international transactions [1].

The integration of international trade (NAFTA, the European Union, and so forth) will further necessitate the use of one common standard worldwide. At the present time, X.12 is mature and relatively more stable than EDIFACT. EDIFACT, however, is catching up. Finally, it is anticipated that X.12 will migrate to or merge with EDIFACT. A survey of industry membership has determined that some 70% are in favor of one common standard for worldwide trade. The ultimate objective would be to establish EDIFACT as the common standard. A highly recognized EDI software company, Premenos, expects UN/EDIFACT to be the universal standard of choice [1].

Six regional boards, consisting of the Pan American, Western Europe, Eastern and Central Europe, Africa, Asia, and Australia/New Zealand regions, administer UN/EDIFACT. The U.S. X.12 committee works closely with the PAEB (Pan America EDIFACT Board) to make sure that X.12 stays in close alignment with UN/EDIFACT.

There are numerous proprietary standards that have been established in various industries such as [31]:

- LIMNET (London Insurance Market Network for insurance industry)
- SWIFT (Society for Worldwide Interbank Financial Transactions for the banking industry)
- ODETTE (Organization for Data Exchange Through Tele-Transmission for European automotive industry)
- DISH (Data Interchange for Shipping for European transportation industries)

- RINET (Reinsurance and Insurance Network)
- TRADCOMS (Trading Data Communication in the United Kingdom)

In addition, there are company-specific standards, such as Ford-Net from Ford of Europe or the proprietary rules from Siemens in Germany.

12-5-6 EDI IMPLEMENTATION

There are basically two types of EDI implementation [1]:

1. *Stand-alone EDI.* In this type of implementation a small pilot project with only microcomputer interface is designed. Transactions are often printed, manually reviewed, and re-keyed for entry into the application system. Thus, there is a small change in the workflow (small audit impact).
2. *Integrated.* In this type of implementation application-to-application EDI with the integration of the receiver's and sender's computer systems (for example, order processing, fulfillment, and payment) will be implemented.

EDI implementation goes through three phases: (1) pre-implementation; (2) implementation; and (3) postimplementation audit [11,22,31].

During the **pre-implementation** phase, the organization current position must be carefully identified. Questions such as the following must be asked:

- Does the organization have any vendors, clients, or business partners that are currently using EDI? If so, the organization can use them to help support its implementation.
- Who is the right person to "champion" the EDI project? Like other information systems projects, someone, preferably from top management group who has fairly broad experience and contacts within the organization should champion the project.

A design team should be organized. This team is similar to the CBIS task force that we discussed in Chapter 9. The team should include at least representatives from the MIS, legal, and accounting departments. Representatives from the production and purchasing departments will add more strength to the team. Whoever leads the team should preferably report to the CFO or another high-level financial executive. This individual should feel that she has a personal stake in making sure that EDI project would be successful. This is because they are the ones who will best be able to quantify and understand the benefits that EDI will bring to the organization.

The final step in pre-implementation is to set a strategic direction and to make an implementation plan. The organization needs to identify the areas of the business that can most benefit from EDI. A plan should be laid out, preferably with dates, to implement the entire project. Tools such as Gantt charts and PERT as discussed in Chapter 9 are very helpful.

There are several ways to implement EDI. The basic process include:

1. Identify the organization potential trading partners.

2. Identify the types of documents the organization is going to exchange with those trading partners.

3. Acquire some expert advice or training in setting up the specific EDI transactions the organization will use.

4. Choose the EDI software. There are many options available, and features and prices vary. Make sure the organization receives what it needs. If one of the organization's trading partners is already using specific software that should be considered. Talking to other companies in the same field and observing what they are using is a good idea. Also, contacting one or more of the EDI consulting firms is a good idea. There are plenty of resources and products available.

5. Choose a communication method. There are three primary ways that communication takes place: direct dial-up, Internet, and VAN (value-added network). As explained earlier, a VAN is a service provider that provides a type of private and secure e-mail box for your corporation. There are a number of commercial VANs available (most of the major telephone companies provide such services). The costs for their services vary, so several options should be examined. The cheapest service is not necessarily the best. A secure and consistent access is of the prime importance.

6. Coordinate setup with your trading partners and make sure you are all using the same version/release of the EDI software, and that the protocol of transmittal and confirmation is agreed upon. The transactions you choose partially dictate what you can and should do. At this stage all the trading partners should be identified. The full benefits of EDI are not realized if the organization only identifies a small number of the trading partners.

7. Prioritize the implementation process. The organization must make sure to identify where the greatest benefits will be gained and implement those areas first. Since EDI is relatively new, the benefits generated from this application may be different from other CBIS applications. It is a new and significantly different way of doing business, and it is going to create a cultural change in the business, not just an improvement project.

The **post-implementation audit** is at least as important as pre-implementation and implementation. The organization should review how things went and plan for the future. The organization should realize that, even though a number of trading partners have been secured and several areas are online, there will be more work in the future. The organization should put together a permanent EDI team to ensure the future growth. This team will be responsible for making sure that EDI continues to run as smoothly as it did during a well-planned implementation.

The organization should review the implementation process and evaluate it and see how the system is working. The team should evaluate how much money is being saved and exactly where it is being saved. They should evaluate the number of transactions that the system processes and evaluate the satisfaction of the trading partners. The team should look for other areas where the organization can use its newfound EDI expertise to continue to improve the organization competitiveness.

12-6 EDI APPLICATIONS

The number and diversity of the EDI applications is well documented throughout the literature. In this section we review some of the popular applications and the organizations that are using these applications [19,20,24]. Table 12-8 lists some of the organizations that have been using EDI successfully.

12-6-1 THE DuPONT CORPORATION

The DuPont Corporation of Wilmington, Delaware, exports 200 shipments originating from many commercial centers within the company. The company's forwarders generate 2000 telex messages and produce a total of 30,000 pages of related information daily. The cost of producing and storing this information is estimated at $20 million annually.

While EDI can serve as a catalyst for operational improvements throughout a company, for many, such improvements need to start with the initial automation of processes and procedures that are still paper- and people-intensive. DuPont's solution is called XT or Export-TRIMS (Transportation Rate/Route Information Management System) with export rating, routing, payment, and shipment information files among other modules. With information provided by the material and logistics department and with shipment specifications, the system presents available routings, including carriers, exit ports, and types of services available. Inquiries can be made based on various parameters such as export control numbers and hazardous material controls, and the system audits for duplicate shipment payments. Compatible with other corporate systems, XT is credited with enhancing the company's competitive position in the global marketplace [29].

12-6-2 THE FEDERAL GOVERNMENT

The federal government is trying to reduce government paperwork by using various applications of EDI. The U.S. Customs Service, for example, is attempting to gain maximum electronic linkage between its headquarters and the import

Table 12-8

A Sample of Organizations Using EDI

Alcoa

BancBoston Mortgage Co

Bank of America

British Airways

Carter Hawley

Chrysler Corp.

Department of Defense

DuPont

Federal Government

Ford Motor Co.

General Electric

General Motors

J.C. Penney

MCI Communications

Mobil

Nestle Distribution Co.

Price Club Canada

RJR Nabisco

Rockwell International

United Parcel Services (UPS)

United States Custom Service

Veterans Administration

Whirlpool Corp.

community, using its Automated Commercial System to exchange trade data. The paperless environment for cargo clearance is an achievable goal. Ultimately, there will be no hard-copy forms involved in the entry of merchandise into the country. Import brokers can use EDI to send entry forms to the agency and get clearance for certain shipments before the ship ever reaches the port. This means that millions of dollars in duties and fees can be sent quickly to the United States.

The Treasury Department can begin earning interest rather than waiting days or even weeks for paperwork to clear. The Defense Department wants to migrate its acquisition and logistics operations to EDI and paperless applications by 2002. The goal is to set up programs that can support electronic data interchange throughout a project's life cycle [6,26].

12-6-3 GENERAL MOTORS

General Motors Corporation has introduced an invoice-less payment system where all invoices will be paid electronically by using EDI and electronic funds transfer (EFT). This is mainly because several financial institutions are setting up third-party EDI networks. EFT, a special type of EDI, is a money transfer system that banking and financial institutions provide worldwide. In addition, the automobile industry was one of the early supporters of EDI and helped promote the number of EDI users by adopting EDI for doing business with its thousands of EDI transactions each day. General Motors sees many advantages for using this technology:

1. *Cost-effectiveness:* an EDI transaction costs less than traditional methods.
2. *Speed:* EDI eliminates five-day mailing time for business documents.
3. *Reliability:* transaction acknowledgements help ensure the delivery of information.
4. *Flexibility:* EDI transactions are not restricted to a paper form. Information may be added or deleted as required.
5. *Expandability:* additional transactions can be easily added.

In the United States, General Motors considered paper reduction a strong motivating factor for EDI introduction. Implementation began in its payments system, where the organization was sending $4 billion per month using 400,000 checks to 2000 suppliers. Complete implementation of EDI was reported to be capable of saving $200 to $500 in costs per vehicle produced [1,28]. In addition, GM began linking suppliers in Germany, Spain, Italy, Belgium, and The Netherlands to the company's central European computer system in Antwerp, Belgium.

12-6-4 THE HEALTHCARE INDUSTRY

The electronic claim has revolutionized the way healthcare organizations conduct business and has provided direction for the next generation of EDI technology in the healthcare industry [23]. In 1995, the state of New Jersey released a report on the Healthcare Information Networks and Technologies (HINT) project. HINT is the only available independent report that details the impact of EDI on the healthcare industry. The HINT survey results support the popular view that provider groups that submit information electronically benefit from:

- A lower average cost per claim than paper-based claims;
- A lower average rejection rate for both initial claims and follow-up claims than paper-based claims;
- A shorter turnaround time on accounts receivable than paper-based claims.

Generally speaking, every segment of the healthcare industry reported cost savings, lower claims rejection rates, and faster payment as a result of using EDI. The survey revealed that hospitals save 15%, pharmacies save 24%, physicians save 35%, laboratories save 37%, and payers save 37% by using EDI. In addition, hospitals reported 47% fewer rejected initial claims and 45% fewer rejected follow-up claims as a result of using EDI. Physicians experienced 21% fewer rejected initial claims and 20% fewer rejected follow-up claims. Laboratories, pharmacies, and payers averaged 27% fewer rejected initial claims and 30% fewer rejected follow-up claims. The survey also concluded that electronic claims were paid considerably faster than paper-based claims. By submitting electronic claims instead of paper-based claims, hospitals saved 29 days in collecting accounts receivable, with a 44% improvement in cash flow; physicians saved 30 days in collecting accounts receivable, with a 52% improvement in cash flow, according to HINT survey results [17].

12-6-5 MOBIL CORPORATION

Proxicom, the leading provider of Internet-based business solutions, and Mobil Corporation recently announced the deployment of a revolutionary Internet-based EDI solution. This will help Mobil Corporation to conduct business more effectively with its more than 300 lubricants distributors. Proxicom implemented an Extranet application adhering to EDI's X.12 standard while allowing for a paperless exchange of business documents using the Internet. (We briefly explained Extranet in Chapter 8.)

Mobil Corporation is a leading oil, natural gas, and petrochemical company with operations in more than 125 countries. Mobil Corporation distributors can now submit purchase orders directly through their Web browsers without the complexity and cost of a traditional EDI system. In addition to placing orders via their Internet connection, distributors will be able to execute product buy-backs, and receive invoices and transaction acknowledgments. This solution is the future of business-to-business electronic commerce. Internet-based EDI is faster and considerably less expensive than traditional systems. Mobil Corporation has secured a competitive advantage by embracing the Internet to create new values for their distributors while incorporating their specific business rules. Through this Extranet, Mobil has strengthened its distribution channels and increased the profit potential for all the involved parties. EDI offers Mobil Corporation and its distributors a tremendous business advantage over the Internet. The Internet vastly extends what they can accomplish compared with more traditional systems. They gain innovative, easy ways to communicate and work with their distributors, while saving time and money. Proxicom has been instrumental in helping Mobil Corporation to define an Internet strategy and in developing a workable solution [3].

12-6-6 THE TRANSPORTATION INDUSTRY

Ocean shipping is becoming a crucial link in all important international trade sectors, and a new EDI network promises to transport the industry's customers into the age of paperless business, while saving time and money. The ocean transport industry is counting on EDI and other information technologies to link all international trade. The difference between booking a cargo with an ocean carrier by phone or by EDI is significant. For example, the cost of a phone and fax booking is around $3, while the same booking by EDI costs 5 cents [9].

In the rail industry, the Industry Reference Files will allow customers to get stationmaster, rail regulations, and rail route information. It will also allow for the information to be passed from company to company along the rail routes of the United States. The rail industry uses 70 transaction sets, which deal with every aspect of rail transport from bills to ways to financial EDI for transaction settlement [8].

The air transportation industry has finished the first year of using a UN/EDIFACT message suite for passenger processing. EDIFACT is the United Nations-sponsored EDI standard for global commerce. The interactive UN/EDIFACT messages being used are connecting computer reservations with the airlines. Also, EDI is used in the fuel and corporate purchasing ends of the airline industry as well as in the air cargo industry [8].

SUMMARY

This chapter provided a detailed discussion of EDI as a growing application of information systems. The chapter provided a definition, and it covered the historical development and the growth of EDI throughout the world, particularly in North America. The chapter introduced six major steps for a proper introduction of EDI in the organization. These included assessing the strategic value of EDI applications, analyzing the advantages and disadvantages, analyzing the costs, choosing a communication interface option, EDI standards, and implementation. The chapter concluded with several popular applications of EDI and introduced several organizations that have been using EDI successfully.

REVIEW QUESTIONS

1. What is EDI? What are some of the differences between EDI and data communications in general? Discuss.
2. How did EDI start?

3. What are some of the important milestones in EDI development?
4. What is the role of the Internet in the further development of EDI applications?
5. What are some of the strategic values of EDI applications?
6. What are the relationships of EDI, TQM, and BPR?
7. What are three main advantages of an EDI system?
8. What are three main disadvantages of an EDI system?
9. Are the advantages and disadvantages of EDI the same for all the applications and organizations? Discuss.
10. What are some of the costs of EDI implementation?
11. How are EDI costs different from other information systems applications? Discuss.
12. When it comes to selecting a communication interface option, how many choices are there? What are some of the advantages and disadvantages of these various options?
13. What are some of the components of an EDI system?
14. What are EDI standards? Why should an organization choose a standard? What are some of the popular options?
15. What are some of the choices for the implementation of EDI? Discuss.
16. List 10 popular applications of EDI.
17. What are some examples of companies that have implemented EDI successfully?
18. What has EDI done for DuPont? For Mobil Corporation?
19. What has EDI done in the transportation industry? In the healthcare industry?
20. In your opinion, will the popularity of EDI increase or decrease in the near future? Discuss.

PROJECTS

1. A new automotive discount retailer in Southern California is planning to use EDI in dealing with its suppliers. They need your help. Provide a detailed cost and benefit analysis statement for this organization. What would be some of the advantages of using EDI for this organization? What are some of the disadvantages? Discuss.
2. Compare and contrast LANs, WANs, MANs, EFT, and EDI. You may want to refer to the materials presented in Chapter 5 for background information.
3. What are some of the advantages of EDI for academic institutions? How is the transportation industry benefiting from EDI? The healthcare industry?

4. What is the relationship between EDI and TQM? How might a properly designed EDI system improve the TQM program? Discuss.

5. How is the implementation of EDI different than other information systems applications? What are some of the similarities? What are some of the dissimilarities? Discuss.

6. How might project management and control tools such as the Gantt chart and PERT improve the implementation phase of an EDI project? Discuss.

KEY TERMS

Business process reengineering, 346
EDI advantages, 350
EDI applications, 341
EDI costs, 352
EDI disadvantages, 353
EDI history, 342–345
EDI implementation, 357–359
EDI standards, 355–357

Extranet, 362
Internet, 362
Point-to-point connection, 352–353
Proprietary networks, 354
Public networks, 351–352
Stand-alone EDI, 357
Total quality management, 346
Value-added networks, 351–353

REFERENCES

[1] American Institute of Certified Public Accountants-AICPA. (1996). *Auditing procedure study: Audit implication of EDI,* pp. 7–21. New York: AICPA.

[2] American Institute of Certified Public Accountants-AICPA (1996), *Auditing procedure study: Audit implication of EDI,* pp. 55–58. New York: AICPA.

[3] Anonymous. (March 10, 1997). Proxicom and Mobil introduce new Internet-based electronic data interchanges. *PR Newswire.*

[4] Anonymous. (March 15, 1997). Electronic data interchange (EDI). *Automatic I.D. News,* 20.

[5] Anonymous. (August 18, 1997). Proprietary UPS EDI system could put customers in a bind. *EDI News,* Vol. 11, No. 17.

[6] Anonymous. (September 1, 1997). Digital or else: Defense Department wants to migrate acquisition and logistics operations to EDI and paperless application by 2002. *Government Computer News* Vol. 16, No. 26, 60.

[7] Anonymous. (September 15, 1997). EDI modeling would change ASC X.12 procedures: Standards groups stake future on IDEF, contemplate implementation. *EDI News* Vol. 11, No. 19.

[8] Anonymous. (October 27, 1997). "EDI News Short Takes . . ." *EDI News,* Vol. 11, No. 22.

[9] Anonymous (October 27, 1997). Ocean shipping gets easy with interactive EDI. Other modes of transportation show interest too. *EDI News,* Vol. 11, No. 22.

[10] Anonymous. (October 27, 1997). "GE Unveils European TradeWeb Web-Based EDI System," *Newsbytes.*

[11] Chan, S., Govindan, M., Pichard, J. Y., Takach, G. S., and Wright, B. (1995). *Information technology division: EDI management, and audit issues,* p. 2. New York: American Institute of Certified Public Accountants (AICPA).

[12] Chan, S., Govindan, M., Pichard, J. Y., Takach, G. S., and Wright, B. (1995). *Information technology division: EDI management, and audit issues,* pp. 7–9. New York: American Institute of Certified Public Accountants (AICPA).

[13] Chan, S., Govindan, M., Pichard, J. Y., Takach, G. S., and Wright, B. (1995). *Information technology division: EDI management, and audit issues,* pp. 22–28. New York: American Institute of Certified Public Accountants (AICPA).

[14] Comaford, C. (October 14, 1996). Taking care of business the Net way: Electronic data interchange. *PC Week,* Vol. 13, No. 41, 69.

[15] Davey, T. (September 22, 1997). They are still sold on EDI. *InformationWeek,* No. 649, 153–157.

[16] Dearing, B. (November 1995). How EDI is driving VAN growth in Europe: Electronic data interchange and value-added network operators: Industry trend or event. *Telecommunications,* Vol. 29, No. 11, 62.

[17] Hansen, B. (January 1996). Electronic data interchange: Exploring the benefits of full-service EDI networks. *Healthcare Financial Management,* Vol. 50, No. 1, 64–66.

[18] Joseph, G. W., and Engle, T. J. (July 1996). Controlling an EDI environment: Electronic data interchange. *Journal of Systems Management,* Vol. 47, No. 4, 42.

[19] Jilovec, N. (August 29, 1997). Call centers using EDI, CTI, imaging and workflow. *Midrange Systems,* Vol. 10, No. 13, 33.

[20] Kerstetter, J. (June 24, 1996). Livermore labs, banks of America debut secure EDI; Electronic Data Interchange; pilot project almost complete; technology information. *PC Week,* Vol. 13, No. 25, 10.

[21] Kumar, R., and Crook, C. W. (March 1996). Educating senior management on the strategic benefits of electronic data interchange. *Journal of Systems Management,* Vol. 47, No. 2, 42.

[22] Lankford, W. M., and Riggs, W. E. (March 1996). Electronic data interchange: Where are we today? *Journal of Systems Management,* Vol. 47, No. 2, 58.

[23] Lummus, R. R. (May 1997). The evolution to electronic data interchange; Are there benefits at all stages of implementation? *Hospital Material Management Quarterly,* Vol. 18, No. 4, 79–83.

[24] Mahabharat, C. T. (September 10, 1997). India-exporters body sets up EDI service center. *Newsbytes.*

[25] Montana, J. (July 1996). Legal issues in EDI; Electronic data interchanges; Legal Issues. *Records Management Quarterly,* Vol. 30, No. 3, 39.

[26] Olsen, F. (August 12, 1996). Electronic data interchange hits a home run; At the Veterans Affairs Department and the Treasury; Government Activity. *Government Computer News,* Vol. 15, No. 20, 1.

[27] Puttre, J. (August 1997). Can Internet standards bring EDI to everyone? Electronic Data Interchange. *Business Communication Review,* Vol. 27, No. 8, 23.

[28] Thierauf, R. J. (1990). *Electronic data interchange in finance and accounting,* pp. 12–16. Westport, Connecticut: Quorum Books.

[29] Thierauf, R. J. (1990). *Electronic data interchange in finance and accounting,* p. 63. Connecticut: Quorum Books.

[30] Tucker, M. J. (April 1997). EDI and the Net: A profitable partnering; electronic data interchange; Includes related article on EDI's detractors; Internet/Web/Online Service Information. *Datamation,* Vol. 43, No. 4, 62.

[31] Whipple, L. C. (June 1997). Electronic data interchange: Making it happen; Discover what EDI is, and what it takes to implement it in your business. *Database Web Advisor,* 48.

[32] Wilde, C. (March 17, 1997). New life for EDI: The Internet may help electronic data interchange finally meet expectations. *InformationWeek.*

Chapter 13

Decision Support and Executive Information Systems

Learning Objectives

After studying this chapter, you should be able to:

- Define a decision support system.
- Elaborate on the costs and benefits of decision support systems.
- Explain the three technologies of a decision support system.
- Introduce the major players in the decision support systems environment.
- Explain the components of a decision support system.
- Highlight some of the applications of the DSS and guidelines for building these systems.
- Define an executive information system.
- Introduce guidelines for successful executive information systems design.
- Discuss successful applications of executive information systems.
- Discuss executive information systems tools and packages.

13-1 INTRODUCTION

This chapter explains decision support and executive information systems in detail. The chapter reviews decision support systems (DSS) taxonomy, and it discusses costs and benefits of a DSS, major players in the DSS environment, and the components of a DSS. We examine three important technologies in the DSS environment as well as several applications of the DSS in functional areas and guidelines for building a DSS. The later part of the chapter introduces executive information systems (EISs) as growing applications of DSSs. The chapter introduces several real-life applications of EISs and concludes with the packages and tools used in the EIS environment.

13-2 WHAT IS A DECISION SUPPORT SYSTEM (DSS)?

For the purposes of this book we define a DSS as [7]:

> A decision support system is an interactive, computer-based information system consisting of hardware, software, data (internal and external), models (mathematical and statistical), and the human element that is designed to assist any decision maker at any organizational level. However, the emphasis is on semistructured and unstructured tasks.

This simple definition underscores several requirements for a DSS.

- A DSS is interactive.
- A DSS requires hardware.
- A DSS requires software.
- A DSS requires data (internal and external).
- A DSS requires models (mathematical and statistical).
- A DSS requires human elements (designers, programmers, and users).
- A DSS is designed to support decision making.
- A DSS should help decision makers at all organizational levels.
- A DSS emphasizes semistructured and unstructured tasks.

Table 13-1

Key Characteristics of DSSs Compared with MISs

Emphasis on semistructured and unstructured decisions versus structured decisions

Emphasis on the present and future versus the past

Emphasis on planning versus control

Emphasis on data and models versus data only

Emphasis on active involvement of the users in all phases of design and utilization

Emphasis on internal and external data usage versus internal data usage

Emphasis on the overall efficiency and effectiveness versus on efficiency only

Decision support systems differ from traditional electronic data processing and management information systems in many ways. For example, Keen and Scott Morton address the distinction between EDP/MIS and a DSS. They describe a DSS as the use of computers to [14]:

- Assist the manager in his/her decision making process for semi-structured tasks;
- Support, rather than replace, managerial judgment;
- Improve the effectiveness of decision making rather than its efficiency.

They describe the characteristics of MISs somewhat differently:

- Efficiency through cost reduction is the key point.
- The emphasis is on structured tasks.
- Data storage, access and report generation are the major processing tasks.

In comparing EDP, MISs, and DSSs one can draw some conclusions regarding their specific differences. Table 13-1 identifies some of the key factors that differentiate DSSs from the other systems. However, you should remember that a DSS is not a disjointed technology. It shares a number of common technologies. One can also say that a DSS is a natural progression or expansion of EDP and MISs.

13-3 DSS TAXONOMY

Steven L. Alter surveyed 56 systems with DSS characteristics. According to their generic operations, he divided them into a 7-category taxonomy [1]:

1. File drawer systems
2. Data analysis systems
3. Analysis information systems

4. Accounting models
5. Representational models
6. Optimization models
7. Suggestion models

He further divided them into two groups: data-oriented systems (the first three) and model-oriented (the last four) systems. DSS software (or generators), commercially available on the market, offer capabilities based on this taxonomy. In the microcomputer environment Microsoft Excel is an example of a modeling software and Microsoft Access is an example of data-oriented software.

The major distinction dividing the two groups (e.g., data-oriented versus model-oriented) is the utilization of modeling analysis by the second group and pure data analysis by the first group. To illustrate the differences consider Tely-Tak, a manufacturer of electronic devices. Tely-Tak has collected the sales data for the past 18 months from corporate headquarters. Using data-oriented analysis we can organize this data based on sales regions (e.g., which region has generated the highest sales, which region has generated the lowest sales) or we can organize it based on the performance of different products (e.g., which product has generated the highest total sales, which product has generated the lowest total sales). Up to this point all we have done is the pure manipulation of data. By looking at these data as they are you cannot say anything about the future. You cannot also establish any possible relationship among these data items.

Now, let us say we create regression model using sales during the past 18 months in order to generate a sales forecast for the next period. In this case we can say we have performed a modeling analysis. By looking at the outcome of this regression model, with relative confidence you can plan for the next period budget based on the results of the forecasting model. For example, you may have to hire new salespeople or you may have to order more raw materials based on this modeling analysis.

Regardless of the type of analysis performed, the objective is providing managerial support for decision making. The findings from this 56-system study show that applications are being developed and used to support decision makers for making, justifying, and implementing decisions, rather than to replace the decision maker. In other words, people in a growing number of organizations are using DSSs to improve their managerial effectiveness. The comprehensive study conducted by Eom and colleagues introduces numerous recent applications of DSSs [9].

13-4 COSTS AND BENEFITS OF DSSs

The costs and benefits of DSSs are difficult to assess, since these systems are aimed at effectiveness rather than efficiency and because it is said to facilitate, but not directly cause improvements. How does one assign monetary values to facilitating interpersonal communication, or expediting and improving problem-solving activities, or receiving information in 15 minutes as opposed to 2 hours?

Peter G. Keen [13] conducted an interesting study of a number of organizations regarding their DSS use. He concluded that the decision to build a DSS appears to be based on value, rather than cost. He outlined the benefits of a DSS as follows:

1. An increase in the number of alternatives examined.
2. A better understanding of the business.
3. Fast response to unexpected situations.
4. The ability to carry out ad hoc analysis.
5. New insights and learning.
6. Improved communication.
7. Improved control.
8. Cost savings.
9. Better decisions.
10. More effective teamwork.
11. Time savings.
12. Making better use of data resources.

As this study indicates, few of the benefits generated by a DSS are tangible ones. The majority of these benefits is intangible and are difficult to assess.

The intangible benefits generated by a DSS can be quantified. However, this quantification may be subjective and different individuals may come up with different figures. For example, the opportunity cost of wasting 2 hours of a manager's time can be measured and transferred into monetary values—the 2 hours spent by a manager looking for information that could have been made readily available by a DSS. A decision maker could have spent this time in a more productive session to make more effective decisions. A less frustrated manager is easier to work for and more productive.

The fact that a DSS increases communication and interaction between clients and organizations, between organizations and employees, and among employees is also a benefit worth mentioning [1]. A DSS can, and is, facilitating the way in which a decision maker views herself, her job, and the way she spends time. In fact, improving communication and expediting learning are among the objectives of a DSS.

A DSS is said to have achieved its goals if employees have found it useful in doing their jobs. Some DSSs have had definite clerical savings while others have caused significant improvements in the decision-making process.

Overall, it seems that the majority of DSSs can be developed from the resources already available in the organization. One may assume that the cost of developing a DSS compared to the benefits generated by these systems is minimal.

13-5 DSS CAPABILITIES

In recent years, DSSs have appeared in a variety of disciplines. These applications can be categorized under the following major functions:

1. *What-if analysis.* Many analyses can be performed using this approach. The effect of a change in one variable over the entire system can be easily illustrated. If, for example, labor costs increase by 4%, what is going to happen to the final cost of a chair? Or if the advertising budget increases by 2%, what is the impact on total sales?

2. *Goal-seeking.* This capability is the reverse of what-if analysis. As an example, you may ask: How much should you charge for a particular unit in order to generate $200,000 profit? Or, How much should you advertise in order to generate $50,000,000 total sales?

3. *Sensitivity analysis.* Using this feature will enable you to perform analysis applying different variables. For example, what is the maximum price that you should pay for raw material and still make a profit, or how much overtime can you pay and still be cost-effective.

4. *Exception reporting analysis.* This feature monitors the performance of variables that are outside of a predefined range. It keys in on the region that generated the highest total sales or the production center that spent more than the preestablished budget.

These are only some of the capabilities of a typical DSS. There are many more analyses and capabilities available, such as graphical analysis, forecasting, simulation, statistical analysis, and modeling analysis.

13-6 THREE LEVELS OF DSS TECHNOLOGY

In the DSS environment there are three levels of technology that must be understood by both DSS users and designers. These include specific DSSs (SDSSs), DSS generators (DSSGs), and DSS tools (DSSTs) [18]. The following is a brief explanation of each technology.

A **specific DSS** is a combination of hardware and software that is used to assist a decision maker with a specific task. This capability may be utilized for any task at any level of the organization. There are many of these systems that have been successfully utilized for many years. These systems are used to support decision makers in a variety of settings. In a typical business organization, these systems may be designed in different functional areas. For example, a SDSS for a manufacturing department assists in manufacturing decisions. This system may provide timely information on different aspects of a manufacturing environment such as production and distribution decisions. A SDSS may provide online sales forecast for a marketing department. A SDSS for a finance department may assist the portfolio analyst with information to minimize the risk of investment by monitoring and providing timely information on stocks, bonds and different financial activities.

DSS generators are a combination of hardware and software used as a package to develop specific DSSs. These generators already include most of the capabilities needed by a specific DSS. A typical DSS generator includes capabilities such as a database management system (DBMS), graphics, built-in functions (predefined formulas), modeling analysis, statistical analysis, optimization, and simulation models. These generators include macro programming, which is more powerful than using high-level languages such as C, FORTRAN, and COBOL. DSS generators continue to gain popularity. Interactive Financial Planning System (IFPS) by Comshare and Express by Information Resource, Inc., are two examples of these generators. Using these generators, many different specific DSS in the areas of finance, marketing, and personnel can be developed.

In the microcomputer environment, spreadsheet programs such as Microsoft Excel, Lotus 1-2-3, and Quattro Pro are becoming powerful generators. The basic requirements for the construction of small-scale specific DSSs are readily available in these packages.

For example, Microsoft Excel includes what-if features, several hundred built-in functions, a goal-seeking option, a scenario manager, and a solver option. Using the *Data Table* option, you can monitor the effect of a change of one or two variables over the entire system. You can construct sophisticated models and then perform various analyses using one or two variables. The *built-in functions* include several categories such as financial, statistical, mathematical, logical, and table search. Even if the desired function is not available among the built-in list, you can develop it yourself. The *macro capabilities* of Excel provide an easy-to-use and a comprehensive programming environment. Programming or macro programming in spreadsheet programs is much easier than using-high level languages. The major reason is that by using macro programming, you can achieve the same task as you do using a high level language with much less code. The *Goal Seek* option allows you to build a model, then adjust the value in a specified cell until a formula dependent on that cell reaches the value you specify. For example, you may develop a sales-forecasting model based on the amount of advertising budget. If you establish a goal for the sales level, then you can manipulate the advertising amount in order to achieve the preestablished sales goal. The *Scenario Manager* feature allows you to create and save different sets of data as separate scenario. You can then use these scenarios to view multiple outcomes based on different assumptions. You can also create a separate summary report that shows the changing cell values and the resulting cell values for each scenario. The *Solver* option allows you to define the problem you want to solve. Using the Solver option, you can solve complex problems by creating a model with multiple

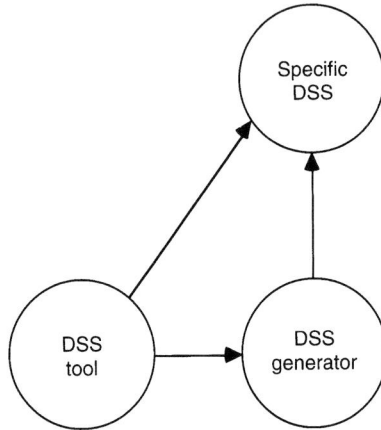

Figure 13-1   Three technologies of DSSs.

adjustable cells. You can impose constraints on your problem that must be satisfied before a solution is reached. The Solver feature allows you to solve optimization type problems (for example, maximizing the profit or minimizing the cost).

DSS tools are computer hardware or software used to develop either a specific DSS or a DSS generator. For example, either a graphics package or COBOL may serve as a DSS tool. A DSS tool deals with part of the DSS, but not all of it. Development of specific DSSs from a DSS generator is faster, and it may be more economical than the development of these systems from DSS tools.

Both hardware and software technology have improved continuously. For example, computer languages have gone through several generations. From machine language to assembly, to high-level languages, to fourth-generation languages, and finally the developers are working on natural language-processing systems. Another example of such improvement is the enhancement of operating systems for microcomputers. Very soon these operating systems should simulate the same level of sophistication first found in larger computers. Hardware technology has improved in parallel with the software technology. For example, graphic terminals, laser printers, and sophisticated modems all are examples of DSS tools. Figure 13-1 illustrates these three technologies of DSSs and their relationships.

13-7 DIFFERENT PLAYERS IN THE DSS ENVIRONMENT

To design, implement, and utilize a DSS, several different groups of individuals must be involved. We recognize three roles for the design, implementation, and utilization of a DSS. These roles are:

- User
- Designer
- Intermediary

The **user** is the individual for whom the DSS is designed. This may be an individual, a department, or an organizational unit. A specific DSS must address and incorporate the specific requirements of the user into its operation. The success and failure of the system are heavily dependent on the user(s).

The **designer** may include two different groups: the managerial designer and the technical designer. A *managerial designer* is the individual(s) who defines the management issues related to DSS design and utilization. This role is very similar to the role of an architect in building a house. The architect provides the general design of a house. Without getting into specifics, he highlights the important aspects of the house. In a DSS environment, this individual may be the MIS specialist in the organization, the decision maker, or anyone else who can define the requirements of the DSS in question. For example, to develop an online forecasting DSS some of the managerial issues may include:

- What data must be collected?
- From what source must the data be gathered?
- How recent must the collected data be?
- How must the data be organized?
- How must the data be updated?
- What should be the balance between aggregated (lump sum) and desegregated (itemized) data?

The *technical designer* usually is not concerned with the issues specified under the managerial designer's domain. Instead, her role is very similar to the role of a construction engineer charged with the task of building a house. The technical designer is concerned with the technical issues related to the DSS design and use. Some of the questions addressed by a technical designer would be:

- How must the data be stored?
- What type of file structure must be implemented (sequential, random or indexed sequential)?
- What type of user access must be implemented?
- What type of response time is required?
- How must the security measures be installed?

The computer specialist or a consultant from outside the company may occupy this role. The technical designer may incorporate these facilities into a specific DSS by using a DSS generator, DSS tools, or by inventing new capabilities from scratch.

An **intermediary** is the liaison between the user and the DSS. This individual(s) may play different roles. For example, during the design phase for the above-cited forecasting DSS, the intermediary may explain the user's needs to the managerial designer or technical designer of the system. This same individual, at a later date, may explain the provided output to the user. This individual may explain the output of the regression analysis provided by the forecasting DSS mentioned earlier. He may tell the user about the assumptions underlying the model, the limitations, and the strengths. He may also suggest new or different applications of the system. Figure 13-2 graphically illustrates these roles in a DSS environment.

13-8 COMPONENTS OF A DSS

A DSS includes three major components: a database, a model base, and dialog management [18]. The **database** component includes both internal and external data. Internal data are either transaction data or data collected internally from other subsystems in the organization. External data may come from various sources. They may come from competitors, the government, or the financial community. Associated with the database is software called a database management system (DBMS). This software creates, modifies, and maintains the database as required by the user. The database component enables a DSS to perform any type of data analysis operation. For a detailed discussion of database and database management systems, see Chapter 3.

The **model base** component includes a series of mathematical and statistical models. These models, in conjunction with the database, enable a DSS to perform various types of modeling analyses. Associated with the model base is software called a model base management system (MBMS), which performs similar task to DBMS in accessing, maintaining, and updating the models in the mode base. Tables 13-2 and 13-3 [4] provide listings of some of the popular models used in DSS environment.

Finally, the **dialog management** component is the user/system interface. This component provides a user with different interface procedures that enable her to access the DSS. This component, from the user's point of view, is probably the most important part. It is imperative that this component be as flexible and as user friendly as possible. Since the majority of DSS users are discretionary in their usage, user-friendliness is even more important consideration in such a situation.

Figure 13-3 illustrates a graphical model for DSS within the organization. As this figure illustrates, a DSS user who may occupy a position in any one of the three management levels of the organization (operational, tactical, or strategic) may be faced with the need to make a decision. The decision process may include the three stages of intelligence (problem definition), design (generation of alternatives), and choice (selection of the best alternative). The user, through the dialog component, may query the database, model base, or both for decision help.

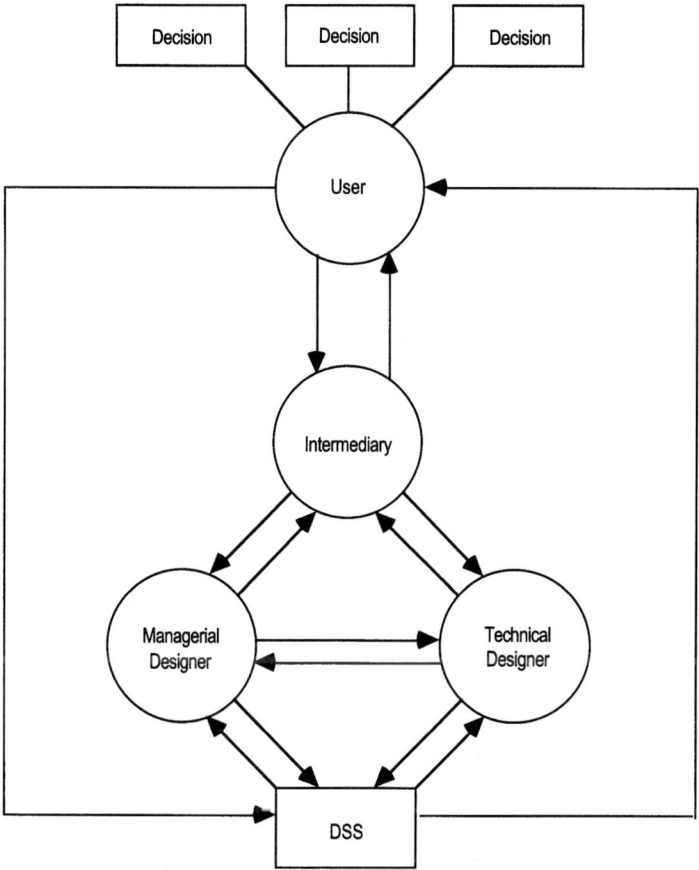

Figure 13-2 Different roles in the DSS environment.

Table 13-2

Examples of Optimization Models

Linear optimization models

    Allocation models
    Assignment models
    Transportation models
    Network models (PERT, CPM, MOST, and LOB)

Inventory optimization models (EOQ and EMQ)

    Portfolio optimization models

Dynamic programming optimization models

Nonlinear optimization models

Table 13-3

Examples of Nonoptimization Models

Forecasting models
   Quantitative (moving average and exponential smoothing)
   Qualitative (delphi and analogy)
Regression models
   Simple linear regression
   Multiple linear regression
Decision tree models
Simulation models

13-9 BUILDING AN EFFECTIVE DSS

Decision support systems can be developed using the methodology introduced in Chapter 9. However, due to the rapid changes in the environment of a DSS, prototyping plays an important role. A sample prototype should always be developed and shown to the user. Based on this sample prototype, the final system should be constructed. Table 13-4 provides guidelines for effective DSS design.

13-10 DSSs IN ACTION

There are numerous real-life applications of DSSs reported in the information systems literature. The recent study conducted by Eom and colleagues [9] identified more than 270 applications of DSSs in various disciplines. Table 13-5 lists several functional areas that have successfully used DSS applications. Table 13-6 lists several companies that are using DSSs.

13-11 DEFINING EXECUTIVE INFORMATION SYSTEMS (EISs)

Executive information systems (EISs), executive support systems (ESSs) or executive management systems (EMSs) are a branch of DSSs that are gaining in popularity. Although some authors have tried to differentiate these various applications, in this text we use them interchangeably and refer to all of them as EISs. For the purpose of this text we define an EIS as:

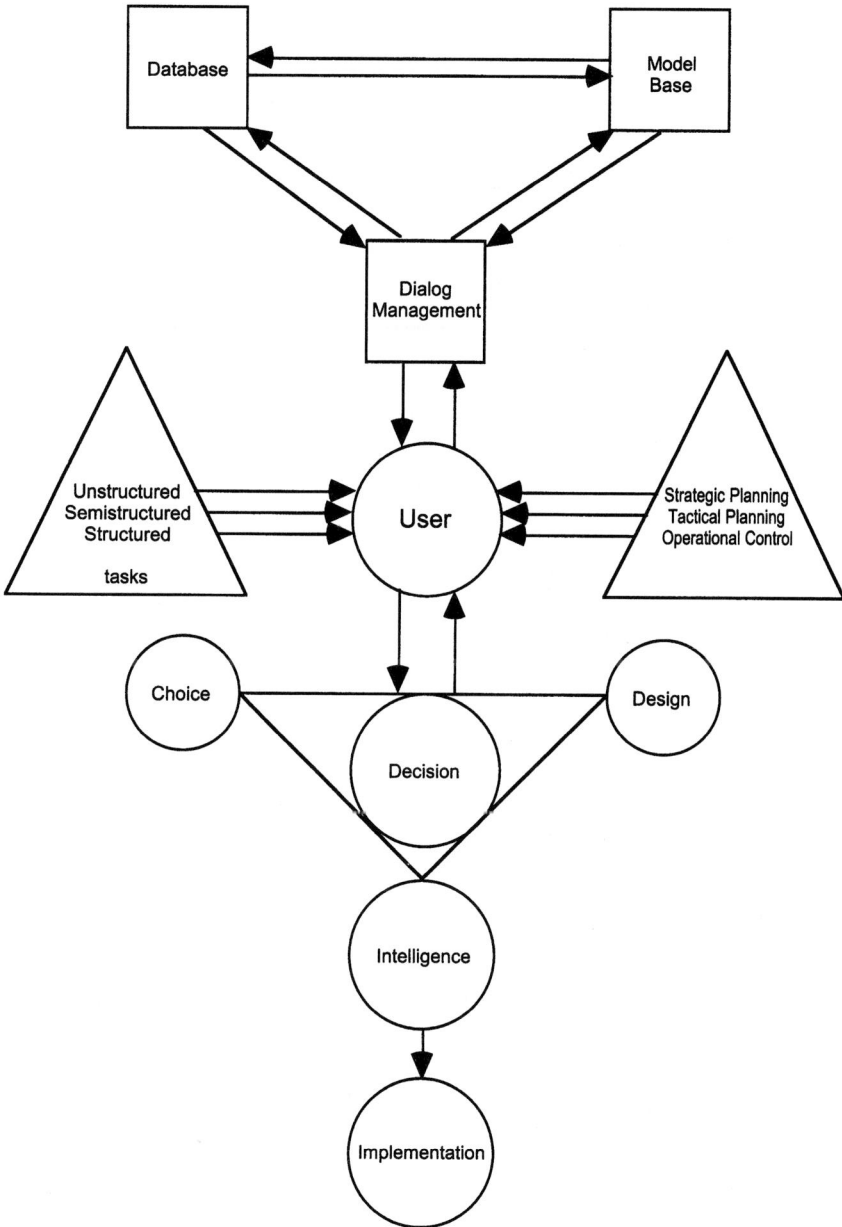

Figure 13-3 DSSs in the organization.

Table 13-4

Guidelines for Effective DSS Design

Clearly define the objectives and the benefits of the system

Identify the information needs of a decision maker

Involve the top management and the user

Form a task force

Design a prototype

Provide a user-friendly interface

Perform evaluation

Table 13-5

**Functional Areas Using
DSS Applications**

Accounting and budgeting

Banking

Facility planning

Finance and investment

Health care management

Human resource management

Insurance

Manufacturing

Marketing

Office automation

Purchasing

Sales

Strategic planning

An interactive, computer-based information system that provides executives with easy
access to internal and external data and information, with drill-down capability related
to the critical success factors for running current and future business operations.

The diagram presented in Figure 13-4 illustrates the key features of an EIS. Let's
briefly explain these important features:

Ease of use plays an important role for the success of an EIS. Since the
majority of EIS users are not computer-trained personnel, simplicity of the system
is crucial. By using various types of user/system interfaces, the designer(s) of
the EIS provide a variety of options for using the system. Graphical user inter-

Table 13-6

**Selected Organizations That Are
Using DSS Applications**

American Airlines

American Petrofina

Central and Southwest Corporation

Champion Petroleum

First United Bankcorporation

FritoLay, Inc.

General Dynamics

Gifford-Hill and Company

Lear Petroleum

Mercantile Texas Corporation

National Gypsum

Southern Railway

Texas-New Mexico Power

Texas Oil and Gas Corporation

Texas Utilities Company

The LTV Corporation

The Western Company

Zale Corporation

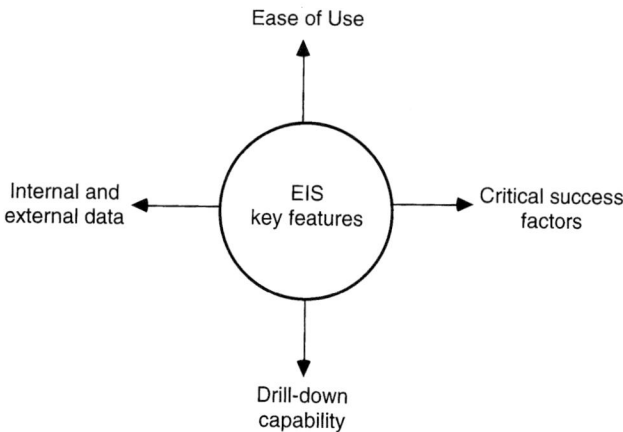

Figure 13-4   EIS key features.

faces (GUIs) have been well received by typical users. Pull-down menus, context-sensitive help, multimedia, virtual reality, and possibly voice input/output can further enhance the ease of use of an EIS.

Access to both internal and external data is a critical consideration for an EIS. To be able to spot trends, and to forecast and analyze various scenarios an EIS should have access to both types of data. As discussed in Chapter 3, external data may come from a variety of sources such as competitors, and government and financial communities. Internal data comes from within the organization itself. The challenge that remains is the collection and proper manipulation of the external data.

Critical success factors are those issues that make or break a business. Different organizations, divisions, and individuals have different types of critical success factors. For example, in a financial institution, the interest rate may be considered the critical success factor. For a car manufacturer, the location of a dealership and style may be considered critical success factors. An EIS should be designed in order to be able to provide related information for the critical success factors of the organization, division, or individual.

The **drill-down capability** of an EIS provides access to multilayer information as well as data (drill-down) on request. For example, at the first level an EIS may report the performance of a company in eight sales regions. In the next layer, a marketing executive may be interested in the northwest region, and this analysis can be further broken down. By doing these types of analyses, an executive is able to zero in on a particular situation and then make an appropriate decision.

To ascertain the features presented in Figure 13-4, the following are some of the important characteristics of an EIS [8,15,20]:

- They are tailored to meet executives' information needs.
- They have the ability to extract, compress, filter, and track critical data.
- They have the capability to provide on-line status access, trend analysis, and exception reporting.
- They can access and integrate a broad range of internal and external data.
- They are user-friendly, and require minimal or no training to use.
- They are used directly by executives without the assistance of intermediaries.
- They provide graphical, tabular, and/or textual information.
- They discover and report relationships among data items.
- They provide statistical-analysis techniques for summarizing and structuring data.
- They perform data retrieval across on a wide range of platforms and data formats.
- They analyze data in a variety of methods.
- They create ad hoc reports.

- They contain customized application-development tools to build an application that automatically performs routine tasks.
- They support electronic communications (e-mail, voice mail, and computer conferencing).
- They include organizing tools such as calendars, automated rolodexes, and tickle files.

In the remaining part of the chapter, we further examine these features and characteristics of EISs.

13-12 A CONCEPTUAL MODEL FOR AN EIS

Executive information systems are popular today because they provide the most crucial information in a usable format. How information relates to the decision maker is very important. Corporate data comes in a number of formats. It can be internal or external data, and it can also be "hard" or "soft" data. *Internal data* is mostly provided by a corporate database. Internal information can also come from operational data, reports and documents, and directly from corporate personnel. *External data* might come from external databases, news services, surveys from customers, information from vendors, trade services, surveys from competitors, or information from vendors. Data from these two sources can be "hard" data, such as database information, or it can be "soft" data, such as rumors, opinions, ideas, or predictions.

To effectively collect and manipulate both internal and external data and to provide critical information in an easy to follow format an EIS may utilize some or all of the following technologies:

- Graphical user interfaces
- Touch-sensitive screens
- Voice input
- Color screens and displays
- Voice and electronic mail
- Local area networks
- Wide area networks
- Metropolitan area networks
- Message distribution systems
- Teleconferencing
- Spreadsheets
- Facsimile and image-transmission systems
- Laptop, notebooks, and hand-held computers

The dialog between the executive and the EIS is one of the most critical elements of a successful EIS. Whether it is through the use of touch-sensitive

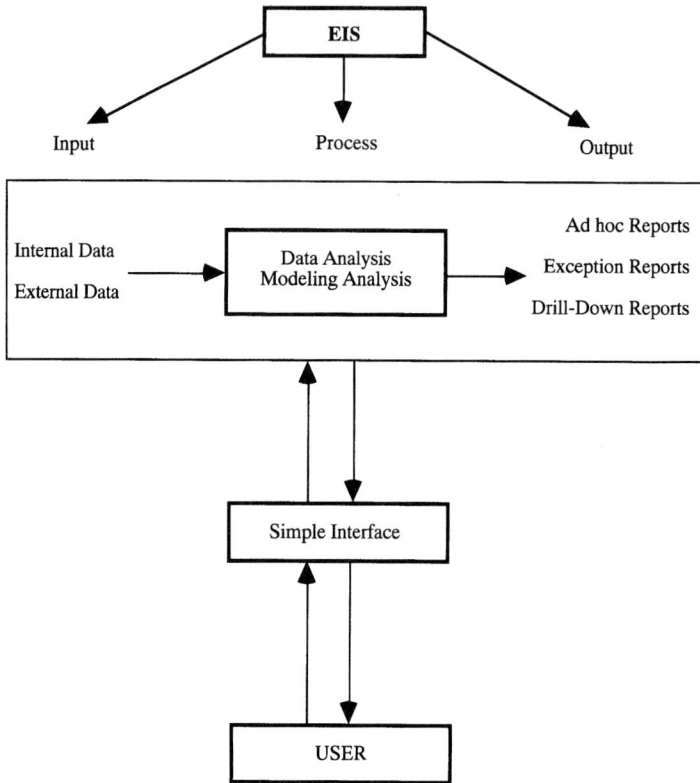

Figure 13-5   A conceptual model for an EIS.

screens or light pens, simplicity of use and access is essential. The diagram presented in Figure 13-5 illustrates a conceptual model for an EIS.

13-13 WHY DO EXECUTIVES NEED AN EIS?

There are many good reasons for executives to use an EIS. An EIS puts a full array of powerful analytical and business decision-making tools at their fingertips. An EIS provides data analysis and graphical presentation functions that enable them to make critical decisions quickly using relevant information. In addition, by using an EIS, executives can share information with others more quickly and easily. All of these features can dramatically increase the efficiency and effectiveness of the decision-making process. This is how:

1. An EIS increases an executive's productivity. This is possible by providing easy access to relevant information in a timely manner.
2. An EIS provides all critical information at the executive's desktop. Information can be transformed to various formats in order to analyze different business scenarios. This will help an executive to see the effect of certain decisions on the organization.
3. An EIS spots trends and reports exception-type situations. For example, from her desktop, an executive can easily get the information on profitability and production costs at a particular manufacturing plant, and she can determine whether closing the plant is more beneficial for the corporation than keeping it open because of low profitability.

A study conducted by Hugh Watson and Kelly Rainer [20] identified a number of specific factors that lead to EIS development. These factors are listed below:

- A need for timely information
- A need for improved communication
- A need for access to operational data
- A need for rapid status updates on different business units
- A need for increased effectiveness
- A need to identify historical trends
- A need for increased efficiency
- A need for access to corporate (internal) databases
- A need for more accurate information
- A need for competing in an increasingly competitive environment
- A need for facing a rapidly changing external environment
- A need to be more proactive in dealing with the external environment
- A need to access external databases
- A need for facing an increasing government regulation

13-14 AVOIDING FAILURE IN EIS DESIGN AND UTILIZATION

Like other management support systems, effective EIS design and implementation require the support of top management, active user involvement, and an appropriate technology. Watson and Satzinger identified several specific factors that lead to failure of an EIS. Among these factors are the following [19]:

1. *Executives themselves.* Many of today's senior executives missed the computer revolution. They may feel uncomfortable using computers. Ongoing education and increasing computer awareness should resolve this issue.

2. *The nature of executive work.* Executives' busy schedules and travel requirements are not amenable to long training sessions, do not permit much uninterrupted time for system use, and do not allow a system to be employed on a daily basis. The result is that senior executives are unlikely to employ systems that require considerable training and regular use to be learned and remembered. A user-friendly interface should encourage executives to use the EIS more extensively.

3. *The nature of provided information.* Many EISs have contained little information of value to senior executives, which is related to a lack of understanding of executive's work. Systems designers who often possessed excellent technical knowledge but little business or "big picture" knowledge have exacerbated this problem. This is why we have recommended all along the use of a task force design team that improves the chances of success by delivering systems that are tailored to the specific needs of the decision maker. The bottom line is that in order to develop a successful EIS, it is necessary to be aware of all functions that are to be touched by the EIS and to be sensitive to the executives' decision-making requirements. An EIS can then be developed that allows information to flow cross-functionally to improve decision making. In order to solve this problem, senior management should use its leadership and influence to achieve this type of cross-functional design. They should involve all departments in the design process, not just the department that the system is being designed for.

Another common mistake is that in acquiring information requirements the interviews of executives are done on an individual basis instead of as a group. This method of interviewing places the executive in a limited position. Having an executive singled out impedes his or her ability to properly react to any inquiries being made. This is why joint application design (JAD) has been recommended. A significant advantage of using JAD is that different functional areas of corporations have different agendas when it comes to creating a new system. Using JAD, an organization can be assured that all executives representing various departments are together in group interviews. This will help to avoid collecting narrow and one-dimensional information requirements [23].

Another common mistake in defining the requirements is that designers usually ask the wrong question such as: What information do you need from the new system? System analysts should not assume that managers know exactly what they need. Instead of being an order taker, the analyst should be a problem solver, asking indirect questions that will help lead to proper information requirement identification. The design team should use a combination of top-down and bottom-up techniques in order to identify the information needs of executives. Examples of such questions are:

- What are the major problems encountered in accomplishing the purposes of the organizational unit that you manage?
- What are good solutions to those problems?

- How can information play a role in any of those solutions?
- What are the major decisions associated with your management responsibilities?

Questions such as these can help in determining what information will be required to ensure that the executives' information needs are met.

Another mistake in information requirement determination is that executives are not permitted to visualize their ideas or plans. This is possible through a trial-and-error type of modeling. With prototyping, specific screens and reports can be produced for management to be examined. Trial and error are important in determining information requirements. Using readily available software and hardware, a prototype of a new system can usually be constructed in a short period and presented to the executive decision makers for their reactions [23].

Glover and colleagues present the results of a detailed study that clearly highlights characteristics of failed EISs. The results of this study are shown in Table 13-7 [11].

Table 13-7
Characteristics of Failed EISs

Corporate culture not ready

Data integrity in doubt

Executives lost interest

Failed to meet objectives

Inability to define information requirements

Inadequate technology

Information requirements too detailed

Insufficient depth of information

Insufficient resources

Lack of sponsorship

Management not committed

Not cost-justified

Not linked to critical success factors

Organizational resistance

Perceived as unimportant

Sponsor turnover

Too complicated

Too much time to develop applications

Unknown objectives

Vendor support discontinued

13-15 GUIDELINES FOR EFFECTIVE EIS DESIGN

Like other management support systems, the goals and objectives of the system should be clearly defined prior to the design of an EIS. After defining the objectives of the system, methodologies similar to the ones discussed in Chapter 9 can be followed. Since the purpose and users of EISs are somewhat different than other computer-based information systems, we summarize the important factors for designing an EIS in Table 13-8 [2,19,21]. Following are brief descriptions of the factors in Table 13-8.

1. *Come from the top.* Support and commitment must come from the top. Without a full commitment from top management, do not build the system because the chances of failure are high.

2. *Clearly define the objectives and the benefits of an EIS.* Since the majority of the benefits of an EIS are intangible, this step is a challenging task. The costs are in hard dollars, while the benefits are qualitative. The design team should spend enough time to identify all the costs and benefits and present a convincing scenario to top management.

3. *Identify the information needs of an executive.* The decision-making process of executives should be examined to find out what kinds of decisions they are making. What are the critical successes factors in meeting those goals or objectives?

4. *Keep the communication line open.* Make sure the communication line is open at all times between developers, executives, and the entire design team who directly and/or indirectly will be the users of the system.

5. *Hide the complexity.* Use common language when talking with executives. Avoid using technical and MIS gorgons. There is no need to explain the technol-

Table 13-8

Guidelines for Effective EIS Design

Come from the top
Clearly define the objectives and the benefits of the system
Identify the information needs of an executive
Keep the communication line open
Hide the complexity
Keep the interface simple
Keep a similar look and feel concept
Design a flexible system
Provide a fast response time

ogies used in the EIS. Executives may lose interest if they perceive the system as too technical. Remember that typical executives are not interested in a particular platform or software. All they are interested in is getting the needed information in the simplest terms and format.

6. *Keep the interface simple.* The system must be simple and intuitive otherwise it would be too difficult for executives to learn and use. Keep in mind that an executive should be able to use an EIS with no training or with a short training session. To a typical executive, the interface is the system. The ease of use of this component is the make-or-break determinant of success or failure.

7. *Keep a similar look and feel concept.* Developers should design standard layouts, formats, and colors through all windows, menus, and dialog boxes. These standards offer many advantages such as a consistency of look and feel. Also, the gained knowledge and training can be transferred to other systems. The Windows environment has achieved this goal to a certain degree.

8. *Design a flexible system.* Almost all aspects of an EIS, including the user interface, change in time. It is quite possible that the system will require some changes a few months after its implementation because of the dynamic business environment, as well as changes in technologies. A flexible system will be able to augment changes in a short time period.

9. *Provide a fast response time.* EIS developers must continually monitor the response time of the system. Executives are intolerant of a slow response time. When the system function takes more than a few seconds, a message should always provide feedback that the system is processing their request.

13-16 EISs IN ACTION

There are numerous companies who have been successfully using EISs. The following is a list of some of these companies:

- ABC News
- AlliedSignal
- Bristol Meyers
- British Airways
- Chase Manhattan Bank
- Citibank
- Compaq Computer
- DuPont
- Duracell
- General Electric
- General Motors
- Hertz Car Rental Company

- J.C. Penney
- Johnson & Johnson
- Kraft
- Motorola
- Pepsi-Cola International
- Phillips Petroleum
- Polaroid
- Sunbelt Systems Concepts, Inc.
- Texas Instruments
- Washington Hospital
- Xerox

In the following pages we briefly introduce in more detail several successful applications of EISs in the real world. For a detailed coverage consult the provided references.

13-16-1 WASHINGTON HOSPITAL CENTER

Different executives at the Washington, D.C., Hospital Center are currently using an EIS. The president can review patient admissions and discharges on his monitor, along with revenue trends to prepare for meetings. Before having the EIS, the president had to use other methods for retrieving valuable information. Information was accessible, but in order for him to obtain it he had to filter through numerous reports. If some information was missing, he had to have someone produce a report for him that could be quite time consuming, not to mention other hassles. Now the information is downloaded daily from the mainframe.

Besides the president being able to use the system, other executives are starting to realize its capabilities. It was estimated that by the second month of its installation, 30 decision makers were expected to use it. A few months later that number was supposed to reach 150 to 200. Ken Samet, president of the organization stated, "All of our managers need data to make decisions and they need it just as fast as I do" [3, 12].

13-16-2 HERTZ CAR RENTAL COMPANY

It is very important for executives in the car-rental business to have the ability to electronically sift through important information. This information can be about cities, climates, holidays, business cycles, tourist activity, past promotions, and market forecasts that allow a company to make immediate marketing decisions.

This kind of decision making has become a requirement for competing in the car rental business.

In order to have a competitive edge, Hertz has implemented a mainframe-based DSS and an EIS, a PC-based front end to the DSS that gives executives the tools to analyze the massive of demographic data and make real-time marketing decisions.

With this EIS, Hertz' DSS now has a front end in the form of tools that executives use to analyze essential information from all over the nation. This includes internal and external information. These include Hertz's own rental agreements, fleet purchases, and computer reservation system reports on the number of calls made to Hertz's 800 number. It also includes airport reports on comparative revenues for the various car-rental companies stationed there.

One way that Hertz has measured the success of its system is by comparing its operations and level of customer service with its competitors. According to the designer of the system this is due to the fact that their executives can maneuver and refine data to be more meaningful and strategically understandable to them. In addition they have the ability to store needed data on their PCs and to perform all sorts of what-if analyses. According to an executive at Hertz, Scott H. Meadow, using an EIS does not ensure prosperity, but "how you use it" will have an impact [16].

13-16-3 TEXAS INSTRUMENTS

Before Texas Instruments (TI) implemented Lightship, information was spread around in a variety of reports, and it was difficult to anticipate problems. With the EIS, managers and engineers at many levels (e.g., cost center, project and site managers, and chemical and hardware engineers) can control spending on both internal and R&D projects.

The main office used to run a series of damage reports to find out what had gone wrong when costs for the process-automation systems were out of line. Since the reports were run after the fact, it was too late to do anything to fix the problems.

Using a hot spot on the screen (i.e., an area that has been programmed to perform other actions when you click on it), managers can "drill down" (in hypertext fashion) from the project level to actual cost elements and compare budgeted dollars to actual costs as they occur. Thus, they can see not just how much money is left in a certain budget but whether or not the money is going too fast.

TI considered several packages before making its final choice to use the Lightship. Reports that used to take days to compile can be generated in few seconds now. The change from damage reports to damage control that Lightship made possible is one of taking control of your information [15].

13-17 EIS PACKAGES AND TOOLS

EISs are generally designed with two or three components: an administrative module, where data access is managed; a builder module, where a developer sets data mapping and builds a sequence of screens; and a run-time module that the executive or knowledge worker runs. Sometimes the first two components are combined. Data access and consolidations vary, depending on the package. Some EISs provide their own data storage system; some only package the data and route it into a more accessible database, usually on a LAN. Finally, almost all of today's EISs come with a standard GUI, such as Windows, Macintosh, or Presentation Manager.

There are generally seven tasks that managers do for which an EIS will be useful: track, flag exceptions, rank, compare, spot trend, and investigate and explore. Most EIS packages provide tools that perform these tasks. They present summarized and consolidated data in both report and chart format, or they allow sequencing of screens to produce executive slide shows. Locations that users can click on to get more information and other drill-down techniques help users navigate through varying levels of detail.

Exception reporting is another extremely useful technique managers use to flag data that is unusual or out of bounds. Variance reporting is the most common form of exception output. Both unusual and periodic events can be defined to trigger visual cues or activate intelligent agents to perform a specific task. Intelligent agents, as introduced in Chapter 1, are smart programs that can carry out specific and repetitive tasks. They can be programmed to make decisions based on pre-specified conditions. Table 13-9 provides a listing of some of the popular EIS products on the market.

13-17-1 DATA WAREHOUSES AND REPLICATION CAPABILITIES

Client/server packages with intelligent agents can automate processes such as warning a financial analyst when a key ratio has been exceeded or sending e-mail to a purchasing manager when an inventory quantity has been reached. Many organizations are meeting the challenge of providing direct access to corporate data on the mainframe by creating LAN-based data warehouses that contain read-only snapshots of host data that is periodically refreshed. A data warehouse is the physical repository where relational data are organized to provide enterprise-wide useable data in a predefined format. Departmental data warehouses are referred to as data marts. Data mining is a technique for looking for specific but unknown

Table 13-9

Selected EIS Products

Product name	Company name
Acumate Enterprise	Kenan Technologies
Business Intelligent Software	SAS Institute, Inc.
Commander EIS	Comshare, Inc.
Cross Target	Dimensional Insight Inc.
Data Interpretation System (DIS)	Metaphor, Inc.
EIS ToolKit	Microstrategy, Inc.
Essbase	Arbor Software Corporation
Express/EIS	IRI Software
Focus/EIS	Information Builders, Inc.
Forest & Trees	Trinzic Corp.
Holos	Holistic Systems, Inc.
LightShip	Pilot Software, Inc.
Monarch	DataWatch, Inc.
On Track	Hyperion
PowerPlay	Cognos Corp.

information in databases. Data mining techniques reveal information to decision makers that is not easily available. LAN-based data warehouses have the advantage of minimizing network traffic, expensive host CPU time, and security headaches. Vendors offer different versions of data warehouses. Some offer a relational database management system that is optimized for queries rather than data entry. Typical clients are firms that need to analyze large amounts of data, such as retailers and financial institutions.

Replication servers are also becoming more widespread. Replication is related to the notion of data warehousing, but data warehouses usually contain only a subset of the data, while replicas are usually copies of an entire database. Vendors sell replication servers that can keep multiple copies of the database up to date, making it easier for users who may be physically dispersed to get fast, local access to data. Lotus Notes was the first to popularize the concept of replication. Since then replication has become a common feature in the majority of EIS products [22].

13-17-2 EVALUATION CRITERIA

Before selecting an EIS product, a detailed evaluation must be conducted in order to select the right package among the competing products. The following are the factors that must be carefully examined before choosing an EIS product [6,11].

Cost
> Software
> Hardware
> Training
> Consulting fees
> Documentation

Features
> Ease of use
> Drill-down capabilities
> What-if analysis
> Goal-seeking capabilities
> Exception reporting
> Ad hoc inquiry
> Multidimensional analysis
> Display format and quality
> Security
> Data integrity
> File and document security

Vendor
> Number of installations
> Vendor size
> R & D expenditures
> Training
> User groups and support

Additional features
> Optimization techniques
> Regression and trend analysis
> Simulation analysis
> AI and explanation capabilities

SUMMARY

This chapter provided a detail discussion of DSSs and EISs. It presented different characteristics of DSSs, costs and benefits of DSSs, different technologies of DSSs, major players, and various capabilities of DSSs. The chapter introduced DSS applications, selected companies using DSSs, and guidelines for building a successful DSS. The later part of the chapter concentrated on EISs as a growing application. The chapter provided definition of an EIS, reasons for developing an EIS, guidelines for successful development of an EIS, and several real-life applications of an EIS. The chapter concluded with a discussion of EIS tools and packages on the market and selection criteria for EIS products.

REVIEW QUESTIONS

1. What is a DSS?
2. What is an EIS?
3. Mention some of the unique characteristics of DSSs and EISs.
4. Are DSSs really something new? Discuss.
5. Give one example of Alter's taxonomy of DSS applications.
6. What is the major difference between data-oriented and model-oriented DSSs?
7. What are some of the costs and benefits of a typical DSS?
8. What is the difference between what-if analysis and goal seeking in the DSS environment?
9. What is sensitivity analysis?
10. Give an example of each of the three types of analyses.
11. Who are the main players in the DSS environment?
12. What are the three main components of a DSS?
13. What are the three technologies of a DSS?
15. How do you compare an EIS with a DSS?
16. Discuss similarities and differences between EDP, an MIS, a DSS, and an EIS.
17. What are some guidelines for building a successful DSS?
18. What is drill-down capability?
19. What are critical success factors (CSFs)? What are some examples of CSFs in automobile industries?
20. What are some of the sources for external data to be used in an EIS environment?
21. What are some of the components of an EIS?
22. What are some of the factors that mandate the implementation of an EIS in a business organization?
23. Why have some EISs failed and how can you guard against failure?
24. What are some of the guidelines for developing an effective EIS?

25. Why does top management involvement increase the chances for success of an EIS design?
26. Why is the user/system interface component so important for a successful EIS design?
27. What is achieved by the EIS in Washington Hospital? In Hertz Car Rental Company? In Texas Instruments?
28. What are some typical capabilities of an EIS package?
29. What are some of the evaluation criteria for an EIS product?

PROJECTS

1. Identify one example of an EDP, an MIS and a DSS application in a typical college or university. What are the bases of your classification? What are the differences in these three applications as far as the user is concerned?
2. What are some DSS and EIS applications in a typical bank? What can a DSS or an EIS do for a loan officer of a bank? What can a DSS do for a stock analyst?
3. Give an example of how inventory control systems such as those used at grocery stores have evolved from the typical EDP to a MIS system. Explain how this could be taken one step further and evolve into a DSS system.
4. The CEO of a major insurance company needs your advice regarding the acquisition and implementation of an EIS. Where should this executive start? What are some of the costs of this EIS? Who are some of the vendors? What should be done to avoid failure? Discuss.
5. Investigate an organization that you are familiar with that has implemented an EIS. What are some of the tasks performed by the system? What types of interfaces exist for using this system? How was the system developed? Discuss.

KEY TERMS

Database, 376
Decision support systems, 368–379
Dialog management, 376
Drill-down capability, 382
DSS generators, 373–374
DSS tools, 374
Executive information systems, 378–395

Intermediary, 375–376
Managerial designer, 375
Model base, 376
Players in the DSS environment, 374–376
Replication capability, 392–393
Specific DSS, 372–373
Technical designer, 375

REFERENCES

[1] Alter, S. L. (1980). *Decision support systems: Current practice and continuing challenges.* Reading, MA: Addison-Wesley Publishing Company.

[2] Barrow, C. (Spring 1990). Implementing an executive information system: Seven steps for success. *Journal of Information Systems Management,* 41–46.

[3] Bergman, R. (September 20, 1994). From the top down: EIS works for everybody. *Hospital & Health,* 68.

[4] Bidgoli, H. (1998). *Intelligent management support systems.* Westport, CT: Quorum Books.

[5] Bidgoli, H. (1997). *Modern information systems for managers.* San Diego, CA: Academic Press, Inc.

[6] Bidgoli, H. (November 1989). DSS product evaluation: An integrated framework. *Journal of Systems Management,* 27–34.

[7] Bidgoli, H. (1989). Decision support systems: Principles and applications. Minneapolis, MN: West Publishing Company.

[8] Cronk, R. (June 1993). EISs Mind Your Data. *Byte,* 121–128.

[9] Eom, S. B., Lee, S. M., Kim, E. B., and Somarajan, C. (1998). A survey of decision support system application (1988–1994). *Journal of the Operational Research Society,* Vol. 49, No. 2, 109–120.

[10] Frolick, M. N., Parzinger, M. J., Rainer, R. K. Jr., and Narender K. Ramarrapu (Winter 1997). Using EISs for environmental scanning. *Information Systems Management,* 35–40.

[11] Glover, H., *et al.* (Winter 1992). 20 ways to waste an EIS investment. *Information Strategy: The Executive's Journal,* 11–17.

[12] Keegan, A. J., and Baldwin, B. (November 1992). EIS: A better way to view hospital trends. *Healthcare Financial Management,* 38–66.

[13] Keen, P. G. (March 1981). Value analysis: Justifying decision support system. *MIS Quarterly,* Vol. 5, No. 1, 1–15.

[14] Keen, P. G., and Scott-Morton, M. S. (1978). *Decision support systems: An organizational perspective.* Reading, MA: Addison-Wesley Publishing Co.

[15] Kinland, J. (June 1992). EIS moves to the desktop. *Byte,* 206–212.

[16] O'Leary, M. (February 1990). Putting Hertz executives in the driver's seat. *CIO,* 62–69.

[17] Overton, K., Frolick, M. N., and Wilkes, R. B. (Summer 1996). Politics of implementing EISs. *Information Systems Management,* 50–57.

[18] Sprague, R. Jr., and Carlson, E. D. (1982). *Building effective decision support systems.* Englewood Cliffs, NJ: Prentice-Hall, Inc.

[19] Watson, H. J., and Satzinger, J. (Fall 1994). Guidelines for designing EIS interfaces. *Information Systems Management,* 46–52.

[20] Watson, H. J., and Rainer, R. K. Jr. (March, April 1991). A manager's guide to executive support systems. *Business Horizons,* 44–50.

[21] Watson, H. W., *et al.* (March 1991). Executive information systems: A framework for development and a survey of current practices. *MIS Quarterly,* 13–29.

[22] Watterson, K. (June 1994). The changing world of EIS. *Byte,* 183–193.

[23] Wetherbe, J. C. (March 1991). Executive information requirements: Getting it right. *MIS Quarterly,* 53–65.

Chapter 14

Group Support Systems: Collaborative Computing Has Started

Learning Objectives

After studying this chapter, you should be able to:

- Define group support systems.
- Explain components of a GSS.
- Define levels of support and GSS tools.
- Classify different types of GSSs.
- Explain the advantages and disadvantages of a GSS.
- Review some of the real life applications of a GSS.
- Review some of the commercial GSSs on the market.

14-1 INTRODUCTION

This chapter provides a comprehensive discussion of group support systems (GSSs) including group decision support systems (GDSSs), electronic meeting systems (EMSs), and GroupWare. It provides definitions, applications, and software support for each category. The chapter also provides a definition of three popular types of teleconferencing and provides several real-life case studies of the applications of GSSs. The chapter concludes with a comprehensive listing of software support for GSSs.

14-2 GROUP SUPPORT SYSTEMS (GSSs): AN OVERVIEW

In today's business environment, decision makers increasingly work in group settings. Group or collective computing is a new buzzword. All major software vendors are competing to either enter this fast-growing market or to increase their market share. Within this collaborative environment, there has been an increase in the use of computer-aided group support technologies. Group decision support systems (GDSSs), a subfield of decisions support systems (DSSs), has evolved over the past decade. More recently, technologies such as electronic meeting systems (EMSs) (teleconferencing) and GroupWare have found their way into the workplace. We call these technologies "group support systems" (GSSs). GSSs are intended to assist a group of decision makers who are working together on a certain task to make a decision or a better decision. These systems utilize computer and communications technologies in order to process, formulate, and implement a decision-making task by a group of decision makers.

Computer-aided decision supports such as GDSSs can be considered a kind of intervention technology that can help to overcome the limitations of group interaction. A GDSS is introduced to support a group's natural decision-making processes. The intervention features of a GDSS reduce communication barriers and introduce order and efficiency into situations that are inherently disorderly and inefficient. Thus, a GDSS facilitates the process of decision making by providing a clear focus for group discussion, minimizing politicking, and organizing attention around the critical issues. The effective outcome of this intervention depends on:

1. Successfully matching the level and sophistication of the GDSS and its collaborative tools with the appropriate size of the group, scope of the task, and proximity of the decision-making environment; and
2. Providing supportive management (especially at the CEO level) who are willing to "champion" the application of GDSSs within the organization.

Other computer-aided technologies that have emerged in the 1990s for group support are EMSs and GroupWare. Even though these systems are not considered to be "full-functionality GDSSs" due to their decision-tool limitations, they are less expensive and they provide communication and problem-solving mechanisms necessary for effective team management in a collaborative environment [8,18].

As discussed in Chapter 13, DSSs are usually designed to be used by a particular decision maker. A decision is made basically from the inputs given by this particular person. Group DSSs are designed to be used by more than one decision maker. These systems are useful for committees, review panels, board meetings, task forces, and decision-making sessions that require the input of several decision makers who may need to decide on for example, the location of a new plant, the introduction of a new product, or participation in an international bid.

14-3 THE COMPONENTS OF A GROUP DECISION SUPPORT SYSTEM (GDSS)

DeSanctis and Gallupe define GDSSs as an interactive computer-based system that facilitates the solution of unstructured and semistructured problems by a group of decision makers working together as a team [9].

By this definition, the components of a GDSS are basically the same as the components of a DSS, meaning hardware, software, people, and procedures. In addition, communications technology is added for group participation from various sites. Let's provide a breakdown of each component.

14-3-1 SOFTWARE AND HARDWARE

The software components may include:

- Database and database management systems
- Modeling capabilities (model base and model-based management systems)
- Dialog management with multiple-user access
- Specialized application programs to facilitate group access

The hardware components of GDSSs may include:

- General purpose I/O devices (dumb terminals, PCs, workstations, and voice I/O)
- Central processing unit
- Common viewing screen (for the group) or individual monitor for each participant
- A network system that links different sites and participants to each other

14-3-2 PEOPLE

In addition to the hardware and software components, a GDSS is composed of people: the facilitator and the decision-making participants. Let's briefly explain these individuals:

14-3-2-1 The Facilitator

The **facilitator** is the individual who must guide the group through the planning process. The facilitator must have sound computer skills and a thorough understanding of the dynamics of group interaction. The level of control the facilitator exercises varies by meeting style. There are three meeting styles: the chauffeured meeting, the supported meeting, and the interactive meeting [10].

In the **chauffeured meeting,** the facilitator is the primary user and controller of the GDSS. The computer and a projector act as an electronic blackboard where the facilitator records and updates key information as the group orally discusses the issues (the participants do not have input devices). The system also can access databases and modeling tools to analyze various alternatives.

A **supported meeting** is similar to the chauffeured meeting except that the participants use input devices, such as a keypad or workstations that are attached to the facilitator's computer. Since all participants have an input device, parallel communication capabilities enable the participants to talk and vote simultaneously, which saves time.

An **interactive meeting** is the most common meeting format where a "meeting room" provides a computer for each participant. In these meetings the "discussion" is done simultaneously through typing rather than verbal exchange. The facilitator's role is to keep the group focused on the issues and direct the momentum derived from the group's synergy. Even though the cost for a facility that can accommodate an interactive meeting requires a major capital investment, the efficiency and effectiveness gained from this style of meeting quickly return the investment.

Regardless of the meeting style, one of the most important duties of the facilitator is to identify the meeting's objectives, to select the appropriate GDSS tools and models, and to make sure the essential databases, both internal and external, will be available during the meeting. The objective of extensive premeeting planning is to minimize the time the participants will need to spend in the formal meeting and to make sure the agenda can be completely covered in the allotted time [10].

14-3-2-2 The Decision-Making Participants

Decision-making participants are the major players in group decision-making processes. The most important factor in a computer-aided group support system is the group of people. The technology must "support the group, not dominate it" [10]. The impact of the technology's support often depends on the size of the group. In an unassisted environment (non-GDSS), as the number of participants increases, the potential for information exchanges rises significantly and the frequency, duration, and intimacy of information exchange declines. Therefore, consensus becomes harder to achieve [7]. Since larger groups have more communication difficulties, the impact of a GDSS is more obvious. However, with small groups, the minimization of "group think" is a major beneficial consideration. Research shows that the parallel communications and voting features were of more benefit for large groups than small groups, while the anonymity feature of a GDSS was of greater benefit for small groups [7,10]. A conceptual model of a GDSS is provided in Figure 14-1 [9].

14-4 LEVELS OF SUPPORT PROVIDED BY A GSS

The features that a GSS provides to facilitate the "decision-making process" can be divided into three distinct levels of support; each suited for different needs [2,3,7,11].

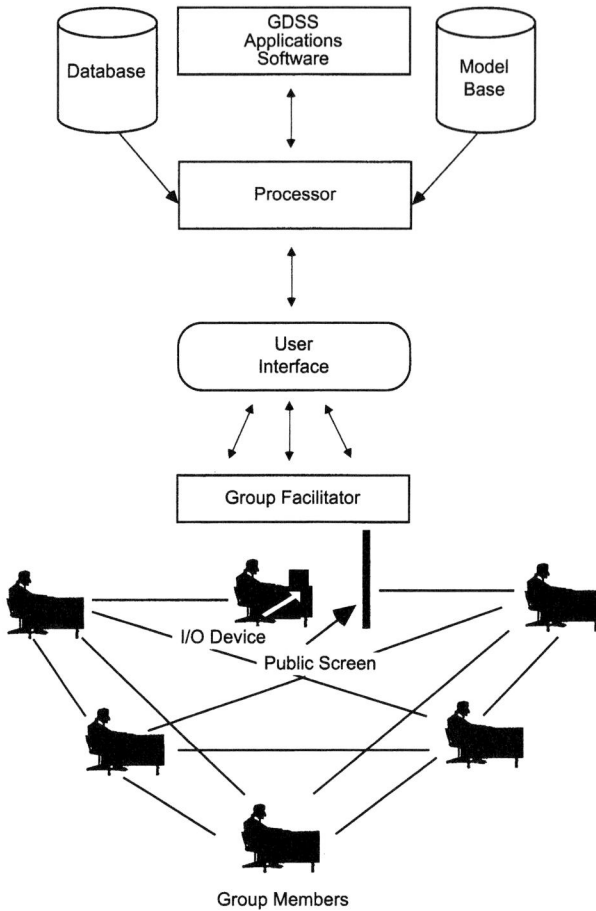

Figure 14-1   A conceptual model for a GDSS.

14-4-1 Level 1 Support

The purpose of a GSS at this level is to improve the decision processes by removing common communication barriers and by providing communication support (i.e., large screen to gather and display ideas, features to anonymously solicit/compile votes and results, and electronic messaging capabilities.) Most GDSSs and EMSs provide this level of support. Some GroupWare products also provide limited capabilities at this level of support.

14-4-2 LEVEL 2 SUPPORT

GSSs at this level are enhanced versions of level 1 because they provide quantitative modeling and planning tools (i.e., Delphi technique, or PERT and CPM). The purpose of level 2 support is to reduce uncertainty, and permit groups to simultaneously work on problem identification and solutions while viewing their analyses. Full-functionality GDSSs such as the University of Minnesota's SAMM, the University of Arizona's (Ventana) GroupSystems, IBM's TeamFocus, Collaborative Technology's VisionQuest, and RONIN Development Corporation's RONIN War Room provide level 2 support [17].

14-4-3 LEVEL 3 SUPPORT

This level of GSSs uses expert systems (ES) and artificial intelligence (AI) technologies. A level 3 GSS can actually control the pattern, timing, and content of group interaction using rule-based features and heuristics to adapt to the meeting environment, changing the interaction patterns as needed. A GSS at this level eventually will provide advice to the group in selecting the most suitable rules for enhancing group discussion. The systems available at this level are experimental, such as Argnoter, an "intelligent" enhancement for Xerox's COLAB to assist decision makers in proposal evaluations [24].

Tables 14-1, 14-2 and 14-3 provide a concise overview of the three levels of GSSs, and the group problems or needs that GSS support.

14-5 GSS TOOLS

Full-functionality GDSSs are differentiated from other group support systems such as an EMS and GroupWare by the sophistication and availability of planning tools and decision models [8]. The following tools, basic and advanced, have been developed for problem identification, deliberation, planning, and problem solving by a group. The basic tools can be found in some GroupWare products. An EMS usually has the basic tools and many of the advanced tools. Full-functionality GDSSs usually include the full range of tools—both basic and advanced.

14-5-1 BASIC TOOLS

Electronic brainstorming and voting, described below, are considered "generic" tools and can be applied to a wide range of problem identification, idea generation, and problem-solving situations:

Table 14-1

GSS Level 1

Group problem or need	GSS feature
Sending and receiving information efficiently among all parties or specific groups members.	Electronic messaging, broadcast or point-to-point communication.
Access to personal data files or corporate data during the course of a meeting.	Computer terminal for each group member; gateway to a LAN or central computer and e-mail systems.
Display of ideas, votes, data, graphs, or tables to all members simultaneously.	Large common viewing screen or "public" screen at each group member's terminal.
Reluctance of some members to speak due to their shyness, low status, or controversial ideas.	Anonymous input of ideas and votes from the participant sites.
Failure of some members to participate due to laziness or "tuning out."	Active solicitation of ideas or votes from each group member.
Failure to efficiently organize and analyze ideas and votes.	Summary and display of ideas; statistical summary and display of votes.
Failure to quantify preferences.	Provide rating scales and/or ranking schemes; solicit and display rankings.
Failure to develop a meeting strategy or plan.	Provide a mock agenda which the group can complete and/or modify.
Failure to stick with the meeting plan.	Continuously display the agenda; provide a time clock; automatically display agenda items at the appropriate time.

Electronic Brainstorming (EBS) supports idea generation by allowing group members to simultaneously share comments in response to a specific question. The anonymity of EBS encourages objectivity and creativity. EBS is based on the manual method, Individual Brainwriting Pool Technique, in which each member of a group writes a comment on a piece of paper and then places it in the center of the table for another member to read before adding a comment. This process continues until the group runs out of comments on the topic that is under consideration [25].

Voting can offer a variety of prioritizing methods, such as true/false, rank ordering, and multiple-choice questions. All the participants cast private ballots, and then the accumulated results are displayed in graphical and tabular formats that are appropriate for the method used. The use of voting techniques results in a listing of prioritized alternatives for further elaboration by the group [10].

Table 14-2

GSS Level 2

Group problem or need	GSS feature
Need for problem structuring, planning, and scheduling.	Planning models, e.g., PERT, CPM, Gantt chart, and responsibility matrix.
Decision-analytic aids for uncertain future events.	Utility and probability assessment models, e.g., decision trees, risk assessment models, and probability models.
Decision-analytic aids for resource allocation problems.	Resource allocation models, such as linear programming and assignment models.
Decision-analytic aids for data-oriented tasks.	Statistical models, multicriteria decision models.
Decision-analytic aids for preference tasks.	Social judgment models.
Decision to use a structured decision technique but insufficient knowledge or time to use the technique.	Automate the Delphi, brainstorming, other idea-gathering and compilation techniques; provide an on-line tutorial for the group or a human facilitator.

Table 14-3

GSS Level 3

Group problem or need	GSS feature
Desire to enforce formalized decision procedures.	Automated parliamentary procedure.
Desire to select and/or arrange an array of rules for discussion.	Rule base; facility for rule selection and application.
Uncertainty about options for meeting procedures.	Automated counselor, giving advice on available rules and appropriate use.
Need to develop meeting rules.	Rule-writing facility.

14-5-2 ADVANCED TOOLS

The next groups of tools offer advanced problem-solving decision models that are often customized to a particular class of problems. Group-decision situations concerning strategic planning, contingency planning, problem formulation, and resource allocation can benefit from these tools [8]. Table 14-4 summarizes these tools. The following is a brief explanation of these tools:

Table 14-4

Advanced Tools Used in GSSs

Stakeholder identification and assumption analysis
Alternative evaluator
Policy formulation
Topic commentor
Idea organizer
Issue analyzer
Questionnaire
Enterprise analyzer
Semantic graphics browser
File reader
Group dictionary

Stakeholder identification and assumption analysis is used to systematically evaluate the implications of a proposed policy or plan. Stakeholders and their assumptions are identified and rated in terms of importance, and then they are presented graphically to the group for discussion and analysis. (Stakeholders are the entities, individuals, or groups of individuals upon whose actions the organization depends, or who will be affected by the organization's proposed plan or course of action) [25].

Alternative evaluator provides multicriteria decision-making support. Alternatives are examined by applying flexible weighted criteria to evaluate decision scenarios and trade-off. Results are displayed in tabular or graphical format.

Policy formation supports the group's development of a policy or mission statement. Sample text is contributed and then edited through group discussion. The process is iterative until a consensus is reached.

Topic commentor facilitates idea solicitation and provisions for additional details in connection with the list of topics that may also include subtopics. Group participants enter, exchange, and review information on self-selected topics.

Idea organizer helps the group to identify and consolidate text of the key items, and also supports the integration of external information to support the identified items.

Issue analyzer helps the group to condense the combined topic list to a manageable size by identifying the topics that merit further consideration.

Questionnaire supports researchers and facilitators to design on-line questionnaires. The questionnaires are "dynamic," meaning that the additional questions are triggered based upon the responses received.

Enterprise analyzer is an organization-modeling tool to support any user-definable approach, by capturing characteristics of a business subsystem such as IBM's Business System Planning [16].

Semantic graphics browser is used to examine information from the enterprise analyzer by allowing the users to "zoom in" on specific areas of interest for more detail [17].

File reader is an efficiency tool that allows the group members to immediately browse (read-only) previously stored material at any point in a group discussion and then return to the discussion at their own discretion.

Group dictionary permits a group to formally define a word or phrase or create references for future group work. The process is iterative to encourage group participation in arriving at a consensus.

14-6 CLASSES OF GSSs

Group support systems (GSSs) can be classified in two ways: input devices and geographic devices [9,12]. Figure 14-2 illustrates this classification.

14-6-1 INPUT DEVICES CLASSIFICATION

There are three major classes of GSSs under the input devices classification: software-only, keypad response, and full-keyboard workstation systems. Let's briefly explain each type [12].

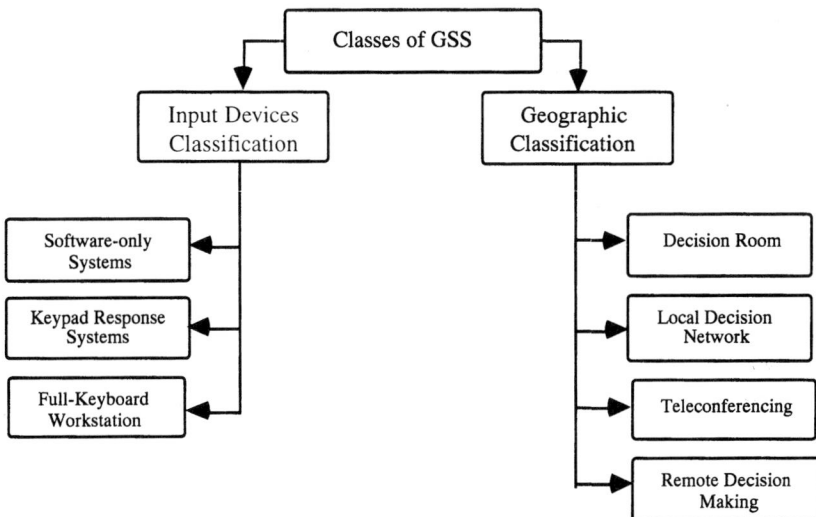

Figure 14-2   GSS classes.

14-6-1-1 Software-Only Systems

The simplest form of GSSs is a single-computer, software-only system. Although these systems often are marketed as GroupWare, they are single-user, decision-support tools that use a video display monitor to allow the meeting participants to view the decision-making outcome. They do not have the anonymous input capabilities of the more sophisticated keypad response and full-keyboard systems, but they are portable, and they are relatively inexpensive.

Decision Pad (Apian Software) and AutoMan (Sterling Software, Inc.) are examples of software-only systems that provide support for evaluating alternatives. For example, a group could evaluate a capital budgeting decision using multiple criteria such as payback, return on investment, and investment risk. The group may assign weights to each criterion, then rate each alternative based on the three criteria. The system manipulates the ratings, considers the criteria's weights, and ranks the alternatives accordingly.

If meeting participants should disagree with the outcome ("we did not put enough weight on investment risk"), what-if analysis can quickly find out how alternative weights might affect the outcome. For instance, the outcome might not change even if the group weighted investment risk four times as heavily as the other two criteria. In this case, the desired alternative is chosen, and the group saves time by avoiding further discussion.

14-6-1-2 Keypad Response Systems

The second level of GSS is the keypad response system, which consists of a host PC and wired or wireless hand-held keypads. Group members respond to questions or evaluate alternatives using the electronic keypads. The host PC processes the participants' input and displays the analysis on a screen.

Keypad response systems have an advantage over software-only systems in that they allow a meeting facilitator to gather participants' input instantly and anonymously. They also have two important advantages over the more sophisticated keyboard-based systems: They are portable, and they are relatively inexpensive.

OptionFinder (Option Technologies, Inc.) and Data-Back system (Macro 4, Inc.) are two commercial keypad response systems. Both systems allow redefined rating scales such as yes/no, multiple choice, and 5-point Likert scales questions. They also allow users to design their own rating scales, and they support graphical display of the data, such as bar charts and line graphs. A keypad response system also can be used in capital budgeting decisions. As an example, consider a group that is considering six investment alternatives. The keypad response systems provide several methods for prioritizing the six alternatives. They could be ranked from one to six by each participant, or each alternative could be evaluated separately using a 5-point Likert scale. It is also possible to evaluate each alternative using multiple criteria, such as return on investment, payback, investment risk, and so forth. Criterion weighting is also possible. The group's input would be tabulated, providing immediate feedback about where the group agreed and disagreed. Thus, the group can save time by bypassing areas of consensus and by concentrating on disagreement.

14-6-1-3 Full-Keyboard Workstation

The third type of GSSs under this group is the full-keyboard workstation system. Typically, these systems are configured in a meeting room with workstations connected using a local area network (LAN). Workstations are arranged around a U-shaped table, with a facilitator station and projector screen at the front of the room. Some companies place file servers, workstation central processing units (CPUs), and printers in a separate room to reduce the noise level and improve room aesthetics.

The full-keyboard workstation systems support:

- Alternative evaluation, rating, and voting
- Brainstorming
- Idea organization
- Issue analysis
- Strategic planning, such as developing mission statements, identification of critical success factors, and developing master plans

Alternative evaluations, rating, and voting tools are similar to keypad response's systems, but full-keyboard systems allow the participants to talk through their computers. Anonymous talking provides an ideal method for involving a heterogeneous, broad-based group in brainstorming and strategic planning activities.

During a brainstorming session, each participant submits an idea to the system, then receives other participants' ideas, comments on them, and sends them back to the system—all via the workstation. This technology improves traditional brainstorming in several ways:

1. Anonymity helps provide a supportive atmosphere: ideas are more likely to be evaluated based on their merit, independent of the source. Thus, criticism is less likely to be seen as a personal attack.
2. There is parallel processing of ideas. No one has to wait to be heard because everyone talks at the same time.
3. By forcing the participants to write their comments, the ideas tend to be more concise and more focused.
4. All comments are captured in memory, so no ideas are lost.

5. Cross talk, side talk, and chitchat are reduced.

After using the brainstorming tool to generate a diverse list of ideas or suggestions, the idea organizer tool can be used to combine similar ideas. Several service organizations use this technique to generate suggestions on how to improve customer satisfaction.

14-6-2 GEOGRAPHIC CLASSIFICATION

There are four major classes of GSSs under the geographic classification: decision room, local decision network, teleconferencing, and remote decision making. Let's briefly explain each type [9].

14-6-2-1 Decision Room

In this type of GSS, decision makers sit around a horseshoe-shaped desk that faces a large screen. Each participant has access to a terminal for individual participant input and at the same time everybody can see the large screen. The large screen is used to summarize the input from different participants. The terminals are used for individual participant input. This configuration is the equivalent to the full-keyboard workstation system.

14-6-2-2 Local Decision Network (LDN)

In this type of GSS, the participants are dispersed in a limited geographical area. They can participate from their own offices and express their views. This configuration includes a central processor with dedicated software for storing the results.

14-6-2-3 Teleconferencing

This architecture enables different decision makers in scattered geographic regions to participate in a group decision-making process. Teleconferencing can include one of the following:

1. **Real-time computer conferencing** allows a group of users, who are either gathered in an electronic meeting room or physically dispersed, to interact synchronously through their workstations or terminals. When a group is physically dispersed, an audio link, such as a conference call, is often established.

There are two basic approaches to implementing real-time computer conferencing system [26]. The first approach is to embed an unmodified single-user application in a conferencing environment that transmits the application's output to each participant's display terminal. Input comes from one user at a time, and floor passing protocol exchanges input control among users. Examples include terminal linking where several terminals are in communication at the same time. The second approach is to design the application specifically to account for the presence of multiple users. Examples are a meeting scheduling system, and a real-time group note-taking system.

2. **Video teleconferencing** is the most familiar example of teleconferencing that requires special rooms and sometimes trained operators. Video teleconferencing approximates face-to-face meetings. Television sets and cameras are used to transmit live pictures and sounds. This is markedly more effective than the telephone and limited image conferencing; however, it is more costly. Newer systems provide workstation-based interfaces to a conference and make the process more accessible. Xerox, for example, established an audio/video link for use by a project team split between Portland, Oregon, and Palo Alto, California. Most video interactions occurred between large common areas at each side, but project members could also access video channels through their office workstations. Video teleconferencing is not only relatively inaccessible, but it also has the disadvantage of not letting participants share text and graphics. Real-time computer conferencing does not offer video capabilities.

3. **Desktop conferencing,** a third type computer-supported conferencing combines the advantages of video teleconferencing and realtime computer conferencing while mitigating their drawbacks. Desktop conferencing still uses the workstation as the conference interface, but it also runs applications shared by the participants. Modern desktop conferencing systems support multiple video windows per workstation. This allows display of dynamic information, and dynamic video images of participants.

An example of desktop conferencing is the MMConf system. MMConf provides a shared display of a multimedia document, as well as communication channels for voice and shared pointers. Another example is the Rapport multimedia conferencing system. Rapport is designed for workstations connected by a multimedia network. The system supports various forms of interaction, from simple telephone-like conversation to multiparty shared-display interaction.

14-6-2-4 Remote Decision Making

This configuration advocates uninterrupted communication on a regular basis in a geographically dispersed organization that includes a fixed number of decision makers [9]. In this type of architecture there is no need to schedule meetings in advance as in video teleconferencing. A participant may send her input to the central database (electronic mailbox), and then the other participants will respond to this input. Eventually a decision is made by consensus.

Figure 14-3 illustrates these four types of configuration [9].

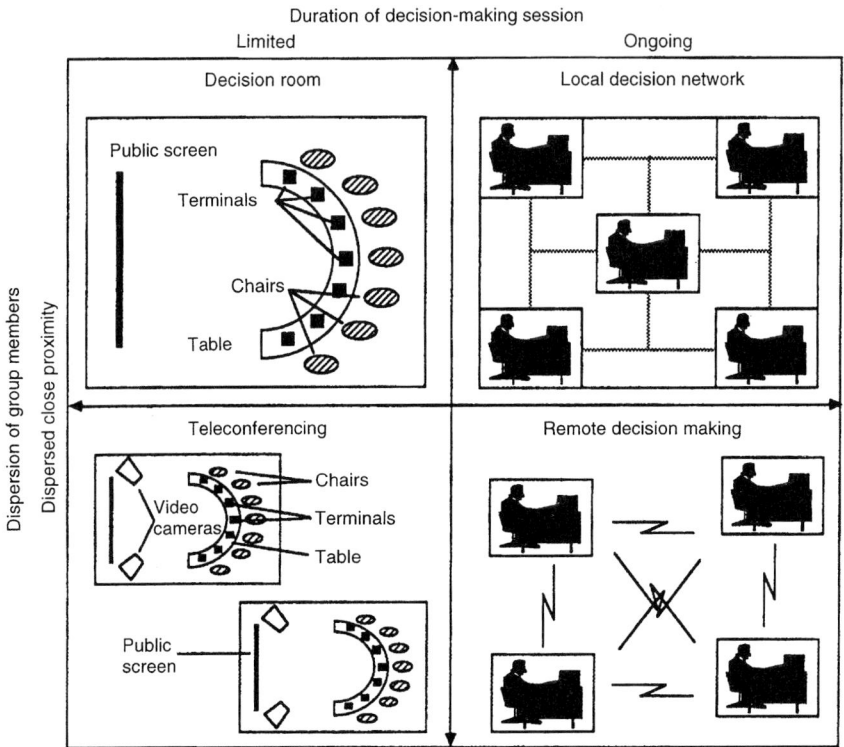

Figure 14-3   GSSs based on geographic classification.

14-7 GROUPWARE: AN OVERVIEW

The goal of GroupWare is to assist groups in communicating, in collaborating, and in coordinating their activities. For the purposes of this book, we define GroupWare as:

> Computer-based systems that support group of decision makers engaged in a common decision-making task by providing access to the same-shared environment and information. The shared environment may be a memo, a single file, or even an entire database. Lotus Notes, Microsoft Exchange, and Novell GroupWise are three popular examples of GroupWare on the market [14,21,23].

Lotus Notes (Lotus Development Corporation) focuses on managing (accessing, collecting, parsing, sorting, storing, and distributing) information. Lotus Notes provides a distributed database support with built-in wide-area connectivity, automated document routing, and e-mail. With these tools, users can easily build databases, data-tracking, and open discussion applications that can be connected via phone lines. A classic example (used in routing of help requests) archives previously handled problems and solutions, support-staff discussions, and distributes messages.

Local area networks (LANs), wide area networks (WANs) and metropolitan area networks (MANs) are the backbone of GroupWare. Recently, the Internet has become a key participant in GroupWare utilization. In turn, the software foundation of GroupWare is electronic mail, in simple terms, the transport of text messages across the network. While e-mail is not GroupWare per se, it is vital for some communications facilities that do have workgroup implications.

Today, GroupWare are in early stages of development. Viable products are here, but businesses are only beginning to adopt them. The available commercial products vary significantly in their functions, complexity, and cost. At one end of the scale, a product like Futurus Team (Futurus Corp.) offers communications with a workgroup twist at an affordable price and minimal setup and administrative demands. At the other end, industrial-strength products, such as CM/1 (Corporate Memory Systems) and Keyfile (Keyfile Corporation) can cost tens of thousands of dollars to implement, often requiring setup procedures and extensive training to run.

14-8 GROUPWARE CLASSIFICATION

GroupWare software can be classified based on two features: types of group meeting and types of software [22,27]. Figure 14-4 shows this classification. Let's briefly explain each type.

14-8-1 TYPES OF GROUP MEETINGS

This class of GroupWare includes four types of software support: the small group, the planetary group, the decision-making group, and the worn-sneakers group.

The small group (or task group) is a group of four or five co-workers who tend to interact extensively on projects. The groups are not necessarily everlasting. They may dissolve and they may be recreated on a per-project basis. Keyfile (Keyfile Corporation) and Office IQ (Portfolio Technologies, Inc.) are suitable software for this type of group. One member of the group may create, copy, or scan an initial set of files or documents. The other team members enhance, adjust, suggest changes, and generally refocus the work. All collaborative notes can appear on one document; the document can have some tracking provision to log

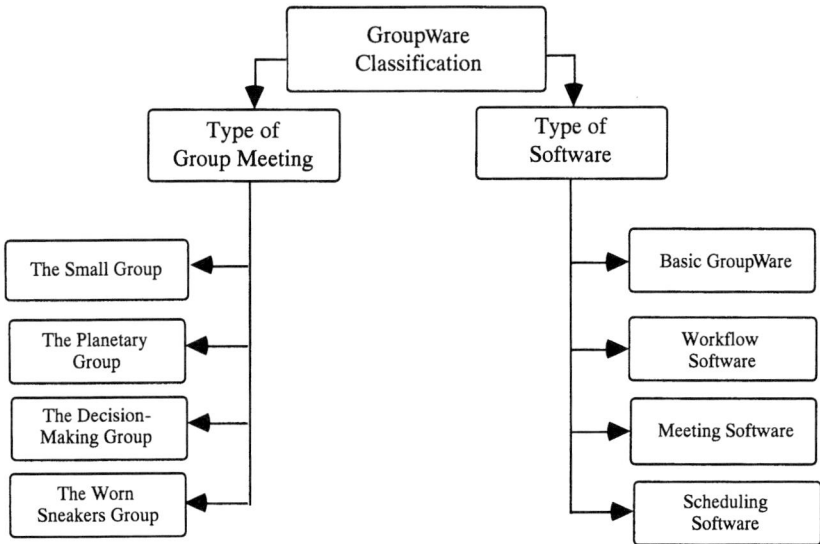

Figure 14-4   GroupWare classification.

whose changes came first, second, third, and so forth. These comments and changes can then be incorporated into the final project.

The planetary group is a group of workers who work in different places. They have to contact each other in order to transfer the information and gain the update information. Lotus Notes (Lotus Development Corporation) is a good example of software support for this type of group. Beyond being a highly successful product, Lotus Notes is rapidly becoming the nucleus of a whole new GroupWare development community, as vendors develop Lotus Notes add-ons and products that work in conjunction with Lotus Notes.

With offices all over the world, a company can have a hard time keeping track of all its wide-reaching information. For example, salespeople in every location need to know whether the account for the XYZ Company, with offices in the United States and Germany, shows that it has agreed to buy peripherals for all its locations. A shared database with some application development tools could be the perfect answer. With this facility, up-to-date customer and account information would be available at all locations. With sales-order tracking tools built into the application development environment, all invoices are automatically filled and copied to the product distribution center.

The decision-making group is the management team that has to make a decision in a specific location. CM/1 (Corporate Memory Systems) is an example of software for this type of group. This is a tool that lets the management team discuss the issues involved from their individual locations (over a proprietary leased-line network) and yet remember past discussions, arguments, and conclusions to save time.

For example, Organization for Petroleum Exporting Countries (OPEC) oil ministers regularly meet to decide whether they should slow production to hike up oil prices. The problem is, they always have to meet face to face and discuss the same issues over and over again every time in different places. This software can assist them significantly by bringing up all the past discussions, arguments, and comments made by each member. By doing this, they can concentrate on the new issues and expedite the decision-making process by attacking fewer issues.

The worn-sneakers group is a group of workers who are in a small business environment. They are constantly hand-delivering goods, products, invoices, messages, and even appointment notices from one desk to another for approval and changes. BeyondMail (Beyond Inc.) is a good software candidate for this type of group. Some small business owners cannot afford secretaries. So when they are out of the office, work may pile up on their desks. They need to automate the workflow from one desk to another (in their absence or when they are busy with other tasks) as necessary. GroupWare with BeyondMail capabilities can significantly improve the productivity of such groups by providing e-mail capability, automated routing slip, form integration, and form delivery.

14-8-2 TYPES OF SOFTWARE

This class of GroupWare includes four types of software support: basic Group-Ware, workflow software, meeting software, and scheduling software.

Basic GroupWare, for which Lotus Notes has almost the entire market share, combines a sophisticated messaging system with an extensive database containing work records and memos. It changes the way information flows in an organization. It creates a kind of corporate on-line service similar to the Internet of the office. Unlike plain e-mail, Notes does not require you to figure out who needs to know a fact or hear an idea. Instead, you simply forward your memo to the appropriate bulletin board. Several hundred large and medium-size organizations, such as Price Waterhouse, Andersen Consulting, Compaq Computer, Chase Manhattan, General Motors, and Texaco, have been successfully using this very powerful software. Since its inception in 1989, Lotus Development Corporation has sold more than 15,000,000 copies of Notes to more than 4,000 companies at around $300 for each PC that uses it.

Workflow software is designed to remake and streamline business processes, especially in paper-clogged bureaucracies. It helps workers understand the steps that make up a particular process and allows them to redesign those steps. It also routes work automatically from one employee to another. The most popular software in this group is Action Works (Action Technologies, Inc.). This software allows a user to draw charts, creates documents, and prints a map of business processes. It identifies process inefficiencies based on prespecified business rules.

Meeting software allows participants in face-to-face or videoconference gatherings to talk simultaneously by typing on PC or workstation keyboards. Since people read faster than they speak, and do not have to wait for others to finish talking, the software can significantly speed up the progress toward consensus. It also ensures that everyone gets a chance to participate. The most prominent software in this group is GroupSystems (Ventana Corporation).

Scheduling software uses a network to coordinate colleagues' electronic datebooks and figure out when they can all get together. This can be a powerful tool, especially when there are several executives involved and they have diverse schedules. There are several software support of this type; Network Scheduler (Powercore International Inc.) is one example.

14-9 WEB-BASED GSSs

The popularity of the Internet has created a growing market for Web-based GSSs. New GSS tools are specifically designed to run on LANs, MANs, WANs, telephone lines via conference calls, the organization private Intranet, and the Internet [1]. In these systems, Internet protocols are used to handle all communication. Web-browser software such as Netscape or Microsoft Internet Explorer is usually used for accessing these systems.

TCBWorks developed at the University of Georgia is one of the first Web-based GDSSs [6]. This GSS provides inexpensive anytime/anyplace decision making support. Like most commercial software, TCBWorks offers features such as brainstorming, voting, ranking, and agenda setting.

The most significant advantage of a Web-based GSS is the use of open network standards, and the most notable disadvantage are the speed and security issues.

The following are three popular examples of Web-based GSS tools. In the near future we should see many more of these types of GSSs on the marketplace. For detailed information regarding the functionality of these systems the perspective vendor should be contacted.

- TCBWORKs: Webware for Teams (Alan Dennis at the University of Georgia, Athens, GA).
- Netscape Communicator (Netscape Communications Corporation, Mountain View, CA)
- Lotus Domino (Lotus Development Corporation, Cambridge, MA)

14-10 ADVANTAGES AND DISADVANTAGES OF TELECONFERENCING AND OTHER GSSs

A teleconferencing system may include some unique advantages [4,5]:

1. Cost savings by not traveling from place to place and paying high costs for planes, hotels, and meals.
2. More contacts are possible. Since the decision makers are not traveling long distances, they may have more time to talk with each other and resolve organizational problems.
3. Issues of shyness may not be as severe in a teleconferencing environment as it is in face-to-face meetings. This is particularly helpful to those decision makers who are shy in face-to-face settings.
4. Less stress because of fewer hours spent traveling. By using a teleconferencing system, the decision makers may be able to spend more time with family and friends, which may improve the morale of these individuals.

Teleconferencing systems, with all the advantages, may include some disadvantages:

1. Lack of human touch. In a teleconferencing system, some of the gestures, face-to-face impressions, handshakes, and eye contacts may be lost. This in turn may hinder the effectiveness of the regular meetings. At this point only two of the five senses, i.e., sound and vision, are present in a teleconferencing system. Taste, smell, and touch are missing in a teleconferencing system. With new development in the Virtual Reality (VR) technologies, some of these shortcomings may be resolved in the near future. We will discuss VR in Chapter 16.
2. Unnecessary meetings. Since it is relatively easy to arrange a teleconference meeting, some of these meetings may not be necessary and time and energy may be wasted.
3. Security problems. Teleconferencing has the same security problems as any other telecommunications system. Some valuable and private organizational information may get into the hands of unauthorized individuals. This issue dictates the implementation of tight security measures that only allow authorized individuals to have access to the data and information being transferred among the participants.

Other types of GSSs include all the advantages and disadvantages of the teleconferencing systems described above. In addition, they include the following specific advantages and disadvantages:

Advantages

- Help improve meeting satisfaction, which may help improve group morale.

- Provide both electronic and hard copy documentation of the meeting activities.
- Save decision-making time by providing online support to the group.
- Save money by requiring fewer people to perform the same task.
- Improve group effectiveness by advancing collaboration.

Disadvantages

- Difficult to reward someone for quality input. An electronic shouting match is no better than a verbal one.
- A strong member who could dominate meetings may lose that power when an anonymous GSS is used.
- More difficult to introduce to an organization than more traditional, less threatening software.
- Costs of GSS implementation are high since the system includes many features. A company must identify its needs before getting into this expensive venture.

14-11 GSSs IN ACTION

There are numerous GSS-related studies that have been performed by academia in conjunction with private businesses. The results are not always successful, as will be illustrated in the Department of Indian Health Services (IHS) case. Overall, however, most cases reveal more successes than outright failures.

The studies are conducted either at the university's campus "meeting room" facilities as was the case with Burr-Brown Corporation, or in a "decision room" installed on-site at the place of business as was the case with the multiple Texaco sites. The Burr-Brown and Texaco cases are representative of the overall positive outcome of companies that have used a GSS. The IHS and IBM cases are discussed to contrast one GSS failure (IHS) and one overwhelming success (IBM). The last case illustrates successful application of a GroupWare in a large corporation.

14-11-1 Burr-Brown Corporation

Burr-Brown Corporation is a Tucson-based international electronics company that used the meeting room at the University of Arizona to develop several divisional 5-year strategic plans and a 1-year action plan. Among the benefits they derived from using a GSS was being able to expand their planning group from an average of 8 to 10 managers to 31 senior managers. Even with a significantly larger group, they achieved their objective in 3 days that usually took months with fewer people. They benefited from more input and from working less time. The company's CEO expressed that the most notable benefit, which is not quantifiable, was the improved understanding of the planning process and direction of the company on the part of his managers [20].

14-11-2 TEXACO, INCORPORATED

The University of Minnesota constructed SAMM (Software Aided Meeting Management) "decision rooms" on the premises of Texaco, Inc., in Houston, Tulsa, and Midland. The 2-year program was evaluated as a success despite the initial user "unfriendliness" of SAMM. (SAMM is not as "friendly" as commercially available software.) The success was measured by the extensive use of SAMM by all levels of management, for issues that ranged from the broad to the highly technical. The voting and brainstorming features were the most popular. The savings of time spent in meetings, the quality and quantity of ideas generated during the meetings, and the completion of meeting agendas were considered major accomplishments. The most important benefit for Texaco was using SAMM for dispersed meetings because they use cross-functional teams extensively within the organization. With SAMM, team members in the Tulsa and Harrison office, for example, did not need to travel to Houston for meetings. The future use of SAMM within the Texaco organization, as well as other GDSS and EMS systems they are testing, is being evaluated [8].

14-11-3 DEPARTMENT OF INDIAN HEALTH SERVICES (IHS), TUCSON

The significance of this case study is that it is an example of a GSS failure due to management resistance and political pressures within a company's environment. In 1988, an IHS doctor saw that the limited productivity of IHS meetings could be assisted with electronic meeting system technology. The University of Arizona supplied GroupSystems on-site at IHS, at no charge. From its inception, myriad difficulties had to be overcome to simply install the system. IHS management did not perceive a need for this technology and were unwilling to commit proper resources. Some of the problems were that fewer chairs arrived than were requested, improper lighting washed out the BARCO (public screen), and getting a dedicated room was a major hurdle since space was a scarce commodity. There were political disagreements concerning equipment liability and a fundamental disagreement between the administrative core (IHS management) and the technical core (the doctor who suggested the GroupSystems idea). Once the system was finally installed, the results were positive. The most noticeable benefit was the increased level of participation. One observation was that Native American participants were quiet during verbal sessions, but contributed actively during the nonverbal sessions. However, due to lack of use over a year's time (less than a dozen times), the system was dismantled and returned to the university [15].

There are two reasons for the failure of this system. First, management did not perceive a need for such a system. Secondly, there was no one to "champion" the system to illustrate how IHS could benefit from its use in the long term. This case illustrates a very important point. Success of any computer-aided group decision system requires that: (1) there be a perceived need for the technology; (2) the technology be well matched with the users' needs; and (3) there be a strong commitment from top management to support the use of the system within the organization.

14-11-4 INTERNATIONAL BUSINESS MACHINES

IBM is a well-documented example of a GSS success story. The benefits that IBM has derived using their system are cited in numerous studies related to computer-aided group decision support. Initially, IBM used the "meeting room" site at the University of Arizona to test the technology by doing some strategic planning. The measurable success of the sessions prompted IBM to work with the university from 1983 through 1989 to develop its own in-house system [16]. The result was a sophisticated EMS named TeamFocus, equipped with extensive planning and modeling tools and remote meeting capabilities. Currently, the company has more than 50 facilities at IBM sites around the world. Each facility can cost approximately $20,000 to $300,000 to develop. Each facility is equipped and designed with the user group in mind (i.e., the differences in needs between metropolitan administrative needs and remote manufacturing site needs). The sites are used by IBM and are frequently leased to outside companies for $2000 to $7000 a session [13].

IBM uses its facilities for strategic planning and problem solving, that is, factors contributing to cost overruns, workload elimination, and functional area data processing needs. The tasks are usually complex, requiring creativity, and have no known right answer, and they require input from a group [16].

The cost–benefit results are astounding and attest to why IBM is committed to making this technology an integral part of its organization. Without the aid of a GSS, it is estimated that managers spend anywhere from 35% to 70% of their time in meetings. IBM wanted to make better use of their managers' time. IBM's use of its facilities, ranging from the administrative to manufacturing orientation, averaged man-hour savings of 55.6% [16]. In addition, administrative costs fell, calendar time was reduced, and the number of meetings necessary to complete a project diminished [16]. The average time an IBM group spent completing a project was reduced by 90% [13]. IBM's data and experience also show that the larger and more difficult the task, the greater the savings realized. During the first year of using TeamFocus, when the costs of development were compared with the savings in time and increases in productivity, IBM indicated they realized a full return of their investment. Some of the success factors cited by IBM are as follows [13]:

- Organizational commitment
- Executive sponsor ("champion")
- Dedicated facilities
- Communication and liaison
- Training
- Cost and benefit evaluation
- Software flexibility
- Meeting managerial expectations

The significance of the IBM case illustrates that, ultimately, GSS success is measured by the way the technology meets the needs of the business. In IBM's case, the technology is appropriately matched with the business needs and the tasks of the decision-making group, and management "champions" the use of this technology throughout the organization.

14-11-5 PRICE WATERHOUSE

Price Waterhouse, one of the largest accounting and consulting firm in the world, used Lotus Notes to win a multimillion-dollar consulting contract [22]. This is how it was done. On Thursday, Price Waterhouse was invited to submit a bid. However, there was a catch: the bid was supposed to be submitted on the following Monday. A Price Waterhouse competitor had been working on its own bid for several weeks. The four executives who were supposed to write the bid were in three different states. However, they were able to work together using Lotus Notes. Lotus Notes allowed them to conduct a four-way dialogue on-screen. First of all they were able to extract major components of the proposal from various databases on Notes. From one end they were able to pull résumés of the Price Waterhouse experts from all over the world who were supposed to work on this assignment. From the other end they were able to borrow passages from similar successful proposals from various Notes databases. Several drafts were generated and all four executives reviewed them carefully, and Notes kept track of all the changes. Other executives were able to review the proposal over the weekend. Price Waterhouse submitted the proposal and won the bid on Monday. Its competitor did not even meet the deadline!

14-12 SOFTWARE SUPPORT FOR A GSS

Table 14-5 provides a comprehensive list of the popular software for group support systems. As you see from this list, the capabilities of these software products vary significantly. An organization should choose the one that meets its specific needs.

SUMMARY

This chapter covered the definition, capabilities, and uses of computer-aided support technology, including group decision support systems (GDSSs), electronic meeting systems (EMSs), and GroupWare. GDSSs, EMSs, and GroupWare provide a wide range of collaborative decision-making support. However, the successful outcome of this technology's use requires that the capabilities of the group support system be appropriately matched with the decision-making group's needs, and that management is supportive and will "champion" its use within the organization.

The "virtual organization" of tomorrow is flat, team-driven, downsized, global, and very competitive. In such a dynamic business environment the winners are those who make complex decisions with input from the key decision makers in a timely manner. With decreasing costs and increasing sophistication in communications and computer technologies GSSs can play a significant role in keeping the organization ahead of the competition. The outlook for the continual development and application of computer-aided group decision support technologies such as GDSSs, EMSs, and GroupWare is very promising [3,19].

REVIEW QUESTIONS

1. What is a group decision support system?
2. What are other computer-based group support systems?
3. What are the differences between a full-featured GDSS and GroupWare?
4. What are some of the components of a GDSS?
5. What is the role of the facilitator?
6. What are the three types of meetings?

Table 14-5

Software Support for GSSs

Software name	Company name	Application
Action Workflow	Action Technologies, Inc.	Allows users to draw, document, and print map of system business processes and its network of workflows. Consists of an analyst, which identifies process inefficiencies, and Application Builder, which allows developer to specify business rules and forms.
AutoMan	Sterling Software, Inc.	Provides supports for evaluating alternatives.
BeyondMail for Windows	Beyond Inc.	E-mail system that offers messaging functionality. Offers ability to automate workflow through BeyondRules. Includes automated routing slip, enhanced rule language, third-party form integration, database access, and image-enabled mail through Watermark Explorer Edition.
CM/1	Corporate Memory Systems	GroupWare communication tool for distributed teams. Provides any time, anyplace virtual meeting that can replace most face-to-face meetings. Combine graphical hypertext interface with object-oriented database to allow groups to collaboratively construct maps of all formal and informal information related to projects or problems.
CRUISER	Bellcore	Supports the users in electronically roaming the hallways by browsing video channels.
CSTaR	Andersen Consulting	Supports group meeting.
Data-Back	Macro 4, Inc.	Enables user to backup and restore VSAM clusters and other VSAM-based datasets to disk or tape. Interfaces with other VSAM products. Copies clusters from one catalog to another, reloads cluster from sequential dataset, compares contents of clusters and lists contents of backup.
FirstClass	SoftArc Inc.	E-mail, group conferencing, access to existing corporate databases, form processing, real-time discussions and on-line communications function.
Decision Pad	Apian Software	Combines facts and opinions in spreadsheet-style matrix. Applications include purchasing, employee evaluations, hiring, vendor evaluation, investing, project prioritization, and sales.

(continues)

Table 14-5 *(continued)*

Software name	Company name	Application
Futurus Team	Futurus Corp.	GroupWare, personal group and resource communication and productivity package. Includes e-mail, on-line chat, phone messages, scheduling, document enclosures, CUA user interface, carbon and blind carbon copy, archiving and keyword search, multiple mailbox, to-do list, spell checker, and print capture engine. Allows user to create and send e-mail messages from within other applications.
GroupSystems	Ventana Corp.	Electronic meeting software, solicits ideas from more than one person simultaneously, automatically captures meeting information in standard PC files and enables users to enter anonymous voice opinions.
Keyfile	Keyfile Corporation	Integrated documents manager, handles paper and electronic documents, client/server architecture. Files, retrieves, shares, and distributes documents using PC network. Windows-based desktop environment includes icons representing in/out bins, filing cabinets, shredder, and other office objects. Supports keyboard document retrieval, database querying, and faxing on desktop.
Lotus Notes	Lotus Development Corp.	Allows large group of users to share information over LANs. Forwards e-mail messages or other correspondence to users. Supports graphic files of any size and CUA-compatible interface that provides 3D icons. Allows remote users to compose messages off line and streamline server-to-server communications.
Network Scheduler	Powercore International Inc.	Enables users to schedule meetings with others on time and other resources such as company equipment or conference rooms for individual or entire group. Provides individual appointment books and shared calendar for group use and enables user to implement any security level.
Office IQ	Portfolio Technologies Inc.	Intelligent workgroup product designed to package diverse types of information by project task and distributes that information among work groups. Features object-oriented desktop, document, folder, and workflow templates, information search and retrieval, information security, workflow information, and document enhancement.

(continues)

Table 14-5 *(continued)*

Software name	Company name	Application
OptionFinder	Option Technologies, Inc.	Interactive group decision support system for meeting management. Allows each meeting participant to vote on issues using numeric keypad connected to PC. Collects and tallies electronic votes and produces graphs of results.
Process-IT	NCR Corp.	Allows user to re-engineer business process in LAN environment. Includes MapBuilder graphical tool that allows user to describe business processes, workview display of to-do for users and tools for monitoring status of projects.
Rapport	Clarity Software, Inc.	Allows user to employ various compound, multimedia documents to construct mail messages, assemble media objects, and send their results. Includes drag-and-drop construction of compound, multimedia documents, automatic conversion of multimedia compound to PC, Macintosh, or UNIX environment and support for HP OpenMail.
TeamFocus	IBM Corp.	Supports meetings by improving productivity.
TeamLinks	Digital Equipment Corp.	Provides functions of x·400 mail service. Can be used to order new mail, save/edit unsent mail, send/receive mail, read new mail, file mail into folders, reply to and forward mail, create/edit distribution lists and personal address book entries and perform address validation.
VisionQuest	Collaborative Technologies	Provides electronic meeting support software to improve productivity of meetings and group consensus. Brainwrite, rating, scoring, allocation, voting, comments, and subgroup tools used in collaboration process. Presentation of group results, instant meeting minutes, and meetings in any time/any place of face-to-face scenarios available.
WorkMAN	Reach Software Corp.	Presents organization of information as form view. Intelligently routes forms through different stages of workflow and processes information and business tasks at each stage. Tools are also available for workflow application.

7. What are the three levels of support provided by a GSS?
8. What are some examples of GSS tools?
9. How do you classify GSSs?
10. What are the GSS types under input devices?
11. What are the GSS types under the geographic dimension?
12. What are three types of teleconferencing?
13. What are some of the advantages and disadvantages of teleconferencing systems?
14. How do you classify GroupWare?
15. What are some of the capabilities of Lotus Notes as one of the most popular GroupWare on the market?
16. What are some the advantages of a GSS? What are some of the disadvantages?
17. What are the applications of a GSS in Burr-Brown Corporation? In Texaco?
18. Why wasn't a GSS all that successful in the Department of Indian Health Services (IHS) in Tucson?
19. What have GSSs achieved in IBM? Discuss.
20. What did Lotus Notes achieve in the Price Waterhouse Corporation?

PROJECTS

1. You have been asked to recommend a GroupWare to the First East Bank. Prepare a cost and benefit analysis to be submitted to the president of the bank. What would be some of the main benefits?
2. By consulting the documentation provided by Lotus Development Corporation on Lotus Notes, investigate the capabilities of this GroupWare. What type of organization will benefit from a GroupWare such as Notes? Discuss. Compare and contrast Lotus Notes with Novell GroupWise and Microsoft Exchange.
3. Consult an organization of your choice that is using a GroupWare. What are the specific applications of this software?
4. By referring to references cited for the Department of Indian Health Services (IHS), discuss why EMS implementation was not all that successful.
5. By referring to the references for IBM's applications of a GSS, discuss the reasons for the successful implementation.
6. By consulting the literature, identify three of the major vendors of GroupWare. Why is Lotus Notes so popular?

7. Major carriers such as AT&T, Sprint, and MCI now provide teleconferencing facilities. By contacting one of these carriers, investigate their offerings. What are some of the strengths and limitations of these teleconferencing systems? In your opinion, what are the main advantages of teleconferencing as compared with regular one-to-one meetings? What are some of the limitations?

KEY TERMS

Chauffeured meeting, 402

Desktop conferencing, 413

Electronic meeting systems, 412–413

Facilitator, 402

Group decision support systems, 401–403

Group support systems, 400–427

GroupWare, 414–418

GSS tools, 405–409

Interactive meeting, 403

Real-time computer conferencing, 412–413

Supported meeting, 403

Video teleconferencing, 413

Web-based GSS, 418

REFERENCES

[1] Adhikari, R. (November 18, 1996). A new twist on Groupware. *Information Week,* 75–80.

[2] Bidgoli, H. (1997). *Modern information systems for managers.* San Diego: Academic Press, Inc.

[3] Bidgoli, H. (July/August 1996). Group support systems: A new productivity tool for the 90s. *Journal of Systems Management,* 56–62.

[4] Baldazo, R., and Diehl, S. (March 1995). Workgroup conferencing. *Byte,* 125–128.

[5] Campbell, T. (July 1990). Technology update: Group decision support systems. *Journal of Accountancy,* 413–50.

[6] Dennis, A. R., Pootheri, S. K., and Natarajan, V. (January 1997). TCBWorks: A first generation Web-Groupware system. Proceedings of Twenty-ninth Annual Hawaii International Conference on Systems Sciences, Wailea, HI.

[7] DeSanctis, G., and Gallupe, B. (May 1987). A foundation for study of group decision support systems. *Management Science,* Vol. 33, No. 5, 589–609.

[8] DeSanctis, G., Dickson, G., and Poole, M. (1992). Texaco University of Minnesota research project: Status report and project summary. *Brainstorm,* Vol. 1, No. 4, 12–16.

[9] DeSanctis, G., and Gallupe, B. (Winter 1985). Group decision support systems: A new frontier. *Data Base,* 3–9.

[10] Dennis, A., *et al.* (1990). A new role for computers in strategic management. *The Journal of Business Strategy,* Vol. 11, No. 5, 38–43.

[11] Dickson, G. W., *et al.* (June 1993). Exploring modes of facilitative support for GDSS technology. *MIS Quarterly,* 173–175.

[12] Donelan, J. G. (March 1993). Using electronic tools to improve meetings. *Management Accounting,* 42–45.

[13] Eisenhart, T. (1990). Systems that support group decision making. *Business Marketing,* Vol. 75, No. 6, 50–51.

[14] Ellis, C. A., *et al.* (January 1991). GroupWare: Some issues and experiences. *Communications of ACM,* 38–60.

[15] George, J. F., *et al.* (1992). Electronic meeting systems as innovation: A study of the innovation process. *Information & Management,* 22, 181–195.

[16] Grohowski, R., *et al.* (December 1990). Implementing electronic meeting systems at IBM: Lessons learned and success factors. *MIS Quarterly,* 369–383.

[17] Hoffman, D. (June 1992). Evolution of SAMM: From theory into practice. *Brainstorm,* 6–7.

[18] Hsu, J., and Lockwood, T. (March 1993). Collaborative computing. *Byte,* 113–120.

[19] Jacob, R. (May 18, 1992). The search for the organization of tomorrow. *Fortune,* Vol. 125, No. 10, 90–98.

[20] Jessup, L. M., and Kukalis, S. (1990). Better planning using group support systems. *Long Range Planning,* Vol. 23, No. 39, 100–105.

[21] King, W. R. (Spring 1996). Strategic issues in GroupWare. *Information Systems Management,* 73–78.

[22] Kirkpatrick, D. (December 27, 1993). GroupWare goes boom. *Fortune,* 99–106.

[23] Miller, M. J., *et al.* (June 14, 1994). The changing office. *PC Magazine,* 112.

[24] Mockler, R. J., and Dologite, D. G. (1991). Using computer software to improve group decision making. *Long Range Planning,* Vol. 24, No. 4, 44–57.

[25] Nunamaker, J. F., *et al.* (1988). Computer-aided deliberation: Model management and group decision support. *Operations Research,* Vol. 36, No. 6, 826–848.

[26] Sarin, S., and Greif, I. (October 1985). Computer-based real time conferencing systems. *IEEE Compute,* 33–45.

[27] Stevenson, T. (June 15, 1993). GroupWare: Are we ready? *PC Magazine,* 261–272.

Chapter 15

Geographic Information Systems

Learning Objectives

After studying this chapter, you should be able to:

- Define a geographic information system (GIS).
- Elaborate on GIS components.
- Outline the steps for developing a GIS.
- Review GIS applications.
- Explore the future applications of GIS.

15-1 INTRODUCTION

This chapter provides an overview of geographic information systems (GIS) as a growing decision support tool both in the public and private sectors. The chapter first provides an overview of the GIS, then it discusses the components of a typical GIS. The chapter provides guidelines for developing a successful GIS, which includes performing a needs assessment and a cost and benefit analysis, and choosing the right platform and implementation. The chapter then concentrates on the popular applications of GIS. It concludes with an outlook for the GIS as a rapidly growing information system.

15-2 WHAT IS A GEOGRAPHIC INFORMATION SYSTEM (GIS)?

Executives in a growing number of organizations are faced with questions such as:

- Where should we locate a new store?
- Where should we locate a fire station?
- Where should we locate a fast food restaurant?
- Where should we locate a new school?
- Where should a new airport be located with a minimum environmental impact?
- What route should our delivery truck follow for a minimum of driving time?

A properly designed geographic information system (GIS) can answer these questions and more.

A GIS utilizes spatial and nonspatial data and specialized techniques for storing the coordinates of complex geographic objects, including networks of lines (roads, rivers, streets) and reporting zones (zip codes, cities, counties, or states).

There are numerous definitions for a GIS. The Environment Systems Research Institute in Redlands, California, one of the major vendors of GISs, defines a GIS as follows:

> A GIS is an organized collection of computer hardware, software, geographic data, and personnel, designed to effectively capture, store, update, manipulate, analyze, and display all forms of geographically referenced information.

Three typical geographic objects utilized by a GIS are:

- **Point.** The intersection of lines in a map. For example, a customer location, a dealership location, the location of a fast food restaurant, a gas station, or the location of an airport.

- **Line.** This is usually a series of points on the map, such as a street, a road, or a river.
- **Area.** This is usually a section of the map. Examples include a particular zip code such as the zip code for the southwest region of the city of Portland, or the San Diego Zoo on the San Diego map.

Digitized maps and spatially oriented databases are two major components of GIS. Imagine a company wants to open a new store in the southwest part of the city of Portland, Oregon. You would like to find out how many people live within walking distance of this new store. With a GIS you can start with the map of the United States, zoom in on the state of Oregon, then zoom in on Portland, and finally end up with a street map on your screen. Your tentative store location becomes a marked point on the map. You can draw a circle around your desired location in order to highlight the area that you feel is within walking distance. Now you can ask for a summary of the U.S. Census data on all the people living inside the circle who meet certain conditions such as income level, age, marital status, and so forth. A GIS can provide all sorts of information that enables you to zero in on individual customers and individual marketing objectives [5, 6,8].

A GIS integrates and analyzes spatial data from a variety of sources. The ever-increasing power of the microcomputer and the significant cost reduction in computing equipment makes a GIS an attractive alternative for a wide variety of organizations.

The GIS has been around for almost 30 years. Its major applications have been in government and utility companies, mostly for analyzing census data. As will be explained later in this chapter, GISs are increasingly utilized by various business organizations, particularly in marketing, manufacturing, insurance, and real estate.

A typical GIS is able to perform the following tasks:

- Enables the user to digitize maps
- Associates spatial attributes with points, lines, and polygons on the maps
- Integrates the maps and database data with queries

The query language available in the GIS supports sophisticated query operations. This includes:

- Single criteria search—all customers with an income more than $40,000.
- Multiple criteria search—all the female customers with income over $40,000 who live in the southwest part of the city.
- Searches with logical operators (AND, OR, and NOT)—all the customers who are either female or have an income below $30,000. All the male customers except those who make more than $100,000.

Geographic information systems are differentiated from database management systems (DBMSs) and CAD/CAM (computer-aided design/computer-aided manufacturing) in addressing fundamental, theoretical, and technical problems that geographic information presents. The spatial interdependence among geographic entities, termed spacing autocorrelation, requires filtering to compensate for the spatial proximity between two entities, which creates interdependency. GIS spatial displays account for the spatial autocorrelation, as required for the statistical analysis of the data in an attempt to identify relationships between independent entities [31]. CAD technology is also designed to deal with spatial objects, and is similar to GISs in this respect. However GISs differ at this level in linking spatial objects with their distinguishing attributes, providing the ability to access records through their geographical locations.

A GIS with analytical capabilities evaluates the impact of decisions by providing interpretation of spatial data. Modeling tools and statistical functions are used for forecasting purposes, including trend analysis and simulations. Multiple windows provide simultaneous viewing of the mapped area and the relative nonspatial data. The display of points, lines, and polygons can be color-coded to the nonspatial attributes. The zoom feature can provide the viewing of geographic areas in varying detail levels. Several maps of varying features can be consolidated with map overlays. A map overlay might be used to view all of the gas lines, all of the public schools, or all of the fast food restaurants in any specified region. A buffering feature creates pin maps by highlighting locations based on queried criteria. The new store location that we just described is a good example of this type of analysis.

Figures 15-1, 15-2, 15-3, and 15-4 display sample outputs from selected commercial GISs on the market.

15-3 COMPONENTS OF A GEOGRAPHIC INFORMATION SYSTEM

A typical GIS consists of the following components:

1. *GIS software.* This component includes one of the commercial GIS software packages available on the market. As you will see later in this chapter, there are several types of software available for virtually all platforms. This includes Macintosh, DOS, Windows, and UNIX operating systems. Some of the popular GIS software include ARC/INFO, Atlas GIS, Tactician, MapInfo, and GeoQuery. Using GIS software, an executive can view the names of customers and competitors overlaid on streets, together with demographic information showing population density, gender, income, age, and ethnicity. Geographic objects such as customers or locations can then be analyzed, evaluated, and presented in maps, tabular reports, and graphs [21].

A GIS software package usually does not include data sets such as demographic and census information, city, county and zip code boundaries, and major

RETAIL

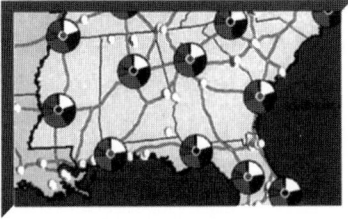

Tactician provides fast, accurate
competitive analysis

DISTRIBUTION

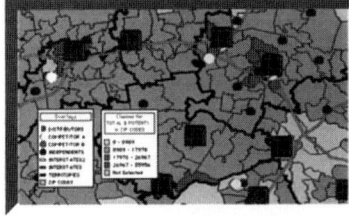

Tactician assists in evaluation and
selecting distribution channels

COMMUNICATIONS

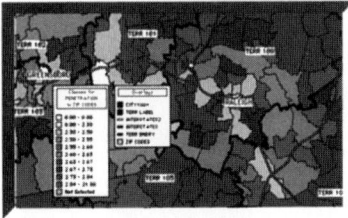

Tactician helps improve cellular market
coverage versus your competitors'

MEDICAL

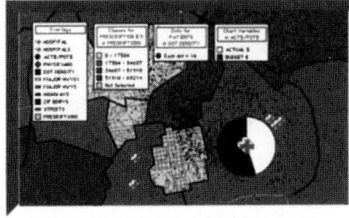

Tactician is a powerful strategy
planning tool for health care

INSURANCE

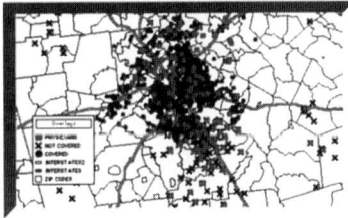

Tactician improves the evaluation of
Health Care Provider Coverage

COMMUNICATIONS

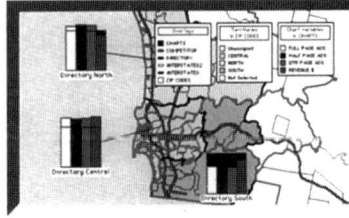

Tactician improves Analysis of, and
response to, Market Penetration data

DISTRIBUTION

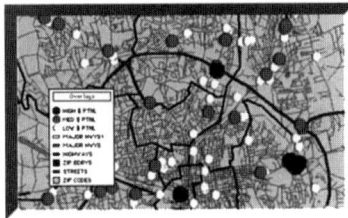

Use Tactician pro-actively to target
new distribution and new business

MANUFACTURING

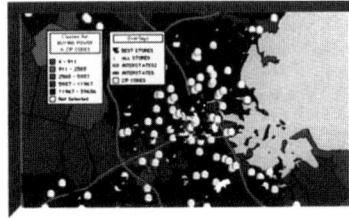

Tactician strengthens retail partnering,
based on market knowledge

Figure 15-1 Tactician micromarketing information systems: turning data into competitive advantage. Courtesy of Tactician Corporation.

BANKING

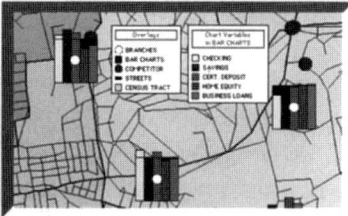

Tactician's Micro-merchandising delivers the right financial products to the market

INSURANCE

Tactician offers seamless access to host-based insurance data

MANUFACTURING

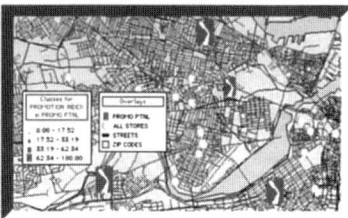

Tactician's 120,000 outlet database cuts promotional waste

DISTRIBUTION

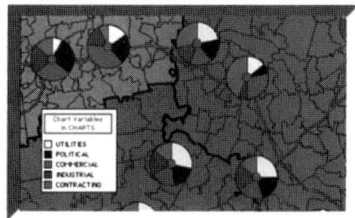

Tactician can expand business for manufacturers and distributors

RETAIL

Tactician delivers site impact analysis with street level precision

RETAIL

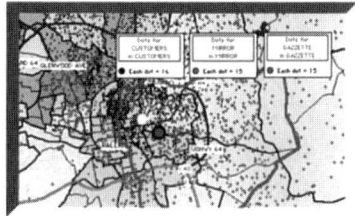

Tactician gets the right advertising message to the right audience

BANKING

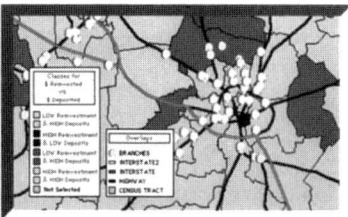

Tactician manages CRA Planning, development, implementation and review needs

MEDICAL

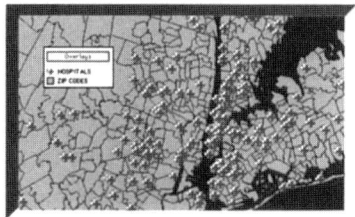

Tactician offers Health Care specific Data Sets

Figure 15-1   *(continued)*

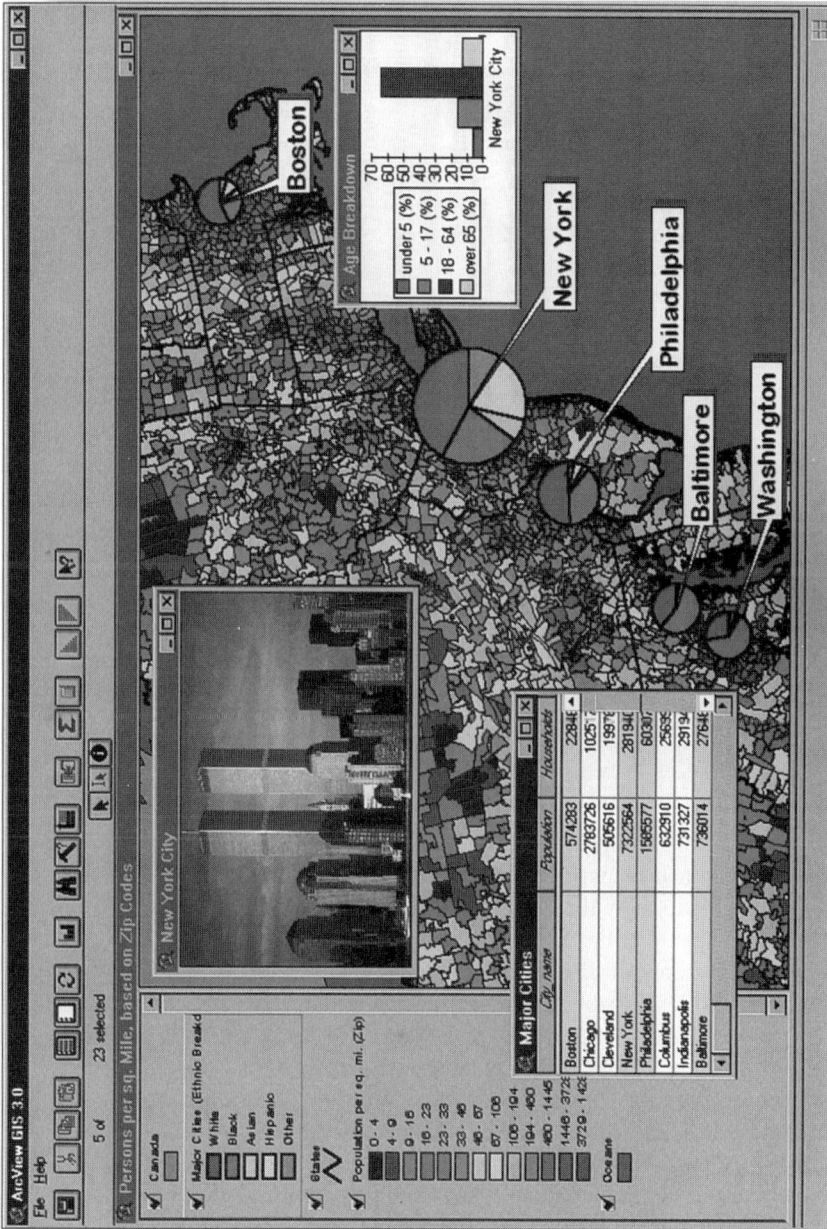

Figure 15-2 Working geographically reveals relationship: among forces that drive your organization. It helps you see patterns you couldn't see before, gain new insights, and make significantly better decisions. Courtesy of ESRI. Copyright © 1996 Environmental Systems Research Institute, Inc.

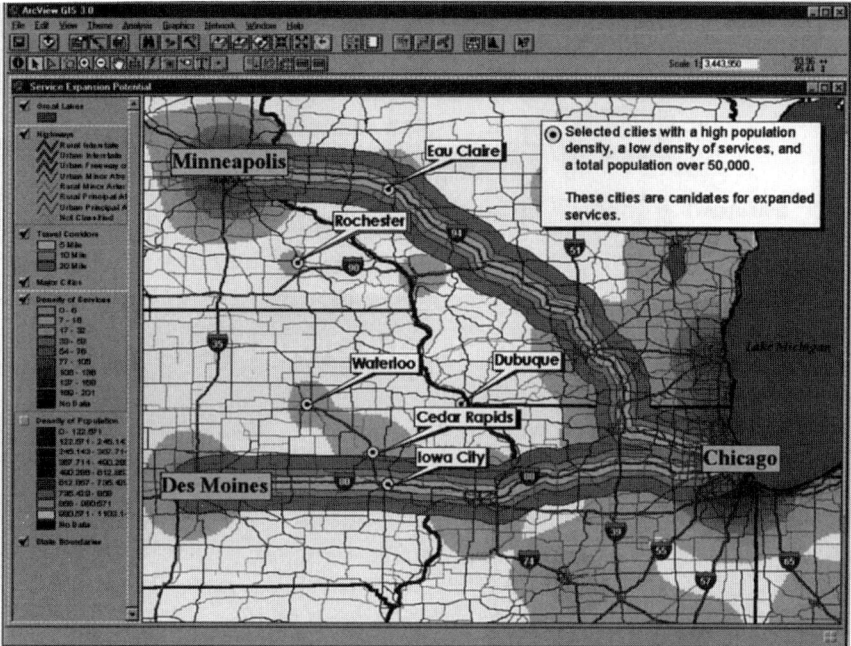

Figure 15-3 Add data to maps to find the geographic factors that drive trends and distributions. Courtesy of ESRI. Copyright © 1996 Environmental Systems Research Institute, Inc.

road systems. This kind of data is purchased from public agencies or private vendors.

2. *Graphics workstation or a high-powered PC.* This component is used for display of data and maps. It should be in color, with a very high resolution in order to be able to view the details of maps and graphs with clarity. The workstation or PC should utilize a CPU that is sufficiently powerful to handle massive data files in a graphical display format. Ideally, the screen should be oversized, for example, 20 or 21 inches, in order to accommodate large viewing areas easily.

3. *Plotter.* This output device is used to generate hard copy maps and drawings in large sheets and 8.5-by-11 inch page-sized formats.

4. *Digitizing tablet.* This component is equipped with conductors that receives electrical signals emitted by a cursor and converts a hard copy map mounted on the surface of the tablet into a digitized map.

5. *A scanner.* Is used to optically read and convert images such as a hardcopy map or photograph into digital format. Scanners vary in price and sophistication.

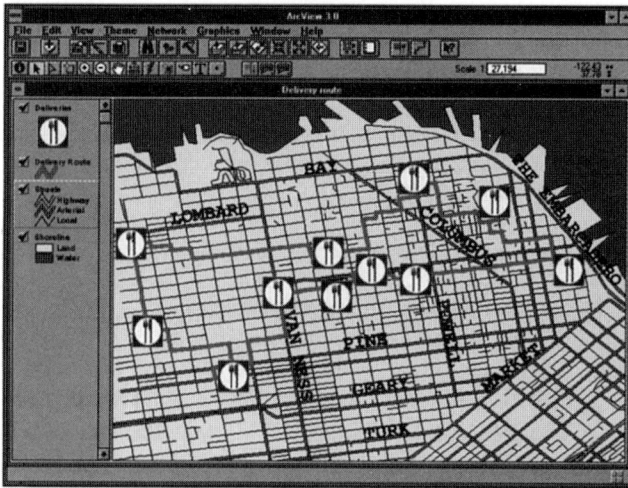

Figure 15-4 ArcView GIS allows you to find the most direct route between two locations or find the best way to visit several locations. Courtesy of ESRI. Copyright © 1996 Environmental Systems Research Institute, Inc.

6. *Vast storage device.* A huge storage device is required to accommodate the immense storage requirements of both spatial and nonspatial data created and used by a GIS. Ten gigabytes or more of storage space is recommended.

7. *CD-ROM* (compact disk read-only memory). Accommodates the distribution of a large GIS database. For example, one CD ROM may include all the maps for the city of Seattle and another one may include all the maps for the city of Los Angeles.

8. *Cursor/puck.* This is a palm-sized input device for digitizing. It consists of a glass or plastic lens with a crosshair target and multiple buttons. It is used with the digitizing tablet to create lines, boundaries around specific areas, and to trace the outline of map objects by tracing over the hard-copy map while it is laying on the digitizing tablet.

9. *Mouse.* This device controls a cursor or pointer on the screen. They come in a variety of shapes with different capabilities. By moving the mouse on the surface of the desk or a mouse pad, the user moves the mouse pointer on the screen. To select an item, after positioning the mouse pointer on the desired location, the user clicks on the left or right mouse button.

10. *Database.* This component includes spatial and nonspatial data with related attributes about the objects. It stores and manipulates the data within the geographic information system. It also includes a query language for various query operations. The spatial database consists of a digitized representation of

maps in cartographic layers. When stored with specific coordinates, the maps can be overlaid to create new maps. For example, let us say that you have started with a map of Chicago. Next, you zoomed in on a particular region of the city, then overlaid the map with the coordinates (locations) of all stoplights within that region. Then you overlaid the map with the coordinates of all emergency roadside call boxes in that same region. This custom map can then be saved in a separate file for later editing or analysis.

Three important elements of data are required for each feature on a map:

- The *location* of each feature in geographic space.
- Each feature's *spatial relationship:* the distance and orientation to other features.
- *What each feature is.* As an example consider the top of Mt. Rainier: its latitude and longitude, how far it is from Mt. St. Helens (what used to be Mt. St. Helens), and that it has all the attributes of a mountain peak (whatever they are).

In the GIS environment, there are two spatial database approaches: raster and vector models. The **raster** structure divides the coverage area into grid cell series in either a detailed or thematic basis. The detailed raster model is generated by remote sensing systems in data acquisition. The thematic model is useful in application-specific analysis projects. A thematic map is a map that displays different quantitative ranges of data by varying colors, textures, symbols, or embedded charts. The **vector** model stores maps as spatial attribute tables for each type of map element, containing the point and line coordinates [16]. The vector model is either unstructured (spaghetti) or topologically structured (intelligent) [24]. The vector model is typically used in data acquisition, and the raster model is useful in the integration of data across multiple sources.

The nonspatial database uses a relational database structure for storing records with reference connections to the spatial database. It is used for queries and provides the basis for examining the relationship among the data elements.

Figure 15-5 provides a conceptual model for a geographic information system.

15-4 DEVELOPING A SUCCESSFUL GIS

The design and implementation of a successful geographic information system, similar to other computer-based information systems, is a multidimensional venture. A methodology similar to the life-cycle approach discussed in Chapter 9 can be utilized. The diagram presented in Figure 15-6 shows the important steps for developing a successful GIS.

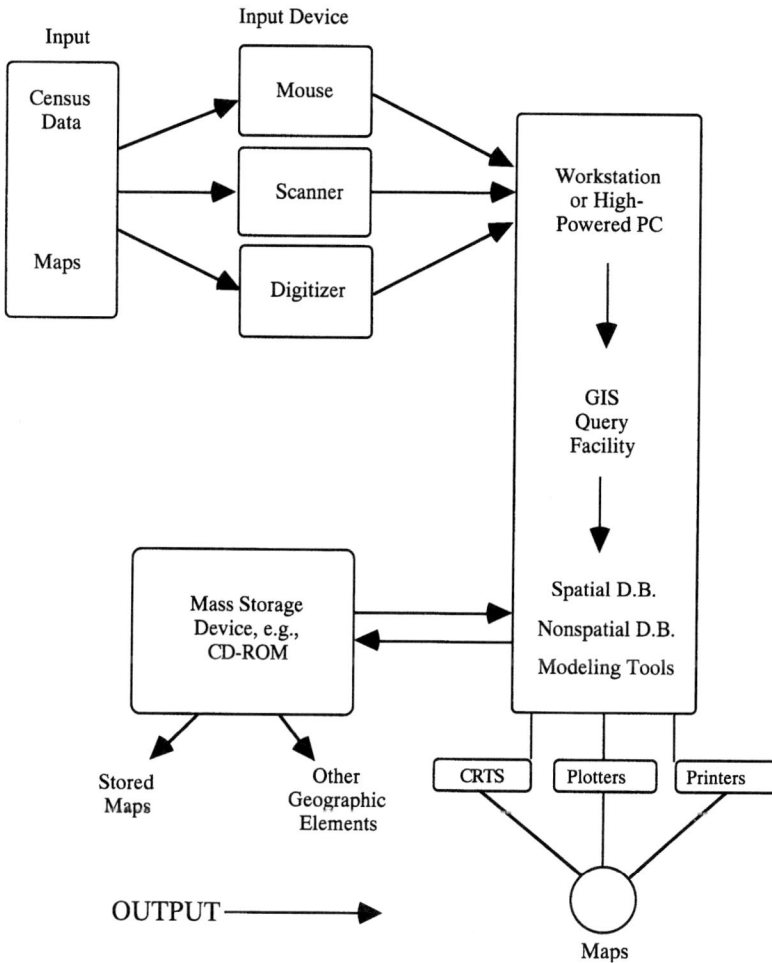

Figure 15-5   A conceptual model for a GIS.

15-4-1 Needs Assessment

The first step before establishing a GIS is to define the mission for the system. The tasks and types of analysis performed by the GIS must be clearly understood. A clear needs analysis should help the design team to create an appropriate system for a particular organization. GISs vary in sophistication. A GIS can be a simple computerized mapping system or a sophisticated decision-support tool for diverse analysis. An organization must decide the following issues:

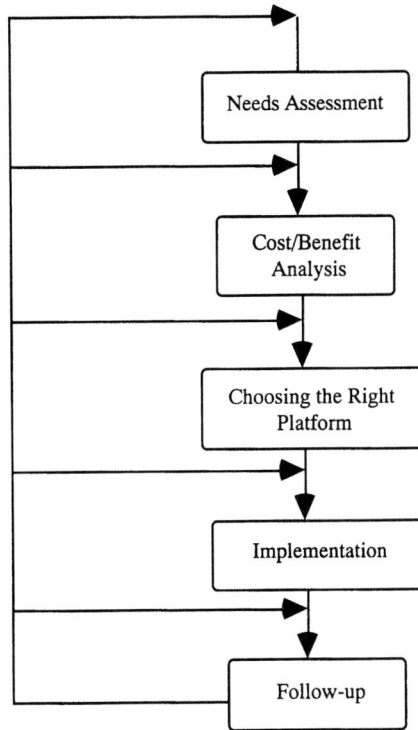

Figure 15-6   Important steps for developing a GIS.

- Storage volume
- Format of the provided output
- Types of data to be included
- Level of sophistication of the end user(s)
- Types of statistical analysis needed
- Types of modeling capabilities needed
- Types of simulation analysis needed

An organization should establish a GIS planning and implementation team. The participants of this team should include individuals with a comprehensive understanding of how geographic data are created, manipulated, interpreted, and distributed throughout the organization. The key users of the proposed GIS should be included in this team. This team is similar to the information systems task force discussed in Chapters 9 and 11.

The selection of a GIS administrator is imperative. Qualifications should include familiarity with mapping and map terminology, superior computer proficiency, and information management experience. Familiarity with the organization's operations is preferred. Because GIS is a relatively new technology, staffing is critical and the development of an effective GIS administrator often entails a year or more of training and experience. The GIS authority must be established within or outside of the control of the information systems department. The relationship of the GIS administrator to the information systems department must be defined.

The initial phase of the project must be clearly defined. One of the most important decisions is the selection of the base map to construct. It is of primary importance to the organization, as it establishes the foundation for further map development. Pertinent decisions include which geographic areas to choose, scale, resolution, and level of accuracy.

The data sources must be identified. This may include in-house development of data, purchasing the data from government agencies, or purchasing it from private companies. Database redundancy control must be established to avoid duplication of central information services. Whether integration of the organizational data is used, a central repository is accessed, or individual vendors are used, conversion requirements must be established.

Data acquisition and conversion require the integration of multisource data and are complicated by varying scales and coordinates, as well as imprecise measurements. The census data offered by private vendors is superior to the government offerings due to data refinements and an improved user interface. The Census Bureau maintains a list of TIGER (Topologically Integrated Geographic Encoding and Referencing) file-related products and services. Digital mapping is faster and more accurate than topographic conversion and reduces costs significantly. Topographic features define elevation information sometimes called third dimension. To achieve particular levels of accuracy specific densities of vertical control points must be available. Digital ortho mapping is based on aerial photographs that have been digitally scanned after airplane tilt and ground relief is rectified. Scaling is possible, unlike U.S. Geological Survey maps [31].

Data acquisition and conversion costs may be reduced in the future by more extensive commercial and governmental database availability, automated digitalization of maps and sharing of data among organizations with similar geographic interests.

15-4-2 Cost and Benefit Analysis

The cost of a GIS, similar to other computer-based information systems, includes hardware and software costs and personnel. Data acquisition is probably one of the most important costs for developing a GIS. As explained in the next section, a GIS may run on the existing hardware or on specialized hardware that might be purchased. The amount of time, energy, and money required to effectively implement a GIS can be significant, in addition to the long-term costs of updating and maintaining the software and data. A leading GIS consulting firm, Plan Graphics, Inc., estimates that data conversion compromises 50 to 60% of implementation costs [31]. The cost of the basic GIS package and optional data files such as street data and geographic detail files, should be evaluated, as each vendor requires proprietary file formats for geographic data. Although most of these data are publicly available from the Census Bureau, the format will differ, requiring conversion, and the third-party vendor often provides enhancements. The U.S. Bureau of Census offers a 44-disk set of street maps and a 17-disk set of population and economic data. Shortly, this data will be available on CD-ROM that makes it cheaper and more compact.

The elements of specialized hardware and software require extensive training and a steep learning curve for users. Sufficient time must be allocated to train users in the full capabilities of the GIS. The hardware requirements should not be compromised. Substantial processing power, immense storage, and an oversized high-resolution monitor are essential.

A properly designed GIS can easily outweigh its cost by improving the efficiency and effectiveness of decision making. A GIS produces informative maps for data analysis prior to making decisions that put resources in jeopardy. A GIS, by performing statistical and modeling analyses, provides new insight for the data prior to its utilization. The manager of marketing analysis at Ostram/Sylvania commented on the use of GIS (they are using Tactician by Tactician Corporation) in presentations to their customers (wholesale distributors):

> Of course, we could have given them the same data on reams of spreadsheet printouts, but illustrating the information with a map is a much more powerful tool.

He referred to the use of a GIS as a "sensory approach to bring customers" [26].

The use of GIS overcomes the drawbacks of using maps for decision analysis. The following are some of the drawbacks of using maps. A GIS eliminates these shortcomings:

1. Images contain limited amounts of information.
2. Requires extensive knowledge of map interpretation due to limited detail.
3. Difficulty in the assessment of multiple maps due to inconsistencies in map sizing and presentation.
4. Complications of overlaying map for information consolidation.
5. Difficulty in updating and manipulation [16,17].

Additionally, electronic storage is more compact than maps and the associated manual records. The capability to obtain data from a variety of sources is improved by the ability to digitize maps.

As discussed in Chapter 3, all database and DBMSs include the following benefits:

1. Automated data entry and retrieval
2. Data consistency enforcement
3. Both logical and physical data views
4. Presentations of data in a format appropriate to specific problems

The unique features of a GIS query identify the power of a geographic information system by offering the following capabilities [24]:

1. The merger of voluminous data sources from dissimilar data models is required.
2. Both spatial and nonspatial data must be interpreted and abstracted.
3. A rapid response time is required.

15-4-3 CHOOSING THE RIGHT PLATFORM

The discriminating factor in assessing GIS software is the task performed by the software. Each has a particular focus and a variety of strengths and weaknesses; thus the needs assessment will narrow the criteria and number of products to evaluate. The annual *International GIS Source Book,* published by GIS World, Inc., includes comprehensive descriptions of hardware, software and suppliers. Additionally, the periodical *GIS World* provides current technical articles.

The market is divided into software for two hardware platforms: workstations and microcomputers. The size of the application determines the necessary hardware. However, due to the ever-increasing power of microcomputers, the gap between these two platforms is narrowing.

15-4-3-1 Workstation-Based GISs

There are more than 150 companies competing in the GIS market. Two software vendors dominate the market with a combined share of approximately 50%: Environmental Systems Research Institute, Inc. (ESRI), and Intergraph [18]. The three major vendors of workstation GIS include ARC/INFO ESRI, Intergraph, and Earth Resources Data Analysis Systems (ERDAS). ARC/INFO ESRI is the leading workstation product. A wide variety of data formats are supported, including TIGER, DLG (Digital Line Graph), ETAK (this format was developed by ETAK corporation to represent street information), and DIME (this format is the predecessor to the U.S. Bureau of the Census' TIGER format). Hardware plat forms include Apollo, Hewlett-Packard, SUN, and DEC-VAX. The ARC product processes vector-based cartographic data; the INFO product is a relational DBMS.

Intergraph of Huntsville, Alabama, provides vector-based turnkey systems for a variety of applications. ERDAS is a raster-based system, typically used for natural resources management and military intelligence applications, requiring remotely sensed data.

15-4-3-2 Microcomputer-Based GISs

ARC/INFO (Environmental Systems Research Institute, Inc.) is a PC-based GIS of complexity and depth, consisting of a cohesive unit of individual modules. Its strengths lies in providing a mapping front end to database queries. An application programming language and compiler is included (Simple Macro Language), which enables command line and shell procedures to be sequenced for application development. The complexity of the product requires a high learning curve; the vendor suggests a 6-month familiarity period.

Atlas GIS (Strategic Mapping, Inc.) focuses on map generation, has a propriety geographic file format, and is vector-based. A map-layering capability is included and maps data from different sources can be combined. Several thematic presentation maps are available:

1. Ranged maps, ranking data by color, symbol, and fill pattern.
2. Proportional maps, representing data with varying fill patterns in proportion to the data value.
3. Dot-density maps proportioned to the data values.

The ease of digitizing new maps and adding detail to existing maps are prominent features. Atlas GIS is not designed as an interface for querying databases; no programming language is provided. However, simple queries by (1) map features, (2) map feature relations, and (3) attribute relations can be performed. A data file format common to dBASE and FoxBase is used, and other database files can be imported with translation utilities.

Site selection is a typical use of Atlas GIS. A model is developed from defined parameters that identify "where stores do best." Electronic scouting for the areas that meet the criteria is performed, producing selected sites for physical review.

Tactician (Tactician Corporation) is a vector-based GIS, designed for sales and marketing applications. It includes superior data retrieval and recompilation speed due to the fact that it was migrated from the DEC VAX/VMS platform. It can integrate with varying hosts and database systems with an Ethernet connection. Foreign cartographic files can be imported. Thematic maps using color and dot density are accompanied by corresponding chart display of the data. All layer data must be of the same type, but when map layering is used, selective, reveal and hide features of the display serves to provide only pertinent geographic data. Tactician is a complex program of considerable difficulty for users lacking technical knowledge [11]. It is available for both the Windows and Macintosh environments.

In 1989, Sears Roebuck and Company implemented Tactician for various analytical applications. Their marketing database contained 70 million households from their retail, credit, insurance, brokerage, and real estate entity marketing files. They performed site location analysis for new and relocated stores, redistricting for reorganization, and physician location for their managed healthcare program [23].

MapInfo (MapInfo Corp.) focuses on map data analysis, combining map drawing and map query features. It is targeted for sales management, and offers two query methods: the user interface (Windows) and the MapBasic programming language. Turnkey applications can therefore be generated. Alternative map sources include (1) those provided with the software; (2) digitized maps; and (3) imported maps in alternative formats. Alternative data source formats that can be imported include ASCII, dBASE, Lotus 1-2-3, and Excel. During data import, the geocoding process assigns relative map locations. If no match exists, a manual assignment is asked for a later assignment or a match can be made in aggregate by an alternative database. Analytical functions are relational with assessment of multilayer relationships. MapInfo is available in both MS-DOS and Windows versions.

GeoQuery (GeoQuery Corp.) is a Macintosh GIS with data analysis emphasis, designed to search preexisting imported databases and maps for details by query. It provides full relational analysis and is supported by the 4th Dimension (Acius) Relational Database Management System (RDBMS). A unique feature is the ability to load and manipulate data from within a custom application, enabled by the use of Apple Events. Map zooming is available by map scale definition.

Table 15-1 provides a summary of popular commercial GIS software [25,30].

15-4-4 IMPLEMENTATION

GIS development requires a multiyear commitment due to an extensive database development process [17]. Massive amounts of data must be compiled, standardized, and input into the system. A major cost can be the development of a customized database if products or services are not available to meet the organization's specific requirements.

GIS software varies in integration capabilities with other database software. This feature greatly extends the usefulness of the software in applications for which retrievable data exist. The lack of data standards and state or nationwide GIS data inventories limits data availability and the resulting cost of collecting data must be factored. A common misconception about a GIS is that the required data "already exist" in a GIS-accessible format. This is not true in the majority of cases. Efforts to overcome the fact that the majority of geographically referenced information does not adhere to common data format standards are being undertaken by the U.S. government's TIGER (Topologically Integrated Geographic Encoding and Referencing) and DLG (Digital Line Graph) data formats. The former was developed by the U.S. Bureau of the Census for use in compiling the 1990 Census of Population; the latter by the U.S. Geological Survey. A data

Table 15-1

Popular GIS Software on the Market

GIS name	Vender	Features
ARC/Info	ESRI, Inc.	Command-line interface Application programming language Screen, digitizer, printer and plotter support Relational database
Atlas GIS	Strategic Mapping, Inc.	Menu-driven Extensive tools for developing thematic maps Digitizer, printer and plotter support dBASE oriented
GeoQuery	GeoQuery Corp.	Macro interface Relational database Strong market analysis and reporting

MapInfo	MapInfo Corp.	Windows interface
		Screen, printer, plotter and Windows
		    device support
		SQL database query
		Full-featured map drawing and
		    query application programming

Tactician	Tactician Corporation	Menu-driven Spreadsheet oriented Strong market analysis and reporting Flexible fitting for external data query and importing

quality issue of the federally provided GIS data has been identified; the accuracy of the first national digital map is only to 200 feet. Vendors offer improved versions that correct and enhance the TIGER and DLG data formats.

The effects of the positioning of a GIS within an organization must be considered. Often, a GIS is considered to be important by small units within an organization, yet not necessarily by information systems departments, which must be relied on for evaluation and implementation. Conversely, the organizational impact of GIS implementation must be evaluated, as individuals may be threatened by the perceived loss of control over information within their arena when organization-wide projects are undertaken. Sufficient resources should be allocated to alter the potential resulting resistive attitude.

The users and designers of GISs should also be aware of some of the possible downsides of this powerful technology. GISs may create ethical and legal issues. Can the organization be sued if it based decisions on data that was incorrect in a

GIS? Who is responsible for such a lawsuit? Does anybody have the right to photograph my property from a satellite and use that information for various purposes without my permission? If an aerial photograph showed someone building bombs on their property, would that be probable cause for an arrest? What if the photograph was false or mistaken? Does the Census Bureau have the right to sell or give away information I provide to them? How does it ensure that information is not combined with other information in such a way that my privacy is invaded? Are there industries (e.g., title search) that may disappear as a result of GISs? How could GISs be used for positive environmental purposes? These are all-important issues and will become more important with the widespread applications of the GIS. Careful planning and considerations are needed in order to minimize the negative impacts of this very powerful technology.

15-5 GIS APPLICATIONS: AN OVERVIEW

Although GIS applications started with government agencies and utility companies, they now covers a diverse spectrum. GIS applications can be broadly classified within the following categories [3,4,7,14,15]:

- Advertising (see section 15-5-1)
- Archeology (e.g., keeping tracks of sites during excavation)
- Control of endangered species (e.g., using special transmitters and satellite receivers to track the migration of endangered species)
- Education planning (e.g., where to build the next school)
- Election administration (e.g., how best to manage the voters and provide services for them)
- Employment opportunities (e.g., looking for a specific job in a specific location)
- Finding products and services
- Government (local, state, and federal; see Section 15-5-5)
- Insurance (see Section 15-5-3)
- Map and database publishing
- Oil, gas, and mineral exploration
- Real estate (see Section 15-5-4)
- Research and education
- Survey and mapping
- Transportation and logistics (see Section 15-5-2)
- Urban and regional planning

The range of public sector applications of GISs is extensive. Operation Desert Storm in the Gulf War used a GIS from Intergraph Corporation to support supply logistics and to determine cruise missile targets.

City and county administrators rely on GISs for dispatching personnel and equipment to crime and fire locations, as well as maintaining crime statistics and locating fire hydrants. GIS education applications include making changes on school district boundaries to alter the total school population and racial diversity. GIS land-use applications include area zoning, boundaries, classification, and taxation. A GIS can track the shifting ridership on local transit systems for analysis purposes. Based on this analysis, new political districts can be developed. Disaster management and recovery can benefit from GIS use. Public services can provide quicker emergency response and insurance companies can provide faster customer response for dispatching services and adjusters to the most devastated neighborhoods.

15-5-1 MARKETING

Marketing and sales applications are extensive. For target marketing purposes, a GIS pinpoints the area of the greatest concentration of a retailer's ideal customers with the display of sales statistics in geographic terms. Evaluating demographic and lifestyle data can identify new markets. New products and services can be targeted at specific population groups. Analysis of customer distribution, including market share and population growth relative to store locations, can be performed. A company's current position in the marketplace based on industry, company size, and geographic location can be evaluated [19,27].

The need for new stores can be determined, based on mapping of the success of existing stores, the location of competitors, and the areas not penetrated. Site selection is a critical application of GISs because stores succeed or fail based mainly on location. By combining data on demographics and traffic patterns, PepsiCo, Inc., uses a GIS to help pinpoint the best locations for new Pizza Hut and Taco Bell outlets.

With a GIS, sales territory management for retail and wholesale products can be improved. Historically, sales territories have remained static due to the complexity of redefinition. Modifications are crucial in response to competitive pressures and productivity improvements. Sales territories are not always contiguous geographic zones nor do they have balanced sales potential. Sales figures can be evaluated in order to balance territory assignments. As sales territories are redefined, the cumulative sales potential and size and shape of the territory are examined to minimize travel time.

Political campaigns present an interesting marketing application for GISs. Marketing in political party organizations and campaigns can be effectively supported with a GIS in the development of target campaigns for promoting contributions and candidates. Census data and voter registration files provide the same data. The Clinton presidential campaign used Atlas GIS from Strategic Mapping to improve volunteer efforts and enhance media efforts [20]. Specific uses of GISs in political campaigns include:

- Securing union endorsement by mapping AFL-CIO members
- Enlisting volunteers from organized labor
- Improving responses to negative advertising by mapping their origination
- Identifying voters who would determine election results

Similar applications include political action committees, labor unions, and grassroots movements.

15-5-2 TRANSPORTATION

The transportation industry and industries that use transportation services and involve logistics can benefit from GIS use. A GIS is used for dispatching and vehicle fleet management as route and scheduling optimization reduces fleet operating costs. Delivery addresses are geocoded, a routing algorithm is applied, and a street network is produced that enables the estimation of actual driving time. Geocode is the key by which one can quickly retrieve a geographic object such as a point, line, or an area. A simple example would be a street address. However, you can generate your own keys from the longitude, latitude, and map layer, or any method that you want. All geocodes within a map must be unique. This is similar to the key in a relational database [25].

Home delivery and taxi company delivery zones can be defined and factored for efficient dispatching. Emergency vehicle, repair, and parcel pickup services can benefit from dynamic dispatching and updating recent knowledge of required service calls. Commercial delivery services, such as Federal Express and United Parcel Service (UPS), have benefited from GIS use. For example, Federal Express uses a GIS to place its drop boxes and estimate the number of trucks and planes it needs during peak periods [1].

The distribution problem of delivery trucks returning to the warehouse empty results in a waste of time and resources. Development of a scheduling system to pick up supplier merchandise on returns from customer deliveries can improve the effectiveness of the system. A GIS can identify the stores and suppliers, develop a map showing those closely related and schedule the routing accordingly.

15-5-3 INSURANCE

Insurance agencies are using GISs for various demographic information. Their most common application is for guarding against classification errors. Insurers and their agents are frequently pressed by market demands to act quickly on a potential new customer's request for coverage. Researching for information such as risk and premium rates mean hours of searching various books and a variety of maps. With GIS, the insurance company can identify an appropriate premium in a few seconds without ever having to pick up a telephone or look at a map. A GIS combines community boundaries, street addresses, postal carrier routes, and zip codes, plus four codes with search capabilities to locate a risk and it provides key hazard information in four areas as follows [13]:

- Windstorm, including wind pool eligibility, proximity to nearest large body of water, historical wind events at the site, extended coverage, as well as group II zones and territory codes for personal and commercial lines.
- Auto rating variables, including territory codes and distance between an insured's home and work address, measured as the probable minimum driving distance.
- Indexes that measure crime rates, including auto theft, robbery, aggravated assault, burglary, crimes against persons and properties, and overall crime hazard index.
- Public fire protection information gives data about the public protection of the community in which specific property is located.

In addition, the system is capable of providing information on earthquakes and brush fires, as well as environment risk data collected from federal and state agencies.

The benefit of an insurance GIS is that it can help insurers to uncover fraudulent application information. In the last 3 months of 1993, GISs uncovered 10 to 15 cases in which information regarding an insured's property address was false and resulted in premium rates that were 80% lower than the predefined rate. The risk factors built into the GIS system are based on information and most often misrepresented in the insured property's proximity to fire hydrants or a fire station [9].

15-5-4 REAL ESTATE

The real estate industry has benefited from GIS use in numerous applications. Real estate agents can use the GIS as a tool to identify a lot for a potential buyer's preferences and price range. The use of a combination of census data, multiple listing files, and mortgage information and buyer profiles can do this. Realtors can establish selling prices of homes, replacing the time-consuming task of finding comparable homes and identifying the sale prices [2].

A GIS can survey the entire city to identify comparable neighborhoods and average sales prices. Real estate market analysis can be performed for appraisal purposes to determine the causal relationships between national, regional, and local economic trends and the demand for local real estate [28]. Additionally, factors that effect the return on real estate investments can be analyzed.

15-5-5 GOVERNMENT

We already mentioned some of the GIS applications in government. Cities and counties have been some of the major users of GISs. The following is another look at these growing GIS applications. With more and more constraints being placed on all forms of governments, cities and local agencies are being forced to become more efficient. The story is always the same, do more with less. In real-life practice the only way this can be done is with increasing use of technology— GISs are an example of such technology. In recent years only the larger cities and agencies could justify the useage of such technologically advanced equipment. Now, not only has cost of GISs lowered to an affordable level, their application is absolutely essential for operating government efficiently. There are three categories of GIS applications in government [29]:

- The conversion of data to information
- The integration of data with maps and CAD
- The ability to provide error-free analysis

Every city and government agency keeps track of volumes of data. These data are mostly found in hard-copy format scattered throughout the organization. Most of these data are valuable and irreplaceable. However, access to them is hampered by the logistics of the data storage systems. Even when data can be located they must be manipulated and merged with all other data from other departments in order to provide the services requested. A GIS eliminates this painstaking search. The database can be sorted and resorted, depending on the information requested. When one department needs information from another department, the inquiring department can use a GIS to simply call it up on the screen—no more inter-departmental memos and lost days waiting for information to be routed back. With a GIS countless hours of sorting, filling, and digging through basement files are eliminated. One benefit of using a GIS is the image projected to the public. Before, if a citizen requested information he was supposed to wait while the clerk sorted through numerous hard-copy reports. Now, the answer is at the fingertips of the person taking the request. All cities and agencies strive for increasing efficiency, and GISs project efficiency.

A GIS also allows this newfound database power to be merged with existing CAD systems. Field crews equipped with a laptop, notebook, or a subnotebook can access almost unlimited information anywhere in the field. At the present time most of the field crews carry large, bulky hard copies to the field. Because of its large size, the hard copy is limited to the needs of only their department. With GISs a street crew could ask for sewer or water grid overlay on their laptop and in seconds they could see the location of all utilities before digging the street. Back in the engineering department drafters could overlay all of the utilities to see the total effect of the design process. When field crews change systems or find differences the problem could be noted and uploaded onto the database. One major improvement as pointed out is the ability to merge written files with CAD systems. With GISs all aspects of information transfer would be greatly improved.

One of the main problems with any large amount of data is human error and the time required to generate and manipulate models. In the absence of GIS data the creations of models for different situations require painstaking hand drawing and tabulation. In this manual process error could cause days of work to be wasted. With a GIS this is reduced to a simple query task, and what used to take days or week now only takes a few minutes. In addition to the obvious speed advantage all work is done error-free. With new GIS techniques numerous models can be designed and simulated. Due to budget constraints, before GISs this would not have been possible. Models could have only been constructed on a few selected variables.

GISs do help government agencies to be more effective and efficient by allowing fewer people to perform more and more difficult tasks. They free much-needed technical personnel for more specific tasks, by permitting less-technical employees to carry out these tasks. In the field every crew has complete and total access to whatever information they need to perform the job at hand. This eliminates down time and backtracking. The system allows for an unlimited flow of information between all interested parties [29].

15-5-6 EMERGING APPLICATIONS

The integration of GISs and expert systems is referred to as an intelligent GIS. Two such systems have been developed for resource management. A prototype that links a GIS, an expert system, and remote sensing equipment has been designed for irrigation scheduling. Plant canopy temperature is considered to be an indicator for the timing of crop irrigation and the sensory equipment provides remote measurement for interpretation by the expert system component. The results are transferred to the GIS, which prioritizes fields in the region by water need and allocates the available water accordingly [22].

A second application, integrated resource management automation (IRMA), links a GIS, an expert system, and a conventional database for forest pest management use. Graphical records of previous defoliation enable the visual analysis of forest stands for the determination of pesticide treatment. The area descriptions, stand conditions, and spatial relationships are transferred to the expert system for treatment recommendation [22].

The integration of GISs and global positioning satellites (GPS) has the potential of transforming the aviation and shipping industries. It enables vehicles or aircraft equipped with a GPS receiver to pinpoint their location as they move [26]. Jepson Corporation of Minneapolis currently utilizes GPS in roving vans with 10 video cameras. Their goal is to record an image of every U.S. city street in digital and video output formats with digital map linking with annual updates [1].

Alliance Retail Information Systems (Englewood, Colorado) is developing GeoStore, a multidepartment GIS for retailers to meet the customized demand. Planned uses include advertising, market research, distribution, transportation, site location, and real estate [3].

Japanese car manufacturers have started offering cars that employ this technology by using a small device on the dashboard. This device can give you directions and help you find needed places in an unfamiliar city or state.

15-6 OUTLOOK FOR GISs

Vehicle navigation systems have potential use in emergency services, utility repair vehicles, and passenger vehicles. Etak, Inc. (Menlo Park, California), has developed The Navigator, a vehicle tracking and navigation system that works with digital street maps. It includes a database of U.S. street centerlines, as well as streets of portions of the developed world [3].

Two factors position geographic information systems for potentially explosive growth. Accessibility to the sources of data is in place, as street maps and economic and population data are offered by the Census Bureau. The technology links spatial databases with traditional alphabetic and numeric databases.

Business applications thus far have comprised only 6% of the GIS market, yet they are the fastest growing segment [26]. Geographic technology can be sold by providing a competitive edge, providing the basis for accelerated expansion of corporate market. Production, marketing, and distribution efficiencies determine business success, and a GIS can support the identification of opportunities and inefficiencies [12].

The task of site location has become more critical, considering higher costs, fewer prime locations to choose from, and the resulting increased risk in opening new stores. A GIS can provide location analysis considering all the important factors.

GISs are already emerging as an embedded technology. The first database software to offer GISs is offered by OneSource Information Services, a Lotus Development Corporation spinoff. Microsoft and Lotus Development Corporation have both incorporated a mapping engine (Strategic Mapping, Inc.) to Excel and Lotus 1-2-3 spreadsheet upgrades.

In the near future, GIS technology will provide business with a better representation of its customers and competition that is similar to the way that spreadsheets provided an improved view of financial information in the 1980s [10]. Technology can influence a firm's competitive ability, and GIS technology can provide access to enhanced information that will support the effort to create and sustain a competitive advantage.

The future of the GIS will undoubtedly contain links to virtual reality and artificial intelligence software. In the near future we should be able to review a home from across the world, while choosing the neighborhood that we want to live in. Included here would be the ability to view the schools our children will attend, the stores we will shop, and the parks and other social and economic necessities that they will have. The everincreasing power and reduction in cost of microcomputers will expedite the adoption of this exciting technology.

SUMMARY

This chapter provided an overview of the GIS as one of the growing applications of decision support systems in both public and private sectors. The chapter examined the components of a typical GIS, it explained important steps for developing a successful GIS, and it introduced an overview of some of the popular applications of GISs in marketing, transportation, insurance, real estate, and government. The chapter concluded with an outlook for GISs. All indications are that GIS applications will continue to grow and will become more affordable to many organizations regardless of their size and financial status.

REVIEW QUESTIONS

1. What is a GIS?

2. What are two types of data used by a GIS?

3. What are three types of geographic objects?

4. Is the GIS relatively new or has it been around for years? Why are GISs gaining in popularity?

5. What is the difference between a GIS, a DBMS and a CAD/CAM system? Discuss.

6. What are some of the components of a typical GIS?

7. What are some of the popular GIS software programs on the market?

8. What is included in the database component of a GIS?

9. What are two spatial database approaches in a GIS environment?

10. What are the major dimensions or issues for developing a successful GIS?

11. What are some of the considerations when performing needs assessment for developing a GIS?

12. What are some of the qualifications of a GIS administrator?

13. What are some of the costs and benefits of a GIS?

14. When choosing a platform for a GIS, what should be considered?

15. What are some of the popular workstation-based GISs? Of microbased GISs?

16. What are some of the issues that must be considered during the implementation of a GIS?

17. What are some of the general applications of a GIS?

18. What are some of the specific applications of GISs in marketing? Transportation? Real Estate? Insurance? Government?

19. What has a GIS done for Federal Express? For PepsiCo?

20. What are some of the emerging applications of the GIS?

21. What are some of the uses of vehicle navigation systems that employ GIS technology?

22. What is the outlook for GIS? Why is the GIS market expanding so rapidly? Discuss.

PROJECTS

1. A government agency in southern California is planning to introduce a GIS into its day-to-day operations. They have asked for a detailed cost and benefit analysis of this new information system application. Prepare a cost and benefit analysis report for this agency. Who would be the main users of the system? In addition to the hardware and software costs, what other costs should be considered?

2. Investigate the applications of a GIS for city planning in your area. What can a GIS do for utility companies?

3. Investigate the applications of a GIS in a local insurance company and in the insurance business in general.

4. Compare and contrast two of the microbased and two of the workstation-based GISs introduced in this chapter. What are some of the advantages of a workstation-based GIS compared with a microbased GIS?

5. By referring to the references provided in this chapter, research the upcoming applications of GISs. What would be the unique applications of these systems?

6. What is an expert GIS? What are some of the applications of this type of GIS?

7. Consult the computer center in your school or an organization that might have one of the GIS software products. Try to do some hands-on work with one of these packages. The majority of them provide a comprehensive online help system. By reading through the help screens investigate some of the features of the software.

KEY TERMS

Components of a geographical information system (GIS), 434, 438–440
Cost and benefit analysis, 443–445
Geographic information systems, 432–434
GIS administrator, 442–443
GIS applications, 449–455

GIS objects, 432–433
GIS software, 448
Implementation issues, 447–449
Microcomputer-based GIS, 446–447
Needs assessment, 441–443
Nonspatial data, 432
Spatial data, 432
Workstation-based GIS, 445

REFERENCES

[1] Anonymous. (July 26, 1993). *Business Week,* 75–76.
[2] Aalberts, R. J., and Bible, D. S. (October 1992). Geographic information system: Application for the study of real estate. *The Appraisal Journal,* 483–492.
[3] Antenucci, J. C. (1990). *Geographic Information Systems: A Guide to the Technology.* New York: Van Nostrand Reinhold.
[4] Barnett, A. P., and Okoruwa, A. A. (April 1993). Application of geographic information systems in site selection and location analysis. *The Appraisal Journal,* 245–254.
[5] Bidgoli, H. (1997). *Modern information systems for managers.* San Diego: Academic Press, Inc.
[6] Bidgoli, H. (May/June 1995). Geographic information systems: A new strategic tool for the 90's and beyond. *Journal of Systems Management,* 24–27, 66–67.
[7] Bibe, D. S., and Hsieh, C.-H. (October 1996). Warehouse buildings and geographic information systems. *The Appraisal Journal,* 416–422.
[8] Celko, J. (November 1991). What you need to know about geobases, *Systems Integration,* p. 39.
[9] Covaleski, J. M. (February 1994). Software help carriers avoid perilous areas. *Best's Review,* 82–83.
[10] Dunn, W. (May 1992). How to talk to a map. *American Demographics,* 8–23.
[11] Eglowstein, H., and Smith, B. (January 1993). Putting your data on the map. *Byte,* 188–190.
[12] Ester, T. G. (May 1992). The next step is called GIS. *American Demographics Desk Reference,* 2–4.
[13] Gilbert, E. (October 4, 1993). GUS guards against costly classification errors. *National Underwriter,* 5.

[14] Goodchild, M. F. (Spring 1991). Geographic information systems. *Journal of Retailing,* Vol. 67, No. 1, 3–15.

[15] Griffin, M., and Hester, J. (December 1990). New opportunities for capital improvement programming using GIS. *Government Finance Review,* 7–10.

[16] Grupe, F. H. (Summer 1992). Can a geographic information system give your business its competitive edge? *Information Strategy,* 41–48.

[17] Grupe, F. H. (Summer 1990). Geographic information systems: An emerging component of decision support. *Technology Outlook,* 74–78.

[18] Kindel, S. (January 19, 1993). Geographic information systems. *Financial World,* 44.

[19] Lewis, R. (August 1992). Putting sales on the map. *Sales & Marketing,* 76–80.

[20] Montague, C. (February 1993). Clinton follows computer maps to White House. *American Demographics,* 13–15.

[21] Moore, M. (June 13, 1994). GIS software proliferates. *PC Week,* 34.

[22] Plant, R. E. (May/June 1993). Expert systems in agriculture and resource management. *Technological Forecasting and Social Change,* 241–247.

[23] Robins, G. (January 1993). Retail GIS use growing. *Stores,* 44–50.

[24] Sinton, D. F. (February 1994). Reflections on 25 years of GIS. *GIS World,* 1–8.

[25] Smith, B. and Eglowstein, H. (January 1993). Putting your data on the map. *Byte,* 188–200.

[26] Tetzeli, R. (October 18, 1993). Mapping for dollars. *Fortune,* 91–96.

[27] Thom, J., and Walters, L. (July 1992). A map for marketing. *Sales & Marketing,* 102–104.

[28] Weber, B. R. (January 1990). Application of geographic information systems to real estate market analysis and appraisal. *The Appraisal Journal,* 127–131.

[29] Wilson, J. P. (May 1995). Reinventing government with GIS. *Public Works,* 38+.

[30] Woodbury, C. (September/October 1996). GIS Software. *Journal of Property Management,* 61–64.

[31] Wright, A. G., *et al.* (October 25, 1993). Going digital: GIS maps out bright future. *EIR,* 27–28.

Chapter 16

Multimedia and Virtual Reality Information Systems

Learning Objectives

After studying this chapter, you should be able to:

- Define multimedia and its related technologies.
- Elaborate on the historical development of multimedia systems.
- Explain several applications of multimedia systems.
- Discuss hypertext and hypermedia systems.
- Explain virtual reality (VR).
- Elaborate on the components of a VR system.
- Define important concepts in VR.
- Discuss successful applications of VR.
- Discuss obstacles in using VR systems.

16-1 INTRODUCTION

This chapter explains multimedia as one of the growing technologies used in information systems. The chapter examines different components of a multimedia system and presents a historical development of this popular technology. Commonly used applications of multimedia are introduced. The chapter investigates hypertext and hypermedia as other multimedia technologies. The latter part of the chapter concentrates on virtual reality, its definition, components, limitations, and strengths. The chapter concludes with a discussion of the obstacles for using VR systems, including virtual legality.

16-2 MULTIMEDIA: AN OVERVIEW

Multimedia is the ability to present and transfer information through more than one medium at a time. This may include voice, data, images, full motion video, and animation. The most compelling reason for utilizing multimedia is that when using traditional methods, chances are that the majority of your audience may not absorb the entire presentation. Multisensory presentations speed and improve understanding, and they can further attract the user attention [4,10].

The use of multimedia is similar to comparing radio to television. While radios distribute information through sound, television can disseminate information through a combination of sounds and visual images. Multimedia popularity is mainly due two factors [16]:

1. Enhancement and popularity of video.
2. The ever-increasing power of computers, particularly microcomputers.

Before we go any further let me share a personal experience with you regarding multimedia applications. A couple of years ago we were trying to teach a group of schoolchildren about various kinds of birds. We began with a canary. First, we wrote on the board a detailed description of a canary. Only a few students understood what kind of a bird a canary was from our description. We were using a CD-ROM-based training package that included the names and descriptions of all birds. We retrieved a textual description of the canary on the monitor, then a picture of the bird appeared on the monitor, then the bird started singing, and finally the bird flew through the monitor.

This is multimedia. By combining text, images, sound, and video the information gets across with minimum difficulty. The old saying, "a picture is worth a thousand words," makes more sense in the multimedia environment. In multimedia you may add color, sound, and motion to the picture. Multimedia technology allows you to condense a large amount of information and package it in a way that makes it more presentable and understandable.

Traditionally, information has been presented in graphical or report-oriented formats. Adding color can enhance reports and graphs. A simple ordered presentation of still images can be enhanced with the addition of captured video. Digitized images add a more natural appearance to a presentation. With a video output board, a regular TV can be used to show various presentations.

The simplest method for adding full-motion video is to have an external device generate the moving video, then piping it into a special board that can display the signal in a window on the computer screen. However, the real power of a full-motion presentation comes when the user can control the external video device. This gives multimedia a powerful feeling of interaction that is only achieved when the presenter or the user controls the path that the presentation follows.

A basic hardware package for a desktop multimedia machine should include the following:

1. A 486 or higher PC with at least 8 megabyte (MB) of RAM expandable to 64 MB or more.
2. A hard disk with a minimum of 300 MB of disk space.
3. A super VGA or higher resolution monitor.
4. A CD-ROM drive with a data transfer rate of 300 kilo byte per second (kbps) and access time under 200 millisecond.
5. A 6-inch wide color scanner or a full-page scanner.
6. Video, graphics, and audio cards.
7. Mouse or trackball.
8. Speakers.
9. Sound board.
10. Video capture and display board for VCR and TV images.

Figure 16-1 illustrates a multimedia system.

Of course, a Pentium-based PC (or MMX chip) with higher RAM, a larger hard disk, and a faster CD-ROM is highly recommended.

A multimedia presentation may utilize one or more of the following technologies:

- MIDI (musical instrument digital interface) music and sound effects generated by synthesizers.
- Digitized audio that may be used for music, voice, or sound effects.
- Digitized photographs.

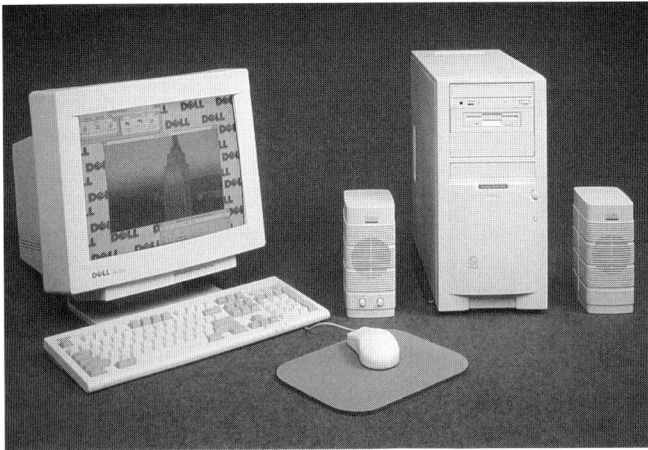

Figure 16-1   A multimedia system. Courtesy of Dell Computer Corporation.

- Drawings and other graphics.
- Animation.
- Full-motion video with synchronized sound.

Creating an interactive multimedia application requires a powerful tool called authoring software, which is similar to a programming language. One such software package is the Windows-based Authorware Professional. It uses icons to represent graphics, sounds, animation, and video. Sound is a key element in making a multimedia presentation interactive and appealing. With Authorware, sound can be played off a laser disk or VCR player, or using a microphone attached to the soundboard of the computer.

The use of video is an entertaining way to present dry yet important information. Not all multimedia-authoring programs can incorporate video or animation. Capabilities vary and continue to improve as more organizations implement multimedia technology. Table 16-1 illustrates some of the popular commercial multimedia development tools on the market. These tools vary in price and sophistication.

16-3 MULTIMEDIA HISTORICAL DEVELOPMENT

Although the origin of multimedia technology can go back as to the origin of computers, there has been certain developments in the computer field that have

Table 16-1

Multimedia Tools

Product	Company
Adobe Presentation	Adobe Systems, Inc.
Authorware Professional	Macromedia, Inc.
Demoshield	Sterling Technologies, Inc.
Freelance Graphics	Lotus Development Corp.
Multimedia Toolbook	Asymetrix Corp.
PowerPoint	Microsoft Corp.
Quest	Allen Communications, Inc.
Visual Basic	Microsoft Corp.

been essential for the popularity of multimedia today. We summarize these important developments in the following paragraphs [6]:

1. The first video game—Pong—was introduced in 1972. Computer games are still popular today and have helped computer users to migrate smoothly from character-based environment such as DOS to a graphical environment such as Windows. Games have been instrumental in acquainting children to the exciting world of computers. Most of the today's games are packaged as a full-featured multimedia product.

2. The introduction of Disco vision interactive laserdisc kiosk by IBM in 1977. This technology was created to provide interactive employee training.

3. The introduction of Apple II computer in 1978. Apple II and Macintosh have been leaders in multimedia development through their graphical user interface (GUI) and introduction of sound to computers in 1981. Many experts believe that most basic tools and concepts of multimedia were introduced with the launch of the Macintosh in 1984.

4. The introduction of the first PC by IBM in 1981. Entering the PC market by the giant computer maker reassured the computing world that PCs were real and were here to stay.

5. The introduction of MacroMind VideoWorks Animation 101 in 1985. This product was among the first multimedia software-authoring tools. This software enabled individuals with minimal computer skills to create animation on-screen.

6. The introduction of Intel 386 microprocessor in 1986. This started a whole series of powerful microcomputer systems leading to today's Pentium, Pentium Pro, MMX, and Pentium II microprocessors.

7. In October 1991, the Multimedia PC Marketing Council was formed to develop hardware standards on which newly developed products would run. The

Table 16-2

Multimedia Applications

Business presentation
Computer assisted surgery
Computer-based training
Education and training
Electronic encyclopedia
Electronic books
Electronic classroom presentation
Electronic newspaper
Full motion video conferencing
Information kiosks
Medical imaging
Sales demos
Surgery simulation

introduction of multimedia PC (MPC) standards not only benefited multimedia product development, it also helped computer manufacturers market new PCs.

8. The introduction of Windows 95 by Microsoft in 1995. This new, enhanced GUI created a lot of excitement in the PC world because of its ease of use and widespread acceptance by millions of users all over the world.

9. The introduction of Harvard graphics in 1996, the first presentations package for PCs.

10. The introduction of Pentium Pro, Pentium II, and MMX microprocessors by Intel Corporation in 1997 further facilitated and enhanced the desktop multimedia applications.

16-4 MULTIMEDIA APPLICATIONS

Multimedia has become a powerful tool in delivering information in an easy-to-understand format. All indications suggest even more popularity for this technology in coming years. Multimedia has been used in various disciplines for diverse applications. Table 16-2 provides a listing of some of these popular applications.

In the following pages we discuss some of these applications in more detail.

16-4-1 MULTIMEDIA PRESENTATION

From sales calls, to product display, to board meetings, presentations are major factors in conducting business. Although effective presentations can be made with regular texts and transparencies, multimedia can add a definite value to the presentation. College students are using a readily available tool such as Microsoft PowerPoint for their various class presentations. The majority of instructors conduct their lectures using multimedia. Lectures are better received if delivered in multimedia format. Multimedia has been a major factor in incorporating technology in teaching.

Multimedia presentations are more lively, colorful, and expressive. Diverse businesses such as Marriott hotel chain, Olympus Cameras, Boston Market fast food, and Florist Transworld Delivery have insisted on interactive demonstrations by agencies participating in their account reviews. In addition, businesses have recognized that their sales representatives have been able to use multimedia to convey a professional image that is superior to their competitors [23].

The following are specific applications of multimedia for sales presentations:

- Customer contracts
- Regular sales
- Sales contracts

One company using multimedia sales presentations is Ingersoll-Rand Corporation. Ingersoll-Rand believes in multimedia because it involves customers in sales calls and allows salespeople to customize presentations in minutes, demonstrate products using video or animation, and bring live customer participation in any sales call. Bill Berg, senior area manager of the air compressor group, is pleased with the new presentation method because it allows him leave boxes of carousels and slides at home. He now carries his entire presentation on a laptop computer. It is the interactive feature of multimedia that impresses Berg the most. For example, his first use of multimedia was supposed to be a 20-minute presentation for two executives from a major customer. As Berg was clicking through the screens customized for that particular customer, the executives began asking questions and requesting changes for what-if analysis. Before long, Berg claims the executives were operating the computer themselves. Although Berg did not make the sale, he was sure he "scored some points" [24].

Keith Waldon, CEO of Earth Preserv, experienced success with his presentation using multimedia to sell his company's products to JCPenney. Waldon was looking to create a partnership with a major company to introduce his environmentally sensitive bath and body products. He knew that he did not have enough capital to take on this venture alone. So he banked his future in a 5-hour multimedia presentation to several senior buyers at JCPenney's Dallas headquarters. Not holding back anything, Waldon overwhelmed the buyers with everything from TV storyboards to full-motion video. To close the presentation, Waldon gave JCPenney a 2-week deadline to respond because he wanted to unveil his products on Earth Day. JCPenney not only responded, they also wanted to be the only retailer store featuring the product line [11].

16-4-2 SALES DEMOS

A large number of companies are now promoting their products through the use of sales demos. For instance, Polaroid corporation promotes sale of its ID-3000 by sending customers a disk that presents a soup-to-nuts pitch for security badges' system, complete with PC speaker audio, animation, and even an interactive game to drive home the product's features [15,23].

A growing number of textbook publishers in the United States send multimedia CD-ROMs to prospective adopters of their books as sales demos. The demo disks highlight some of the key features of these publications. The user can examine some of the features in an interactive fashion.

This method of sales presentation helps companies to reduce their sales force and it lets the technology sell their products using the customer's own computer.

16-4-3 INFORMATION KIOSKS

Another method for reaching customers in an inexpensive way is through information kiosks. Kiosks can demonstrate a company's products and allow the customers to sell themselves without pressure from a salesperson. These kiosks can be very convenient if they are located within the reach of the prospective customers. The buyer can interact with the kiosk in a flexible time frame and she can examine the feature(s) of the product as many times as she wishes.

Allstate Insurance Company of Canada has a network of interactive multimedia kiosks in convenient locations throughout four provinces of Canada. These systems provide advice on how to save money on various insurance options, and they provide quotes on auto, home, and life insurance. They can also sell certain products [16]. PRO Tix has created a network of multimedia kiosks that sell and deliver tickets for sporting events such as basketball, baseball, and hockey as well as concerts and other public events. These systems not only allow the customers to choose among the available seats, they can also preview their actual seats in the seating area before they actually purchase the ticket. This gives them a pretty good idea if the investment is worthwhile.

Real estate companies are using kiosks to provide a tour to the perspective buyers through all their offerings. A customer can reach one of these kiosks and by going through a series of interactive multimedia menus to find out about her desired home. Shopping malls and tourist attractions in places such as Disneyland and Sea World are also using these kiosks to guide tourists through their facilities. Because of the downsizing and cost reduction pressures that all companies are facing, these kiosks are expected to become even more popular in the near future.

16-4-4 COMPUTER-BASED TRAINING (CBT)

Organizations throughout the world are spending billions of dollars to train and educate their employees regarding new developments in technology, new product offerings, and new procedures introduced in the organization. Computer-based training (CBT) can significantly benefit from multimedia. Using CBT, more employees can be trained with less cost and added flexibility. CBT can reduce training costs because employees no longer have to travel to expensive seminars. Multimedia CBT allows trainees to set their own pace and repeat the instructions as many times as needed. When the training materials are designed, countless employees can go through the same program with same initial cost.

Dominick's Finer Foods, in Northlake, Illinois, has installed a CBT system that incorporates color graphics, audio, and full-motion video. Each system connects with the company's mainframe at headquarters so that the personnel department can track the trainee's progress. The first of Dominick's CBT applications included training for produce identification and cash register utilization. Dominick's claimed that CBT succeeded in cutting formal training from 24 to 6 hours, and time allocated to live training from 4 hours to 2. Dominick's also claimed that their employees actually learned better through the interactive training environment provided by CBT. Dominick's is sure that CBT has made its training program more efficient, and they expect to implement as many as 60 more CBT modules [9].

Duracell International is another company that uses CBT. In this organization video clips of executives expressing company goals are being used as a training vehicle. Other items in the training package include information related to the organizational structure, product backgrounds, and corporate culture. The main objective of this training program is to provide employees with a consistent representation of the company's goal and message [17].

16-4-5 INTERACTIVE TELEVISION

Interactive television is another application of multimedia and the information superhighway. The digitization of phone and TV analog signals and digital compression are the technologies that will make it possible. Integrated services digital network (ISDN) will allow voice, data, and video to be sent over the same line. Digital compression will increase the transmission capacity of a single analog TV channel to 10 channels with the same bandwidth. This will increase the number of channels that are available for use. In addition, the conversion to fiber optics will exponentially expand capacity as one fiber optic cable can transmit thousands of times as much information as a single telephone line.

Expanded channel capacity will pave the way for new television services: video-on-demand, video malls, games, voting, educational programming, and special interest niche channels. Consumers will be able to select and play movies from a large library in the privacy of their own homes. Fancy department stores such as Nordstrom and Macy's have expressed interest in entering the video mall business. Nintendo-like games will be available via television. Educational programs with channels categorized by subject matter and grade level will be included. Also, special interest channels will focus on such topics as travel, politics, weather, cooking, comedy, the courtroom, and so forth.

Assumptions have been made that presume success for these ventures. One such assumption is that buying television time will cost less as channel capacity expands and that television marketing will cost less than direct mail. However, channels may expand to the point that audience fragmentation may result. As 500 channels may be possible. Human limitations dictate that a person can only view so many channels. Therefore, marketing may be a hit-and-miss proposition with so many consumer options available [19].

Savvy businesspersons such as Bill Gates project that people will want these services provided on interactive TV. However, human nature is such that people do things in the easiest way possible. Therefore, the interface will have to be non-computer-like and it will have to provide appealing features such as product demonstrations. A perceived need for change will be necessary for people to overcome the inertia of learning a new system. Most people cannot even program their own VCRs!

It has been predicted that ordering merchandise will be as easy as pushing a button on a remote control. Real-time assignment of inventory to a customer order is imperative for customer satisfaction. Nonavailability must be communicated to the customer immediately. Database access and compatibility will be required in order to match the level of service currently available via telephone ordering. How an order or service is paid for is yet another hurdle. Many of the proposed systems incorrectly assume that consumers will willingly place their credit card number in a master database and automatically pay for all items ordered via interactive TV. An alternative is the inclusion of a built-in credit card reader with each future television. Cost ramifications may make this alternative less attractive to consumers. The simplistic "one-button merchandise ordering" approach does not consider services such as expedited delivery, delivery to an alternate address, and so forth [19].

Conversing with a television is another problem that has to be resolved. Natural language processing is a challenge due to different frequencies of voices, similar-sounding words, accents, regional dialects, and so forth. What experts believe will happen is that a telephonic function will be included in future TVs. A button on the remote control would automatically dial a merchant whose product is on the screen whereby consumers can then order by voice or by using a remote control keypad [19].

Utilization of the information superhighway primarily for interactive television assumes that people want to "computerize" their private lives and replace telephone and television systems that are working just fine for them now. The information superhighway may be paved to their neighborhood but not to their door. Significant personal expense will be required to upgrade communications wiring within the home as well as from homes to public lines.

16-5 STRENGTHS AND LIMITATIONS OF MULTIMEDIA TRAINING

Like any other technology multimedia training includes a series of advantages and disadvantages. With the popularity of this technology it seems that the advantages outweigh the disadvantages. Table 16-3 lists strengths and Table 16-4 identifies the limitations of multimedia training.

Table 16-3

Strengths of Multimedia Training

It is interactive.

It improves communications.

It is self-paced.

It cost less over a long period.

Complex concepts are explained better by using animation.

Table 16-4

Limitations of Multimedia Training

Lack of standard for multimedia hardware and software.

High initial development cost.

High maintenance cost.

Limited bandwidth for downloading and uploading multimedia products.

Most multimedia software are proprietary.

16-6 HYPERTEXT SYSTEMS

Hypertext is an approach to data management in which data are stored in network of nodes connected by links. The nodes are designed to be accessed through an interactive browsing system. A hypertext document includes node links and supporting indexes for a particular topic. A hypertext document may include data, voice, and images. This type of document is usually called hypermedia. In hypertext documents the physical and logical layouts are usually different. This is not the case in a paper document. In a paper document the author of the paper establishes the order.

A hypertext system provides users with nonsequential paths to access information. This means that information does not have to be accessed sequentially as in a book. A hypertext system allows the user to make any request that the author or designer of the hypertext provides through links. These links choices are similar to lists of indexes. They also can be links within information nodes. The user chooses which choice best suits his needs [22].

Some hypertext systems define their links as directed or directed-hierarchical. In this format the links have a direction between source and destination nodes. In this type of arrangement it is much easier for the user to navigate through the system. However, they are not as flexible as in a network of interrelated links. In a network system, links point in both directions. The system is not organized into a hierarchical format. This type of arrangement may be difficult for the user to navigate or traverse.

There is a similarity between a hypertext document and an encyclopedia-type document. In an encyclopedia you may read a topic and then look for more information on this topic in another section of the encyclopedia. Hypertext documents are designed for this type of access [21].

A good example of a hypertext document is the online help provided by the majority of Windows applications. When you click the Help menu option, a context-sensitive help screen will be provided. You can read about a topic and then find out more about other related topics by simply clicking on any of the related topic icons. The internal links will quickly take you to the requested topic. Also, in addition to text, you may see images as well. These images provide more visual support that in turn makes it easier to retrieve information. Figure 16-2 shows an example of a hypertext system. We should see many applications of hypertext technology in the future, particularly in the expert systems and executive information systems environments.

16-6-1 HYPERMEDIA

In the last section, we explained hypertext technology as a sophisticated method for retrieving information from a variety of sources. Hypermedia is an

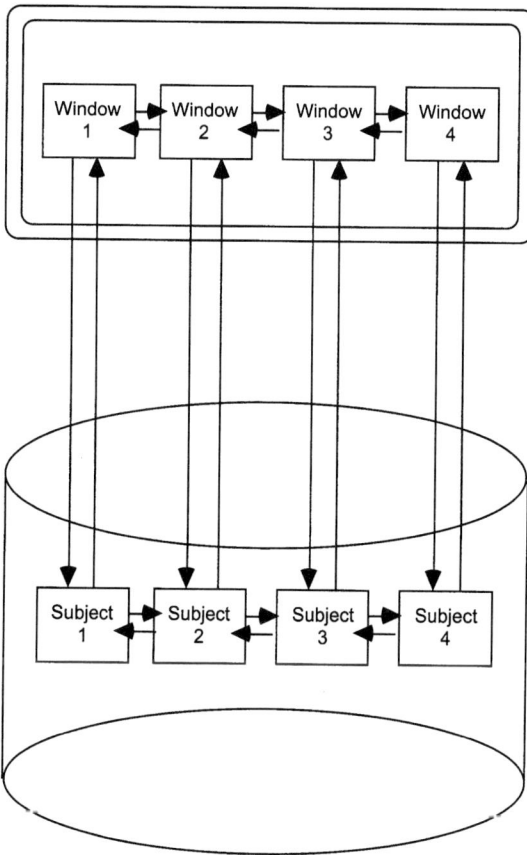

Figure 16-2 A Hypertext system.

extension of hypertext. It combines text, images, sounds, and full-motion video in the same document. It allows information retrieval with a click of a button.

The graphics used with hypermedia can either be scanned images or object-oriented pictures. Hypermedia is encoded digitally on CD-ROM-type media and played back through a highly interactive PC or workstation.

Hypermedia technology has been successfully utilized in executive information systems (EIS). (We discussed EIS in detail in Chapter 13.) A hypermedia-based EIS offers several advantages to executives and allows them to accomplish four basic needs [13]:

1. They can quickly track the information behind reports.
2. They have user-friendly access to information.

3. They can retrieve filtered and compressed information that focuses on critical data behind reports.
4. They can experience hands-on navigation through detailed organizational information, which eliminates the use of subordinates to search for detailed information.

16-7 VIRTUAL REALITY (VR): AN OVERVIEW

The goal of virtual reality (VR) is to provide an environment in which a user can interact and participate as she does in the real world. Jaron Lanier, a pioneer scientist who later founded VPL Research, first coined the term, virtual reality. For the purposes of this book, we define VR as:

> A technology that uses computer generated, three-dimensional images, to create an illusion of interaction in a real-world environment. It can be integrated with stereo sound and tactile sensations to give the user the "feel" of being immersed in a three-dimensional real world.

Virtual reality has been referred to by other names such as virtual environments and simulation, artificial reality, synthetic environment, augmented reality, and telepresence. However, the most commonly used name for this growing technology is VR.

Prior to VR technology, we viewed three-dimensional objects in a two-dimensional environment. Even the best of graphics programs, including computer-aided design (CAD) and computer-aided manufacturing (CAM), used a two-dimensional environment to illustrate a 3-D object. With VR, we no longer have to view images in a two-dimensional world. They can now be seen in a true three-dimensional environment.

The three dimensionality is not the only feature that makes VR an exciting new technology. With VR, a user can also interact with various objects in a way that has never been possible before. A user can now "enter" into a "virtual world" and interact with graphical objects as if they were real. As Thomas Furness, a notable pioneer of VR states, "the distinction between immersion in a VR world and analyzing the same information using blueprints, numbers or text, is the difference between looking at fish in an aquarium and putting on your scuba gear and diving in with them" [2].

The day-to-day physical and symbolic worlds in which we live, work, and interact are referred to as information environments (IEs). The hypermedia (discussed earlier) and virtual reality systems are the front runners of information environments. In this environment users of information technology should be able to freely interact with the system and with one another. In other words, no barrier should oppose the free format interaction between people and information technology [14].

Virtual reality has its origin in military flight simulation. The earlier VR simulators had limitations but they were improved gradually. Matsushita, a Japanese company, built a "virtual kitchen." Using this virtual kitchen, customers could change different designs, fixtures, and appliances on a computer then "walk around" in the kitchen space. If they are not satisfied with certain arrangements, they can move things around. After complete satisfaction, the new arrangement becomes the blueprint for the final actual design of the kitchen. It has been estimated that there are more than 100 companies in the United States alone that specialize in some aspect of VR, and the number, by all estimates, is growing.

One future application of VR would be in site selection. A simulation model combined with VR capabilities may allow decision makers to walk down the street into the new plant and examine the important components before its construction. This should provide a far more realistic view of the plant than looking at maps and blueprints.

16-8 TYPES OF VIRTUAL ENVIRONMENTS

There are two major types of user environments in VR: egocentric (total immersion) and exocentric (window view). An **egocentric** environment in VR is one in which the user is totally immersed. This can be accomplished by the use of a head mounted display (HMD). By using this device, the user becomes a part of the environment that he or she is viewing. In reality, the user steps into a computer generated world. Using an HMD, the world is presented in 3-D right before the user's eyes.

The **exocentric** environment is nearly similar to the total immersion environment. In this environment, data also are rendered in 3-D, but they can only be viewed on screen. They cannot be interacted with in the same way as in an egocentric environment. The main type of enabling technology used in this environment is 3-D graphics.

Another enabling technology that allows the user to become totally immersed in an environment is made possible through the use of a laser beam. Through a technology called the virtual retinal display (VRD) developed by Joel Kollin at HITL, a very low-power laser beam is shot into the user's eye. The laser beam carries with it an image that is projected onto the back of the eye. This technology works on a principal that is similar to an HMD. It allows users to move their heads in any direction, without losing sight of the image that they are viewing. Although the idea of having a laser beam shot into the eye may put some people off, its creators swear by its harmlessness. As Kollin puts it, "you could stare into this thing all day . . . I have" [18].

There are four categories of movement that VR systems use [1]:

1. *No movement.* In this VR system a person can walk through the VR environment but cannot have any interaction.
2. *Movement.* This VR system allows each object to react according to the natural laws of physics. For example, if a ball is dropped it will bounce back and it eventually stops.
3. *Behavioral control.* This VR system allows objects to detect and react to certain circumstances. The user can visualize complex and dynamic processes such as movement of parts through a factory, movement of smoke or fluid, and interaction between the user and the virtual word.
4. *Artificial intelligence.* This VR system allows the complete and unrestrained movement and interaction of objects within the environment.

16-9 COMPONENTS OF A VR SYSTEM

There are three major components for an operational VR system [3]:

1. *Visual and aural systems, through which the user sees and hears the virtual world.* A HMD is an example. The other part of the HMD is its aural system. By adding stereo sound to a VR environment, it becomes more natural. Not only is a user able to see objects that move as if they were real, she is also able to hear them as though they really have sound. By adding sound to 3-D graphics, a virtual environment can become so convincingly real, some people forget that it is just VR. A HMD contains two small TV screens. One is placed in front of each eye along with a magnifying lens to generate the view. There are also sensing devices on the top of the helmet to determine the orientation and position of the user's head. The information is reported to the computer, which then generates two pictures as slightly different views for each eye, just as is the case in the real world.

2. *A manual control for navigating through the virtual world.* The most commonly used device here is the DataGlove. Using the DataGlove, the user can perform navigation. The DataGlove also allows a user to grasp objects in a virtual world, and to some extent, it simulates limited tactile sensation. While wearing a DataGlove, a user can point to objects, pick them up to examine them, and even throw them in the VR environment. The DataGlove can also be used as an input device, such as a mouse. With a DataGlove, a user can point to, call up a window, a dialog box or pull down a menu. However, the main purpose of the DataGlove is for navigation, and also to represent the user's hand in the virtual world. It is a device that allows interaction.

The DataGlove is made of a glove that is covered with optical sensors. Whenever a user moves his hand or finger, the sensors send this information to a computer that reconstructs this movement graphically. The agent representing his hand in the virtual world duplicates whatever movements are performed by the user's hand. Some DataGloves have limited tactile sensation. A user can pick up an object in the virtual world and he is able to distinguish, to some extent, its shape and size, just by mere touch. As in the real world, the user is able to tell the difference between something round, square, hard, or soft just by touching it.

3. *The central coordinating processor and software system.* This component of a VR system generates and manipulates high-quality graphics in real time. To achieve this, an extremely fast processor is needed. This is because with 3-D images, the refresh rate of each screen has to be extremely fast in order to display images in real time.

16-10 IMPORTANT CONCEPTS IN VR ENVIRONMENTS

To better understand the world of VR the following concepts should be understood [12]:

1. *Simulation.* In a system that simulates an environment you can see 3-D images with texture and shading. This type of VR system started with flight simulators and is now being used in medicine, entertainment, education, and training. This VR environment is usually accompanied with 3-D sound.

2. *Interaction.* The interactive systems allow the user to manipulate and interact with the environment. For example, using a mouse on a computer desktop to throw away a computer file in a trash can can represent interaction. Later the user may change his mind and grab the file in the trash can and bring it back to the original application. While these tasks are being performed, they seem real.

3. *Artificiality.* This feature allows the analysis and examination of different variables in an environment for further action. As an example, purchasing habits are analyzed to tell retail stores which department should be placed in which area of the store and which items should be placed along the aisles. These types of analyses may be performed to maximize the exposures of different products to perspective buyers.

4. *Immersion.* As discussed earlier immersion uses special hardware and software technologies to completely immerse a person's senses in the environment. With immersion the surrounding real world is blocked out and all attention is focused selectively on a particular environment. This feature was first used by the U.S. Air Force.

5. *Telepresence.* This feature is provided when the user seems to be present at a distant location and is able to manipulate objects in the environment as if she were really there. These systems use HMDs, DataGloves and communication links. However, these systems are very expensive and require sophisticated equipment for optimum use.

6. *Full body immersion.* This technology combines interactive environments with cameras, monitors, and other devices that allow a user to move around without the hindrance of specific gear. The person's body can interact with all other images in the environment by manipulating objects.

7. *Networked communications.* This technology allows the connection of virtual worlds where two or more users in different locations can interact and manipulate the same world at the same time.

As you can see these technologies overlap somewhat, but they are being examined and further developed by different companies and for different applications.

16-11 VR APPLICATIONS

To date, the most popular applications of VR have been in the military for flight simulation, in medicine for "bloodless" surgery, and in the entertainment industry. With further development in VR technology, we should see more business applications and the use of VR as a prominent user-interface in the CBIS environment [5]. Table 16-5 lists some of the popular applications of VR.

As discussed in Chapter 2, some of the most popular types of software tools used in CBISs are spreadsheet packages such as Lotus 1-2-3 and Excel. Using these packages, various types of graphics can be generated. With VR, the presentation of the outputs of these packages will be perceptually enhanced. By adding

Table 16-5

VR Applications

Applications for disabled

Architectural design

Computer-aided design (CAD)

Education

Flight simulation

Housing market

Marketing

Medicine

Recreation and games

Science and engineering

Simulation of dangerous situations such as space walk

Training (e.g., training pilots, surgeons, and skiers)

3-D graphics to various charts, a decision maker is better able to distinguish crucial information. As Coul and Rothman state [8]:

> The application of virtual reality to decision support systems with a focus on the powerful functionality of multidimensional presentation of data, dynamic interaction with data, and multi-user networking in a shared virtual space, lets the technology emerge as an alternative to the standard ways in which we understand and visualize complex and changing data.

Using VR, a decision maker will better be able to comprehend the information that is presented by a typical CBIS. Users better comprehend true 3-D charts and graphs than numbers in the rows and columns format.

Another possible use in business is in the area of teleconferencing and group support systems (GSSs). Teleconferencing today is conducted by way of the television screen. Without saying that this is not the most effective way to bring several people together who are in different physical locations, there is something lacking in this method. The sense of a missing presence exists.

One could argue that a face-to-face meeting, as opposed to a teleconference, is a better way for people to communicate; there is certainly the increased capability of interaction. With today's teleconferencing, people are not able to physically touch each other, extend handshakes, or look directly at each other. When several people are looking at the same screen, they are not able to tell if the person talking is looking at them or at the person next to them. This is where today's teleconferencing technology is weak.

With VR, these obstacles can be overcome. By putting all of the participants in one VR environment, true interaction can be achieved. All of the participants will be in the same computer-generated world, so to speak. By using their DataGloves, they can physically touch each other. Instead of just saying hello to an image on a television screen, people will be able to actually shake hands with the other participants in the VR environment, although they may be physically thousands of miles apart. This may sound like science fiction, but this technology already exists. VR participants have been able to interact with one another in the same environment for some time now. Imagine playing a video game, where there is another participant playing along with you; the same principle applies to VR, where two or more people can easily be in the same environment. Because of this, teleconferencing will be given the capability of interaction that was never possible with the old technology. It gives a new meaning to the old AT&T phrase, "reach out and touch someone." It enables people thousands of miles apart to confer in a shared virtual experience. Instead of flying to London, you and your British colleague would sit across a virtual table from each other and exchange information.

One major obstacle that has kept this technology from being instituted is that there is not enough fiber optic cable lines in existence to carry the data transmission that is needed for a shared VR environment of this size. Because people will be in different geographical locations, high-speed transmission capability will be needed in order for participants to interact in real time. This is very important in a teleconference situation; people need to be able to share information in a timely manner. Imagine how frustrating it would be to have to wait a few seconds each time someone made an action in a VR environment. It could be quite confusing.

16-12 OBSTACLES IN USING VR SYSTEMS

VR systems have generated a lot of excitement in recent years. However, a number of issues and factors must be resolved before this technology can be utilized in its fullest capacity. Let's introduce these problems.

1. *Confusion between VR and the actual environment.* Some users may come to the point where they cannot distinguish reality from virtual reality and may believe that anything they do in the virtual environment is all right to do in the real world. This becomes dangerous with some of the computer games that allow the user to torture or even kill the victim.

2. *Problems with HMD.* At the present time, the user is connected to one place when wearing a HMD, and it is difficult to switch tasks if need arises. This is because the HMD must be removed to be able to do any other tasks outside the virtual world. There is also some distortion using HMD. The refresh rates are not fast enough. This may cause visual distortion.

3. *Sound representation.* It is difficult to represent 3-D sound if it requires the sound to move. Stationary sound is relatively easy to achieve, but if, for example, a screeching bird were flying overhead in the VR world, the sound may not necessarily follow or be associated with the bird [20].

4. *Additional power.* Today, the VR programs require a lot of memory and speed to manipulate large graphic files and provide instantaneous response time to give the impression of the real world. Drawing continuous frames and refreshing these frames in a millisecond do need super fast computers with a large memory.

All indications show that the majority of these problems are going to be resolved in the near future and VR will become an active decision making companion in business organizations.

16-13 VIRTUAL LEGALITY

Virtual reality and the information superhighway together may create the so-called virtual legality issue. Virtual legality occurs when people act on and react to the virtual world without regard for the law. When users online ignore the legal issues that occur in regular day-to-day human interaction, they have entered the realm of virtual legality. As mentioned earlier, because the virtual environment comes so close to the real and actual environment, some people may become confused. Without authentication, offering and accepting contracts via e-mail is most likely not legally enforceable because of the potential for counterfeit. Contrast this with the non-Internet world where enforceable contracts are regularly created by letters of offer and acceptance. Offline, people would think twice about defaming others in a public forum. However, on the Internet, flaming occurs regularly with little regard for the consequences. Employers should be aware as they may be responsible for their employees' activities on the Internet. A mentality of using the old rules of contract law when convenient and ignoring the libel law may soon have dangerous consequences. At the present time, legal rights and obligations are unclear. Technology seems to precede corresponding law by significant degrees. The best advice to businesses is to treat the virtual world like the real world. To believe otherwise makes the likelihood of encountering virtual legality a virtual certainty [7].

SUMMARY

This chapter explained multimedia as one of the growing applications of computer technology in information systems. The chapter examined different components of a multimedia system and presented the historical development of this popular technology. Popular applications of multimedia were introduced. The chapter explained hypertext and hypermedia as two other multimedia-related technologies. The last part of the chapter concentrated on virtual reality—its definition, components, limitations, and strengths. With the ever-increasing power and sophistication of PCs and the reduction in price both multimedia and VR will become affordable alternatives for organizations regardless of their size and financial status. We should see more business applications of these technologies in the near future.

REVIEW QUESTIONS

1. What is multimedia?
2. What are some of the components of a multimedia system?
3. What are the minimum requirements of a multimedia system?
4. What is the role of CD-ROM in a multimedia system?
5. How was multimedia started?

6. What are some of the major events that have contributed to multimedia development?

7. What is the role of Apple computer and Macintosh in the popularity of multimedia?

8. If you want to mention one company that has been very crucial in the multimedia development what would be that company? Discuss.

9. Why are multimedia presentations more effective than regular presentations?

10. What are some of the applications of multimedia in sales? In information kiosks?

11. What are some of the companies that have successfully utilized multimedia technology? Discuss.

12. What is hypertext?

13. How is information retrieved in a hypertext system?

14. What is the difference between a hypertext search and sequential search?

15. What is hypermedia?

16. What is virtual reality (VR)?

17. How was VR started?

18. What are some of the components of a VR system?

19. What are two types of VR environments? What is the difference between these two types of environments?

20. What are some of the important concepts in a VR environment?

21. What are some of the obstacles in using a VR system?

22. Why will VR and multimedia become more popular in the near future? Discuss.

23. What is virtual legality? Discuss.

PROJECTS

1. First State Grocery chain is planning to use multimedia training for new employees. The training materials will concentrate on the chain operations and cash register functions. Prepare a detailed cost and benefit analysis for this company regarding multimedia use. What are some of the limitations of this type of training program?

2. Product demonstration is a popular application of multimedia. What are some of the advantages and disadvantages of this type of presentation? What about

information kiosks? What type of business would benefit the most from these kiosks?

3. Most online helps for popular software are presented in hypertext format. What are some of the unique advantages of presenting data in this format? What is the difference between this type of presentation and regular text? Discuss.

4. Virtual reality systems have been used by many organizations, including the U.S. Air Force. What are some of the strengths and limitations of these systems? What are some of the components of a VR system?

5. What is virtual legality? How might virtual legality and actual legality become confused? Discuss.

KEY TERMS

Computer-based training (CBT), 469
DataGlove, 476
Hypermedia, 472–474
Hypertext, 472
Head mounted display (HMD), 476

Information environment, 474–475
Information kiosk, 468
Multimedia, 462–464
Virtual legality, 480–481
Virtual reality, 474–475

REFERENCES

[1] Andrew, I., and Ellis, S. (May 1994). Bringing virtual worlds to life. *AI Expert,* 15 17.
[2] Anonymous (February 22, 1992). Trial of a cyber-celebrity. *Business Week,* 95–97.
[3] Arthur, C. (May 1992). Did reality move for you? *New Scientist,* 22–27.
[4] Bidgoli, H. (1997). Modern information systems for managers. San Diego: Academic Press, Inc.
[5] Briggs, J. C. (September/October 1996). The promise of virtual reality. *Futurist,* 13–18.
[6] Calico, B., and Gillian, N. (January 2, 1996). When did you get multimedia. *New Media,* 48+.
[7] Cosentino, V. (March 1994). Virtual legality. *Byte,* 278.
[8] Coul, T., and Rothman, P. (Fall 1993). Virtual reality for decision support systems. *Virtual Reality Special Report,* 31–34.
[9] Fox, B. (December 1994). Dominick's employees train with multimedia computers. *Chain Store Age Executive,* 71–72.
[10] Frank, A. (July 1996). Multimedia LANs and WANs. *LAN,* 81–86.
[11] Greco, S. (October 1995). The five-hour multimedia sales presentation. *Inc.,* 108.
[12] Heim, M. (1993). The metaphysics of virtual reality, New York: Oxford University Press.
[13] Inmon, W. (July 9, 1986). Building the best database. *Computerworld,* 73–75.
[14] Jacobson, B. (April 1992). The ultimate user interface. *Byte,* 175–182.
[15] Kay, A. S. (June 15, 1995). The business case for multimedia. *Datamation,* 55–56.
[16] O'Hara, F. (November 1994). Interactive multimedia. *Journal of Systems Management,* 16–19.
[17] Ouellette, T. (October 2, 1995). Multimedia jolts Duracell training program. *Computerworld,* 64.
[18] Pope, G. T. (September 1992). The beam in your eye. *Discover,* 26.

[19] Segel, J. (February 1994). The information superhighway—Separating hype from reality. *Direct Marketing,* 16–21.

[20] Sheridan, T. B., and Zeltzer, D. (October 1993). Reality check. *Technology Review,* 21–28.

[21] Smith, J. B., and Weiss, S. F. (July 1988). Hypertext. *Communications of the ACM,* Vol. 31, No. 7, 816–819.

[22] Swift, M. K. (June 1991). Hypertext: A tool for knowledge transfer. *Journal of Systems Management,* 35–37.

[23] Taylor, T. C. (April 1994). It's better to show than tell. *Sales & Marketing Management,* 47–48.

[24] Trumfio, G. (November 1994). The future is now. *Sales & Marketing Management,* 74–80.

Part V

Emerging Technologies and Applications in the Information Systems Environment

In Part V several recent issues related to information systems design and utilization are discussed. We examine artificial intelligence, expert systems, neural computing, fuzzy logic, and natural language processing systems. Research data show that these issues and technologies are becoming more popular. A thorough treatment of these topics should prepare information systems users for the challenges of tomorrow.

Chapter 17

Applied Artificial Intelligence: What Is Really Involved?

Learning Objectives

After studying this chapter, you should be able to:

- Explain what is artificial intelligence
- Discuss various methods for measuring the intelligence
- Review various fields within AI discipline
- Outline some of the successful applications of AI
- Explain expert systems and their applications
- Outline the possible contribution of AI to DSS
- Review some of the integrated systems on the market

17-1 INTRODUCTION

This chapter provides an overview of artificial intelligence (AI) and its related technologies. AI as a concept is discussed, and general problems, including a lack of training and understanding for AI users, associated with the AI field, are explained. Also among these problems are maintenance issues that may be overcome in the near future. As one of the most important areas in the AI field expert systems are discussed in detail. The architecture, applications, and types of expert systems are explored. The chapter concludes with a discussion regarding the possible contribution and integration of the AI field with decision support systems and traditional CBISs. The integration should enhance the power and versatility of traditional information systems.

17-2 WHAT IS ARTIFICIAL INTELLIGENCE?

AI refers to a series of related technologies that try to simulate and reproduce human behavior, including thinking, speaking, feeling, and reasoning.

AI technology applies computers to areas that require knowledge, perception, reasoning, understanding, and cognitive abilities. To achieve this, computers must:

- Understand common sense
- Understand facts and manipulate qualitative data
- Deal with exceptions and discontinuity
- Understand relationships among the facts
- Interface with humans in a free-format fashion
- Be able to deal with new situations based on previous learning

The idea behind what AI is can stir debate. There are basically three groups whose different interests in artificial intelligence specify their definitions. The most controversial group are the humanists. Their objective is to create computers that use human processes to solve problems. The problems arise when common sense is needed to successfully conclude a problem, something the humanists have failed to create.

Another group, called logicists, is trying to install mathematical theory in a "nonmonotonic" sense, which basically means a program that is capable of learning from its own mistakes. The logicists are also faced with the problem of the computer's lack of ability to cope with failure. They have not been successful in either area.

The last group, called the structuralists, is probably considered the most practical. They focus on programs that perform small-specialized tasks of only limited intelligence. They have been successful as far as credit approval programs, simple blood disease diagnostics, and redirection of system control [7].

While CBISs are concerned with storage, retrieval, manipulation and display of data, AI-systems are concerned with the reproduction and display of knowledge and facts.

In traditional CBISs, programmers and systems analysts design and implement systems that help decision makers by providing timely, relevant, accurate, and integrated information. In the AI field, "knowledge engineers" are trying to discover "rules of thumb" that will enable computers to perform tasks usually performed by humans. Rules employed in AI technology may come from a diverse group of experts in such areas as mathematics, psychology, economics, anthropology, medicine, engineering, and physics.

Some AI experts believe that AI is more of a concept than a solid field. AI encompasses a group of related technologies. Among these technologies are:

- Expert systems (ESs)
- Fuzzy logic
- Intelligent agents
- Natural language processing (NLP)
- Neural networks
- Robotics
- Speech recognition
- Vision recognition

Figure 17-1 illustrates AI-related technologies. Intelligent agents and robotics were introduced in Chapter 1. Expert systems will be explored in this chapter and in Chapter 18. Chapters 19 and 20 will discuss fuzzy logic and neural networks, respectively, in detail. Chapter 21 will elaborate on natural language processing as an ideal language for a typical end user.

17-3 GENERAL PROBLEMS ASSOCIATED WITH AI TECHNOLOGIES

Conceptually, AI has been around since the 1950s. Although we have experienced some success in several areas of AI, such as ES, NLP, and, to some degree, robotics, there are still some significant issues that must be resolved before we can implement AI technologies on a broader scale. A summary of these general problems follows [1,7]:

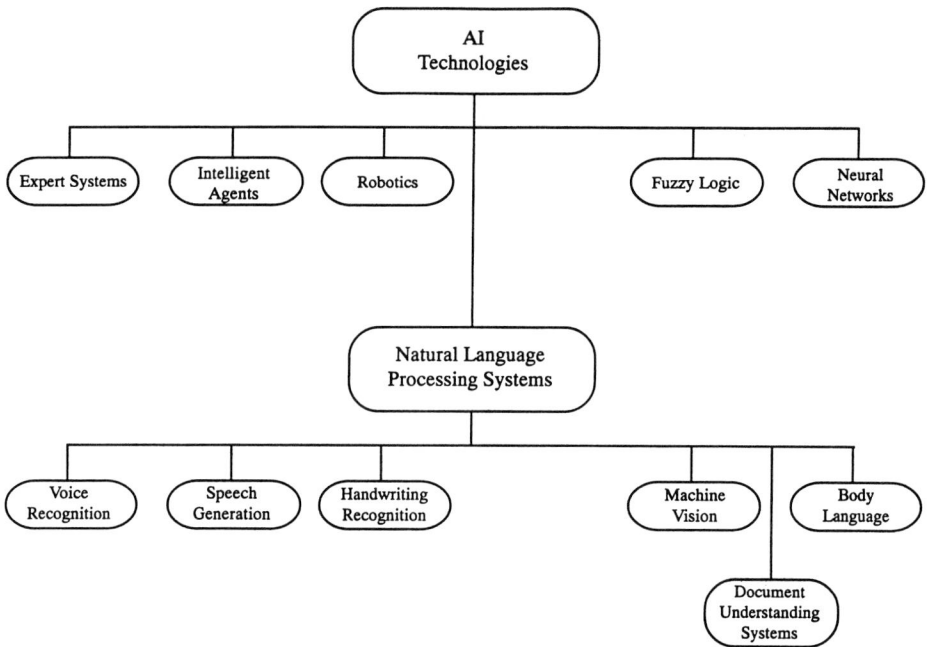

Figure 17-1   AI-related technologies.

1. *Misunderstanding of the AI domain.* Various AI users and designers have different views of AI. This lack of a common understanding may generate false expectations regarding the real strengths and weaknesses of AI technologies.

2. *Fear of replacement by AI.* Many workers feel AI technologies are being designed to replace them in their jobs. This fear may cause an obstacle in the further development of AI technologies. Robotics has already replaced many workers on assembly lines in the United States and particularly in Japan.

3. *Cost-effectiveness.* The development and design of AI-related technologies (except robotics and expert systems) may not be cost-effective at this time. Many resources may be spent on something that does not have a tangible economic value. Management is reluctant to invest valuable resources in projects that do not promise a positive economic value.

4. *Lack of training for the user.* Many workers are still not familiar with even traditional computer technology, to say nothing of AI fields. Lack of training may be another obstacle to AI use in the workplace.

5. *Maintenance.* Because AI technologies are still new and evolving, it is difficult for designers and particularly for users to effectively maintain them. More has to be learned about AI technologies before they can be efficiently maintained.

Data Processing Systems ——————————————————————→ Intelligence

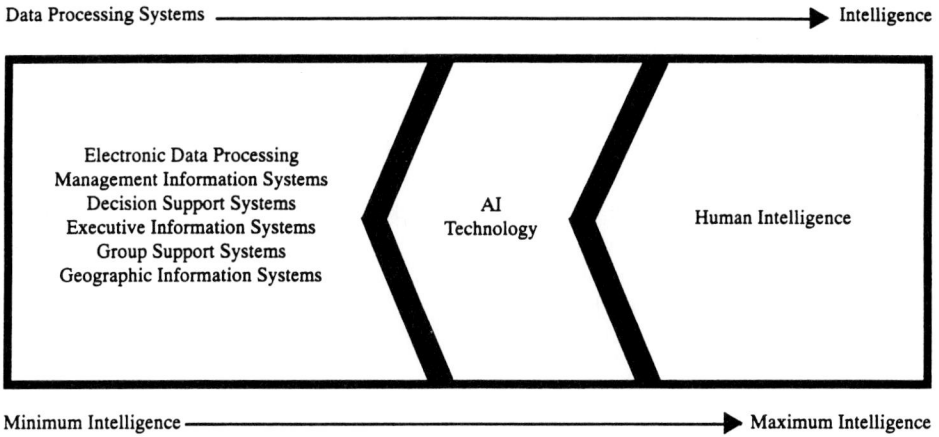

Electronic Data Processing
Management Information Systems
Decision Support Systems
Executive Information Systems
Group Support Systems
Geographic Information Systems

AI
Technology

Human Intelligence

Minimum Intelligence ——————————————————————→ Maximum Intelligence

Figure 17-2   Comparison of the AI technologies with traditional information systems technologies.

6. *Transportability.* At this time, the AI technology, developed in one discipline, may not be able to be used in another discipline. This again may consume valuable resources. It may be necessary to first explore the real potential of AI and then start the development of these systems on a broader scale.

At this time, one can conclude that computers that work with AI technologies are smarter than other computer-based information systems; however, they do not approach the human intellect. Figure 17-2 shows this conclusion graphically.

17-4 HOW DO WE MEASURE INTELLIGENCE?

The debate on what intelligence is, how we measure it, and what a machine should do to be called intelligent has been around since the early 1950s. However, there are two tests or experiments that have received a lot of attention and have been debated seriously. One is the Alan Turing test and the other is the Chinese Room experiment. Let's briefly explain these two tests for measuring intelligence.

17-4-1 THE ALAN TURING TEST

Alan Turing, a British mathematician and one of the founders of modern computing suggested a test as follows: if we propose a question in a written form and pass it to a separate room with a human and a computer, and request an answer in written form from the human and the computer, and if we cannot differentiate the two answers, then we can call the computer an intelligent computer.

Interestingly enough, on November 8, 1991, in Boston, Massachusetts, the Turing test was put into practice. A panel of judges interrogated a number of programs. A program called PC Therapist III won a prize for being judged the least indistinguishable from a human by the interrogators. On November 16, the *New York Times* wrote the following as a headline: "A computer mistaken for a human." Does this mean that the PC Therapist III really is intelligent [10]? We believe the answer to this question is No! The Chinese experiment presented in the next section will make this more clear.

17-4-2 THE CHINESE ROOM EXPERIMENT

In 1980, John Searle, a professor at the University of California, Berkeley, published his well-known "Chinese room" experiment. He put a person who did not have any Chinese background in a room equipped with dictionaries and a filing system. Written questions in Chinese were passed to the room and the person in the room, with the help of the dictionaries and filing system, provided answers in Chinese and passed them out. Professor Searle argues that the answers coming from the room might be indistinguishable from those that would be generated by a native Chinese speaker, even though the person does not understand what the question and answers mean. Then, Searle argues that apparently intelligent behavior cannot be taken to indicate true intelligence.

These two tests lead us to the question "do computers think?" As mentioned earlier, the issue of computer intelligence has been around since the early 1950s. This is a controversial issue, and different experts have different opinions. Computers play chess and can even win a game against the best (as mentioned in Chapter 1). The question remains the same: When a computer plays a chess game, is it thinking?

Generally speaking, when a computer prints a paycheck and plays a chess game, there is more intelligence involved in the latter case, but is this really thinking? In our opinion, no. The algorithm, or road map, for thinking has been given to the computer. Because computers possess extensive memory and are extremely fast, they can play a chess game and win when facing a human player.

Deep Thought II, the most powerful computer chess player, can examine five million positions (called nodes) per second. Humans use intuition and insight to eliminate all moves on the board that do not pertain to the immediate position or current line of play. IBM has completed a VLSI chess chip, and using a 10-processor prototype expected to be capable of examining 30 to 50 million nodes per second. The new generation of computer chess player has been named Deep Blue. It is a 1000-processor machine with a goal of reaching the processing of one billion nodes per second. With parallel architecture, there is theoretically no limit on the number of processors that can be put into work [9].

To make a computer a thinking machine, it must behave and simulate the human brain. To date, we have not been able to fully understand how the brain functions, let alone how to design a computer that operates similarly to the human brain.

AI research in both the United States and Japan has been steady. Billions of dollars are being spent on it throughout the world. The result of this research undoubtedly will assist us to design more intelligent computers. The outcome of this research will improve the quality and effectiveness of robots, natural language processors and expert systems.

17-4-3 THE CYC PROJECT

The CYC (cyclopedia) project started in 1994 in an attempt to convey common sense to a machine. Dr. Douglas B. Lenat is the instigator of CYC as a part of the MCC (Microelectronics & Computer Technology Corp.) effort for designing intelligent machines. CYC includes approximately 10 million interconnected facts. Dr. Lenat hopes that CYC will soon be able to do a number of things that current AI systems cannot do. These include translation of new ideas into concepts with which it is already familiar, and therefore help to teach itself. With all these facts CYC has a view of its surrounding, but the view is a strange one! According to Patrick Hayes, "CYC knows that here is the thing called CYC and that CYC is a computer program," but it has no idea that it is CYC.

The system that possess so many millions of facts and more than 27 different special purpose inference engines does not come even close to what a child can do. In parallel with this project, Edward Feigenbaum and his colleagues at Stanford's Knowledge Systems Laboratory are taking a different approach to making intelligent computers. Instead of transferring all the knowledge that a human might have, they want to enable a machine simply to share the knowledge that other computers already have. It has yet to be seen if any of these approaches will generate a real intelligent computer [7].

17-5 WHAT IS AN EXPERT SYSTEM?

Among all the AI-related technologies, expert systems have achieved a relatively high degree of success. For successful ES design and implementation, the system must be applied to an activity that has already been successfully performed by human experts, such as endeavors in the fields of medicine, geology, or electronics. Expert systems mimic human expertise in a particular discipline in order to solve a specific problem in a well-defined area.

For the purposes of this book we define expert systems as follows:

> An expert system is a series of computer programs that attempt to mimic human thought behavior in a specific area that has successfully been solved by a human expert.

While decision support systems generate information by using data and models and well-defined algorithms, expert systems work with heuristic data.

The Random House *Webster's College Dictionary* defined heuristic as:

1. Serving to indicate or point out; stimulating interest as a means of furthering investigation.
2. Encouraging a person to learn, discover, understand, or solve problems on his or own, as by experimenting, evaluating possible answers or solutions, or by trial and error.

In other words, heuristic is not formal knowledge, but it helps find a solution to a problem without following a rigorous algorithm. Heuristics sometimes refer to "rules of thumb" or general knowledge available in a discipline.

Expert systems have been around since the 1960s. These systems have continually improved during the past 30 years. The first expert system was introduced in the mid-1960s at Stanford University, and was called DENDRAL. Today, there are a variety of them on the market. Table 17-1 illustrates a number of successful expert systems on the market.

As this table indicates, expert systems have already been applied to a diverse area of science and technology. The remaining parts of this chapter should reinforce this claim and explore the ever-increasing potential of these systems in diverse areas.

News about expert systems is kept somewhat secret. Developers of these systems do not reveal detailed information regarding the technical capabilities of these systems until the product's final release. Practitioners and companies who are using these systems are also reluctant to reveal successes achieved by these systems due to the competitive advantages that may be gained by other users of these systems. In spite of all the secrecy, significant savings and success are reported in the literature.

The usage of expert systems (ESs) will increase as additional applications for the technology are discovered. Expert systems are already in use in many businesses. Not only will these systems grow in number and complexity in business firms, they also will make a greater impact on the lives of consumers in the future.

Large companies such as Texas Instruments and American Express are using ESs in such fields as capital investments and credit authorization. These are only two of the application areas. With expert systems, expert knowledge is retained. When an employee retires or passes away, his or her expertise can be gathered

Table 17-1

Popular Expert Systems on the Market

Name	Specific area
AALPS	Advises U.S. Army's 82nd Airborne for loading cargo
BUGGY	Teaches medical diagnoses
CADUCEUS	Internal medicine
CALISTO	Project management
CART	Computer faults
CRYSALIS	Protein crystallography
DELTA	Locomotive troubleshooting
DENDRAL	Chemistry
DIPMETER ADVISOR	Gives oil field log interpretation
ELAS	Analyzes oil well logs
EMPRESS	A planning and scheduling tool for NASA
GUIDON	Medical diagnoses
IMS	Automated factory management
MECHO	Mechanical problems
MEDAS	Critical care medicine
ONCONCIN	Recommends therapy for cancer patients
PHOENIX	Oil well log modeling
PROSPECTOR	Geology
PUFF	Lung disorder
TAX ADVISOR	Provides estate planning
TAXMAN	Evaluates the tax consequences of proposed projects for organizations
XCON/R1	Computer system configuration
XSEL	Computer sales
VISIONS	Vision analysis

in advance and stored in the computer for future use. ESs can also make job training more efficient, improve worker productivity, and distribute information and expertise to more regions and throughout the entire organization at a faster speed.

One area where ESs may prove valuable is in computer technology that is already in operation, particularly in database management systems (DBMSs). The integration of expert systems with existing databases will improve the efficiency and effectiveness of the computer systems already installed. This is possible by rule-based capability added to existing DBMS functions.

Another exciting frontier for ESs is the consumer market. Some systems are already available for applications such as tax advice, statistical analysis, and stock market trading. As the technology is refined and mass production becomes more feasible, we should see consumer products of ESs under $100 price range.

To date approximately half of the Fortune 500 companies are either using or experimenting with ESs. As technologies such as hypertext and neural networks are developed further, making ESs more powerful, more companies will invest in these systems. Soon we may see an increasing number of ES created for the microcomputer, with sophisticated shell programs to make using the systems easier and more effective [13].

17-6 SURVEY OF SUCCESSFUL APPLICATIONS OF EXPERT SYSTEMS

In addition to the applications that we just introduced, there are numerous other applications of expert systems that have proven to be successful. This section overview these successful applications.

Expert systems software began to emerge in 1965. Feigenbaum and Buchanan developed DENDRAL, for determining the chemical structure of molecules. In 1969, Martin and Moses at MIT developed MACSYMA, a math expert system. The development and application of expert systems expanded in the 1970s with MYCIN for medical diagnosis of blood infections. Today, various companies are engaged in the research and development of ESs. Expert systems have been utilized in such areas as:

- *Aerospace technology* (e.g., when NASA launched the space shuttle Discovery in 1988, Mission Control used expert systems to make flight control decisions).
- *The airline industry* (e.g., American Airlines has developed an expert system to manage frequent flier transactions).
- *Banking and finance* (e.g., Manufacturers Hanover Trust Company developed a foreign currency trades expert system to assess historical trends, new events, and buying and selling factors).
- *Criminology* (e.g., the FBI has developed several expert systems to create personality profiles of violent criminals).
- *Education* (e.g., Arizona State University has developed an expert system to teach and evaluate the math skills of children).
- *The food industry* (e.g., Campbell's Soup Company developed an expert system to capture the knowledge of a highly specialized, long-time employee who possessed all knowledge of plant operations and sterilizing techniques).
- *Healthcare management* (e.g., the British National Health Service developed an expert system to evaluate the performance of national healthcare providers. This system has more than 11,000 rules, which qualifies it as one of the largest ES applications in the world).
- *Manufacturing design and assembly* (e.g., Northrop Corporation has developed an expert system to assist in the planning process of manufacturing jet

fighters, reducing the planning and assembly stages by a factor of between 12 and 18).

- *Oil exploration* (e.g., Texaco has developed an expert system to help drilling engineers diagnose and manage drilling-fluid problems, and Schumberger Corporation developed Dipmeter Adviser for oil exploration purposes).
- *Personnel management* (e.g., IBM has developed their own expert system to assist in the training of technicians, which has reduced training time from between 14 and 16 months to between 3 and 5 months).
- *Security* (e.g., Canadian Trust Bank has developed an expert system to track their credit card holders' purchasing trends, and to report deviations such as unusual activity on the card. The system has saved more than $1.2 million in losses since it was installed).
- *Tax planning* (e.g., Coopers & Lybrand developed an expert system to assist in tax planning analysis).
- *The U.S. government* (e.g., expert systems have been developed to monitor nuclear power plants and to assist such departments as the IRS, INS, U.S. Postal Service, Department of Transportation, Department of Energy, and Department of Defense in decision-making processes).

Other interesting applications of ESs have been developed and utilized in such recognizable companies as Hewlett-Packard, DuPont, General Dynamics, Nippon Steel, Dun & Bradstreet, The Swiss Bank, and many more.

To understand the true impact that an expert system may have on an organization, let's take a closer look at specific case applications in the areas of criminology, education, oil exploration, and tax planning from the list above.

The U.S. Federal Bureau of Investigations has developed more than 20 expert systems. The Behavioral Science Unit of the FBI has developed an ES to create personality profiles of violent criminals by consolidating information from reports acquired from crime scene investigators, victim data, the media, crime research statistical data, pattern analysis, and activity analysis. The ES then processes the database on its programming in expert criminology reasoning and knowledge, and develops its own psychological hypothesis about the profile and type of person who committed the crime. Another ES developed by the FBI is in the area of arson investigation. The Arson Information Management System (AIMS), designed similarly to the violent crime ES, is used to analyze an arsonist's psychological profile and activity to help forecast the possible locations the arsonist may strike next.

At the local law enforcement level, burglary detectives in Baltimore County were the first to get a look at an ES prototype developed to analyze information about burglary sites and identify a possible list of suspects. Information about 300 burglary cases that had been solved, and 3000 records about unsolved cases and known burglars, was loaded into the system. Eighteen detectives were interviewed for their insight into local burglaries and came up with 397 ES input statements, including categorical information such as characteristics of the residence, its environment, the type of entry used, behavior, types of property stolen, and possible means of transportation to or from the scene. The residential burglary prototype system was successful, and is now used in other police departments around the United States [22].

In the field of education, Arizona State University has developed and implemented a three-part interactive, multimedia expert system to educate and evaluate the math skills of children. The user interface aspect of the ES was programmed using IBM's Info Windows and M-Motion video platforms. The system also incorporates laserdisk and touch screen technologies. The expert system tracks and interprets student mathematical progress from kindergarten to twelfth grade. The system predicts, diagnoses, plans and monitors, and instructs these students through off-site learning center nodes placed in various local schools. It can quiz a student and analyze why a student missed a particular question or set of questions, as well as identify strengths and weaknesses to develop customized learning plans. Students may select English or Spanish audio on-screen instructions. This project, named the Hispanic Math Project, is funded by the National Science Foundation and is equipped with all-IBM hardware [17].

In the field of oil exploration, Texaco originally set out to build a "Question and Answer" expert system to help engineers detect drilling-fluid problems and make recommendations. However, Texaco has now expanded its ES, called the Exsys system. The user has a choice of two screens, either a question-driven screen or a word and/or numeric input screen. After a 10-minute question-and-answer session, the ES reaches a conclusion and makes recommendations to the engineers on possible solutions to drilling problems. The system has proved to be an invaluable training tool, and has helped to uncover weaknesses in Texaco's well-drilling operations [17].

And finally, in the field of tax planning, Coopers & Lybrand, a world-renowned accounting firm, has developed an expert system called—ExperTax—which assists auditors with client firm tax planning. ExperTax's purpose is to provide junior auditors with senior-level tax expertise, and replace a 200-page tax-planning questionnaire previously used. The system analyzes income, assets, liabilities, and so on, and makes recommendations to the auditor about the best approach to improve the client's tax liability position. ExperTax contains more than 3000 rules developed by the senior-level partners and runs on IBM-compatible hardware. It has proven invaluable to Coopers & Lybrand in providing completeness, accuracy, and consistency to its customer service, as well as increased production and training for their lower-level auditors [18].

In the above examples of companies that have incorporated ES technology in their day-to-day business activities, it is clear that expert systems can play an important role related to training and education, data analysis and interpretation,

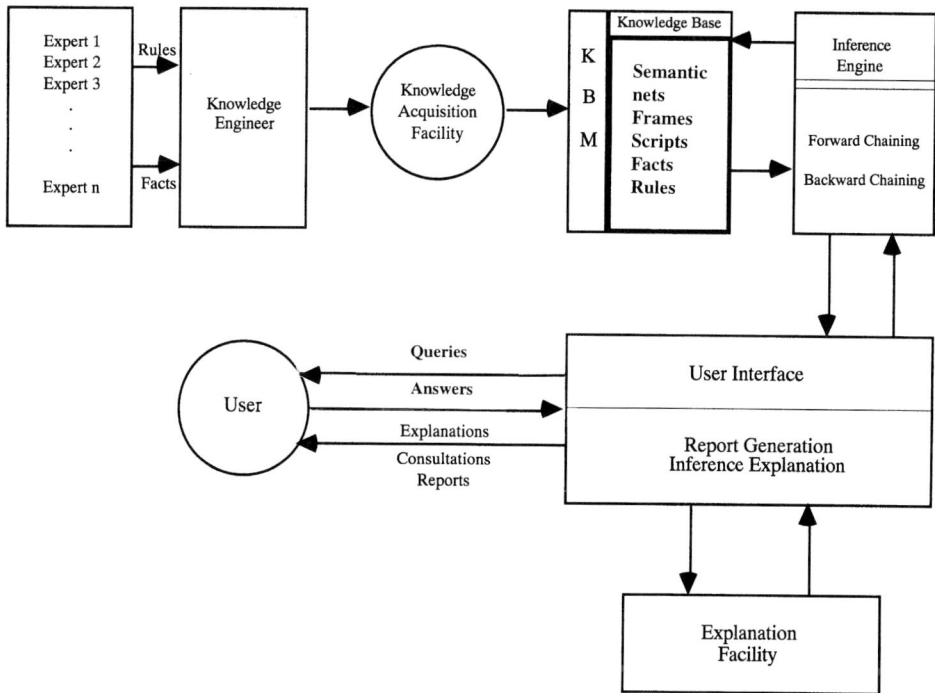

Figure 17-3   A conceptual model for an expert system.

planning, forecasting, and identification of strengths and weaknesses. When utilized properly, an ES can help an organization attain a competitive advantage in its particular field, whether it is criminology, oil exploration, tax planning, or some other disciplines. For additional applications of expert systems consult the comprehensive study conducted by EOM [13].

17-7 COMPONENTS OF AN EXPERT SYSTEM

A typical expert system includes the following components (see Figure 17-3):

- Knowledge acquisition facility
- Knowledge base (rule base and database)
- Knowledge-base management system (KBMS)
- Inference engine
- User interface
- Explanation facility

Let's briefly explain these components.

A **knowledge acquisition facility** is needed to assure the growth of the system. This subsystem should provide methods to acquire new rules and facts. The availability of new facts creates the opportunity for the KBMS to modify the existing rules and incorporate the new facts into the knowledge base. The knowledge acquisition facility and KBMS work in conjunction with each other to keep the knowledge base in its most updated form. Manual, automated, or a combination of both techniques may be used to acquire knowledge for the expert systems construction.

The **knowledge base** is very similar to the database of an information system. However, a knowledge base not only stores facts and figures, it also keeps track of a series of rules and explanations associated with the facts. For example, the knowledge base of a financial expert system may keep track of all the figures that constitute the current assets. This may include cash, deposits, accounts receivable, and so forth. It also keeps track of the fact that the current assets are the type of assets that can be converted to cash within one year.

An expert system in an academic environment may include all the facts regarding a classified graduate student, such as number of deficiencies, GMAT score, and GPA. At the same time, it may include a rule that indicates that a student may be classified only if he or she has no deficiencies, has a GMAT of 600 or better, and has a GPA of 3.40 or better.

The knowledge base of an expert system must include three types of knowledge to be considered a true expert system. These include [16]:

- Factual knowledge
- Heuristic knowledge
- Meta-knowledge

Factual knowledge consists of facts related to a specific discipline, subject or problem. An example is all the facts related to kidney problems, such as size, blood components, pain duration, and location. **Heuristic knowledge** consists of the rules related to a particular problem or discipline. An example is all the general rules that indicate that a patient has a kidney problem such as a serious pain in the lower left or lower right of the abdomen.

Incorporation of **meta-knowledge** in an expert system may be the ultimate goal of ES designers. This knowledge enables an ES to use and examine the facts, extract those facts, and direct the path used to obtain a solution. In simple terms, meta-knowledge suggests the ability for an expert system to learn from experience. This is the area that has not been fully developed and is yet to be seen in future expert systems. The integration of expert systems and neural networks is one approach for achieving this goal.

A **knowledge base management system** (KBMS) is similar to a DBMS in an information system environment. Its major task is to keep the knowledge base updated with all the facts, figures, and rules. If new facts become available or new rules are added to the existing system, it is the job of KBMSs to update the knowledge base of an expert system.

An inference engine is similar to the model base of a decision support system. Through different techniques, such as forward and backward chaining (explained later in this section), an inference engine manipulates a series of rules. In forward chaining, a series of "If-Then" pairs are performed. The condition "If," is evaluated first, then the appropriate "Then" is performed. For example, if the temperature is less than 80 degrees Fahrenheit and the grass is three inches long, then cut the grass. In a medical diagnostic ES, the system may ask:

- What is the body temperature of the patient?
- Does the patient have a headache?

The system then may conclude it is very likely (95%) the patient has the flu.

In backward chaining, the expert system first starts with the goal; the "Then" part, and backtracks in order to find the right solution, (i.e., to achieve this goal what conditions must be met?)

As an example consider a financial expert system that provides advice for financial investment for different investors [19]. In forward chaining, the system may ask 50 questions in order to determine which of the five categories of investments is more suitable for a perspective investor as follows:

- Oil-gas
- Bonds
- Common stocks
- Public utilities
- Transportation

Let us further assume a particular investor is in a given tax bracket and each investment scenario provides her with a different tax shelter.

In forward chaining the system evaluates through all the "If-Then" conditions then makes the final recommendation. In backward chaining, the system starts with the goal, the "Then" part. In this example, let us say investment in public utilities is under investigation by an investor. The expert system starts with this goal and then backtracks through the entire "If" conditions needed to achieve this goal to see if a particular investor qualifies for this type of investment. The backward chaining inference engine may be faster in a particular situation by not considering the irrelevant rules to a given situation. However, the solution recommended by the system may not be the optimum one.

Some inference engines work from a matrix of facts. The matrix may include several rows of conditions and rules. This is similar to a decision table. In this case, a number of rules are evaluated at a time and then the advice is provided. Also, some inference engines learn from doing. In addition to if-then rules there

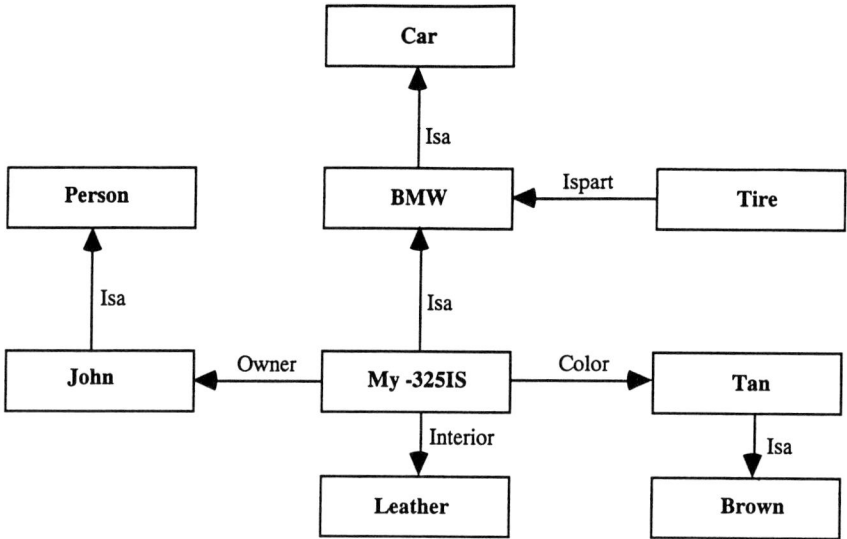

Figure 17-4   An example of a semantic network.

are other techniques used for representing knowledge in the expert system knowledge base. Among the popular techniques are semantic networks, frames, and scripts. The following is a brief description of each technique.

Semantic (or associative) networks were initially developed to represent the meanings of words in a sentence and gained their first wide spread use in the study of natural language. Information is represented as a set of links and nodes. Nodes contain objects (Figure 17-4). Arcs that represent relationships between the nodes connect nodes to each other. Each arc is a one-way link. Each arc represents only one type of relationship. To store bi-directional relationships it is necessary to store two links separately. Representation with semantic networks is easily understandable because interrelationships between concepts can be easily determined.

The term "frame" or "schematic" has been applied to several slot-and-filler representation schemes. A frame-based system stores situations or objects that are to be encountered in the problem domain. The situation or object to which the frame refers is a large chunk of knowledge. The frames are arranged in a hierarchy, with the most general frame at the top. Frames on lower levels of the hierarchy inherit the characteristics of their parents. Figure 17-5 illustrates an example of frames.

A script is another knowledge representation technique, which describe a sequence of events. Going to a picnic or setting up a birthday party are examples of events. Some of the elements of a typical script are entry conditions, roles, and scenes. The entry conditions describe situations that must take place or be satisfied

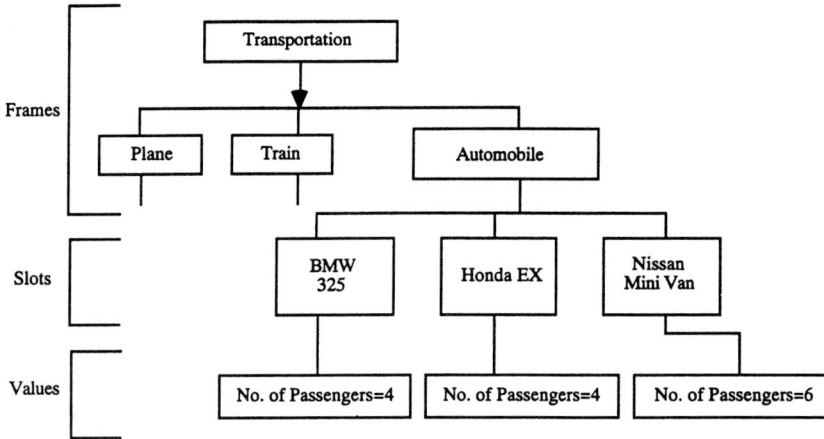

Figure 17-5   An example of frames.

before events in the script can occur or be valid. Roles are the individuals involved in the event and scenes describe the actual sequence of events.

User interface is the same as dialog management of a DSS. It provides a method of user-friendly access to the ES for the user. The goal of AI technology is to provide a natural language for the user interface. As will be discussed in Chapter 21, natural language processing is the ideal goal for the user/system interface for any computer-based information system. There are many problems associated with natural language processing that must be overcome before a full-featured NLP can be introduced. However, with the introduction of the graphical user interface (GUI) this component of expert systems has been significantly improved.

Explanation facility performs tasks similar to a human expert. It explains to the end user(s) how recommendations are derived. For example, in a loan evaluation expert system, the explanation facility will tell you why an applicant was approved and another applicant was not approved. In a medical expert system such as MYCIN, this component explains why the system concluded that the patient has a kidney stone. The explanation facility is important for ES success because having explanations assures the user of results and provides a feeling of confidence.

17-8 THREE TECHNOLOGIES OF AN EXPERT SYSTEM

The development process of an expert system parallels closely the development of a DSS. An expert system can be developed in-house or by using commercial packages. We will introduce several packages (shells) for the construction of expert systems in the next chapter. As with a DSS, in an ES environment we can identify three technologies as follows:

- ES tools
- Specific ES (SES)
- ES shells or generators (ESS)

Expert systems tools include AI languages such as LISP, PROLOG, ROSIE, or OPS. These languages can be used directly to develop either a specific expert system or an ES shell. However, other languages such as C, Pascal, or even COBOL can be used in the development process. Due to the special requirements of ES, symbolic languages such as LISP or PROLOG are more suitable than the usual high-level languages. If this alternative is chosen, the developmental period may be long and costly, but at the same time, the final product may be closer to the ES users' needs.

The second group of technologies in the ES environment includes specific expert systems. These systems, developed from either ES tools or shells, are designed to perform a specific task within a particular discipline. For example, a medical expert system that only does blood analysis falls into the category of specific expert systems. XCON, XSEL, and XSITE, developed by Digital Equipment Corporation and Carnegie-Mellon University to configure VAX computers, are also examples of specific ES. Dipmeter Advisor by Schlumberger, Inc., which interprets data from oil logs to determine the amount of oil resources or the possibility of oil resource, is another example of a specific ES. Prospector, developed by SRI International to provide consultation in mineral exploration, is another specific expert system.

The third technology, the most versatile, includes ES shells. These systems are readily available for a variety of applications. Three micro products from Human Edge Software Corporation in Palo Alto, California, are examples of ES shells. These products include Negotiation Edge, Communication Edge, and Management Edge for the IBM PC and Apple. Based on facts fed into the system, these products provide consultation to the user regarding the type of responses to be expected from a prospective customer.

Some ES shells are integrated. They may run on a company's existing computer system and utilize the corporate database. A good example of this type is the Knowledge Workbench by Silogic, Inc., in Los Angeles. This system incorporates a knowledge base, a inference engine, a natural language, and a universal database interface.

Which tool should be chosen depends on a particular application and the availability of the user(s) and knowledge engineer(s) in an organization. Shells offer a more attractive alternative because of their versatility and relatively low cost. Since a majority of the tools needed to develop a specific ES are already available

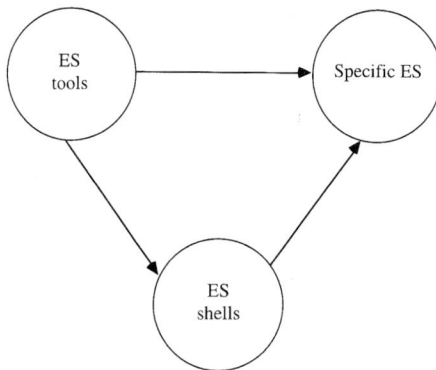

Figure 17-6   Three technologies of expert systems.

within the shell, the developmental period is relatively shorter than that needed to develop a specific ES from ES tools.

Figure 17-6 illustrates the relationship among these three technologies.

17-9 TYPES OF EXPERT SYSTEMS ARCHITECTURES

There are two types of expert system architectures.

- Rule-based
- Example-based (frame-based or case-based)

The rule-based ES, as its name implies, operates based on a series of rules. In a specific situation a series of rules are evaluated, then a conclusion is drawn. A typical rule-based system includes a variety of rules related to a particular discipline. The inference engine compares a given situation by using a series of if-then statements and provides consultation to the user. The number and complexity of rules depend on the particular system and can be anywhere from under 100 to more than several thousand.

In an example-based ES comparing a specific situation to an existing example stored in the knowledge base draws a conclusion. These examples have been collected from an expert or a number of experts throughout years of practice within a discipline. For example, a kidney of normal size and normal density with an irregular contour denotes a kidney stone.

Another example of an example-based expert system would be a loan-processing system. The system will keep a knowledge base of all previous loan applications as individual cases. When the system is used to process a new loan, the data for the new loan is input to the system and matched, based on preestablished criteria. When a match is made, the match is output to the user to act as a basis for judgment on the matter (approving or rejecting the loan).

One of the main differences between a rule-based and an example-based expert system is the adaptability of the system. Rule-based expert systems can be adapted, as new knowledge becomes available, by changing the rules within the knowledge base. In example-based systems, the examples in the knowledge base cannot be altered. The evaluation criteria used to determine if there is a match can be altered but the actual example cannot. If the evaluation criteria are matched, it appears that it would affect the validity of the actions associated with the cases (examples) in the knowledge base.

For example, if the financial requirements for loan qualification were altered, would that not affect the validity of the actions taken in previous cases stored in the knowledge base? Loans that were previously granted may not be under the new guideline [8].

These two types of systems can be further classified as one of the following [3].

1. *Assistant type.* This type of system helps a user make a decision by providing routine analysis and pointing out those areas for which human experience is needed. Dipmeter Advisor falls into this group. This system performs a series of tedious tasks and summarizes its findings, then the human expert takes over.

2. *Colleague type.* This type of system works jointly with the human expert to reach a conclusion. For this type of system the "why" and "how" features of the ES may be very helpful to the human expert. The system may provide a recommendation regarding a particular situation. The human expert may then ask why this recommendation was given. The ES will explain why it made the recommendation, and it may also state how the recommendation was generated. From this information, the human expert may gain insight about the problem under investigation. MYCIN is a good example of this type, especially when it is used for training purposes.

3. *Ideal expert system.* In this type, the user accepts the advice of the ES and, based on this advice, a decision will be implemented.

At this point in time the majority of ES fall in the first two groups. An ideal ES should possess the following criteria:

- Must possess common sense
- Must understand exceptions
- Must learn structuring knowledge and rules
- Must learn to revise and reproduce rules

As you see, humans only possess the above four features. It is yet to be seen if computers can ever possess such human traits.

17-10 APPLICATION AND NONAPPLICATION SITUATIONS OF EXPERT SYSTEMS

An expert system should be used if one or a series of the following conditions exists [3,5]:

1. *A great degree of human expertise is needed.* This is the case when one expert is not able to investigate all the dimensions of a problem. An ES, by integrating the experience and expertise of several experts, may be a more viable option compared with consulting the human expert.

2. *Situations that are not oriented toward mathematical models.* As mentioned earlier in this chapter, an ES usually works based on heuristics. Heuristics is a suitable option in the absence of a well-defined algorithm. Therefore, whenever knowledge can be represented as rules or heuristics, an ES becomes a viable candidate.

3. *Situations that have been successfully solved by human experts.* Since an expert system is trying to mimic human expertise, that expertise must be made available to an ES. At this point, the problems that have not been solved previously by human experts are not candidates for ES application.

4. *Situations that require consistency and standardization.* Since computers are more accurate and will not fail to follow a series of standard tasks, in these situations an ES may be superior to humans who tend to vary solutions or tasks based on irrelevant elements in the problem-solving setting.

5. *Limited subject domain.* Expert systems are successful if the problem under investigation is narrow.

6. *Under uncertainty.* If a situation involves a degree of uncertainty (e.g., 90% probability or 75% probability and/or some degree of fuzziness) an ES may present a viable option.

7. *Many rules.* Whenever there are several hundred to several thousand rules or the logic of the problem is complex, an ES may present a more viable option. Usually, an ES is suitable where there are between 100 and 10,000 rules.

8. *"Why" and "How" situations.* For those situations that require some explanation (e.g., "Why did you choose this answer?" or "How was this conclusion drawn?") an ES presents an attractive alternative.

9. *Scarcity of experts.* For those situations where there are not enough experts to go around, an ES can closely replace and duplicate the scarce knowledge resource.

10. *Key experts are retiring.* If this is the case, an ES may replicate the expertise of retirees.

11. *Hazardous situations.* To avoid the loss of human life, an ES may present an attractive alternative.

If these situations are not present, the expert system may not provide any advantages compared with the human expert. To be more specific, at the present time the following problem areas are unsuitable for expert systems:

1. *Problems that include very few rules (e.g., less than ten).* It is more cost effective to solve these types of problems using human experts.

2. *Problems that include too many rules (e.g., more than 10,000).* It may take a long time to develop a system to solve a problem of this magnitude. At the same time, the processing time may be slow.

3. *Well-structured numerical problems.* These types of problems may be solved by standardized data processing methods more quickly and economically. For example, payroll processing is a good candidate for an EDP application.

4. *Problems in areas that are "too wide and shallow."* This means the problem area covers a broad range and at the same time there are not that many rules involved, as opposed to problems that are "deep and narrow."

5. *Problem areas in which there is disagreement among the experts.*

6. *Problems that are solved by human experts better than ESs.* This may include areas that involve the five senses, (i.e., taste, smell, touch, sight, and hearing.)

Using an expert system for performing different tasks compared to humans for the same task may include the following advantages:

- An ES never becomes distracted.
- An ES never forgets.
- An ES never becomes tired.
- An ES never loses its train of thought.
- An ES can be used for tedious, monotonous tasks with no objection.
- An ES can be used for hazardous tasks with no risk of losing life.
- An ES duplicates the expertise of scarce experts.
- An ES can utilize the expertise of more than one expert.
- An ES improves decision making by nonexperts.
- An ES creates consistency in decision making.
- An ES disseminates rare expertise throughout the organization.

17-11 DECISION-MAKING SETTINGS AND COMPUTER TECHNOLOGY SUPPORT

The application of computer technology in various stages of decision making is well supported throughout the literature. The most recent developments, in AI technologies, promise new areas of decision making processes support. *Business Week* in its March 2, 1992, issue, under the heading "Smart Programs Go to

Table 17-2

Various Applications of Computer Technologies

Application area	Agency	Specific applications
Energy	Arco & Tenneco	Neural networks used to help pinpoint oil and gas deposits
Finance	Shearson Lehman	Neural networks used to predict the performance of stocks and bonds
Government	Internal Revenue Service	Testing software to read tax returns and spot fraud
Human services	Merced County in California	Expert systems used to decide if applicants should receive welfare benefits
Marketing	Spiegel	Neural networks used to determine most likely buyers from a long list
Telecommunications	NYNEX	Software support to assist unskilled workers to diagnose customer phone problems
Transportation	American Airlines	Expert systems used to schedule the routine maintenance of its airplanes

Work" presents an interesting report regarding various applications of computer technologies. The summary of this report is presented in Table 17-2.

In the dynamic business world decision makers seek help from a CBIS in the following decision-making settings [4]:

- What-is setting
- What-if setting
- Why setting
- What does it mean setting
- What to do setting
- When to do it setting

The "what-is" setting has been well supported by the typical electronic data processing (EDP) and management information systems (MIS). You may key in a customer account number, and your system displays his current balance. These systems report after-the-fact information and lack the flexibility required to tell the user what is going on now and what may happen in the near future. A better example would be reports generated by most accounting information systems. These systems provide historical reports regarding the financial status of the organization after the fiscal period has expired. In this type of setting the decision maker is not really able to do much about a particular situation, since the event is passed.

The "what-if" setting is supported by decision support systems. By using "what-if" a decision maker can monitor the effect of change over a given business decision by changing one or more variables. This feature is easily available in spreadsheet programs such as Microsoft Excel and in DSS generators such as IFPS (interactive financial planning system).

The real challenge remains for the last four settings: why, what does it mean, what to do, and when to do it. Various AI technologies may be integrated with DSS and traditional CBIS in order to support these additional decision scenarios.

17-12 DECISION SUPPORT AND ARTIFICIAL INTELLIGENCE INTEGRATION

AI-related technologies, such as expert systems, natural language processing, and voice and pattern recognition can improve the quality of today's DSS. While a DSS presents a "What-if" capability to a decision maker, AI technologies can add "Why, How, What to do, When to do it, and What does it mean" capabilities to a DSS. You can easily see the advantages of the integration. The result is a much more powerful DSS than is presently available. AI technologies particularly expert systems and natural language processing can be integrated to all or one of the following components of a DSS:

- Database
- Model base
- Dialog management (user/system interface)

The benefits to be achieved from the integration of ES into the database component are as follows [4, 20,27]:

- Adding deductive reasoning to the traditional DBMS functions.
- Improvement of the access speed.
- Improvement of the construction and maintenance of the database.
- Providing the ability to handle uncertainty and fuzzy knowledge.
- Representation of data symbolically.
- Simplification of the query operations in complex environment through the use of heuristic search algorithms.

The contribution of AI to the model base component of a DSS would be [4,20,27]:

- ES for improving sensitivity analysis.
- ES for reasoning and explanation of model base output.
- ES to add heuristics to the existing analysis capability of the model base.
- Improving the validation and verification process and also providing advice regarding debugging models.

- Possibly an ES can incorporate imprecise representation (fuzzy sets) into the model-building process. This should help the user/designer of a DSS to build a model that represents a more realistic view of a real-life situation.
- Providing expert assistance to novice users.
- Providing modeling experiments, similar to human expert.
- Providing the opportunity to incrementally modify the initial modeling structure supplied by the DSS.
- Reducing computational times and cost.
- Selection of the right model for the problem at hand.

One area, that may improve the quality and user friendliness of the existing DSS, would be the integration of ES capability into the dialog component (user/system interface) of the DSS. This feature should improve and incorporate:

- Explanation capability to the DSS. This facility may explain in a nontechnical term what a particular response means.
- Symbolic presentation
- Terminology more similar to user's native language

The integration of vision recognition, speech recognition, and NLP into the dialog component of a DSS should immensely improve the effectiveness of these systems. Natural language processing will be discussed in detail in Chapter 21.

Another approach that shows promising signs for improving the user-system interface is visual interactive approach (VIA) [2].

Through AI technology, the expressive power of the dialog management component can be augmented to create a symbiotic relationship between human and computer known as the visual interactive approach. The DSS takes on the role of an active partner, "relying" on its human counterpart to supply input that will lead to joint decision making. Design principles of this approach are (1) usability prior to functionality and (2) active cooperation [2].

The focus is on first designing a friendly, communicable environment that the human can identify with, and then determining its underlying functions. Most traditional systems use the opposite approach, in that the friendly interfaces are added at the end of the process. This proactive design means that problems to be solved do not have to be that well defined beforehand. The user is free to use mental representations through manipulation of objects, relations, and constraints directly on the screen. These building blocks, known as primitives, form the structure for visual interactive modeling (VIM).

Another benefit of VIM is that the human and the system "communicate" with each other by exchanging examples based on the cognitive style of the user. This approach is also known as modeling by example (MBE). The user need only be concerned with those model components that are relevant to him or her. Also, MBE helps build the model incrementally in a series of interactive steps. This process accomplishes two objectives: (1) it gradually increases the user's knowledge about the problem and (2) it makes it possible to use the updated model or solution as a platform for further analysis and exploration.

It can be stated, then, that a combination of AI-based visual languages and object-oriented principles can greatly enhance the dialog management capabilities of DSSs. Without a doubt it will increase user acceptance and transform the role of a DSS from passive to active. The benefits of this integration are summarized below [2]:

- Improves dialog capability
- Inspires creativity
- Offers tutoring and guidance
- Promotes usability prior to functionality
- Provides a symbiotic relationship and active cooperation between the user and the system
- Provides reasoning and explanations to the user

17-13 HAS INTEGRATION ALREADY STARTED?

Integration has already started in a number of directions. A review of the literature shows promising signs for further integration between CBIS, DSS, and AI technologies. Let us briefly introduce some of the existing examples of integrated systems.

1. GURU by Micro Data Base Systems, Inc., combines ESs, DBMSs, spreadsheet, graphics, communication, and word processing programs. This package can be used for development of numerous DSS/ES type systems. GURU extends the conventional AI notions of knowledge representation and processing to embrace business-computing methods. Conversely, it can be viewed as an integration of traditionally alien AI techniques into a unified business problem-solving environment. This integration significantly enhances prior business computing methods [15].

2. Knowledge Workbench by Silogic Corporation integrates a comprehensive database and a natural language processing interface.

3. KEE by Intellicorp integrates various modeling and simulation techniques, by using AI technology [24].

4. REVEAL by Decision Products, Inc., works based on "fuzzy sets" theory for financial and corporate planning. This system helps to represent fuzzy words such as "fairly high," "reasonably important," or "adequate progress." This presentation should add more flexibility to the model-building process.

5. IFPS Optimum by Comshare helps to identify the nature of a problem under investigation. For example, is a particular problem a linear optimization or a nonlinear optimization? It also offers answers to "why" scenarios. For example, you may ask why the sales for the northwestern region have increased by 32%.

6. Promoter by Management Decision Systems, Inc., is used with EXPRESS (a 4GL by the same company). This package analyzes the effects of promotional activities on sales in the packaged goods industry.

7. STRUDL (Structural Design Language) developed by Terry Winograd [23]. This system and its added components help the engineers during the design process by telling them what data to input what action to take and so forth.

8. Logistics Management System (LMS) by IBM combines DSSs, MISs, ESs, simulation, computer-aided manufacturing, and DDP. This system is used by IBM's Burlington Plant manufacturing management team as a tool for resolving crises and providing accurate planning.

9. Lambda 2x2 Plus by LISP Machines, Inc., combines and supports both DSS and ES users. This system is equipped with a LISP processor, and UNIX processor, and has the capability of adding a PROLOG processor.

10. Explorer LX by Texas Instruments provides access to UNIX and LISP files [24].

11. HP Workstations combine C, Pascal, FORTRAN, UNIX, LISP, and PROLOG [24].

12. Stratex was developed to analyze the market situation according to user's parameters. Developed for Norwegian fishing exporters, the system is used for strategic marketing and planning [6].

13. KBES for grain farmers was developed to assist grain farmers grow, market, and sell grain [20].

14. DSS/ES for cabinet makers was developed to assist cabinet makers in bidding jobs [25].

15. EXBEST in three levels (EXBEST1, EXBEST2, and EXBEST3) was developed to solve inventory problems. This system assists inventory managers to accomplish such goals as uninterrupted material flow, reduced operating costs, improved productivity, and it makes decision making more consistent [2].

16. OPASA was developed for Chevron Corporation's Richmond, California, refinery in order to advise and train process operators. This system assists production improves product qualities, and helps keep operating costs at their minimum level [26].

17. MDS was developed to use smart alarms with expert system technology to warn the driller of unexpected circulation events so that action can be advised and taken regarding offshore oil drilling [12].

18. KB was developed for use in selecting controls and displays in large and complex control systems such as those involved in nuclear power plants [28].

SUMMARY

This chapter reviewed artificial intelligence and its related disciplines. Progress in the AI field will have a direct impact on CBIS, DSS, and ES design and utilization. Among the AI-related disciplines, expert systems and natural language processing are the most important areas as far as a CBIS is concerned. The chapter discussed expert systems in detail. The last part of the chapter reviewed the possible integration of AI technologies and CBISs and DSSs. Several examples of integrated systems were introduced.

REVIEW QUESTIONS

1. What is AI?
2. Is AI a solid discipline or just a concept? What is the Turing test? The Chinese room experiment?
3. What are some AI-related technologies?
4. Among the AI-related technologies, which one has a direct impact on CBISs and DSSs? Why?
5. What is an expert system? What are some examples of expert systems applications?
6. What have expert systems done in the field of education? In oil exploration?
7. What are four of the major components of an expert system?
8. What is the role of the explanation capability component?
9. What is the inference engine?
10. What is heuristic knowledge?
11. What are the differences between forward and backward chaining?
12. What are the three technologies of expert systems?
13. What is the difference between expert systems tools and shells? Which one may be faster for developing a specific expert system?
14. What are the two major types of expert systems architectures?
15. What are some situations and/or applications that are prime candidates for expert systems implementation?
16. What are some applications that are not suitable for expert systems implementation?
17. What are the five decision-making scenarios outlined in this chapter?

18. What is the difference between the "what is " and "what if" scenarios?
19. What are some contributions of AI technologies to the database component of a CBIS or DSS?
20. What are some contributions of AI technologies to the model base component of a CBIS or DSS?
21. What is visual interactive approach? What is its role and impacts on the user/ system interface of a DSS?
22. What are some examples of integrated systems introduced in this chapter?

PROJECTS

1. Research the strengths and weaknesses of AI computers. Are they really intelligent? What does "intelligent" mean?
2. Research the function of the brain and the function of computers. How are they similar? How are they dissimilar?
3. Research two of the expert systems presented in this chapter. What are their strengths? Their weaknesses?
4. Compare and contrast the architecture of a DSS and an expert system. What are the similarities? What are the differences?
5. By referring to the references at the end of the chapter further investigate two of the integrated systems introduced in this chapter. What are some of the strengths of these systems? What are their weaknesses? Is integration really needed? Discuss.
6. With all possibilities the CYC project should be completed by now. Research this project and find out if any of the stated goals has been achieved by this project. Is a machine ever able to teach itself? Discuss.

KEY TERMS

Artificial intelligence, 488–489
Backward chaining, 501
Chinese room experiment, 492–493
CYC project, 493
ES shells (ESS), 504–505
ES tools, 504–505
Example-based ES, 505–506
Expert systems, 493–499

Explanation facility, 503
Forward chaining, 501
Heuristics, 494
Inference engine, 501–503
Knowledge acquisition facility, 500
Knowledge base (rule base and
 database), 500

Knowledge-base management system
  (KBMS), 500
Natural language processing, 503
Rule-based ES, 505–506
Specific ES (SES), 504–505

Turing test, 491–492
User interface, 503
Visual interactive approach (VIA),
  511–512

REFERENCES

[1] Andriole, S. J. (July 1985). The promise of artificial intelligence. *Journal of Systems Management,* 8–17.

[2] Angehrn, A. A., and Luthi, H-J. (November-December 1990). Intelligent decision support systems: A visual interactive approach. *Interfaces,* 17–28.

[3] Anonymous. (April 1995). Expert systems resource guides, products and services directory. *AI Expert,* 26.

[4] Bidgoli, H. (1993). Integration of technologies: An ultimate decision-making aid. *Industrial Management & Data Systems,* No. 1, 10–17.

[5] Bidgoli, H. (1997). *Modern information systems for managers.* San Diego: Academic Press, Inc.

[6] Borch, H. (January 1991). Knowledge-based systems for strategic market planning in small firms. *Decision Support Systems,* 143–157.

[7] Browning, J. (March 14, 1992). A survey of artificial intelligence. *The Economist,* 5–24.

[8] Buta, P. (February 1994). Mining for financial knowledge with case-based reasoning. *AI Expert,* 344.

[9] Coles, L. S. (April 1994). Computer chess: The Drosophila of AI. *AI Expert,* 25–31.

[10] Collins, H. (June 20, 1992). Will machines ever think? *New Scientist,* 36–40.

[11] Dudleson, Arnold, and McCann. (October 1990). Early detection of drillstring washouts reduces fishing jobs. *World Oil,* 43–47.

[12] Ehrenberg, D. (July 1990). Expert systems for inventory control. *Decision Support Systems,* 293–298.

[13] Eom, S. B. (September/October 1996). A survey of operational expert systems in business (1980–1993). *Interfaces,* Vol. 26, No. 5, 50–70

[14] Griesser, J. W. (May 1992). Expert among us: Computer systems that aid in decisions. *Business Horizons,* Vol. 35, No. 3, 77–80.

[15] Holsapple, C. W., and Whinston, A. B. (1987). *Business expert system,* Irwin Homewood, IL, No. 15, 34.

[16] Keim, R. T., and Jacobs, S. (December 1986). Expert systems: The DSS of the future? *Journal of Systems Management,* 6–14.

[17] Kestelyn, J. (May 1991). Application witch. *AI Expert,* 71.

[18] Kneale, D. (November 1986). How Coopers & Lybrand put expertise into its computers. *Wall Street Journal.*

[19] Luconi, F. L., Malone, T. W., and Scott-Morton, M. S. (1986). Expert systems: The next challenge for managers. *Sloan Management Review,* 3–13.

[20] Martin, J., and Oxman, S. (1988). *Building expert systems: A tutorial,* p. 117. Englewood Cliffs, NJ: Prentice-Hall.

[21] Metzler, S. (October 1987). Knowledge-based system designed by Purdue University helps grain farmers. *Computers and People,* 22–27.

[22] Newquist III, H. P. (March 1990). In practice: Bloodhounds and expert systems. *AI Expert,* 67–69.

[23] Patent, D. H. (1986). *The quest for artificial intelligence,* pp. 70–72. New York: Harcourt, Brace and Jovanovich Publishers.

[24] Raunch-Hindin, W. (August 1987). Hardware dynamos power AI deployment. *Mini-Micro Systems,* 75–85.

[25] Sullivan and Shiverly. (January 1989). Expert system software in small business decision making. *Journal of Small Business Management,* 17–26.

[26] Touchstone, Blackwell, Carter, and Kramer. (February 1990). Expert systems trains, advises process operators. *Oil and Gas Journal,* 41–44.

[27] Turban, E., and Watkins, P. R. (June 1986). Integrating expert systems and decision support systems. *MIS Quarterly,* 121–136.

[28] Wang and Teh. (July 1991). A knowledge-based system for controls-displays selection. *Decision Support Systems,* 195–191.

Chapter 18

Expert Systems Construction: Putting Theory to Work

Learning Objectives

After studying this chapter, you should be able to:

- Define the knowledge acquisition process for expert system (ES) construction.
- Explain the knowledge representation process for ES construction.
- Define the process of constructing an ES.
- Explain the various steps taken to construct an ES.
- Compare and contrast ES construction with other CBIS construction.
- Review important shells for the ES construction.
- Review the important issues regarding the ES construction including the legal issues.

18-1 INTRODUCTION

This chapter provides a detailed discussion regarding the construction of expert systems. It first reviews knowledge acquisition and knowledge representation processes as two key components for ES construction; it then puts these two important phases into practice. Expert systems construction follows a methodology similar to the life-cycle approach discussed in Chapter 9; however, there are some differences. Important phases for the construction of an expert system include: problem definition, organizational readiness, expert selection, tool selection, design team selection, prototype design, final construction, validation, and postimplementation audit. Naturally, the basic mission of an expert system is different than that of a traditional CBIS. Also, the domain expert plays a very important role in the construction of an expert system. These differences mandate that a slightly different life-cycle approach to be followed for ES construction. The chapter also provides a listing of some of the popular ES shells on the market. The chapter will conclude with important considerations for ES construction that must be carefully examined before releasing the system for general use.

18-2 THE KNOWLEDGE ACQUISITION PROCESS

Knowledge acquisition involves extracting, structuring, and organizing the knowledge from a human expert or experts and representing it in machine-readable forms. In some cases, the knowledge may be in documented forms. This may be in books, films, videos, newspapers, and so forth. In such cases, the knowledge engineer does not need to involve the expert. The knowledge engineer plays a similar role to a programmer/analyst in a CBIS environment. The knowledge engineer must have an extensive computer background, communication skills, and general knowledge about the field [2,3].

The knowledge engineer will use a series of techniques and tools in order to extract the expert knowledge. After extracting the knowledge and performing the validation process it will become the basis for the knowledge-base component of the expert system.

Experts in the field believe that knowledge acquisition is the "bottleneck" in the development of expert systems. Although an expert or experts may know precisely how a particular problem is solved, it is often difficult to transfer this expertise to others. Many issues that are obvious to the expert may not be as obvious to others.

Knowledge includes all the facts that have been accumulated regarding a particular problem or task. There are two types of knowledge: undocumented and documented. Undocumented knowledge resides on the experts' minds. Documented knowledge comes from books, notes, brochures, databases, films, movies, stories, songs, research projects and so forth.

The knowledge acquisition process involves the following three activities [12]:

1. The knowledge engineer uses various communication techniques to elicit data and information from the expert.
2. The knowledge engineer interprets these data and information in order to draw conclusions on what might be the expert's underlying knowledge and reasoning processes.
3. The knowledge engineer uses his or her conclusions to direct the construction of a model, which describes the expert's knowledge and processes for solving a particular problem. The knowledge engineer and the expert carry out an iterative process as the expert system model evolves into a functional system.

18-3 STEPS IN THE KNOWLEDGE ACQUISITION PROCESS

Practitioners in the expert systems field generally agree on five distinct steps for acquiring knowledge [4].

1. Identification
2. Conceptualization
3. Formalization
4. Implementation
5. Testing and validation

Let's briefly explain each step:

1. *Identification.* During this phase the problem and its major characteristics are identified. Subproblems, participants, and resources are clearly defined. The knowledge engineer learns about the problem and the goal of the expert system is agreed upon. The scope of the problem and its relationship to the organization as a whole is defined.

Hayes-Roth and colleagues [10] provide a comprehensive list of questions designed to help define the problem:

- What class of problems can be solved by the expert system?
- How can these problems be characterized or defined?
- What are important subproblems and partitioning of tasks?
- What are the data and information to be gathered and analyzed?
- What are the important objects and their interrelations?
- What aspects of the human expertise are essential in solving these problems?
- What is the nature and extent of "relevant knowledge" that underlies the human solution?
- What situations are likely to impede solutions?
- How will these impediments affect the expert system?
- What is the problem that the expert system is intended to solve? The active participants (expert, knowledge engineer, user and sponsoring manager) are also identified and their roles are defined.

2. *Conceptualization.* The knowledge important to the decision process can vary. Care must be taken to determine the concepts and the relationships to be used. What is the necessary information? What is the best way to extract it? Which tool should be used?

3. *Formalization.* This step determines the format in which knowledge is to be represented and organized. In rule-based systems knowledge must be organized in terms of rules. During this stage, knowledge acquisition is actually integrated with knowledge representation. It is also a difficult stage in that it is here that most of the extraction of the expert's knowledge occurs.

Questions that must be answered during this phase include:

- Are the data sparse and insufficient or plentiful and redundant?
- Is there uncertainty attached to the data?
- Does the logical interpretation of data depend on their order of occurrence over time?
- What is the cost of data acquisition?
- How are the data acquired or elicited? What types of questions need to be asked to obtain the data?
- Are the data reliable, accurate and precise?

4. *Implementation.* This stage involves the actual programming of knowledge into the expert system. Refinements may occur in the acquired knowledge. A prototype expert system is being developed during this stage.

5. *Testing and validation.* As the final stage, the knowledge engineer tests the system by subjecting it to examples. In this stage the rules are revised if necessary.

Knowledge validity is examined at this stage. Usually there are three activities in this phase: evaluation, validation, and verification. Although the terms are often used interchangeably elsewhere, each has a distinct meaning in the context of the knowledge acquisition process. Evaluation refers to the assessment of the ES's overall value. The emphasis is on its usability, efficiency, and cost effectiveness. Validation concerns the system's performance. Usually, tests are given to verify the accuracy of the ES's response relative to that of human experts. Rolston [20] developed three principles to be used for this purpose. The first principle is that for many of the domains addressed by an ES, it is impossible to identify an answer that is "absolutely correct" for any given problem. Second, in ES evaluation, the correct response is taken to be that given by a human expert given the same question. Finally, an ES's response should be evaluated relative to the domain expert's and then relative to the responses given by a group of experts. Verification is focused on the system implementation activities, that is, how the system was built, and how closely the implementation was carried out based on the specifications. Validation and verification are dynamic and repetitive. Any changes in each of the ES components will result in another round of validation and verification.

18-3-1 SELECTED KNOWLEDGE ACQUISITION TECHNIQUES

There are several techniques used for knowledge acquisition for expert systems construction. The following is a brief definition of some of the popular knowledge acquisition techniques.

The **observation** technique allows simply observing the expert when he/she is performing a specific task in his/her comfortable environment without interruption by the knowledge engineer.

Protocol analysis requires that the expert "think aloud" while solving a problem. Protocol analysis, originated in clinical psychology is a form of data analysis using problem scenarios to stimulate the experts' thinking process.

Discourse analysis is similar to protocol analysis. Interview sessions are tape-recorded and the tapes are transcribed and analyzed later.

Interviews are effective technique for knowledge acquisition. There are two types of interviews used as knowledge acquisition tools: unstructured, and structured. Open, unstructured, or free-form interviewing is one of the most commonly used methods for knowledge acquisition. The knowledge engineer may start by asking a question such as "How do you solve this problem?" The advantage of the free-form interview is that the knowledge engineer can elicit unanticipated information. The disadvantage is that experts become less aware of the cognitive processes they use in performing a task. They cannot explicitly describe the reasoning used. There are also biases and fallibility in human reasoning. They tend to leave out certain components since it may be so obvious to them. The structured interview is goal-oriented. It forces the expert to be organized and interpretation problems are reduced.

The **voting** technique is used to generate consensus among the experts. After identification of various alternatives, experts are asked to vote on a desired alternative.

Brainstorming is an effective technique for generating ideas. Special attention areas can be uncovered in this process. Inhibiting behavior and confrontation can be reduced with multiple experts working together as a team. The experts must be sufficiently stimulated by a question, a scenario, or a demonstration of a system similar to the one under investigation. Each expert must submit one idea as a resolution to the problem. This idea is given to another expert to see if he or she can follow the same train of thought. This process continues until the experts have no more ideas. These interactions among multiple experts provide an enriched domain of expertise.

The **Delphi** technique uses a series of questionnaires used to aggregate knowledge, judgments, or opinions from multiple experts. This is usually done anonymously. This technique reduces the influence of dominant experts, preventing undue influence of strong personalities and it allows strangers to communicate effectively. Integration of some of the group support systems tools such as idea organizer, voting and ranking can significantly improve the Delphi process. (For detailed discussion of these various tools consult Chapter 14.)

18-4 KNOWLEDGE REPRESENTATION: AN OVERVIEW

Knowledge representation (KR) is a key component of expert systems construction. KR is a part of the knowledge engineering discipline that assists a knowledge engineer to program and store the knowledge gathered from the expert(s) and other sources into some types of computer codes.

Knowledge representation is writing down in some language or communication medium, descriptions and facts, objects, or pictures that correspond to a real-world situation. KR is the process of structuring knowledge about a problem in a way that makes a problem easier to solve [9].

Knowledge is the ultimate input into expert system software packages and provides the basis for the intelligent and problem-solving capabilities of these systems. How that knowledge is represented into a workable program, and what methods are used for the representation, is the focus of knowledge representation process. If knowledge can continue to be defined for use in expert systems, then the future of this technology is wide open.

To represent knowledge is one of the major differences that lie between ESs and other CBISs. The knowledge of an expert, including facts and rules of thumb, must be implemented into software to comprise a knowledge-based system. This knowledge can be symbolically represented in various forms of logic and object relationships [21].

The idea of representing knowledge in a computer using a computer programming language, or an ES shell, does not seem to be a difficult task. The definition of KR used earlier suggests that you simply write down the knowledge in some language acceptable to a computer. This, however, is the easy part. The difficult part as Ringland and Duce suggest is to represent knowledge so that a computer can come to new conclusions about its environment by manipulating the representation. They break down the problem of KR into three components [19, p. 3]:

1. Finding a knowledge representation language in which the domain of knowledge can be described.
2. Finding a knowledge representation language that can perform automatic inferences for the user.
3. How to capture the detailed knowledge base that represents the system's understanding of its domain.

This may not seem so difficult to accomplish, but when you evaluate how much is being spent on KR in the United States you begin to get a better picture of the scope of these projects.

Goel [7] sites a study that estimates that U.S. companies spent $5 to $10 billion exploring AI and used as much as 4% of their information technology budget on ESs alone. By 1999, U.S. companies plan to spend 15% to 20% of their information technology budgets on ES. If companies are spending that much on AI and ESs and plan to spend more, KR cannot be taken as a simple or unimportant aspect of AI and ESs. Goel goes on to explain why costs are so high. According to Goel, only a small fraction of the ES applications developed has been implemented in a production environment. The literature is rich with stories of magnificent failures, brilliant ideas as yet untested, systems that might have worked, and systems that will be available soon.

KR applications failures are the result of many problems such as a lack of standards and technology limitations. Goel suggests that lack of software standards and development methodology have caused companies to incur higher systems development cost and risk. KR suffers from technological limitations as well. All knowledge presentation forms (e.g., production rules, frames, etc.) are based on predicate calculus. This approach has proven to be inadequate for expressing various assertions, disjunctions, inequalities, and existentially qualified statements, for example, as well as metalevel propositions, which include such things as a company's beliefs, attitudes, goals, value systems, cultural situations, and purpose [7].

18-4-1 SELECTED KNOWLEDGE REPRESENTATION TECHNIQUES

Knowledge representation can be broadly classified into declarative and procedural methods. Declarative methods represent facts about the domain in a modular fashion. The rules are stated explicitly and independently of one another. The knowledge regarding how to use the facts resides separately in an inference engine. In our day-to-day lives we use declarative methods most of the time. For example, this book has 21 chapters or John is a carpenter. These are examples of declarative methods. Declarative methods include semantic networks, scripts, frames, and object-oriented representation methods. The advantages of declarative techniques stem from the modularity aspect. Each fact needs to be stored only once regardless of the ways it can be used. Adding or modifying facts is easily accomplished without changing other facts or procedures.

A procedural representation is essentially a plan for the use of the information. Procedural knowledge may be such that a routine waits for conditions to trigger the procedure. If the conditions are met then an action takes place. Another example of procedural representation is the ordering of rules. If rules are independent, then the order in which the rules are applied should be of no consequence. However, if the order of application is specified and that specification leads to additional knowledge, then the knowledge is embedded in the procedure and is not separately available to the system. Simple examples of procedural methods would be changing gears in a car or building a house.

Procedural representation is used to represent knowledge about how to do things or knowledge that does not fit well into declarative schemes. Knowledge such as heuristic or probabilistic reasoning can also be represented using procedural representation. **Production rules** are perhaps the most popular way to represent knowledge. Let's briefly explain this popular technique for KR.

Sometimes it is referred to as the classic way to represent knowledge. A system of IF-THEN rules is used to move from condition(s) to action(s). The IF is a list of premises, and THEN is the conclusion. To use a rule-based system it is usually assumed that the data, facts, or information consist of small, modular chunks of knowledge that can be expressed in a rule format. A production system can be in one of the following formats:

IF   (antecedents)   THEN   (consequences)
IF   (condition)   AND   (condition)   AND . . . THEN   (action)

Rule-based systems are often referred to as production systems. Three main components must be present to have a minimum working system [19].

1. *Working memory*—this is where the observed data enters the system.
2. *Rule memory*—data are passed to the rule memory for comparison with the stored rules to form a match.

3. *The interpreter or inference engine*—it selects the rules that were matched in the rule memory and performs the appropriate action(s). This is the action part of the system.

In addition to these three components, a fourth component is often used in more sophisticated systems. A meta rules component can be added to store new rules that result from the processing of existing rules. Rules are distinguished from conventional conditional statements by two factors:

1. The conditional part is expressed as a pattern not a Boolean expression, and
2. Each rule is determined separately by the interpreter and is not passed from one rule to the next in lexical sequence.

Forward and backward chaining describe the flow of data from input to output. In forward chaining the system moves from the origin and by checking a series of if-then statements, tries to achieve the goal. In this case let's say a passenger is trying to go to Istanbul, Turkey, from Los Angeles, California. In forward chaining all the planes leaving the Los Angeles airport will be checked until it reaches Istanbul. In backward chaining the goal is know and the system backtracks in order to achieve the goal. In our example, the system starts from Istanbul (the goal) and checks all the planes that land in Istanbul and keep working until it reaches to Los Angeles.

An example of dealing with a car problem will be used to demonstrate how these components interact. The following is a simple model of forward chaining in a rule based system [19].

The observed data is sent to working memory:

(Complaint: The car won't turn on)
(No battery)

The above-observed data is sent to rule memory to be matched with the rules stored in the rule memory.

Rule: No battery = dead battery
IF   (Complaint: The car won't start)
AND   (No battery)

The inference engine then selects the matched rule from rule memory that matches the contents of working memory. This is called firing (or taking an action).

THEN   (assert (replace the battery))
IF   (remedy (car turns on))
AND   (Customer is happy)
THEN   (Thanks for your business)

If the customer is happy the output would be, "Thanks for your business." If the remedy does not work, then the inference engine goes back to working memory for more data or a modification of data and the process starts all over again until the customer is happy.

The above case is typical example of how a forward-chaining data-directed production system would work to solve a problem. The system starts from observed data and proceeds to working memory for a match of the data with the existing rules. It then "fires" this to the inference engine. The inference engine will take action, either to deliver output or go back to working memory for more data. This process will continue until all data and rules are exhausted or an answer is found.

In backward chaining a goal is defined and the search is directed to accomplish the goal. In this example the goal was to make the customer happy. The interpreter would select rules to match the data that would make the customer happy. This is where the meta rules component would come into play. The solution replace the battery might not correct the problem. The starter might be the problem and so on.

18-5 EXPERT SYSTEMS CONSTRUCTION: AN OVERVIEW

The construction of an expert system, similar to other CBISs, is a multifaceted and complex task. A series of well-defined steps must be followed in order to deliver a final product that is an operational expert system.

Each step of ES construction is not a step or activity all to itself nor must they be completed in sequence. Problem definition should be completed first, but could be done more than once if the prototype fails to solve the problem. The problem at hand may have to be redefined, modified, or even abandoned. Organizational readiness may have to take place right after the problem definition phase, but may be just as effective if done during the entire project.

Expert selection and tool selection are separate issues, but can be done at the same time. The knowledge engineer may need to select the tools or shells to fit the expert or the type of domain knowledge under consideration. Design team selection must take place but not all members need to be chosen at the start of the project.

Prototype design and revision are very important and must be performed carefully. Final construction will be the last step before the postimplementation audit. Many factors will affect the actual sequence in which the ES is to be constructed, and should be given some consideration before starting the project.

18-6 EXPERT SYSTEMS CONSTRUCTION: FROM THE BEGINNING TO THE END

The construction of an ES is more than the mechanics of implementing a system. It is not enough to buy the hardware and software, hire the necessary personal, and build the system. According to Meador and Mahler, choosing a strategy that fits your company's culture and structure has a lot to do with your chances for ultimate success [14]. To have an effective and efficient system you must consider many factors. These factors will be discussed in detail in this chapter. Construction can be carried out using the various methods that a typical system analyst would use while implementing any project. A top down, bottom up or a combination approach may be used. The important point is that each of the nine following steps must be given consideration while implementing the project. Some steps can be done during the project and even after the project is finished. ES construction similar to the CBIS construction is never finished because there is always room for improvement. Figure 18-1 highlights the nine phases involved in the construction of an ES.

18-6-1 PROBLEM DEFINITION

The first step in the construction of an ES is to define the scope and the nature of the problem. In another words the domain of the expert system must be specified. This means that the organization must decide if an ES will solve the problem under investigation. An ES may be the most effective way to solve the problem, but not the most efficient. It can be a very expensive way to solve a problem that can be solved in some other, less expensive manner. (See the applications and nonapplication situations of expert systems in Chapter 17, Section 17-10).

A basic feasibility study should be conducted to determine the costs and benefits of the project. The feasibility study in the ES environment is similar to the feasibility study described in Chapter 9 for a CBIS with some minor variations. As you may recall, the feasibility study first investigates the costs and benefits of the system. In other words, its economic desirability, then its social, technical, and time dimension are carefully analyzed. The various dimensions of feasibility study for expert system development are summarized bellow:

- Economic
- Social
- Technical
- Time

Let's briefly explain these various dimensions of a feasibility study for ES development.

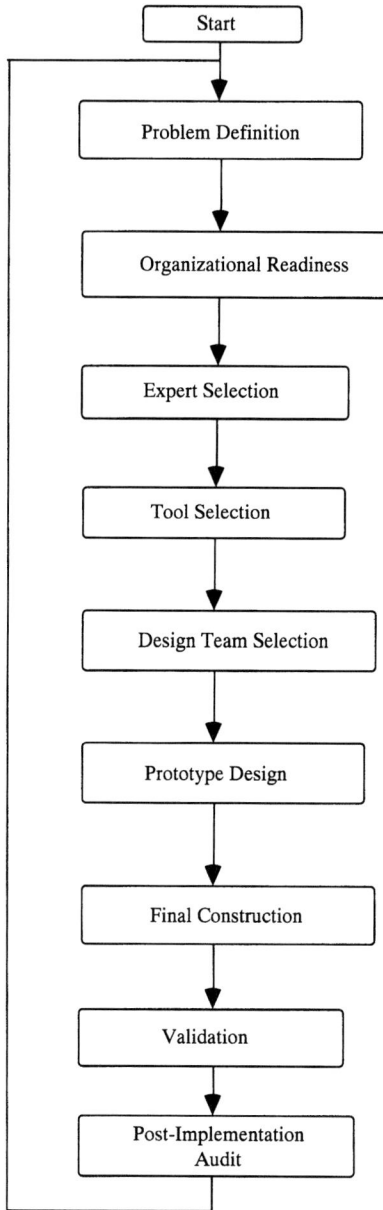

Figure 18-1   Expert systems construction life cycle.

The economic dimension usually is concerned with all the costs and benefits of the system. Both costs and benefits include tangible and intangible items. The assessment of tangible costs and benefits is relatively straightforward. The most noticeable benefit of an expert system is the preservation and distribution of rare expertise throughout the organization. As an example, consider the expert system developed in Campbell's Soup Company. This system has recorded 44 years of the expertise of a rare expert in the organization. The benefit of such a system is tremendous. In addition to tangible benefits, an ES may include numerous intangible benefits such as improving communication, a better problem-solving process, improving customer service, and so forth. The tangible cost of an expert system involves the cost of hardware, software, and personnel. The cost of personnel in an ES environment is somewhat different than the cost of personnel in the CBIS environment. In an ES environment the personnel costs not only include the cost of programmers, knowledge engineers, and support staff, but also the cost of the expert whose expertise will become the core of the system development process. The expert's time is very expensive, and in some cases, the expert may request additional compensation.

The social feasibility is also somewhat different than the social feasibility in the CBIS environment. The design team not only should consider user acceptance of the system, they should carefully investigate the reaction of the expert(s) and the user(s) toward the system. Expert systems are associated with the notion that they may replace the expert(s). Widespread education and participation are needed in order to alleviate these problems. The user(s) and the expert(s) must be actively involved in the entire ES development process. The user(s) and expert(s) must be responsible for both the success and the failure of the system. Careful planning should minimize some of the social issues of expert systems development.

The technical dimension investigates the required expertise, organizational readiness, and the availability and willingness of the key expert(s) to be used for the ES development. The time dimension investigates the availability of the system within the required time frame. If the system will not be ready within the desired time frame, we conclude that the system is not feasible from the time dimension standpoint. Other types of feasibility do not matter.

The problem definition phase should include a survey of the rules to be used in the ES. It is more cost effective to choose another method of solving the problem if the rules are few, say less than 10. On the other hand, if there are too many rules (more than 10,000) it may cost too much and take too long to develop an ES. If the problem can be solved numerically, there may be no need for the ES. A complete understanding of the quantity and quality of the rules to be used will help in deciding if an ES is the right application.

The suitability of the problem at hand for expert system implementation is very important. It is important that a specific problem domain be narrowly defined.

Too broad a domain will make the coding of the rules to apply to the knowledge base a time-consuming task. In other words the efficiency might be at risk. Expert systems perform well when they are applied to a narrow and deep area. This means a limited problem area that we know a lot about it. The design team must make sure that the problem at hand falls into one of the following categories:

- A high degree of human expertise is needed.
- Available experts are retiring or scarce.
- The problem area does not call for extensive mathematical modeling, such as those found in the CBIS environment.
- There is always some degree of uncertainty.
- The existing experts are willing to share their expertise for the ES construction.
- Recognized experts exist.
- Experts agree on solutions.
- The task under investigation requires reasoning and informed judgments, as opposed to just common sense.
- The task is well understood.
- Typical example cases or situations are readily available.
- The task requires symbolic manipulation.

Richardson and Defries [18] use the following two considerations to determine the suitability of a problem for ES implementation:

1. Does the task have such a quantitative or procedural content or structure that would best be solved by using a more conventional computer tool, such as a spreadsheet or a database management application?
2. When a situation involves a decision or task encountered only a few times a year, then it is probably best handled by a human expert.

Just as in the number of rules, the type of rules to be used is very important. Time and money can be associated with each type and this must be taken into consideration [15].

- *Completely innumerable rules.* These are usually limited in number and are completely known. They are simple and do not have many arguments.
- *Partially innumerable rules.* This is a situation where many rules are known, but many others are not known. This may require additional rule development with a human expert involved.
- *Unknown rules.* This is the most complex of the three. There is no way to know the magnitude of the number of rules. This type of system must be developed in a way to be able to easily modify as new information comes to light.

18-6-2 ORGANIZATIONAL READINESS

Management support and user readiness must be taken into consideration before attempting to construct an ES. Management and users may have no understanding of how an ES works. They will need a minimum level of general computer understanding and some understanding and appreciation of what an ES will do for them. Management must be committed to the project. They must be able to justify the expenditures in terms of the benefits. The users must be able to see the importance of the system and how it will affect them. The same involvement that is needed when developing any CBIS should be provided. Management and the users must be involved in every step of the project from the beginning to the end. This gives them a sense of commitment to the project. Both management and users can cause the project to be a failure, even if the system functions according to the specifications.

The best method of providing organizational readiness is through education and on-going education. All the impacted personnel should be told about the functions of the new ES, its costs and benefits, and its overall impact on the organization as a whole. When the system is put to work, the management should provide on-going education in order to expose the user group to the new features and the overall effectiveness of the system. By doing this, the management is significantly improving the chances of success.

18-6-3 EXPERT SELECTION

During this stage of ES development the domain expert(s) must be selected. The expert(s) could be a collection of knowledge available in documented forms such as books, notes, manuals, or videos, or an actual human expert. The expert has the knowledge that is being transferred to the expert system. If the knowledge of the experts has been written down and collected in some manner as to make it compatible with the ES, then very little, if any, involvement of the human expert will be needed. This is usually not the case. Not only will the human expert need to be involved, there may be more than one expert needed to complete the acquisition of knowledge.

Knowledge acquisition occurs at this stage as discussed earlier. Knowledge acquisition involves eliciting, analyzing, organizing, and interpreting the knowledge that the expert possesses. The knowledge engineer uses techniques such as structured interviews and protocol analyses to extract the expert's knowledge. The expert will not always be able to articulate his or her knowledge accurately. The expert will work with the knowledge engineer to develop the knowledge needed for the ES. It is important to note that the proper knowledge acquisition method is very important to the development of a successful ES and cannot be taken lightly. The knowledge engineer must be chosen as carefully as the expert.

Various tools and techniques must be examined in order to choose the right tool for a given situation. The knowledge engineer may have to utilize a combination of tools for optimum results.

Expert identification can be a complex task in some situations. In some cases it may be a simple task because many fields have a small number of people who are clearly world-class experts. This is very true in fields such as medicine and it certainly was true in the case of Campbell's Soup Company.

But, in many cases the selection of the expert may be difficult. The task under investigation may require expertise in more than one area. No outstanding expert may be available. Choosing one expert over another may present a problem due to status or standing in that field of expertise. The expert may not be willing to share and communicate his or her expertise. There are two types of experts: the expert with the theoretical knowledge and the expert with practical, hands-on knowledge [17]. The expert with theoretical knowledge usually has extensive education and practical, high-level experience. The hands-on expert has apprentice-style training, little formal education, but many years of experience. The expert should stand out from the norm and bring some personal motivation to the project. If several experts must be used because the project scope overlaps several areas of expertise, a different set of criteria should be applied to select the experts. Experts should be able to communicate what they know. They should be able to work with abstract concepts. They should be able to use their knowledge to solve problems. The level of detail at which the expert works should correspond to that of the user. A familiarity with computers or a willingness to learn is very helpful.

The involvement of the expert can range from total control to limited participation with the system development process. A complex situation may require total control. In a situation where large amounts of past experience are available, the involvement of the expert could be minimal, using the expert only to review and modify the rules if needed.

18-6-4 TOOL SELECTION

The selection of a specific type of ES tool or ES shell must be carefully considered. An ES tool is a programming language. An ES shell is the product of a programming language, which allows for a comparatively easy-to-use format in which to construct the ES. Shells provide a ready-made interpreter that allows a fast design, edit, prototype design, revision and run for the debug cycle. Most tools will fit into one of the following four-type [15]:

1. *Algorithmic programming languages.* These can be any standard procedural computer languages such as C, FORTRAN, BASIC, or PASCAL. The code is

written to record if-then rules. These languages allow for portability between applications and sites. Using any of these languages requires an experienced programmer. For example, PUFF, a pulmonary function expert system, was developed using BASIC.

2. *Symbolic programming languages.* These languages include LISP, PROLOG or some dialect of these languages. These languages process symbols. They can reach conclusions on a logical level unlike the algorithmic languages. Symbolic languages can categorize, analyze, and reach conclusions with symbols. Generally speaking, these languages are more suitable for ES development than algorithmic languages. Developing expert systems using algorithmic programming and symbolic languages may be more expensive than using shells. It usually takes a longer time to develop expert systems using the first two groups of tools; however, the final product will be more customized and it usually fits closely to the specific user's requirements.

3. *Shell-based expert system.* Shells are relatively easy to use. The system provides all the tools necessary for developing an expert system. These are like empty expert systems. For example, EMYCIN, a popular ES shell, was used to develop MYCIN. Two methods of development are usually found in these systems: deductive and inductive. The deductive method uses a decision tree rule structure and by examination of a series of If-Then rules reaches the conclusion. In the inductive approach, a number of actual examples whose results or conclusions are known, are examined using some standard algorithm to drive efficient branching rules. An ES shell usually includes word processing, graphic, spreadsheet and tracing components. Exsys and Exsys Pro by Exsys Corporation are good examples of a PC-based ES shell.

4. *Knowledge-engineering environment.* This approach usually is done through an elaborate multiwindow, icon and graphic, blackboard-like environment. They are expensive and require high-powered PCs or workstations. KEE and ART are two examples of this environment. KEE, the Knowledge Engineering Environment (by IntelliCorp, Mountain View, California), is a large hybrid expert system development environment that requires at least the power of a workstation. KEE has rule-based and object-oriented representations, and has image-processing and windowing capabilities. It also has a number of functions that allow the developer to control the inference process. ART, Adaptive Resonance Theory, has been successfully utilized for neural network construction. It was developed by Stephen Grossberg in 1976, and later was used in ART 1, ART 2, and ART 3 neural networks (developed by Stephen Grossberg and Gail Carpenter in 1987 and 1989).

When a programming method is chosen, the hardware must be taken into consideration also. The computer must be able to work with the software and grows as the system grows. Careful consideration must be given to the hardware.

Depending on what is already available in an organization, the selected language or shell may or may not run on the existing hardware. If the selected language or shell does not run on the existing hardware, then a line of budget must be devoted for the acquisition of the hardware. The availability of one type of hardware may dictate (in some cases) which software (shell or language) must be chosen.

18-6-5 DESIGN TEAM SELECTION

The design team includes programmers, systems analysts, knowledge engineers, experts, users, and top management. This is similar to the CBIS task force discussed in Chapter 9. In some cases, it may not be a bad idea to involve a representative of the vendor community at least for the first couple of meetings. These representatives may be able to provide some insight regarding the suitability of the project at hand and the commercial platform that will be used to design and implement the system. Each member must have a commitment to the project. Programmers and systems analysts may not be needed depending on the type of ES. Most ES projects will need them in some capacity. The top management role is his or her commitment to the project. This is very important to the success of the project. Without top management support, the project may not even get off the drawing board. Top management participation can improve the chances of success for the ES development by providing both financial support and a sense of commitment. This, in turn, encourages others in the organization to be committed to the project as well. The user is another very important participant of the design team. The ES must be designed with the user in mind. The user may not be able to contribute much in the technical areas, but can contribute to the overall success of the project. They will be using the system and can make or break a project if they feel the project is not of much value to them. Having the user on the team will help to ensure that the project will be accepted by the company and will be a useful tool. Knowledge engineers and experts are unique to the ES. Knowledge engineers, experts and users must all be involved and actively participate in the design team. The knowledge engineer works with the expert and the user to transfer the knowledge, rules, and data to the knowledge base of the ES. The expert should have the knowledge and the know how about the rules and facts about the problem domain.

18-6-6 PROTOTYPE DESIGN

As discussed in Chapter 9, a prototype is a small-scale version of the larger system. The prototype should be constructed before the final system is implemented. Although the prototype is not the entire system, it is significant enough to provide the user with a good representation of the actual system. This allows all members of the design team to view the system. It also allows for a demonstration to the user and management. This is a good way to discover any flaws in the system, or misconceptions about its purpose and operation. The prototype should be revised until all possible corrections have been made. This should be an ongoing effort throughout the process of implementation of the system.

As we discussed in Chapter 9, there are several kinds of prototypes. In the ES environment either a throwaway or an evolving prototype should be used. Initial problem definition should take place, knowledge acquisition and knowledge representation should be performed. The cycle should continue until a workable system is developed. Figure 18-2 illustrates this process.

Prototyping should be used as a rapid system development process. This means the prototyping process phase could be done with little or no programming. Using a shell will allow for a much faster prototype design. When a shell is used it allows a wider range of individuals to test the system. Each time the prototype is revised it becomes more complete and complex. This problem is further complicated if a dedicated programming language is used. Not all the rules need to be defined at this time, only enough to test the design. However, at a later point the programming of all the identified rules will be needed to control and test the inference engine, runtime efficiency, customized graphical interface, interface with other external software and hardware applications, and any other issues that may arise from the testing of the prototype [17].

One of the major similarities of expert systems with transaction-processing systems is that both systems try to model the real world, consider users' cognitive limitations in handling complexity, leave room for future growth, and accommodate the heterogeneity of the computing environment [11]. This implies that rapid prototyping and incremental growth are essential elements of both systems. Logical and physical designs are needed in both systems.

18-6-7 FINAL CONSTRUCTION

This phase is the transformation of the final prototype into the final product. Some experts also call this system integration. The final product is either the final result of the evolving prototype or a brand new system constructed based on the throwaway prototype.

Although an expert system construction is never really finished and it will always go through changes, this is the point where the system is delivered to the user as a finished product.

As mentioned earlier, the majority of expert systems evolve over time. This is mainly because of all the new exposure that the system receives after the initial construction. A good example is XCON developed by Digital Equipment

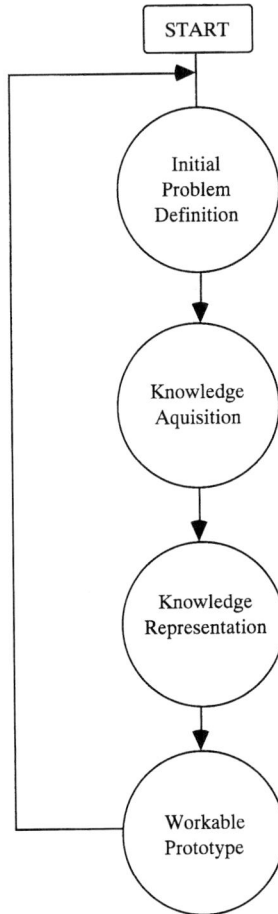

Figure 18-2   Rapid prototyping process.

Corporation and Carnegie Melon University. The system initially started with a few hundred rules and has gone through several revisions. At the present time the system includes more than 10,000 rules.

To continue with the construction of the expert system we should examine its architecture once again as illustrated in Figure 18-3. We explained these various components in detail in Section 17-7.

Depending on which tool is selected, either some of these components are readily available or they must be coded from scratch. The knowledge acquisition facility is designed for acquiring rules and facts. It is essential for the growth of

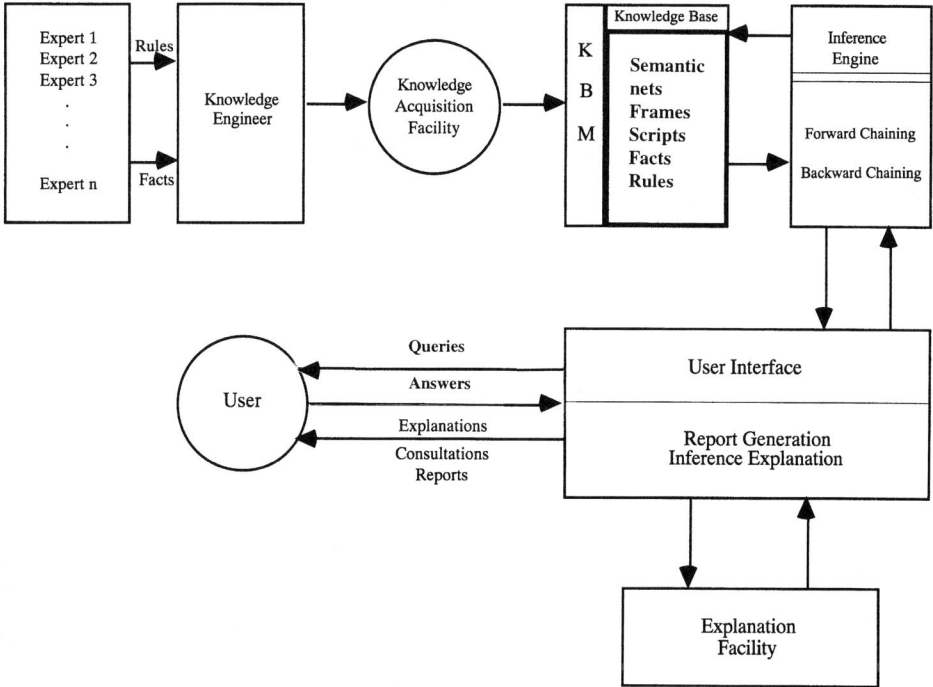

Figure 18-3   A conceptual model for an expert system.

the system. The knowledge engineer uses this facility to capture the expertise of the domain expert.

The knowledge base is where all the knowledge, facts, and rules are stored. It usually includes three types of knowledge. These are factual knowledge, heuristic knowledge, and meta-knowledge. Using the selected tool, this component must be coded.

The knowledge base management system (KBMS) is usually available within the majority of ES shells. If an algorithmic programming or symbolic programming language is used, then this component must be developed. Its purpose is similar to DBMS in the CBIS environment. It allows the creation, manipulation, and maintenance of the knowledge base.

The inference engine applies rules to the knowledge and facts available in the knowledge base. Again, ES shells provide a readily available inference engine. In the case of the first two classes of tools, this component must also be developed.

The last component, the user interface, is probably the most important component from the user's standpoint. It is the goal of ES designers that this component be very userfriendly. That is why some types of natural language with GUI will be ideal. Again, this component is readily available in ES shells and must be constructed in the case of algorithmic or symbolic programming languages.

18-6-8 VALIDATION

Validation is the process of analyzing the knowledge and decision-making capabilities of the expert system. There are several approaches to validation that deal with different aspects of the expert system. As a holistic approach, you can treat the system as a black box and test it on cases to determine if it makes the right decisions for the right reasons. Or, you can evaluate each of the components of the system. You can analyze the knowledge base for accuracy, analyze the knowledge base for completeness, test the inference engine, analyze condition-decision matches for decision quality and condition-decision matches to determine whether the right answers were found for the right reasons. When test cases fail, the explanation or trace facility will point to the problem component (e.g., knowledge base or inference engine). Then the design team should fix the particular component and continue the test [16].

The testing process should provide enough test cases to demonstrate the variety of knowledge needed by the expert. This can be a difficult task. Usually, cases where the decisions are evenly spaced between the two extremes provide the coverage of knowledge. Or, in situations where a discreet number of decisions are possible then you must ensure that each decision is represented. It is also advisable to include multiple cases for each decision where the starting conditions are different.

The most important component of an expert system that must pass all the tests is the knowledge base. Direct examination is the best way to analyze the accuracy of the knowledge base for relatively small systems. For large systems, analyzing the most important rules or frames can adequately test the accuracy of the knowledge base.

The validation and delivery of an expert system is much like any other system. The system must be approved or validated by the expert, the end-user, and the management team. The system will be put into use for final acceptance in much the same way as any other information systems. Training the user, installing the user interface, setting up the hardware platform, and dealing with any software issues are all part of the final construction. Validation of the system should include the following:

1. *Testing.* This should be done to make sure that the system is usable outside the prototype environment. The more complete testing, the fewer problems will be discovered after the system is in the hands of the user. After all the testing,

real-world problems will still arise. Testing can take several forms and shapes. You may test the system based on an existing case and see how close the system generates responses. Although experts believe that no system is fully debugged, testing will minimize a lot of future problems that may occur after the final release of the system.

2. *Expert validation.* The system answers should be compared with the answers given by the expert. All incorrect answers or advice by the system should be recorded in detail. If the system logic breaks down under certain conditions and cannot be corrected immediately, the system should inform the user that the advice may not be correct. It may also be useful to request other experts who have not been involved in the construction of the system to validate the system.

3. *End-user validation.* This is testing of the system's overall usability. It should be done by a few selected users and after the expert has validated the system. The goal is to detect any deficiencies in the user interface and determine training requirements. This stage of the testing is mostly concerned with the usability of the system and its soundness as it appears to the user with a minimal computer background.

18-6-9 POSTIMPLEMENTATION AUDIT

This is the stage in which the system has been up and running for some time. The validation and testing are finished. The users are working with the system. This is the real test that determines the true value of an ES. No system is ever perfect; there is always room for improvement. At this stage, an audit of the system is performed to find any possible areas for improvement. These improvements can be to any component of the system. Some areas to look for when performing the postimplementation audit are listed below [7].

1. *Operational performance.* This can include any area in which the user is involved. Is the system easy to use? Does it respond quickly enough to be effective? These are the same types of operational performance issues found in any information systems.

2. *Face validity.* This is much like the expert validation found during the construction phase. It differs in that the system has been running for a while and should have developed a level of experience. This means the system should be able to remember and use previous case experience in solving a problem or providing an answer, then be able to use this past experience to solve a similar case at the present time. This should be done without any bias that may have been built in by the expert(s). The expertise of the system should be tested to confirm the results after some running time has elapsed.

3. *Objectivity.* The objectivity of the system should be examined by using a library of test cases and scenarios to test for average cases, boundary conditions,

and error conditions. This is to ensure that expert bias and difference in judgment have not become part of the system.

4. *Reliability.* Reliability is not a question of system performance. System performance and reliability are performed when operational performance issues are addressed. Reliability refers to the solution that the ES generates. The stability of the system and its ability to generate identical solutions should be tested when given identical input. Changing input variables and parameters to see the effect on system performance should perform a systematic sensitivity analysis.

5. *Economics.* Economics should be evaluated to see if the system would indeed pay for itself. Is the system cost-effective? Are the solutions given by the ES cost-effective and will it put the company at risk? More emphasis should be placed on the cost of the solutions and answers from the ES than on the cost of implementation. System-implementation cost should have already been evaluated in the feasibility study before final construction.

18-7 SELECTED EXAMPLES OF ES SHELLS

The following are examples of expert systems shells on the market. For detailed descriptions and capabilities of these systems, the specific vendor should be contacted [1].

1. ACQUIRE (Acquire Intelligence, Inc.) offers a set of knowledge-based products designed for nonprogrammers. The knowledge-acquisition system creates knowledge bases, and the expert system shell tests them on actual cases. Finished applications can be delivered as stand-alone systems using Acquire-RTS (run-time system) or fully embedded using Acquire-SDK (software development kit).

2. DPL (Applied Decision Analysis) offers a decision-analysis software program that combines decision trees and influence diagrams to create a complete modeling environment. DPL uses the logical framework of decision analysis to make decisions based on what the user knows, can do, and prefers. Features include: spreadsheet links, automated sensitivity analysis, policy summaries, and more.

3. FORECAST PRO (Business Forecast Systems) offers a business-forecasting application using AI. The program does not require any background in statistical forecasting. Instead, an expert system examines the data, and the program guides users to exponential smoothing, Box-Jenkins, or regression: whatever method suits the data best. A standardized set of diagnostic screens helps users compare and evaluate models.

4. BUSINESS INSIGHT (Business Resource Software, Inc.) offers an expert system for strategic analysis, gathers information about the desired prospect, the product or service, and competition. Then, using the knowledge of over 30 busi-

ness experts, it identifies strengths, weaknesses, and inconsistencies, and gives a thorough explanation. Service Industry Knowledge Base, software used with Business Insight, contains the rules and data relationships from business planning and marketing experts in the services industry.

5. DCLASS (CAM Software) offers an expert system development tool used to capture and process logic for manufacturing applications. It uses decision trees, including features for controlling decision points, manipulating variables, calculating and calling other subsystems.

6. PENSION PLANNER (Foundation Technologies, Inc.) offers an expert system facilitating the establishment of employee-benefit management programs. The system validates and speeds the input process, ensures completeness of data, outputs administrative documents for defined contribution and defined benefit programs. Additional software integrates Pension Planner to manage employee health and welfare benefits as well.

18-8 IMPORTANT CONSIDERATIONS FOR EXPERT SYSTEMS CONSTRUCTION

Expert systems have proved to be cost-effective for the majority of organizations that have properly introduced them. The number of experts systems in use has been steadily increasing in recent years [8]. The increasing power and sophistication of PCs and their very affordable cost will expedite this transition and the adoption of this powerful technology. However, organizations must be aware of several issues before they commit large budgets to this technology.

1. First and foremost, an organization must choose a strategy that fits best into its culture and specific environment. A well-known example is the case of DuPont and Digital Equipment Corporation [14]. Both of these companies share a fundamental goal in implementation of ES to improve decision making and decision implementation throughout the organization by putting relevant and scarce information into the hands of key decision makers. But each company chose a route specific to its organizational culture.

DuPont uses a "dispersed" approach for developing expert systems. This means that end users develop their own systems using standard, low-cost tools. From the other end Digital Equipment Corporation uses a centralized development center with trained knowledge engineers and programmers. These systems are more complex, involve more rules, and solve higher level problems than the ones solved by DuPont using the dispersed approach. Each approach has advantages and disadvantages. For example, the dispersed approach usually is fast, has a low cost, and enjoys broader support throughout the organization. However, the final product may not have the highest possible quality. On the other hand, the centralized approach is more costly and takes more time; however, the final product is of a higher quality.

2. The integration of ES technology into the existing information systems technology may also be a challenging task. More or less, ESs will utilize some of the existing data resources available in the organization. This may create a compatibility problem. Expert systems applications have many of the same requirements as conventional applications, including the need to access databases, to interface with external systems, and to operate efficiently in a network-intensive computing environment [7]. The issue of compatibility forces organizations to take a more comprehensive look at the entire information systems resources before committing large budgets to expert systems technology.

3. Regardless of the type of product that is introduced to the market, there is always a need to consider its legal ramifications. The same holds for expert systems. In the case of expert systems this issue is even more important. This is because ESs are used as decision-making tools, and when people use them to make a decision, there is always the chance that an action taken by someone based on what was given by the ES can have detrimental effects on the company. Of course, this in turn means that someone must become liable for any damages done. But the challenging question is who is liable? Is the knowledge engineer? The domain expert? The sponsoring manager or the user? Who exactly is at fault? This is one of the major issues that must be examined very carefully. At this point, this issue has not been resolved [13].

4. Another important issue that must be considered is cost. Expert systems are not cheap. Not only it is time consuming to build one, but many of the components of an expert system cannot be built with existing hardware and software. Although some applications can be written in low-level languages such as BASIC, COBOL, PASCAL, or C, most are written in symbolic languages such as LISP and PRO-LOG. Hardware and software that can run these languages will be needed.

From what we have seen, we can conclude that expert systems have a bright future. According to John Gressier [8] the worldwide growth of expert systems will continue in both the public and private sectors. American businesses have seen the payoff of using expert systems. Many are now looking toward this technology in order to be able to stay competitive in today's highly competitive environment.

18-9   FUTURE TRENDS IN EXPERT SYSTEMS

Expert systems usage has been steadily increasing, particularly in recent years. As research efforts continue in the field of intelligent systems, the future trends in ES technology appear to be in two main areas. Advancements in ES interfacing and integration technologies have moved to the forefront of future expert systems.

Recently, many ES software packages have been developed to interface with multiple sources such as users, other databases, spreadsheets, and remote and direct data feeds [5]. Also, as we will discuss in Chapter 19, expert systems are being combined with fuzzy logic, neural networks, and genetic algorithms. These new expert systems are becoming even user-friendlier and require fewer computer skills to run them. An example of such new systems is EASE, an expert system mainframe applications generator that integrates the use of voice and fax database connections to access data from various software, such as dBase, Clipper, and FoxPro, and provides "client users" access to the resulting ES processed data via in the telephone.

Another future trend in expert systems is the integration of ES with other AI technologies. These recent combinations of technologies have helped advance computer capabilities as a whole. Examples of such combinations include:

- *Scanning technology combined with ES technology.* As an example, CypherScan's Scan-a-List is the latest technology in creating database records, address lists, and mailing labels via a handheld scanner and ES that automatically deciphers the scanned data and formats it according to its possible uses.
- *Robotics technology combined with ES technology.* As an example, Aaron is an expert system equipped with its own robotics-painting machine. Aaron can create its own original images, mix and match color dyes, and paint with the finesse of a fine artist.
- *Neural network technology combined with ES technology.* As an example, TriStar Corporation has developed a system, called INVESTAR, that signals a commodities broker when to buy and sell mutual funds, stocks, bonds, and so forth.

Professor Grossberg, at Boston University, is developing a concept of unassisted, internal system feedback. This feedback allows the system to reexamine its own previous decisions with each new case input. As the system gains knowledge it refines its own decision processes for the next time it has a similar case [6].

Biophysicist Michael Conrad is developing a concept for chemical analysis whereby a computer is based on living tissue. Living tissue enzymes are used as pattern recognizers in interaction with other chemicals. These enzymes release different molecules in reaction to different chemicals that can be identified and digitized by a linked processor [6].

Finally, intelligent agents discussed in Chapter 1 are another growing application of expert systems. These intelligent agents appear on the monitor as cartoon dogs that assist the user with prioritizing tasks, such as e-mail receiving, scheduling meetings, calendar events, arranging day-to-day activities, and so forth. What makes these agents so special is that they learn by experience and interaction with their environment, without special programming. Through interaction with their master user, as well as observation of other users on its network, the agent evolves and becomes more and more intuitive to its individual users' needs, responsibilities, scheduling desires, work priorities, and daily routine [6]. We briefly introduced several types of intelligent agents in Chapter 1.

SUMMARY

This chapter provided a detailed discussion on the construction of an expert system. After knowledge acquisition and knowledge representation, ES construction is the third phase in the sequence. The chapter introduced a methodology similar to the life-cycle approach introduced in Chapter 9. Since uncertainty and human knowledge play an important role in construction of expert systems, the life-cycle approach should be modified accordingly. The phases introduced for the construction of an expert system included problem definition, organizational readiness, expert selection, tool selection, design team selection, prototype design, final construction, validation, and postimplementation audit. The chapter introduced several popular ES shells and it concluded with several important considerations for ES construction and releasing it to the public as a "product."

REVIEW QUESTIONS

1. What are some of the popular knowledge-acquisition techniques? Knowledge-representation techniques?

2. What questions are usually asked to determine the suitability of a problem for ES application?

3. Why is ES construction never final?

4. What are the nine phases introduced in this chapter used for the construction of an ES?

5. How are these phases different from those introduced in Chapter 9?

6. What is the objective of the feasibility study? Is the economic feasibility the only type of feasibility involved here? What are other types of feasibility? What is an ideal situation or problem for expert system application?

7. If the number of rules are too low (less than 10) or too high (more than 10,000), is this a good case for ES application? Discuss.

8. What is organizational readiness? Why is it important to perform this task before the introduction of the ES?

9. How do you select an expert? Is the expert always a human or are there other sources of expertise?

11. What are the four available tools for ES construction?

12. What is the advantage of algorithmic programming languages for ES construction? What are their disadvantages?

13. What are some of the advantages of ES shells?

14. Generally speaking, using shells makes it easier to develop an ES. Why is this true?

15. Who are the major participants of the design team for ES construction? How do these members differ from the members of the CBIS task force discussed in Chapter 9?

16. Designing a prototype during the ES construction is a critical issue. Why is this claim true?

17. What are the objectives behind designing a prototype?

18. What are the steps in the rapid prototyping process?

19. What are some of the activities performed during the final construction phase of an expert system?

20. What are the goals of the validation phase?

21. How do you measure the accuracy and completeness of an ES?

22. What is the difference between expert validation and end-user validation?

23. What are some of the activities performed in the postimplementation audit phase? Why is this phase important?

24. What is face validity?

25. What are some of the important considerations that must be carefully examined before releasing an ES as a "product"?

26. What are some of the legal ramifications of ESs?

PROJECTS

1. By referring to the source mentioned in the chapter, compare and contrast the "route" chosen by Digital Equipment Corporation and DuPont. What are these specific cultures? Why is it important to choose a game plan that is suited to the specific culture of a company?

2. The AION Development System by AION Corporation, EXSYS by EXSYS, Inc., and PENSION PLANNER by Foundation Technologies Inc., are three of the popular ES shells on the market. By acquiring the documentation from

these vendors, compare and contrast these products. What are the strengths and weaknesses of each product?

3. Compare and contrast the phases introduced for ES construction in this chapter with those for CBIS construction in Chapter 9. What are some of the specific differences? What are the similarities?

4. MYCIN is one of the well-known ES applications on the market. Investigate the approach used for the construction of this system. Do the same thing for XCON.

5. ExperTax by Coopers & Lybrand is a well-known tax planning expert system on the market. Investigate the strengths and weaknesses of this system. What are some of the unique features of this system that are not offered by a human expert? How many rules are used by this system?

6. The United States government has been a major user of expert systems. Investigate these various applications. In which areas have these systems been successful? What are some of the current and future applications of expert systems in Internal Revenue Service? Discuss.

KEY TERMS

Algorithmic languages, 534–535
Design team selection, 536
Expert selection, 533–534
Expert systems shells, 535, 542–543
Face validation, 540–541
Knowledge acquisition, 520–524
Knowledge engineering environment, 535
Knowledge representation, 524–528

Legal and liability issues, 544
Organizational readiness, 533
Postimplementation audit, 541–542
Problem definition, 529–532
Prototype design, 536–537
Symbolic languages, 535
Tool selection , 534–536
Validation, 540–541

REFERENCES

[1] Anonymous (April, 1995). Expert systems resource guides, products and services directory. *AI Expert,* 26.
[2] Bidgoli, H. (1997). *Modern information systems for managers.* San Diego: Academic Press, Inc.
[3] Bidgoli, H. (1998). *Intelligent management support systems.* Wesport, CT: Quorum Books.
[4] Byrd, T. A., *et al.* (March 1992). A synthesis of research on requirements analysis and knowledge acquisition techniques. *MIS Quarterly,* 118–138.
[5] Foltin, G. L., and Smith, M. L. (November 1994). Accounting expert systems. *The CPA Journal,* 64(11),46.
[6] Freedman, D. H. (February, 1994). Profile in artificial intelligence. *Omni Magazine,* 17(5), 62.

[7] Goel, A. (Winter 1994). The reality and future of expert systems: A manager's view of AI research issues. *Information Systems Management,* 53–61.

[8] Griesser, J. W. (May-June 1992). Experts among us, *Business Horizons,* 77–80.

[9] Gum, R., and Blank, S. C. (August 1990). Designing expert systems for effective delivery of extension programming. *American Journal of Agricultural Economics,* Vol. 72, 540.

[10] Hayes-Roth, F.D., *et al.* (1983). *Building expert systems.* Reading, MA: Addison Wesley.

[11] Jih, W.J. K. (May 1990). Comparing knowledge-based and transaction processing systems development. *Journal of Systems Management,* 23–28.

[12] Kidd, A. (1987). *Knowledge acquisition for expert systems.* New York, NY: Plenum Press.

[13] Lynn, M. P., and Bockanic, W. N. (November 1993). Legal liability of the domain expert. *Journal of Systems Management,* 6–10.

[14] Meador, L., and Mahler, E. (August 1990). Choosing an expert systems game plan. *Datamation,* 64.

[15] Nelson, C., and Balanchandra, R. (1991). Choosing the right expert system building approach, *Decision Sciences,* 354–368.

[16] O'Leary, D. E. (November-December 1988). Methods of validating expert systems. *Interface,* 72–79.

[17] Payne, E. C., and McArthur, R. C. (1990). Developing expert systems. *A Knowledge Engineer's Handbook for Rules & Objects.* New York, NY: John Willey & Sons.

[18] Richardson, J. J., and Defries, M. J. (1990). *Intelligent systems in business: Integrating the technology.* Norwood, New Jersey: Ablex Publishing Corporation.

[19] Ringland, G.A., and D.A. Duce (1983). Approaches to knowledge representation: An introduction. New York: John Wiley & Sons, Inc.

[20] Rolston, D. W. (1988). *Principles of artificial intelligence and expert systems development.* New York: McGraw Hill Book Company. 9–10.

[21] Slater, J. R. *et al.* (October, 1993). On selecting appropriate technology for knowledge systems. *Journal of Systems Management,* 10–15.

Chapter 19

Fuzzy Logic and Hybrid Systems: Managing Imprecise Data

Learning Objectives

After studying this chapter, you should be able to:

- Define fuzzy logic and trace its origin.
- Discuss the working process of a fuzzy logic system.
- Discuss the advantages and disadvantages of fuzzy systems.
- Define expert systems, genetic algorithms, and neural networks.
- Discuss advantages of hybrid systems.
- Discuss the outlook for fuzzy systems.

19-1 INTRODUCTION

This chapter discusses fuzzy logic as one of the growing concepts within the CBIS field. The chapter introduces commonly used fuzzy logic terminology and explains the working process of a fuzzy logic system. The chapter introduces the advantages and disadvantages of fuzzy logic and reviews the hybrid systems that can significantly benefit from fuzzy logic. The chapter introduces several popular applications of fuzzy logic and concludes with an outlook for further development of fuzzy logic systems.

19-2 BACKGROUND FOR FUZZY LOGIC

In our day-to-day life we hear and use terminology that is not "yes" and "no," but within a context we understand the statement. Examples include, phrases such as "it depends," "most likely," "he is tall," "she is short," " I did pretty well on the exam," "the weather is fairly cold," and "the movie was crowded." What do we really mean by these phrases? How tall is tall? How short is short? Is 6'2" tall? What about a 6'8" person [5]?

Have you ever been given a questionnaire that asks ambiguous questions and then expects you to give a straightforward yes or no response? Did you wish that you could use words such as "usually," "often," "sometimes," it depends," "probably," "only if," or "most likely"? You probably have had this feeling, but you still answered the questions with "yes" or "no" because you know that the survey could not be analyzed if only descriptive answers were given. Even the survey did not give such an option. You must answer yes or no, or at best leave it blank. The computers and software that the surveyor uses to analyze the questionnaire simply cannot deal with anything but clear-cut, crisp, black-and-white, yes-and-no answers. Today, this is no longer true; computers can analyze information to whatever degree of accuracy you wish. It is done with the help of fuzzy logic.

The computer industry has been dominated by digital computers. These binary machines only understand a clear-cut, yes-no answer. Our day-to-day life involves numerous situations that deal with vocabulary that is not simply yes or no. Fuzzy logic allows a slow and smooth transition between our vocabulary and the ones used by computers. Fuzzy logic can deal with linguistic terms by using a degree of membership. For example, you might consider someone who is 6 feet tall as a tall person, a 6'3" tall individual is taller still, but what about person who is 6'8"? Fuzzy logic is designed to help computers simulate the various types of vagueness and uncertainty in our everyday lives.

When fuzzy logic is applied to computers, it accommodates the complex approximation of the human reasoning process and it provides a crisp conclusion. Professor Lotfi A. Zadeh invented fuzzy logic at the University of California at Berkeley, where he was a professor and chairman of the electrical engineering department. He developed fuzzy logic theory by using a form of mathematics called fuzzy sets. This theory allows precise computations using approximations that then deal with vagueness. Professor Zadeh explained how in conventional computers everything is crisp and is a 0 or a 1, but fuzzy logic can deal with items that are between 0 and 1.

According to Zadch, the trouble with classical approaches is that the classes or categories that one is allowed to deal with have boundaries that are clear-cut, but most real-world classes do not have clear boundaries [28]. Aristotelian logic can only deal with true and false boundaries; however, highly complex systems, such as those concerned with power distribution, transportation, air traffic controllers, and economic modeling, do not lend themselves to precise analysis. They include many variables and uncertainties.

Zadeh found that he could use a branch of mathematical set theories and membership functions to develop a solution to recognize handwriting problems. According to Zadeh, membership in a set is a matter of degree. For example, a 6' tall individual may have a .8 membership in a tall people set and a .15 membership in a short people set. Based on this principle, the programmers do not need to make thousands of rules to make computers "think"; computers could "judge" by themselves, using fuzzy logic. According to this theory, computers can deal with the vagueness in our lives, rather than just manipulating clear-cut items.

At the beginning, fuzzy logic was not accepted by most American scientists. In the 1970s Ebrahim Mamdani at Queen Mary College in London introduced the first industrial application of fuzzy logic. Mamdani and coresearchers began studying ways to use fuzzy rules of thumb directly in automating process controls. They applied their algorithm to control the speed and pressure in industrial process control, automating engine control, and other fields.

In the 1970s fuzzy logic was also utilized in an industrial application with expert systems. By applying fuzzy rules of thumb with If-Then rules, the expert system can solve complex problems somewhat like human experts do (for example: when the temperature is over 82°, turn the temperature down a little bit). In 1980 F.L. Smidth & Co. of Copenhagen began marketing the first commercial fuzzy expert system: a fuzzy logic controller that controlled the fuel-intake rate and gas flow of a rotating kiln used to make cement.

During 1980s, the scientists in United States and Europe seemed less enthusiastic about fuzzy logic because some thought that uncertainty and imprecision can be solved by use of the probability theory. Only NASA used fuzzy logic as part of its space program. In Japan, fuzzy logic received widespread attention and in the mid-1980 the first industrial applications were developed.

19-3 FUZZY LOGIC TERMINOLOGY

When dealing with fuzzy logic, a number of terms are commonly used. To be able to understand a fuzzy logic discussion you should be familiar with the following terminology [3,28,29].

1. *Crisp logic.* Another name for traditional logic to differentiate it from fuzzy logic. In crisp logic, the three logical operations AND, OR, and NOT return either a 1 or a 0 (true or false). Example: pass or fail, accepted or rejected, hot or cold, dry or wet, dark or light.

2. *Crisp set.* Traditional, classical, or crisp sets have strict membership criteria in which an object is either completely included or excluded from the set. They are mathematical sets with definitive boundary points. Example: the score of 70 is passed; less than 70 is failed.

3 *Defuzzification.* A process in which fuzzy output is converted into crisp, numerical results. Example: most likely means 70% of the time.

4. *Fuzzification.* The process of fuzzifying an element by combining actual values (e.g., the temperature of a liquid) with stored membership functions to produce fuzzy input values.

5. *Fuzziness.* A term that expresses the ambiguity that can be found in the definition of a concept or the meaning of a word or phrase. Example: usually, regularly, most often, or rarely.

6. *Fuzzy logic.* A kind of logic using graded or qualified statements rather than ones that are strictly true or false. The results of fuzzy reasoning are not as definite as those derived by strict logic, but they cover a larger field of discourse.

Warm   **Hot**

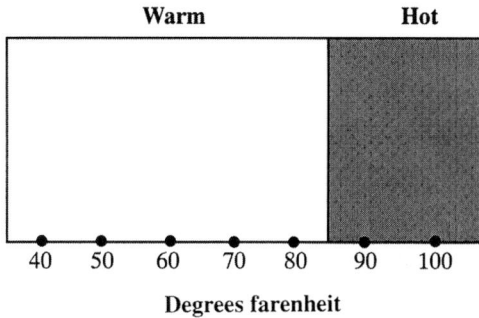

Degrees farenheit

Figure 19-1 An example of a conventional set.

7. *Fuzzy modifiers.* Operations that change the membership function of a fuzzy set by spreading out the transition between full membership and nonmembership, by sharpening that transition, or by moving the position of the transition region.

8. *Fuzzy sets.* Sets that do not have a clearly defined membership but rather allow objects to have grades of membership from 0 to 1.

9. *Fuzzy inference.* The process of using the degree of truth in production rule premises to select an appropriate rule to execute. Production rules are a series of If-Then statements. They are commonly used in expert systems.

10. *Membership.* The degree of inclusion in a set. Fuzzy sets have values between 0 and 1 that indicate the degree to which an element has membership in the set. At 0, the element has no membership; at 1, it has full membership.

11. *Set.* A collection of objects. For example heights of 4', 5', 6', and 7' may constitute the set of heights for a population.

To better understand the membership functions consider Figure 19-1. This is an example of a conventional set or crisp set. Based on this diagram, 84.9° is warm, and 85.1° is hot. A small change in the temperature could cause a large response in the system.

Figure 19-2 shows the same set using fuzzy logic conventions. For example, in this figure 80° has a membership degree of .30 in the fuzzy set warm and .40 in the fuzzy set hot. All temperatures between 40 and 100° are the universe of discourse.

19-4 WHAT IS FUZZY LOGIC?

As explained earlier, traditional logic categorizes everything as being "yes" or "no"; "on" or "off"; "one" or "zero"; "pass" or "fail." Fuzzy logic allows the computer to reason in a fashion similar to humans. Traditionally, a computer

556 Chapter 19 Fuzzy Logic and Hybrid Systems: Managing Imprecise Data

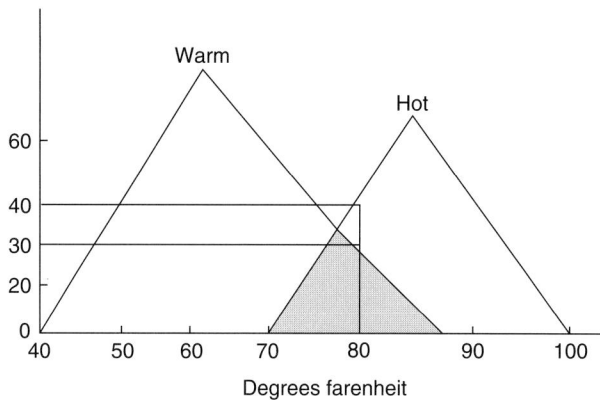

Figure 19-2   Degree of membership in a fuzzy system.

would analyze problems using straightforward AND, OR, and NOT functions, providing true or false or 0 or 1 answers from clearly defined inputs. With fuzzy logic, one can use approximations and vague data, and yet produce clear, definable answers. Fuzzy systems use three steps for solving a problem: fuzzification, rule evaluation, and defuzzification.

In the first step, **fuzzification** takes actual values (e.g., room temperature) and combines them with stored membership functions to create fuzzy input values. In step two, **rule evaluation,** also known as fuzzy inferencing, decides which rules are appropriate to a given situation. In step three, **defuzzification** analyzes all of the possible outputs, finally providing a crisp output (an actual number).

According to Ruggiero there are three parts to a fuzzy operator as [17]:

• *Membership functions.* Relates the data to the concept of each rule.
• *Fuzzy rule logic.* Performs the reasoning and thought processes.
• *Defuzzifier(s).* Map the fuzzy answers back into identifiable "real-world" answers.

You should bear in mind that fuzzy logic could produce exact results. Fuzzy logic can deal with any degree of precision from input data, and it can react just as precisely in returning the results or processed information. As you will learn later in this chapter, numerous commercial applications of fuzzy logic confirm this claim.

19-5 FUZZINESS VERSUS PROBABILITY

Mathematicians and scientists who still have not been convinced by the notion of fuzzy logic have argued that fuzzy logic is merely an extension of traditional probability functions. Bart Kosko, one of the pioneers in fuzzy logic development, disproves that uncertainty is not the same as randomness, and that being unsure about something is not the same as being left to chance [11]. He proceeds to discuss the differences between ambiguity and randomness; and whether versus how much. The premise of his argument is based on "whether an event occurs is random," but "to what degree it occurs is fuzzy." For example, if the possibility of John's passing his computer course is .75, this is random. However how well he will pass the course (with which grade) is fuzzy.

Probability is concerned with undecidability in the outcome of clearly defined and randomly occurring events such as customers' arrival in a service station. Fuzzy logic is concerned with the ambiguity or undecidability inherent in the description of the event itself such as a tall person, a warm room, or a sweet drink [26].

19-6 IMPLEMENTING A FUZZY SYSTEM

To implement a fuzzy system, the following six steps are usually recommended [3].

- Analyze and understand the problem
- Identify degrees of membership
- Define a rule or a series of rules
- Identify a procedure to fuzzify and process the problem
- Interpret and evaluate results
- Fine-tune results

Implementing a fuzzy logic system is essentially a learning process. Relatively simple applications will not need much refining, and this does not create a problem. The time saved in reduced programming far outweighs the time taken to fine-tune the rules and membership sets. Also, the ability to keep ambiguous and contradictory rules in a system allows much more flexibility in analysis. Moreover, it allows every avenue of thought to remain open instead of closing off possibilities using traditional straightforward logic. Designing the rules and membership functions can, however, become quite complicated if a system requires a high level of complexity. Under these circumstances the front-end learning processes will become the most significant part of implementation.

To better understand this process, consider the following example of a fuzzy logic application, which tries to balance an inverted pendulum [1]. This problem can be likened to trying to balance a broomstick in the palm of one's hand.

The first step in implementing the system is to make sensible, logical rules that will manage the control of the pendulum movement. If regular programming were to be used, this program could add up to hundreds of lines of coding, all with specific "clear" parameters being identified. In this example, only seven simple rules are needed. Each rule outlines a simple rule of thumb, or expected behavioral characteristic for the system. These production rules are If-Then statements, which are broken down into the If (antecedent) block, and the Then (consequent) block. They are as follows:

Rule 1	If the stick is inclined moderately to the left and is almost still	Then move the hand to the left quickly
Rule 2	If the stick is inclined a little to the left and is falling slowly	Then move the hand moderately to the left a little quickly
Rule 3	If the stick is inclined a little to the left and is rising slowly	Then don't move the hand much
Rule 4	If the stick is inclined moderately to the right and is almost still	Then move the hand moderately to the right quickly
Rule 5	If the stick is inclined a little to the right and is falling slowly	Then move the hand moderately to the right a little quickly
Rule 6	If the stick is inclined a little to the right and is falling slowly	Then don't move the hand much
Rule 7	If the stick is almost not inclined and is almost still	Then don't move the hand much

From the set of rules, one can see that there are only two variables that need to be controlled. The first is the angle from the vertical (that is, the voltage input from a potentiometer), and the second is the rate of change of the angle due to the speed of the corrective movement. Both can be positive or negative, and both are governed by ambiguous words stated in the production rules.

Once the production rules have been identified, membership functions must be constructed. The membership functions partially quantify the ambiguity in the production rules. Words such as "moderately," "slowly," "quickly," and "a little" are all modifiers in controlling the two variables. The system developer must decide how each word is represented in special codes, or labels. "A little" to the left could be translated as -1 to -3 volts, or "vertical" (zero position) could be allowed between a range of -1 to $+1$, depending on the degree of accuracy set by the developer. Everything is set at the discretion of the developer. If more accuracy is required, more rules with tighter constraints could be added.

After establishing the rules and membership functions, the system can be put to the test. The developer will be able to see how each rule affects the system by adding or deleting one rule at a time. If a rule appears to have no effect whatsoever, it can be permanently deleted from the system. Perhaps the system will not be accurate enough, so the developer will make smaller ranges for each label. Finally, the developer will be happy with the system after much trial and error, and the system will be ready for implementation. Trial and error, and the reliance on the developer's judgment, is the only way to get to the finished product because there is no specific benchmark that can say what is right or wrong. The lack of rigidity can be analyzed as being both positive and negative, depending on which stance a person wishes to take [1].

19-7 ADVANTAGES OF FUZZY SYSTEMS

The applications of fuzzy logic systems can be seen in many different facets of business and society. The improvements that fuzzy logic has offered to appliances and products have already proved its worth beyond doubt. Fuzzy logic has been applied in so many shapes and forms that defining why it is advantageous would require recognizing every triumph that it has had. Products and successes will be discussed later, but for now we will weigh up the pros and cons associated with fuzzy logic in general. The following are some of the advantages of fuzzy logic.

19-7-1 SIMPLICITY

Fuzzy logic eliminates the difficulties of mathematical modeling. It allows the designer to describe inputs, rules, and outputs in a natural language. Overall, there are less rules required compared with traditional logic. This was shown in the inverted pendulum example discussed in Section 19-6: Seven rules versus hundreds or more lines of codes. Generally speaking, fuzzy logic systems require up to ten- times fewer rules than do many conventional systems; coding is reduced and therefore the efficiency and effectiveness of the system can be improved.

19-7-2 CONTRADICTION

One of the most unusual characteristics of programming with fuzzy logic is the ability to include contradictory statements. Rules can be completely contradictory and yet exist side by side without any problems. If traditional logic were given two opposing instructions, the computer would not be able to decide which path to branch on and the problem would be unresolved. Using fuzzy logic a certain degree of tolerance and compromise is allowed. For example, a member in the membership function can belong to two sets. However, the degree of membership will be different. Membership functions allow degrees of membership to many fuzzy sets. Rather than having an item or state belong to only one set (as in traditional logic); the item or state can have a belonging of .65 to one set, .45 to another, and .15 to yet another. For example a 6' tall person may have a .70 belonging to a tall set a .45 belonging to a medium set, and a .01 belonging to a short set. The number of sets that an item belongs to can depend on the degree of accuracy and sensitivity. Also, fuzzy logic is a precise problem-solving methodology with the designer having complete control over the accuracy (by choosing the degrees and number of rules required).

19-7-3 REDUCING DEVELOPMENT TIME AND INCREASING FLEXIBILITY

The analysis phase is reduced because designers can begin work without most of the information required. Functional objectives can be focused on without having to worry about the underlying mathematical concepts. The ability to evaluate multiple rules and to grade multiple inputs simultaneously reduces the time spent in design. Also, part of the reduction in development time, tools, and applications can be reassessed and redesigned much faster than before. Components of the fuzzy inference process function independently, so systems can be easily modified.

19-7-4 SYSTEM AUTONOMY

Fuzzy systems consist of a number of rules that function independently of one another. One rule could be faulty and the others will still compensate for the error. Removing one rule at a time can test the robustness of the system. Using fuzzy systems eliminates the tradeoff between robustness and sensitivity; sensitivity will actually increase as a system becomes more robust. Rules will continue to work even in circumstances in which the whole system is completely changed [10].

19-7-5 REDUCED COSTS

One of the major reasons that businesses take an interest in any product is its cost. The processors that use fuzzy logic can be much smaller and are still more powerful than the traditional processors that would be too costly for use in home appliances.

19-7-6 USER FRIENDLINESS

Natural languages and commonly used jargon in many cases provide phrases with which we are familiar. This in turn provides an easy to understand user/system interface, avoiding much of the number crunching and formula solving.

19-8 FUZZY LOGIC SHORTCOMINGS

Fuzzy systems with all the advantages mentioned in the last section include some disadvantages and shortcomings. The following are some of these shortcomings:

1. A difficult task in fuzzy logic implementation is determining the *optimal* membership functions. Presently there is no precise mathematical method for verifying the correctness of a membership function.

2. Fuzzy logic currently is not capable of optimizing the efficiency of a fuzzy system. Fuzzy logic probably cannot reach optimal efficiency, say 100%, but it can achieve 95% efficiency, which is still better than the traditional systems. Modeling and simulation are the ordinary method for verifying a system using fuzzy logic, but this has not been enough to gain the confidence of mathematicians and control engineers [25].

3. Fuzzy logic can be an obstacle in verifying a system's stability and reliability, especially in a safety-related area. However, using simulation can complement this obstacle. In fine-tuning and improving a fuzzy system, however, there is no substitute for simulation. Where classical control systems demand a lot of work to establish the model in advance before doing the design, fuzzy systems require a large amount of simulation and tuning to optimize their performance and verify their reliability [24].

4. Front-end design becomes increasingly more time consuming when the complexity of a system increases. It can become almost impossible to know if the correct rules are being kept during fine-tuning. Redefining membership functions is a process that has no guidelines or set examples that can be easily followed. As a result, users do not always know if they are improving their systems or moving away from a better solution [3].

5. Fuzzy systems lack learning capabilities and have no memory. This is why hybrid systems (discussed later in this chapter), particularly neuro-fuzzy systems, are becoming popular for certain applications.

6. A general misconception of the term "fuzzy" as meaning imprecise or imperfect. Many practitioners believe that fuzzy logic represents some magic solution without concrete mathematical models.

7. Finally, other problems arise simply because people try to apply fuzzy logic to situations that are far more suited to traditional reasoning. People see that fuzzy logic has helped others, and thus try to throw a solution at a problem without stopping to think about their needs.

19-9 FUZZY LOGIC HYBRIDS: INTEGRATING THE STRENGTHS OF COMPLEMENTARY SYSTEMS

Fuzzy logic can be integrated effectively with other technologies such as expert systems, neural networks, and genetic algorithms. By applying one or more of these techniques in unison, the hybrid system can increase speed, fault tolerance, and overall effectiveness. It is also possible to choose the strongest feature of each application and add it into the integrated system. The integrated system should be stronger than any of the contributing system. In the following pages we briefly explain the hybrid systems of fuzzy logic, neural networks, expert systems, and genetic algorithms.

19-9-1 NEURAL NETWORKS

In Chapter 20 we will discuss neural networks in detail. Neural networks attempt to bring a learning capability into computer applications. A combination of fuzzy logic and neural networks used in National Semiconductor's Neufuz is a popular example of the integration of these two applications [3]. Input and output data, and application parameters are fed into the neural networks, which then pass on knowledge and data to a fuzzy-rule and membership function generator. These rules are then verified and optimized before the process moves to an automatic code generator that produces microcontroller assembly code.

Neural networks and fuzzy logic have complementary strengths [18]. Neural networks, which save countless hours of work for the developer, easily handle the front-end processing that sorts out fuzzy logic's rules and membership functions. Neural networks learn the importance of each rule, and given time (and sometimes some help) will readjust those rules that need to be changed or that need to have their weights adjusted. Neural networks can work on all levels of a fuzzy-based tool, working toward being perfectly self-maintaining. Specific advantages that a neural network adds to a neural-fuzzy hybrid are [17]:

- Prediction capabilities
- Selection capabilities
- Mechanical subjective analysis

These properties are especially useful in financial analysis, as will be discussed later.

19-9-2 EXPERT SYSTEMS

Expert systems and fuzzy logic make incredibly powerful hybrids. Expert systems add to a hybrid the following:

- A knowledge base
- Working memory
- Inference engine

By using fuzzy logic, expert systems can make predictions with degrees of certainty, instead of making bold, sweeping statements. Several authors underscore the importance of expert systems that can now learn and adapt to an ever-changing environment [20,30]. Before hybrids were used, an expert system would work well until crashing catastrophically. Now, an expert system can learn from past experiences, but it can also cope with unforeseen exceptions that would otherwise lead to its demise. Expert traders can now be utilized on stock markets without a huge fear of becoming undone.

19-9-3 GENETIC ALGORITHMS

Although not as widely accepted, genetic algorithms (GAs) are becoming more recognized as a form of artificial intelligence that lets machine thought processes evolve. As with natural selection and evolution, GAs reproduce in various recombinations, each time hoping to find a new recombinant that will be better adapted than its predecessors. GAs are emerging as a new way of looking at problems in their entirety or in large chunks instead of one piece at a time [12].

John Holland originated the concept of genetic algorithms in the 1940s while he was working at MIT. The term genetic algorithm applies to a set of adaptive procedures used in a computer system that are based on Darwin's theory of natural selection and survival of the fittest. It can put complicated items of information into a simple bit string that represents a solution to the current problem. The GA then refines the solution through an evolutionary process until an acceptable solution is found. The original bit strings are just a "guess at a solution," and the evolutionary process imitates the processes of reproduction and natural selection [7].

GAs can examine complex problems without any assumptions of what the correct answer or solution should be. There is no one best way to start and the computer does not need vast amounts of variables to be input by the user. It is an interactive process and can adapt quickly to reach an acceptable solution [15]. GAs are already being used in conjunction with neural nets and fuzzy computing systems to solve problems in areas such as scheduling, engineering design, and marketing. For example, a docking truck algorithm uses neural net and fuzzy functions in conjunction with a GA to find the best and shortest route for a robot to take around obstacles and between walls to reach a docking bay [23]. Metropolitan Insurance uses a GA called Evolver from Axcelis to solve insurance financial problems [15].

To begin a discussion of GA you should know how a GA is set up, and what basic operations are carried out. The first and most basic item is a chromosome. It is a list of items shown as a binary number that represents a solution to the problem. Each item in the chromosome is called a gene and is one part of the solution. A creator operation starts the GA by developing an initial population of chromosomes that are possible solutions [13].

An evaluator or fitness function rates the chromosomes on their ability to solve the problem and passes the best ones on to a generator. The generator or genetic operator carries out mutations and crossovers on the chromosomes that were passed on. These are then recombined with selected mates to create new chromosomes. A replacement strategy is then carried out to keep the population size constant. Finally, the generation cycle is repeated [13].

GAs cannot be used for every type of optimization problem. A prerequisite to using a GA is that the correct solution must be able to be represented as a bit string. Also, one must note that rules used in one situation may not work in another, even if the two problems are very similar. To overcome this problem a technique called "breeding" can be used. It is a method of getting the computers to learn how to solve problems for themselves. However, to breed correct solutions there must be reproduction and crossover breeding (crossbreeding) [19].

Reproduction (the breeding cycle) creates a new generation of possible solutions that are "more fit" by selecting answers that have a high weight figured by the fitness function. In crossbreeding, nodes are randomly selected from each of two potential solutions; the nodes are then switched [23].

Mutation occurs in a single chromosome in one following two ways: (1) order based, where mutation occurs when two genes within the same chromosome switch places; (2) position based, where mutation occurs when one gene is placed in front of another within the same chromosome [13]. The chromosomes are then evaluated by a fitness function that determines the best solution of the population by assigning weights. The solutions with the worst fitness score are eliminated to make room for the new offspring chromosomes, and the chromosomes with the highest or above average fitness scores are allowed to contribute more than one copy of themselves to the offspring chromosomes. The GA then starts the process over with reproduction and crossover, focusing the majority of its activity on the chromosomes that are most closely related to the solutions with the highest fitness scores [23].

There are some precautions to take when setting up or coding a GA problem. There are a few parameters that have a major effect on how quickly the optimal solution is found. The first parameter is population size. If you have a large population size it takes a longer time to carry out the process, but there is a wide range of diversity. A population size of 10 seems to be an optimal size; fewer than 10 does not work well, and greater than 10 takes a long time with no visible advantage [22].

Table 19-1

Hybrid Products on the Market

Acquire (Acquired Intelligence, Inc.)
Analyzer (Attar Software)
Esteem (Esteem Software, Inc.)
Flex Hybrid Expert System (Logic Programming Associates)
Goldworks (Gold Hill, Inc.)
Mahogany Professional (Emerald Intelligence)
O'INCA Design Framework (Intelligent Machines, Inc.)

The other parameters that have a major effect are mutation, crossbreeding, and number of tests or iterations. Mutations should only be used to make sure that duplication of members does not occur. Care must be taken to ensure the right amount of crossbreeding. If no crossbreeding is done, no new structures will be created. If all crossbreeding is done, good genes will disappear. It has been recommended that approximately 90% of the population be crossbred. The number of test or iterations of the GA also needs to be regulated. The more tests there are, the slower the GA will be in coming to an optimal solution, but the more accurate it will be [22].

As mentioned earlier, genetic algorithms have been put to work on real-life problems and are paying valuable dividends. For example, D.E. Goldberg of the University of Illinois has developed algorithms that learn to control a gas pipeline system modeled on the one that carries natural gas from the Southwest to the Northeast [7]. In addition, researchers at General Electric and Rensselaer Polytechnic Institute have used a genetic algorithm to design a better jet engine turbine. The genetic algorithm produced a design with three times the improvement of a manually produced model in one-fourth the time. It improved the design by 50% over the use of an expert system that, after initial achievement, failed to keep up with the exponential variables involved with different multiple changes. Finally, R.L. Riolo of the University of Michigan has already observed genetic algorithms that display latent learning, which is a key ingredient if man is to be able to create true artificial intelligence. Table 19-1 provides a listing of some of the popular hybrid products on the market. For details on features, the respective vendor should be contacted.

19-10 FUZZY LOGIC APPLICATIONS

Fuzzy logic, in a relatively short period, has established itself as a successful concept. In the next few pages we provide a listing of some of the successful applications of fuzzy logic.

19-10-1 MICROELECTRONICS

Motorola, Intel Corporation, Hitachi, National Semiconductor Corporation, and VLSI Technology are all actively working on their own microprocessors that implement fuzzy logic [16]. Intel and Hitachi made the news in 1992 by launching their fuzzy logic processors 32-bit controllers. VLSI Technology also made the headlines in the same year when they teamed up with Togai Infralogic to design their new embedded controllers on 32-bit processors. The new controllers can be designed in the size of a 10-bit configuration, but can range from 8-bit to 32-bit in performance [14]. The activity in designing these new embedded controllers is the backbone to all of the appliances and electronic applications for which fuzzy logic has been utilized successfully. Without these new controllers, fuzzy logic would not be as cheap or as powerful.

19-10-2 TRANSPORTATION

The underground train in Japan was the breakthrough that stirred a more concerted interest in fuzzy-based control systems. Other systems have mimicked this application on a smaller scale, allowing transportation to be controlled without the need for human drivers. Other areas of transportation in which fuzzy logic is applied include many parts of new automobiles. Antilock braking systems, automatic transmissions, and smart airbags that are released only in potentially harmful conditions are just some examples of the ways in which fuzzy logic has entered the automobile industry. Canon, Mitsubishi Chemical, Hewlett-Packard, Hitachi and General Electric Corporation are actively using fuzzy logic for various process control operations.

19-10-3 GOVERNMENT

The military is a natural user of fuzzy logic. As with many new sciences, progress and research can depend heavily on the amount of money a government spends on its own projects. Fuzzy logic could be harnessed in numerous areas of the military, from expert systems to using intelligent missiles. NASA is also a major investor and user of fuzzy-based control systems in various areas of space programs.

19-10-4 HOME APPLIANCES

Home appliances have sneaked fuzzy logic into our homes without many consumers even knowing that it is there. Washing machines that know what settings to use from soil content in the water and toasters that refuse to burn bread are just the tip of the iceberg. Perhaps these applications do not appear to be that clever, but these products would not be able to perform such intricate functions for such low costs without the aid of fuzzy controllers. The following are other applications of fuzzy systems in homes:

1. *Air conditioner.* Prevents overshoot, undershoot temperature oscillation and consumes less on-off power.
2. *Dryer.* Converts load size, fabric type, and flow of hot air to drying times and conditions.
3. *Elevator control.* Reduces waiting time based on passenger traffic.
4. *Humidifier.* Adjusts moisture contents to room conditions.
5. *Microwave oven.* Sets and tunes cooking conditions.
6. *Refrigerator.* Sets defrosting and cooling times based on usage.
7. *Rice cooker.* Sets cooking time and method based on steam, temperature, and the amount of rice in the pot.
8. *Shower system.* Suppresses variations in water temperature.
9. *Still camera.* Finds object anywhere in the frame and adjusts autofocus.
10. *Television set.* Adjusts screen color and texture for each frame and stabilizes volume based on viewer's location in the room.
11. *Vacuum cleaner.* Sets motor-suction condition based on dust quantity and floor type.
12. *Video camcorder.* Eliminates handheld jittering and adjusts autofocus and lighting.

19-10-5 ROBOTICS AND APPLIANCES

Artificial intelligence has struggled for years to simulate human walking. Scientists have been unable to mimic what appears to be a simple process. Omron Corporation of Japan uses fuzzy technology to drive an eight-motor, two-legged robot. Numerically programmed set patterns have never been able to smooth out the motion of robotic legs. Fuzzy sensors in the biped allow intuitive decisions from approximately 20 commands. The robot can even adjust its gait according to changes in the surface it is walking on. This achievement is all that more remarkable when one realizes that a human leg uses 400 muscles to produce the same movement [21].

19-10-6 FINANCIAL MANAGEMENT

Artificial traders using traditional methods were known to work perfectly before crashing as soon as any extenuating circumstances arose. This was not acceptable, and so people began to shun the idea of an expert system of any type managing billions of dollars. The hybrid fuzzy-neural-expert systems can now learn from the past, and they also react to a continuously changing environment. If the conditions change, the rules change, making the system utilize its superior processing power while it emulates human responses in times of volatility. Artificial traders incorporate risk assessment, forecasting, and decision support.

The world of finance has also utilized fuzzy logic to do detective work [8]. The London Stock Exchange is poised to implement a fraud detection system that blends neural networks with fuzzy logic. The networks are used to spot patterns in insider dealing, unveiling all of the techniques used to aid illegal activities. Fuzzy logic helps the system by allowing for contingencies when actions do not follow a perfect pattern but are still highly suspicious. A system called Monitors can even work by itself, setting its own parameters. The legal sector will be very interested to see how trials are performed for those who are caught by the artificial system.

19-10-7 DATABASE MANAGEMENT SYSTEMS

Despite much cynicism and skepticism, fuzzy logic has already moved into relational database management systems. Fuzzy words stored in databases appear to be useless and unmanageable. Many people express scorn for the idea of trying to make statistical analyses about tall, middle aged, and other data items. The tool described in the section on the future shows that this is not too far away, and when systems become more mature, the limits for this application will be boundless.

19-10-8 SYSTEMS DEVELOPMENT

Hyperlogic Corporation released Rulemaker in April 1995 to add on to an existing fuzzy based tool called CubiCalc. This tool uses:

- Statistical analysis
- Heuristic methods
- Edge enhancement
- Data filtering
- Center emphasis
- User defined manipulation options

These features make it possible to work with sparse data and in other ad hoc situations [2].

19-10-9 SOFTWARE DEVELOPMENT

Byte Dynamics, Inc., markets a CASE tool that creates portable C code for rule-based analysis applications. Graphical capabilities of this tool allow:

- Contour planes
- Surface plots
- Three-dimensional simulation modes

MATLAB is paired with the Fuzzy Logic Toolbox to create an intuitive software environment that combines easy-to-use fuzzy logic modeling for practical engineering design. This package allows:

- A comparison of fuzzy and traditional methods
- An evaluation of fuzzy designs
- The use of a fuzzy inference system
- Inclusion of a membership function editor
- Inclusion of a rule editor

19-10-10 DECISION SUPPORT

FuziWare Incorporated has two tools on the market that enable decision makers to use a decision support aid that can deal with fuzzy inputs. FuziQuote includes a number of capabilities. Decision makers must program the package with the operating environment and the tool will then learn to make rapid decisions based on past history and other changing parameters. FuziCalc allows decision makers to manipulate fuzzy inputs and outputs as graphs that are easy to understand, and that can be related back to a spreadsheet. FuziCalc allows users to run simultaneous What-If analyses on vast amounts of data and it can run under a regular Windows environment.

The following are other tools and platforms used for fuzzy system development:

- Fuldex (TSI Enterprises)
- Fuzzy Decision Maker (Fuzzy Systems Engineering)
- MultiFuzz (MSI Corporation)
- TILShell (Togai Infralogic)

Other decision-making applications of fuzzy logic are listed below:

- Capital budgeting
- Facility layout
- Labor scheduling

- Make or buy decisions
- Medical decisions

19-11 THE OUTLOOK FOR FUZZY LOGIC

Before making a forecast of what the future holds for fuzzy logic, it would seem pertinent to discuss an application that, although it has not been implemented, would appear to be a very realistic probability. An article written by Lance Eliot in *AI Expert* entitled "Data Highway Needs Fuzzy Logic" discusses the implications of a recent proposal made by H. Hosmer.

There is no question that the information superhighway is expanding almost exponentially and the number of people using it nearly doubles every year. More than 40 million people use it already in the United States. We live in the information age, with the industrial age past its maturity and into decline. Consequentially, information and data now flies through networks and highways whether you want it or not. Hosmer's proposal predicts that fuzzy logic could be the answer to the rising issue of security on the information superhighway. As Hosmer argues [6]:

> Wherever a continuum is found, fuzzy classes may be appropriate. For example, business-sensitive data like strategic plans and financial data may be a company proprietary to higher or lower degree. Employees and customers may have a varying requirement for privacy for their data. Both integrity and availability are measured along one or more continua.

Using the traditional method of classification, security restrictions would still have to specify if something is accessible or not within each category of security clearance. Fuzzy logic, however, could change this by allowing varying degrees of membership within security specifications. Information that was therefore private from particular individuals could be changed on a daily basis to be accessible if circumstances were to change. This could be done without having to work through a bureaucracy that might prevent important changes from being made.

To clarify this discussion, and to provide a foreseeable real-life application, Eliot's article examines the health-care industry. Here, there is private-sensitive data about employees, hospital-privileged information about finance and plans, integrity-sensitive information for accounting and payroll, and, of course, private and sensitive data about patients [6]. A patient's name might be rated as low for security but high as a medical record. Rules could determine accessibility, but rules would also allow exceptions to be made. Patient information could be protected, but in the case of emergencies a healthcare provider might need to know everything about a patient who needs immediate attention. The healthcare industry is just an example; the same principles apply to many industries that have ever-changing security needs in an ever-changing environment.

19-11-1 FORCES INFLUENCING FUZZY LOGIC DEVELOPMENT

Maytag and Admiral Products have been extremely successful with their IntelliSense product that is used in fuzzy-based washing machines. These companies see certain factors that have pushed them toward developing smarter products. Energy will become more expensive, and therefore washing machines and dishwashers that can work effectively while using less energy will become more valuable. More importantly, water management will become the most important constraint, according to Richard Hains, president of Maytag and Admiral Products. Water shortages in the western United States will create an even bigger need for more efficient, fuzzy-based machines that can make decisions to use water more sparingly without hurting performance. The government is also indirectly helping fuzzy-based product development by pushing water and energy regulations that demand ever-increasing standards [4].

The most obvious force acting on the future is money. If fuzzy logic allows a company to install a more powerful processor at a lower cost, it is bound to be accepted. Using a fuzzy-based tool in the design, development, and redesign processes can now help companies to provide new products more quickly. Motorola has given the name "natural computing" to fuzzy logic, neural networks, genetic algorithms, and their integration. Jim Huffman from Motorola adds that these technologies allow us to "deal with the real world in natural ways." The end result is that natural computing means more cost-effective, high-performing products for every type of user or consumer [9].

19-11-2 TRAINING AND SUPPORT FOR FUZZY LOGIC

Fuzzy logic development tools are approximately one-fifth as costly as their CASE tool counterparts in today's marketplace. To educate a work force in the new technology does, however, initially offset some of these advantages. Costs for training and support will rise in both real terms and as a percentage of sales [27].

19-11-3 PAYOFF IN FUZZY LOGIC DEVELOPMENT

The time and money saved by companies and individuals who utilize fuzzy logic development tools cannot be quantified exactly because such savings depend on each user and each specific application. If an expert knows exactly what a system needs, then fuzzy-based tools will continue to reduce development time to as little as one-fifth of the traditional cycle. Traditional mathematical models will not become extinct, but fuzzy logic will provide a better working environment when systems are ambiguous, qualitative, and when a high degree of complexity is involved.

Today, fuzzy logic provides a competitive edge for companies that have already applied many of its capabilities. In the future, fuzzy logic and fuzzy hybrids will become a natural part of business applications and product design. Fuzzy logic has paved the way to a future with intelligent machines.

SUMMARY

This chapter discussed fuzzy logic systems as one of the growing concepts within the CBIS field. It provided a definition, commonly used terminology, and a description of the working process of a fuzzy logic system. The chapter introduced the advantages, disadvantages, and popular applications of fuzzy logic systems. The chapter reviewed hybrid systems that can benefit from fuzzy logic, including expert systems, neural networks, and genetic algorithms. It concluded with an outlook for future development of fuzzy logic systems.

REVIEW QUESTIONS

1. What is fuzzy logic? What is the main difference between a fuzzy-based computer and a traditional computer?
2. Who invented fuzzy logic? When was it introduced?
3. Why has fuzzy logic gained so much popularity?
4. What is a fuzzy set?
5. What is a crisp set? What is fuzzification?
6. What is the difference between fuzziness and probability? Give an example.
7. What are some of the advantages of fuzzy logic systems? What are the disadvantages?
8. Why and how do fuzzy systems require shorter programming time? How can they improve performance?
9. How and why are fuzzy systems more user-friendly?
10. How and why are neural networks integrated with fuzzy logic?
11. What are genetic algorithms? What is the benefit of integrating genetic algorithms with fuzzy logic?
12. What are some of the applications of fuzzy logic in microelectronics? In transportation?

13. What are some of the applications of fuzzy logic in robotics? In home appliances?

14. What are some of the factors that may influence the future of fuzzy logic?

15. What are some the possible applications of fuzzy logic in healthcare management?

16. What are some of the possible contributions of fuzzy logic to the information superhighway?

17. What are some examples of software packages for fuzzy logic that were introduced in this chapter?

PROJECTS

1. By consulting the literature, identify some of the popular applications of fuzzy logic in Japan. What are some of the transportation applications of fuzzy logic in Japan?

2. By obtaining relevant documentation from the vendor of FuziCalc, compare and contrast this product with a typical spreadsheet product such as Excel or Lotus 1-2-3. What are some of the unique features of FuziCalc?

3. By referring to the sources introduced in this chapter, identify popular applications of genetic algorithms (GAs). What are some of the unique applications of GAs?

4. Hybrid systems including fuzzy logic, expert systems, neural networks, and genetic algorithms are gaining in popularity. Why is this claim true? What are some of the strengths of these hybrid systems?

5. Motorola Corporation is among the U.S. corporations which are very active in fuzzy logic development. Research this company and identify some of the products that have been introduced using fuzzy logic.

6. Axcelis, Inc., American Heuristics Corp., Attar Software, and BioComp Systems are among the major suppliers of genetic algorithm and hybrid software. Investigate these companies and find out about the major customers for these products.

KEY TERMS

Crisp logic, 554	Genetic algorithms, 563–565
Crisp set, 554	Hybrid systems, 562–565
Fuzziness, 554	Membership function, 555
Fuzzy logic, 552–557	Neural networks, 562
Fuzzy sets, 555	Probability, 556–557

REFERENCES

[1] Anderson, G. (October 1994). Fuzzy logic: What it is, what it does, what it can do. *Production,* Vol. 106; No. 10, 38.

[2] Anonymous. (April 1995). Adapt that fuzzy system: Hyperlogics rule maker add-on for Cubi-Calc. *AI Expert,* 46.

[3] Barron, J. (April 1993). Putting fuzzy logic into focus. *Byte,* 111–118.

[4] Beatty, G. (November 28, 1994). Future shock: Consumers remain wary of high tech appliance features. *HFD—The Weekly Home Furnishings Newspaper,* Vol. 68, No. 48, 50.

[5] Bidgoli, H. (1998). *Intelligent management support systems.* Westport, CT: Quorum Books.

[6] Eliot, L. B. (January 1994). Data highway needs fuzzy logic. *AI Expert,* 9.

[7] Holland, J. H. (July 1992). Genetic algorithms. *Scientific American,* 66–72.

[8] Houlder, V. (September 29, 1994). Tackling insider dealing with fuzzy logic. *Financial Times,* 16.

[9] Huffman, J. (February 1994). Natural computing is in your future. *Appliance Manufacturer,* interface 10.

[10] Kong, S. G., and Kosko, B. (March 1991). Adaptive fuzzy systems for baking up a truck-and-track. *IEEE Transaction on Neural Networks,* 211–233.

[11] Kosko, B. (1993). *Fuzzy thinking: The new science of fuzzy logic.* New York: Hyperion Publishing Company.

[12] Lane, A. (December 1993). Programming with genes. *AI Expert,* 23–27.

[13] Lawton, G. (May 1991). Genetic algorithms for schedule optimization. *AI Expert,* 23–27.

[14] Lineback, R. J. (July 20, 1992). VLSI technology to use fuzzy logic from Togai Infralogic in ASIC line. *Electronic News,* Vol. 38, 134.

[15] Rubkin, B. (February 22, 1993). Applying principles of biology to business problems. *National Underwriter, Property & Casualty/Risk and Benefit,* 39–40.

[16] Rice, V. (November 1992). You want your coffee how? No problem for fuzzy logic. *Electronic Business,* 122–126.

[17] Ruggiero, M. (September 1994). How to build an artificial trader. *Futures: Management Commodities & Options,* Vol. 23, 56.

[18] Shandle, J. (March 21, 1994). Fuzzy logic is shoddy its halfbaked image; Easy-to-use tools and a symbolic relationship with neural networks will make the difference. *Electronic Design,* 75.

[19] Sibigotroth, J. M. (April 1992). Implementing fuzzy expert rules in hardware. *AI Expert,* 25–31.

[20] Stein, J. (August 1991). Expert systems enter gray area of gray matter. *Futures,* 16–18.

[21] Ven, S. (December 16, 1993). Clear grains for fuzzy logic. *Innovation & Technology,* 15.

[22] Wayner, P. (January 1991). Genetic algorithms. *Byte,* 361–364.

[23] Wiggins, R. (May 1992). Docking a truck: A genetic fuzzy approach. *AI Expert,* 28–35.

[24] Williams, T. (April 1992). Fuzzy logic is anything but fuzzy. *Computer Design,* 113–127.

[25] Williams, T. (March 1, 1991). Fuzzy logic simplifies complex control problems. *Computer Design,* 90–102.

[26] Williams, T. (July 1993). Fuzzy logic to make rapid inroads in the next five years. *Computer Design,* 43.

[27] Wong, F.S., *et al.* (January–February 1992). Fuzzy neural systems for stock selection. *Financial Analysts,* 47–52.

[28] Zadeh, L. A. (June 1987). Yes, no, and relatively, part I. *Chemtech,* 340–344.

[29] Zadeh, L. A. (July 1987). Yes, no and relatively part 2. *Chemtech,* 406–410.

[30] Zadeh, L. A. (November 1983). The role of fuzzy logic in the management of uncertainty in expert systems. *Fuzzy Sets and Systems,* Vol. II, No. 3, 199–228.

Chapter 20

Neural Networks: Computers That Learn by Doing

Learning Objectives

After studying this chapter, you should be able to:

- Define neural networks.
- Compare and contrast neural computing with digital computing.
- Compare and contrast neural networks with expert systems.
- Understand how a neural network operates and learns.
- Discuss the advantages, disadvantages, and applications of neural networks in different areas.
- Discuss the outlook of neural computing.

20-1 INTRODUCTION

This chapter provides a detailed discussion of neural networks. It compares and contrasts neural computing with digital computing. It discusses the similarities and dissimilarities of neural networks and expert systems. The chapter explains various types of pattern recognition as it is being applied in the real world. The chapter discusses in detail the working fundamentals of a neural network and various learning techniques. The advantages and disadvantages of neural networks and different applications of these systems will be discussed. The chapter concludes with a sample listing of products and services for neural networks design and utilization.

20-2 NEURAL COMPUTING: AN OVERVIEW

As we briefly discussed in Chapter 1, neural computing or neural networks is one of the new multidisciplinary research fields that has grown because of the study of the brain and its potential for solving ill-structured business problems. Neural networks are capable of performing tasks that conventional computers find difficult. Neural computing technology is also known as connectionism, and parallel distributed processing. The reason behind these names comes from the fact that a neural network connects a number of independent CPUs to perform a task in a way that is very similar to the human brain, which uses numerous neurons to perform a task. The computers that we come in contact with in our daily lives are based on the architecture laid down by John Von Neuman.

Like expert systems, neural computing is used for poorly structured problems. Unlike expert systems, neural computing is not able to explain its solution. This is because neural computing uses "patterns" versus "rules" used by expert systems. A neural network uses a large number of connected microprocessors and software that tackle a problem in a unified, rather than a sequential manner. A neural network learns by doing various tasks. Neural networks achieve the learning process by creating a model based on its input and output.

For example, in a loan application problem the input data are income, assets, and number of dependents, job history, and residential status. The acceptance or rejection of the loan applications is the output data. By using many of these loan applications, the neural network establishes a pattern for an application to be approved or rejected [24]. Other areas of applications for neural computing are characteristics of potential oil fields, diagnosing automobile engine problems, and analysis of price and volume patterns in stock trading. Generally speaking, neural computing is suitable in applications in which data are fuzzy and uncertainty is involved.

To be precise, a neural network is the complex system of interconnected nerve cells, which communicates, processes, and stores information in all animals. While natural neural networks form the conceptual basis for the current research into this subcategory of the broad field of artificial intelligence, it is artificial neural networks (ANN) that are the real focus of this attention. Indeed, while the natural neural network is composed of the brain as well as the skeletal nervous system, current research in artificial neural networks seems to have completely focused on imitating brain functions [16].

Artificial neural networks, which we will simply refer to as neural networks, are an attempt to imitate the structure and function of a natural neural network in computer hardware and/or software. Many authors equate neural networks with "neural computers," on the basis of their apparent belief that special purpose computers (typically multiprocessor based) are required to implement neural networks. To others, neural networks are a form of a logical information processing architecture that can be implemented on any computer. For practical real-world applications, the business requirements will dictate the processing speed that is necessary to accomplish the desired task (such as detecting explosives in airport baggage or detecting the fingerprint of a suspect among millions of criminals' fingerprints stored in a database). This speed or throughput requirement will dictate the processing power needed to drive the network hardware and software. Any computer that can provide the necessary power can be considered a candidate for implementing the neural network. By this description we can say that intensive parallel processor computers would be a reasonable candidate for the implementation of neural computing.

20-3 NEURAL COMPUTING VERSUS DIGITAL COMPUTING

For the basis of discussion, a neural network can be said to be a computer with an internal structure that imitates the human brain's interconnected system of neurons (nerve cells). In neural networks, transistor circuits are the hardware analogue of neurons, and variable resistors represent the synapses (interfaces) between contiguous neurons [10]. Electric signals received by the transistor circuits are either inhibited or enhanced (depending on the task the neural network is performing) when they are passed on to neighboring circuits. This inhibit/enhance process is performed in a manner that is analogous to the way in which the brain's neurons pass on electrochemical signals.

Neural networks are similar to the human brain in that they do not follow rigidly programmed rules, as the typical digital computer does. Instead, the network builds an information base through an exhaustive series of trial-and-error sessions. As an example, a "trainer" (a programmer in the broadest sense) may input the digital representation of a photographic image for the neural network to identify. The network will "guess" which circuits to "fire" (activate) in order to identify the photograph and output the correct answer. If the "trainer" determines that the answer is correct, a positive indication will be given to the network (a form of virtual reward) and having the resistance will strengthen the pathways that were used to come up with the correct answer. In this manner, the neural network learns from its successes and this positive feedback further increases the probability that the network will respond correctly the next time the same image is presented.

If the network responds incorrectly, as it almost certainly will until its knowledge base is well developed, a negative indication will be given to the network (a form of virtual punishment). This will cause the pathways that were used to come up with the wrong answer to be weakened by having the resistance turned up. This process will decrease the probability that the network will respond with the same wrong answer the next time the same image is presented, therefore increasing the likelihood that the correct answer will be given the next time. In this way, a neural network "learns" from its mistakes (as indicated by feedback from its "trainer") and gives more accurate output with each repetition of a task [19, 28].

This dependence on trial-and-error learning for developing the correct output for a given set of inputs is a unique characteristic of neural networks. Virtually all other applications of digital computers involve one form of programming or another in which a human programmer dictates in a step-by-step fashion how the computer is to process the input data. With neural networks, the process is not defined—only the results of the operation are fed back to the network with positive or negative connotation [25]. Indeed, many neural networks are designed to learn from positive and negative feedback stated in terms of degrees of rightness and wrongness ("very nearly correct," "way off," "close, but not exact"). In this way, neural networks can be considered black boxes whose inner workings do not need to be understood in order for the trainer to make them work. In fact, the knowledge base of a neural network is stored as variations in the resistance along pathways connecting the input processors to the output processors learned as the

Table 20-1

A Comparison between Digital and Neural Computing

Digital computers	Neural networks
Process digital data that are written in 1s and 0s for mathematical precision	Process analog signals that fluctuate continuously, providing a range from, say, black through all shades of gray to white
Make yes/no decisions, using mathematical and logical functions	Make weighted decisions on the basis of fuzzy, incomplete, and contradictory data
Handle data in a rigidly structured sequence so that operations are always under control and results are predictable	Independently formulate methods of processing data, often with surprising results
Find precise answers to any problem, given enough time	Find good, quick but approximate answers to highly complex problems
Sort through large databases to find exact matches	Sort through large databases to find close matches
Store information so that specific data can be retrieved easily	Store information so that retrieving any piece of information automatically calls up all related facts

result of various trials fed back to the network [22]. With this approach, the knowledge base is actually stored within the network itself. This is in contrast to the typical information system that is made up of "hard coded" programs and an external database wherein input data is stored exactly as it was input for later retrieval.

Table 20-1 provides a concise comparison between digital and neural computers [1].

20-4 EXPERT SYSTEMS VERSUS NEURAL NETWORKS

As we have said all along, expert systems are rule-based systems that have proved to be successful where the domain is "narrow" and the knowledge about the domain is available. In other words, a human expert has previously successfully solved the problems addressed by expert systems. On the other side, neural networks deal with problems that are not rule-based and have not been solved by a human expert. There are available numerous cases of these kinds of problems. Table 20-2 provides a comparison of rule-based and neural network systems [11].

Table 20-2

Rule-Based versus Neural Network Systems

Rule-based systems	Neural-network systems
Excellent explanation capability	Little or no explanation capability
Requires an articulate expert to develop	Requires many examples, but no expert is needed
Many turnkey shells are available	Few turnkey shells available; most must be customized for the specific application
Average development time is 12 to 18 months.	Development time is as little as a few weeks or months.
Preferred system when examples are few and an expert is available	Preferred system when examples are plentiful or an expert is not available
Many successful, fielded systems are available for public reference	Few successful, fielded systems are available for public reference
Large systems can be unwieldy and difficult to maintain if not carefully developed and designed	Large networks can't be built today; smaller networks can be hierarchically linked for more complex problems, making them more maintainable
Systems built through knowledge extraction and rule-based development	Systems built through training using data examples
Accepted validation procedures for completed system	Validation of completed system is dependent on statistical analysis of performance
Works fine on ordinary digital computers	For all but the smallest networks, best performance comes from use with accelerator-assisted or specialized parallel chip boards

20-5 PATTERN RECOGNITION: AN OVERVIEW

At the present time, neural networks are the most useful in the analysis and recognition of patterns. Ongoing and future research may identify additional applications for neural networks. In this context, pattern recognition refers to the analysis of the complex processes involved in recognizing patterns in input data. In humans, the sense organs input data from the outside world as well as sensations originating within the body. This data is then transmitted across the skeletal nerve network to the brain for processing. The field of artificial pattern recognition is involved with the design and manufacture of artificial systems that achieve similar results, whether utilizing the same methods or not. In particular, the vast majority of current interest in the field is in mimicking sight (optical pattern recognition) and hearing (sound pattern recognition). In addition, much interest is currently being focused upon the recognition of patterns in data (data pattern recognition), a process that appears to be without an analogue in natural systems. This is probably the most important area as far as business decisions are concerned [25].

20-5-1 OPTICAL PATTERN RECOGNITION

There are three stages in optical pattern recognition: image processing, pattern classification, and scene analysis. Image processing takes many forms (depending on the type of image) but is concerned with sharpening the edges of patterns to make classification easier, quicker, and more accurate [30]. Pattern classification interprets specific items in the processed image such as facial features, letters of the alphabet, numbers, or other characteristics of interest. Many applications of neural networks for optical pattern recognition have been reported and several are in wide use.

The most successful neural network application to date appears to be in the area of optical character readers (OCR) or scanners [25]. These applications recognize hand-written characters, both printing and script, as well as machine-generated characters. In the military, neural networks have been developed to analyze radar images to detect friendly and unfriendly aircraft. Law enforcement agencies use optical pattern recognition to match fingerprints taken from arrested individuals and found crime scenes with prints that were recorded previously in order to identify criminals [14]. A widely discussed goal is the development of machine or robotic vision systems that could allow moving images to be analyzed and recognized with a high degree of accuracy. This application would be useful in space or in situations that are hazardous, unsafe, or otherwise not suitable for a human.

20-5-2 SOUND PATTERN RECOGNITION

In order for sound patterns to be recognized by a digital computer, the continuous wave form of the sound must be translated from its analog representation into a digital form that can be analyzed by a computer. Virtually all current applications of sound pattern recognition are implemented using digital computers that "slice" sounds into their discrete elements [22]. The slow speed typical of these applications is adequate for most uses involving the recognition of human speech, because humans speak rather slowly and the information content of their speech is relatively low. New applications of speech recognition that utilizes neural networks offer much greater accuracy and throughput [29]. Some researchers hope to achieve even higher performance by utilizing analog computers for their neural networks applications. By eliminating the need to convert the sound to its digital representation, technologists hope to achieve levels of performance comparable to that currently found in some mammals (whales and bats) that use sound as a primary source of information about their environments. This research is currently hampered by the relatively poor performance of current analog computers that have been virtually ignored in the recent race to maximize the performance of digital devices [5].

Current examples of voice recognition systems are capable of recognizing a very limited vocabulary. Virtually all existing systems are limited to recognizing sounds made by a single individual when spoke at no more than one sound per second [29]. However, the capabilities of these systems are steadily increasing. The physical condition of the speaker as well as the type and volume of background noise further influence the ability of artificial devices to recognize speech. Advances in programming techniques made possible by neural networks as well as the massive parallelism usually found in these systems seem to offer researchers a level of performance that was previously unavailable.

20-5-3 ADDITIONAL FORMS OF PATTERN RECOGNITION

It is widely known that animals possess the ability to recognize patterns in stimuli that enter the brain through media other than sight and sound. Principle among these additional input media in animals is the sense of smell (a form of chemical pattern recognition) and touch (tactile pattern recognition). Anecdotal evidence also suggests that some animals possess the ability to recognize patterns caused by gravity, air pressure, and magnetic fields, as well as various types of polarized and nonpolarized radiation [26]. While there are few references in the literature to attempts at developing neural networks to exploit these sources of data, there is little reason to doubt that we will be able to do so in the near future.

20-5-4 RECOGNIZING PATTERNS IN DATA

While the study of neural networks got its start in attempts by humans to mimic biological processes, the application of this technology to recognizing patterns in stored data—a capability not well developed in animals—may offer the greatest benefits. As enormous volumes of stored data recording past events become available in computer-readable form, the desire to utilize these data to predict future events becomes virtually unbearable. The potential financial and social rewards, which would accrue to those who can anticipate the future, have been a key element of mankind's folklore and dreams since the beginning of recorded history. The ability of neural networks to process huge amounts of data in search of patterns without having to be told what to look for makes these devices remarkably well suited to this endeavor. Although some reports of attempts to use neural networks to predict future events can be found in the literature, we can expect any real successes that result in financial gain to be kept very quiet [20, 27].

Some researchers have found that banks that are prone to failure exhibit similar characteristics [27]. Others have found that neural networks can identify patterns that allow credit applications to be processed with lower default rates than in the case with conventional techniques [20]. Still other applications of neural networks for financial decision making involve the search for patterns that provide insights into asset valuations and investment decisions [14]. *The Wall Street Journal* and other financial publications frequently entertain their readers with stories about computer experts turned investment advisors or vice versa who have utilized neural networks to quickly analyze reams of real-time financial data. Armed with identifiable patterns and calculated risk factors derived from analyzing historical information, these systems are said to identify arbitrage opportunities and investment options in real time. This technology, in the hands of experts, is said to allow split-second investment decisions to be reached and orders placed before humans or slower computers know what is going on.

20-5-5 RECOGNIZING HIDDEN PATTERNS

While much good will certainly come from the use of neural networks in identifying and processing known types of patterns, it is very likely that the discovery of patterns that are so subtle that we neglect to even consider their existence will offer the greatest rewards for mankind. Because neural networks, once constructed, are capable of correlating events whose relationships are very small, "pure research"—devoid of predetermined goals—may offer discoveries in areas where we would never think to look. For example, by analyzing the genetic code and identifying patterns in health, behavior, education, social contribution, and a myriad of other factors, insights into the successes and failures of our social systems can be determined [26]. In addition, the ability to utilize conventional statistical analysis to further process and quantify the patterns identified by neural networks will allow even the most skeptical of researchers to feel comfortable with the results.

The key to the unique ability of neural networks to identify patterns in data without having to be specifically programmed to do so lies in their architecture. Whereas virtually all information systems (including artificial intelligence applications) are based on predefined heuristic processes, neural networks are designed to recognize and identify stochastic process [13]. A stochastic process is a mechanism of a phenomenon that evolves or occurs randomly in time, such as the flow of traffic at a signal-controlled intersection. As compared to heuristic events, which are inherently predictable (if you know the rules), the characteristic feature of a stochastic process is its inherent randomness and apparent immunity to predictive rules.

With a stochastic process, at each instant in time there is a random variable that describes the current state of the process—the number of cars waiting at the intersection, for example. A stochastic process is defined by the collection of random variables, one for each distinct instant in time. The most basic example of a stochastic process (and the one most frequently cited in the literature) is the random walk [23]. This is the motion of a particle that at a sequence of times is moved one unit to the right or to the left with probabilities that do not change.

Through the use of neural networks, enormous quantities of data can be analyzed in order to isolate events or conditions that are correlated in some manner with the particular events under study. Neither causal relationships nor rules need to be established if the neural network is capable of identifying related (hopefully preceding) events. Only a pattern with a certain probability of occurrence is required for some predictive capability to be present. If correlating one or more seemingly random and unpredictable events can identify a legitimate predictive capability, the benefits may be enormous. This capability of neural networks to find patterns where none were thought to exist give them a potential power that is difficult to fully comprehend [10]. It is now easy to see, however, the recent interest being shown in financial markets in neural networks (as well as the scarcity of literature documenting the degree of success being achieved in their use as market prognosticators).

20-6 HOW NEURAL NETWORKS WORK: AN OVERVIEW

Typical information systems excel at raw number crunching and often possess the power to store and retrieve large amounts of data in seconds, tasks that humans do poorly. This is the source or their great value to business organizations. It is ironic that these systems perform poorly tasks at which humans excel—the ability to utilize inductive reasoning and the ability to draw inferences by recognizing subtle patterns. Neural networks attempt to address the shortcomings of conventional information systems by utilizing a unique architecture [23]. They attempt to model and replicate human intuition by simulating the physical processes on which intuition is based. To accomplish this, neural networks simulate the processes of adaptive learning utilized by biological organism—on a much smaller scale. A neural network is theoretically capable of giving the proper response (or the best response if more than one response is applicable) to a given problem even when there is no previously defined procedure for solving the problem. In addition, neural networks are capable of doing this even when the input information is noisy and/or incomplete [14].

Because of this seeming ability to find order within disorder, neural networks are much better suited to support semistructured and unstructured decisions than are conventional systems. They are able to do this because they are modeled after the form and function of the human nervous system. Neural networks possess the ability to learn through repetition—a uniquely biological trait. They do this by mimicking the structure and the basic function of the human brains—the neuron or nerve cell [15]. Artificial neurons serve as the basic functional element of the neural network in much the same way as binary electronic switches serve as the basic elements in digital computers.

A biological neuron is a relatively simple structure that is capable of performing only three basic functions—they can input signals from the environment, they can process the signals, and they can output the signals to another neuron or to a structure that can act on the signal (like a muscle). The input components (called dendrites) receive electrochemical impulses from the output components of other neurons (called axons) directly from sensory organs. Dendrites are similar to roads and highways that connect various towns (neurons). In the human brain, each neuron may be connected to a thousand or more neurons through a complex network of dendrites and axons. It is in this network of interconnections that the brain achieves its remarkable speed [2].

The central processing unit of the neuron (the nucleus) operates very simply. The neuron's many dendrites (input structures) receive impulses from other contiguous neurons and transfer these impulses to the nucleus. The nucleus collects these impulses, sums them and then compares the sum to an output threshold— called an "action potential." This action potential is the level of stimulation ("activation level") necessary for the neuron to "fire" or send an impulse through its axon to other neurons to which it is connected. Research on neurons indicates that, as a rule, they are about 1000 times slower than the digital switches in conventional computers. Since neurons are not getting any faster, and computer processors are, the already wide speed gap between natural and artificial neurons is getting wider each year.

Even with this speed deficit at the neuron level, the brain is able to resolve difficult pattern recognition problems (such as vision and language) in about one-half second. This is in contrast to conventional digital computers that are incapable of resolving even simple pattern recognition tasks. The brain is able to achieve its remarkable speed and processing power because a very large number of inherently slow neurons are linked together into highly complex networks. This network allows many individual neurons to operate (almost) simultaneously on the same task. In reality, the connected neurons earlier in the network (closer to the input) stimulating neurons later in the network (closer to the output) to begin processing the impulse before the earlier neurons have finished. In this way the operation of the individual neurons in the network is overlapped, not truly simultaneous [13].

20-6-1 HARDWARE ASPECTS

Notwithstanding this minor inaccuracy, both the brain and neural networks are characterized as exhibiting a processing mode referred to as "parallel distributed processing" (PDP). This term seems to be given to any device or system that subdivides tasks into separable elements for simultaneous completion [16, 28]. While overlapped processing does not truly represent parallelism in its pure form, this minor distinction is generally overlooked in the literature. Since neural networks are modeled after the structure and function of the brain, it is not surprising that neural networks, too, derive their speed and processing power from the simultaneous functioning of its individual neural processors. In most applications, neural networks are implemented using computer hardware based on parallel processors. This is not because conventional serial computers are functionally incapable of supporting the required processing, but because single threading is too slow. Indeed, some applications of neural networks such as predicting bank failures and reviewing credit applications perform adequately with serial processors. Even workstations and personal computers have been successfully used for neural network applications [3].

20-6-2 LAYERED ARCHITECTURE

Because neural networks are constructed in layers (input layer, one or more middle layers, and output layer) very special hardware is needed to really achieve the benefits of this unique architecture [28]. Figure 20-1 illustrates this simple architecture [8].

These special-purpose computers are referred to as neurocomputers, as compared to neural network applications being run on conventional computers. In a neurocomputer, there is a "front-end" processor that captures the input signal, one or more identical "middle-layer" processors that process the input signal and make inferences, and a "back-end" processor that formulates the best output based on inferential data. The "front-end" processor itself is made up of a matrix of individual processing units, each capable of accepting input information from a sensing device or directly from a digital source such as a database. With applications that are oriented to processing data from the environment in a manner that mimics the sensory processors of animals (vision, sound, etc.) the sensing device would typically capture analog signals. These signals would be digitized and then fed into one of the processors that make up the "front-end" processor or input layer. In order to increase throughput, a matrix of sensors would be used, each one feeding its digitized signal into a processor in the input layer dedicated to receiving and processing its input.

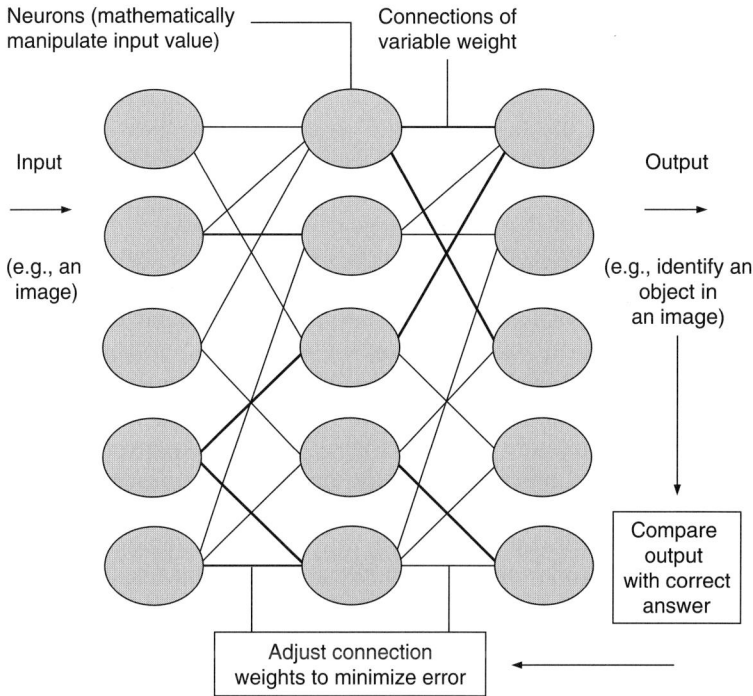

Figure 20-1 A neural network architecture.

Each processor in the input layer is, in turn, connected to every processor in the first of the middle layers if more than one middle layer exists (again each layer is a matrix of individual processing units). If more than one middle layer is required to process the input information, each processor in each level is connected to every processor in the adjacent layer. Multiple middle layers are required if the input information is very ambiguous, very complex, or if the number of possible inferences that can be reached is very large. In the literature, the number of processors in each layer and the number of middle layers, taken together, is a measure of the "robustness" of the neural network. This apparently is considered to be an indication of the inherent power of the system. As with the input layer, each processor in the output layer is connected to every processor in the last of the middle layers (if more than one exists). This architecture makes the neurocomputer more or less symmetrical, although the input layer and the output layer do not need to contain the same number of individual processors (see Figure 20-1).

20-6-3 INPUT LAYER

An interesting feature of neurocomputers is the structure of the input and the output layers. In the input layer, the number of individual processing units is determined by the number of "pieces" or segments the input signal is to be divided into and the speed with which the network is required to operate. Typically, the more pieces, the quicker the processing. In recognizing individual printed or hand-written characters 24 segments may be sufficient to adequately recognize the character and provide speeds greater than a few characters per second. In attempting to recognize the faces of people exiting a commercial airliner, many more individual processing units in the input layer would be required. The human retina is made up of more than 10,000 sensory cells, for example [30]. This explains our visual acuity (the degree of image resolution). To achieve the same acuity a neurocomputer would have to have the same number of processing units in its input layer. In a commercial example, the largest number of processing units in the input layer of a neurocomputer was found to be 512 [2]. While this is a very large number, and the network is very robust, it pales in comparison to even simple biological networks. Most working networks described in the literature contained 64 or fewer processing units in their input layers. This allows input signals to be split into 64 individual segments that can be processed in parallel, an adequate number for many applications, but still primitive in comparison to biological systems.

20-6-4 MIDDLE LAYERS

The identical middle layers of neurocomputer process signals from the input layer, make inferences concerning the values or characteristics of those signals and transmits the single "best" answer (the strongest inference) to the output layer. Inferences are simply based on summing the weights assigned to the signals transmitted from each individual segment of the input layer as these signals pass through each of the middle layers of the network. As the input signals pass through the middle layers, a weight is assigned by each processor in each layer to each signal. These weights accumulate as the signal propagates through each of the middle layers of the network. When the signal reaches the output layer, the weights of each of the original signals are compared to values previously stored in a knowledge base. The output layer simply finds the object in the knowledge base that most closely matches the pattern of weights, which has been assigned to the input signal.

20-6-5 OUTPUT LAYER

The function of the output layer is to match the final values given to the processed signal, which originally entered the neural network via the input layer, to a database or previously stored values. While it is conceivable that a neural network could output a "not found" condition if the processed signal correlated very weakly with the base of stored values, most networks are designed to output a "best guess." For example, a network that is designed to perform optical character recognition of machine-generated characters may have in its knowledge base the letters A through Z, lower case a through z, numbers 0 through 9, and a space. Characters input into the network (even if the image is distorted or blurred) will cause the network to output the character in its knowledge base that most closely resembles the original image. This matching will proceed even if portions of the original character are missing or if the input image is partially masked by "noise" (external data). Neural networks that must produce highly accurate output, such as those that scan hand-written addresses as input to automated letter sorters, may be programmed to output an error signal if the network cannot make an inference that is within predetermined confidence levels. Input that cannot be recognized with confidence will require manual intervention to identify the questionable characters in the address. Eventually unrecognizable addresses will be sorted manually [25].

20-7 LEARNING IN NEURAL NETWORKS: AN OVERVIEW

As compared to expert systems and virtually all other examples of artificial intelligence applications that require that knowledge be entered into the system before processing begins, neural networks begin without a knowledge base. Through the iterative process of the neural network, the knowledge base grows as the network is taught correct responses to input signals. Unlike virtually all CBISs, neural networks are not provided with quantitative descriptions of objects or patterns to be recognized. Neither are they provided with IF-Then rules that would allow them to distinguish individual objects from similar objects. Instead, neural networks are presented with repetitive examples that attempt to display variety in approximately the same way that the universe or real objects display variety [19].

In order for the network to learn to recognize automobiles, images of all automobiles would have to be processed through the network until the network "learned" or "was taught" the correct name for each automobile image. With this learning accomplished, the network could begin to recognize images of automobiles that were distorted, or had missing features. After sufficient learning, the network could learn to identify moving vehicles and those viewed at unusual angles.

Through the teaching process, neural networks discover or infer the relationships between various occurrences of inputs by processing the image and progressively developing and refining and internal matrix of weights. These weights are assigned to each attribute of the input image in relation to the degree to which that attribute correlates with the "right" output pattern. Through this process, the neural network learns through adaptation, similar to the way biological systems learn. This capacity for adaptive learning is the characteristic that most distinguishes neural networks from expert systems applications. Expert systems rely on inference that is based on an accurate representation of the domain of the problem. Traditional expert systems do not have adaptive capability. However, expert networks (a hybrid of neural networks and expert systems) are considered to be a very promising area of research and development activity [11]. These expert systems do possess learning capability.

20-7-1 TRAINING NEURAL NETWORKS

Because neural networks are designed to mimic biological processes in function as well as structure, it is not surprising that they are trained by rewarding desired (typically correct or nearly correct) responses and punishing undesired (wrong and not even close) responses. When the system responds with the correct output response to an input pattern, the "reward" consists of a strengthening of the current matrix of signal weights [23]. This is the key to understanding how neural networks learn to discriminate. It is the weight of the processed signal that is compared to the previously stored weights of "right" answers that allows the network to select the "best" (closest fitting) pattern from its knowledge base. This is compared to virtually all other CBISs that utilize previously determined If-Then rules as their basis for discriminating among the universe of potential "right" answers. If the network selects the correct response to an input pattern, the weight of the processed signal (actually a matrix of weights corresponding to the number of processing elements in the output layer) goes into the knowledge base with a pointer to the "right" output pattern. In addition, an inference weight is established for the connection that corresponds to the frequency that the particular processed signal points to the particular output pattern.

The first time a connection between a processed pattern weight and a (correct) response is input into the knowledge base, the inference strength connecting the pattern and response is set to 100%. When this same connection is found to produce a "wrong" answer, indicating an inability to accurately discriminate, the inference weight is decreased as a form of punishment. This method of increasing the weights of correct answers makes it more likely that a similar response will be produced by similar inputs in the future. When the system responds incorrectly, the "punishment" entails the adjustment of the inference weight downward so that the system will respond differently when the same input is received again.

20-7-2 ADAPTIVE LEARNING IN NEURAL NETWORKS

Since the selection of the "right" output pattern is relative (the best match of options currently in the knowledge base), further learning may lead to an even better match. In this way, a response that was "right" yesterday because it was the best match currently in the knowledge base may be "wrong" tomorrow. This would occur if an even "better" response to the input pattern were learned today and added to the knowledge base. This adaptive learning capability is the feature of neural networks that seems to offer the greatest potential benefit to business decision making. It is evident that a system that is capable of virtually unlimited learning capacity can, in a relatively short time, outpace the discriminating ability of other types of CBIS (such as expert systems) that must be "taught" through additional programming. (e.g., adding more If-Then rules).

Another feature of the more sophisticated neural networks is the ability to increase the speed of the adaptive learning through the feature of "back propagation" [13]. Using this technique, when a "wrong" response to an input pattern is given, the network is not only told that the response is incorrect, but the system is also given the "right" answer. For example, a system designed to identify pictures of automobiles may respond with a "98 BMW IS" to an input pattern of a "98 Mercedes Benz 280 C Class." A response from the system's trainer of "wrong" would weaken the inference weight of that response, reducing the probability of the same incorrect response to the same pattern—this is an inherent feature of all neural networks. In a system with back propagation, the system answer to the same incorrect response would be "Wrong—that is a 98 Mercedes Benz 280 C Class." By providing both the signal of "wrong" and the "right" response the network is given two valuable pieces of information. In this manner the inference weight of the incorrect answer can be decreased and the inference weight of the correct answer can be increased in a single processing cycle. This approach, which reminds us of how human learning occurs, greatly accelerates the rate of learning and adaptation in neural networks.

Another method of adaptive learning in neural networks is a technique whereby the trainer responds to the system's output not simply with a binary "right/wrong" response, but rather with a range of responses that identify the degree of "rightness or wrongness." Gradations of responses may be simply "right," "very close," "close," "not close," and "way off." In very sophisticated systems the range of feedback responses could become quite large. In such a system a range of numeric responses would probably be employed [10]. In any case, the more the categories of feedback responses, the greater the ability of the neural network to "tune" its inference weights, resulting in more rapid adaptive learning.

If a human trainer is employed to "educate" the network, the capability of the network to learn from the fewest repetitions is a definite advantage. Overall, in neural networks as well as in biological systems, the more information that can be gained from a processing cycle, the better. As in all education, the more "enriched" the learning experience is, the more benefit it provides to the "students" (learner) whether they be biological or artificial.

20-7-3 SUPERVISED TRAINING

A neural network can be trained by using a supervised or unsupervised methodology. In **supervised training** (most examples given in this chapter refer to this type) an input pattern is explicitly paired with a specific output response. While much iteration may be required to accomplish this, the learning experience is not complete until the system produces the correct response. For example, the input may be a series of numbers and the desired output may be the product of the numbers. The objective of the training process would be for the network to discover, through inference, the underlying pattern that forms the relationship between the input and the output patterns [14]. Prior to this training, the network is presumed to have no "a priori" knowledge of numbers, their relative magnitudes, or mathematical operations. Through repetitive training sessions the neural network would have to infer that 20 was twice the magnitude of 10 and that multiplying numbers together produced a quantity greater than that achieved by adding them together (with a few notable exceptions). The key to this technique is the presence of a trainer capable of providing the correct answer. In this mode, the network only needs to infer the internal "rules" of relationships that connect the input pattern to the correct output pattern. It should be noted that supervised learning does not require a human trainer. Several successful neural networks utilize computers, video tape players, or other mechanized devices to provide the correct responses to input patterns.

20-7-4 UNSUPERVISED TRAINING

In unsupervised training the neural network is presented with only the input pattern; no "correct" output or target pattern exists. The objective of the system is to detect, isolate, and identify patterns in the input. To accomplish this the neural network must parse through the input information in a repetitive manner, organizing it until a consistent output (not necessarily the "right" output) is achieved each time the same input pattern is received. This is the equivalent of unstructured decision making. The characteristics of the output may be entirely unpredictable prior to training. It is for the human researcher to determine any value in the network's output. As with any repetitive process, conventional statistical methods may be utilized to determine if the pattern is intrinsic, random, or just noise. As with supervised training, the system in an unsupervised training mode discovers recurring patterns in the input information, but it must accomplish this without information about the expected, desirable, or correct output [14].

While this undirected approach seems inherently inefficient, results that are not expected, intuitively obvious, or even perceived to be possible can be achieved. Using this approach, a neural network could be trained to recognize patterns in financial data that could be shown to have statistically significant predictive capabilities. Identifying patterns in stock market data, either for investment, speculation, or arbitrage purposes could easily provide the user of a neural network with profound economic advantages. This advantage may be in the form of insights that are not available to others, or just plain speed in identifying momentary imbalances that could be exploited through arbitrage transactions. Technical stock market analysis attempts to identify patterns in financial data and capitalize on investment opportunities not available to those who do not use this technique (or whose interpretations of the patterns result in different insights). The use of neural networks for this type of research appears to offer considerable advantages over traditional, manual analytical techniques. The availability of enormous volumes of data in computer-readable form, much available on-line and even in real time (if one is willing to pay for it), would seem to indicate that the use of neural networks in unsupervised training mode could provide insights and advantages well beyond the scope of most people's imagination.

20-8 THE ADVANTAGES OF NEURAL NETWORKS

In addition to the benefits derived from providing inferences and insights not readily available through the use of other techniques and technologies, neural networks have other advantages over alternative CBISs [19, 26]. These include:

- Able to avoid explicit programming and detailed If-Then rules
- Able to generalize from information context or other clues
- Able to process erroneous, inconsistent, and incomplete data
- Creates abstractions from diverse data
- Dynamic system that continues to improve with use
- Inherently adaptable, no need to update the system when input changes

- No need for troublesome and expensive "experts"
- No need to input a predefined knowledge base
- Uses "common sense" to make educated guesses

20-9 THE DISADVANTAGES OF NEURAL NETWORKS

Like other CBISs, neural networks are not without their drawbacks. These shortcomings include [19, 26]:

- Black box approach makes it hard to determine reliability and accountability.
- A certain amount of trust is involved.
- Hard to trace steps taken in process of making inferences. In other words, there is no explanation capability.
- Many repetitive training steps may be required.
- May require special purpose computers not commercially available.
- One must monitor output in order to deliver correct results.
- Scarcity of available talent and expertise.

20-10 APPLICATIONS OF NEURAL NETWORKS: AN OVERVIEW

Neural networks are theoretically capable of any information-processing task we can perform. Currently, however, neural networks have been most effectively applied to three tasks within the broad field of pattern recognition—classification, associative memory, and clustering [14]. Classification involves the assignment of input patterns to predefined groups or classes based upon patterns within the input data itself. Recent applications of neural networks to classification tasks include:

- Grouping financial instruments by risk class. This may be used for capital structure analysis.
- Identification of plastic explosives in luggage.
- Optical recognition of handwritten and printed characters. This may prove to be a very significant step for automating the source data.
- Target recognition and acquisition of radar and sonar images.

Associative memory (also called a content-addressable memory) involves the ability to retrieve a complete pattern from the knowledge base using only an element or subset of the original pattern. Recent applications of neural networks to associative memory tasks include:

- Identification of fingerprints based on incomplete images
- Prediction of movements in financial markets

Clustering involves the ability to compress or filter input data without losing important information. Recent applications of neural networks to clustering tasks include:

- Clustering bonds into homogeneous (but not predefined) risk classes based on financial statements
- Grouping loan applications into risk classes

20-11 NEURAL NETWORKS IN ACTION

There are numerous real life applications of neural networks reported in the literature. The following is a listing of some of the areas in which neural networks have been successfully employed [4,9,12,17,18,21]:

- Bankruptcy prediction
- Credit rating
- Data validation
- Financial forecasting
- Industrial process control
- Investment analysis
- Machine diagnostics
- Material usage optimization
- Medical field
- Oil and gas exploration
- Production and manufacturing scheduling
- Quality control
- Risk management
- Sales forecasting
- Speech and pattern recognition
- Stock market
- Target marketing

20-12 OUTLOOK FOR NEURAL COMPUTING

With the possession of learning capabilities, neural networks offer remarkable opportunities to explore and enhance our own capabilities. Because they are designed to do the same tasks that we do well, these systems may provide benefits to mankind in a different way than other forms of automation and mechanization.

While neural networks are new and the technology is immature, the potential for exploring our own limitations as humans using these surrogate brains is currently unimaginable. In the future these systems will undoubtedly serve us well as powerful assistants to whom we delegate repetitive tasks and mundane jobs. But, their greatest potential benefit to us will probably be in two areas: identifying fundamental patterns in our universe that we have so far overlooked and in their integration with expert systems to form expert networks [11].

In the task of identifying fundamental patterns, the tireless work of parallel processors will almost certainly identify patterns and relationships in our lives and environment that will provide insights into new ways to improve our lives. A well-designed neural network operating in unsupervised training mode with access to the enormous databases available to us could identify patterns that are, even now, beyond our comprehension. In addition, the integration of the inferential capabilities and speed of neural networks with the user-friendliness of expert systems could allow us to benefit from the strong features of both technologies. These developments will open up new areas for research and development efforts and will allow us to learn more about our own intellectual and perceptive capabilities as well as providing greater insights about our environment.

20-13 SELECTED NEURAL NETWORKS PRODUCTS AND SERVICES

The following are selected examples of products in the neural networks environment. For detailed information, you should contact the vendor of the particular service or product [6].

1. *CAD/Chem Modeling and Optimization System* (AI Ware) is a product design tool for chemists. CAD/Chem automatically develops neural network models of formulation data, discovering the underlying relationships between ingredients, processing, and product properties. Genetic algorithms are used for finding optimal formulations according to current design preferences and constraints expressed with fuzzy logic. Two- and three-dimensional graphics help visualize relationships and sensitivity.

2. *IDIS Predictive Refinement Module* (Information Discovery, Inc.) analyzes predictive modes such as neural networks for success and failure and pinpoints where the model works best. The modules automatically build a hit-and-miss database and a critique database for analysis and suggests where to improve the neural predictive model or that a different model should be used on some data segment.

3. *Neural Network Toolbox* (MathWorks, Inc.) is a collection of MAT-LAB functions for designing and simulating neural networks. It also includes unsuper-

vised training functions that use associative learning rules for competitive layers, feature map layers, and Hopfield networks. The Toolbox integrates with MATLAB, a numeric computing visualization environment, and runs under various platforms.

4. *NeurOn-Line* (Gensym Corp.) is graphical, object-oriented neural network software capable of online adaptive learning, which is integrated with an expert system shell.

5. *NeuroSolutions* (NeuroDimension Inc.) is a Windows-based neural network simulation environment that supports static, fixed-point, and trajectory learning through backpropagation, recurrent backpropagation, and backpropagation through time. Because of its object-oriented design, NeuroSolutions provides the flexibility needed to construct a wide range of learning paradigms and network topologies.

6. *Propagator* (ARD Corp.) is a neural network development system with a graphical interface. It has three dynamic graphs, up to five layers (32,000 nodes/layer), data scaling, and C/C++ source code generation.

7. *Stock Prophet version* (Future Wave Software) is designed to perform the preprocessing of data for application of neural networks to market timing. It also performs evaluation of neural network indicators for your choice of markets through profitability testing. It can generate larger training files, it includes new indicators, and it has several other features that make the development of neural network trading systems even easier.

8. *VantagePoint* (Mendelsohn Enterprises, Inc.) is a pretrained trading system that uses neural networks to perform synergistic market analysis, combining technical, intermarket, and fundamental data inputs. VantagePoint also gives the strength of the move and forecasts whether or not the market is about to make a top or bottom.

SUMMARY

This chapter provided a detailed discussion of neural networks (neural computing) as one of the growing applications of AI and CBIS. It compared and contrasted neural computing with digital computing and neural networks with expert systems. The chapter explained various types of pattern recognition and the working fundamentals of neural networks. The chapter introduced various types of learning in a neural network environment and presented several advantages and disadvantages of neural networks. The chapter concluded with several applications of neural networks and a selected listing of commercial products and services for neural networks design and implementation.

REVIEW QUESTIONS

1. What is a neural network?
2. What are some of the differences between a neural computer and a digital computer?
3. What are some of the similarities and dissimilarities of neural networks and expert systems?
4. What is pattern recognition?
5. What are some examples of pattern recognition types? What is optical pattern recognition? Sound pattern recognition?
6. How do we recognize patterns in data?
7. What are some applications of recognizing patterns in data?
8. Describe in your own terms how a neural network works.
9. What are various dimensions that must be recognized in order to be able to understand the working fundamentals of a neural network?
10. What is layered architecture? The input layer? The middle layers?
11. How does a neural network learn?
12. What is the difference between supervised training and unsupervised training?
13. What are some applications of these two types of training?
14. What is adaptive learning in neural networks?
15. What are some advantages of neural networks? What are some disadvantages?
16. What are some business applications of neural networks?
17. What is the outlook for neural networks?
18. What are some examples of neural network shells on the market? What are some of the basic capabilities of these systems?

PROJECTS

1. Select one of the ES shells introduced in Chapter 18 and one of the neural network shells introduced in this chapter. Compare and contrast the basic capability of each product.
2. By analyzing the materials presented in Section 20-5 and by referring to the references in this section, who would benefit the most from pattern recognition applications? Discuss.

3. By analyzing the materials presented in Section 20-7, compare and contrast various types of learning for neural networks. Which type of training is more promising?

4. By referring to the references in this chapter, investigate financial applications of neural networks. What have neural networks done in the stock market and in commodity training? What are some of the possible obstacles for using neural networks in these areas in a broader scale? Discuss.

5. The majority of vendors outlined in Section 20-13 offers demo disks for their products. Contact one of these vendors and request a demo disk. Do some hands-on activities with the demo. What are some of the similarities and dissimilarities of these types of software with other types of software that you have used before? Discuss.

KEY TERMS

Back propagation, 591–592
Digital computing, 577–579
Expert systems, 579–580
Input layer, 588
Layered architecture, 586–587
Learning in neural networks, 589–590
Middle layers, 588

Neural computing, 576–577
Optical pattern recognition, 581
Output layer, 581
Pattern recognition, 580–584
Sound pattern recognition, 581–582
Supervised training, 592
Unsupervised training, 592–593

REFERENCES

[1] Anonymous. (June 2, 1986). Computers that come awfully close to thinking. *Business Week,* 93.

[2] Anonymous. (May 2, 1987). What the brain builders have in mind. *The Economist,* 94–96.

[3] Anonymous. (June 17, 1991). Software developed for using neural network technologies in problem solving. *Aviation Week and Space Technology,* 216.

[4] Azoff, E. M. (January/February 1995). Extracting meaning from a neural network solution. *Neurove$ Journal,* 7–10.

[5] Barron, J. J. (November 1990). Chips for the nineties and beyond. *Byte,* 342–350.

[6] Berg, T. D. (June 1995). Neural networks resource guide. *AI Expert,* 35–42.

[7] Bidgoli, H. (1998). Intelligent management support systems. Westport, CT: Quorum Books.

[8] Brady, H. (August/September 1990). The neural computer. *Technology Review,* 45.

[9] Brockett, P. L., *et al.* (1994). A neural network method for obtaining an early warning of insurance insolvency. *The Journal of Risk and Insurance,* Vol. 61, 402–428.

[10] Brunak, S., and Lautrup, B. (1984). Neural networks—computers with intuition. New York: Times Book.

[11] Caudill, M. (October 1991). Expert networks. *Byte,* 110.

[12] Enrado, P. (June 1995). Application watch. *AI Expert,* 48.

[13] Gabriel, M., and Moore, J. (1990). Learning and computational neuroscience: Foundations of adaptive networks. Cambridge, MA: MIT Press.

[14] Hawley, D. D., *et al.* (December 1990). Artificial neuron systems: A new tool for financial decision making. *Financial Analysis Journal,* 63–72.

[15] Jubak, J. (January 1989). Think like a bee. *Venture,* 48–52.

[16] Khanna, T. (1990). Foundations of neural networks. Reading, MA: Addison-Wesley Publishing Company.

[17] Kestelyn, J. (February 1991). Application watch. *AI Expert,* 71–72.

[18] Kestelyn, J. (May 1991). Application watch *AI Expert,* 72.

[19] Kirrane, D. E. (December 1990). Machine learning. *Training and Development Journal,* 24–29.

[20] Klein, E. (February 1992). Thinking machines and new expertise. *Savings Institutions,* 37–38.

[21] Li, E. Y. (1994). Artificial neural networks and their business applications. *Information Management,* 27, 303–313.

[22] Meiklejohn, I. (November 1989). This does not compute—yet. *Management Today,* 181–184.

[23] Pao, Y.-H. (1989). *Adaptive pattern recognition and neural networks.* Reading, MA: Addison-Wesley Publishing Company.

[24] Rochester, J. B. (February 1990). New business uses for neuro computing. *I/S Analyzer,* 1–12.

[25] Schantz, H. E. (Spring 1991). An overview of neural OCR networks. *Journal Information Systems Management,* 22–27.

[26] Stein, R. M. (January 1991). Real artificial life. *Byte,* 289–298.

[27] Tam, K., and Kiang, M. (July 1992). Managerial applications of neural networks: The case of bank failure predictions. *Management Science,* 926–927.

[28] Touretzky, D. S., and Pomerleau, D. (August 1989). What's hidden in the hidden layers? *Byte,* 227–233.

[29] Waibel, A., and Hampshire, J. (August 1989). Building blocks for speech. *Byte,* 235–245.

[30] Wright, D. P., and Scofield, C. L. (April 1991). Divide and conquer. *Byte,* 207–210.

Chapter 21

Natural Language Processing: The Ultimate User/System Interface

Learning Objectives

After studying this chapter, you should be able to:

- Define natural language processing (NLP) systems.
- Explain some of the advantages and applications of NLP.
- Discuss some of the problems associated with NLP.
- Explain natural language input and output technologies.
- Explain how a natural language processing system works.
- Explain various parsing techniques.
- Review natural language interfaces, machine translation, and document understanding systems.

21-1 INTRODUCTION

This chapter provides a detailed discussion on natural language processing (NLP). It provides definitions, advantages, applications, problems, and an explanation of popular natural language input and output technologies as they relate to CBISs. The chapter explains natural language understanding systems, including syntax, semantic, and pragmatic analysis. The chapter explains how a natural language system works in conjunction with different parsing techniques and approaches. The chapter highlights several popular natural language interfaces available on the market and explains in detail machine translation and document-understanding systems. This chapter should give you an understanding and appreciation for an ideal "interface" for a CBIS that is easier and more powerful than traditional user-system interfaces. As you will see in this chapter, there is still a long way to go in order to see a natural language that is comparable to the way in which humans are able to communicate with each other. However, progress has been steady and will continue well into the future.

21-2 NATURAL LANGUAGE PROCESSING (NLP): AN OVERVIEW

Computer-based information systems have been designed for users who are somewhat computer literate. No matter how flexible and user-friendly they are, a specific method must be followed in order to operate these systems or perform queries.

As discussed in Chapter 2, four classes of computer languages have evolved: machine language, assembly language, high-level language, and fourth-generation language (4GL). The fifth class, natural language, is the ideal language from a user's point of view. This language is supposed to enable a computer user to communicate with the computer in his or her native language. The goal of NLP is to provide a method for interface that is very similar to our native language. A NLP provides a free-format, question-and-answer situation for a typical user. There are a number of NLP systems available on the market. Table 21-1 provides a listing of some of the more successful NLP on the market.

At the time of this writing, none of these products are capable of providing a dialog that is comparable to one between humans. However, progress has been steady. There are numerous commercial applications of NLP. These are summarized in Table 21-2 [2,6,7, 8,13].

In this chapter we explore all types of natural language systems, including voice, text, handwriting, and machine translation. When we want to communicate with computers, we have to do it on their terms, in their language, and in their media. We have to learn Assembler, BASIC, COBOL, FORTRAN, or some other programming languages. These languages tend to be unforgiving. For example, if we put a period in the wrong spot or leave out a parenthesis or some other minute detail, our command to the computer simply won't work. There are currently some attempts to alleviate the communication problem with interfaces, such as menus, online help facilities, and graphic icons. Graphical user interface (GUI) environments have indeed simplified this process up to some degree. However, these are still somewhat cumbersome, require some training, and tend to be system or application dependent. Natural language systems can accommodate our native tongues, such as German, English, Japanese, Chinese, Persian, and French.

There are numerous definitions of NLP. However, all "point" to the same basic concept of being able to interface or communicate with the computer in a natural or human language as opposed to machine or artificial language. An artificial language is a language based on a prescribed set of rules that are established prior to their usage. A natural language, on the other hand, is defined as a language that we as humans use to communicate with each other, such as English, Japanese, Chinese, German or French. NLP can provide a front end for other computer programs, especially database management systems.

Table 21-1

Natural Language Systems on the Market

NLP name	Area of use
BROKER	Standard and Poor's data
CLOUT	Database management system
DragonBusiness	Business data retrieval
DragonDictate	Voice dictation system
DragonLaw	Legal document processing
DragonMed	Medical and emergency room applications
DragonPro	Professional dictation system
EXPLORER	Map generation and display
INTELLECT	Database management system
Kurzweill VoicePad	Voice dictation system
LADDER	Ship identification and location
MARKATEER	Market analysis
NATURALLINK	Dow Jones data retrieval and display
Naturally Speaking	Voice dictation system
POLITICS	Ideological belief system simulation
Q & A	Interface with database, word processing and report generator
SAM	Generic story understanding
SHRDLU	Location and manipulation of three-dimensional pictures
STRAIGHT TALK	Interface with word processing and spreadsheet
TDUS	Electromechanical repair
TEAMS	Database management system

Although far from being completely solved, the NLP problem may be the most important task that AI can solve because once solved, it opens the door for direct human-computer dialogues, bypassing normal programming and operating system conventions.

NLP is a viable target project, but the size and complexity of human language has kept it from being fully accomplished. NLP does exist and is generally divided into six major categories. These categories are [17]:

1. Natural language interface to databases.
2. Machine translation, that is, from one natural language to another.
3. Text scanning and intelligent indexing programs for summarizing large amounts of text.
4. Text generation for automated production of standardized documents.

Table 21-2

Natural Language Processing Applications

Automatic paraphrasing

Bond trading

Call routing

Computer-aided instruction

Dictation

Document or text understanding

Information retrieval

Interaction with complex programs for process control

Interface to CBIS

Inventory control

Knowledge acquisition

Knowledge compilation

Machine translation

Order entry

Quality inspection

Question and answering systems

Robotics

Speech control for automobile cruise controls

Speech output

Speech understanding

Story understanding

Telephone banking

Text or document generation

User directory

Video games

Writing assistance

5. Speech systems to allow voice interaction with computers.
6. Tools for developing NLP systems for specific applications.

NLP is the technology that permits computers to "understand" human languages. To understand means that a computer can perform two specific types of activities. One activity is to accept ordinary human language as input, execute the corresponding command, and generate the proper output. This activity is called interfacing. The second kind of activity is called knowledge acquisition. Knowledge acquisition involves using the computer to read huge amounts of text and understand information well enough to summarize points of importance and store information so it can respond to inquiries about the content [22]. A natural language interface allows users to communicate with the computer through their language rather than the computer's, thus eliminating many of the inherent difficulties of "low-level" computer languages such as BASIC or C.

21-3 ADVANTAGES OF NLP

The advantages of using NLP are numerous. The first and foremost is the elimination or reduction of the barriers to computer use. Hence, productivity is improved because [11]:

- A larger population has access to the data and expert information that different programs can provide.
- Access to computer data is expedited.
- It will promote further usage of computers, especially in the decision support systems area.
- Large amounts of text can be quickly transformed into a knowledge base.
- The user's ability to handle complex tasks is increased.
- User training requirements are minimized.

21-4 PROBLEMS WITH NATURAL LANGUAGE PROCESSING

Many workers are not using computers simply because they do not know how to operate them. Many do not even know how to type. According to senior executives, it would be wonderful to be able to talk to the computer and have the computer talk back to you. Although with the graphical user interface (GUI), user-friendliness has improved significantly, specific training is still needed to use computers. A natural language interface can immensely increase the effectiveness of a computer-based information system. However, there are several serious obstacles that have to be overcome before a true natural language interface can be developed [1].

1. *Ambiguity in our native language.* Human communications contain many ambiguities. Nowhere is this more evident than in language. A word can have many different meanings, depending on the context in which it is used. The context in which a word is used can vary widely due to differences between people. We all have different training and backgrounds. Everyone knows people of different backgrounds and status.

2. *Problems with ellipses.* Incomplete sentences, or ellipses, can also present difficulties to computers. These may occur when a word or words are left out, creating grammatical incompleteness. As examples consider:

- If late, don't come (meaning if you are late, do not come)
- If possible, pay the bill (meaning if it is possible, you pay the bill)
- They have fun in Hawaii, me too (meaning you had fun also)

3. *Problems with metaphors.* Metaphors may also create problems for NLP. Metaphor problems occur when you say something and you mean something else. Consider the sentence, "He is on top of the world." This sentence usually means the man is happy; it does not mean the man is on the highest point of the world. Consider the following sentences:

He is straight as an arrow (meaning he is conventional, honest, etc.)
After the race started, I died (meaning I became exhausted)

4. *Confusion between questions and action.* When a statement requests an action, not just a yes or no answer, still more problems are encountered by NLP systems. Consider the following questions:

- Can you give me a ride?
- Can you hold my briefcase?

In these cases, the yes or no answer is not the goal; you are asking for an action. Hold my briefcase or answer the phone for me, please, or give me some sugar, please.

5. *Idioms in our language.* Idioms and slang also present serious problems to NLP systems. Consider the word "run" as a verb and as a noun. The word run as a verb has at least 16 meanings, and when you use it as slang, the number of meanings becomes very large. Some examples are: run up, run down, run out, and run on.

Another interesting example is all the slang made with the word go: go around, go far, go at, go down, go into, go off, go over, go to, go under, go with, and so on. The English language is full of slang such as this.

6. *Similar sounding words and phrases.* Humans have problems distinguishing similar sounding words and phrases. The same is true about computers. Consider:

Bear	Bare
Chip	Cheap
Fortunes	Four tunes
Flour	Flower
Grade	Great
Night	Knight

Read   Red
Sent   Scent

21-5 NATURAL LANGUAGE INPUT AND OUTPUT TECHNOLOGIES

Natural language inputs and outputs are achieved through both text and sound, but other forms of natural input are on the horizon. Communication via text is accomplished with traditional hardware mechanisms—keyboards, printers, plotters, and video monitors. Natural language communication via sound is accomplished with hardware mechanisms packaged as speech recognition and synthesis systems. Some of these recognition and synthesis systems are supported by AI technologies that interpret spoken input or generate humanlike audible speech output.

Natural language is an umbrella term for communication with computers using our native languages. In actuality, there are several branches within the field of natural language processing. It includes language input, output, and understanding. "Natural language" is also sometimes used in a more restrictive sense to refer to the text branch of the language problem. "Speech understanding" refers to the ability of computers to respond correctly to spoken language. And "speech generation" refers to the ability of computers to output spoken language. Commercial products are already available in two of the areas of natural language communication: speech generation and natural language interfaces. Other goals, particularly speech understanding, require a great deal more research before they will become widely used in commercial settings.

In order for a computer to achieve full natural language processing capabilities it must be able to cope with all forms of natural input technologies, including voice and handwriting recognition and gesture interpretation as well as traditional text input. The computer must then be able to process these various forms of input and then produce natural output, which could take the form of text displayed on a monitor, printed reports, speech, expressive, rational gestures and motions, and virtual reality environments.

Because we do not yet understand how human beings are able to make sense of the stream of sound that is spoken, it is not surprising to find that this area of natural language communication is not yet in its maturity. Early techniques involved storing the sound patterns of a selection of words relevant to a problem domain and comparing the input signal with these patterns, attempting to make matches. Let's briefly explain these various areas of natural language processing that have a direct impact on the successful design of CBISs.

21-5-1 VOICE RECOGNITION

Achieving accurate speech-to-text conversation with a natural-speech input system brings up some special problems. Most systems to date can recognize a single speaker using a limited vocabulary once they are trained on that speaker's voice pitch, frequency, tone, accent, and pronunciation. But if another individual tries to use this system, the computer has difficulty recognizing even simple one-syllable words. To train a system to recognize words in a speaker-dependent format, you must provide it with samples of a person's speech. While there is some variation in the way one or more individuals pronounce consonants, there is huge variation in the pronunciation and diction speed for vowels. These factors require the training to include many varying samples. Attempting to enable a system to understand connected or continuous speech adds difficulty to the problem. Syllables of adjacent words may blend or cause some sounds to be dropped. Since connected speech bears little resemblance to the stream of sound made if each word in the string is pronounced individually, it does not suffice to simply match patterns, word-for-word. Difficulties for speech understanding systems also arise with homonyms, words that sound the same and may or may not have the same spelling but have different meanings, such as:

- I threw a ball.
- I went through the door.
- I am through with the test.

A closely related difficulty is presented by similar sounding phrases such as "I scream" and "ice cream." Connected speech is easier for a system to interpret when rules of conversation are provided to help predict which words can legally follow each other.

Regional accents can also confuse computers. For example, people in different parts of the United States may say the same word or sentence in totally different dialects and tones. Letters of the alphabet are also pronounced differently in different states. How can computers be programmed to understand dialects and accents?

Another problem with speech recognition is the variety of human speech patterns. Women tend to have high voices and men low ones. Some people speak fast, some speak slowly. Even the same person may have different voice patterns during different hours of the day. In the morning or late afternoon, people will have different frequencies in their voices. How can all this be taught to a computer?

The limited success achieved to date on voice recognition is in those areas that are very precise. A voice recognition system can be trained to understand one particular voice. Even when trained for a particular individual, the system may get confused when this person catches a cold, when it is early in the morning and the voice has a different quality, or late in the afternoon when the voice is tired. There are voice-independent commercial products on the market; however, their capabilities are limited.

Limiting the vocabulary to certain words within a domain also helps, reducing the processing time for pattern matching. Research is now being done on providing systems with knowledge about the world that will help them predict what expressions might mean, based on the context in which they are used.

Systems in use at the present time vary in several respects. Some are speaker-independent (anyone can use the system without having to train the system to recognize their voice pattern), while some recognize only a particular individual's speech. Some can recognize only isolated words, while others can pick a particular word out of a stream of connected speech, and some even understand connected speech within certain narrow limits. Systems also vary in the size of their vocabularies.

Teuvo Kohonen of the Helsinki University of Technology developed one of the most well-known voice recognition systems in the mid-1980s [3]. His "voice typewriter" was a marriage of digital signal processing, neural networks, and a rule-based expert system. Together, these technologies produced surprisingly accurate (92 to 97%) results when tested against multiple speakers, continuous speech, and a large vocabulary, with only about a quarter of a second delay for a spoken word to be displayed on a monitor. Even with these results, however, most businesses would still consider it to be too slow and error prone for acceptable commercial use.

Raymond Kurzweil, founder of Kurzweil Applied Intelligence, is also a forerunner of voice recognition systems. He began his career in the mid-1970s with a "Reading Machine" that could distinguish printed text and generate digitized speech. His company markets a product called "Voice-system" that recognizes any speaker, without the need for voice pattern training, and has a vocabulary of 30,000 words [14]. His product was so successful that it enabled him to gain control of 75% of the speech recognition market. Other manufacturers of similar products include Dragon Systems, Digital Equipment Corporation, IBM, and ITT Voice Processing Corporation.

On the cutting edge of voice recognition technology are research teams at MIT, Carnegie Mellon's School of Computer Science, and private industry such as AT&T and SRI International [15]. The group at MIT has developed a street map system that gives directions and shows the shortest route between two points when asked in conversational English. If your question is ambiguous it will rephrase your query to solicit more information from you. The Carnegie group is developing a system that stores key parts of sentences during a conversation, such as noun phrases, in order to clarify the context sensitive statements. AT&T has installed voice recognition systems to augment its service to customers without access to touchtone service. These customers do not have the option to press a number to select from a menu of options. SRI International is attempting to use the tonal qualities of human speech, such as loudness, pitch and timing as forms of punctuation during conversation. They hope this will help language understanding systems grasp context and intent [15].

21-5-2 SPEECH GENERATION

Speech generation is the term for a machine reading text aloud. The speech is the audible production of the output of a system, whose text has already been determined, in correctly pronounced speech. This part of the natural language problem has been solved with the arrival of commercially available speech-generation devices.

Text-to-speech output has been with us for quite some time in the form of telephone directory assistance, over-the-phone banking services, and automated voice mail. Most of these systems use a form of digitized and then edited human voice recordings coupled with special mixing controls to produce a natural-sounding voice. One successful application of these systems has been for training blind students. You simply put the printed text facedown on a monitor-type device, and the system then generates computer speech based on the typed text. If the student does not understand the generated speech the first time, the process can be repeated as many times as needed. Speech generation also has its own special problems. Many words in the English language have different pronunciations depending on the context in which they are used. Syntactic and semantic analysis must be performed to sort out these variations. Also, once the phonetic translation of source text has been performed, the system must alter these objects into a form that the speech synthesizer can process. This processing has a tendency to give the output an artificial sounding quality. Some systems use a rule-based model to help correct this and other problems, such as differing duration of phonemes in words and sentences. This gives the output a more natural, flowing quality.

A truly sophisticated speech-generating system must pronounce phrases the way a human reader would. As an example, a simple device would read $965.60 as "dollars nine six five point six zero." But more advanced systems read it as is should be read: "nine hundred sixty-five dollars and sixty cents." Conventional speech systems have pronunciations that are preset at the factory. But the incorporation of AI technologies allows for a flexible user interface in which the end user can specify details. An important feature is a choice of many natural-quality speaking voices with variable speaking rates and intonations, a choice between male and female voices, and other special effects.

Many companies in the insurance industry are using speech synthesis systems to give a wide assortment of policy, coverage, and claims information over the phone. It is hoped that these systems will speed up customer service, increase productivity, lower costs, and provide for better communication and information flow. Some examples of these systems include Syntellect's Infobot, which is being used by Prudential Property and Casualty Insurance Co., Preferred Risk Mutual Insurance Co., and Erie Insurance Exchange. AT&T's Conversant Voice System is being used at Travelers Insurance [14].

21-5-3 HANDWRITING RECOGNITION

Besides spoken language, the written word is one of the most natural forms of communication available to us. So it comes as no surprise that handwriting recognition is another important form of natural input. Many systems have been developed with this capability over the past several years, all with varying degrees of usefulness and success. Dynamic recognition and static recognition are the two most widely used methods for a system that can recognize handwriting [3]. In dynamic recognition, the system follows each pen stroke as you form individual characters. This process makes it easier for the system to distinguish between characters with similar shapes. Static recognition, on the other hand, only looks at the character after it has already been formed. This method is more problematic in that clues such as stroke order and the location of where characters begin and end are missing. Also, handwritten characters can be poorly shaped, overlapping, and even illegible at times because individual writing styles vary so dramatically. For this reason most systems will only recognize printed text. Some systems have been designed with neural network technology, but these systems are extremely complex, it can take weeks to train an individual user (not to mention several users), and the systems can be prohibitively expensive due to the newness of this technology and the large amounts of processing power needed to run them.

21-5-4 BODY LANGUAGE

During the course of a typical conversation between two individuals, many things are said that can take on completely different meanings depending on the speaker's body language. Products are currently on the market that allow a computer to receive and interpret your body language as you input data. Interfaces range from a body suit or dataglove attached to the system by fiber optic cables to a system that uses intelligent machine vision to actually watch your movements. The dataglove or body suit interface uses a series of sensors that measure the movements of your hand and fingers, arms, legs or other body parts. In VPL's

Dataglove, sensors detect the timing of light passing through a short fiber-optic cable that is aligned over two knuckles of each finger [3]. As each finger bends, the light passing through the cable dims, which allows the system to measure the precise angle of your fingers. There are drawbacks to this interesting technology, however. In order for the dataglove subsystem to determine the overall position of your hand in space you must keep your hand within a magnetic field which induces a current in special coils on the back of the glove. A microprocessor then uses these currents to determine the location of your hand within the field. The dataglove's subsystem must also be attached to a large computer that monitors and interprets each movement. Portability does not seem to have been a determining factor when this system was designed. The system also has inherent inconsistencies and inaccuracies in measuring and interpreting data.

21-5-5 MACHINE VISION

A seemingly simpler way for a computer to accept and interpret body language would be for it to watch you as you move. But machine vision is one of the most complex areas of artificial intelligence. As soon as you see an object, your brain instantly gives it a meaning. This is also true of hearing. When somebody talks to you, your brain instantly identifies the person as male, female, an old friend, and so on. Hearing and sight share certain features that are difficult for computers to simulate. Both hearing and sight are responses of the nervous system to the environment. When we see and hear, the stimulation of our nervous system is usually continuous. Our eyes see the entire scene; our brain effectively separates the scene into individual, understandable objects. Our ears do the same thing with sound stimulation. A continuous stream of sound is received, but the brain can determine where one word starts and ends and where a sentence is finished and a new one starts. Visual or pattern recognition is one small element of human behavior that requires an enormous amount of data to be processed swiftly and efficiently when done by a computer. The system must perform massive computations using some type of heuristics in order to be able to create and correlate the object with what it has in the database. Heuristics are rules of thumb, representing knowledge in a given field. For example, a heuristic in the real estate field is that if money is an issue, you should buy the cheapest house in the most expensive neighborhood.

One example of such a system is the Thirsty Saber project, which is a defense project. It is a new cruise missile that uses 70,000 processor chips that process images as the missile flies at 400 MPH over enemy territory. The images are a series of pixels that direct the missile to a predefined target [5]. The ability to detect or match a pattern will not make computers intelligent, but when they work fast enough on pattern matching, the computer will look intelligent. Pattern recognition has numerous commercial applications such as bank check scanning, analysis of handwriting, scanning of written materials, and searching fingerprint databases for crime detection. This technology has already been successfully utilized for security protection. MIT researchers have invented a method to identify faces stored in a computer with 16 key features such as eye, nose, and chin measurements. The query may start by asking a question such as: Do you know this face? The computer answers the question by comparing the face to the ones in its database, using a formula for resemblance.

Still, several approaches for developing a practical system are currently in progress. A dynamic machine vision system has been developed by two German scientists, Ernest Dieter Dickmanns and Volker Graefe, that uses humanlike characteristics to interpret stationary and moving objects [3]. Their systems process images in frames and uses a localized search area in each frame to prevent the need for searching the entire frame for an object each time. The search area in each frame is slightly larger than the target object. If the object is not located, the search area is expanded until the object is found. This method significantly reduces the search time needed to find a specific object when compared with a system that searches the entire frame each time. Although Dickmanns and Graefe's system has not been used for interpreting body language input, it seems ideally suited for that purpose.

21-6 NATURAL LANGUAGE-UNDERSTANDING SYSTEMS

When we say that a computer "understands" language, we mean that it is able to process the plain language of the user, carry out the command, and generate appropriate output. Applications of natural language understanding systems include:

- Document-understanding systems that enable a computer to read and understand the information well enough to summarize and redirect points of importance to various recipients and to organize and store information in order to answer questions on the contents.
- Interfaces to systems such as databases or operating systems, expert advisory systems, or robots.
- Machine translation systems to translate written materials from one language to another.

Three kinds of analyses are performed on the input to the natural language-understanding systems. One focuses on syntax (how words are structured in expressions), one focuses on semantics (the meaning of words within expressions), and the third focuses on pragmatics (the meaning of sentences when taken into context with other sentences). These analyses together allow natural language systems to generate a paraphrase of the input expression in an internal representation language. Let's further explain these three types of analyses.

21-6-1 SYNTAX ANALYSIS

Syntax is the way in which words are ordered to form a grammatically correct and meaningful sentence. Each word or group of words falls into a particular class known as parts of speech. Rules of grammar are derived from the proper ordering of the parts of speech. Syntax analysis tests a sentence to see that it follows these rules and then builds a representation of the sentence structure. The syntax analyzer interacts continuously with a dictionary in order to assign each word to a set of word classes. The problem with syntax analyzers is that most sentences may have hundreds or even thousands of possible syntactic analyses. Most of them have no plausible meaning [19].

21-6-2 SEMANTIC ANALYSIS

Semantic analysis focuses on the meaning of words and phrases that is needed to clarify the system's understanding. Semantic analysis proceeds by associating words and their roles in an input sentence with information about the problem domain stored in the system's data or knowledge base. This knowledge can constitute a background context of expectations against which to interpret the input. The stored knowledge might be descriptions of objects, events and relationships in the problem domain, descriptions of typical situations that might be encountered in the problem domain, or chains of events or procedures that occur given certain conditions in the problem domain [19].

21-6-3 PRAGMATIC ANALYSIS

The final stage of analysis in a language understanding program is pragmatic analysis. This is an analysis of context. Every sentence is embedded in a particular setting, it comes from a particular speaker at a particular time, and it refers, at least implicitly, to a particular body of understanding. Some of the embedding is straightforward. For instance, the pronoun "I" refers to the speaker; the adverb "now" refers to the moment at which the sentence is spoken. Yet even these can be problematic. Consider the use of "now" in a letter I write today expecting you to read it three or four days later. Still, fairly uncomplicated programs can draw the correct conclusion most of the time. Other types of embedding are more complex. The pronoun "we" is an example. "We" might refer to the speaker and the listener or to the speaker and some third party. For example, "we" as a nation must agree on this issue. Which of these it is (and who the third party might be) is not explicit and in fact is a common source of misunderstanding when people converse.

In addition to using the information in the system's knowledge structures to analyze the input, the system can store the input itself in knowledge structures, increasing and refining its knowledge as processing goes along. This helps the system to understand the input in context larger than single sentences. The stored information provides a way to link references in one sentence to references in another.

Natural language systems can combine information from the syntactic, semantic, and pragmatic analyses to generate formalized representations of input sentences. The formalizations generated by the analyses can be stored in the knowledge base for comparison to other input or they may set off some activity in the system, such as responding to a database query.

21-7 HOW A NLP WORKS

In a typical natural language system, a user either types a sentence or chooses a sentence or a group of sentences from a menu. At this point, we are talking about text input. When the request is typed or selected through an input device, the NLP follows the following steps:

1. The parser figures out how a sentence is parsed together. (Various types of parsing techniques and approaches will be discussed in the next section.) As an example, consider a user who has typed:
"Alan drew a picture"
The parser may parse this sentence as follows:
"Alan" as noun phrase.
"Drew a picture" as verb phrase.
In the next round the verb phrase is parsed further to:
Drew
A picture
This process will continue until the entire sentence is parsed. The result of this process is a parse tree.

2. Then the NLP starts semantic analysis. The verb is translated first because the verb states the action. Then the modifiers of an action are translated, and finally the nouns are translated. In this process, the NLP compares the itemized tree with its dictionary in order to figure out the meaning of a statement.

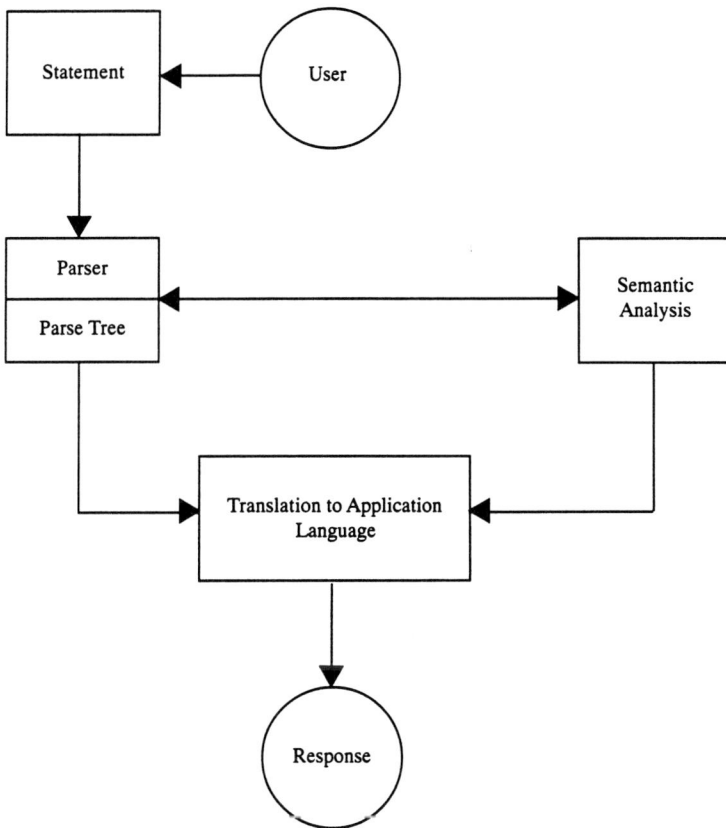

Figure 21-1 The function of a natural language processing system.

3. If there is any ambiguity, an expert system is used to clear up the ambiguity. As will be discussed later, this process is not as easy as it sounds. Figure 21-1 [9] illustrates this process.

21-8 DIFFERENT PARSING APPROACHES

The purpose of applying NLP to computer usage is to transpose or paraphrase conceivably ambiguous statements into the internal representation necessary for processing. This transposition or parsing is how NLP begins to work. Parsing is usually a process of combining the symbols and components of a phrase into a group that can be replaced by another more general symbol. This new symbol can in turn be combined into another group, and so on, until an allowable structure evolves [17].

Five different types of parsers or parsing approaches have evolved from the extensive research that has been done in NLP. They are [17]:

1. Pattern-matching parsing
2. Grammar-based parsing
3. Semantic parsing
4. Knowledge-based parsing
5. Neural network parsing

Although all of these methods have a similar goal, they each provide a dissimilar approach to NLP.

21-8-1 PATTERN-MATCHING PARSING

Pattern-matching approaches were used in early natural language programs. The idea behind this kind of parser is relatively simple. These programs look for recurring linguistic patterns in a sentence without using any grammatical formalism. While performing the sentence analysis, the system merely looks for a possible match with a fixed number of patterns. If a match is found the program performs certain action (e.g., rearranges the input according to another pattern and so on) until the necessary internal command is derived. ELIZA, a program written by Joseph Weizenbaum in 1966, is the most well-known pattern-matching program. ELIZA was written to simulate the conversation with a psychiatrist of the Carl Rogers School might carry on with a patient (the user). These programs do not have a grammatical base and have thus proved to be of limited use. Pattern-matching programs are useful only if partial analysis is required or if other components of the system can make up for the loss of syntactic information.

21-8-2 GRAMMAR-BASED PARSING

The second approach to NLP uses grammar-based parsers. Grammar refers to a set of rules that defines the parts of sentences of a particular language. This set of rules is called the rewrite rules or production. Examples of two simple rewrite rules are:

$$S \rightarrow NP + VP$$
$$S \rightarrow VP.$$

These rules state that a sentence (S) must have a noun phrase (NP) and a verb phrase (VP) or simply a verb phrase. These rules allow a tree structure to be constructed that shows clearly how the words in a sentence interact.

Noam Chomsky, an eminent linguist, formulated four types of grammar based on the types of rules they used. The simplest is termed TYPE 3, or finite-state or regular grammar, and is capable of producing only simple sentences. In TYPE 2, or context-free grammar, the left side of each rewrite rule can consist of only a single nonterminal symbol (e.g. S, VP, DET (determinant), ADJ (adjective), N (noun), and so forth). The next more complex grammar is TYPE 1, or context-sensitive grammar. In this type, more than one symbol can appear on the left side of the rewrite rule. The only requirement for these rules is that there be more symbols on the right side than on the left. Finally, the most complex grammar, TYPE 0, has rules that do not follow any set pattern or requirements [17].

Chomsky has asserted that a natural language such as English cannot be completely described by a context-free grammar. He argues that English requires a context-sensitive or Type 0 grammar.

21-8-3 SEMANTIC PARSING

The semantic approach to NLP parser was developed because meaning has a principal function in the comprehension of language. The researchers of this semantic rather than syntactic approach do not deny the necessity for some structural processing but use it to complement their semantic considerations. There are two semantically oriented approaches to NLP: case grammar and semantic grammar. C. Fillmore developed case grammar in 1968. This theory of grammar asserts that every sentence has an underlying representation of its meaning. The representation consists of the verb and the various noun phrases related to the verb. For example, "Alan hit the nail with the hammer" designates Alan as the agent, nail as the object, and hammer as the instrument. The cases remain identical for the sentence. "The nail was hit with the hammer by Alan" because the meaning is the same.

Semantic grammar consists of lexicon and a series of rewrite rules. It is similar to syntactic grammar except that word classes are replaced by specific semantic classes, e.g. NOUN, ADJ, for OFFICE, OFFICE PROPERTIES. The advantage of this approach is that the size of these semantic classes is much smaller than the size of the equivalent word class. The disadvantage is that there is a difficulty of transferring rewrite rules from one domain of applications to another [17].

21-8-4 Knowledge-Based Parsing

The fourth approach to parsing involves a knowledge-based parser or an actual expert system built into the program. So instead of relying solely on the structural or semantic information of a sentence, the NLP system has access to a knowledge base for a specific domain of knowledge. There are two approaches of knowledge-based parsing: word-expert parsing and the conceptual dependency theory.

In **word-expert parsing** the word is considered the basic linguistic unit. Linguistic knowledge is distributed among a group of procedural "experts" that know how the interpretation of a word changes in particular contexts. The argument in favor of this approach is that words have a rich linguistic and conceptual structure and that language cannot be reduced solely to a number of rewrite rules as implied by most grammar-based theories [17].

The **conceptual dependency theory** desires to create canonical representations of sentences based on certain semantic primitives. A canonical representation is simply a basic way of representing the meaning of a sentence. Different sentences that mean the same thing will all have the same common canonical representation. For example, "wolf eats sheep" and "sheep is eaten by wolf" are both canonically represented by wolf—INGEST—sheep.

In this theory, semantic primitives are the most basic entities used to describe the world. Individual words can always be analyzed further, but semantic primitives cannot. Roger Schank has done the most well-known work on this theory. His idea of representing a sentence is to postulate primitive actions to represent semantic relationships. There are seven primitive actions, five of which describe physical actions and two of which describe state changes. These seven are [17]:

- PROPEL
- MOVE
- INGEST
- EXPEL
- GRASP
- PTRANS (physical transfer of location)
- MTRANS (mental transfer of information)

In 1977, Schank integrated this theory of conceptual dependencies into his script theory. A script is a set of standardized, perhaps oversimplified knowledge, used for processing natural language. For example, a script for a restaurant would contain certain basic facts, such as [17]:

S→ Customer
Entry conditions:
S is hungry
S has money

Results:
S has less money
S is not hungry
S is pleased (optional)

21-8-5 NEURAL NETWORK PARSING

In Chapter 20 we examined neural computing in detailed. Here we introduce neural networks as a parsing approach. This approach involves setting up a network of neuron-like computing units. Each unit has a certain number of inputs, i.e. a small set of possible states, and an output that is a function of the inputs. When a computing unit is activated, it evaluates all of its inputs and examines them according to their respective confidence values. If certain conditions are met the computing unit generates an output value that is used as input by other computing units. The fundamental premise of this approach is that the individual units do not transmit large amounts of data but compute simply by being connected to a large number of similar units.

The neural-network parsing model contains three levels of "neurons," the lexical, the wordsense, and the case logical. The lexical level serves as the input level of the network. The neurons are mapped to particular words. The wordsense level receives the input from the lexical level and activates neurons that represent the meaning of the words. Finally, in the case-logical level, the meanings derived from the second level are combined to form predicates and objects. The neural network parsing comes closest to modeling human linguistic information processing. It is still at the beginning stage of development, but it shows promising signs.

21-9 PARSING TECHNIQUES

Once an approach to parsing has been selected, a parsing technique must be chosen. Parsing techniques fall into two categories: deterministic and nondeterministic. Nondeterministic parsers are further subdivided into two subgroups: top-down and bottom-up parsers.

Top-down parsers try to match the grammar rules against the input, starting at topmost rewrite rule (which usually involves the start symbol or sentence symbol S) and recursively moving toward lower, more specific rewrite rules. The parsing is successful if a sentence can be constructed that matches the input sentence. This type of parser is easy to write and change as necessary. Productions that are more likely to be used can be easily placed ahead of those that are less likely to be used. This factor can greatly enhance performance [17].

The disadvantage of a top-down parsing is that it can be slow. For example, if the rules at a certain level fail, it will backtrack up to a previous level to try another rule. This means that the same constituents may be analyzed many times over.

Bottom-up parsing on the contrary, starts by combining the lowest level elements first and then building up larger constituents. It can also at least partially parse poorly formed input. However, since this type of parsing is not goal-directed, it can generate numerous bogus parses, and the appropriateness of the parse can only be determined after all parses are performed.

Deterministic parsing differs from the top-down and bottom-up parsing in that there is no backtracking. It is sometimes referred to as WASP (wait and see parsing). This technique creates new modes in bottom-up fashion but narrowly looks ahead to determine which node to use. The greatest advantage of this technique is increased speed because it avoids the combinatorial explosion of possible parses. However, the disadvantage is that the algorithm is based only on syntactic information.

There are two types of deterministic parsing techniques: augmented transition networks (ATNs) and recursive transition networks (RTNs). A transition network consists of a series of states connected by arcs. A word category (e.g., noun or verb) or a specific word labels each arc. The program starts at a given state and then checks the next word in the input string for a match with one of the arcs. If a match is found, the program proceeds to the next arc, and thus traverses the network. The advantage of this type of network is that it can be easily implemented on a computer [17].

Augmented transition networks (ATNs) are similar to RTNs, but include three additional features: registers, which can store conditions or information on a global basis, regardless of which particular subnetwork is being processed; conditions, which let arcs be selected if registers indicate certain conditions; and actions, which let arcs modify the structure of data [17].

ATNs are the most widely used technique for NLP because they are very flexible and powerful. They do, however, experience problems with ungrammatical sentences for which no relevant networks have been provided. In this case, the program simply stops.

Figure 21-2 illustrates these various techniques.

21-10   NATURAL LANGUAGE INTERFACES

Natural language interfaces allow people to use subsets of their native languages to communicate with computers in specific domains. It is expected that a major use of the technology will be in organizations that query databases. In fact,

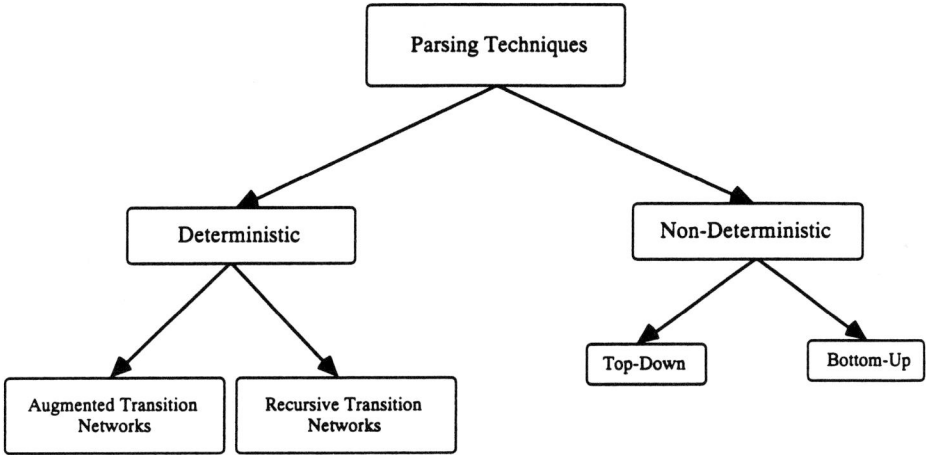

Figure 21-2 Parsing techniques.

many organizations are already using natural language processing interfaces on a limited basis, for that very purpose. Managers, office workers, and technical professionals will be able to get needed information from the computer without going either to data processing courses or through the data processing department. This will make it worthwhile to pose ad hoc questions that may not warrant the development of full-fledged programs but that do contribute useful information to the problem at hand. A long-range goal is to make it easier and more comfortable for people to use their home computers and to program and control robots. Several commercial natural language interfaces to databases are already on the market. Let's briefly introduce few of the popular ones.

21-10-1 INTELLECT

One of the earliest of the commercial products is INTELLECT, developed by Artificial Intelligence Corporation, Waltham, Massachusetts. INTELLECT is intended for use as a front-end interface to information retrieval applications such as finance, marketing, manufacturing, and personnel. INTELLECT parses the user's natural language query into an internal representation that sets off a database search. To do this, in addition to using a grammar, the system also draws on knowledge of the database structure, database contents, a built-in data dictionary, and an application specific dictionary. When the query results in the generations of more than one possible interpretive paraphrase, INTELLECT resolves the ambiguity by assigning preference ratings to the different paraphrases, choosing the one most highly rated due to its consistency with information in the database. If necessary, INTELLECT even asks the user which of several interpretations is correct [14].

Steelcase, Inc., a $1.5 billion manufacturer of office furniture, found INTEL-LECT ideal for keeping track of its inventory and allowing end-users direct access to its database. This was a necessity in Steelcase's move toward a just-in-time (JIT) inventory system [12]. Before INTELLECT was installed at the Albert Einstein Medical Center in Philadelphia, the information systems department was being swamped by requests for custom reports that would take a programmer two full days to complete. Now managers are using INTELLECT to develop custom reports to meet ever-changing medical reporting requirements [21].

21-10-2 Q & A

Unlike INTELLECT, which runs on a mainframe system, Symantec Corp's Q&A was designed for a microcomputer implementation. Introduced in 1985, Q&A has gone through several releases. Queries can be in short or long sentences, including articles such as "a" and prepositions such as "in," and it can accurately interpret hundreds of variations of the same question" [18].

21-10-3 DOSTALK

DOSTALK from SAK Technologies is used as a natural language front-end for MS-DOS-based computers. DOSTALK translates English sentences into DOS commands and then executes them. For example, "Instead of having to type in such cryptic commands as COPY C:\TEST*.DOC C:\BACKUP, you can simply enter the phrase "copy all the files in the TEST directory that have the extension DOC to the BACKUP directory" (capitalizing only the names of files and directories) [20]. Anyone with absolutely no experience with DOS might find this package appealing.

21-10-4 OTHER PRODUCTS

As mentioned earlier an approach to interfaces that emphasizes semantics has been taken by Professor Roger C. Schank, chairman of Yale University's computer science department, and the director of Yale's artificial intelligence laboratory and founder of Cognitive Systems, Inc., New Haven, Connecticut. Cognitive

Systems has developed natural language interfaces to databases and conversational advisory systems. Cognitive Systems' products "map" natural language input into conceptual representations based on Schank's theory of conceptual dependencies, which capture the meaning of the input. In addition to storing information about meaning in conceptual representations, these systems incorporate information about the problem domain in various knowledge structures, such as scripts. These knowledge structures aid interpretations by providing the system with expectations, contexts in which to understand input. A script, for instance, is a description of what happens in a situation that conforms to a stereotype. When a scripted topic is presented to a system employing this knowledge structure, it has a set of expectations that helps it resolve ambiguity [24].

Some products also combine expert systems with natural language systems. These natural language systems set up a context and keep track of it during a conversation. This adds to the system's fund of expectations, helping to resolve ambiguity. It is also possible to build into the system profiles of the user's goals, so that the system can retrieve not only the specific information requested, but also related information that would be of interest to the user. And again, the profiles provide a context that helps the system decide how to interpret a request: one person's "year," for instance, might be fiscal, while another's might be the calendar year.

Natural language interfaces vary in how much users must conform their input to the structure of the system, some allowing for the use of language that is more natural than others. Most allow users to modify the dictionaries with which the systems are equipped and to add their own entries, with varying degrees of ease and allowing varying kinds of definitions. Some systems handle sentences in which words have been omitted by proposing a fleshedout interpretation to the user and asking if this was the correct reading. On encountering a spelling error some natural language systems ask for a correction, some automatically correct the word, and others simply stop processing the sentence. At the present time, individual language interfaces must be specialized for particular subject matter contexts in order to interpret words and phrases correctly.

It should also be noted that most natural language and AI systems are usually not aware of these limits. Unlike people, the systems "assume" that they operate in a closed world, that their knowledge of the domain is complete and adequate. When a natural language system responds "no" to a query, it may really mean that the system does not know the answer. In reality, objects and relationships pertaining to most real-world domains change or are not modeled in the system. Another problem is that an appropriate response frequently depends on knowledge of the user's motivation in asking a question, and current systems are naive in this area. Nevertheless, natural language interfaces are now available that successfully lessen communication obstacles to problem solving in some computing tasks and speed up access to information.

21-11 MACHINE TRANSLATION

Work in machine translation from one natural language to another has revealed that the delicacy of human language does not easily yield to computerization. The word-for-word translation systems of 30 years ago just did not work. Research in machine translation has made it increasingly clear that human language cognition is a very complex ability that requires many kinds of knowledge, including knowledge of the structure of sentences, the meaning of words, the patterns of conversation, the expectations, goals and beliefs of the partner with whom you are conversing, and a great deal of knowledge about the world as well as knowledge about the particular topic of conversation.

Current implementations that most closely approach automatic translation may use syntactic and semantic information in order to translate words in context. Different systems require varying degrees of human assistance to edit machine-translated drafts or to assist in translating elements outside the bounds of the systems' abilities. In addition, systems described as "fully automatic" are, at this time, restricted to small domains. The speed of translation may be as slow as 600 words per hour for output that requires little editing or as fast as 60,000 words per hour for output that is likely to need considerable editing. Faster speeds are achieved in some systems by constraining the input to shorter sentences or by setting lower standards for the quality of the output. As with all natural language systems, the more highly constrained the domain of discourse, the better the translation [23]. Let's briefly describe some of the popular machine translation programs.

21-11-1 LOGOS

The LOGOS system, from Logos Corporation, Waltham, Massachusetts, is designed for business use. LOGOS works in partnership with a human translator. Before LOGOS begins a translation, the system examines the document for words it does not know. The translator then provides the system with information about these words, expanding the general dictionary. After the dictionary is complete for the purposes of the particular translation, LOGOS generates a draft of the document, which the translator edits. Customizing the dictionary with multiple definitions of words for various contexts does not make the system unable to accept new releases of the vendor's dictionary.

21-11-2 PC-BASED SYSTEMS

Traditionally a mainframe-based application, machine translation software is now making its move toward desktop PCs. While some of the older mainframe-based machine translation software is being rewritten to run on PCs, many vendors are offering new products written specifically for the PC platform. Products typically range in price from $70 to $1000 and include a wide range of languages such as: Arabic, Danish, Dutch, Finnish, French, German, Greek, Italian, Japanese, Korean, Russian, Spanish, and Swedish. While many systems translate in only one direction, for example, English to Spanish, a few products are bi-directional, English to Spanish and Spanish to English. The Language Assistant Series from MicroTac Software and GTS-Basic and GTS-Professional from Globulin are a few of these bi-directional products [16].

Performance figures for machine translation software varies with the speed of your PC, how much RAM you have, if you use disk-caching hardware or software, and even with the machine translation software itself. The typical PC will translate anywhere from 10,000 to 30,000 words per hour. Translation speed will increase if more of the programs will fit in RAM. If you are using some form of cache, or increase the DOS buffer size, the software will store previously found words in the cache or buffer and speed up the translation process [16].

The quality of machine translation output is dependent on the dictionaries (also called lexicons) included with the software. Most products come with a single-word (no phrases) dictionary containing anywhere from 20,000 to 100,000 word listings. Some packages even come with a multiple-word dictionary that stores group of words and colloquial expressions. More advanced packages, such as PC-Translator by Linguistic Products, allow you to make use of several context-specific single-word and phrase dictionaries simultaneously. This feature is useful if you regularly translate documents from an assortment of technical areas that use specialized technical jargons. The ability to create your own dictionary or customize the one included in the package is essential for adding your own ter minology to the program. PC-Translator can simplify this process by importing lists of terms in ASCII format directly into its dictionary [16].

The ability to import and export ASCII text files is an important feature offered in all machine translation products. Some systems can even link directly into your word processing software via a menu to assist in converting text to and from ASCII format. A few systems can even process formatted text from popular word processing programs such as WordPerfect or Microsoft Word. Even more systems will retain (but not process) the formatting codes from the original document. This can be an important time-saving feature, because formatting codes such as boldface, italic, underlining, and charts and tables are restored in the output without the need to repeat these steps.

21-11-3 ALPS

The ALPS system from Automated Language Processing Systems, Inc., Provo, Utah, takes a slightly different approach in that the translation process operates in an interactive, rather than batch, mode [10]. This system goes a bit further in that the interactive mode not only finds unknown words but also words with ambiguous meanings in context. In general, the ALPS dictionary is somewhat more sophisticated, accommodating word strings or phrases, such as idioms, as well as single words. Instead of one large dictionary, ALPS utilizes several reference dictionaries and, moreover, builds a separate dictionary for each document. The document dictionary can be fine-tuned for the document's specific context without affecting dictionary definitions that will be applied to documents written in other contexts.

Experimental systems are beginning to incorporate more semantic information in knowledge structures such as conceptual dependencies and scripts that provide the system with knowledge that helps to resolve ambiguities in interpretation. For instance, semantic elements are being included in EUROTRA, a system being developed under the support of the European Economic Community [10].

21-12 DOCUMENT-UNDERSTANDING SYSTEMS

So far, we have described systems for inputting natural language, generating natural language output, processing natural language queries, and translating between different natural languages. But none of these systems actually generates questions in natural language. There are currently systems on the market, termed document-understanding systems, that read printed text, provide summaries of that text, and comment on the author's writing style, word usage, and grammar. Let's briefly introduce two such systems [4].

21-12-1 WRITER'S WORKBENCH

Colorado State University provides its freshmen English-composition students with access to one such system named Writer's Workbench. This system analyzes a first draft composition; notes spelling and grammatical errors; comments on words, phrases and punctuation marks; and makes suggestions for deleting, changing, or at least thinking about these. The system then assigns a readability grade to the composition (a number equal to the years of schooling a reader could be expected to need to understand the writing, as determined by a standard formula). The students then consider the analyses, make corrections and turn in a final draft to their instructor [24].

Writer's Workbench has been in use at Colorado State since 1981 and the general consensus is that it has definitely helped students improve their writing skills. Instructors also seem to like the system, if for no other reason than it saves them time in teaching and grading papers. Some instructors have even adapted the system to help students who are taking English as a second language and students who are developing their business writing skills.

Writer's Workbench was developed initially for academia by AT&T Bell Laboratories in 1981 as an experiment, to see if this type of system could actually improve someone's writing skills. Their system was so successful that it spread to more than 60 high schools and universities across the country. Now AT&T offers a new version aimed at technical writers. This system is marketed to business rather than institutions. Both versions require the UNIX operating system and more memory than is available in a typical PC. Taking advantage of this limitation, computer entrepreneurs have developed PC-based style-analyzers. Two such programs, Grammuk II and Punctuation and Style, are both based on Writer's Workbench [24]. The grammar component of popular word processing programs such as Microsoft Word and WordPerfect now offers similar features.

21-12-2 SMART EXPERT EDITOR

The Smart Expert Editor system, Max, developed by Smart Communications, Inc., is another document-understanding system. Like the second version of Writer's Workbench, this system was developed for technical writing— writing that is concise, clear, and to the point. Smart Communications, Inc., customizes Max for each company that buys it. Max is currently in use in the technical-writing department at the Murry Ohio Manufacturing Company, which manufactures lawn mowers. In their case, Max was customized to edit owner's and repair manuals and to make certain that they earned a readability grade of no higher than eight (eighth-grade education level). If Max rejects a document it must be revised and then sent back through the system until Max approves it.

Max's company-specific customized dictionary contains anywhere from 2500 to 7500 words. Most of these words have exactly one definition to avoid ambiguity. A company's technical writing department may use any of these words, but no others. Max will recognize any word not found in its dictionary and promptly reject it. This specialized, limited vocabulary makes it very easy for Max-approved documents to be translated into other languages. Smart Communications offers companion programs for Max that will automatically translate Max-approved English into five languages [24].

Document understanding systems such as those we have just described make it possible for computers to summarize text and generate responses based on content. They also make it possible for computers to store and retrieve information based on concepts, rather than just key words.

SUMMARY

This chapter provided a detailed discussion on natural language processing systems. The coverage included definitions of NLP, advantages, applications, problems, natural input/output systems, and natural language understanding systems. The chapter explained in detail how a natural language system works and various techniques and approaches used for parsing. As you see, the technology has come a long way. The chapter presented numerous commercial applications of these various natural language processing systems. Several commercial natural language interfaces were introduced and the chapter concluded with a discussion on machine translation and document understanding systems. Further development in this area should expedite and enhance the applications and acceptance of CBIS in all types of organizations.

REVIEW QUESTIONS

1. What is a natural language? What is the difference between a natural language and a high-level computer language?
2. What are some of the applications of natural language processing systems? What are some of the problems with our natural language that are difficult to overcome?
3. What are the six major categories of NLP applications?
4. What are some of the advantages of NLP?
5. What are some examples of natural language input and output systems?
6. What have we achieved so far in the area of voice recognition? What are some obstacles that must be overcome in this area?
7. How accurate is the "voice typewriter" introduced in this chapter? What are some of the difficulties involved in using the device as it now stands?
8. What are some of the successful applications of speech generation systems? Who will benefit the most from this technology?
9. What has been achieved so far by handwriting recognition systems? What are some of the obstacles that must be overcome before developing a full-featured handwriting recognition system?
10. What is body language? How is it implemented?
11. Explain the three types of analyses: syntax, semantic, and pragmatic.
12. How does a natural language system work?
13. What is parsing? How many different approaches and techniques are available for parsing?

14. Which parsing technique is the most accurate type? Explain.

15. What is semantic parsing? Neural network parsing?

16. What is the difference between top-down and bottom-up parsing? Deterministic and nondeterministic?

17. What are two of the popular natural language interfaces? What are some of their applications?

18. What does DOSTALK as a natural language interface do?

19. What is machine translation? What has been achieved in this area?

20. What are some of the popular commercial products of machine translation?

21. What are document-understanding systems? What has Colorado State University been doing with Writer's Workbench?

22. What are some of the unique applications of document-understanding systems?

PROJECTS

1. By referring to the sources introduced in this chapter, investigate in detail why developing a full-featured NLP system is difficult. What are some of the obstacles that must be overcome? How close are we in this development?

2. By referring to the references provided in the chapter, investigate the applications of NLP in the insurance industry and in retail. What has AT&T done with NLP?

3. By contacting the vendors of Q&A and INTELLECT, compare and contrast these two natural language interfaces. What are the strengths of each? What are some of their limitations?

4. Compare and contrast LOGOS and ALPS as two popular machine translation programs. What are the strengths and limitations of each?

5. In addition to a university setting, what are other commercial applications of a package similar to Writer's Workbench?

6. There are a number of voice-activated software products that work with Windows applications. Some experts believe that using a voice synthesizer can effectively perform tasks such as word processing. Investigate this claim. What are some popular products on the market for performing such tasks? Have they been able to solve the problem of continuous speech?

7. Compare and contrast the IBM and Dragon dictation systems. Prepare a cost and benefit analysis for a company that is trying to purchase 100 pieces of such

software for their publications department. What are some of the actual gains? What would be the limitation of these systems? Discuss.

KEY TERMS

Body language, 612–613
Document-understanding systems, 628–629
Grammar-based parsing, 618–619
Handwriting recognition, 612
Knowledge-based parsing, 620–621
Machine translation, 626
Machine vision, 613–614
Natural language processing, 603–608

Neural network parsing, 621
Parsing techniques, 621–623
Pattern matching parsing, 618
Pragmatic analysis, 615–616
Semantic analysis, 615
Semantic parsing, 619
Speech generation, 611–612
Syntax analysis, 615
Voice recognition, 609–611

REFERENCES

[1] Bidgoli, H. (July 1990). Designing a user-friendly Interface for a DSS. *Journal of Information Age,* Volume 12, No. 3, 148–154.

[2] Boyle, E. (August 1996). Chase Bank on voice verification. *Communication News,* Volume 33, 46–47.

[3] Caudill, M. (April 1992). Kinder, gentler computing. *Byte,* 135–150.

[4] Cowie, J. (January 1996). Information extraction. *Communication of the ACM,* Volume 39. 80–91.

[5] Churbuck, D. (December 23, 1991). The computer as detective. *Forbes,* 150–155.

[6] Diehl, S. (May 1994). Desktop dictation. *BYTE,* 145–146.

[7] Dieterich, R. (March 1996). I will talk to you soon. *BYTE,* Volume 21, 36.

[8] Elliot, K. (March 1996). In plain English please. *Journal of Accountancy,* 43–46.

[9] Fresko-Weiss, H. (November 1985). Natural language: The dialog has begun. *Personal Computing,* 93–96.

[10] Hovy, E. (January 1993). MT at your service. *Byte,* 160–164.

[11] King, K. G., and Elliott, R. W. (March 1990). In plain English please. *Journal of Accountancy,* 43–48.

[12] Latamore, B. G. (February 1988). Getting in touch with JIT. *Computer & Communications Decisions,* 280.

[13] Lewis, D. D. (January 1996). Natural language processing for information retrieval. *Communication of the ACM,* Volume 39. 92–102.

[14] May, K. M. (October 1991). The next wave in AI. *Best's Review,* 118–127.

[15] McWilliams, G. (November 1, 1993). Computers are finally learning to listen. *Business Week,* 101–101.

[16] Miller, C. L. (January 1993). Babelware for the desktop. *Byte,* 177–183.

[17] Obermeir, K. K. (December 1987). Natural language processing. *Byte,* 225–231.

[18] Pitta, J. (July 1990). Talk to your computer, *Forbes.* 281–282.

[19] Ray, P. J., and Doukidis, G. I. (August 1986). Further developments in the use of artificial intelligence techniques which formulate simulation problems. *Journal of the Operational Research Society,* No. 8, 787–810.

[20] Sheldon, K. (April 1989). Talk to me DOS, talk to me. *Byte,* 104.

[21] Stevens, L. (April 22, 1986). Getting data in plain english. *Computer Decisions,* 42–47.

[22] Sweeney, R. (October 1989). PC: What did we learn last year? *Management Accounting,* 31–35.

[23] Vasconcellos, M. (January 1993). Machine Translation. *Byte,* 155–156.

[24] Wallraff, B. (January 1988). The literate computer. *The Atlantic Monthly,* 64–71.

Index